The Installation and Getting Started Guides for Red Hat Linux 6.0

FIRST EDITION
FIRST PRINTING 1999

Linux Press
P.O. Box 220
Penngrove. CA 94951

Phone: (707) 773-4916
Fax: (707) 765-1431
Web: http://www.linuxpress.com
E-mail: sales@linuxpress.com

International Standard Book Number: 0-9659575-3-5

Printed in Canada

Linux Press Acknowledgements

Copy Editor **Dale Scheetz**

Proofreading **Les Villanyi**

Cover Art **Folio Creative Services of Glen Ellen, California**

The Installation Guide
for
Red Hat Linux 6.0

Red Hat Software, Inc.
2600 Meridian Parkway
Durham, NC 27713
P. O. Box 13588
Research Triangle Park, NC 27709
(919) 547-0012
redhat@redhat.com
http://www.redhat.com

Table of Contents

Preface

Welcome! And thanks for your interest in Red Hat Linux. We have what we think is the best Linux distribution on the market today, and we work hard to keep it that way. Red Hat Linux 6.0 is the latest in a long line of software from Red Hat Software. We hope you like it, and that you enjoy using Red Hat Linux as much as we've enjoyed making it for you

While Linux is popular and well-known by a certain segment of the computer-using population, there are many people out there that are only now hearing about Linux. For this group of people, the following section should provide enough background to help you get acquainted with Linux and Red Hat Software.

What is Linux?

Back in August of 1991, a student from Finland began a post to the *comp.os.minix* newsgroup with the words:

> Hello everybody out there using minix - I'm doing a (free) operating system (just a hobby, won't be big and professional like gnu) for 386(486) AT clones.

The student was Linus Torvalds, and the "hobby" he spoke of eventually became what we know today as Linux. A full-featured POSIX-like operating system, Linux has been developed not just by Linus, but by hundreds of programmers around the world. The interesting thing about this is that this massive, world-wide development effort is largely uncoordinated. Sure, Linus calls the shots where the kernel is concerned, but Linux is more than just the kernel. There's no management infrastructure; a student in Russia gets a new motherboard, and writes a driver to support a neat feature the motherboard has. A system administrator in Maryland needs backup software, writes it, and gives it away to anyone that needs it. The right things just seem to happen at the right time. Another interesting thing is that Linux can be obtained for absolutely no money. That's right, most of the software is available (at no charge) to anyone with the time and inclination to download it. But not everyone has that much time...

What is Red Hat Linux?

Enter a group of programmers based in North Carolina. Their goal was to make it easier for people to give Linux a try. Like many other such groups, their approach was to bundle all the necessary bits and pieces into a cohesive distribution, relieving "newbies" from some of the more esoteric aspects of bootstrapping a new operating system on their PCs. However, unlike other distributions, this one was fundamentally different. The difference? Instead of being a snapshot of a hard disk that had a working copy of Linux on it, or a set of diskettes from which different parts of the operating system could be dumped, this distribution was based on packages. Software development in the Linux world is fast-paced, so new versions of old software come out continually. With other distributions, upgrading software was painful — a complete upgrade usually meant deleting everything on your hard drive and starting over. Each package provided a different piece of software, fully tested, configured, and ready to run. Want to try a new editor? Download the package and install it. In seconds, you can give it a try. Don't like it? Issue a single command, and the package is removed. If that was all there was to it, this distribution would be pretty nifty. But being package-based meant there was one additional advantage: This Linux distribution could be easily upgraded. By now you've probably guessed that the group of programmers in North Carolina is Red Hat Software, and the package-based distribution is Red Hat Linux. Since Red Hat Linux's introduction in the summer of 1994, Linux and Red Hat Software have grown by leaps and bounds. Much has changed: support for more esoteric hardware, huge increases in reliability, and the growing use of Linux by companies around the world. But much still remains the same. Linux is still developed by people world-wide; Linus is still involved. Red Hat Software is still located in North Carolina; still trying to make Linux easier for people to use. And Red Hat Linux is still package-based; always has been, always will be. Since the release of version 4.0, Red Hat Linux runs on three leading computing platforms: Intel compatible PCs, Digital Alpha computers, and Sun SPARC equipment. Our unified source tree and the benefits of RPM (Red Hat Package Management) technology enable us to deploy Red Hat Linux for each platform with a minimum of effort. This in turn enables our users to manage and port software between these platforms as easily as possible. We make Red Hat Linux available by unrestricted FTP from our site and many mirror sites on the Internet. Red Hat Linux is also available on CD-ROM. For current information on our product offerings and links to other Linux resources please check Red Hat Software's web site at *http://www.redhat.com*.

On most systems, Red Hat Linux is easy to install; the installation program can walk you through the process in as little as 15 minutes. The system itself is very flexible. With RPM, you can install and uninstall individual software packages with minimal effort. Because of RPM, Red Hat Linux is also easy to maintain — package installations can be verified and corrected, and packages can be installed and uninstalled simply and reliably. Furthermore, Red Hat Linux is easy to administer. Included are a rich set of administrative tools which reduce the hassle of everyday system administration. Complete source code is provided for the freely distributable components of the system.

An Overview of This Manual

This manual is organized to guide you through the process of installing Red Hat Linux quickly and easily. Toward that goal, let's take a quick look at each chapter to help you get acclimated:

Chapter 1, *New Features Of Red Hat Linux 6.0*
: contains information concerning new functionality that has been added to Red Hat Linux 6.0.

Chapter 2, *Before You Begin*
: contains information on tasks you should perform prior to starting the Red Hat Linux installation.

Chapter 3, *Starting the Installation*
contains detailed instructions for starting the Red Hat Linux installation process.

Chapter 4, *Local Media Installations*
contains instructions on installing Red Hat Linux from a CD-ROM or hard drive.

Chapter 5, *Network Installations*
contains instructions on installing Red Hat Linux via NFS, FTP, or HTTP.

Chapter 6, *Finishing the Installation*
contains instructions on the last steps required to complete the installation process.

Chapters 7 – 11
explain how to find documentation on your system, and how to use the various system management and administration tools which accompany Red Hat Linux. They also include an explanation of what's special about your Red Hat Linux system, including where special files live and more.

Appendixes
contain extra information about Red Hat Linux, including an explanation of Red Hat Software's support offerings, packages lists, and more.

Quick Start Information

Those of you that have installed Red Hat Linux/Intel before and are in a hurry to get started need only boot from a boot diskette (or the Red Hat Linux/Intel CD-ROM, if your computer supports booting directly from CD-ROM). There are two separate boot disks, one for CD-ROM and hard drive installations and another for NFS, FTP, and HTTP installations.[1]

Next, select the desired installation method. If you will be using a PCMCIA device during the installation, you will need to use the PCMCIA support disk.[2]

1 If you need a boot disk for network type installations, you will have to create one. See section 2.5 for that information.

2 If you will be using a PCMCIA device during the install you will need to create a PCMCIA support disk. Section 2.6 will describe how that disk is made.

Upgrading from a Prior Version of Red Hat Linux

The installation process for Red Hat Linux 6.0 includes the ability to upgrade from prior versions of Red Hat Linux (2.0 through 5.2, inclusive) which are based on RPM technology. Upgrading your system installs the modular 2.2.x kernel as well as updated versions of the packages that are installed on your machine. The upgrade process preserves existing configuration files using a .rpmsave extension (e.g., `sendmail.cf.rpmsave`) and leaves a log telling what actions it took in `/tmp/upgrade.log`. As software evolves, configuration file formats can change, so you should carefully compare your original configuration files to the new files before integrating your changes.

A Word From the Developers

We would like to thank all our beta testers for entrusting their systems to early versions of Red Hat Linux and for taking the time to submit bug reports from the front, especially those of you who have been with Red Hat since the "Halloween" release and earlier. We would also like to thank Linus Torvalds and the hundreds of developers around the world for creating, truly, one of the wonders of distributed development. And, again, we'd like to thank you for your interest in Red Hat Linux!

The Red Hat Development Team

Notes from the Editor

Red Hat's evolutionary process of expanding the scope of this Installation Guide continues. As before, they have updated the chapters related to the actual installation process. They also updated the New Features chapter to reflect all the good stuff that's been added to Red Hat Linux 6.0. This is "business as usual." As the linuxconf system configuration tool continues to mature, they have created a new system configuration chapter containing task-based linuxconf documentation, as well as those vestiges of the control-panel tools that still remain.

Their goal is to continue adding linuxconf documentation; what you see here is just a first step in that process. The package list has proven to be quite popular; this time they have improved it by adding icons showing whether a given package is part of a pre-defined set of packages. All of this has resulted in the Installation Guide putting on a little weight. This is a trend that is expected to continue.

I Couldn't Have Done it Without...

Many thanks go out to the past authors of this manual. A great deal of their work is still here. Thanks also go out to the developers and testers who have patiently listened to my questions and even more patiently given me answers. Without their help, I wouldn't have been able to put this manual together. A "BIG" thank you also goes out to two of the members of the documentation team. Paul Gallagher, our editor, has done a wonderful job of proof reading and editing this manual. He has also written the GnoRPM chapter of this book and the Official Red Hat Linux Getting Started Guide. Edward Bailey, "fearless leader" and head of the documentation team, has done a fabulous job at keeping me up to speed and helping me go in the right direction. He is also credited with the new partition appendix in this Installation Guide. Without his leadership and guidance, this would have been an impossible task for me. You both have been wonderful to work with and I just can't say thank you enough. Thanks are also due to all the readers of past Installation Guides. Without their corrections, suggestions and even occassional praises, I wouldn't know if I were on the right track. Your feedback has been incorporated as much as possible (pagecount and deadlines permitting). Please keep the feedback coming. Many thanks to Cynthia Dale for updating the Frequently Asked Questions chapter and Jeff Goldin for correlating it for publication. Unfortunately, we could not print it due to lack of space in the manual. However, you can find the most up-to-date FAQ at http://www.redhat.com/knowledgebase/index.html. Finally, thanks goes out to the support group at Red Hat Software. They have given many insightful suggestions regarding this manual, based on extensive experience with thousands of Red Hat Linux customers. If you find yourself going through this Installation Guide with greater ease, a large part of that is due to all of their effort. Thank you to everyone at Red Hat Software for your help and support.

Sandra A. Moore

1 New Features of Red Hat Linux 6.0

This chapter describes features that are new to Red Hat Linux 6.0.

Installation-Related Enhancements

Here is a list of the many changes which have been made in order to make the Red Hat Linux installation process even easier:

- New HTTP Installation Method
- "Out-of-the-Box" Processor Optimized Kernel Support
- New Boot Disks
- Improved Package Selection Screen
- New Authentication Configuration Screen
- Xconfigurator Now Part of Install

Let's take a look at each one in a bit more detail.

New HTTP Installation Method

The Red Hat Linux 6.0 installation program has added HTTP to its available list of network-class installations. Similar to the way you would perform an FTP installation, you are now able to log in to a website and install Linux. For more information on network-class installations, please refer to Chapter 5.

'Out-of-the-Box' Processor Optimized Kernel Support

Optimized kernels for the Pentium Pro, Pentium II, and Pentium III processors and APM enabled kernels are now supported. Additionally, the Red Hat Linux 6.0 installation now has SMP motherboard support. The installation process will probe your system and if more than one processor is detected, an SMP enabled kernel will be automatically installed.

New Boot Disks

There are now two boot disks for Red Hat Linux. One is for installing from local media (CD-ROM installs, hard drive installs) and the other is for network based installs (NFS, FTP, or HTTP). Additionally, the supplemental disk has been replaced by the PCMCIA support disk. All install methods now require only one disk, unless you need PCMCIA support during the install. If needed, you will be prompted for the PCMCIA support disk.

Improved Package Selection Screen

Individual package selection has been improved, with collapsible and expandable tree menus to allow easy selection of packages during the installation process.

New Authentication Configuration Screen

The Authentication Configuration screen gives you the option of enabling three different types of passwords:

- **Enable NIS** — allows you to run a group of computers in the same Network Information Service domain with a common password and group file. There are two options here to choose from:

  √ **NIS Domain** — this option allows you to specify which domain or group of computers your system will belong to.

  √ **NIS Server** — this option causes your computer to use a specific NIS server, rather than "broadcasting" a message to the local area network asking for any available server to host your system.

- **Enable Shadow Passwords** — provides a very secure method of retaining passwords for you.

- **Enable MD5 Passwords** — allows passwords up to 256 characters, rather than the standard eight.

Xconfigurator Now Part of the Install

Xconfigurator is now run at the very end of the install, after all file system components have been installed. In the past, if Xconfigurator were to hang, you would likely have to start the installation over. Now it is possible to boot Red Hat Linux and configure X after the installation has completed. Additionally, Xconfigurator tests X during the installation to make sure it is configured correctly for your system. Xconfigurator also offers you the option of booting into the X Window System immediately after the installation.

Desktop and Window Managers

Red Hat Linux 6.0 provides additional choices in graphical user interfaces.

- GNOME with Enlightenment Included
- KDE Included

GNOME with Enlightenment Included

GNOME is now included in Red Hat Linux 6.0 as the default desktop manager. GNOME features a graphical interface which enables users to easily use and configure their systems. GNOME also supports Drag and Drop protocols which help you use applications that are not GNOME-compliant. Enlightenment is included as the default window manager. Enlightenment provides a window manager with a great graphical interface, and is designed to allow the user to manipulate it in any way fashionable.

KDE Included

Red Hat Linux 6.0 also includes KDE. A very popular and powerful desktop environment, KDE offers a great graphical interface, window manager, file manager and much more.

Miscellaneous New Features

Other miscellaneous features of Red Hat Linux 6.0 are:

Enhanced Font Support

Enhanced Init scripts

Switchdesk Feature

Latest Stable 2.2 Kernel Included

Enhanced Font Support

TrueType fonts are now supported in Red Hat Linux 6.0. Dynamic font loading is now supported and can be used as a font-server on a local machine.

> **Please Note:** Those of you who upgrade will not have this feature until you edit your font paths. To do this you must edit the /etc/X11/XF86Config file. Scroll down until you see font paths listed. Replace them all with FontPath "tcp/localhost:7100". You must also verify that xfs, the X Font Server, is running. By issuing the command /sbin/chkconfig —add xfs you will insure that it starts at system boot time.

Enhanced Initscripts

While booting and shutting down the system, Red Hat Linux 6.0 users are now able to easily see if a service has failed by displaying OK, PASSED or FAILED at the right-hand side of the screen.

Switchdesk Feature

Switchdesk, just as the name implies, allows you to easily switch between different desktop environments such as GNOME, Another Level or KDE. Simply run "switchdesk" and choose your desired interface.

Latest Stable 2.2 Kernel Included

Red Hat Linux 6.0 includes the latest stable version of the 2.2 Linux kernel.

2 Before You Begin

While installing Red Hat Linux is a straightforward process, taking some time prior to starting the installation can make things go much more smoothly. In this chapter, we'll discuss the steps that should be performed before you start the installation. **Please Note:** If you are currently running a version 2.0 (or greater) Red Hat Linux system, you can perform an upgrade. Skim this chapter to review the basic issues relating to installation, and read the following chapters in order, following the directions as you go. The upgrade procedure starts out identically to the installation procedure; you will be directed to choose an installation or upgrade after booting the installation program and answering a few questions. There are five things you should do prior to installing Red Hat Linux:

1 Make sure you have sufficient documentation to effectively use your Red Hat Linux system after the installation.

2 Make sure you have access to the Red Hat Linux components required for installation.

3 Make sure you know your computer's hardware configuration and networking information.

4 Decide, based on the first two tasks, what method you will use to install Red Hat Linux.

5 Determine where on your hard drive(s) Red Hat Linux will reside.

Let's start by making sure you have the documentation you'll need after you install Red Hat Linux.

Getting Documentation

Red Hat Linux is a powerful, full-featured operating system. Unless you're a Linux wizard, you're going to need additional documentation to make the most of your Red Hat Linux system. We strongly suggest reading over the Red Hat Linux Getting Started Guide to see what it can offer you in terms of both use and support. It has been written to guide you through using Red Hat Linux once the installation has been completed. Everyone should review the Red Hat Linux Getting Started Guide for more information on available Linux documentation as well as using Red Hat Linux 6.0 to its full potential. While many people will find the resources described in the Getting Started Guide to be very helpful, people who are just starting to use Linux will likely need additional information. The information that will be most helpful to you depends on your level of Linux expertise:

New To Linux — If this is your first time using Linux (or any Linux-like operating system, for that matter), you'll need solid introductory information on basic UNIX concepts. For example, O'Reilly and Associates (*http:// www.ora.com/*) produce a wide variety of Linux and UNIX-related books. Give their more general titles a try.

Some Linux Experience — If you've used other Linux distributions (or a Linux-like operating system), you'll probably find what you're looking for in some of the more in-depth reference material available. For example, O'Reilly's more specialized titles are valuable when you need a lot of information on a particular subject.

Old Timer — If you're a long-time Red Hat Linux user, you probably don't need us telling you what documentation to read. Thanks for reading this far!

The Red Hat Linux 6.0 Components

The Red Hat Linux 6.0 set that you are currently learning about contains the one volume manual that includes the *Red Hat Linux 6.0 Getting Started Guide* and the *Red Hat Linux 6.0 Installation Guide* as well as 2 CD-ROMs

Installation Guide

The Red Hat Linux Installation Guide is what you're currently reading. It contains the information necessary to install Red Hat Linux. In addition, it contains information about aspects of the operating system that are unique to Red Hat Linux.

Red Hat Linux Getting Started Guide

The Red Hat Linux Getting Started Guide contains information on what to do after the installation has taken place. It will be referred to on many occasions in this text. We believe it is both well written and informative, and will guide you through the necessary steps of actually using your system once the install is in place. The Red Hat Linux Getting Started Guide covers topics ranging from learning the basics of your system, to navigating your system, to Gnome.

CDs 1 and 2

These two Compact Discs contain the entire Red Hat Linux distribution, including source code. CD 1 contains all the binary packages built for your Intel computer. CD 2 contains the source packages that were used to build the binary packages on CD 1.

Boot Diskette

This diskette is used to start the installation process for Red Hat Linux/ Intel. Depending on your computer's configuration and the type of installation you select, you may or may not need the boot diskette. In addition, you may require a *support* diskette, again depending on your system's hardware configuration, and the installation method you choose. When we discuss the different installation methods later in this chapter, we'll explain which diskettes are needed for each type of installation, and give you instructions for producing any diskettes you require.

Checking for Updated Diskette Images

From time to time, we find that the installation may fail, and that a revised diskette image is required in order for the installation to work properly. In these cases, we make special images available via the Red Hat Linux Errata. Since this is a relatively rare occurrence, you will in general save time if you try to use the standard diskette images first, and then review the Errata only if you experience any problems completing the installation. There are two ways to review the Errata:

1 **World Wide Web** — By pointing your web browser at *http://www.redhat.com/errata*, you can read the Errata on-line, and download diskette images easily.

2 **Electronic Mail** — By sending an empty mail message to `errata@redhat.com`, you will receive a mail message containing the complete Errata. Also included

are URLs to each updated package and diskette image in the Errata. By using these URLs, you can then download any necessary diskette images. Remember to use binary mode when transferring a diskette image!

For now, concentrate only on the Errata entries that include new diskette images (the file names always end in .img). If you find an entry that seems to apply to your problem, get a copy of the diskette images, and create them using the instructions in Appendix A.

Things You Should Know

In order to prevent any surprises during the installation, you should collect some information before attempting to install Red Hat Linux. You can find most of this information in the documentation that came with your system, or from the system's vendor or manufacturer. **Please Note:** The most recent list of hardware supported by Red Hat Linux can be found at Red Hat Software's World Wide Web site at *http://www.redhat.com/hardware*. It's a good idea to check your hardware against this list before proceeding.

Basic Hardware Configuration

You should have a basic understanding of the hardware installed in your computer, including:

- **hard drive(s)** — Specifically, the number, size, and type. If you have more than one, it's helpful to know which one is first, second, and so on. It is also good to know if your drives are IDE or SCSI. If you have IDE drives, you should check your computer's BIOS to see if you are accessing them in LBA mode. Please refer to your computer's documentation for the proper key sequence to access the BIOS. Note that your computer's BIOS may refer to LBA mode by other names, such as "large disk mode". Again, your computer's documentation should be consulted for clarification.

- **memory** — The amount of RAM installed in your computer.

- **CD-ROM** — Most importantly, the unit's interface type (IDE, SCSI, or other interface) and, for non-IDE, non-SCSI CD-ROMs, the make and model number. IDE CD-ROMs (also known as ATAPI) are the most common type in recently manufactured, PC-compatible computers.

- **SCSI adapter (if one is present)** — The adapter's make and model number.
- **network card (if one is present)** — The card's make and model number.
- **mouse** — The mouse's type (serial, PS/2, or bus mouse), protocol (Microsoft, Logitech, MouseMan, etc.), and number of buttons; also, for serial mice, the serial port it is connected to.

On many newer systems, the installation program is able to automatically identify most hardware. However, it's a good idea to collect this information anyway, just to be sure.

Learning About Your Hardware With Windows®

If your computer is already running Windows 9x, you can use the following procedure to get additional configuration information:

- With Windows running, click on the "My Computer" icon using the secondary (normally the right) mouse button. A pop-up menu should appear.
- Select "Properties." The "System Properties" window should appear (see Figure 2-1). Note the information listed under "Computer:" — in particular the amount of RAM listed.

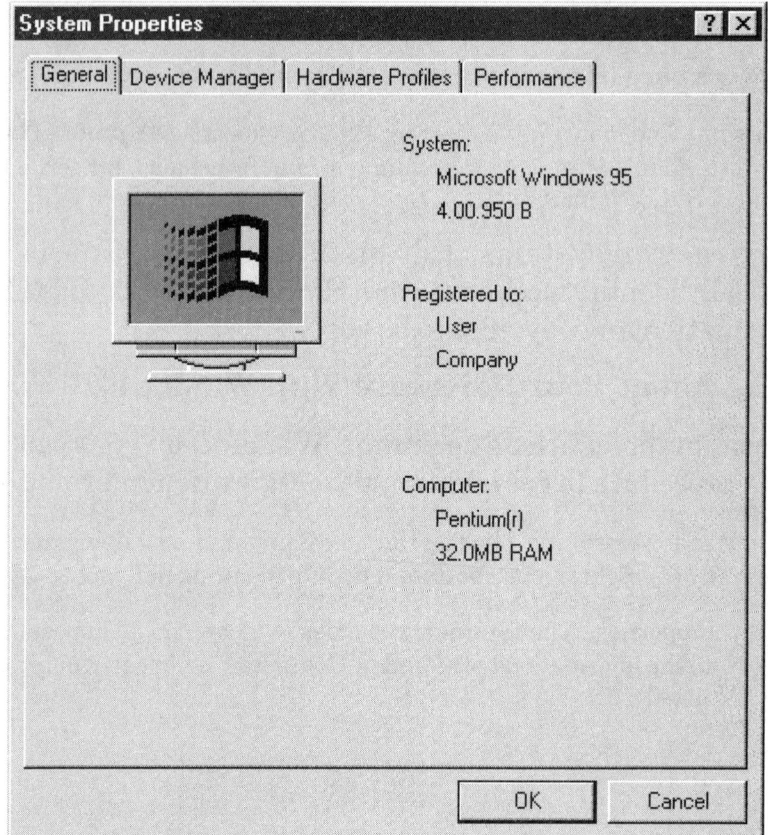

Figure 2-1: Windows System Properties Window

- Click on the "Device Manager" tab. You will then see a graphical representation of your computer's hardware configuration. Make sure the "View devices by type" button is selected.

At this point, you can either double-click on the icons (or single-click on the plus sign [+]) to look at each entry in more detail (see Figure 2-2). Look under the following icons for more information:

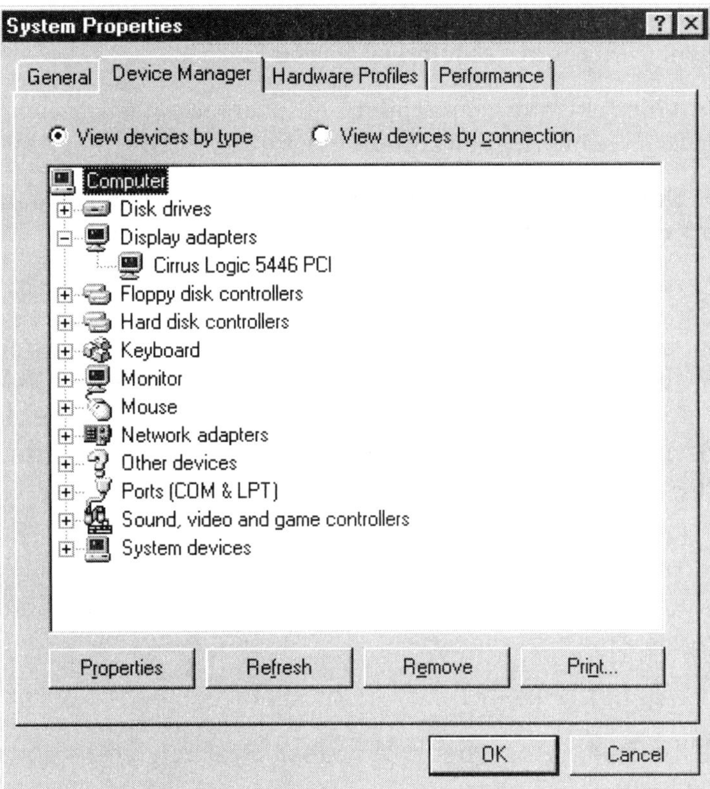

Figure 2-2: Device Manager Under Windows 95

- **Disk drives** – You will find the type (IDE or SCSI) of hard drive here. (IDE drives will normally include the word "IDE," while SCSI drives won't.)

- **Hard disk controllers** – You can get more information about your hard drive controller here.

- **CDROM** – Here is where you'll find out about any CD-ROM drives connected to your computer. **Please Note:** In some cases, there may be no CD-ROM icon, yet your computer has a functioning CD-ROM drive. This is normal, depending on how Windows was originally installed. In this case, you may be able to learn additional information by looking at the CD-ROM driver loaded in your computer's config.sys file.

- **Mouse** – The type of mouse present on your computer can be found here.

- **Display adapters** – If you're interested in running the X Window System, you should write down the information you find here.
- **Sound, video and game controllers** – If your computer has sound capabilities, you'll find more information about that here.
- **Network adapters** – Here you'll find additional info on your computer's network card (if you have one).
- **SCSI controllers** – If your computer uses SCSI peripherals, you'll find additional info on the SCSI controller here.

While this method is not a complete substitute for opening your computer's case and physically examining each component, in many cases it can provide sufficient information to continue with the installation.

> **Please Note:** This information can also be printed by clicking on the "Print..." button. A second window will appear, allowing you to choose the printer, as well as the type of report (the "All Devices and System Summary" report type is the most complete).

Video Configuration

If you will be installing the X Window System, you should also be familiar with the following:

- **your video card** – The card's make and model number (or the video chip set it uses), and the amount of video RAM it has. (Most PCI-based cards are auto-detected by the installation program.)
- **your monitor** – The unit's make and model number, along with allowable ranges for horizontal and vertical refresh rates.

Network-related Information

If you will be connected to a network, be sure you know your:

- **IP address** – Usually represented as a set of four numbers separated by dots, such as 10.0.2.15.
- **netmask** – Another set of four numbers separated by dots. An example netmask would be 255.255.248.0.

- **gateway IP address** — Yet another set of four dot-separated numbers. For instance, 10.0.2.254.
- **one or more name server IP addresses** — One or more sets of dot-separated numbers. 10.0.2.1 might be the address of a name server.
- **domain name** — The name given to your organization. For instance, Red Hat Software has a domain name of redhat.com.
- **hostname** — The name of your computer. A computer might be named pooh, for instance.

Please Note: The information given above is an example only! Do not use it when you install Red Hat Linux! If you don't know the proper values for your network, ask your network administrator.

Installation Methods

You can install or upgrade Red Hat Linux via any of several different methods. Each method works best in different situations, and has different requirements. But before we discuss each installation method, let's take a look at an issue that may affect some of you.

PCMCIA Support During the Installation

Most Intel-based laptop computers support PCMCIA (also known as PC Card). Computers that support PCMCIA devices contain a controller having one or more slots in which a PCMCIA device can be installed. These devices may be modems, LAN adapters, SCSI adapters, and so on. When installing Red Hat Linux/Intel on a PCMCIA-capable computer, it is important to note if a PCMCIA device will be used during installation. For example, if you want to install Red Hat Linux/Intel from a CD-ROM, and your CD-ROM drive is connected to a PCMCIA adapter, the installation program will require PCMCIA support. Likewise, if you are going to use one of the network-based installation methods, you will need PCMCIA support if your network adapter is PCMCIA-based.

Please Note: You don't need install-time PCMCIA support if you're installing Red Hat Linux on a laptop, and using the laptop's built-in CD-ROM drive. PCMCIA support is dependent on two things:

1 The type of PCMCIA controller in your computer system.

2 The type of PCMCIA device that you wish to use during the installation.

While nearly every PCMCIA controller and most popular PCMCIA devices are supported, there are some exceptions. For more information, please consult the Red Hat Linux Hardware Compatibility List at *http://www.redhat.com/hardware*. The main thing to keep in mind is that if you require install-time PCMCIA support, you will need a support diskette. We'll show you how to do this after you've determined which installation method is best for you.

Installing From a CD-ROM

If you have a Red Hat Linux CD-ROM, and your computer has a supported CD-ROM drive, you should consider this installation method. Installing directly from CD-ROM is the most straightforward approach. When installing from CD-ROM, the packages you select are read from the CD-ROM, and are installed on your hard drive.

How To Do It

As the name implies, you'll need a Red Hat Linux CD-ROM, a supported CD-ROM drive, and a means of starting the installation program. Intel systems will need to use the boot diskette (and the PCMCIA support diskette if a PCMCIA device is used during the install). There is an alternate method of installing from CD-ROM that uses no diskettes, but requires that the system be running DOS. We'll discuss this approach (known as `autoboot`) in **Booting the Installation Program**. For now, note that PCMCIA support is not available when using `autoboot`.

Please Note: The Red Hat Linux/Intel CD-ROM can also be booted by newer computers that support bootable CD-ROMs. Not all computers support this feature, so if yours can't boot from CD-ROM, you'll have to use a boot diskette (or autoboot from DOS) to get things started. Note that you may need to change BIOS settings in your computer to enable this feature.

If you've determined that this installation method is most applicable to your situation, please skip ahead to **Need a PCMCIA Support Diskette?**.

Installing From an FTP Site

If you don't have a Red Hat Linux CD-ROM or a CD-ROM drive, but you do have network access, then an FTP installation may be for you. When installing via FTP, the Red Hat Linux packages you select are downloaded (using FTP) across the network to your computer, and are installed on your hard drive.

How To Do It

When doing an FTP install, you'll need LAN-based access to a network; a dialup connection via modem won't cut it. If your Local Area Network has Internet access, you can use one of the many FTP sites that mirror Red Hat Linux. You can find a list of mirror sites at *http://www.redhat.com/mirrors.html*. If your LAN doesn't have Internet access, all is not lost. If there is a computer on your LAN that can accept anonymous FTP requests, simply put a copy of the Red Hat Linux distribution on that system, and you're ready to go. **Please Note**: Your FTP server must be able to handle long file names. For an FTP installation, you must use the network installation boot diskette specific to, and a PCMCIA support diskette if using a PCMCIA device during the installation. You will need to have a valid name server configured or you must specify the IP address of the FTP server you will be using. You will also need the path to the Red Hat Linux directory on the FTP server. If you've determined that this installation method is most applicable to your situation, please skip ahead to **Need a PCMCIA Support Disk?**.

Installing From an HTTP Site

If you don't have a Red Hat Linux CD-ROM or a CD-ROM drive, but you do have network access, then an HTTP installation may be for you. When installing via HTTP, the Red Hat Linux packages you select are downloaded (using HTTP) across the network to your computer, and are installed on your hard drive.

How To Do It

For an HTTP installation, you must use the network installation boot disk and if you are using a PCMCIA device during the installation, a PCMCIA support diskette. You will need to have a valid name server configured or you must specify the IP address of the HTTP server you will be using. You will also need the path to the Red Hat Linux directory on the HTTP server. If you've determined that this installation method is most applicable to your situation, please skip ahead to **Need a PCMCIA Support Diskette?**.

Installing From an NFS Server

If your system doesn't have a CD-ROM drive, but you do have network access, then an NFS installation may be for you. When installing via NFS, the Red Hat Linux packages you select are NFS-served to your computer from an NFS server system. The packages are then installed on your hard drive.

How To Do It

If you wish to perform an NFS installation, you will need to mount the Red Hat Linux CD-ROM on a machine that supports ISO-9660 file systems with Rock Ridge extensions. The machine must also support NFS. Export the CD-ROM file system via NFS. You will need to have a name server configured, or know the NFS server's IP address, as well as the path to the exported CD-ROM. **Please Note:** Your NFS server must be able to handle long file names. For an NFS installation, you'll need a boot diskette only. If you've determined that this installation method is most applicable to your situation, please skip ahead to **Need a PCMCIA Support Diskette?**.

Installing From a Hard Drive

If none of the other installation methods will work for you, but you have some means of getting the Red Hat Linux package files written to your system's hard drive, you can install from your hard drive. In this installation method, the Red Hat Linux packages you select are read from one partition on a hard drive, and are installed on another partition (or set of partitions).

How To Do It

The hard drive installation method requires a bit of up-front effort on your part, as you must copy all the necessary files to a partition before starting the Red Hat Linux installation program. You must first create a Red Hat directory at the top level of your directory tree. Everything you will install should be placed in that directory. First copy the base subdirectory and its contents. Next, copy the packages you want to install to another subdirectory called RPMS. You can use available space on an existing DOS partition or a Linux partition that is not required in the install procedure (for example, a partition that would be used for data storage on the installed system). If you are using a DOS file system, you will not be able to use the full Linux file names for the RPM packages. The installation process does not care what the file names look like, but it is a good idea that you keep track of them. You'll need a boot diskette, and if using a PCMCIA device during the installation, a PCMCIA support diskette, when installing from a hard drive.

Need a Network Boot Disk?

If you are performing an installation via FTP, HTTP, or NFS you will need to create your own network boot diskette. The network boot diskette image file is bootnet.img, and is located in the images directory on your Red Hat Linux/Intel CD. Please turn to Appendix B and follow the instructions there. Then, return here, and read on.

Need a PCMCIA Support Diskette?

Here's a checklist that you can use to see if you'll need to create a PCMCIA support diskette:

- Installing From a PCMCIA-Connected CD-ROM — If you'll be installing Red Hat Linux from a CD-ROM, and your CD-ROM drive is attached to your computer through a PCMCIA card, you'll need a support diskette.
- Installing using a PCMCIA Network Card — If you will be using a PCMCIA network adapter during the installation, you'll need a support diskette.

If you have determined you will need a support diskette, you will have to make one. The PCMCIA support diskette image file is pcmcia.img, and is located in the images directory on your Red Hat Linux/Intel CD. Please turn to Appendix B and follow the instructions there. Then, return here, and read on.

Installation Classes

Red Hat Linux includes defines three different classes, or types of installations. They are:

- Workstation
- Server
- Custom

These classes give you the option of simplifying the installation process (with some loss of configuration flexibility), or retaining complete flexibility with a slightly more complex installation process. Let's take a look at each class in more detail, so you can see which one is right for you. Only the custom-class install allows you complete flexibility. The workstation-class and server-class installs automatically goes through the installation process for you and omits certain steps.

The Workstation-Class Installation

A workstation-class installation is most appropriate for you if you're new to the world of Linux, and would like to give it a try. By answering very few installation questions, you can be up and running Red Hat Linux in no time!

What Does It Do?

A workstation-class installation removes any Linux-related partitions on all installed hard drives (and uses all free unpartitioned disk space) to create the following partitions:

- A 64MB swap partition.
- A 16MB partition (mounted as /boot) in which the Linux kernel and related files reside.
- A variable-sized (the exact size is dependent on available disk space) partition (mounted as /) in which all other files are stored.

This approach to disk partitioning results in the simplest file system configuration possible. **Please Note:** You will need approximately 600MB of free disk space in order to perform a workstation-class installation. If your system already runs Windows, a workstation-class installation will automatically configure your system to dual-boot using LILO. **Please Note:** A workstation-class installation will remove any existing Linux partition on any hard drive on your system. It will also attempt to set up a dual boot environment automatically on your system.

The Server-Class Installation

A server-class installation is most appropriate for you if you'd like your system to function as a Linux-based server, and you don't want to heavily customize your system configuration.

What Does It Do?

A server-class installation removes all existing partitions on all installed hard drives, so choose this installation class only if you're sure you have nothing you want saved! When the installation is complete, you'll find the following partitions:

- A 64MB swap partition.
- A 16MB partition (mounted as /boot) in which the Linux kernel and related files are kept.
- A 256MB partition (mounted as /).

- A partition of at least 512MB (mounted as /usr).
- A partition of at least 512MB (mounted as /home).
- A 256MB partition (mounted as /var).

This approach to disk partitioning results in a reasonably flexible file system configuration for most server-class tasks. **Please Note:** You will need approximately 1.6GB of free disk space in order to perform a server-class installation. **Please Note:** A server-class installation will remove any existing partitions of any type on all existing hard drives of your system. All drives will be erased of all information and existing operating systems, regardless if they are Linux partitions or not.

The Custom-Class Installation

As you might guess from the name, a custom-class installation puts the emphasis on flexibility. During a custom-class installation, it is up to you how disk space should be partitioned. You have complete control over the packages that will be installed on your system. You can also determine whether you'll use LILO to boot your system. For those of you with prior Red Hat Linux installation experience, you've already done a custom-class installation — it is the same installation procedure we've used in past versions of Red Hat Linux.

Disk Partitions

Nearly every modern-day operating system uses disk partitions, and Red Hat Linux is no exception. When installing Red Hat Linux, it will be necessary to work with disk partitions. If you have not worked with disk partitions before (or would like a quick review of the basic concepts) please read Appendix B before proceeding.

Please Note: If you intend to perform a workstation- or server-class installation, and you already have sufficient unpartitioned disk space, you do not need to read this section, and may turn to **A Note About Kernel Drivers**. Otherwise, please read this section in order to determine the best approach to freeing disk space for your Red Hat

Linux installation.

In order to install Red Hat Linux, you must make disk space available for it. This disk space needs to be separate from the disk space used by other operating systems you may have installed on your computer, such as Windows, OS/2, or even a different version of Linux. This is done by dedicating one or more partitions to Red Hat Linux.

Before you start the installation process, one of the following conditions must be met:

- Your computer must have enough unpartitioned disk space available to install Red Hat Linux.
- Your computer must have one or more partitions that may be deleted, thereby freeing up enough disk space to install Red Hat Linux.

Let's look at how this can be done.

Making Room For Red Hat Linux

There are three possible scenarios you may face when attempting to repartition your hard disk:

- Unpartitioned free space is available.
- An unused partition is available.
- Free space in an actively used partition is available.

Let's look at each scenario in order. **Please Note:** The figures in this section are based on those used in Appendix B, and represent the sequence of events necessary to free disk space for Red Hat Linux. If these figures do not make sense to you, you should read Appendix B before proceeding any further. Keep in mind that these illustrations are simplified in the interest of clarity, and do not reflect the exact partition layout that you will encounter when actually installing Red Hat Linux.

Using Unpartitioned Free Space

In this situation, the partitions already defined do not span the entire hard disk, leaving unallocated space that is not part of any defined partition. Figure 2-3 shows what this might look like.

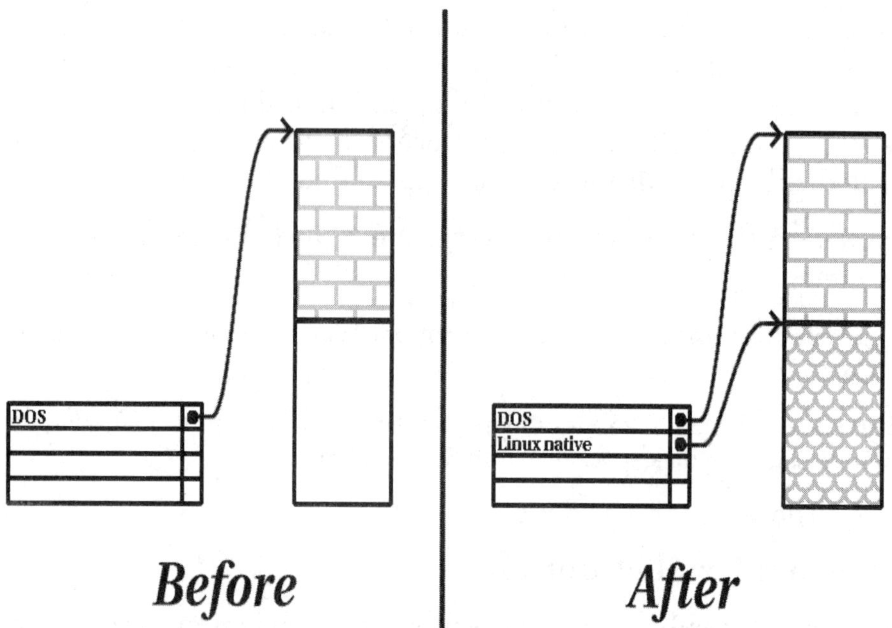

Figure 2-3: Disk Drive with Unpartitioned Free Space

If you think about it, an unused hard disk also falls into this category; the only difference is that all the space is not part of any defined partition.

In any case, you can simply create the necessary partitions from the unused space. Unfortunately, this scenario, although very simple, is not very likely (unless you've just purchased a new disk just for Red Hat Linux).

Let's move on to a slightly more common situation.

Using Space From An Unused Partition

In this case, maybe you have one or more partitions that you just don't use any longer. Perhaps you've dabbled with another operating system in the past, and the partition(s) you've dedicated to it never seem to be used anymore. Figure 2-4 illustrates such a situation.

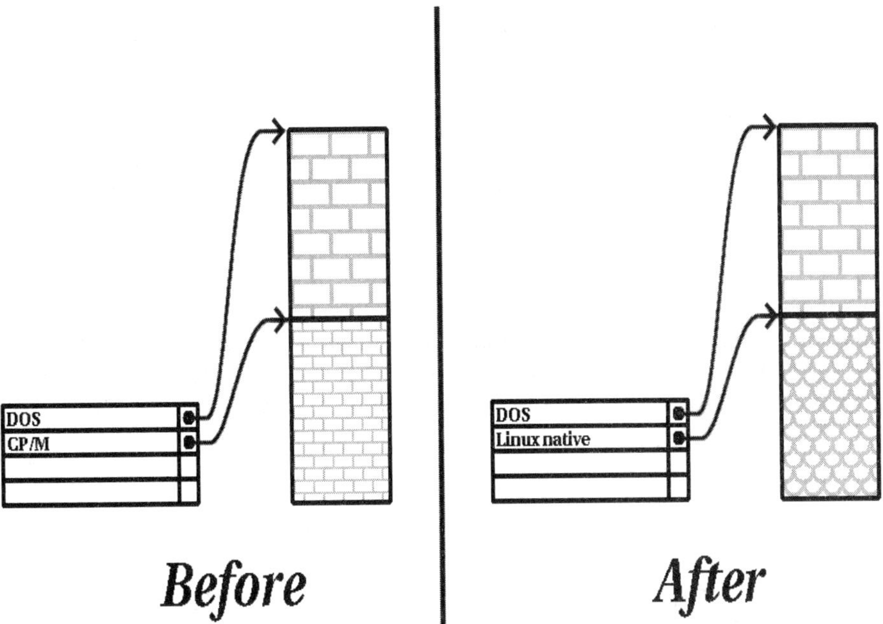

Figure 2-4: Disk Drive With an Unused Partition

If you find yourself in this situation, you can use the space allocated to the unused partition. You'll first need to delete the partition, and then create the appropriate Linux partition(s) in its place. You can either delete the partition using DOS fdisk, or you'll be given the opportunity to do so during a custom-class installation.

Using Free Space From An Active Partition

This is the most common situation. It is also, unfortunately, the hardest to work with. The main problem is that, even if you have enough free space, it's presently allocated to a partition that is in use. If you purchased a computer with pre-installed software, the hard disk most likely has one massive partition holding the operating system and data.

Aside from adding a new hard drive to your system, you have two choices:

Destructive Repartitioning — Basically, you delete the single large partition, and create several smaller ones. As you might imagine, any data you had in the original partition is destroyed. This means that making a complete backup is necessary. For your own sake, make two backups, use verification (if available in your backup software), and try to read data from your backup before you delete the partition. Note also that if there was an operating system of some type installed on that partition, it will need to be reinstalled as well. After creating a smaller partition for your existing software, you can reinstall any software, restore your data, and continue with your Red Hat Linux installation. Figure 2-5 shows this being done.

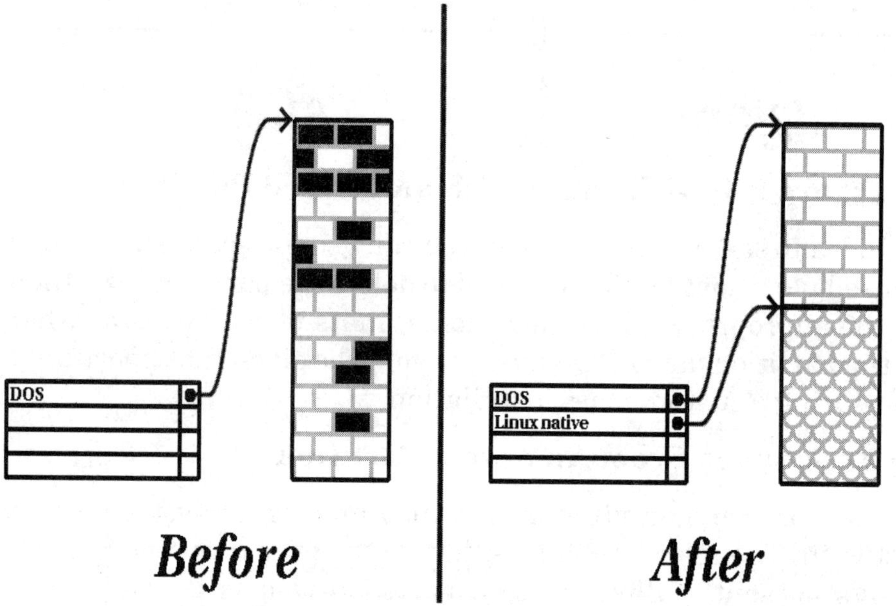

Figure 2-5: Disk Drive Being Destructively Repartitioned

Please Note: As Figure 2-5 shows, any data present in the original partition will be lost without proper backup!

Non-Destructive Repartitioning — Here, you run a program that does the seemingly impossible: it makes a big partition smaller without losing any of the files stored in that partition. Many people have found this method to be reliable and trouble-free. What software should you use to perform this feat? There are several disk management software products on the market; you'll have to do some research to find the one that is best for your situation.

While the process of non-destructive repartitioning is rather straightforward, there are a number of steps involved:

- Compress existing data
- Resize partition
- Create new partition(s)

Let's take a look at each step in a bit more detail.

Compress existing data — As Figure 2-6 shows, the first step is to compress the data in your existing partition. The reason for doing this is to rearrange the data such that it maximizes the available free space at the "end" of the partition.

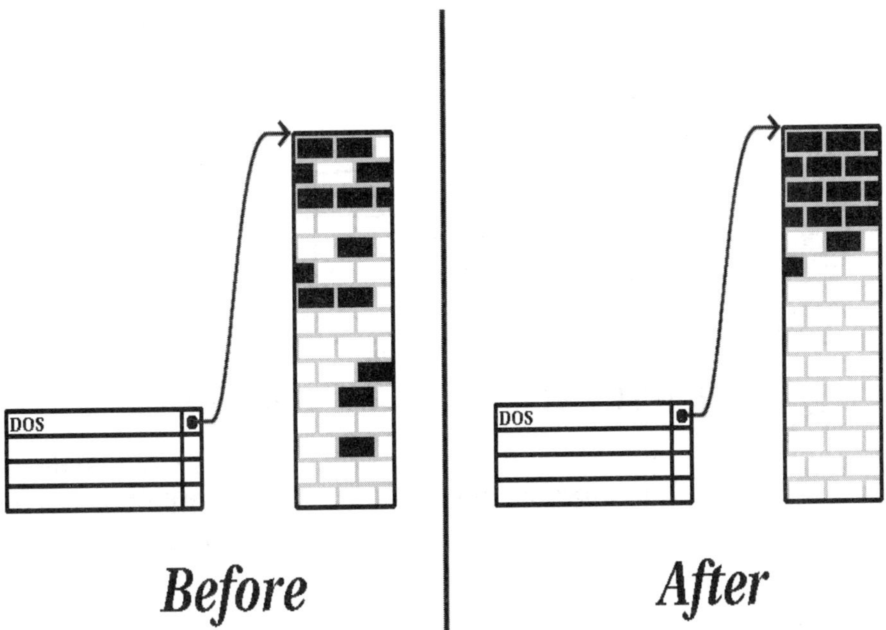

Figure 2-6: Disk Drive Being Compressed

This step is crucial; without it, it is possible that the location of your data could prevent the partition from being resized to the extent desired. Note also that, for one reason or another, some data cannot be moved. If this is the case (and it restricts the size of your new partition(s)), you may be forced to destructively repartition your disk.

Resize partition – Figure 2-7 shows the actual resizing process. While the actual end-product of the resizing operation varies depending on the software used, in most cases the newly freed space is used to create an unformatted partition of the same type as the original partition.

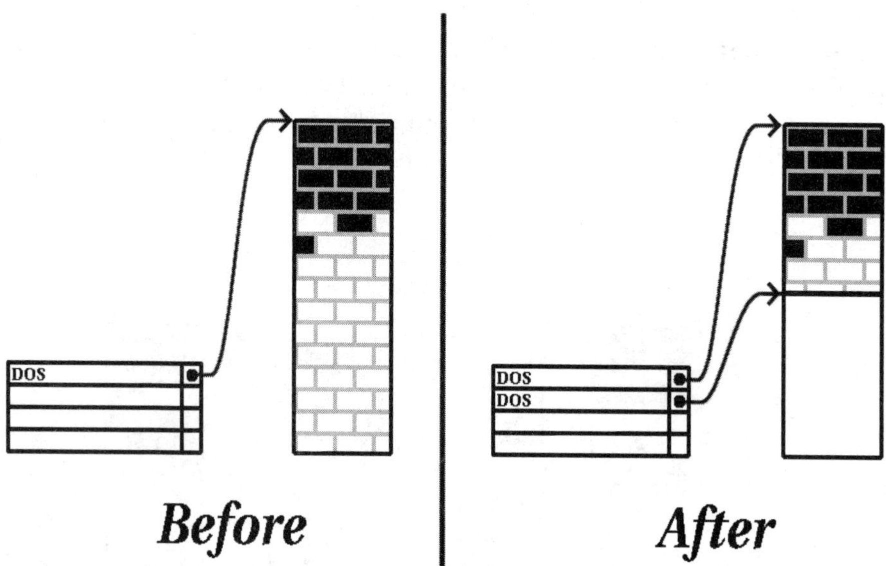

Figure 2-7: Disk Drive with Partition Resized

It's important to understand what the resizing software you use does with the newly freed space, so that you can take the appropriate steps. In the case we've illustrated, it would be best to simply delete the new

DOS partition, and create the appropriate Linux partition(s).

Create new partition(s) – As the previous step implied, it may or may not be necessary to create new partitions. However, unless your resizing software is Linux-aware, it is likely you'll need to delete the partition that was created during the resizing process. Figure 2-8 shows this being done.

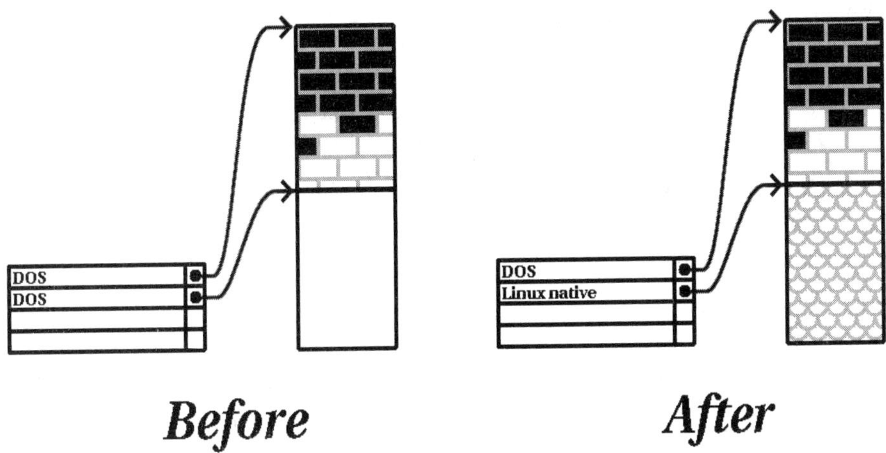

Figure 2-8: Disk Drive with Final Partition Configuration

As a convenience to our customers, we provide the fips utility. This is a freely available program that can resize FAT (File Allocation Table) partitions. It's included on the Red Hat Linux/Intel CD-ROM in the dosutils directory. **Please Note:** Many people have successfully used fips to repartition their hard drives. However, because of the nature of the operations carried out by fips, and the wide variety of hardware and software configurations under which it must run, Red Hat Software cannot guarantee that fips will work properly on your system. Therefore, no installation support whatsoever is available for fips; use it at your own risk.

That said, if you decide to repartition your hard drive with fips, it is vital that you do two things:

- **Perform a Backup** — Make two copies of all the important data on your computer. These copies should be to removable media (such as tape or diskettes), and you should make sure they are readable before proceeding.
- **Read the Documentation** — Completely read the fips documentation, located in the /dosutils/fipsdocs subdirectory on Red Hat Linux/Intel CD 1.

Should you decide to use fips, be aware that after fips runs you will be left with two partitions: the one you resized, and the one fips created out of the newly freed space. If your goal is to use that space to install Red Hat Linux, you should delete the newly created partition, either by using fdisk under your current operating system, or while setting up partitions during a custom-class installation.

Partition Naming Scheme

Linux refers to disk partitions using a combination of letters and numbers which may be confusing, particularly if you're used to the "C drive" way of referring to hard disks and their partitions. In the DOS/ Windows world, here is how partitions are named:

- Each partition's type is checked to determine if it can be read by DOS/Windows.
- If the partition's type is compatible, it is assigned a "drive letter." The drive letters start with "C".
- The drive letter can then be used to refer to that partition as well as the file system contained on that partition.

Red Hat Linux uses a naming scheme that is more flexible and conveys more information than the approach used by other operating systems. The naming scheme is file-based, with file names in the form:

```
/dev/xxyN
```

Here's how to decipher the partition naming scheme:

/dev/ — This string is the name of the directory in which all device files reside. Since partitions reside on hard disks, and hard disks are devices, the files representing all possible partitions reside in /dev/.

xx — The first two letters of the partition name indicate the type of device on which the partition resides. You'll normally see either hd (for IDE disks), or sd (for SCSI disks).

y — This letter indicates which device the partition is on. For example, /dev/hda (the first IDE hard disk) or /dev/sdb (the second SCSI disk).

N — The final number denotes the partition. The first four (primary or extended) partitions are numbered 1 through 4. Logical partitions start at 5. E.g., `/dev/hda3` is the third primary or extended partition on the first IDE hard disk; `/dev/sdb6` is the second logical partition on the second SCSI hard disk.

Please Note: There is no part of this naming convention that is based on partition type; unlike DOS/Windows, all partitions can be identified under Red Hat Linux. Of course, this doesn't mean that Red Hat Linux can access data on every type of partition, but in many cases it is possible to access data on a partition dedicated to another operating system. Keep this information in mind; it will make things easier to understand when you're setting up the partitions Red Hat Linux requires.

Disk Partitions and Other Operating Systems

If your Red Hat Linux partitions will be sharing a hard disk with partitions used by other operating systems, most of the time you'll have no problems. However, there are certain combinations of Linux and other operating systems that require extra care. Information on creating disk partitions compatible with other operating systems is available in several HOWTOs and Mini-HOWTOs, available on the Red Hat Linux CD in the `doc/HOWTO` and `doc/HOWTO/mini` directories. In particular, the Mini-HOWTOs whose names start with Linux+ are quite helpful. If Red Hat Linux/Intel will coexist on your machine with OS/2, you must create your disk partitions with the OS/2 partitioning software—otherwise, OS/2 may not recognize the disk partitions. During the installation, do not create any new partitions, but do set the proper partition types for your Linux partitions using the Linux fdisk.

Disk Partitions and Mount Points

One area that many people new to Linux find confusing is the matter of how partitions are used and accessed by the Linux operating system. In DOS/Windows, it is relatively simple: If you have more than one partition, each partition gets a "drive letter." You then use the drive letter to refer to files and directories on a given partition. This is entirely different from how Red Hat Linux deals with partitions and, for that matter, with disk storage in general. The main difference is that each partition is used to form part of the storage necessary to support a single set of files and directories. This is done by associating a partition with a directory through a process known as mounting. Mounting a partition makes its storage available starting at the specified directory (known as a mount point). For example, if partition /dev/hda5 were mounted on `/usr`, that would mean that all files and directories under /usr would physically reside on `/dev/hda5`. So the file `/usr/doc/FAQ/txt/Linux-FAQ` would be stored on /dev/hda5, while the file `/etc/X11/gdm/Sessions/Gnome` would not. Continuing our example, it is also possible that one or more directories below `/usr` would be mount points for other partitions. For instance, a partition (say, `/dev/hda7`) could be mounted on `/usr/local`, meaning that, for example, `/usr/local/man/whatis` would then reside on `/dev/hda7` rather than `/dev/hda5`.

How Many Partitions?

At this point in the process of preparing to install Red Hat Linux, you will need to give some consideration to the number and size of the partitions to be used by your new operating system. The question of "how many partitions" continues to spark debate within the Linux community and, without any end to the debate in sight, it's safe to say that there are probably as many partition layouts as there are people debating the issue. Keeping this in mind, we recommend that, unless you have a reason for doing otherwise, you should create the following partitions:

- **A swap partition** — Swap partitions are used to support virtual memory. If your computer has 16 MB of RAM or less, you must create a swap partition. Even if you have more memory, a swap partition is still recommended. The minimum size of your swap partition should be equal to your computer's RAM, or 16 MB (whichever is larger). The largest useable swap partition is roughly 127 MB, so making a swap partition larger than that will result in wasted space. Note, however, that you can create and use more than one swap partition if your system requires more than 127MB of swap. The following partition is specific to Red Hat Linux/Intel installations.

- **A /boot partition** — The partition mounted on /boot contains the operating system kernel, along with a few other files used during the bootstrap process. Due to the limitations of most PC BIOSes, creating a small partition to hold these files is a good idea. This partition should be no larger than 16MB. **Please Note:** Make sure you read **Disk Partitions and Other Operating Systems** — the information there applies to the /boot partition!

- **A root partition** — The root partition is where / (the root directory) resides. In this partitioning layout, all files (except those stored in /boot) reside on the root partition. Because of this, it's in your best interest to maximize the size of your root partition. A 500MB root partition will permit the equivalent of a workstation-class installation (with very little free space), while a 1GB root partition will let you install every package.

One Last Wrinkle: Using LILO

LILO (the LInux LOader) is the most commonly used method to boot Red Hat Linux on Intel-based systems. An operating system loader, LILO operates "outside" of any operating system, using only the Basic I/O System (or BIOS) built into the computer hardware itself. This section describes LILO's interactions with PC BIOSes, and is specific to Intel-compatible computers.

BIOS-Related Limitations Impacting LILO

LILO is subject to some limitations imposed by the BIOS in most Intel-based computers. Specifically, most BIOSes can't access more than two hard drives and they can't access any data stored beyond cylinder 1023 of any drive. Note that some recent BIOSes do not have these limitations, but this is by no means universal. All the data LILO needs to access at boot time (including the Linux kernel) are located in the `/boot` directory. If you follow the partition layout recommended above, or you are performing a workstation- or server-class install, the `/boot` directory will be in a small, separate partition. Otherwise, it will reside in the root partition. In either case, the partition in which /boot resides must conform to the following guidelines if you are going to use LILO to boot your Red Hat Linux system:

On First Two IDE Drives — If you have 2 IDE (or EIDE) drives, /boot must be located on one of them. Note that this two-drive limit also includes any IDE CD-ROM drives on your primary IDE controller. So, if you have one IDE hard drive, and one IDE CD-ROM on your primary controller, /boot must be located on the first hard drive only, even if you have other hard drives on your secondary IDE controller.

> **On First IDE or First SCSI Drive** — If you have one IDE (or EIDE) drive and one or more SCSI drives, /boot must be located either on the IDE drive or the SCSI drive at ID 0. No other SCSI IDs will work.
>
> **On First Two SCSI Drives** — If you have only SCSI hard drives, /boot must be located on a drive at ID 0 or ID 1. No other SCSI IDs will work.
>
> **Partition Completely Below Cylinder 1023** — No matter which of the above configurations apply, the partition that holds /boot must be located entirely below cylinder 1023. If the partition holding /boot straddles cylinder 1023, you may face a situation where LILO will work initially (because all the necessary information is below cylinder 1023), but will fail if a new kernel is to be loaded, and that kernel resides above cylinder 1023.

As mentioned earlier, it is possible that some of the newer BIOSes may permit LILO to work with configurations that don't meet our guidelines. Likewise, some of LILO's more esoteric features may be used to get a Linux system started, even if the configuration doesn't meet our guidelines. However, due to the number of variables involved, Red Hat Software cannot support such extraordinary efforts. **Please Note:** Disk Druid as well as the workstation- and server-class installs take these BIOS-related limitations into account. However, if you decide to use fdisk instead, it is your responsibility to ensure that you keep these limitations in mind.

A Note About Kernel Drivers

During installation of Red Hat Linux, there are some limits placed on the file systems and other drivers supported by the kernel. However, after installation there is support for all file systems available under Linux. At install time the modularized kernel has support for (E)IDE devices, (including ATAPI CD-ROM drives), SCSI adapters, and network cards. Additionally, all mice, SLIP, CSLIP, PPP, PLIP, FPU emulation, console selection, ELF, SysV IPC, IP forwarding, firewalling and accounting, reverse ARP, QIC tape and parallel printers, are supported.

Please Note: Because Red Hat Linux supports installation on many different types of hardware, many drivers (including those for SCSI adapters, network cards, and many CD-ROMs) are not built into the Linux kernel used during installation; rather, they are available as modules and loaded as you need them during the installation process. If necessary, you will have the chance to specify options for these modules at the time they are loaded, and in fact these drivers will ignore any options you specify for them at the boot: prompt.

After the installation is complete you may want to rebuild a kernel that includes support for your specific hardware configuration. See **Building a Custom Kernel** for information on building a customized kernel. Note that, in most cases, a custom-built kernel is not necessary.

If You Have Problems...

If you have problems before, during, or after the installation, check the list of Red Hat Linux Frequently Asked Questions. You can find the FAQ at: http://www.redhat.com/knowledgebase/index.html In many cases, a quick check of the FAQ can quickly get you back in action.

One Last Note

Please read all of the installation instructions before starting; this will prepare you for any decisions you need to make and should eliminate potential surprises.

3 Starting the Installation

This chapter explains how to start the Red Hat Linux 6.0 installation process. We'll cover the following areas in this chapter:

- Getting familiar with the installation program's user interface;
- Starting the installation program;
- Selecting an installation method.

By the end of this chapter, the installation program will be running on your system, and the appropriate installation method will have been selected.

The Installation Program User Interface

The Red Hat Linux installation program uses a screen-based interface that includes most of the on-screen "widgets" commonly found on graphical user interfaces. They may look a little different than their more graphical counterparts; Figures 3-1 and 3-2 are included here to make them easier to identify. Here's a list of the most important widgets:

- **Window** — Windows (also referred to as dialog boxes in this manual) will appear on your screen throughout the installation process. At times, one window may overlay another; in these cases, you may only interact with the window on top. When finished with that window, it will disappear, allowing you to continue with the window that was underneath.
- **Text Input** — Text input lines are regions where you can enter information required by the installation program. When the cursor rests on a text input line, you may enter and/or edit information on that line.
- **Check Box** — Check boxes allow you to select or deselect a particular feature offered to you by the installation program. When the cursor rests within a check box, pressing [Space] causes the check box to toggle between a selected and unselected state.

- **Text Widget** – Text widgets are regions of the screen that are devoted to the display of text. At times, text widgets may also contain other widgets, such as check boxes. It is possible that a text widget may contain more information than could be displayed at one time. In these cases, the text widget will have a scroll bar next to it; if you position the cursor within the text widget, you can then use the [\uparrow] and [\downarrow] keys to scroll through all the information available.

- **Scroll Bar** – Scroll bars provide a visual indication of your relative position in the information being displayed in a text widget. Your current position is shown by a # character, which will move up and down the scroll bar as you scroll back and forth.

- **Button Widget** – Button widgets are the primary method of interacting with the installation program. By "pressing" these buttons, you will progress through the series of windows that make up the installation process. Buttons may be pressed when they are highlighted by the cursor.

- **Cursor** – Although not a widget, the cursor is used to select (and interact with) a particular widget. As the cursor is moved from widget to widget, it may cause the widget to change color, or you may only see the cursor itself positioned in or next to the widget. In Figure 3-1, the cursor is positioned on the Ok button. Figure 3-2 shows the cursor on the first line of the text widget at the top of the window.

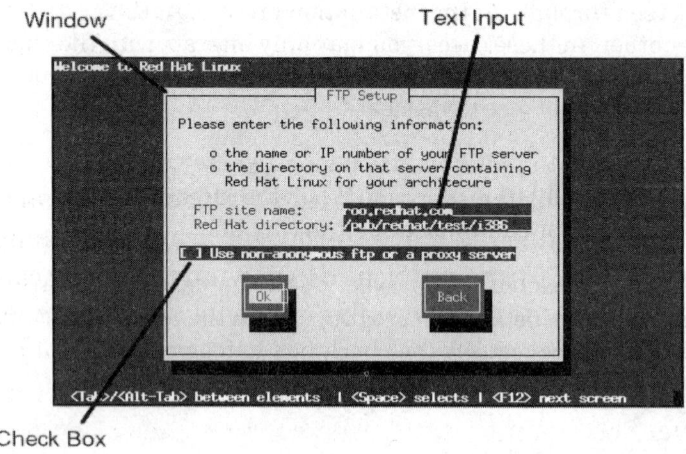

Figure 3-1: Installation Program Widgets

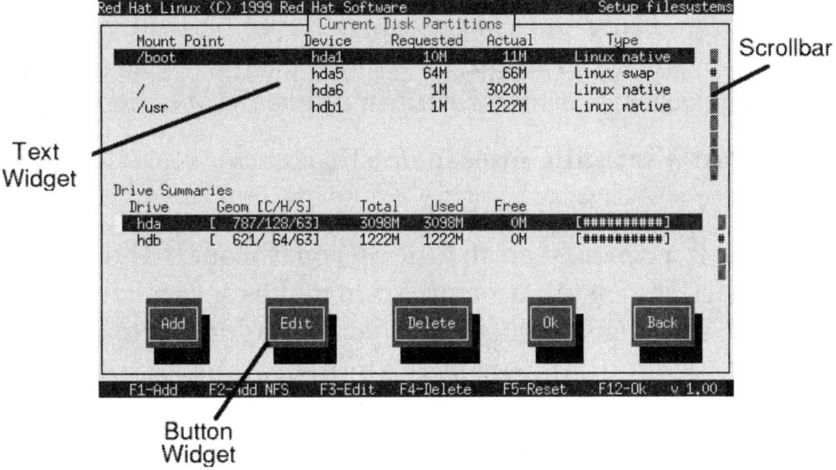

Figure 3-2: More Installation Program Widgets

As you might have guessed by our description of these widgets, the installation program is character-based, and does not use a mouse. This is due to the fact that the installation program must run on a wide variety of computers, some of which may not even have a mouse. The following section describes the keystrokes necessary to interact with the installation program.

Using the Keyboard to Navigate

You can navigate around the installation dialogs using a simple set of keystrokes. You will need to move the cursor around by using various keys such as [<-], [->], [\uparrow], and [\downarrow]. You can also use [Tab], and [Alt]-[Tab] to cycle forward or backward through each widget on the screen. In most cases, there is a summary of available function keys presented at the bottom of each screen. To "press" a button, position the cursor over the button (using [Tab], for instance) and press [Space] (or [Enter]). To select an item from a list of items, move the cursor to the item you wish to select and press [Enter]. To select an item with a check box, move the cursor to the check box and press [Space] to select an item. To deselect, press [Space] a second time. Pressing [F12] accepts the current values and proceeds to the next dialog; it is usually equivalent to pressing the **Ok** button. **Please Note:** Unless a dialog box is waiting for your input, do not press any keys during the installation process — it may result in unpredictable behavior.

A Note about Virtual Consoles

There is more to the Red Hat Linux installation program than the dialog boxes it presents as it guides you through the installation process. In fact, the installation program makes several different kinds of diagnostic messages available to you, in addition to giving you a way to enter commands from a shell prompt. It presents this information on five virtual consoles which you can switch between using a single keystroke. These virtual consoles can be very helpful if you encounter a problem while installing Red Hat Linux. Messages displayed on the install or system consoles can help pinpoint the problem. Please see Figure 3-3 for a listing of the virtual consoles, the keystrokes to switch to them, and their contents.

Console	Keystroke	Contents
1	[Alt]-[F1]	installation dialog
2	[Alt]-[F2]	shell prompt
3	[Alt]-[F3]	install log (messages from install program)
4	[Alt]-[F4]	system log (messages from kernel, etc.)
5	[Alt]-[F5]	other messages

Figure 3-3: Virtual Console Information

In general, there should be no reason to leave virtual console #1 unless you are attempting to diagnose installation problems. But if you are the curious type, feel free to look around.

Starting the Installation Program

Now it's time to start installing Red Hat Linux. To start the installation, it is first necessary to boot the installation program. Before we start, please make sure you have all the resources you'll need for the installation. If you've already read through Chapter 2, and followed the instructions, you should be ready.

Booting the Installation Program

To start installing Red Hat Linux, insert the boot diskette into your computer's first diskette drive and reboot (or boot from the Red Hat Linux CD-ROM, if your computer supports it). Your BIOS settings may need to be changed to allow you to boot from the diskette or CD-ROM. After a short delay, a screen containing the boot: prompt should appear. The screen contains information on a variety of boot options. Each boot option also has one or more help screens associated with it. To access a given help screen, press the appropriate function key as listed in the line at the bottom of the screen. You should keep two things in mind:

- The initial screen will automatically start the installation program if you take no action within the first minute. To disable this feature, press one of the help screen function keys.
- If you press a help screen function key, there will be a slight delay as the help screen is read from diskette.

Normally, you'll only need to press [Enter] to boot. Watch the boot messages to see whether the Linux kernel detects your hardware. If it does not properly detect your hardware, you may need to restart the installation in "expert" mode. Expert mode disables most hardware probing, and gives you the option of entering options for the drivers loaded during the installation. Expert mode can be entered using the following boot command:

```
boot: expert
```

Please Note: The initial boot messages will not contain any references to SCSI or network cards. These devices are supported by modules that are loaded during the installation process. Options can also be passed to the kernel.

For example, to instruct the kernel to use all the RAM in a 128 MB system, enter:

```
boot: linux mem=128M
```

However, with most computers, there is no need to pass this argument to the kernel. The kernel will detect the amount of memory your system has in most cases. To be sure that all of your memory has been detected, at a shell prompt type:

```
cat /proc/meminfo
```

This will display the amount of memory detected by the kernel in the form of total, used, free, etc. If MemTotal is not correct for your system, you will need to modify your lilo.conf to pass that amount of memory to the kernel at boot time. Such as, if your computer has 96 megabytes of RAM, you will add:

```
append="mem=96M"
```

After entering any options, press [Enter] to boot using those options. If you do need to specify boot options to identify your hardware, please make note of them — they will be needed later.

Installing Without Using a Boot Diskette The Red Hat Linux/ Intel CD-ROM can also be booted by newer computers that support bootable CD-ROMs. Not all computers support this feature, so if yours can't boot from the CD-ROM, there is one other way to start the installation without using a boot diskette. The following method is specific to Intel-based computers only. If you have MS-DOS installed on your computer, you can boot the installation system directly from the CD without using any diskettes. To do this (assuming your CD is drive d:), use the following commands:

```
C:\> d
D:\> cd \dosutils
D:\dosutils> autoboot.bat
```

Note that this method will not work if run in a DOS window — the `autoboot.bat` file must be executed with DOS as the only operating system. In other words, Windows cannot be running. If your computer can't boot directly from CD-ROM (and you can't use a DOS-based `autoboot`), you'll have to use a boot diskette to get things started.

Beginning the Installation

After booting, the installation program begins by displaying a welcome message. Press [Enter] to begin the installation. If you wish to abort the installation process at this time, simply eject the boot diskette now and reboot your machine.

Choosing a Language

After the welcome dialog, the installation program asks you to select the language to be used during the installation process (see Figure 3-4). Using the [\uparrow] and [\downarrow] keys, select the appropriate language. A scroll bar may appear to the right of the languages — if present, it indicates that there are more entries than can be displayed at one time. You'll be seeing scroll bars like this throughout the installation program.

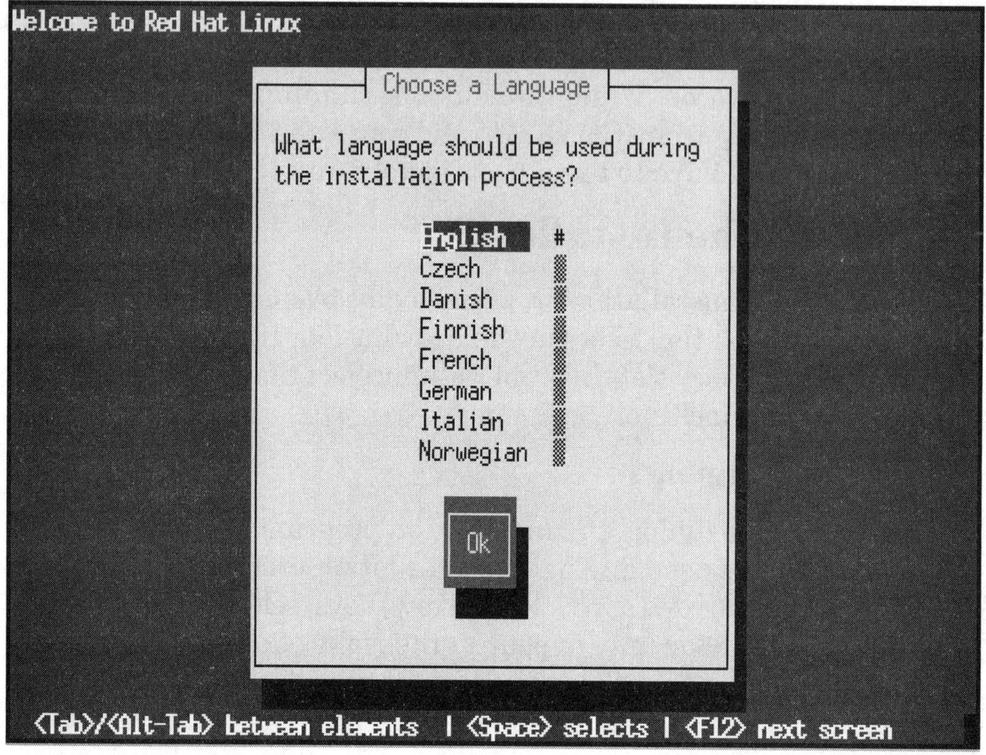

Figure 3-4: Selecting a Language

Selecting a Keyboard Type

Next, the installation program gives you an opportunity to select a keyboard type (see Figure 3-5). You may navigate this dialog box the same way you did with the language selection dialog.

After selecting the appropriate keyboard type, press [Enter]; the keyboard type you select will be loaded automatically both for the remainder of the installation process and each time you boot your Red Hat Linux system.

If you wish to change your keyboard type after you have installed your Red Hat Linux system, you may use the `/usr/sbin/kbdconfig` command or you may type setup at the root prompt.

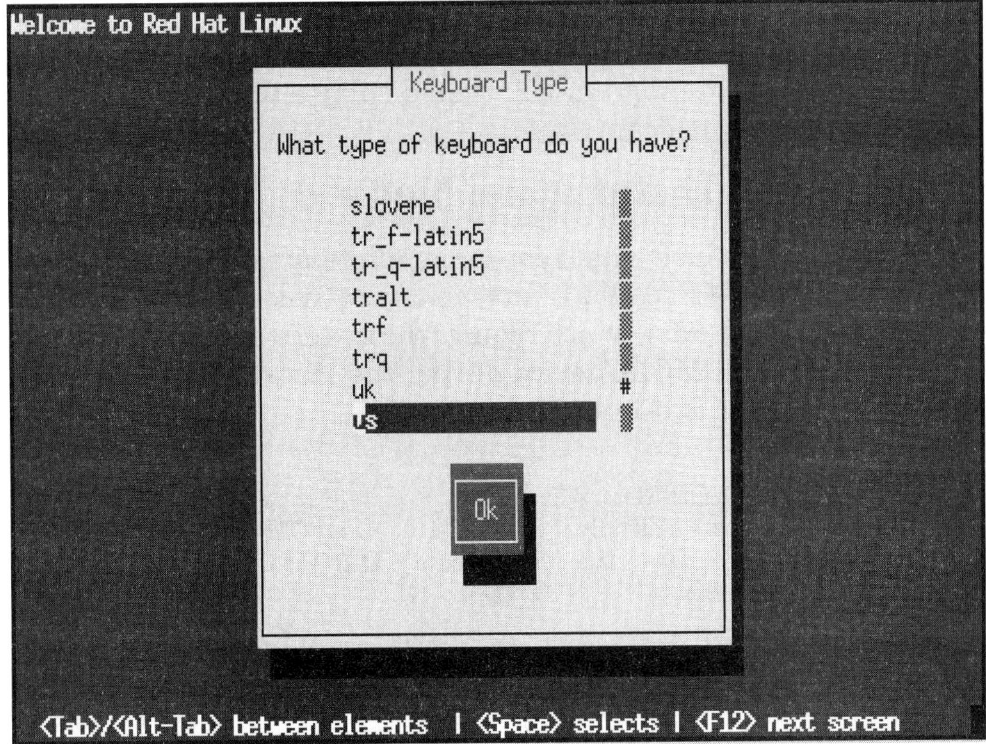

Figure 3-5: Selecting a Keyboard Type

PCMCIA Support

Next, the installation program will probe your system to determine if your system requires PCMCIA (also known as PC Card) support. If a PCMCIA controller is found, you'll be asked if you require PCMCIA support during the installation. If you will be using a PCMCIA device during the installation (for example, you have a PCMCIA ethernet card and you'll be installing via NFS, or you have a PCMCIA SCSI card and will be installing from a SCSI CD), you should select **Yes.** **Please Note:** This question applies only to PCMCIA support during the actual installation. Your installed Red Hat Linux system will still support PCMCIA, even if you say **No** here (assuming that you do not deselect the kernel-pcmcia-cs package during the subsequent installation). If you require PCMCIA support, you will then be asked to insert the PCMCIA support diskette. Select **Ok** when you've done so. The installation program will then display a progress bar as the support diskette is loaded.

Selecting an Installation Method

Next, you will be asked what type of installation method you wish to use. You can install Red Hat Linux via any of five basic methods (see **Installation Methods**), which require the use of a support diskette if you are using a PCMCIA device during the install. To summarize, you can install Red Hat Linux from:

CD-ROM

— If you have a CD-ROM drive and the Red Hat Linux CD-ROM. Requires a PCMCIA support disk only if you will be using a PCMCIA device during the install. Please refer to **Installing from CD-ROM** to select the CD-ROM installation method.

Hard Drive

— If you copied the Red Hat Linux files to a local hard drive. Requires a PCMCIA support disk only if you will be using a PCMCIA device during the install. Please refer to **Installing from a Hard Drive** to select the hard drive installation method.

NFS Image

— If you are installing from an NFS Image server which is exporting the Red Hat Linux CD-ROM or a mirror image of Red Hat Linux. Requires a PCMCIA support disk only if you will be using a PCMCIA device during the install. Requires a network boot disk. Please refer to **Installing via NFS** to select the NFS installation method.

FTP

— If you are installing directly from an FTP server. Requires a PCMCIA support disk only if you will be using a PCMCIA device during the install. Requires a network boot disk. Please refer to **Installing via FTP** to select the FTP installation method.

HTTP

— If you are installing directly from an HTTP Web server. Requires a PCMCIA support disk only if you will be using a PCMCIA device during the install. Requires a network boot disk. Please refer to **Installing via HTTP** to select the HTTP installation method.

If you choose to perform a CD-ROM or a hard drive install, please refer to Chapter 4 for those installation instructions.

If you choose to perform a network-based install (NFS, FTP, or HTTP), please refer to Chapter 5 for those installation instructions.

4 Local Media Installations

Selecting an Installation Method

Now you must decide what type of installation method you wish to use (see Figure 4-1). Highlight the appropriate choice and select **Ok**, or press [Enter].

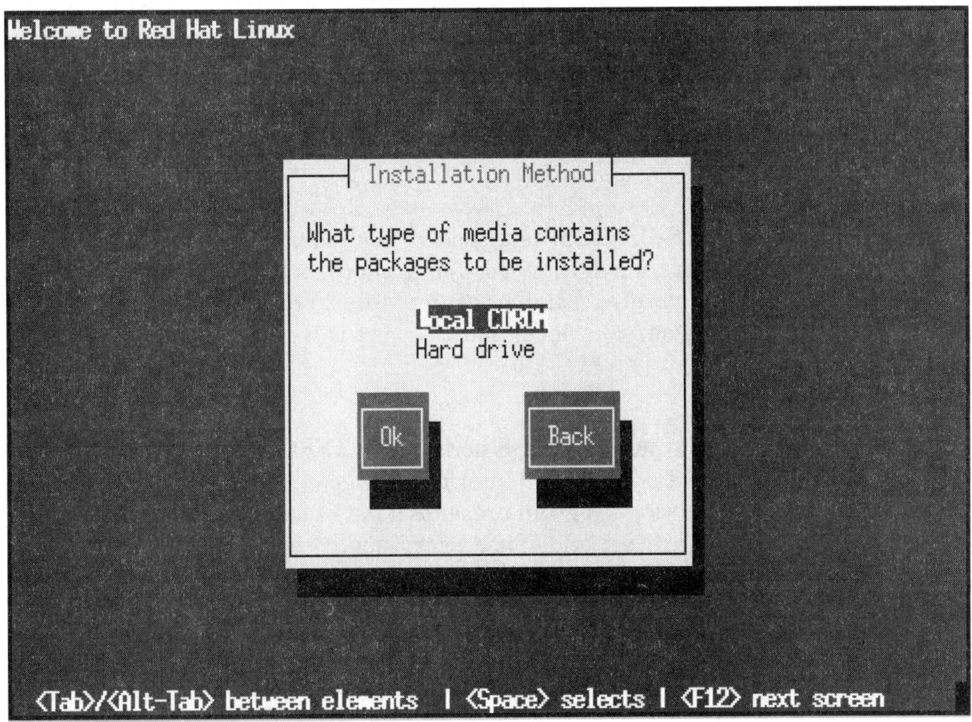

Figure 4-1: Selecting an Installation Method

If you are not performing a local media type installation (CD-ROM or hard drive), then please skip ahead to Chapter 5 for network type installations.

If you are planning to do a local media type installation, please read on.

Installing from CD-ROM

If you are going to install Red Hat Linux from CD-ROM, choose "CD-ROM," and select **Ok**. The installation program will then prompt you to insert your Red Hat Linux CD-ROM into your CD-ROM drive. When you've done so, select **Ok**, and press [Enter]. The installation program will then probe your system and attempt to identify your CD-ROM drive. It will start by looking for an IDE (also known as ATAPI) CD-ROM drive. If one is found, the installation will continue. If the installation program cannot automatically detect your CD-ROM drive, you will be asked what type of CD-ROM you have. You can choose from the following types:

SCSI

Select this if your CD-ROM is attached to a supported SCSI adapter; the installation program will then ask you to choose a SCSI driver. Choose the driver that most closely resembles your adapter. You may specify options for the driver if necessary; however, most drivers will detect your SCSI adapter automatically.

Other

If your CD-ROM is neither an IDE nor a SCSI CD-ROM, it's an "other." Sound cards with proprietary CD-ROM interfaces are good examples of this CD-ROM type. The installation program presents a list of drivers for supported CD-ROMs — choose a driver and, if necessary, specify any driver options.

Please Note: A partial list of optional parameters for CD-ROMs can be found in Appendix D. If you have an ATAPI CD-ROM and the installation program fails to find it (in other words, it asks you what type of CD-ROM you have), you must restart the installation, and enter linux hdX=cdrom. Replace the X with one of the following letters, depending on the interface the unit is connected to, and whether it is configured as master or slave:

- **a** — First IDE controller, master
- **b** — First IDE controller, slave
- **c** — Second IDE controller, master
- **d** — Second IDE controller, slave

(If you have a third and/or fourth controller, simply continue assigning letters in alphabetical order, going from controller to controller, and master to slave.) Once your CD-ROM drive has been identified, you will be asked to insert the Red Hat Linux CD-ROM into your CD-ROM drive. Select **Ok** when you have done so. After a short delay, the next dialog box will appear. Continue to **Upgrading or Installing** for upgrade or full-installation instructions.

Installing from a Hard Drive

If you are going to install Red Hat Linux from a locally-attached hard drive, highlight "hard drive" and select **Ok**. Before you started the installation program, you must first have copied all the necessary files to a partition on a locally-attached hard drive. If you haven't done this yet, please refer to **Installing from an HTTP site**. Continue to **Upgrading or Installing** for upgrade or full-installation instructions.

Upgrading or Installing

After you choose an installation method, the installation program prompts you to either install or upgrade (see Figure 4-2).

Figure 4-2: Upgrading or Installing

Installing

You usually install Red Hat Linux on a clean disk partition or set of partitions, or over another installation of Linux.

Please Note: Installing Red Hat Linux over another installation of Linux (including Red Hat Linux) does not preserve any information (files or data) from the prior installation. Make sure you save any important files! If you are worried about saving the current data on your existing system (without making a backup on your own), you should consider performing an upgrade instead.

If you wish to perform a full install, choose **Install**, and skip to **Installation Class**.

Upgrading

The installation process for Red Hat Linux 6.0 includes the ability to upgrade from prior versions of Red Hat Linux (version 2.0 and later) which are based on RPM technology. Upgrading your system installs the modular 2.2.x kernel as well as updated versions of the packages which are currently installed on your machine. The upgrade process preserves existing configuration files by renaming them using a .rpmsave extension (e.g., sendmail.cf.rpmsave) and leaves a log telling what actions it took in /tmp/upgrade.log. As software evolves, configuration file formats can change, so you should carefully compare your original configuration files to the new files before integrating your changes. If you wish to upgrade your Red Hat Linux system, choose **Upgrade**.

> **Please Note:** Some upgraded packages may require that other packages are also installed for proper operation. The upgrade procedure takes care of these dependencies, but it may need to install additional packages which are not on your existing system.

> **Please Note:** If you already have the X Window System (and possibly an older version of GNOME) on your machine you may see a screen that prompts you to install the latest version of GNOME included in this release.

Installation Class

If you chose to perform a full install, the installation program will ask you to choose an installation class (see Figure 4-3). You will not see this screen if you chose to perform an upgrade. You may choose from the following installation classes:

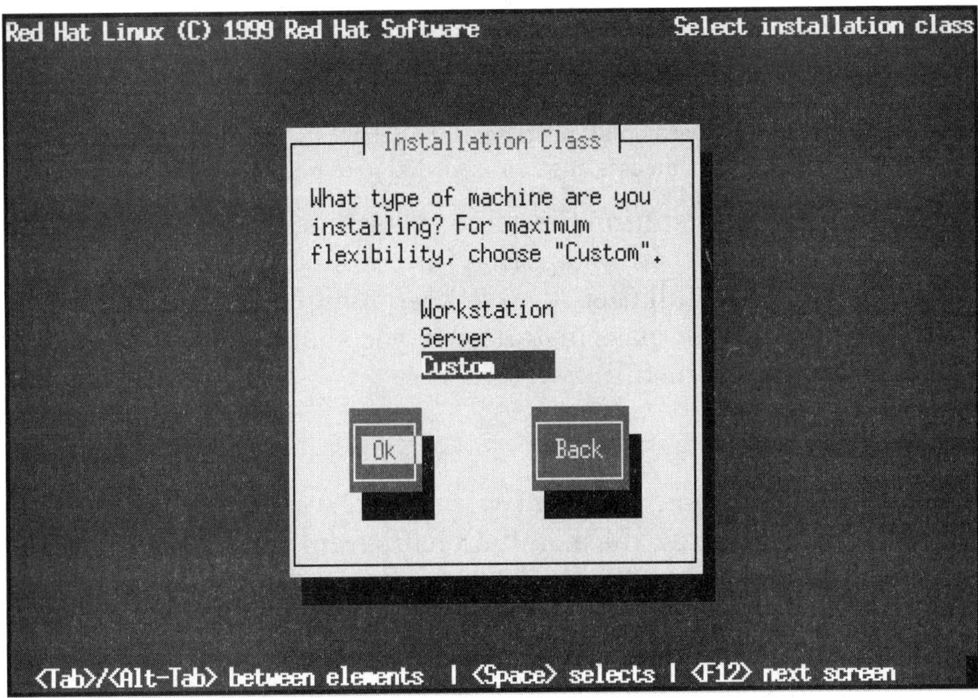

Figure 4-3: Installation Class

- **Workstation** — A workstation-class installation will automatically erase all Linux partitions from your computer's hard drive(s). This installation type will also attempt to set up a dual boot environment automatically.
- **Server** — A server-class installation will automatically erase all partitions (Linux or others) from your computer's hard drive(s).
- **Custom** — A custom-class installation gives you complete control over partitioning-related issues. If you have installed Red Hat Linux in the past, the custom-class installation is most similar to past installations.

Please Note: If you choose either Workstation or Server, part (or all) of your computer's stored data on all drives will be erased! You will be asked to confirm your decision; however, please keep in mind that once the installation program receives your confirmation, the erasure is irrevocable.

Please Note: WARNING — If you choose to perform a workstation-class or server-class installation, data erasure will be irrevocable. The severity of erased data varies according to type of installation:

- **Workstation-class** — Data on any existing Linux partition on any hard drive on your system will be erased
- **Server-class** — Data on all partitions of all drives will be completely erased, regardless if it is on an existing Linux partition or not.

If you choose a workstation- or server-class installation, you will be able to skip over some of the steps that the custom-class install requires. For a hard drive installation, please keep reading. For the CD-ROM workstation- or server-class installation, you should turn to Chapter 6 to continue with the install..

SCSI Support

Next, the installation program will probe your system for SCSI adapters. In some cases, the installation program will ask you whether you have any SCSI adapters. If you choose **Yes**, the next dialog presents a list of SCSI drivers. Choose the driver that most closely resembles your SCSI adapter. The installation program then gives you an opportunity to specify options for the SCSI driver you selected; most SCSI drivers should detect your hardware automatically, however.

Creating Partitions for Red Hat Linux

At this point, it's necessary to let the installation program know where it should install Red Hat Linux. This is done by defining mount points for one or more disk partitions in which Red Hat Linux will be installed. You may also need to create and/or delete partitions at this time.

Please Note: If you have not yet planned how you will set up your partitions, please turn to **Disk Partitions**, and review everything up to

A Note About Kernel Drivers. As a bare minimum, you'll need an appropriately-sized root partition, and a swap partition of at least 16 MB.

If you're still unsure on how to set up your partitions, please refer to Appendix B.

The installation program then presents a dialog box that allows you to choose from two disk partitioning tools (see Figure 4-4). The choices you have are:

- **Disk Druid** — This is Red Hat Linux's install-time disk management utility. It can create and delete disk partitions according to user-supplied requirements, in addition to managing mount points for each partition.
- **fdisk** — This is the traditional Linux disk partitioning tool. While it is somewhat more flexible than Disk Druid, the downside is that fdisk assumes you have some experience with disk partitioning, and are comfortable with its somewhat terse user interface.

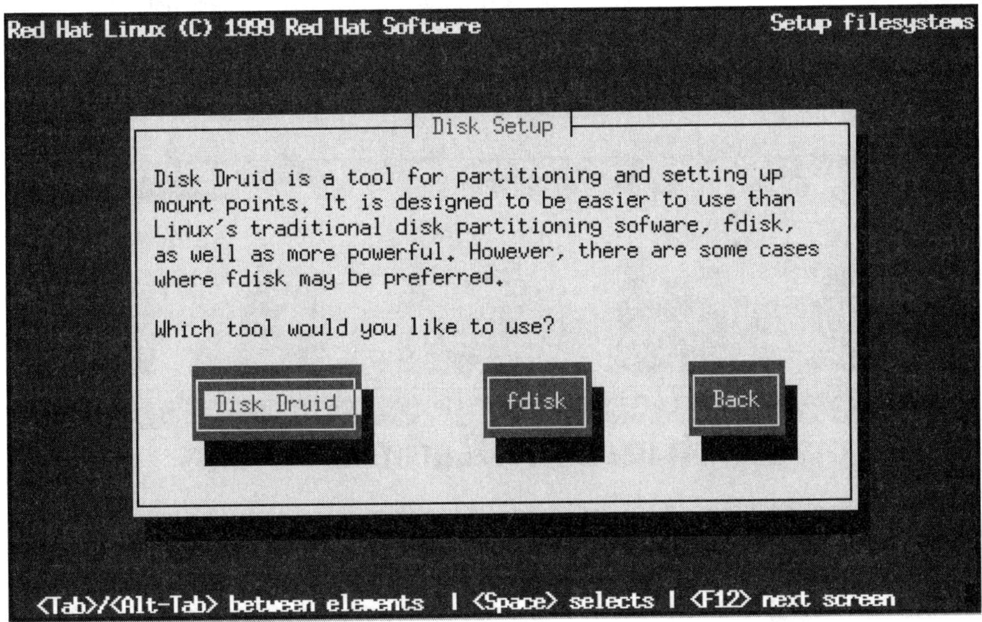

Figure 4-4: Selecting Disk Setup Method

With the exception of certain esoteric situations, Disk Druid can handle the partitioning requirements for a typical Red Hat Linux installation.

Select the disk partitioning tool you'd like to use, and press [Enter]. If you choose Disk Druid, continue reading. If you'd rather use fdisk, please turn to **The "Drive Summaries" Section**.

Using Disk Druid

If you selected Disk Druid, you will be presented with a screen that looks like figure 4-5. While it may look overwhelming at first, it really isn't. Let's go over each of Disk Druid's three sections.

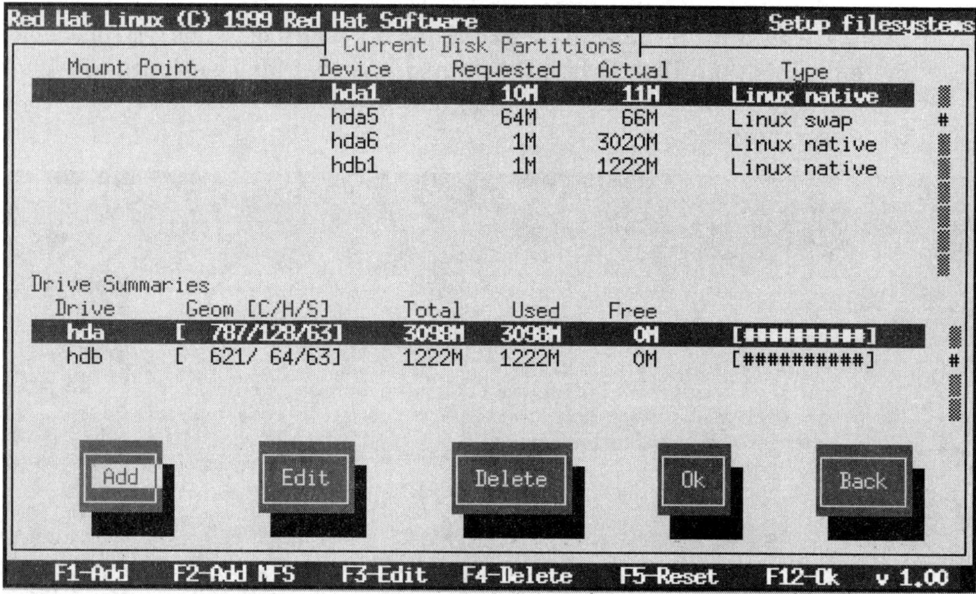

Figure 4-5: Disk Druid Main Screen

The "Current Disk Partitions" Section

Each line in the "Current Disk Partitions" section represents a disk partition. You'll note that this section has a scroll bar to the right, which means that there might be more partitions than can be displayed at one time. If you use the [\uparrow] and [\downarrow] keys, you can see if there are any additional partitions. Each line in this section has five different fields:

Mount Point — This field indicates where the partition will be mounted when Red Hat Linux is installed and running.

Device — This field displays the partition's device name.

Requested — The "Requested" field shows the minimum size requested when the partition was defined.

Actual — The "Actual" field shows the space currently allocated to the partition.

Type — This field shows the partition's type.

Another Type of Partition

As you scroll through the "Current Disk Partitions" section, you might see an "Unallocated Requested Partitions" title bar, followed by one or more partitions. As the title implies, these are partitions that have been requested but, for one reason or another, have not been allocated. A common reason for having an unallocated partition is a lack of sufficient free space for the partition. In any case, the reason the partition remains unallocated will be displayed after the partition's mount point.

The "Drive Summaries" Section

Each line in the "Drive Summaries" section represents a hard disk on your system. Each line has the following fields:

Drive — This field shows the hard disk's device name.

Geom [C/H/S] — This field shows the hard disk's geometry. The geometry consists of three numbers representing the number of cylinders, heads and sectors as reported by the hard disk.

Total — The "Total" field shows the total available space on the hard disk.

Used — This field shows how much of the hard disk's space is currently allocated to partitions.

Free — The "Free" field shows how much of the hard disk's space is still unallocated.

Bar Graph – This field presents a visual representation of the space currently used on the hard disk. The more pound signs there are between the square braces, the less free space there is. In Figure 4-5, the bar graph shows no free space.

Please Note: The "Drive Summaries" section is displayed only to indicate your computer's disk configuration. It is not meant to be used as a means of specifying the target hard drive for a given partition. This is described more completely in the **Adding a Partition**.

Disk Druid's Buttons

These buttons control Disk Druid's actions. They are used to add and delete partitions, and to change partition attributes. In addition, there are buttons that are used to accept the changes you've made, or to exit Disk Druid entirely. Let's take a look at each button in order.

Add – The "Add" button is used to request a new partition. When selected, a dialog box will appear containing fields that must be filled in.

Edit – The "Edit" button is used to modify attributes of the partition currently highlighted in the "Current Disk Partitions" section. Selecting this button will cause a dialog box to appear. Some or all of the fields in the "Edit Partition" dialog box may be changed, depending on whether the partition information has already been written to disk or not.

Delete – The "Delete" button is used to delete the partition currently highlighted in the "Current Disk Partitions" section. Selecting this button will cause a dialog box to appear asking you to confirm the deletion.

Ok – The "Ok" button causes any changes made to your system's partitions to be written to disk. You will be asked to confirm your changes before Disk Druid rewrites your hard disk partition table(s). In addition, any mount points you've defined are passed to the installation program, and will eventually be used by your Red Hat Linux system to define the filesystem layout.

Back – This button causes Disk Druid to abort without saving any changes you've made. When this button is selected, the installation program will take you back to the previous screen, so you can start over.

Handy Function Keys

While there is some overlap between Disk Druid's buttons and the available functions keys, there are two function keys that have no corresponding buttons:

- **[F2] (Add NFS)** – This function key is used to add a read-only NFS-served filesystem to the set of mount points on your Red Hat Linux system. When selected, a dialog box will appear containing fields that must be filled in.
- **[F5] (Reset)** – This function key is used to discard all changes you may have made while in Disk Druid, and return the list of partitions to those read from the partition table(s) on your hard disk(s). When selected, you'll be asked to confirm whether you want to discard the changes. Note that any mount points you've specified will be lost, and will need to be reentered.

  Please Note: You will need to dedicate at least one partition to Red Hat Linux, and optionally more. This is discussed more completely in **Partition Naming Scheme**.

Now let's see how Disk Druid is used to set up partitions for your Red Hat Linux system.

Adding a Partition

To Add a new partition, select the **Add** button, and press [Space] or [Enter]. A dialog box entitled "Edit New Partition" will appear (see Figure 4-6). It contains the following fields:

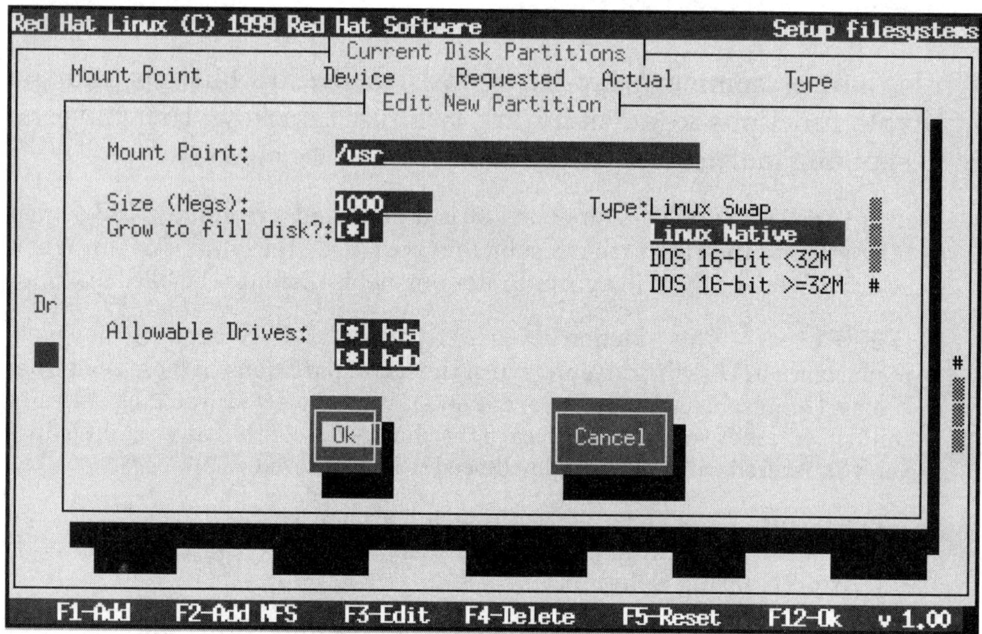

Figure 4-6: Creating a New Partition

- **Mount Point** – Highlight this field and enter the partition's mount point. For example, if this partition should be the root partition, enter /; enter /usr for the usr partition, and so on.

- **Size (Megs)** – In this field, enter the size (in megabytes) of the partition. Note that this field starts with a "1" in it, meaning that unless you change it, you'll end up with a 1 MB partition. Delete it using the [Backspace] key, and enter the desired partition size.

- **Growable?** – This check box indicates whether the size you entered in the previous field is to be considered the partition's exact size, or its minimum size. Press [Space] to check and uncheck the box. When checked, the partition will grow to fill all available space on the hard disk. In this case, the partition's size will expand and contract as other partitions are modified. Note that you can make more than one partition growable; if you do so, the additional free space will be shared between all growable partitions.

- **Type** – This field contains a list of different partition types. Select the appropriate partition type by using the [\uparrow] and [\downarrow] keys.

- **Allowable Drives** – This field contains a list of the hard disks installed on your system, with a check box for each. If a hard disk's box is checked, then this partition may be created on that hard disk. If the box is not checked, then the partition will never be created on that hard disk. By using different check box settings, you can direct Disk Druid to place partitions as you see fit, or let Disk Druid decide where partitions should go.

- **Ok** – Select this button and press [Space] when you are satisfied with the partition's settings, and wish to create it.

- **Cancel** – Select this button and press [Space] when you don't want to create the partition.

Problems When Adding a Partition

> **Please Note:** If you are having problems adding a partition, you may want to reference Appendix B to get more information.

If you attempt to add a partition and Disk Druid can't carry out your request, you'll see a dialog box like the one in Figure 4-7. In the box are listed any partitions that are currently unallocated, along with the reason they could not be allocated. Select the Ok button, and press [Space] to continue. Note that the unallocated partition(s) are also displayed on Disk Druid's main screen (though you may have to scroll the **Current Disk Partitions** section to see them).

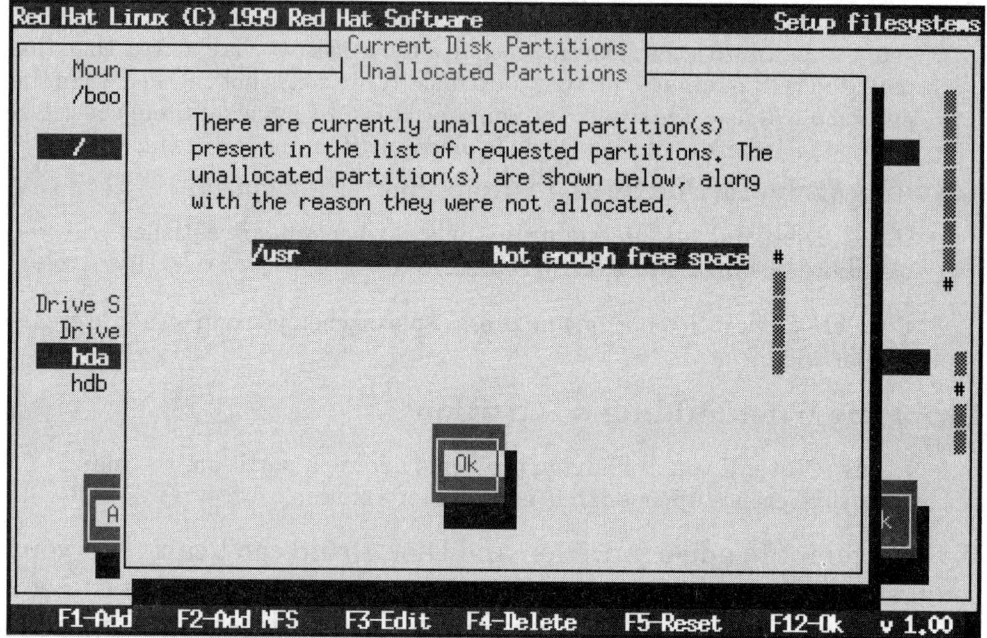

Figure 4-7: Unallocated Partition Warning

Deleting a Partition

To delete a partition, highlight the partition in the **Current Disk Partitions** section, select the **Delete** button, and press [Space]. You will be asked to confirm the deletion.

Editing a Partition

To change a partition's settings, highlight the partition in the **Current Disk Partitions** section, select the **Edit** button, and press [Space]. You will be presented with a dialog box very similar to the one shown in Figure 4-7. Make the appropriate changes, select **Ok**, and press [Space].

> **Please Note:** If the partition already existed on your hard disk, you will only be able to change the partition's mount point. If you want to make any other changes, you will need to delete the partition and recreate it.

Adding an NFS Mount

To add a read-only NFS-served filesystem, press [F2]. If you have not selected a network-related installation method, you will be presented with several dialog boxes concerning network configuration (turn to **Network Drivers Configuration** for more information). Fill in the boxes appropriately. You will then see a dialog box entitled, "Edit Network Mount Point" (similar to the one in Figure 4-12). In this dialog box you will need to enter the NFS server name, the path to the exported filesystem, and the mount point for the filesystem. Select the **Ok** or **Cancel** button as appropriate, and press [Space].

Starting Over

If you'd like to abandon any changes you've made while in Disk Druid, and would rather use fdisk instead, you can select the **Back** button, and press [Space]. If you want to continue using Disk Druid, but would like to start over, press [F5], and Disk Druid will be reset to its initial state.

When You're Finished....

Once you've finished configuring partitions and entering mount points, your screen should look something like the one in Figure 4-8. Select Ok, and press [Space]. Then turn to **Installing Swap Space**.

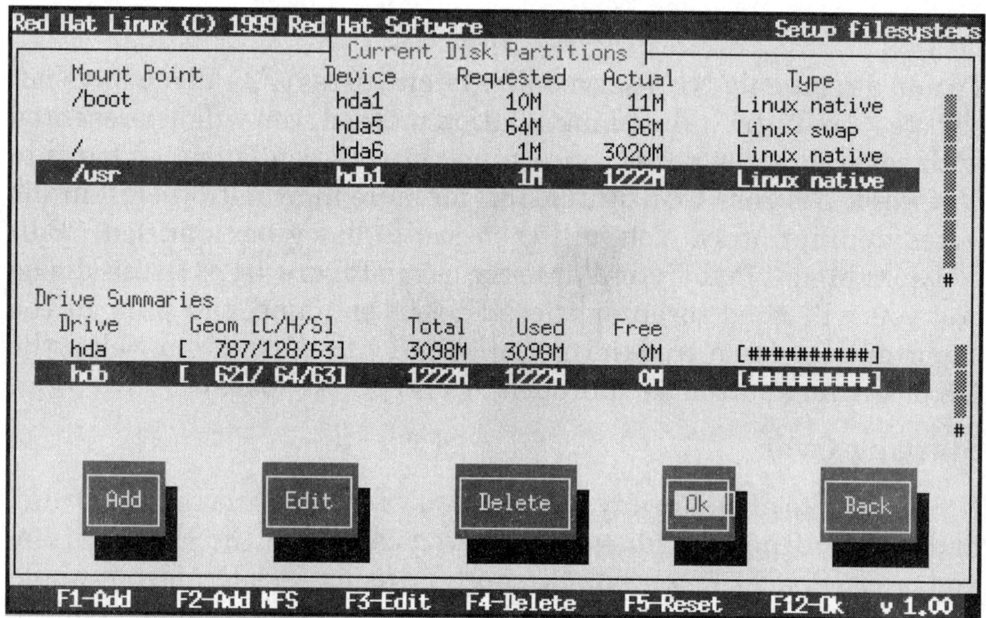

Figure 4-8: Partitions and Mount Points Defined

Using fdisk

If you'd rather use fdisk to manage partitions, this is the section for you. Once you've selected fdisk, you'll be presented with a dialog box entitled "Partition Disks" (see Figure 4-9). In this box is a list of every disk on your computer. Move the highlight to the disk you'd like to partition, select **Edit**, and press [Space]. You will then enter fdisk and can partition the disk you selected. Repeat this process for each disk you want to partition. When you're done, select "Done."

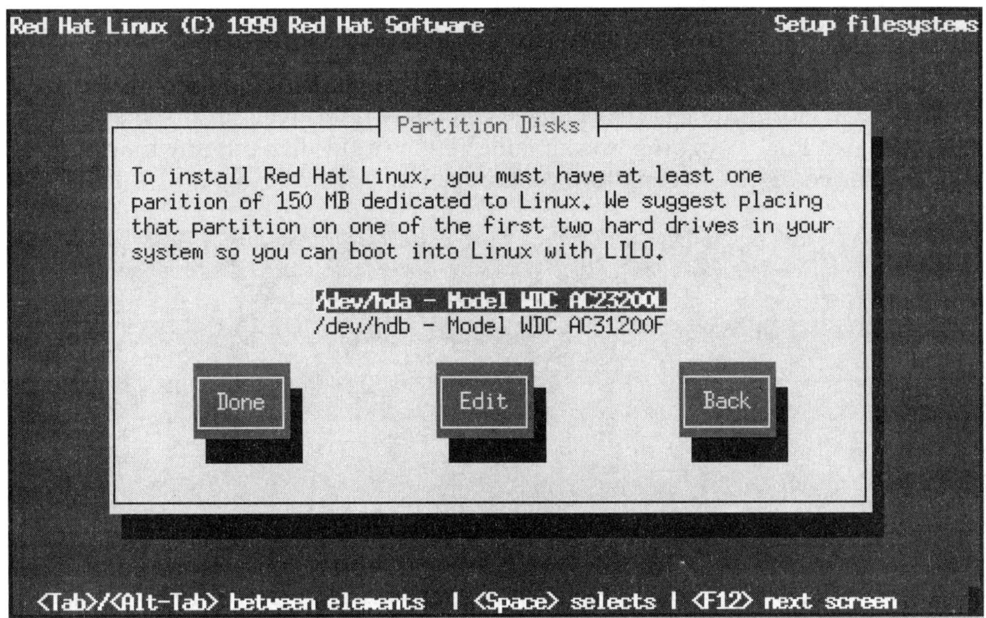

Figure 4-9: Selecting a Disk for Partitioning

An Overview of fdisk

`fdisk` includes online help which is terse but useful. Here are a few tips:

- The command for help is `m`.
- To list the current partition table, use the `p` command (see Figure 4-10).
- To add a new partition, use `n`.
- Linux fdisk creates partitions of type Linux native by default. When you create a swap partition, don't forget to change it to type Linux swap using the `t` command. The value for the Linux swap type is 82. For other partition types, use the l command to see a list of partition types and values.
- Linux allows up to four (4) partitions on one disk. If you wish to create more than that, one (and only one) of the four may be an extended partition, which acts as a container for one or more logical partitions. Since it acts as a container, the extended partition must be at least as large as the total size of all the logical partitions it is to contain.

- It's a good idea to write down which partitions (e.g., `/dev/hda2`) are meant for which filesystems (e.g., `/usr`) as you create each one.
- **Please Note:** None of the changes you make take effect until you save them and exit fdisk using the w command.You may quit fdisk at any time without saving changes by using the `q` command.

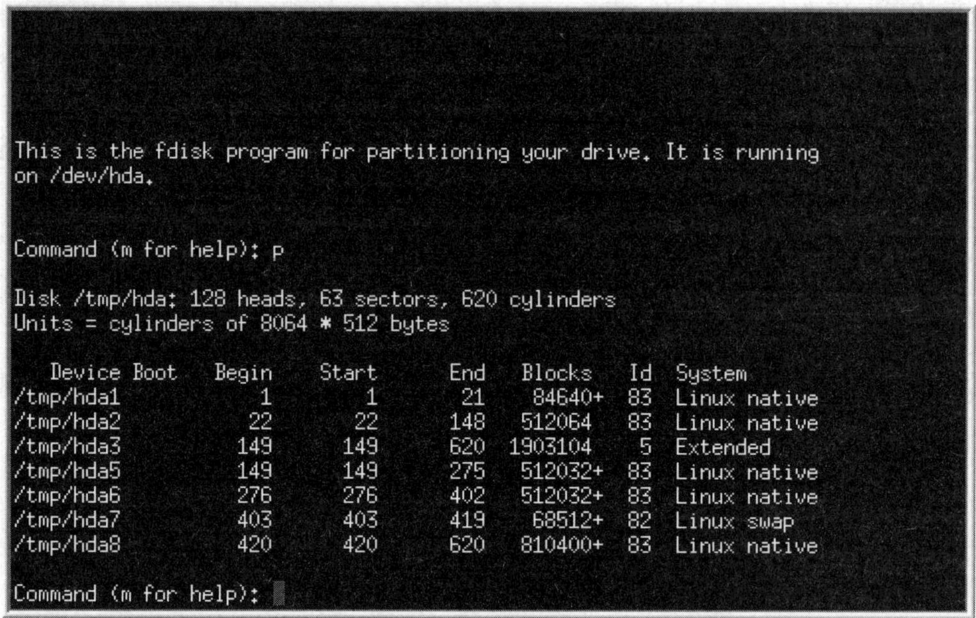

```
This is the fdisk program for partitioning your drive. It is running
on /dev/hda.


Command (m for help): p

Disk /tmp/hda: 128 heads, 63 sectors, 620 cylinders
Units = cylinders of 8064 * 512 bytes

   Device Boot   Begin    Start      End   Blocks   Id  System
/tmp/hda1            1        1       21    84640+  83  Linux native
/tmp/hda2           22       22      148   512064   83  Linux native
/tmp/hda3          149      149      620  1903104    5  Extended
/tmp/hda5          149      149      275   512032+  83  Linux native
/tmp/hda6          276      276      402   512032+  83  Linux native
/tmp/hda7          403      403      419    68512+  82  Linux swap
/tmp/hda8          420      420      620   810400+  83  Linux native

Command (m for help):
```

Figure 4-10: Sample Output From fdisk

Changing the Partition Table

When you are finished partitioning your disks, press **Done**; you may see a message indicating that the installation program needs to reboot. This is a normal occurrence after changing a disk's partition data; it usually happens if you created, changed or deleted any extended partitions. After you press **Ok**, your machine will reboot. Follow the same installation steps you did up until **Partitioning Disks**; then simply choose **Done**.

Filesystem Configuration

The next dialog box contains a list of all disk partitions with filesystems readable by Red Hat Linux, including partitions for MS-DOS or Windows. This gives you the opportunity to assign these partitions to different parts of your Red Hat Linux filesystem. The partitions you assign will be automatically mounted when your Red Hat Linux system boots. Select the partition you wish to assign and press [Enter] (or choose **Edit**); then enter the mount point for that partition, e.g., /usr (see Figure 4-11).

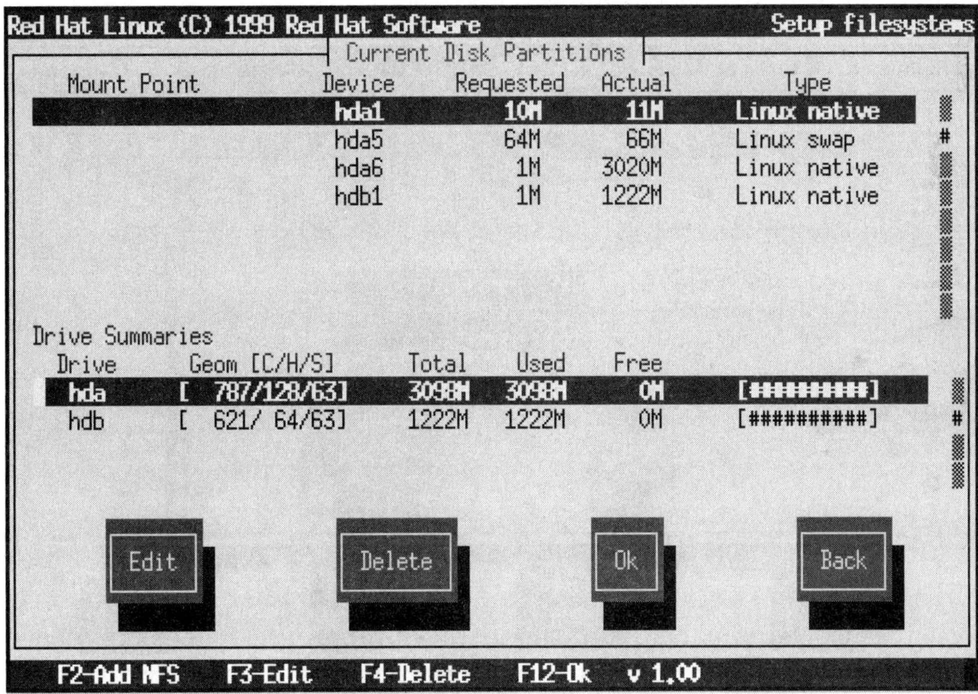

Figure 4-11: Filesystem Configuration

If you are performing an upgrade, the installation program tries to find your root partition automatically; if it does, it obtains all this information automatically, and goes on to the next step.

Adding an NFS Mount

Red Hat Linux also allows you to mount read-only NFS volumes when your system boots; this allows directory trees to be shared across a network. To do so, press [F2]. If you have not selected a network-related installation method, you will be presented with several dialog boxes concerning network configuration (turn to **Configuring TCP/IP Networking** for more information). Fill them in appropriately. You will then see a dialog box entitled "Edit Network Mount Point." Enter the NFS server's hostname, the path to the NFS volume, and the local mount point for that volume (see Figure 4-12).

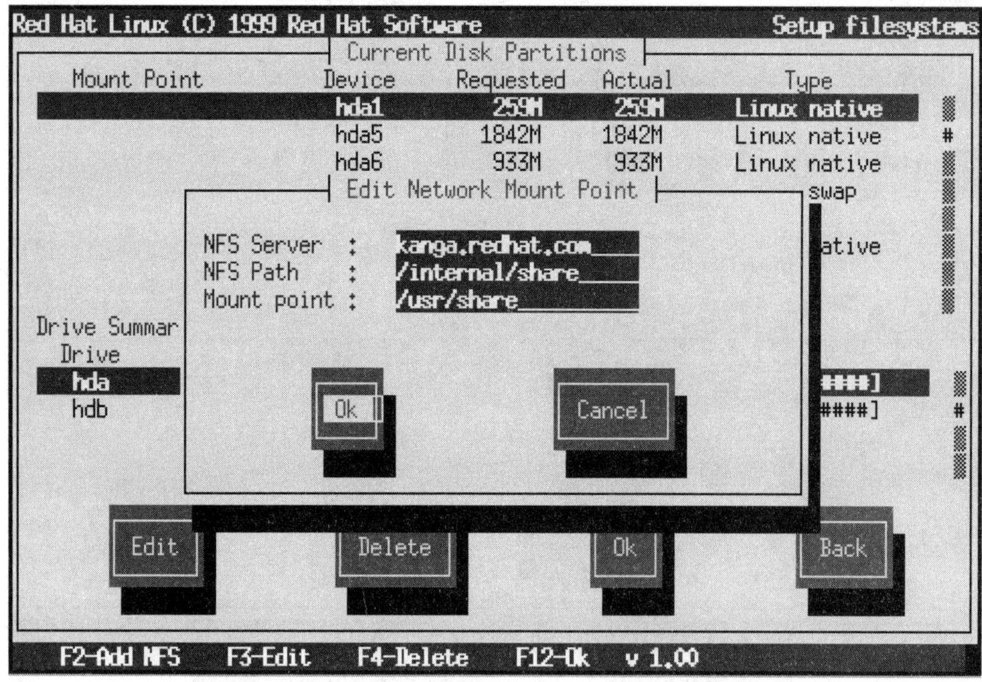

Figure 4-12: Adding an NFS Mount

Initializing Swap Space

Now the installation program will look for swap partitions (see Figure 4-13). If it finds any, it asks whether you want to initialize them. Select the partition(s) you wish to initialize as swap space using [Space]; if you wish to check the partitions for bad blocks, select the **Check for bad blocks during format** box. Choose **Ok**, and press [Space].

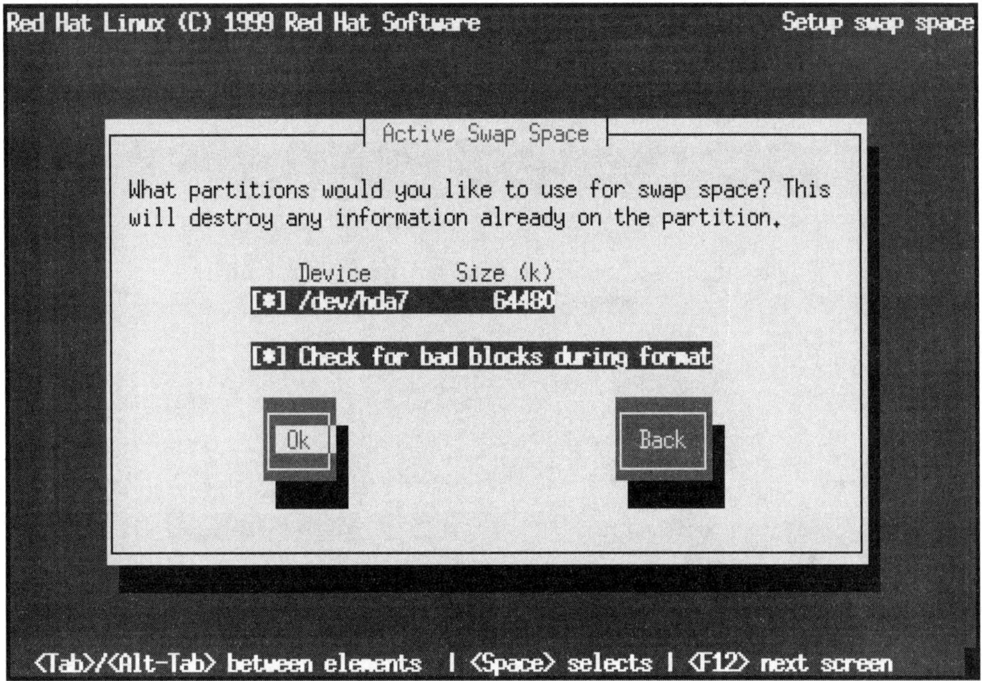

Figure 4-13: Initializing Swap Space

If the installation program can't find a swap partition and you're sure one exists, make sure you have set the partition type to `Linux swap`; see **Creating Partitions for Red Hat Linux** for information on how this is done with Disk Druid or `fdisk`.

For Hard Drive Installations Only...

If you are not performing a hard drive installation, please skip ahead to **Formatting Partitions**. Otherwise, read on.

At this point, a dialog box entitled "Select Partition" is displayed (see Figure 4-14). Enter the device name of the partition holding the RedHat directory tree. There is also a field labelled "Directory." If the RedHat directory is not in the root directory of that partition (for example, `/test/new/RedHat`), enter the path to the RedHat directory (in our example, `/test/new`).

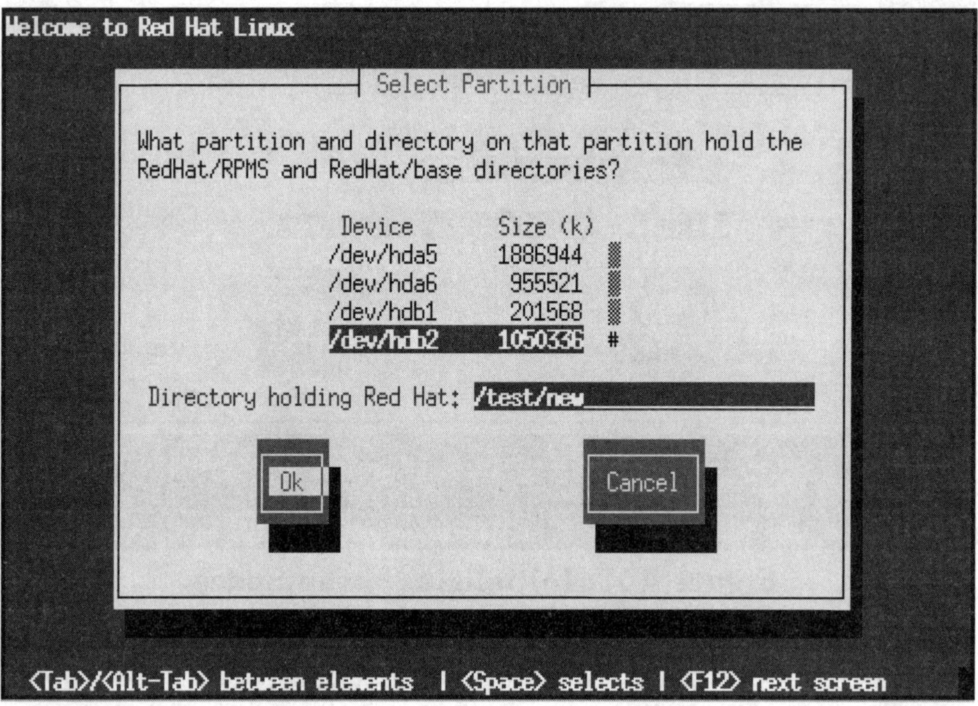

Figure 4-14: Selecting Partition for Hard Drive Install

If the installation program was unable to find the necessary files on the partition and directory you've specified, you'll be returned to the "Select Partition" dialog box to make the necessary corrections.

If everything has been specified properly, you should see a message box indicating that the packages are being scanned.

If you are doing a workstation- or server-class installation, please turn to Chapter 6. Move on to the next section to continue the custom installation of Red Hat Linux.

Formatting Partitions

The next dialog box presents a list of partitions to format (see Figure 4-15). All newly-created partitions should be formatted. In addition, any existing partitions that contain old data you no longer need should be formatted. However, partitions such as `/home` or `/usr/local` must not be formatted if they contain data you wish to keep. Select each partition to format and press [Space]. If you wish to check for bad blocks while formatting each filesystem, select **Check for bad blocks during format**. Select **Ok**, and press [Space].

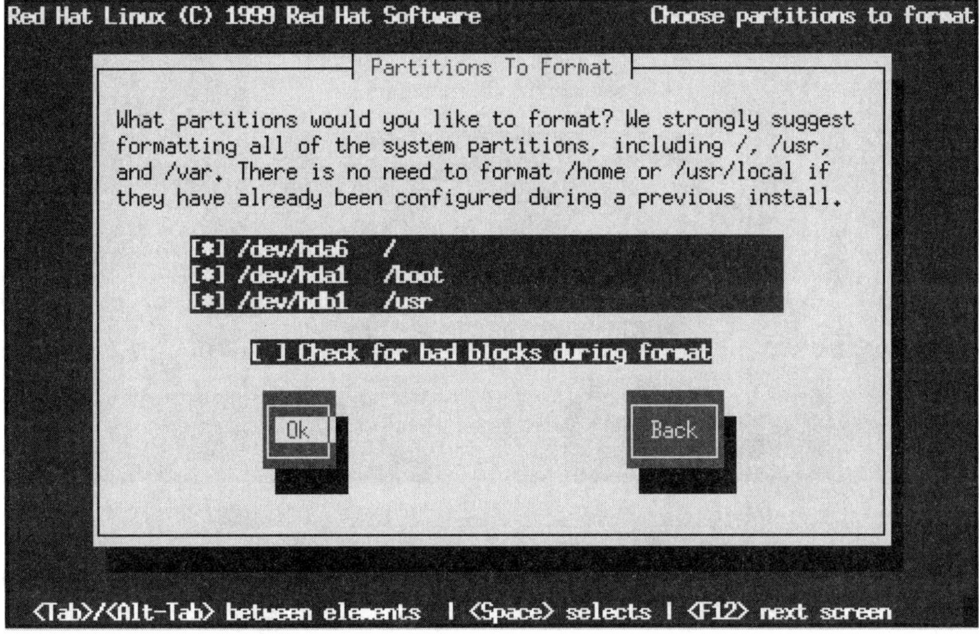

Figure 4-15: Formatting Partitions

Selecting and Installing Packages

After your partitions have been configured and selected for formatting, you are ready to select packages for installation. You can select components, which group packages together according to function, individual packages, or a combination of the two.

Selecting Components

Components group packages together according to the functionality they provide. For example, **C Development, Networked Workstation**, or **Web Server**. Select each component you wish to install and press [Space]. Selecting **Everything** (which can be found at the end of the component list) installs all packages included with Red Hat Linux (see Figure 4-16). Selecting every package will require close to 1 GB of free disk space.

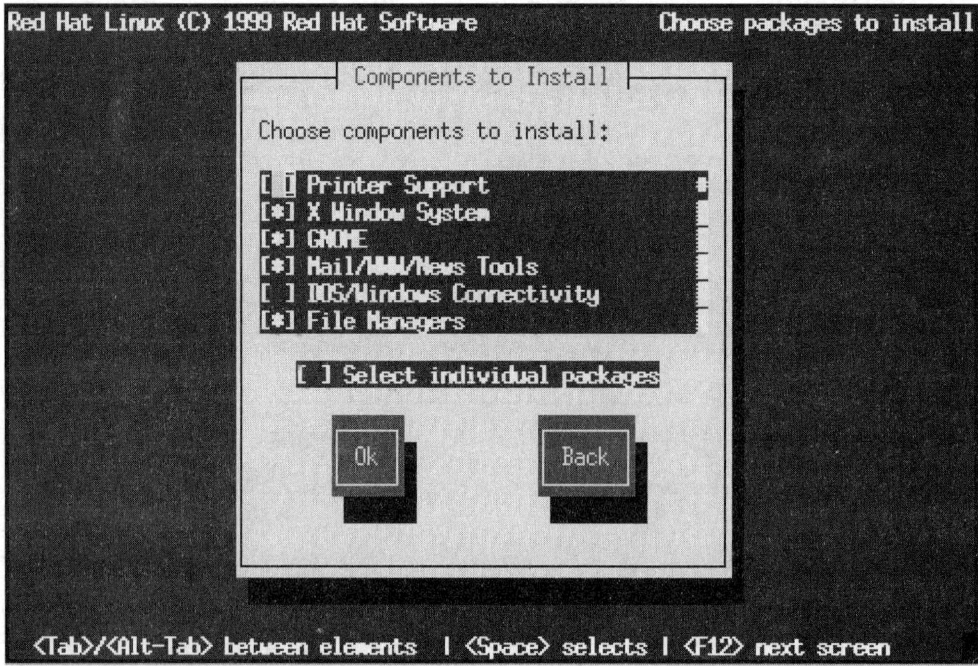

Figure 4-16: Selecting System Components

If you wish to select or deselect individual packages, check the **Select individual packages** check box.

Selecting Individual Packages

After selecting the components you wish to install, you may select or deselect individual packages. The installation program presents a list of the package groups available; using the arrow keys, select a group to examine and press [Enter] or [Space]. The installation program presents a list of the packages in that group, which you may select or deselect by using the arrow keys to highlight a package, and pressing [Space] (see Figure 4-17).

> **Please Note:** Some packages (such as the kernel and certain libraries) are required for every Red Hat Linux system and are not available to select or deselect.

Quick Keys

- [o] — shows that at least one of the packages in that component group has been selected.
- [*] — shows that all the packages of a component group has been selected.
- [—] — removes all packages in a component group.
- [*] — selects all packages in a component group.

> **Please Note:** In the upper right-hand corner of the screen you will see the approximate system size of the components you have selected to install.

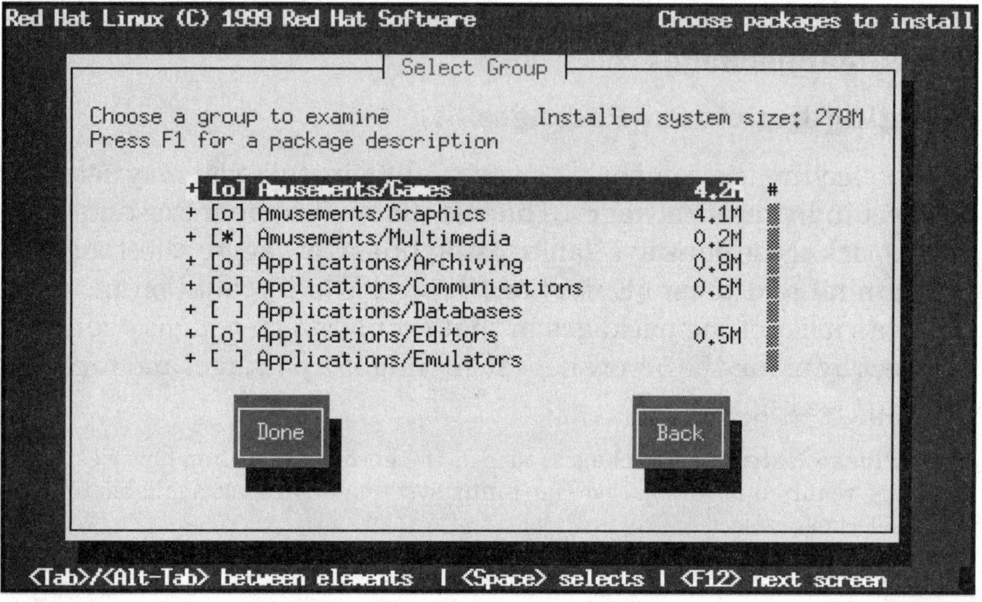

Figure 4-17: Selecting Packages

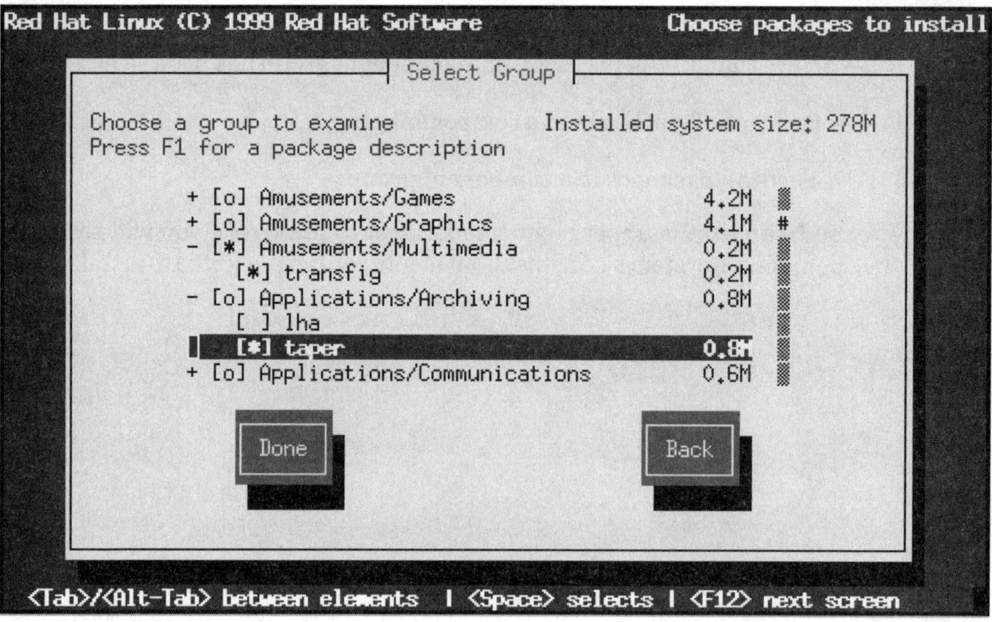

Figure 4-18: Selecting Packages — Expanded View

When you are finished selecting individual packages, press **Ok** in the **Select Group** dialog box.

etting Information about a Package

You may view a detailed description of the currently-highlighted package by pressing [F1]. A dialog box will appear containing a description of the package. You can use the arrow keys to scroll through the description if it cannot fit on the screen. When you're done reading the description, press **Ok**, and the box will disappear. You can then continue selecting packages.

> **Please Note:** If you'd rather read the package descriptions on paper, please turn to Appendix C.

Package Dependencies

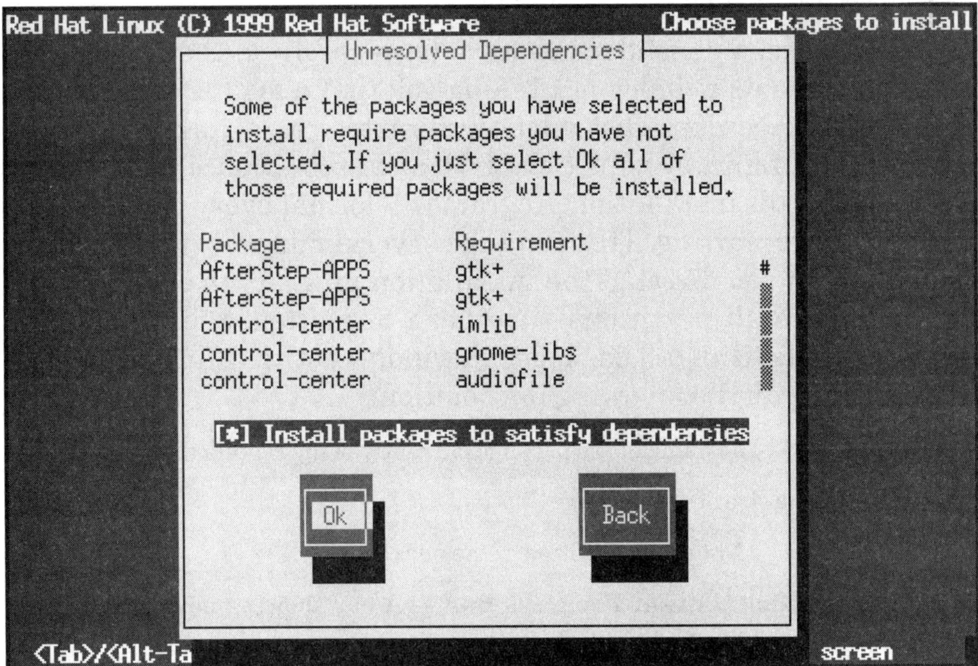

Figure 4-19: Unresolved Dependencies

Many software packages, in order to work correctly, depend on other software packages or libraries that must be installed on your system. For example, many of the graphical Red Hat system administration tools require the python and pythonlib packages. To make sure your system has all the packages it needs in order to be fully functional, Red Hat Linux checks these package dependencies each time you install or remove software packages. After you have finished selecting packages to install, the installation program checks the list of selected packages for dependencies. If any package requires another package which you have not selected to install, the program presents a list of these unresolved dependencies and gives you the opportunity to resolve them (see Figure 4-19). If you simply press **Ok**, the program will resolve them automatically by adding all required packages to the list of selected packages.

Package Installation

After all package dependencies have been resolved, the installation program presents a dialog box telling you that a log file containing a list of all packages installed will be written to `/tmp/install.log` on your Red Hat Linux system. Select **Ok** and press [Space] to continue. At this point, the installation program will format every partition you selected for formatting. This can take several minutes (and will take even longer if you directed the installation program to check for bad blocks). Once all partitions have been formatted, the installation program starts to install packages. A window entitled "Install Status" is displayed with the following information:

Package — The name of the package currently being installed.

Size — The size of the package (in kilobytes).

Summary — A short description of the package.

Package Installation Progress Bar — A bar showing how complete the current package installation is.

Statistics Section — This section has three rows labeled "Total," "Completed," and "Remaining." As you might guess, these rows contain statistics on the total number of packages that will be installed, statistics on the number of packages that have been completely installed, and statistics on the packages that have not yet been installed. The information tracked on these three rows includes:

Packages — The number of packages.

Bytes — The size.

Time — The amount of time.

Overall Progress Bar — This bar changes color showing how close to completion the entire installation is.

At this point there's nothing left for you to do until all the packages have been installed. How quickly this happens depends on the number of packages you've selected, and your computer's speed. Once all the packages have been installed, please turn to Chapter 6 to finish your installation of Red Hat Linux.

5 Network Installations

Selecting an Installation Method

Now you must decide what type of installation method you wish to use (see Figure 5-1). Highlight the appropriate choice and select **Ok**, or press [Enter].

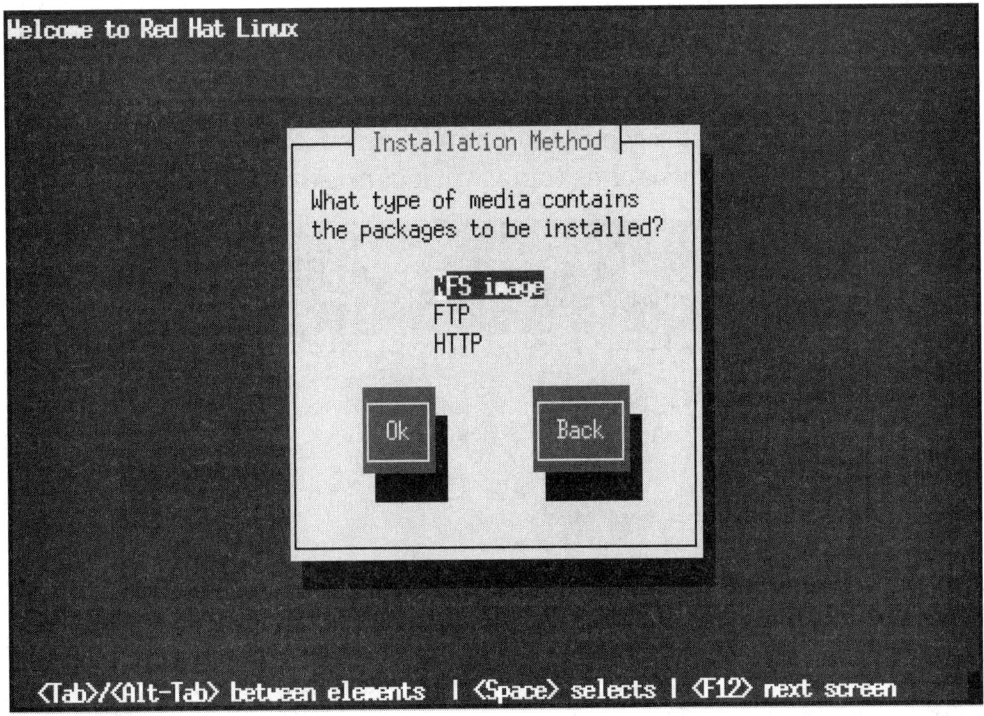

Figure 5-1: Selecting an Installation Method

If you are not performing a network type installation (NFS, FTP, or HTTP) then please skip ahead to Chapter 6 to finish the installation process, or back to Chapter 4 if you need to perform a CD-ROM or hard drive installation.

If you are planning to do a network type installation, please read on.

Network Driver Configuration

Next, the installation program will probe your system and attempt to identify your network card. Most of the time, the driver can locate the card automatically. If it is not able to identify your network card, you'll be asked to choose the driver that supports your network card and to specify any options necessary for the driver to locate and recognize it.

Configuring TCP/IP Networking

After the installation program has configured your network card, it presents several dialogs for configuring your system's TCP/IP networking. The first screen (shown in Figure 5-2) allows you to select from one of three approaches to network configuration:

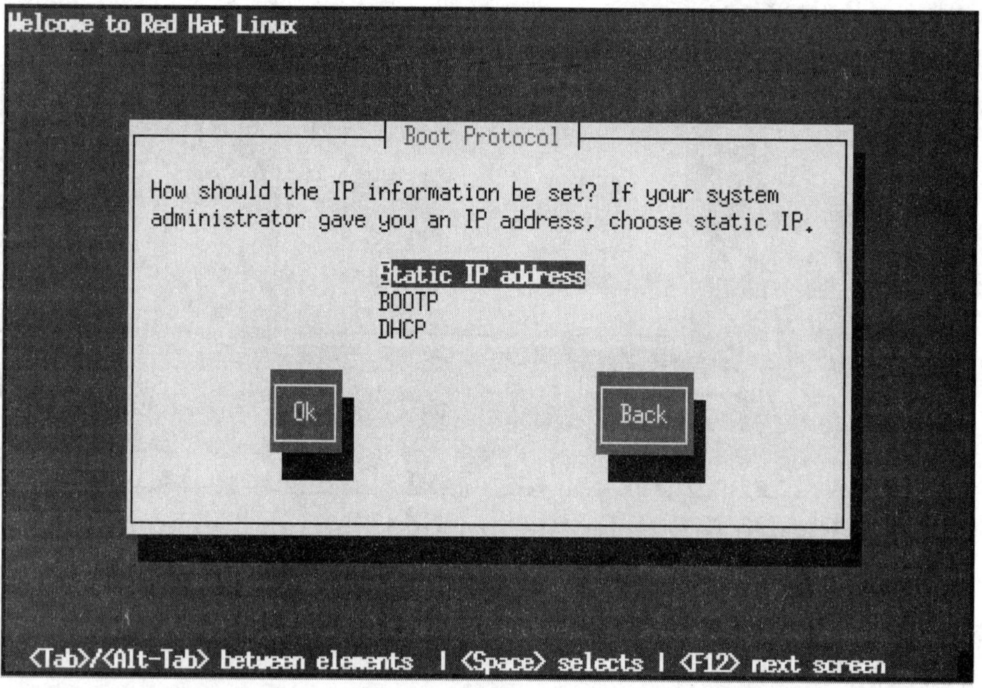

Figure 5-2: Selecting Method of Network Configuration

- **Static IP address** — You must supply all the necessary network-related information manually.

- **BOOTP** — The necessary network-related information is automatically provided using a bootp request.
- **DHCP** — The necessary network-related information is automatically provided using a dhcp request.

Please Note: The **BOOTP** and **DHCP** selections require an active, properly configured bootp (or dhcp) server running on your local area network.

If you choose **BOOTP** or **DHCP**, your network configuration will be set automatically, and you can skip the rest of this section. If you've selected **Static IP address**, you'll need to specify all the networking information yourself. Figure 5-3 contains an example of networking information similar to what you'll be needing.

Field	Example Value
IP Address	10.0.2.15
Netmask	255.255.255.0
Default Gateway	10.0.2.254
Primary Nameserver	10.0.2.1
Domain Name	redhat.com
Hostname	pooh.redhat.com

Figure 5-3: Sample Networking Information

Please Note: The information in figure 5-3 is a sample only! You should obtain the proper information for your network from your network administrator.

The first dialog asks you for IP and other network addresses (see Figure 5-4). Enter the **IP address** you are using during installation and press [Enter]. The installation program attempts to guess your **Netmask** based on your IP address; you may change the netmask if it is incorrect. Press [Enter]. The installation program guesses the **Default gateway** and **Primary nameserver** addresses from your IP address and netmask; you may change them if they are incorrect.

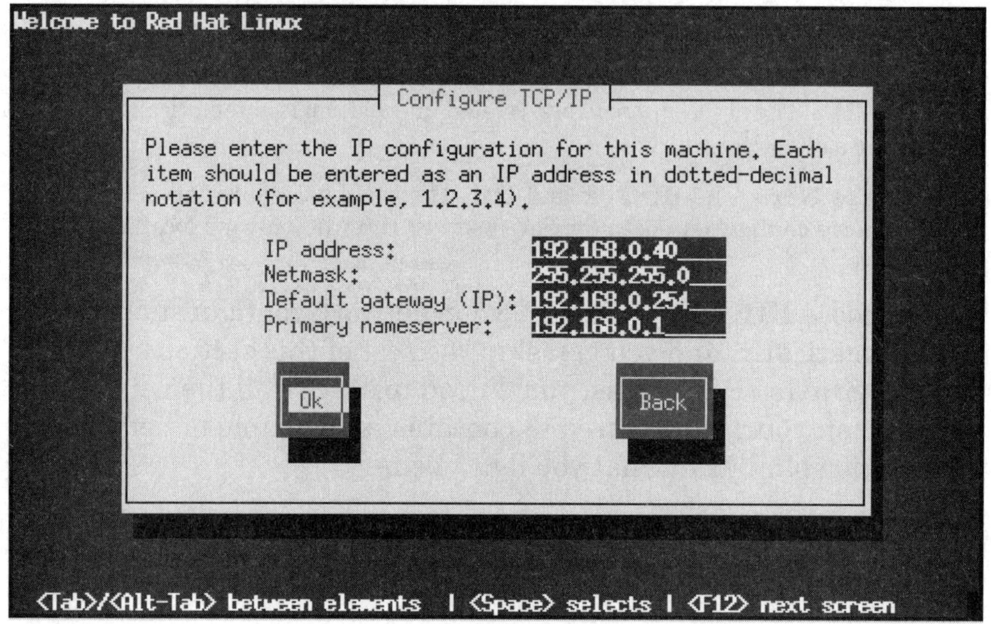

Figure 5-4: Configuring TCP/IP

Choose **Ok** to continue.

After the first dialog box, you may see a second one. It will prompt you for a domain name, a hostname, and other networking information (see Figure 5-5). Enter the **Domain name** for your system and press [Enter]; the installation program carries the domain name down to the **Host name** field. Enter the hostname you are using in front of the domain name to form a fully-qualified domain name (FQDN). If your network has more than one nameserver, you may enter IP addresses for additional nameservers in the **Secondary nameserver** and **Tertiary nameserver** fields.

Choose **Ok** to continue.

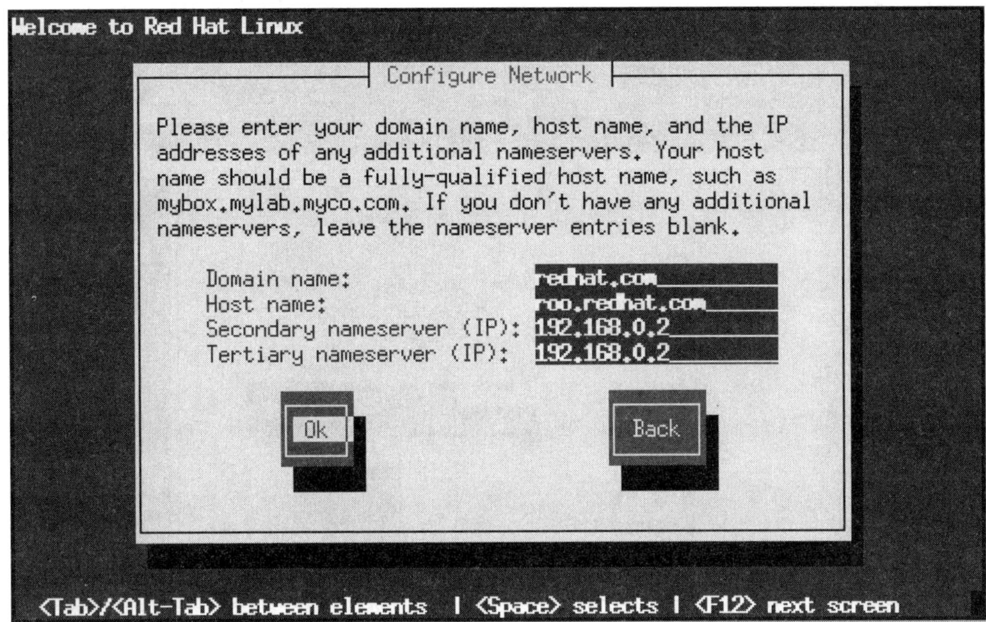

Figure 5-5: Configuring Networking

Please Note: If you're performing an FTP installation, go to **Installing via FTP** and continue from there. If you're doing an NFS installation, read on.

Installing via NFS

If you are installing Red Hat Linux 6.0 via NFS, you will now need to configure your NFS server information.

NFS Server Information

The next dialog requests information about the NFS server (see Figure 5-6). Enter the name (which must be a fully-qualified domain name) or IP address of your NFS server, and the name of the exported directory that contains the Red Hat Linux CD. For example, if the NFS server has the Red Hat Linux CD mounted on `/mnt/cdrom`, enter `/mnt/cdrom` in the **Red Hat directory** field. If the NFS server is exporting a mirror of the Red Hat Linux installation tree instead of a CD, enter the directory which contains the RedHat directory. For example, if your NFS server contains the directory `/mirrors/redhat/i386/RedHat`, enter /mirrors/redhat/i386.

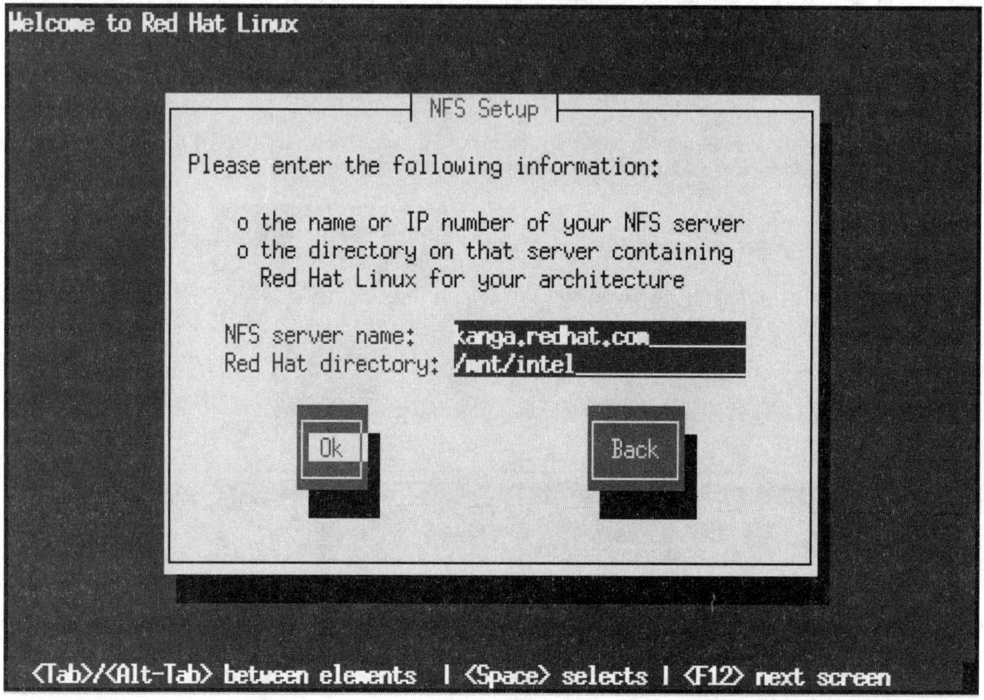

Figure 5-6: Installing via NFS

After a short delay, the next dialog box will appear.

> **Please Note:** An NFS install does not require a support diskette in the installation process, unless you are using a PCMCIA device to complete the installation. If so, you will need to use the PCMCIA support disk when prompted.

Installing via FTP

You should now be looking at the "FTP Setup" dialog box. Here's where you point the installation program at the FTP site of your choice (see Figure 5-7). Enter the name or IP address of the FTP site you are installing from, and the name of the directory there which contains the RedHat directory for your architecture. For example, if the FTP site contains the directory /pub/mirrors/redhat/i386/RedHat, enter /pub/mirrors/redhat/i386. If you are not using anonymous FTP, or if you need to use a proxy FTP server (if you're behind a firewall, for example), check the check box, and another dialog box will request the FTP account and proxy information.

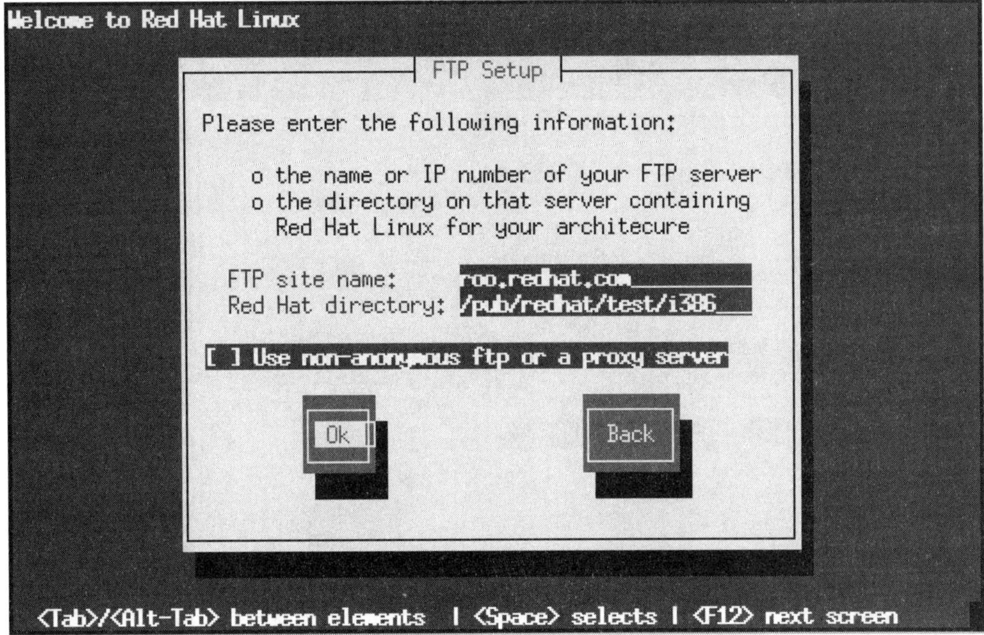

Figure 5-7: Installing via FTP

If everything has been specified properly, you should see a message box indicating that base/hdlist is being retrieved.

Continue to **Upgrading or Installing** for upgrade or full-installation instructions.

Installing via HTTP

You should now be looking at the "HTTP Setup" dialog box. Here's where you point the installation program at the HTTP site of your choice. Enter the name or IP address of the HTTP site you are installing from, and the name of the directory there which contains the RedHat directory for your architecture. For example, if the HTTP site contains the directory /pub/mirrors/redhat/i386/RedHat, enter /pub/mirrors/redhat/i386. If you are not using anonymous HTTP, or if you need to use a proxy HTTP server (if you're behind a firewall, for example), check the check box, and another dialog box will request the HTTP account and proxy information.

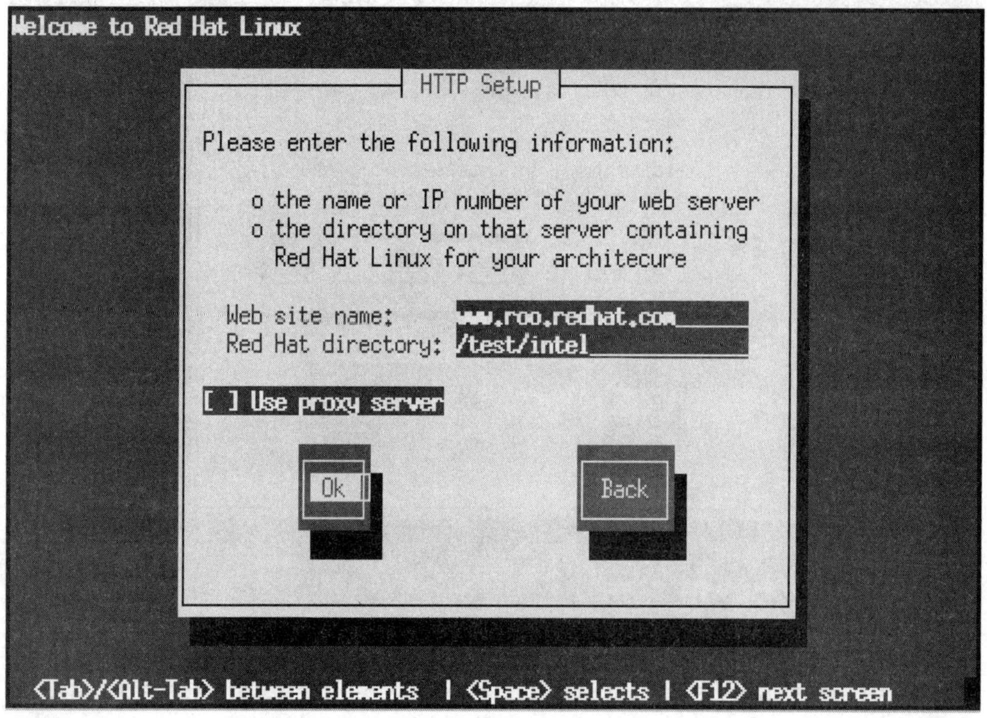

Figure 5-8: Installing via HTTP

If everything has been specified properly, you should see a message box indicating that base/hdlist is being retrieved. Continue to **Upgrading or Installing** for upgrade or full-installation instructions.

Upgrading or Installing

After you choose an installation method, the installation program prompts you to either install or upgrade (see Figure 5-9).

Figure 5-9: Upgrading or Installing

Installing

You usually install Red Hat Linux on a clean disk partition or set of partitions, or over another installation of Linux.

> **Please Note:** Installing Red Hat Linux over another installation of Linux (including Red Hat Linux) does not preserve any information (files or data) from the prior installation. Make sure you save any important files! If you are worried about saving the current data on your existing system (without making a backup on your own), you should consider performing an upgrade instead.

If you wish to perform a full install, choose **Install**, and skip to **Installation Class**.

Upgrading

The installation process for Red Hat Linux 6.0 includes the ability to upgrade from prior versions of Red Hat Linux (version 2.0 and later) which are based on RPM technology. Upgrading your system installs the modular 2.2.x kernel as well as updated versions of the packages which are currently installed on your machine. The upgrade process preserves existing configuration files by renaming them using an .rpmsave extension (e.g., sendmail.cf.rpmsave) and leaves a log telling what actions it took in `/tmp/upgrade.log`. As software evolves, configuration file formats can change, so you should carefully compare your original configuration files to the new files before integrating your changes. If you wish to upgrade your Red Hat Linux system, choose **Upgrade**.

> **Please Note:** Some upgraded packages may require that other packages are also installed for proper operation. The upgrade procedure takes care of these dependencies, but it may need to install additional packages.

> **Please Note:** If you already have the X Window System (and possibly an older version of GNOME) on your machine you may see a screen that prompts you to install the latest version of GNOME included in this release.

Installation Class

If you chose to perform a full install, the installation program will ask you to choose an installation class (see Figure 5-10). You will not see this screen if you chose to perform an upgrade. You may choose from the following installation classes:

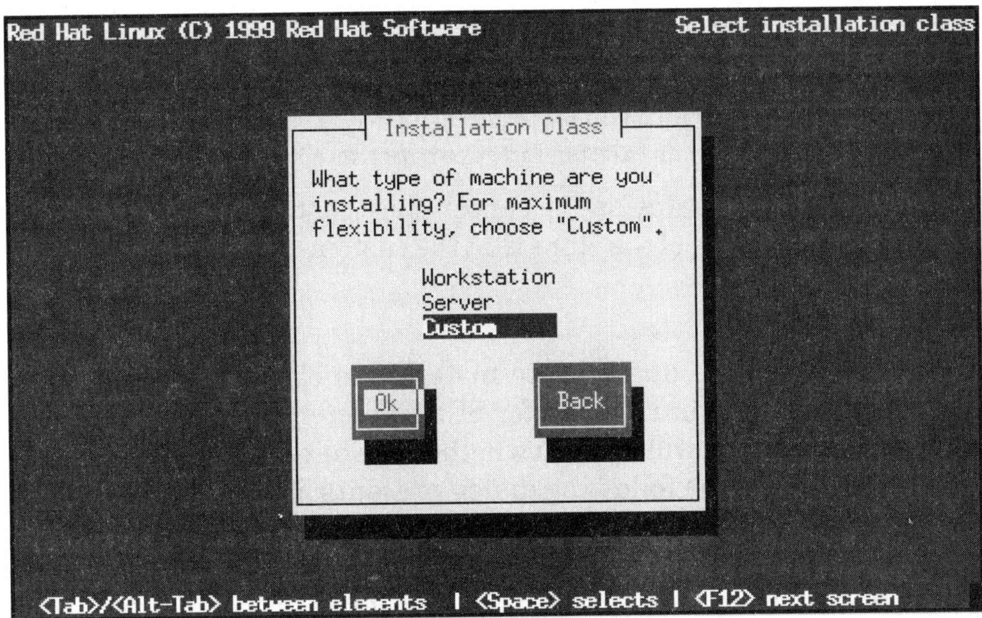

Figure 5-10: Installation Class

- **Workstation** — A workstation-class installation will automatically erase all Linux partitions from your computer's hard drive(s). This type of installation will attempt to set up a dual boot environment automatically.
- **Server** — A server-class installation will automatically erase all partitions from your computer's hard drive(s).
- **Custom** — A custom-class installation gives you complete control over partitioning-related issues. If you have installed Red Hat Linux in the past, the custom-class installation is most similar to past installations.

  Please Note: If you choose either **Workstation** or **Server**, part (or all) of your computer's stored data on all drives will be erased! You will be asked to confirm your decision; however, please keep in mind that once the installation program receives your confirmation, the erasure is irrevocable.

  Please Note: WARNING — If you choose to perform a workstation-class or server-class installation, data erasure will be irrevocable.

The severity of erased data varies according to type of installation:

- **Workstation-class** — Data on any existing Linux partition on any hard drive on your system will be erased.
- **Server-class** — Data on all partitions of all drives will be completely erased, regardless if it is on an existing Linux partition or not.

If you choose a workstation- or server-class installation, you will be able to skip over some of the steps that the custom-class install requires.

SCSI Support

After you choose the appropriate installation class, the installation program will probe your system for SCSI adapters. In some cases, the installation program will ask you whether you have any SCSI adapters. If you choose **Yes**, the following dialog presents a list of SCSI drivers. Choose the driver that most closely resembles your SCSI adapter. The installation program then gives you an opportunity to specify options for the SCSI driver you selected; most SCSI drivers should detect your hardware automatically, however. For either the workstation- or server-class installation, you should turn to Chapter 6 to finish the installation process.

Creating Partitions for Red Hat Linux

At this point, it's necessary to let the installation program know where it should install Red Hat Linux. This is done by defining mount points for one or more disk partitions in which Red Hat Linux will be installed. You may also need to create and/or delete partitions at this time.

> **Please Note:** If you have not yet planned how you will set up your partitions, please turn to **Disk Partitions**, and review everything up to **A Note About Kernel Drivers**. As a bare minimum, you'll need an appropriately-sized root partition, and a swap partition of at least 16 MB.

If you are still unsure about how to set up your partitions, please refer to Appendix B for more information. The installation program then presents a dialog box that allows you to choose from two disk partitioning tools (see Figure 5-11). The two choices you have are:

- **Disk Druid** — This is Red Hat Linux's install-time disk management utility. It can create and delete disk partitions according to user-supplied requirements, in addition to managing mount points for each partition.
- **fdisk** — This is the traditional Linux disk partitioning tool. While it is somewhat more flexible than Disk Druid, the downside is that fdisk assumes you have some experience with disk partitioning, and are comfortable with its somewhat terse user interface.

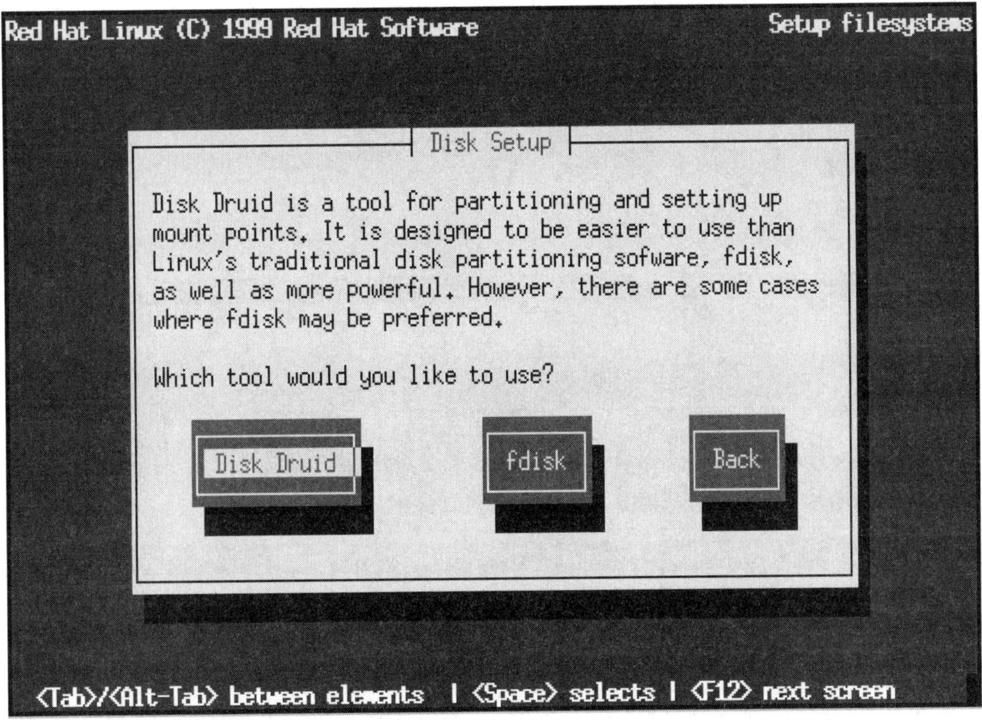

Figure 5-11: Selecting Disk Setup Method

With the exception of certain esoteric situations, Disk Druid can handle the partitioning requirements for a typical Red Hat Linux installation.

Select the disk partitioning tool you'd like to use, and press [Enter]. If you choose Disk Druid, continue reading. If you'd rather use `fdisk`, please turn to **Using Space From An Unused Partition**.

Using Disk Druid

If you selected Disk Druid, you will be presented with a screen that looks like figure 5-12. While it may look overwhelming at first, it really isn't. Let's go over each of Disk Druid's three sections.

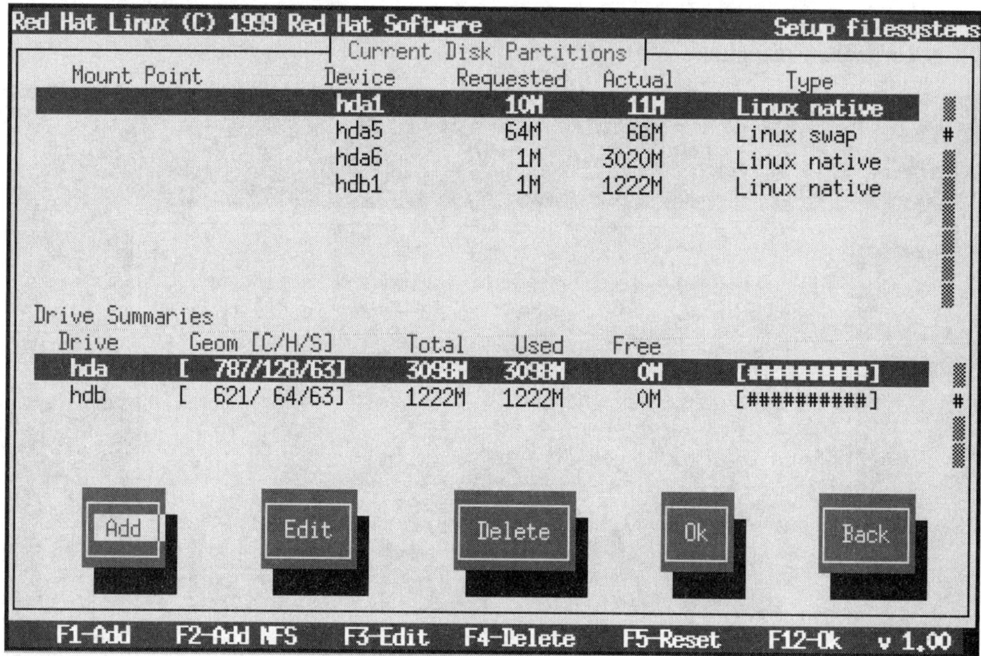

Figure 5-12: Disk Druid Main Screen

The "Current Disk Partitions" Section

Each line in the **Current Disk Partitions** section represents a disk partition. You'll note that this section has a scroll bar to the right, which means that there might be more partitions than can be displayed at one time. If you use the [\uparrow] and [\downarrow] keys, you can see if there are any additional partitions there. Each line in this section has five different fields:

Mount Point — This field indicates where the partition will be mounted when Red Hat Linux is installed and running.

Device — This field displays the partition's device name.

Requested — The "Requested" field shows the minimum size requested when the partition was defined.

Actual — The "Actual" field shows the space currently allocated to the partition.

Type — This field shows the partition's type.

Another Type of Partition — As you scroll through the **Current Disk Partitions** section, you might see an "Unallocated Requested Partitions" title bar, followed by one or more partitions. As the title implies, these are partitions that have been requested but, for one reason or another, have not been allocated. A common reason for having an unallocated partition is a lack of sufficient free space for the partition. In any case, the reason the partition remains unallocated will be displayed after the partition's mount point.

The "Drive Summaries" Section

Each line in the **"Drive Summaries"** section represents a hard disk on your system. Each line has the following fields:

Drive — This field shows the hard disk's device name. Geom [C/H/S] — This field shows the hard disk's geometry. The geometry consists of three numbers representing the number of cylinders, heads, and sectors as reported by the hard disk.

Total — The "Total" field shows the total available space on the hard disk.

Used — This field shows how much of the hard disk's space is currently allocated to partitions.

Free — The "Free" field shows how much of the hard disk's space is still unallocated.

Bar Graph — This field presents a visual representation of the space currently used on the hard disk. The more pound signs there are between the square braces, the less free space there is. In Figure 5-12, the bar graph shows no free space.

Please Note: The **"Drive Summaries"** section is displayed only to indicate your computer's disk configuration. It is not meant to be used as a means of specifying the target hard drive for a given partition. This is described more completely in **Adding a Partition** later in this section.

Disk Druid's Buttons

These buttons control Disk Druid's actions. They are used to add and delete partitions, and to change partition attributes. In addition, there are buttons that are used to accept the changes you've made, or to exit Disk Druid entirely. Let's take a look at each button in order.

Add – The "Add" button is used to request a new partition. When selected, a dialog box will appear containing fields that must be filled in.

Edit – The "Edit" button is used to modify attributes of the partition currently highlighted in the **"Current Disk Partitions"** section. Selecting this button will cause a dialog box to appear. Some or all of the fields in the "Edit Partition" dialog box may be changed, depending on whether the partition information has already been written to the disk.

Delete – The "Delete" button is used to delete the partition currently highlighted in the **"Current Disk Partitions"** section. Selecting this button will cause a dialog box to appear asking you to confirm the deletion.

Ok – The "Ok" button causes any changes made to your system's partitions to be written to disk. You will be asked to confirm your changes before Disk Druid rewrites your hard disk partition table(s). In addition, any mount points you've defined are passed to the installation program, and will eventually be used by your Red Hat Linux system to define the filesystem layout.

Back – This button causes Disk Druid to abort without saving any changes you've made. When this button is selected, the installation program will take you back to the previous screen, so you can start over.

Handy Function Keys

While there is some overlap between Disk Druid's buttons and the available functions keys, there are two function keys that have no corresponding buttons:

- **[F2] (Add NFS)** – This function key is used to add a read-only NFS-served filesystem to the set of mount points on your Red Hat Linux system. When selected, a dialog box will appear containing fields that must be filled in.
- **[F5] (Reset)** – This function key is used to discard all changes you may have made while in Disk Druid, and return the list of partitions to those read from the partition table(s) on your hard disk(s). When selected, you'll be asked to

confirm whether you want the changes discarded or not. Note that any mount points you've specified will be lost, and will need to be reentered.

Please Note: You will need to dedicate at least one partition to Red Hat Linux, and optionally more. This is discussed more completely in **Partition Naming Scheme**.

Now let's see how Disk Druid is used to set up partitions for your Red Hat Linux system.

Adding a Partition

To add a new partition, select the **Add** button, and press [Space] or [Enter]. A dialog box entitled "Edit New Partition" will appear (see Figure 5-13). It contains the following fields:

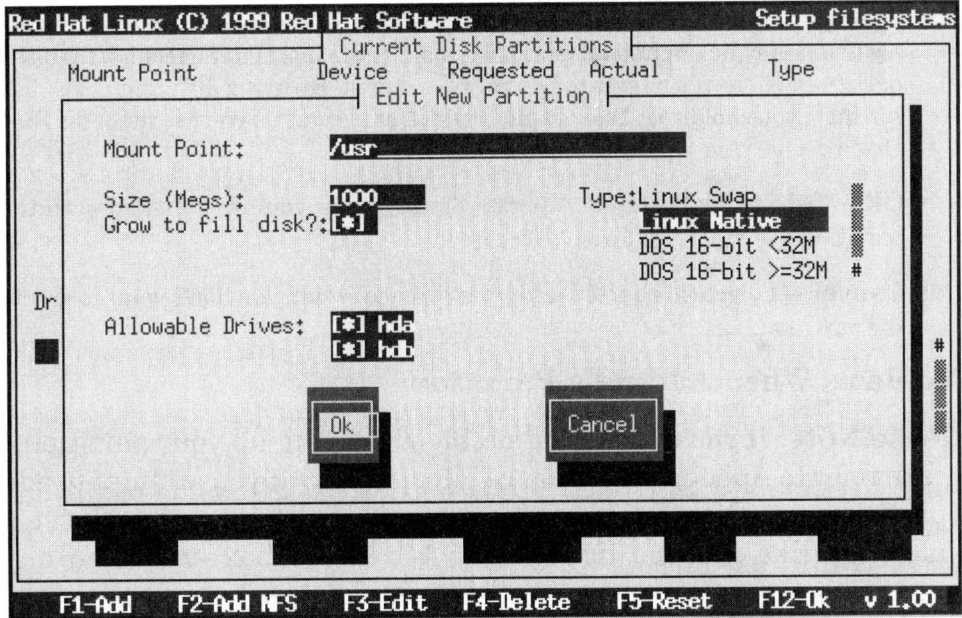

Figure 5-13: Creating a New Partition

- **Mount Point** — Highlight this field, and enter the partition's mount point. For example, if this partition should be the root partition, enter /; enter /usr for the usr partition, and so on.
- **Size (Megs)** — In this field, enter the size (in megabytes) of the partition. Note

that this field starts with a "1" in it, meaning that unless you change it, you'll end up with a 1 MB partition. Delete it using the [Backspace] key, and enter the desired partition size.

- **Growable?** — This check box indicates whether the size you entered in the previous field is to be considered the partition's exact size, or its minimum size. Press [Space] to check and uncheck the box. When checked, the partition will grow to fill all available space on the hard disk. In this case, the partition's size will expand and contract as other partitions are modified. Note that you can make more than one partition growable; if you do so, the additional free space will be shared between all growable partitions.
- **Type** — This field contains a list of different partition types. Select the appropriate partition type by using the [\uparrow] and [\downarrow] keys.
- **Allowable Drives** — This field contains a list of the hard disks installed on your system, with a check box for each. If a hard disk's box is checked, then this partition may be created on that hard disk. If the box is not checked, then the partition will never be created on that hard disk. By using different check box settings, you can direct Disk Druid to place partitions as you see fit, or let Disk Druid decide where partitions should go.
- **Ok** — Select this button and press [Space] when you are satisfied with the partition's settings, and wish to create it.
- **Cancel** — Select this button and press [Space] when you don't want to create the partition.

Problems When Adding a Partition

Please Note: If you are having problems setting up your partitions, please refer to Appendix B for more information. If you attempt to add a partition and Disk Druid can't carry out your request, you'll see a dialog box like the one in Figure 5-14. In the box are listed any partitions that are currently unallocated, along with the reason they could not be allocated. Select the **Ok** button, and press [Space] to continue. Note that the unallocated partition(s) are also displayed on Disk Druid's main screen (though you may have to scroll the **"Current Disk Partitions"** section to see them).

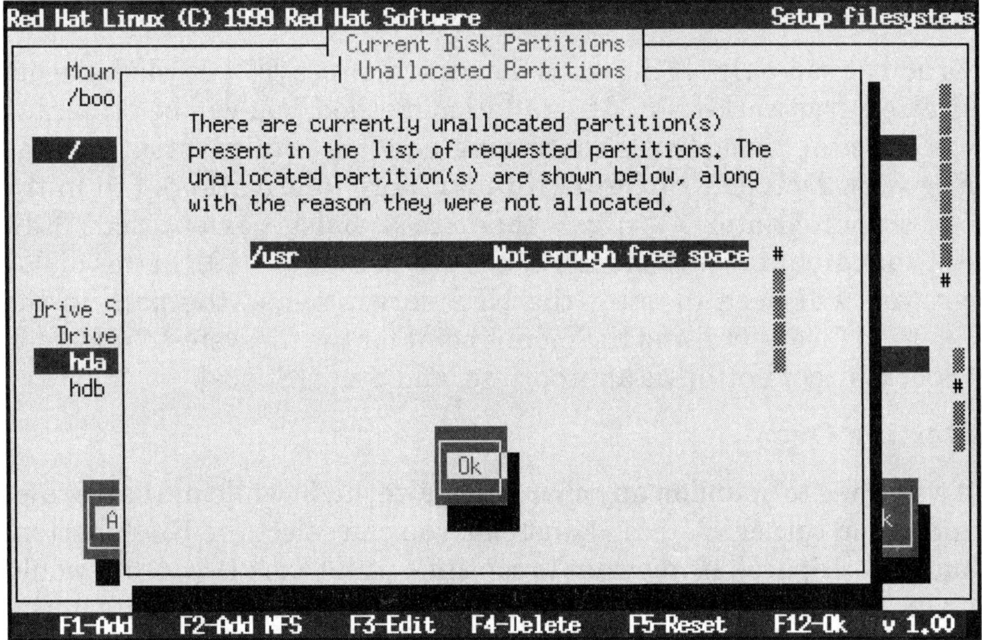

Figure 5-14: Unallocated Partition Warning

Deleting a Partition

To delete a partition, highlight the partition in the **"Current Disk Partitions"** section, select the **Delete** button, and press [Space]. You will be asked to confirm the deletion.

Editing a Partition

To change a partition's settings, highlight the partition in the **"Current Disk Partitions"** section, select the **Edit** button, and press [Space]. You will be presented with a dialog box very similar to the one shown in Figure 5-13. Make the appropriate changes, select **Ok**, and press [Space].

> **Please Note:** If the partition already existed on your hard disk, you will only be able to change the partition's mount point. If you want to make any other changes, you will need to delete the partition and recreate it.

Adding an NFS Mount

To add a read-only NFS-served filesystem, press [F2]. If you have not selected a network-related installation method, you will be presented with several dialog boxes concerning network configuration (turn to **Network Driver Configuration** for more information). Fill in the boxes appropriately. You will then see a dialog box entitled, "Edit Network Mount Point" (similar to the one in Figure 5-19). In this dialog box you will need to enter the NFS server name, the path to the exported filesystem, and the mount point for the filesystem. Select the **Ok** or **Cancel** button as appropriate, and press [Space].

Starting Over

If you'd like to abandon any changes you've made while in Disk Druid, and would rather use `fdisk` instead, you can select the **Back** button, and press [Space]. If you want to continue using Disk Druid, but would like to start over, press [F5], and Disk Druid will be reset to its initial state.

When You're Finished...

Once you've finished configuring partitions and entering mount points, your screen should look something like the one in Figure 5-15. Select **Ok**, and press [Space]. Then turn to **Initializing Swap Space**.

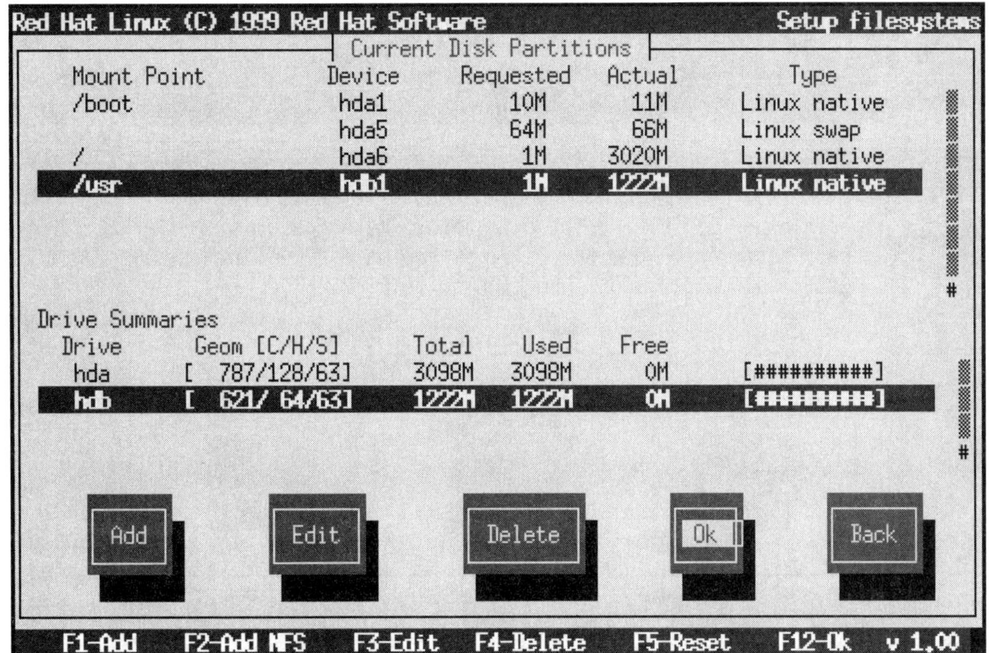

Figure 5-15: Partitions and Mount Points Defined

Using fdisk

If you'd rather use fdisk to manage partitions, this is the section for you. Once you've selected fdisk, you'll be presented with a dialog box entitled "Partition Disks" (see Figure 5-16). In this box is a list of every disk on your computer. Move the highlight to the disk you'd like to partition, select **Edit**, and press [Space]. You will then enter fdisk and can partition the disk you selected. Repeat this process for each disk you want to partition. When you're done, select "Done."

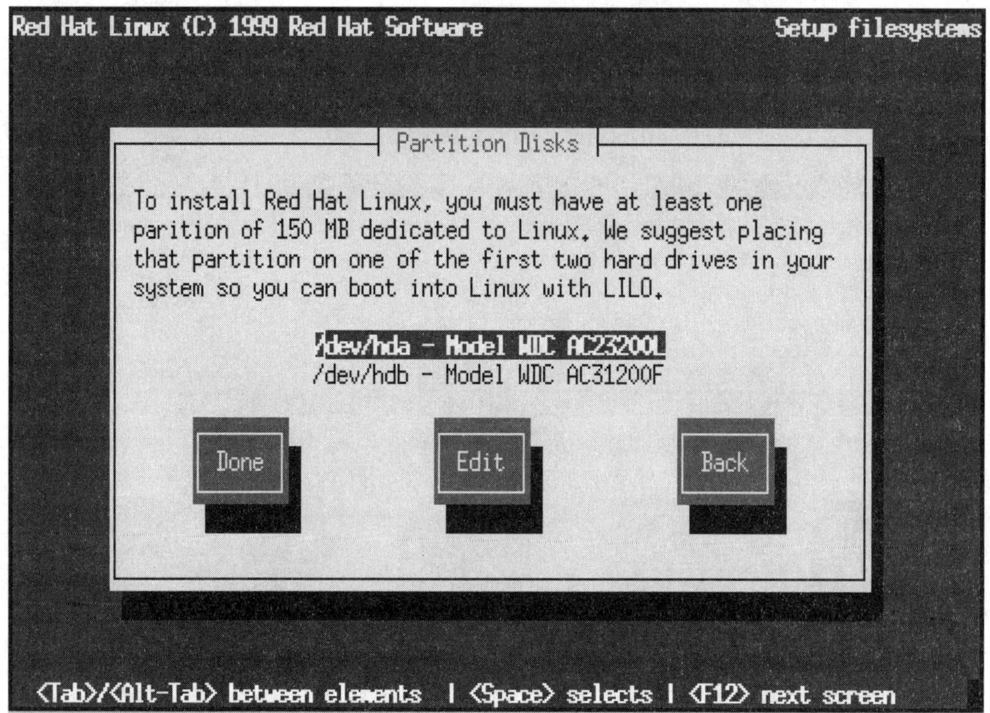

Figure 5-16: Selecting a Disk for Partitioning

An Overview of fdisk

`fdisk` includes online help which is terse but useful. Here are a few tips:

- The command for help is `m`.
- To list the current partition table, use the `p` command (see Figure 5-17).
- To add a new partition, use `n`.
- Linux fdisk creates partitions of type `Linux native` by default. When you create a swap partition, don't forget to change it to type Linux swap using the `t` command. The value for the Linux swap type is 82. For other partition types, use the `l` command to see a list of partition types and values.
- Linux allows up to four (4) partitions on one disk. If you wish to create more than that, one (and only one) of the four may be an extended partition, which acts as a container for one or more logical partitions. Since it acts as a container,

the extended partition must be at least as large as the total size of all the logical partitions it is to contain.

- It's a good idea to write down which partitions (e.g., `/dev/hda2`) are meant for which filesystems (e.g., `/usr`) as you create each one.
- **Please Note:** None of the changes you make take effect until you save them and exit fdisk using the w command. You may quit fdisk at any time without saving changes by using the `q` command.

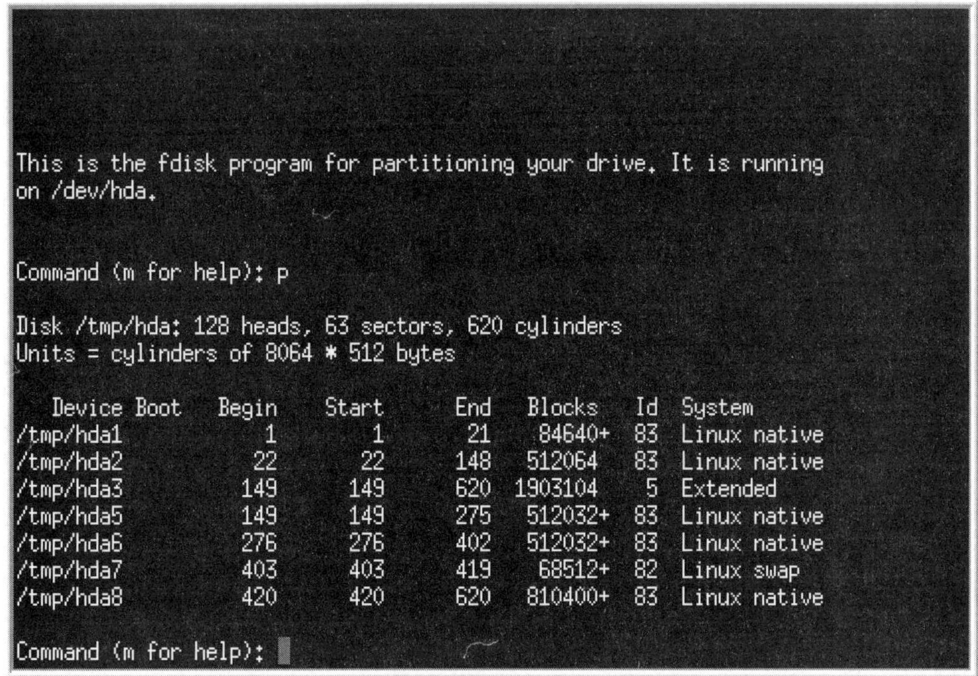
This is the fdisk program for partitioning your drive. It is running
on /dev/hda.
Command (m for help): p
Disk /tmp/hda: 128 heads, 63 sectors, 620 cylinders
Units = cylinders of 8064 * 512 bytes
Device Boot Begin Start End Blocks Id System
/tmp/hda1 1 1 21 84640+ 83 Linux native
/tmp/hda2 22 22 148 512064 83 Linux native
/tmp/hda3 149 149 620 1903104 5 Extended
/tmp/hda5 149 149 275 512032+ 83 Linux native
/tmp/hda6 276 276 402 512032+ 83 Linux native
/tmp/hda7 403 403 419 68512+ 82 Linux swap
/tmp/hda8 420 420 620 810400+ 83 Linux native
Command (m for help):

Figure 5-17: Sample Output from fdisk

Changing the Partition Table

When you are finished partitioning your disks, press **Done**; you may see a message indicating that the installation program needs to reboot. This is a normal occurrence after changing a disk's partition data; it usually happens if you created, changed, or deleted any extended partitions. After you press **Ok**, your machine will reboot. Follow the same installation steps you did up until **Partitioning Disks**; then simply choose **Done**.

Filesystem Configuration

The next dialog box contains a list of all disk partitions with filesystems readable by Red Hat Linux, including partitions for MS-DOS or Windows. This gives you the opportunity to assign these partitions to different parts of your Red Hat Linux filesystem. The partitions you assign will be automatically mounted when your Red Hat Linux system boots. Select the partition you wish to assign and press [Enter] (or choose **Edit**); then enter the *mount point* for that partition, e.g., `/usr` (see Figure 5-18).

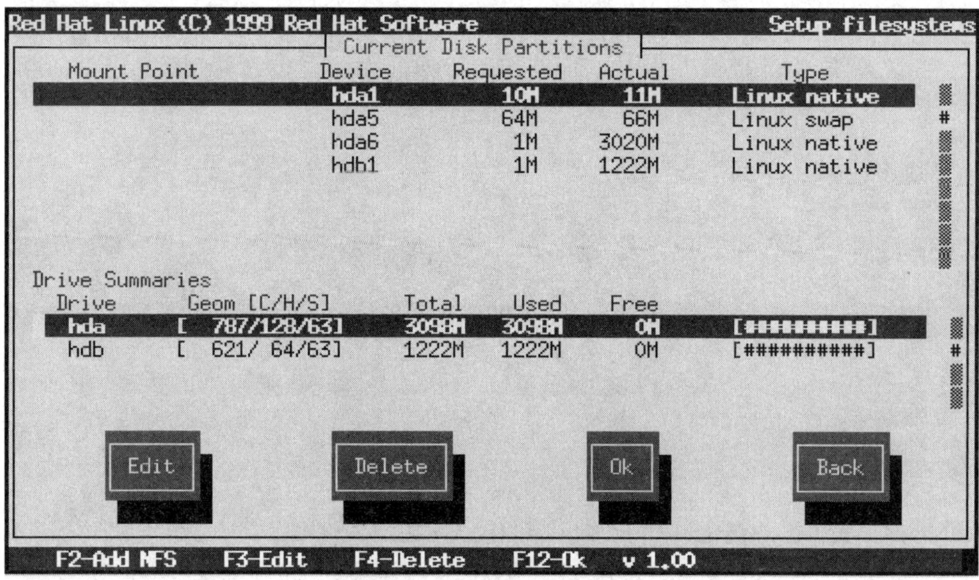

Figure 5-18: Filesystem Configuration

If you are performing an upgrade, the installation program tries to find your root partition automatically; if it does, it obtains all this information automatically, and goes on to the next step.

Adding an NFS Mount

Red Hat Linux also allows you to mount read-only NFS volumes when your system boots; this allows directory trees to be shared across a network. To do so, press [F2]. If you have not selected a network-related installation method, you will be presented with several dialog boxes concerning network configuration (turn to **Configuring TCP/IP Networking** for more information). Fill them in appropriately. You will then see a dialog box entitled "Edit Network Mount Point." Enter the NFS server's hostname, the path to the NFS volume, and the local mount point for that volume (see Figure 5-19).

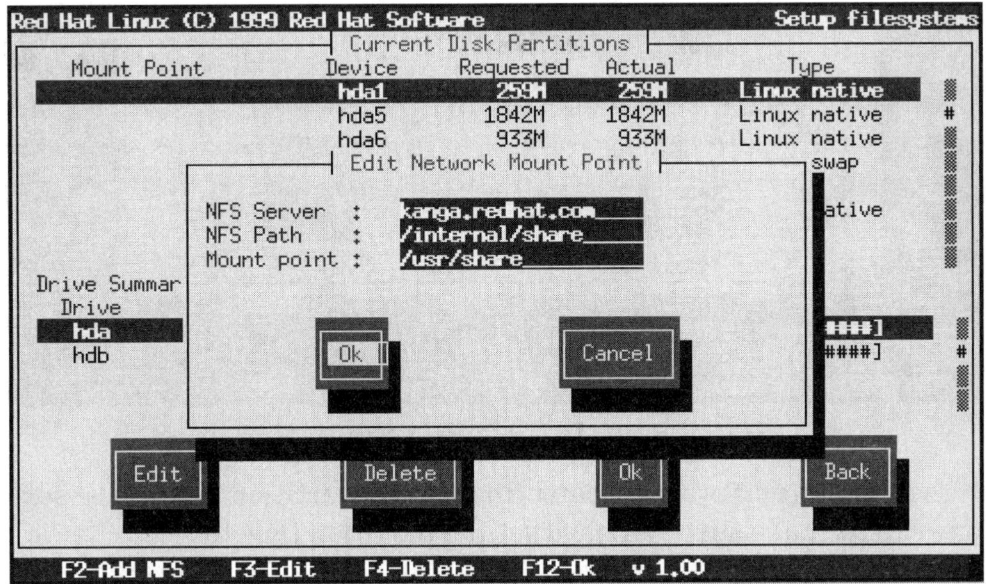

Figure 5-19: Adding an NFS Mount

Initializing Swap Space

After you've created partitions for Red Hat Linux, the installation program looks for swap partitions (see Figure 5-20). If it finds any, it asks whether you want to initialize them. Select the partition(s) you wish to initialize as swap space using [Space]; if you wish to check the partitions for bad blocks, make sure the **Check for bad blocks during format** box is checked. Choose **Ok**, and press [Space].

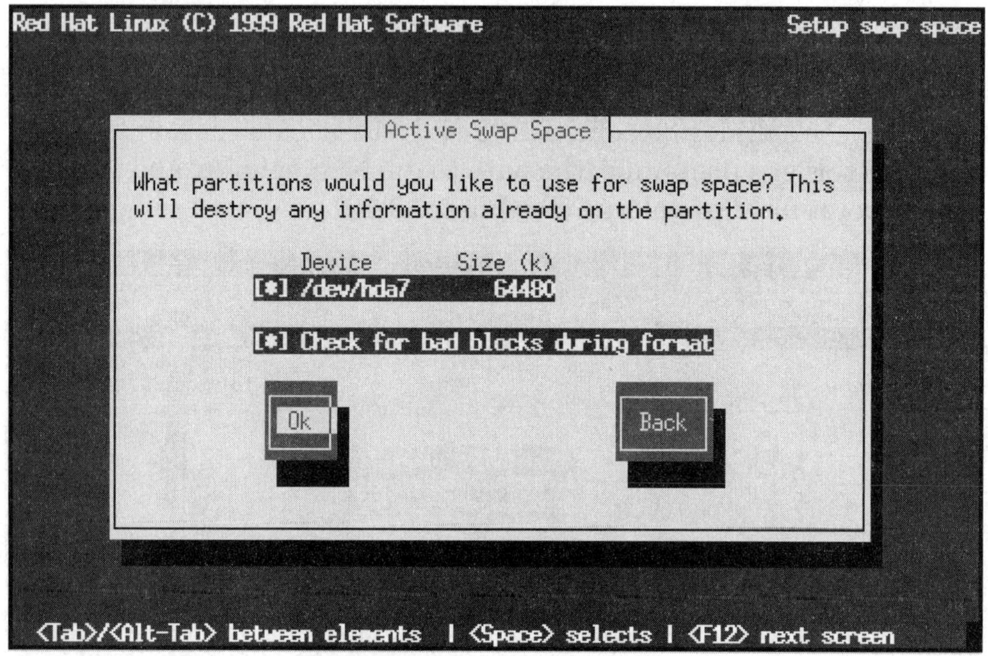

Figure 5-20: Initializing Swap Space

If the installation program can't find a swap partition and you're sure one exists, make sure you have set the partition type to `Linux swap`; see **Creating Partitions for Red Hat Linux** for information on how this is done with Disk Druid or `fdisk`.

Formatting Partitions

The next dialog box presents a list of partitions to format (see Figure 5-21). All newly created partitions should be formatted. In addition, any existing partitions that contain old data you no longer need should be formatted. However, partitions such as `/home` or `/usr/local` must not be formatted if they contain data you wish to keep. Select each partition to format and press [Space]. If you wish to check for bad blocks while formatting each filesystem, select Check for bad blocks during format. Select Ok, and press [Space].

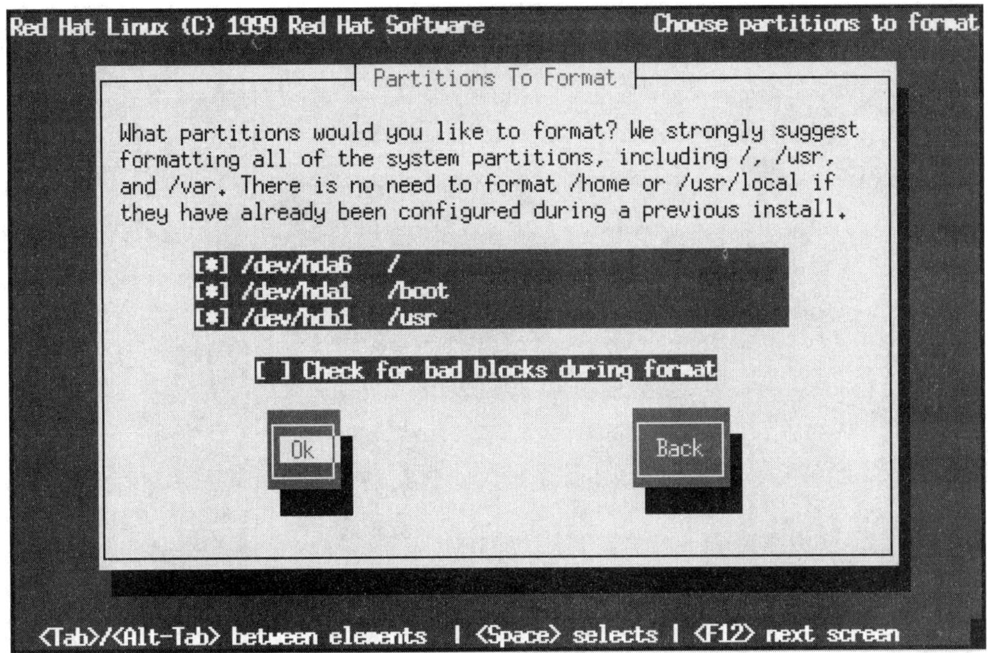

Figure 5-21: Formatting Partitions

Selecting and Installing Packages

After your partitions have been configured and selected for formatting, you are ready to select packages for installation. You can select components, which group packages together according to function, individual packages, or a combination of the two.

Selecting Components

Components group packages together according to the functionality they provide. For example, **C Development, Networked Workstation**, or **Web Server**. Select each component you wish to install and press [Space]. Selecting Everything (which can be found at the end of the component list) installs all packages included with Red Hat Linux (see Figure 5-22). Selecting every package will require close to 1 GB of free disk space.

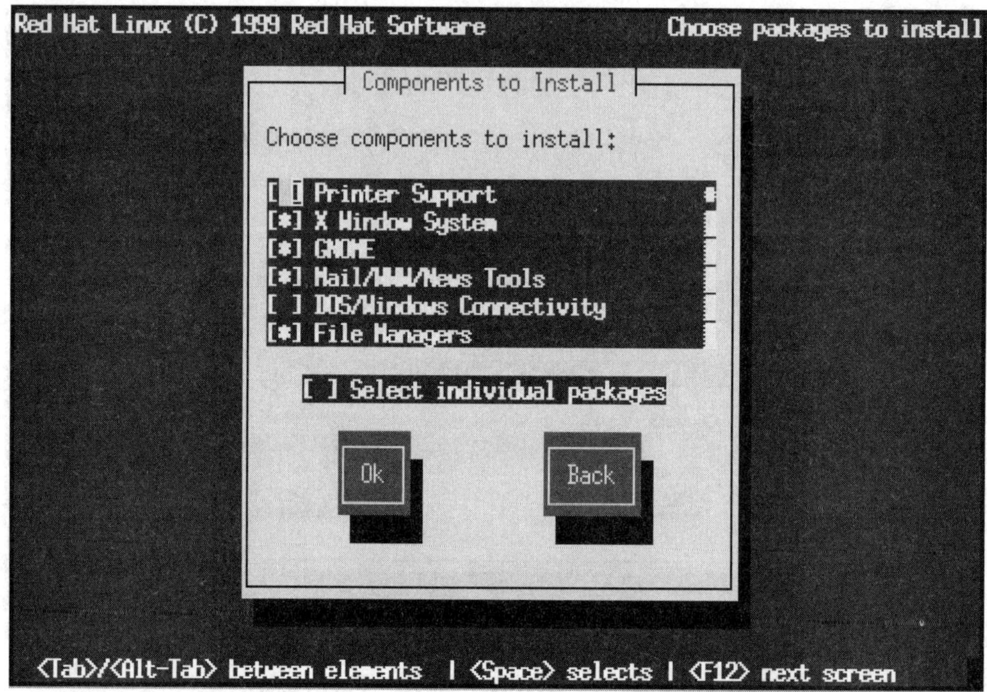

Figure 5-22: Selecting System Components

If you wish to select or deselect individual packages, check the **Select individual packages** check box.

Selecting Individual Packages

After selecting the components you wish to install, you may select or deselect individual packages. The installation program presents a list of the package groups available; using the arrow keys, select a group to examine and press [Enter] or [Space]. The installation program presents a list of the packages in that group, which you may select or deselect by using the arrow keys to highlight a package, and pressing [Space] (see Figure 5-23).

> **Please Note:** Some packages (such as the kernel and certain libraries) are required for every Red Hat Linux system and are not available to select or deselect.

Quick Keys

- [o] — shows that at least one of the packages in that component group has been selected.
- [*] — shows that all the packages of a component group have been selected.
- [—] — removes all packages in a component group.
- [*] — selects all packages in a component group.

Please Note: In the upper right-hand corner of the screen you will see the approximate system size of the components you have selected to install.

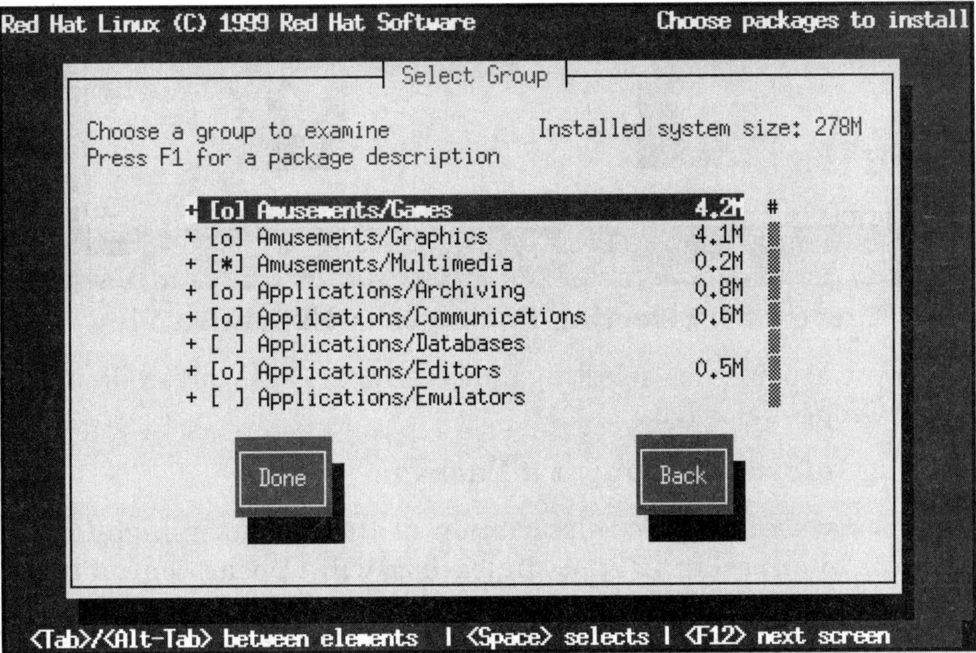

Figure 5-23: Selecting Packages

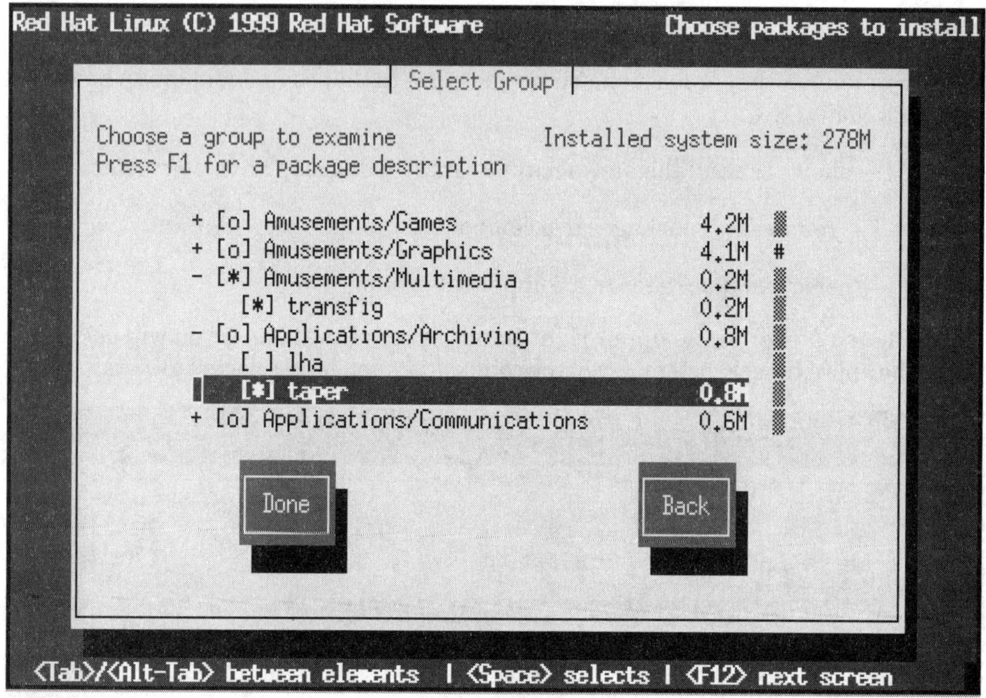

Figure 5-24: Selecting Packages — Expanded View

When you are finished selecting individual packages, press Ok in the Select Group dialog box.

Getting Information about a Package

You may view a detailed description of the currently highlighted package by pressing [F1]. A dialog box will appear containing a description of the package. You can use the arrow keys to scroll through the description if there is more than can fit on the screen. When you're done reading the description, press **Ok**, and the box will disappear. You can then continue selecting packages (and viewing their descriptions).

> **Please Note:** If you'd rather read the package descriptions on paper, please turn to Appendix C.

Package Dependencies

Many software packages, in order to work correctly, depend on other software packages or libraries that must be installed on your system. For example, many of the graphical Red Hat system administration tools require the python and pythonlib packages. To make sure your system has all the packages it needs in order to be fully functional, Red Hat Linux checks these package dependencies each time you install or remove software packages. After you have finished selecting packages to install, the installation program checks the list of selected packages for dependencies. If any package requires another package which you have not selected to install, the program presents a list of these unresolved dependencies and gives you the opportunity to resolve them (see Figure 5-25). If you simply press **Ok**, the program will resolve them automatically by adding all required packages to the list of selected packages.

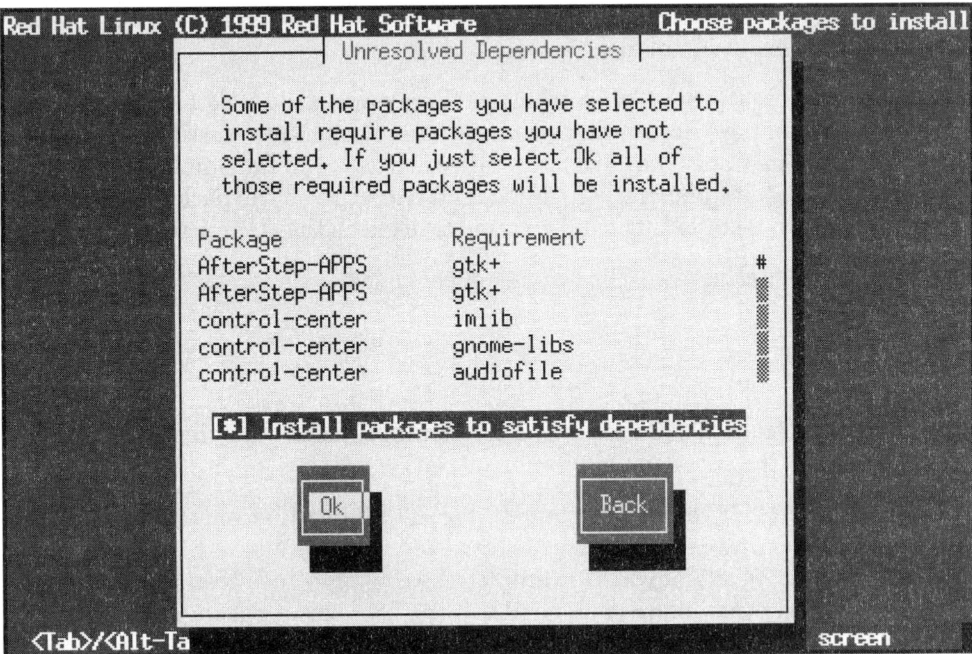

Figure 5-25: Unresolved Dependencies

Package Installation

After all package dependencies have been resolved, the installation program presents a dialog box telling you that a log file containing a list of all packages installed will be written to `/tmp/install.log` on your Red Hat Linux system. Select **Ok** and press [Space] to continue. At this point, the installation program will format every partition you selected for formatting. This can take several minutes (and will take even longer if you directed the installation program to check for bad blocks). Once all partitions have been formatted, the installation program starts to install packages. A window entitled "Install Status" is displayed with the following information:

Package — The name of the package currently being installed.

Size — The size of the package (in kilobytes).

Summary — A short description of the package.

Package Installation Progress Bar — A bar showing how complete the current package installation is.

Statistics Section — This section has three rows labeled "Total," "Completed," and "Remaining." As you might guess, these rows contain statistics on the total number of packages that will be installed, statistics on the number of packages that have been completely installed, and statistics on the packages that have not yet been installed. The information tracked on these three rows includes:

> **Packages** — The number of packages.
>
> **Bytes** — The size.
>
> **Time** — The amount of time.

Overall Progress Bar — This bar changes color showing how close to completion the entire installation is.

Please Note: If you're doing an FTP or HTTP installation, a message box will pop up as each package is retrieved from the site. At this point there's nothing left for you to do until all the packages have been installed. How quickly this happens depends on the number of packages you've selected, and your computer's speed. Once all the packages have been installed, please turn to Chapter 6 to finish your installation of Red Hat Linux.

6 Finishing the Installation

Configuring a Mouse

Next, your system will be probed to find a mouse. Some mice may be detected automatically; in this case, a dialog box is displayed showing the port on which the mouse was found. You may then be asked to give additional information, such as whether you have a two-button mouse, and would like it to emulate a three-button mouse. Make the appropriate selections, and continue to the next section. More commonly, you will see a screen similar to the one in Figure 6-1.

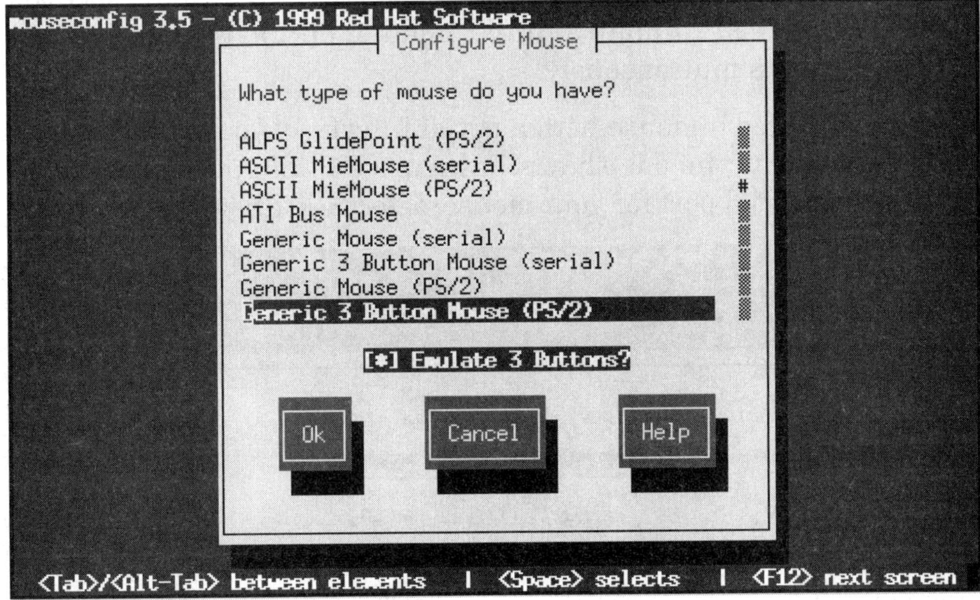

Figure 6-1: Mouse Configuration

The installation program's "best guess" as to your system's mouse type will be highlighted. If the mouse type is not accurate, use the [\uparrow] and [\downarrow] keys to scroll through the different mouse types. In general, you should use the following approach to selecting your system's mouse type:

- If you find an exact match for your mouse in the list, highlight that entry.

- If you find a mouse that you are certain is compatible with your mouse, highlight that entry.
- Otherwise, select one of the Generic entries, based on your mouse's number of buttons, and its interface. To determine your mouse's interface, follow the mouse cable back to where it plugs into your system. If the connector at the end of the mouse cable plugs into a rectangular connector, you have a serial mouse. On the other hand, if the connector is round, you have a PS/2 mouse. If you are installing Red Hat Linux on a laptop computer, in most cases the pointing device will be PS/2 compatible.

The **Emulate 3 Buttons** check box allows you to use a two-button mouse as if it had three buttons. In general, it's easiest to use the X Window System if you have a three-button mouse. If you select this check box, you can emulate a third, "middle" button by pressing both mouse buttons simultaneously.

If you've selected a mouse with a serial interface, you will then see a screen similar to the one shown in Figure 6-2. Simply highlight the appropriate serial port for your mouse, select Ok, and press [Space].

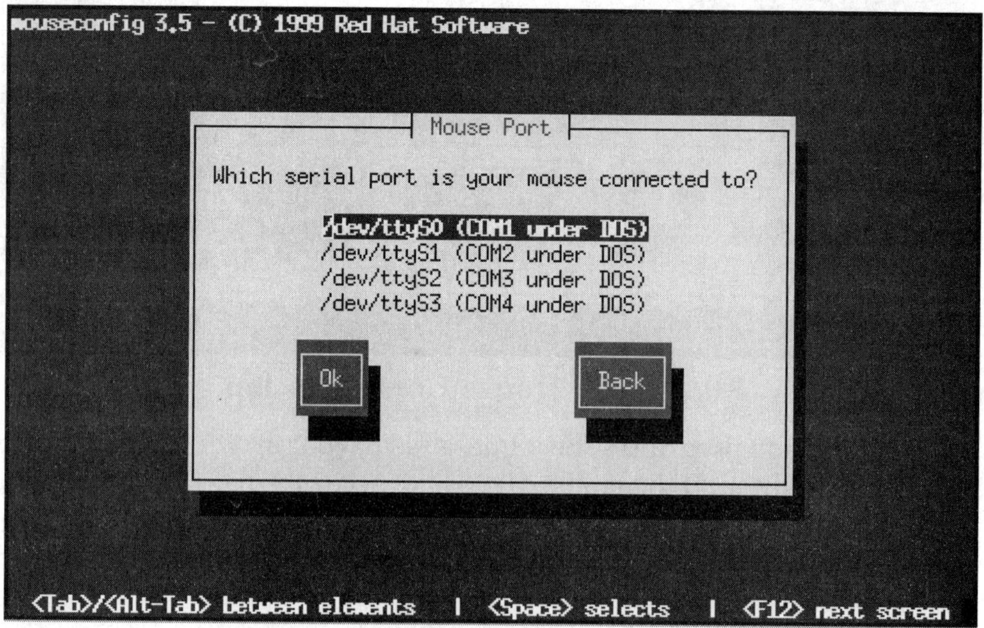

Figure 6-2: Serial Mouse Port Selection

If you wish to change your mouse configuration after you have booted your Red Hat Linux system, you may use the /usr/sbin/mouseconfig command. If wish to configure your mouse as a left-handed mouse, you can reset the order of the mouse buttons. This may be done after you have booted your Red Hat Linux system, by typing `gpm -B 321`.

Configuring Networking

Next, the installation program gives you an opportunity to configure (or reconfigure) networking. If you are installing from CD-ROM or from a local hard disk, the installation program asks if you want to configure networking. If you choose **No**, your Red Hat Linux system will be a standalone workstation. If you choose **Yes**, you may configure networking as described below. If you are installing via network media you have already entered temporary networking information that was used during the installation. The install program offers you three choices (see Figure 6-3 and 6-4):

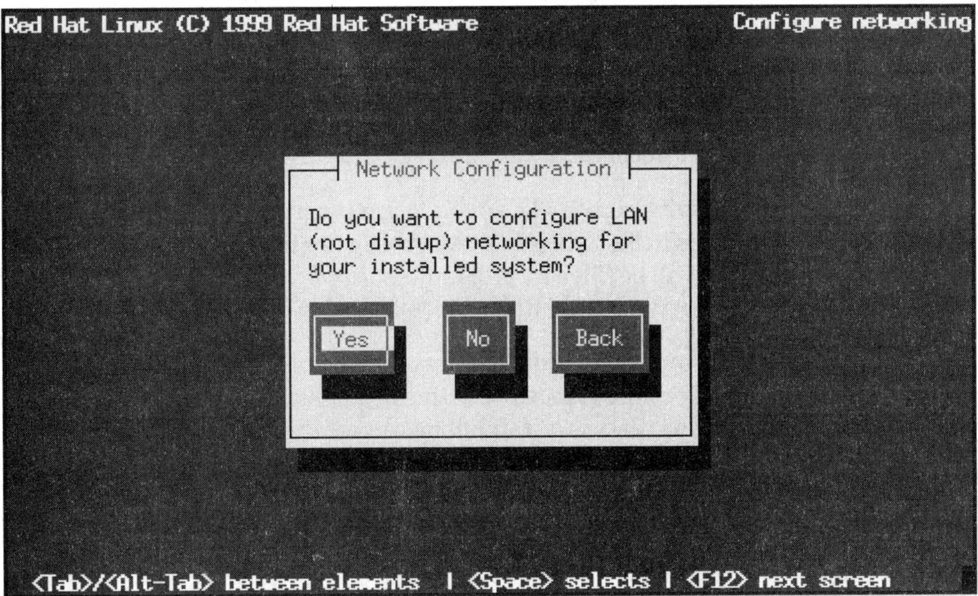

Figure 6-3: Network Configuration Options – Local Media Install

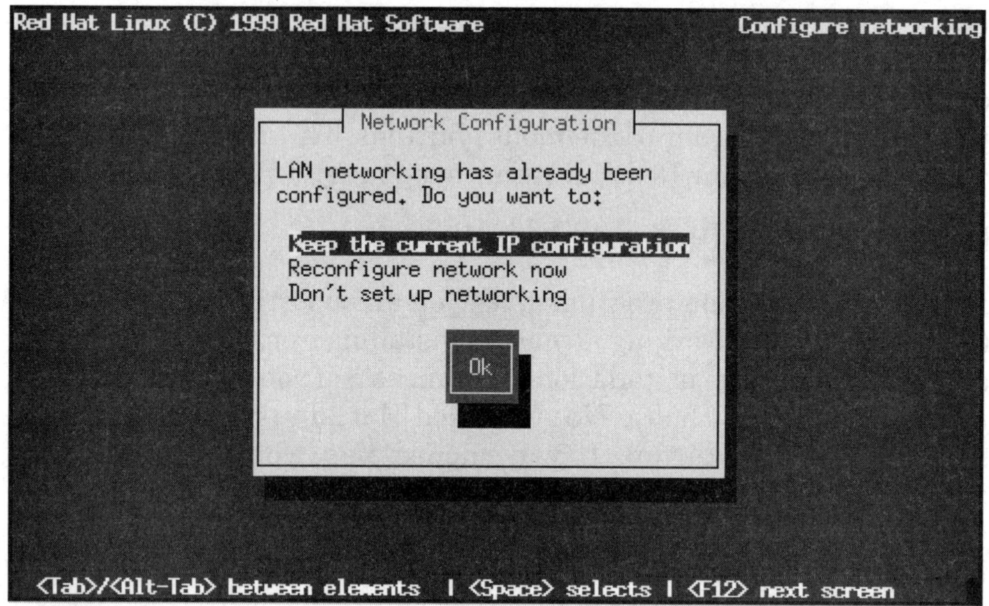

Figure 6-4: Network Configuration Options — Network Install

- **Keep this setup** — Keeps the network configuration you used during the installation. All the networking information you entered previously becomes part of your system's permanent configuration.
- **Reconfigure network now** — The installation program presents the network configuration dialogs in **Network Driver Configuration**. The values you used during installation will be filled in as defaults. Choose this if your system will be installed on a network other than the one you used to install Red Hat Linux.
- **Don't setup networking** — Don't set up networking at all. Your system will not have networking configured. Choose this if you installed your system over a network, but it will be used as a standalone workstation.

Network Configuration Dialogs

If you elected to configure networking at this time, you will be presented with a series of dialog boxes. Please turn to **Configuring TCP/IP Networking** for more information.

Configuring the Time Zone

Next, the installation program presents a dialog to help you configure your system's time zone (see Figure 6-5).

If you wish to set the hardware (CMOS) clock to GMT (Greenwich Mean Time, also known as UTC, or Coordinated Universal Time), select **Hardware clock set to GMT**. Setting it to GMT means your system will properly handle daylight saving time, if your time zone uses it. Most networks use GMT.

> **Please Note:** If your computer runs another operating system from time to time, setting the clock to GMT may cause the other operating system to display the incorrect time. Also keep in mind that if more than one operating system is allowed to automatically change the time to compensate for daylight saving time, it is likely that the time will be improperly set.

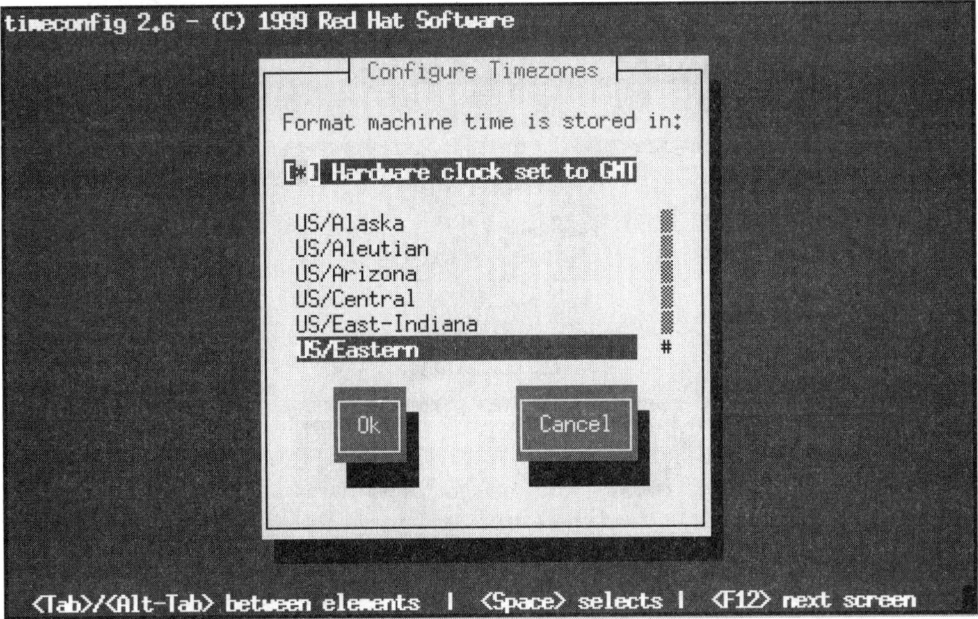

Figure 6-5: Configuring Time Zones

Select the time zone your system will be operating in from the list, and press [Enter].

If you wish to change your time zone configuration after you have booted your Red Hat Linux system, you may use the `/usr/sbin/timeconfig` command.

Selecting Services for Start on Reboot

Please Note: If you're performing a workstation- or server-class installation, this part of the installation is automatically done for you. Please skip ahead to **Configuring a Printer**.

Next you'll see a dialog box entitled "Services" (see Figure 6-6). Displayed in this box is a list of services with a check box by each. Scroll through this list, and check every service that you would like automatically started every time your Red Hat Linux system boots. If you're not sure what a particular service is, move the highlight to it and press [F1]. You'll then get a brief description of the service.

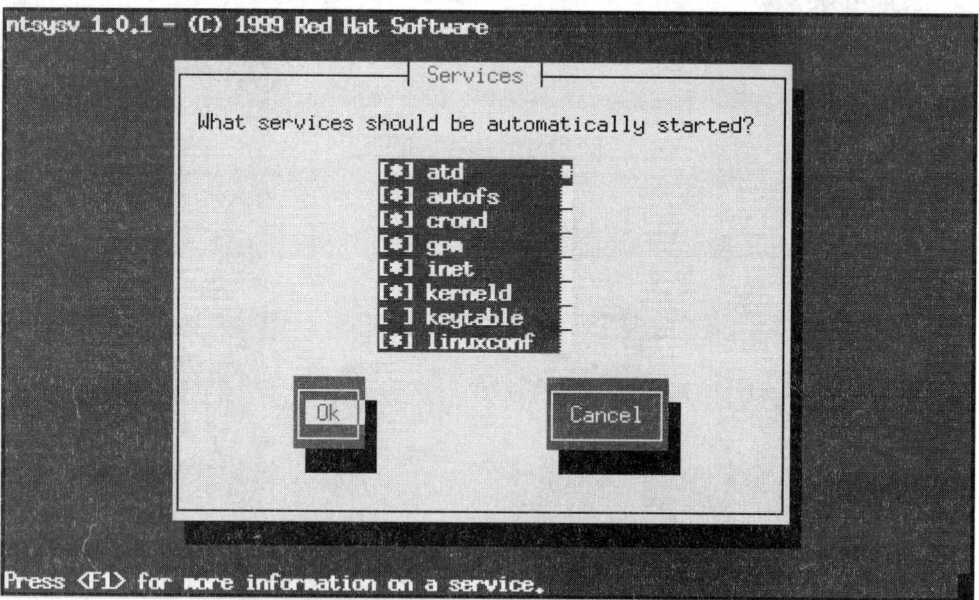

Figure 6-6: Selecting Services

Note that you can run `/usr/sbin/ntsysv` or `/sbin/chkconfig` after the installation to change which services automatically start on reboot.

Configuring a Printer

Next you will be asked if you want to configure a printer. If you choose Yes, a dialog box will ask you to indicate how the printer is connected to your computer (see Figure 6-7).

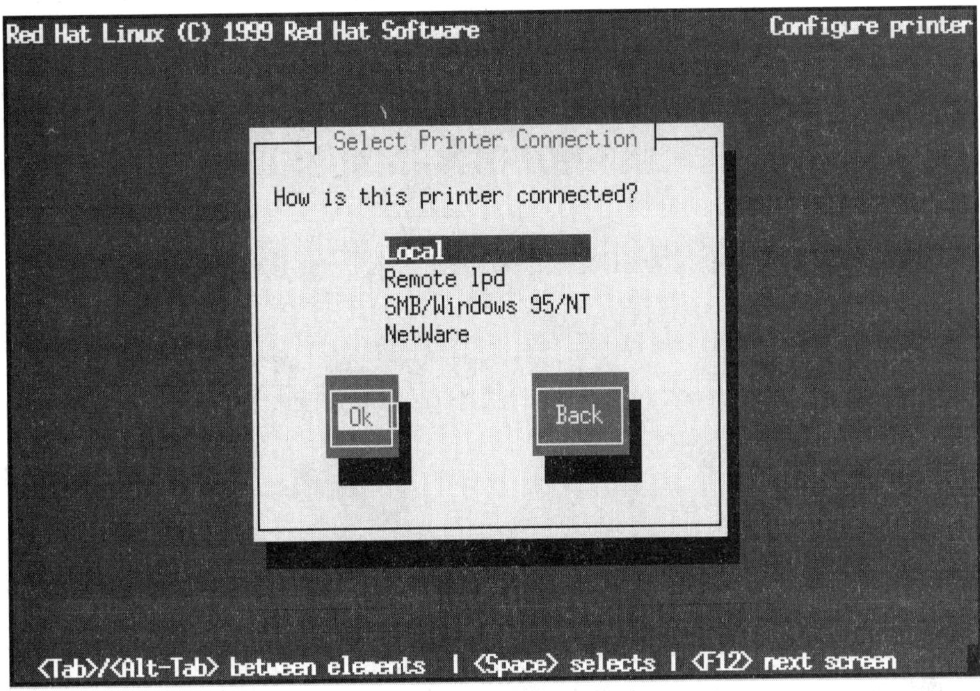

Figure 6-7: Selecting Printer Type

Here is a brief description of the three types of printer connections available:

Local — The printer is directly connected to your computer.

Remote lpd — The printer is connected to your local area network (either through another computer, or directly), and is capable of communicating via lpr/lpd.

SMB/Windows 95/NT — The printer is connected to another computer which shares the printer via SMB networking, such as a printer shared by a Windows 95 or Windows NT computer.

Netware – The printer is connected to another computer which shares the printer via Novell NetWare.

After selecting a printer type, you'll be presented with a dialog box entitled "Standard Printer Options" (see Figure 6-8). Enter the name of the queue and the spool directory you'd like to use, or accept the default information.

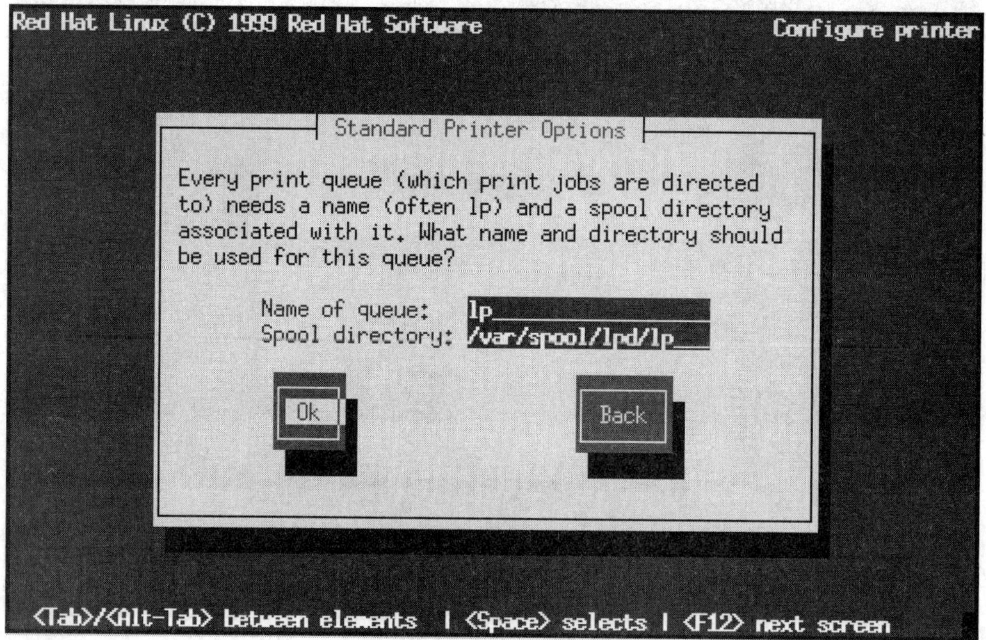

Figure 6-8: Standard Printer Options

The dialog box you'll see next depends on the printer connection type you selected.

Locally Attached Printers

If you selected "Local" as your printer's connection type, you'll see a dialog box similar to the one in Figure 6-9.

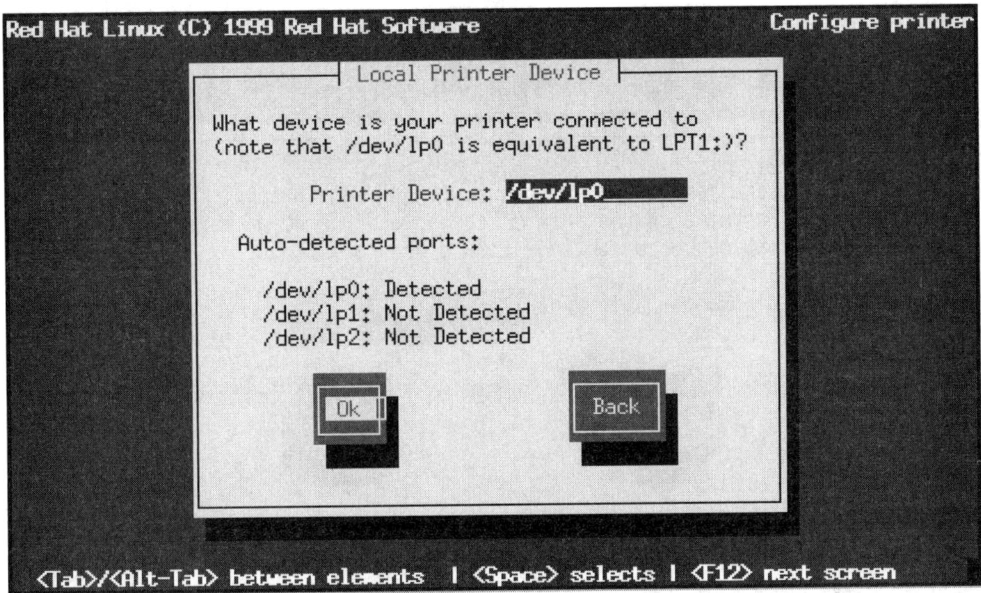

Figure 6-9: Local Printer Device

Enter the printer device name in the field provided. As a convenience, the installation program attempts to determine which printer ports are available on your computer. Select Next, and press [Space]. Now turn to **Finalizing Printer Setup** to continue.

Remote lpd Printers

If you selected "Remote lpd" as your printer's connection type, you'll see a dialog box similar to the one in Figure 6-10.

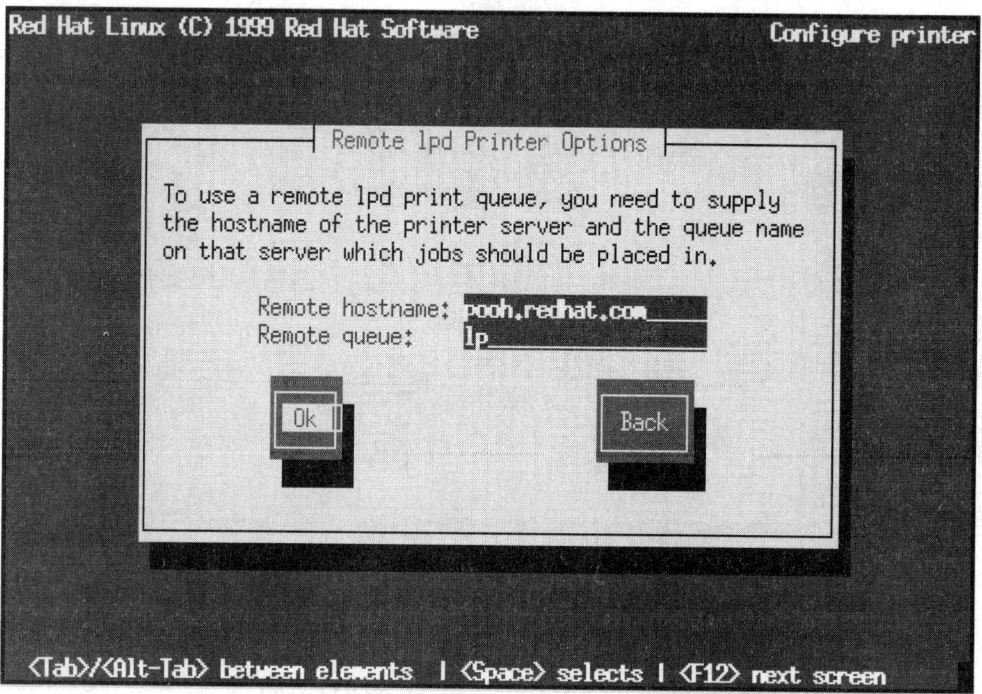

Figure 6-10: Remote lpd Printer Options

Enter the name of the computer to which the printer is directly connected in the "Remote hostname" field. The name of the queue on the remote computer that is associated with the remote printer goes in the "remote queue" field. Select Next, and press [Space]. Now turn to **Finalizing Printer Setup** to continue.

SMB, Windows 95/NT Printers

If you selected "SMB, Windows 95/NT" as your printer's connection type, you'll see a dialog box similar to the one in Figure 6-11.

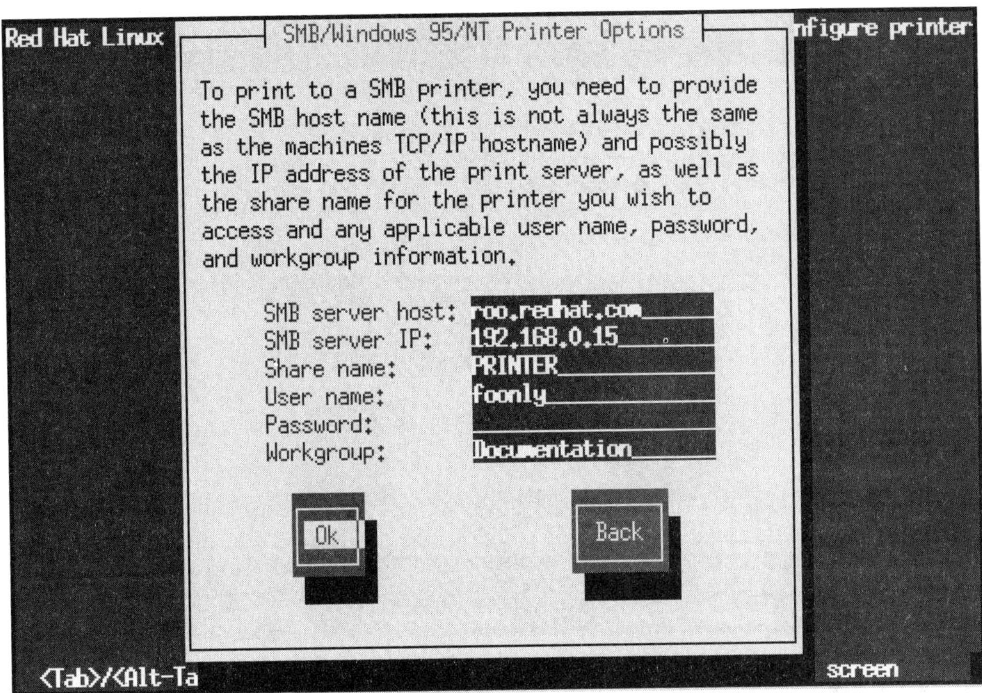

Figure 6-11: SMB and Windows95/NT Printer Options

Enter the necessary information in the fields provided. Select **Next**, and press [Space].

NetWare Printers

If you selected "NetWare" as your printer's connection type, you'll see a dialog box similar to the one in Figure 6-12.

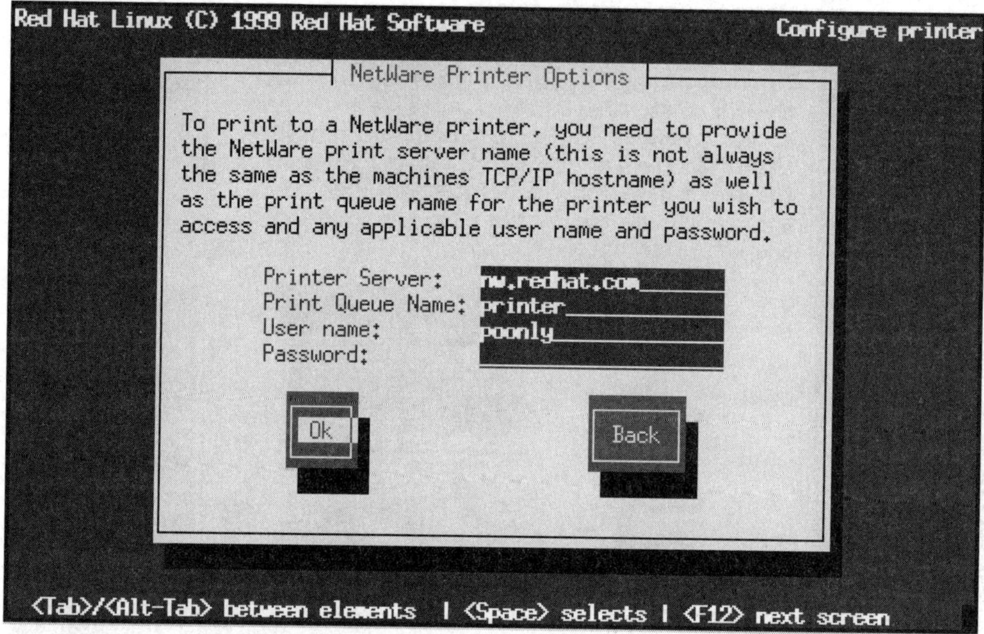

Figure 6-12: Netware Printer Options

Enter the necessary information in the fields provided. Select **Next**, and press [Space].

Finalizing Printer Setup

Next, you'll see a dialog box entitled "Configure Printer" (see Figure 6-13). Select the printer type that most closely matches your printer. Select **Next**, and press [Space] to continue.

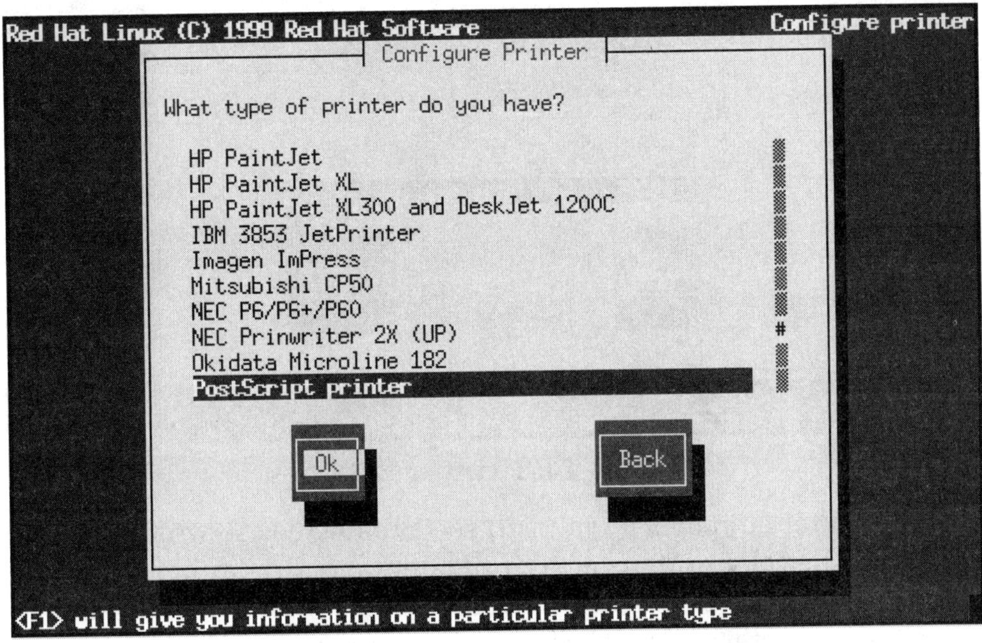

Figure 6-13: Configure Printer

After selecting the printer type, you will see a dialog box similar to the one in Figure 6-14. Set the paper size and resolution appropriately. The **Fix stair-stepping of text** check box should be checked if your printer does not automatically perform a carriage return after each line.

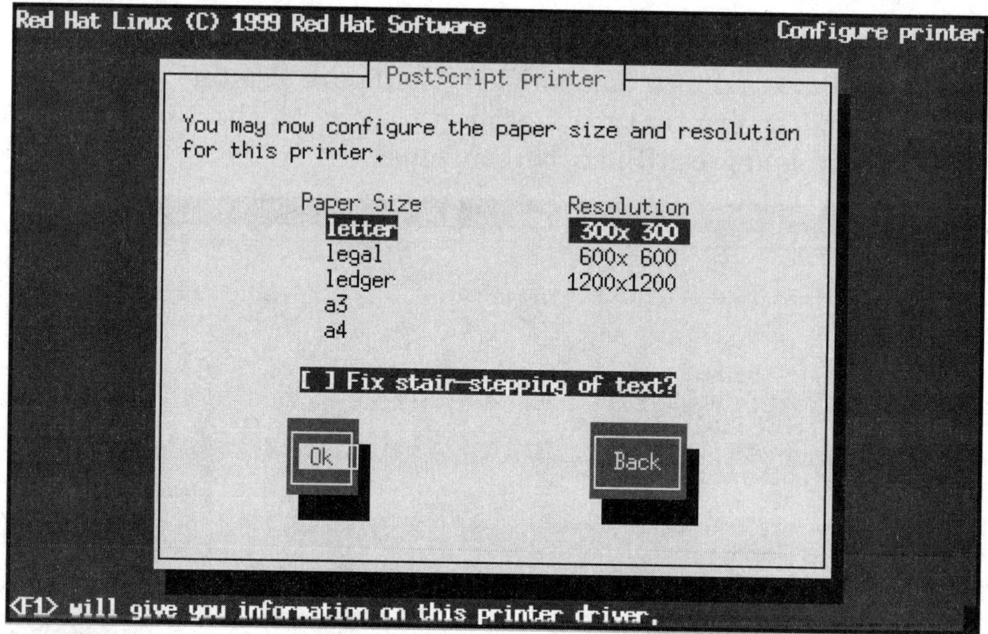

Figure 6-14: Printer Settings

If your printer supports it, you will see a dialog box in which you can configure the color options of your printer, or a similar one, in which you can configure the color and resolutions options of the uniprint driver your printer uses. Set these options appropriately.

Finally, you'll see a dialog box that contains all the information pertaining to your printer (see Figure 6-15). Verify that the information is correct. If everything looks OK, select **Done**. If you need to make changes, select **Edit**. You can also select **Cancel** if you'd rather not configure a printer at this time.

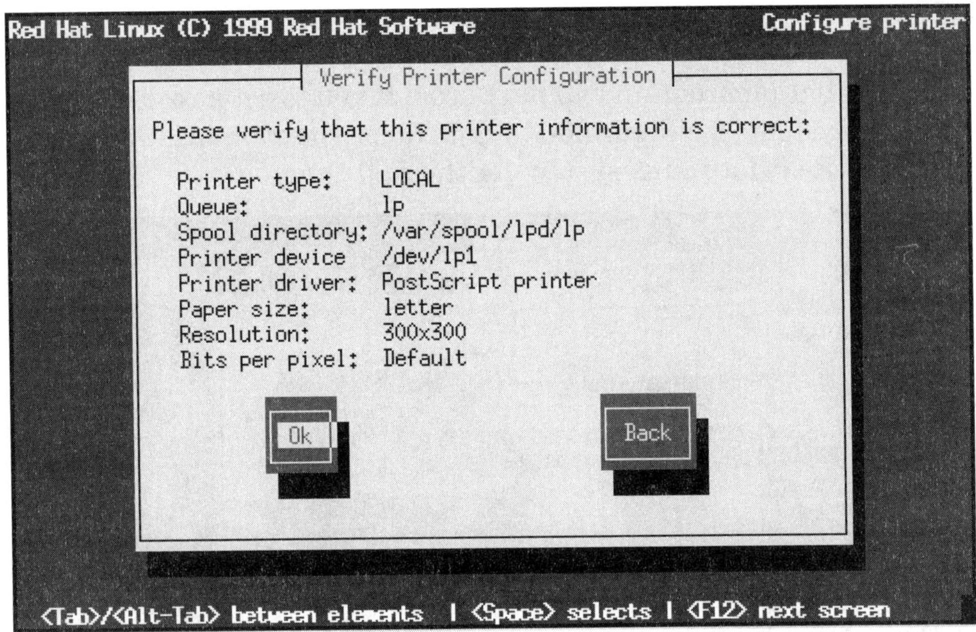

Figure 6-15: Verifying Printer Information

If you select **Done**, you will be given the option to configure another printer, or you may continue with the installation.

Setting a Root Password

The installation program will next prompt you to set a root password for your system (see Figure 6-16). You'll use the root password to log into your Red Hat Linux system for the first time.

Figure 6-16: Root Password

The root password must be at least six characters long; the password you type is not echoed to the screen. You must enter the password twice; if the two passwords do not match, the installation program will ask you to enter them again.

You ought to make the root password something you can remember, but not something that is easy for someone else to guess. Your name, your phone number, qwerty, password, root, 123456, and anteater are all examples of poor passwords. Good passwords mix numerals with upper and lower case letters and do not contain dictionary words: Aard387vark or 420BMttNT, for example. Remember that the password is case-sensitive. Write down this password and keep it in a secure place.

> **Please Note:** The root user (also known as the superuser) has complete access to the entire system; for this reason, logging in as the root user is best done only to perform system maintenance or administration. Please see Chapter 8 for instructions on how to add a user account for yourself after you reboot your system. A more basic method of creating a new user account can also be found in the Red Hat Linux Getting Started Guide in the Welcome to Linux chapter.

Authentication Configuration

After you have set up your root password, you will have the option of setting up different network password authentications:

- **Enable NIS** — allows you to run a group of computers in the same Network Information Service domain with a common password and group file. There are two options here to choose from:
  - √ **NIS Domain** — this option allows you to specify which domain or group of computers your system will belong to.
  - √ **NIS Server** — this option causes your computer to use a specific NIS server, rather than "broadcasting" a message to the local area network asking for any available server to host your system.
- **Enable Shadow Passwords** — provides a very secure method of retaining passwords for you. The /etc/psswd file is replaced by /etc/shadow which is only readable by root.
- **MD5 Password** — allows a long password to use up to 256 characters, instead of the standard eight letters or less.

> **Please Note**: To configure the NIS option, you must be connected to an NIS network. If you are unsure whether or not you are connected to an NIS network, please ask you system administrator. Unless you are setting up a NIS password, you will notice that both Shadow password and MD5 are selected. We recommend you use both to make your machine as secure as possible (see Figure 6-17).

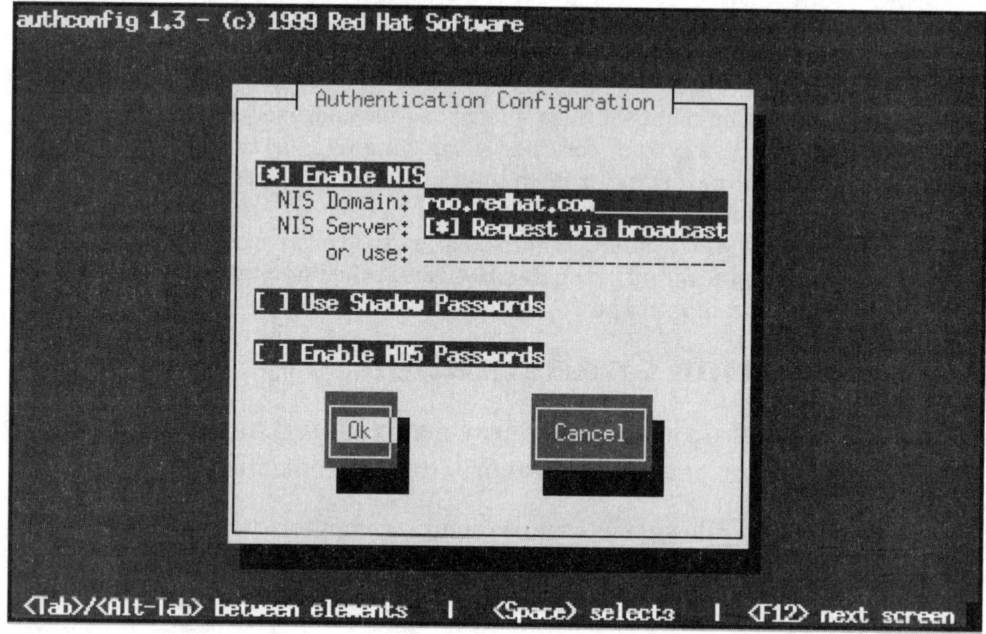

Figure 6-17: Authentication Configuration

Creating a Boot Diskette

Next, you'll be given the opportunity to create a customized boot diskette for your Red Hat Linux system (see Figure 6-18).

Red Hat Linux (C) 1999 Red Hat Software
Create bootdisk
Bootdisk
A custom bootdisk provides a way of booting into your Linux system without depending on the normal bootloader. This is useful if you don't want to install lilo on your system, another operating system removes lilo, or lilo doesn't work with your hardware configuration. A custom bootdisk can also be used with the Red Hat rescue image, making it much easier to recover from severe system failures.
Would you like to create a bootdisk for your system?
Yes
No
Back
<Tab>/<Alt-Tab> between elements | <Space> selects | <F12> next screen

Figure 6-18: Creating a Boot Diskette

A boot diskette can be handy for a number of reasons:

- **Use It Instead of LILO** — You can use a boot diskette instead of LILO. This is handy if you're trying Red Hat Linux for the first time, and you'd feel more comfortable if the boot process for your other operating system is left unchanged. With a boot diskette, going back to your other operating system is as easy as removing the boot diskette and rebooting.

- **Use It In Emergencies** — The boot diskette can also be used in conjunction with a rescue disk, which will give you the tools necessary to get an ailing system back on its feet again.

- **Use It When Another Operating System Overwrites LILO** — Other operating systems may not be as flexible as Red Hat Linux when it comes to supported boot methods. Quite often, installing or updating another operating system can cause the master boot record (originally containing LILO) to be overwritten, making it impossible to boot your Red Hat Linux installation. The boot diskette can then be used to boot Red Hat Linux so you can reinstall LILO.

Given these reasons to create a boot diskette, you should seriously consider doing so. Select Yes and press [Space] to create a boot diskette. Next, you'll see a dialog box directing you to insert a blank diskette in your computer's diskette drive. Select Ok, and press [Space] when you've done so.

After a short delay, your boot diskette will be done. After removing it from your diskette drive, label it clearly. Note that if you would like to create a boot diskette after the installation, you'll be able to do so. If you boot your system with the boot diskette (instead of LILO), make sure you create a new boot diskette if you make any changes to your kernel. For more information, please see the mkbootdisk man page, by typing man mkbootdisk at the shell prompt.

Installing LILO

> **Please Note:** If you are performing a custom-class installation, please keep reading. If you are performing a workstation-class or server-class installation, this part of the installation process is automatically done for you. Please skip ahead to **Configuring the X Windos System**.

In order to be able to boot your Red Hat Linux system, you usually need to install LILO (the LInux LOader). You may install LILO in one of two places:

The Master Boot Record (MBR)
: is the recommended place to install LILO, unless the MBR already starts another operating system loader, such as System Commander or OS/2's Boot Manager. The master boot record is a special area on your hard drive that is automatically loaded by your computer's BIOS, and is the earliest point at which LILO can take control of the boot process. If you install LILO in the MBR, when your machine boots, LILO will present a boot: prompt; you can then boot Red Hat Linux or any other operating system you configure LILO to boot (see below).

The first sector of your root partition
: is recommended if you are already using another boot loader on your system (such as OS/2's Boot Manager). In this case, your other boot loader will take control first. You can then configure that boot loader to start LILO (which will then boot Red Hat Linux).

A dialog box will appear that will let you select the type of LILO installation you desire (see Figure 6-19). Select the location where you wish to install LILO and press **Ok**. If you do not wish to install LILO, press **Skip**.

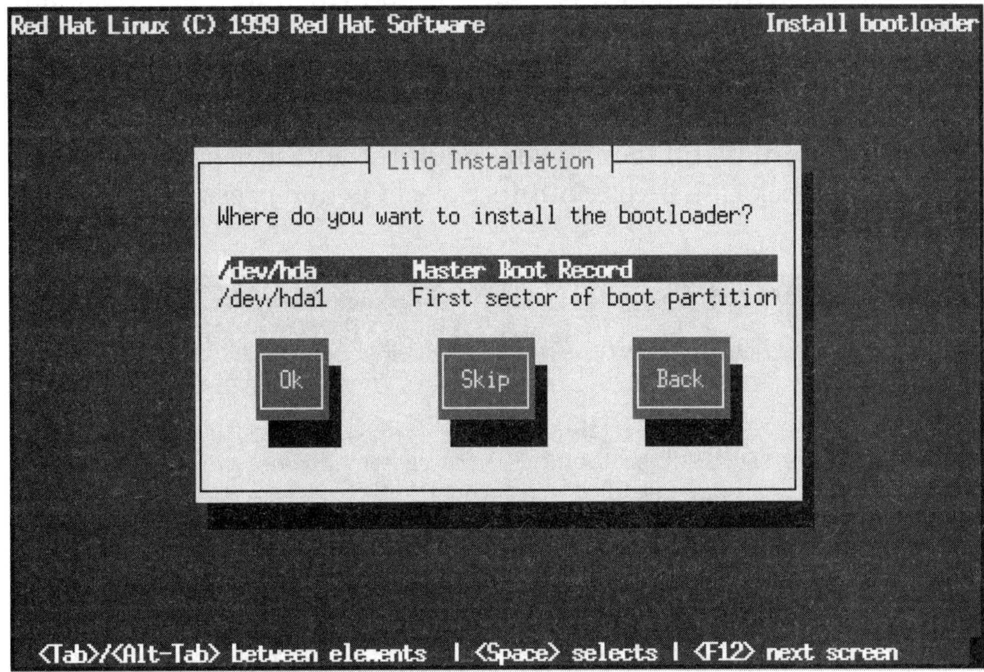

Figure 6-19: Installing LILO

Please Note: If you choose **Skip**, you will not be able to boot your Red Hat Linux system directly, and will need to use another boot method (such as a boot diskette). Use this option only if you know you have another way of booting your Red Hat Linux system!

SMP Motherboards and LILO

This section is specific to SMP motherboards only. If the installer detects an SMP motherboard on your system, it will automatically create two lilo.conf entries as opposed to the usual single entry. One entry will be called smp and the other will be called linux. The smp will boot by default. However, if you have trouble with the smp kernel, you can elect to boot the linux entry instead. You will retain all the functionality as before, but you will only be operating with a single processor.

Adding Options to the LILO Boot Command Line

Next, the installation program will ask if you wish to add default options to the LILO boot command (see Figure 6-20). Any options you enter will be passed to the Linux kernel every time it boots. When you reviewed your computer's BIOS settings in **Basic Hardware Configuration**, if you found your computer accesses a hard drive in LBA mode, check **Use linear mode**. Select **Ok** and press [Space] when finished.

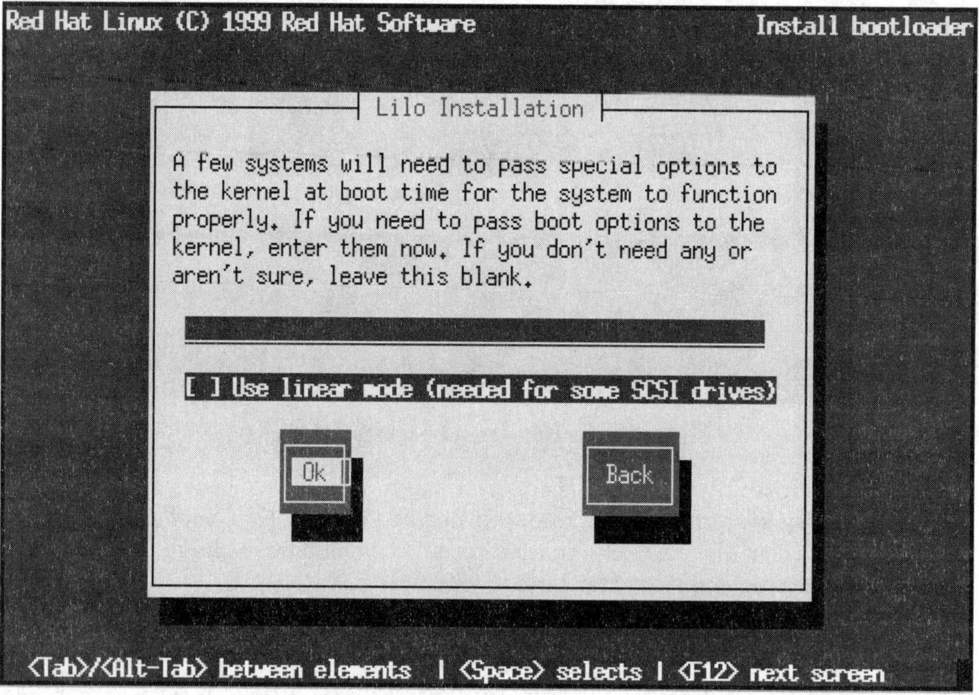

Figure 6-20: LILO options

Finally, the installation program will display a screen similar to the one in Figure 6-21. Every partition that may be bootable is listed, including partitions used by other operating systems. The "Boot label" column will be filled in with the word "linux" on the partition holding your Red Hat Linux system's root filesystem. Other partitions may also have boot labels. If you would like to add boot labels for other partitions (or change an existing boot label), use the arrow keys to highlight the desired partition. Then use the [Tab] key to select the **Edit** button, and press [Space]. You'll then see a small dialog box permitting you to enter/modify the partition's boot label. Press **Ok** when done.

> **Please Note:** The contents of the "Boot label" column will be what you will need to enter at LILO's Boot: prompt in order to boot the desired operating system. However, if you forget the boot labels defined on your system, you can always press [?] at LILO's Boot: prompt to display a list of defined boot labels.

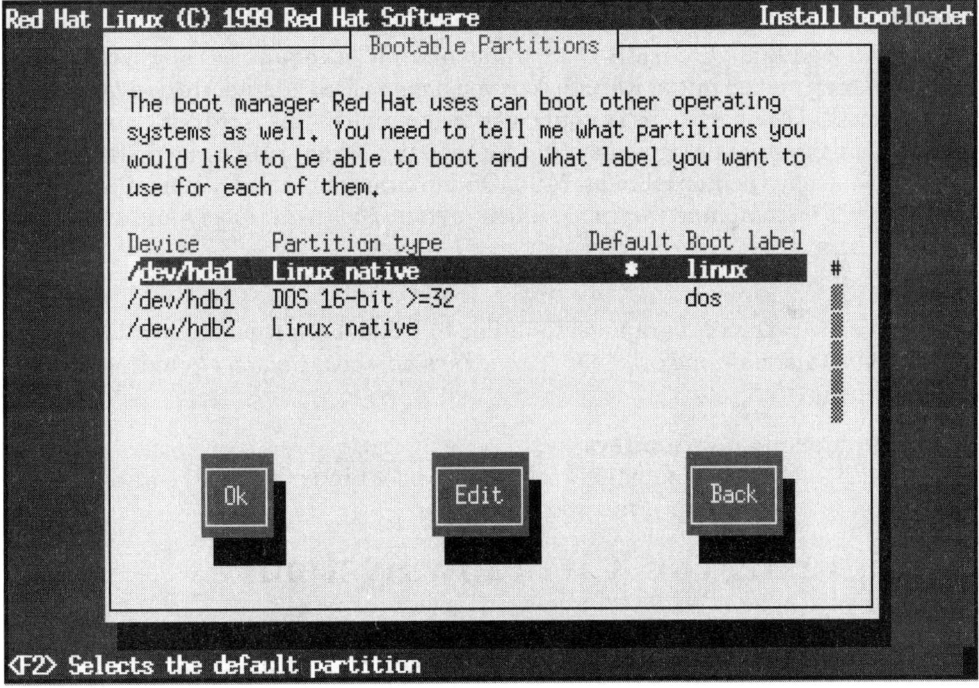

Figure 6-21: Selecting Bootable Partitions

There is also a column labeled "Default." Only one partition will contain an asterisk under that column. The partition marked as the default will be the partition LILO will boot if there is no user input during the boot process. Initially the root partition for your Red Hat Linux installation will be selected as the default. If you'd like to change this, use the arrow keys to highlight the partition you'd like to make the default, and press [F2]. The asterisk should move to the selected partition. When you've finished, select **Ok**, and press [Space].

Alternatives to LILO

If you do not wish to use LILO to boot your Red Hat Linux system, there are a few alternatives:

Boot Diskette
: You can use the boot diskette created by the installation program (if you elected to create one).

LOADLIN
: can load Linux from MS-DOS; unfortunately, it requires a copy of the Linux kernel (and an initial RAM disk, if you have a SCSI adapter) to be available on an MS-DOS partition. The only way to accomplish this is to boot your Red Hat Linux system using some other method (e.g., from LILO on a diskette) and then copy the kernel to an MS-DOS partition. LOADLIN is available from *ftp://metalab.unc.edu/pub/Linux/system/boot/dualboot/* and associated mirror sites.

SYSLINUX
: is an MS-DOS program very similar to LOADLIN; it is also available from *ftp://metalab.unc.edu/pub/Linux/system/boot/loaders/* and associated mirror sites.

Some commercial bootloaders,
: such as System Commander, are able to boot Linux (but still require LILO to be installed in your Linux root partition).

Configuring the X Window System

If you decided to install the X Window System packages, you now will have the opportunity to configure X server for your system. If you did not choose to install the X Window System packages, you may skip ahead to **Finishing Up**.

Configuring an XFree86 Server

If you wish to use XFree86, the installation program launches the Xconfigurator utility. Xconfigurator first probes your system in an attempt to determine what type of video card you have. Failing that, Xconfigurator will present a list of video cards. Select your video card from the list and press [Enter]. If your video card does not appear on the list, XFree86 may not support it. However, if you have technical knowledge about your card, you may choose **Unlisted Card** and attempt to configure it by matching your card's video chipset with one of the available X servers. Once you have selected your video card, the installation program installs the appropriate XFree86 server, and Xconfigurator presents a list of monitors. If your monitor appears on the list, select it and press [Enter]. Otherwise, select **Custom**. If you do select **Custom**, Xconfigurator prompts you to select the horizontal sync range and vertical sync range of your monitor (these values are generally available in the documentation which accompanies your monitor, or from your monitor's vendor or manufacturer). **Caution:** It is not recommended to select a monitor "similar" to your monitor unless you are certain that the monitor you are selecting does not exceed the capabilities of your monitor. If you do so, it is possible you may overclock your monitor and damage or destroy it. Next, Xconfigurator prompts you for the amount of video memory installed on your video card. If you are not sure, please consult the documentation accompanying your video card. It will not damage your video card by choosing more memory than is available, but the XFree86 server may not start correctly if you do. If the video card you selected might have a video clockchip, Xconfigurator presents a list of clockchips. The recommended choice is **No Clockchip Setting**, since XFree86 can automatically detect the proper clockchip in most cases. Next, Xconfigurator prompts you to select the video modes you wish to use; select one or more modes by pressing [Space]. Xconfigurator then writes a configuration file containing all of your choices to `/etc/X11/XF86Config`. Finally, you will see a screen which gives you the option of running the X

Windows System when you reboot. If you choose to have X run, GNOME will be the default desktop manager you see.

Finishing Up...

After you have configured the X Windows System, the installation program will prompt you to prepare your system for reboot (see Figure 6-22). Don't forget to remove any diskette that might be in the diskette drive, or CD that might be in the CD-ROM drive if your system is able to boot from the CD-ROM (unless you decided to skip the standard LILO installation, in which case you'll need to use the boot diskette created during the installation).

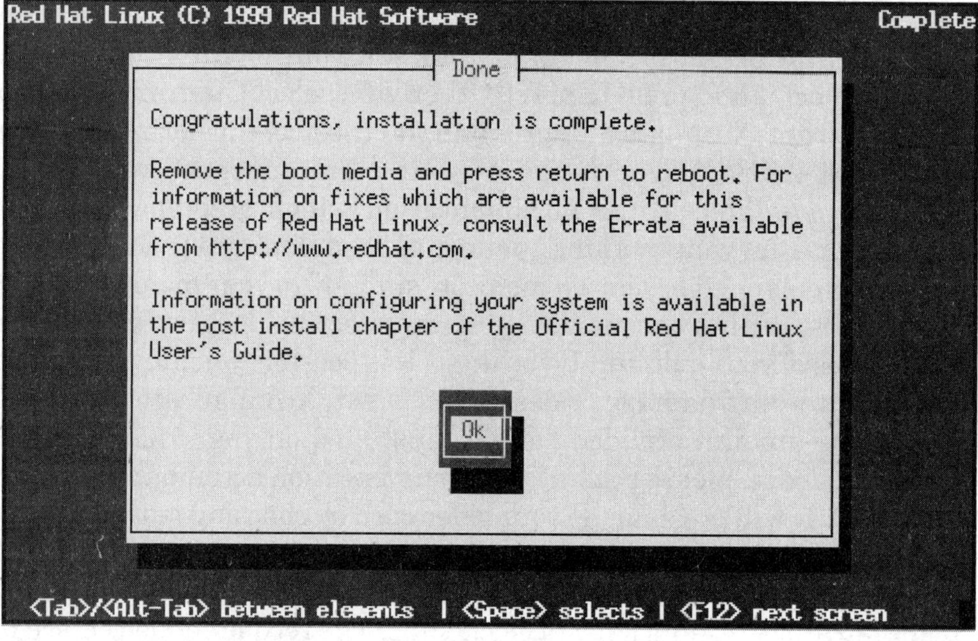

Figure 6-22: Ready for Reboot

After your computer's normal power-up sequence has completed, you should see LILO's standard prompt, which is boot:. At the boot: prompt, you can do any of the following things:

Pressing [Enter] — Causes LILO's default boot entry (as defined by the dialog box shown in Figure 6-21) to be booted.

Entering a Boot Label, followed by [Enter] — Causes LILO to boot the operating system corresponding to the entered boot label.

Doing Nothing — After LILO's timeout period, (which, by default, is five seconds) LILO will automatically boot the default boot entry.

Do whatever is appropriate to boot Red Hat Linux. You should see one or more screens worth of messages scroll by. Eventually, you should see a `login:` prompt.

Congratulations! Your Red Hat Linux installation is complete!

If you're not sure what to do next, we suggest you begin with the Red Hat Linux Getting Started Guide as an introduction to using Linux. The Red Hat Linux Getting Started Guide covers topics such as "learning the basics of your system" to "navigating your system" and much more.

7 Finding Documentation

Red Hat Linux includes thousands of pages of online documentation to help you learn how to use the system. The man pages, info documents, and plain text files included provide information on almost every aspect of Linux. If you've installed it, Red Hat Linux also includes documentation produced by the Linux Documentation Project.

Online Help

When you are looking for general help on commands and error messages, the best place to start is right on your system. There are several different sources of information at your fingertips:

- **Man Pages** — Authoritative reference material for commands, file formats, and system calls.
- **Package Documentation** — Many packages include additional documentation; RPM can help you find it.
- **HOWTOs and FAQs** — Helpful information from the Linux Documentation Project.
- **The locate Command** — A command that can help bridge the gap between a command and its documentation.
- **info Pages** — Hypertext documentation without the Web.

Let's take a look at each information source.

Man Pages

Almost every command on your system has an associated "man" page. This is documentation that you can get to instantly should you have questions or problems. For example, if you were having trouble with the `ls` command, you could use man to get more information by entering `man ls`. This will bring up the man page for `ls`. The man page is viewed through the `less` program (which makes it easy to page forward and backward screen by screen), so all of the options to `less` will work while in a man page. The more important keystrokes for `less` are:

- [q] to quit
- [Enter] to page down line by line
- [Space] to page down page by page
- [b] to page back up by one page
- [/] followed by a string and [Enter] to search for a string
- [n] to find the next occurrence of the previous search

There are times when it's just a lot more convenient to read something from a sheet of paper. Providing you have a working printer, you can print man pages as well. If you don't have PostScript printing capability and just want to print ASCII, you can print man pages with:

```
man COMMAND | lpr
```

If you do have a PostScript printer, you will probably want to print with:

```
man -t COMMAND | lpr
```

In both of those commands substitute "COMMAND" for the command you are trying to get help for.

Sometimes you'll find that certain system components have more than one man page. Here is a table showing the sections that are used to divide man pages:

Section	Contents
1	user commands
8	system commands
2	system calls
3	library calls
4	devices
5	file formats
6	games
7	miscellaneous
9	kernel internals
n	Tcl/Tk commands

This is also the order in which the sections are searched. This can be important; here's an example: Let's say that you want to see the man page for the swapon system call. So, you type man swapon. You will actually get the man page for `swapon(8)`, which is the command used to control swapping. Using the chart above, you can see that what you want is a "system call" and is located in section 2. You can then type `man 2 swapon`. All of this is because man searches the man directories in the order shown above, which means that the `swapon(8)` man page would be found before the `swapon(2)` man page. You can also search the man pages for strings. You do this using:

```
man -k string_to_search_for
```

This won't work, however, unless the makewhatis database has been created. Under Red Hat Linux, this is done by a cron job overnight. If you don't leave your system running overnight the database won't get created. If that is the case, run the following command as the root user:

```
/etc/cron.weekly/makewhatis.cron
```

Once you've done that (note that it might take a while), you could enter `man -k swapon`. That command would return:

```
# man -k swapon
swapon, swapoff (2) - start/stop swapping to
file/device
swapon, swapoff (8) - enable/disable devices and
files for paging and swapping
```

So you can see that there are pages in section 2 and 8 both referring to swapon (and swapoff in this case).

How to Read a Man Page

Man pages provide a great deal of information in very little space. Because of this, they can be difficult to read. Here's a quick overview of the major sections in most man pages:

- **Name** — The name of the program or programs documented in the man page. There may be more than one name, if the programs are closely related.
- **Synopsis** — An overview of the program's command syntax, showing all options and arguments.
- **Description** — A short description of the program's function.
- **Options** — A list of all options, with a short description of each (often combined with the previous section).
- **See Also** — If present, lists the names of other programs that are related in some way to this program.
- **Files** — If present, contains a list of files that are used and/or modified by the program.
- **History** — If present, indicates important milestones in the program's development.
- **Authors** — The people that wrote the program.

If you are new to Linux, don't expect to be able to use man pages as tutorials; they are meant as concise reference material. Trying to learn about Linux using the man pages is similar to trying to learn how to speak English from reading a dictionary. But there are other sources of information that may be more useful to those people just starting out with Linux; let's continue our search for documentation...

Package Documentation

Many packages have README files and other documentation as part of the source package. Packages built for Red Hat Linux define a standard place to install those documents so that you don't have to search through the sources to find the documents. Every package containing documentation (other than man pages, and files that need to be in specific locations) places their documentation in a subdirectory of `/usr/doc`. The name of the subdirectory depends on the package name and version number. For example, the tin package might be at version 1.22. Therefore, the path to its documentation would be `/usr/doc/tin-1.22`. For the most part, the documents in `/usr/doc` are in ASCII. You can view them with `more` *`filename`* or `less` *`filename`*. Having this special documentation area can be handy, but what if you're looking for documentation on a specific command (or file), and you don't know what package that command came from? No problem! Take, for example, the file `/usr/bin/rtin`. You're not sure what package it's part of, but you'd like to learn a bit more about it. Simply enter:

```
rpm -qdf /usr/bin/rtin
```

This command will return a listing of all the documentation (including man pages) from the package containing the file /usr/bin/rtin. RPM is capable of a lot more than this simple example. For more information on RPM, turn to Chapter 9.

Of course, maybe this kind of information is not exactly what you're looking for. Maybe you're more interested in task-oriented documentation. If so, read on...

HOWTOs and FAQs

If you elected to install it, most of the contents of the Linux Documentation Project (LDP) are available in /usr/doc on your system. The directory `/usr/doc/HOWTO` contains the ASCII versions of all the available HOWTOs at the time your Red Hat Linux CD-ROM was mastered. These files are viewable by using the `less` command.

```
less Installation-HOWTO
```

You may also encounter files that end with `.gz`. They are compressed with `gzip` to save space, so you'll need to decompress them before reading. One way of reading compressed HOWTOs without cluttering your disk with uncompressed versions is to use `zless`:

```
zless 3Dfx-HOWTO.gz
```

The `zless` command uses the same keystrokes as `less`, so you can easily move back and forth through a HOWTO.

`/usr/doc/HOWTO/mini` contains the ASCII versions of all the available mini-HOWTOs. They are not compressed and can be viewed with `more` or `less`. `/usr/doc/HOWTO/other-formats/html` contains the HTML versions of all the HOWTOs and the *Linux Installation and Getting Started* guide. To view things here, just use the web browser of your choice. `/usr/doc/FAQ` contains ASCII versions (and some HTML versions) of some popular FAQs, including the RedHat-FAQ. They can be viewed using more or less, or (in the case of HTML files) with the web browser of your choice.

The "locate" Command

When you don't know the full name of a command or file, but need to find it, you can usually find it with locate. locate uses a database to find all files on your system. Normally, this database gets built from a cron job every night. This won't happen, however, if your machine isn't booted into Linux all the time. So, if that is the case, you may occasionally want to run the following command:

```
/etc/cron.daily/updatedb.cron
```

You will need to be root on your system when doing that. That will allow locate to work properly. So, if you know you need to find all the "finger" files, you could run:

```
locate finger
```

It should return something like:

```
/usr/bin/finger
/usr/lib/irc/script/finger
/usr/man/man1/finger.1
/usr/man/man8/in.fingerd.8
/usr/sbin/in.fingerd
```

One thing to note, however, is that locate not only returns hits based on file name, but also on path name. So if you have a `/home/djb/finger/` directory on your system, it would get returned along with all files in the directory.

"info" Pages

While man is the most ubiquitous documentation format, info is much more powerful. It provides hypertext links to make reading large documents much easier and many features for the documentation writer. There are some very complete info documents on various aspects of Red Hat (especially the portions from the GNU project). To read info documentation, use the info program without any arguments. It will present you with a list of available documentation. If it can't find something, it's probably because you don't have the package installed that includes that documentation. Install it with RPM and try again. If you're comfortable using emacs, it has a built-in browser for info documentation. Use the [Ctrl-h] [i] key sequence to see it. The info system is a hypertext based system. Any highlighted text that appears is a link leading to more information. Use [Tab] to move the cursor to the link, and press [Enter] to follow the link. Pressing [p] returns you to the previous page, [n] moves you to the next page, and [u] goes up one level of documentation. To exit info, press [Ctrl-x] [Ctrl-c] (control-x followed by control-c). The best way to learn how to use info is to read the info documentation on it. If you read the first screen that info presents you'll be able to get started.

Help from the Internet Community

Red Hat Mailing Lists

If you can't find help for your problem on line and you have WWW access, you should see *http://www.redhat.com/support/mailing-lists/* . Here you can search the archives of the redhat-list. Many questions have already been answered there. The subscription addresses for Red Hat's lists follow this format

```
<list-name>-request@redhat.com
```

Simply replace `<list-name>` with one of the following:

```
apollo-list
applixware-list
axp-list blinux-list
cde-list
gnome-announce
gtk-list
hurricane-list
linux-alert
linux-security
m68k-list
pam-list
redhat-announce-list
redhat-devel-list
redhat-install-list
redhat-list
redhat-ppp-list
rpm-list
```

```
sound-list
sparc-list
```

To subscribe, send mail to the address of the list you want to subscribe to with `subscribe` in the `Subject:` line. To unsubscribe, send mail to the address of the list you want to unsubscribe from with `unsubscribe` in the `Subject:` line. Then to send mail to the list, you just send it to the address above without the `-request` in the name.

USENET Newsgroups

Another good source of help is the comp.os.linux hierarchy on USENET. If you are familiar with news, you should check it out.

Red Hat-Specific Newsgroups

Red Hat Software currently hosts a number of newgroups specifically for users of Red Hat's software. You can either read these groups directly from news.redhat.com, or ask your news admin to add the redhat.* hierarchy to their news server.

8 System Configuration

After installing your Red Hat Linux system, it's easy to think that the decisions you made during the installation are engraved in granite, never to be changed again. Nothing could be further from the truth! One of the main strengths of Linux is that the operating system can be configured to do just about anything. At Red Hat Software, they try to make system configuration as easy and accessible as possible. To that end, they have worked hard on two fronts:

- By developing system configuration tools in-house;
- By working with outside developers of world-class system configuration tools.

Anyone familiar with Red Hat Linux over the years has probably seen what they call their "control panel" system configuration tools. These tools have been developed by Red Hat Software to make system configuration easier. And while these tools do make life easier for the Red Hat Linux user, they began a search for a system configuration tool with even more flexibility and power. Their search ended with the inclusion of Linuxconf into Red Hat Linux 5.1 in June 1998. Now, with this version of Red Hat Linux, they have been able to more fully document the popular aspects of system configuration using Linuxconf. Note the term "popular aspects." One of Linuxconf's greatest strengths — the incredible range of configuration options under its control — is actually a liability when it comes time to document them all. Rest assured, however, that Red Hat will continue to expand Linuxconf documentation as new versions of Red Hat Linux are released. But what about the control panel tools? They're still there. While Linuxconf at present can do nearly everything the control panel tools can, there are two areas in which the control panel still holds the upper hand:

- Printer configuration
- Kernel daemon control

To that end, the control panel documentation has been left in this manual as the second half of this chapter. But now, let's take a look at Linuxconf...

System Configuration With Linuxconf

Linuxconf is a utility that allows you to configure and control various aspects of your system, and is capable of handling a wide range of programs and tasks. Fully documenting Linuxconf could be a separate book in its own right and certainly more than we can cover in this chapter. So we'll focus on those areas that address common tasks such as adding new users and getting connected to a network.

More information on Linuxconf, including its status, most recent release, and more can be found at the Linuxconf Project homepage:

http://www.solucorp.qc.ca/linuxconf/

This website includes fairly extensive information on Linuxconf including description, rationale, history, list of contacts and a lot of other information in addition to the software itself. It is maintained by Linuxconf's creator, Jacques Gelinas, so it's the best source of Linuxconf information on the Internet.

Notation

Accurately describing the location of specific screens within Linuxconf is easy, but lengthy given Linuxconf's hierarchical nature. If the structure is a family tree, most of the data entry screens are in the fourth generation. To describe the path to the screen where you would add new users to your system, we could write this out as:

> "Select the Config option from the main screen, then the users accounts option from that; on the users accounts screen that appears, select the normal option and then select the user accounts option."

Rather lengthy and not immediately accessible. Given the structural similarity to a family tree, we could write it as:

> "main window beget Users accounts tab, beget Normal tab..."

But that's an awful lot of begets. Instead, we'll use the following format:

```
[Config] -> [Users accounts] -> [Normal] -> [User accounts]
```

It's much more concise and clear. It assumes as its base the Linuxconf entry screen. The other advantage to this approach is that it's not interface specific, so regardless of which interface you're using, you know exactly where the information is. You're happy, we're happy, and the trees which lobbied against lengthy descriptions are happy. What could be better?

Running Linuxconf

To run Linuxconf you must have root access. If you are logged in as something other than root, there is an easy way to handle this situation. Use the su command to become root. In case you aren't familiar with it yet, type su at the shell prompt and hit [Enter]. The password it asks you for is the root account's. Once you've entered that correctly you'll have phenomenal cosmic power! Well, complete control of your system at any rate. Anyway, type `linuxconf` at the shell prompt to begin the program. Linuxconf has the following user interfaces:

- **Command line** — Linuxconf's command-line mode is handy for manipulating your system's configuration in scripts.
- **Character-Cell** — Using the same user interface style as the Red Hat Linux installation program, the character-cell interface makes it easy to navigate your way through Linuxconf, even if you aren't running X.
- **X Window-Based** — Linuxconf can take advantage of X, and give you an easy-to-use "point and click" tree menu interface. This form of navigation is new in Linuxconf! Please see the **Tree Menu Interface** subsection for more information. This is the interface we'll use for illustrations throughout this chapter.
- **Web-Based** — A Web-based interface makes remote system administration a breeze. The Web interface will even play nice with the Lynx character-cell Web browser!

Linuxconf will normally start in either character-cell or X mode, depending on the DISPLAY environment variable. The first time you run Linuxconf, an introductory message will be shown; although it is only displayed once, accessing help from the main screen will give you the same basic information.

Linuxconf has context-specific help available. For information on any specific aspect of Linuxconf, please select **Help** from the screen you'd like help with. Note that not all help screens are complete at this time; as help screens are updated, they will be included in subsequent versions of Linuxconf.

Tree Menu Interface

The new version of Linuxconf comes complete with a tree menu interface.

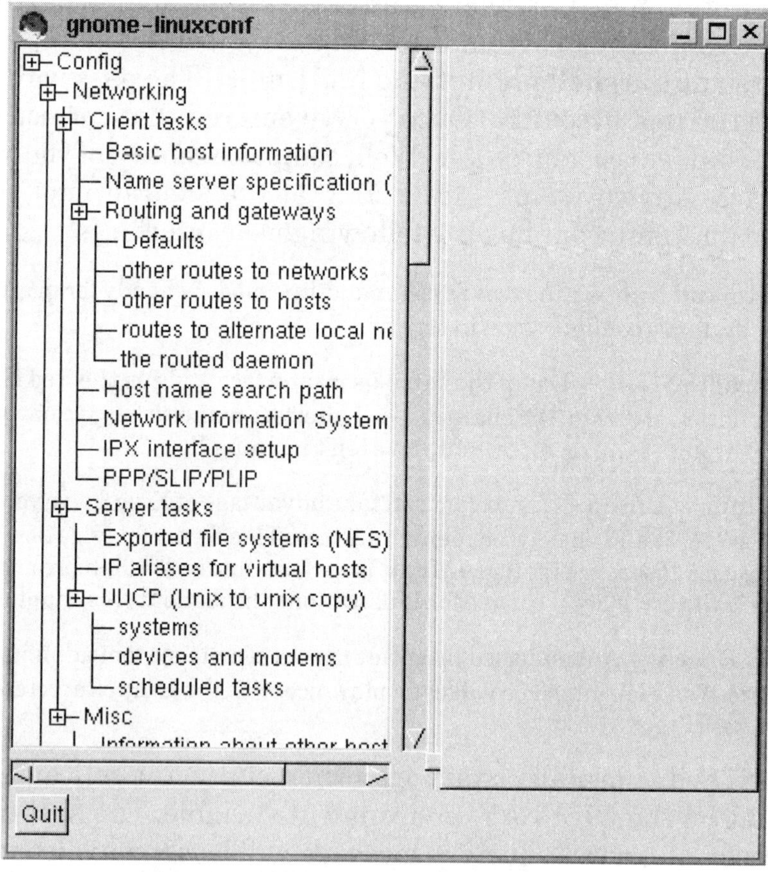

Figure 8-1: Linuxconf Entry Screen

Finding the appropriate panel should be simple and fast. You can collapse and expand sections by clicking on the menu item icons. Click the icon once to activate it for that particular sub-menu. A single click will then collapse it; another single click will expand it again. Selected entries will appear as tabs in the right-hand panel and will remain there until closed. This will greatly reduce the clutter of windows on your desktop that Linuxconf has typically caused. If you end up with more tabs open than you like, just hit **Cancel** on the bottom of each tab to close it without making any changes, or **Accept** to implement them.

Please Note: If you've grown fond of your previous X Window System interface, it's still available. To return to it:

1 Start Linuxconf by typing linuxconf at the shell prompt

2 Open [Control] -> [Control files and systems] -> [Linuxconf modules]

3 De-select the This module is active check box for the treemenu module.

4 Click Accept

5 Click Quit

6 Restart Linuxconf

Enabling Web-Based Linuxconf Access

For security reasons, Web-based access to Linuxconf is disabled by default. Before attempting to access Linuxconf with a Web browser, you'll need to enable access. Here's how to do it from the text-mode interface:

1 Start Linuxconf by typing linuxconf at the shell prompt

2 Open [Config] -> [Networking] -> [Misc] -> [Linuxconf network access]

3 In the **Linuxconf html access control** dialog box, enter the hostname of any computers that should be allowed access to Linuxconf. This would also include your own system, if you wish to use the Web-based interface locally. Web accesses related to Linuxconf may be logged to your system's htmlaccess.log file by selecting the check box shown.

4 Select the **Accept** button and press [Space]. Then select the **Quit** buttons on

each dialog box to back out of the menu hierarchy. When you come to a dialog box labeled **Status of the system**, press [Enter] to take the default action, which is to apply the changes you've made.

At this point, Web-based access has been enabled. To test it out, go to one of the systems that you added to the access control list. Launch your Web browser, and enter the following URL:

http://<host>:98/

(Replacing *<host>* with your system's hostname, of course.)

You should see the main Linuxconf page. Note that you will need to enter your system's root password to gain access beyond the first page.

Adding a User Account — Quick Reference

1 Start Linuxconf by typing linuxconf at the shell prompt

2 Open [Config] -> [Users accounts] -> [Normal] -> [User accounts]

3 Select Add

4 Enter the account's login and full names

5 Enter information in other fields only as necessary

6 Select Accept

7 Enter the initial password for the account

8 Reenter the initial password for the account in the Confirmation field

9 Select Accept

Adding a User Account — General Overview

Adding a user is one of the most basic tasks you will encounter in administering your system. To add a user:

- Start Linuxconf by typing linuxconf at the shell prompt.
- Open [Config] -> [Users accounts] -> [Normal] -> [User accounts] This will open the **Users accounts** tab (see figure 8-3).
- If you have more than 15 accounts on the system, Linuxconf will provide you with a filter screen (see figure 8-2). You can use this to select a smaller range of

accounts than the full list. To get the full list, select **Accept** without changing any of the parameters. For detailed information on the various filters, select the **Help** button on the **Filter control** screen.

- Select **Add**. This will open the **User account creation** tab (see figure 8-4).

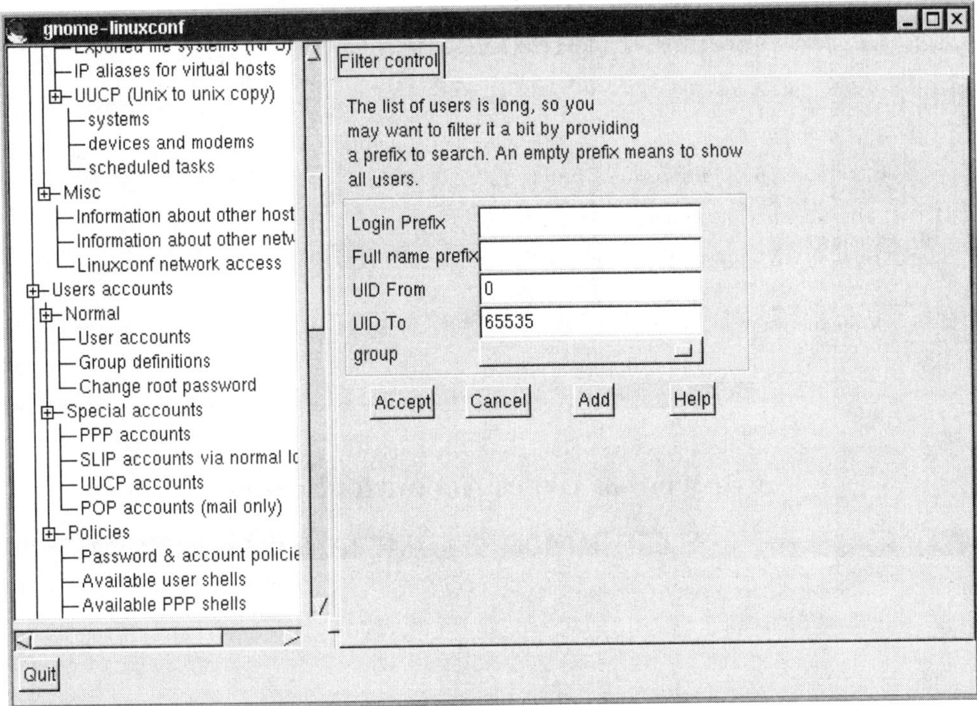

Figure 8-2: Filter Control Screen

The **User account creation** tab is where you enter all the information on the new account. There are a number of fields you should be aware of, some required, some optional.

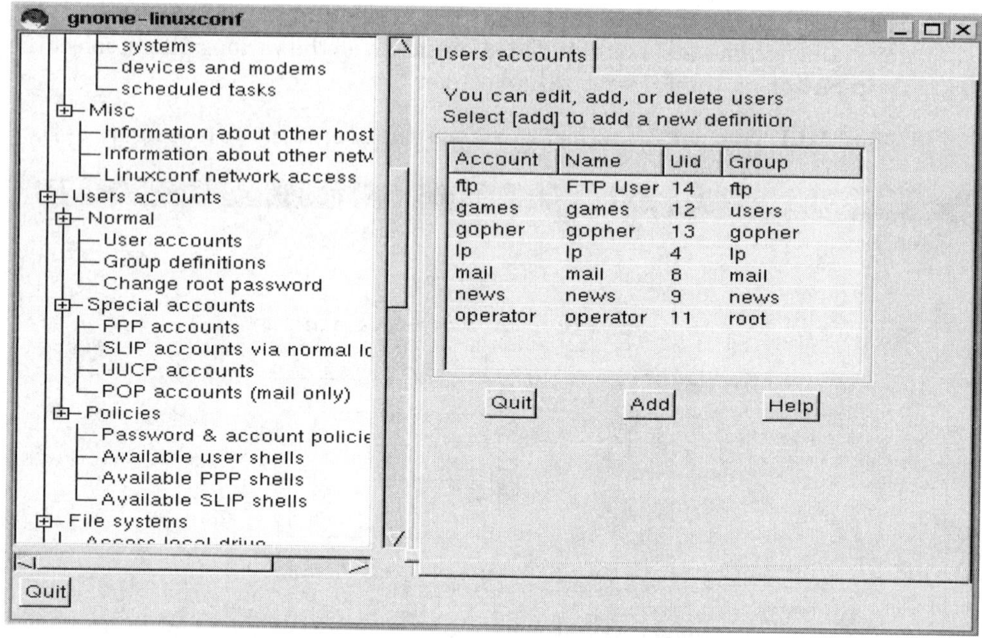

Figure 8-3: Users Accounts Screen

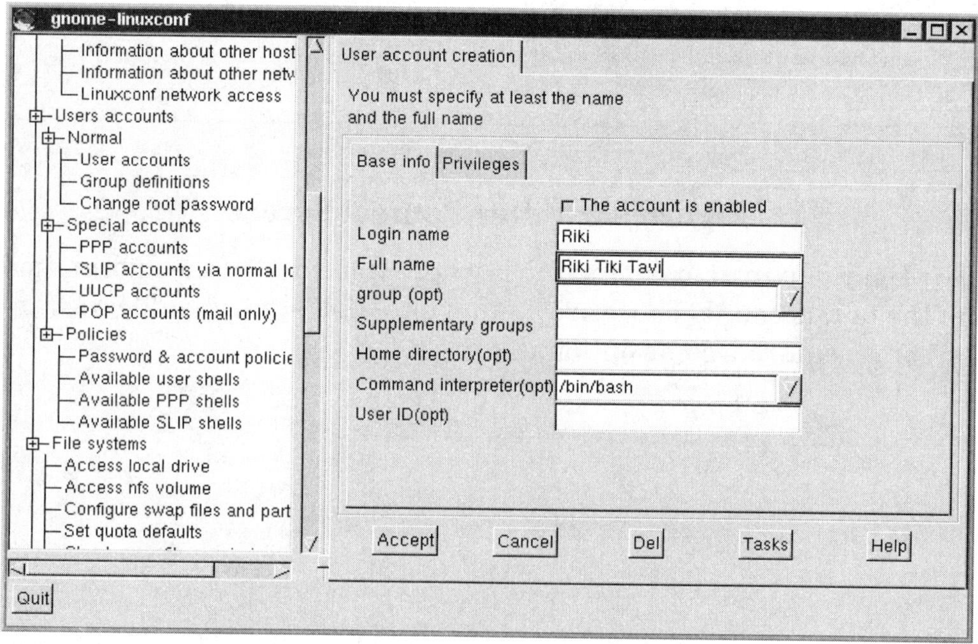

Figure 8-4: User Account Creation

Required Fields:

- **Login name** — the name of the account. Usually all lowercase letters. First or last names, initials or some combination thereof are fairly common login names. For a user named John T. Smith, "smith," "john," "jts," or "jsmith" would be common user names. Of course "spike" or something else works just fine, too. You can also use numbers, so "jts2" would be fine if you had a second person with the same initials. There is no default for this field.

Optional Fields:

- **Full name** — this is the name of the user or the account. For an individual, it would be their name, "John T. Smith" for example. If the account represents a position rather than a person, the full name might be the title. So an account called "webmaster" might have a full name of "Red Hat Webmaster" or just "Webmaster." There is no default for this field.

- **group** — here you can specify the group associated with the account. The default is a group that's the same as the login name. So "jsmith" would have the group "jsmith."

- **Supplementary groups** — here is where you can specify any additional groups. We suggest that if you want to add a user to a group or groups, you do so here, rather than changing the group field. Group names should be separated by spaces. The default for this field is blank, meaning no supplementary groups.

- **Home directory** — specifies the home or login directory for the account. The default is /home/login, where login is replaced by the login name. A home directory is your starting point in the directory structure when you log in, or if in X, for each xterm window opened. This is also where account specific preference files are stored.

- **Command interpreter** — specifies the location of the command interpreter. Command interpreters are usually referred to as shells. The default is displayed in the drop down box.

- **User ID** — the number associated with each user account. This is automatically generated by the system when the account is created.

The **User account creation** screen has a number of fields; only the login name is required, though filling in the **Full name** field is strongly recommended. Once you have entered the login name and any other desired information select the **Accept** button at the bottom of the screen. If you decide against creating a new user, hit **Cancel** instead.

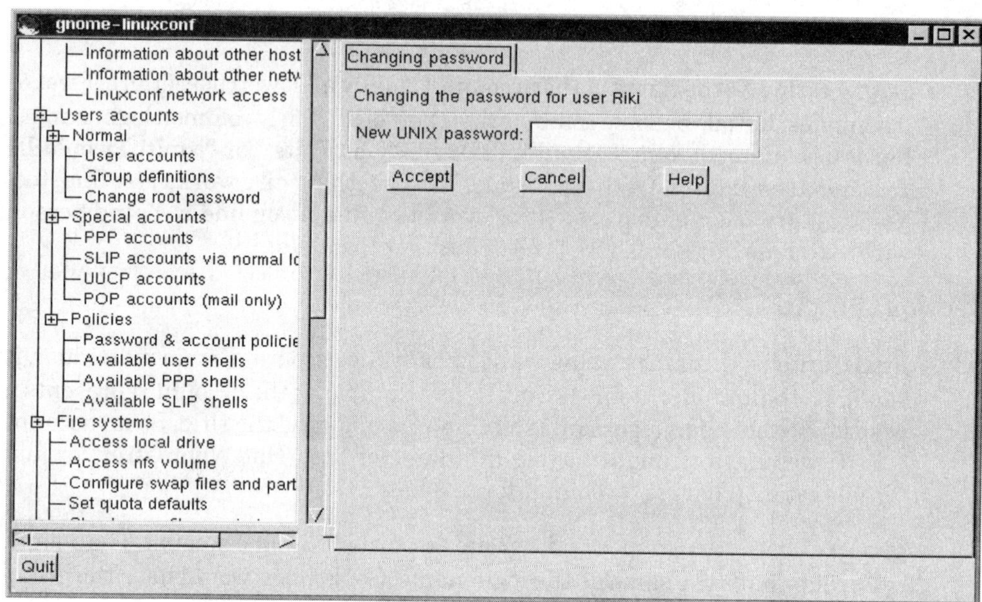

Figure 8-5: Change Password Screen

Upon hitting **Accept** Linuxconf will prompt you to enter the password. There is also a field called **Confirmation** where you will need to type the password again. This is to prevent you from mistyping the password. Passwords must be at least 6 characters in length. They may contain numbers as well as a mix of lowercase and uppercase letters. Hit **Accept** when finished.

Modifying a User Account – Quick Reference

Please Note: Although you can change the settings in any user account, it is usually a bad idea to change the settings in a pre-created account. It is best to change settings and explore options in an account that you have created yourself.

1 Start Linuxconf by typing linuxconf at the shell prompt.

2 Open [Config] -> [Users accounts] -> [Normal] -> [User accounts].

3 Select the user account.

4 Modify entries as desired.

5 Select Accept.

Modifying a User Account — General Overview

- Start Linuxconf by typing linuxconf at the shell prompt.
- Open [Config] -> [Users accounts] -> [Normal] -> [User accounts]. This will open the Users accounts tab (see figure 8-3).
- If you have more than 15 accounts on the system, Linuxconf will provide you with a filter screen (see figure 8-2). You can use this to select a smaller range of accounts than the full list. To get the full list, select Accept without changing any of the parameters. For detailed information on the various filters, select the Help button on the Filter control screen.
- Select the account you wish to modify. This will open the User information tab.

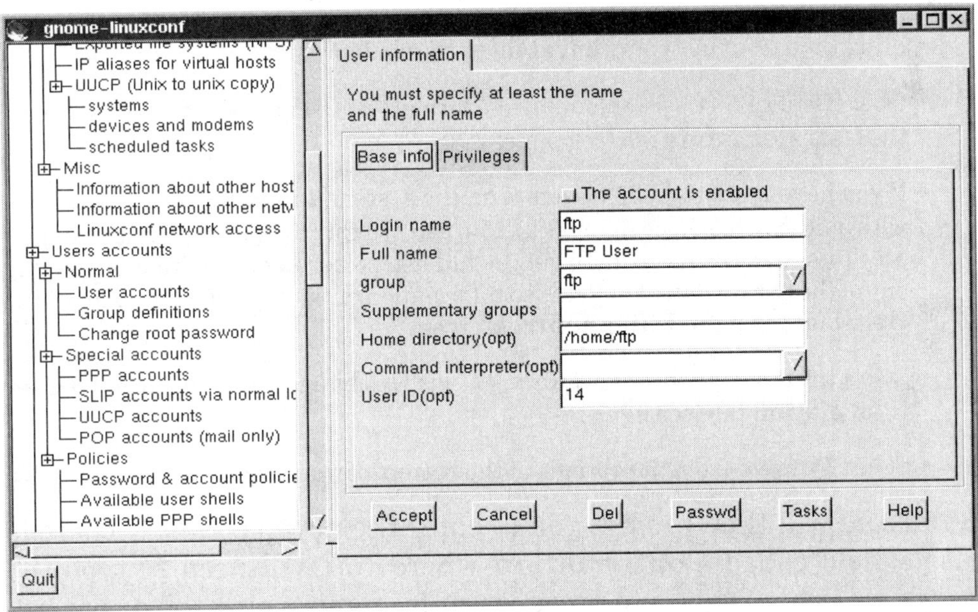

Figure 8-6: User Information Screen

On the **User information** screen, the information can be changed as desired. To implement the changes select **Accept**. If you decide against making any changes select **Cancel**. This guarantees that no changes are made.

Changing a User's Password — Quick Reference

1 Start Linuxconf by typing linuxconf at the shell prompt.

2 Open [Config] -> [Users accounts] -> [Normal] -> [User accounts].

3 Select the user account.

4 Select Passwd.

5 Enter the user's new password.

6 Reenter the user's new password in the Confirmation field.

7 Select Accept.

Changing a User's Password — General Overview

- Start Linuxconf by typing linuxconf at the shell prompt.
- Open [Config] -> [Users accounts] -> [Normal] -> [User accounts]. This will open the **Users accounts** tab (see figure 8-3).
- If you have more than 15 accounts on the system, Linuxconf will provide you with a filter screen (see figure 8-2). You can use this to select a smaller range of accounts than the full list. To get the full list, select **Accept** without changing any of the parameters. For detailed information on the various filters, select the **Help** button on the **Filter control** screen.
- Select the account whose password you wish to change. This will open the **User information** tab (see figure 8-6).
- Select **Passwd** from the options at the bottom of the screen.

Linuxconf will then prompt you to enter the new password. There is also a field called **Confirmation** where you will need to type the password again. This is to prevent you from mistyping the password. Passwords must be at least 6 characters in length. They may contain numbers as well as a mix of lowercase and uppercase letters. If you decide against changing the password, just hit **Cancel**. Once you have entered the new password select **Accept**.

Changing the root Password – Quick Reference

1 Start Linuxconf by typing linuxconf at the shell prompt.

2 Open [Config] -> [Users accounts] -> [Normal] -> [Change root password].

3 Enter the current root password.

4 Select **Accept**.

5 Enter the new root password.

6 Reenter the new root password in the **Confirmation** field.

7 Select **Accept**.

Changing the root Password – General Overview

Changing the roots password isn't handled in the same manner as changing a user's password. Because of both the importance and security considerations surrounding root access, Linuxconf requires you to verify that you currently have access to the root account.

- Start Linuxconf by typing linuxconf at the shell prompt.
- Open [Config] -> [Users accounts] -> [Normal] -> [Change root password].

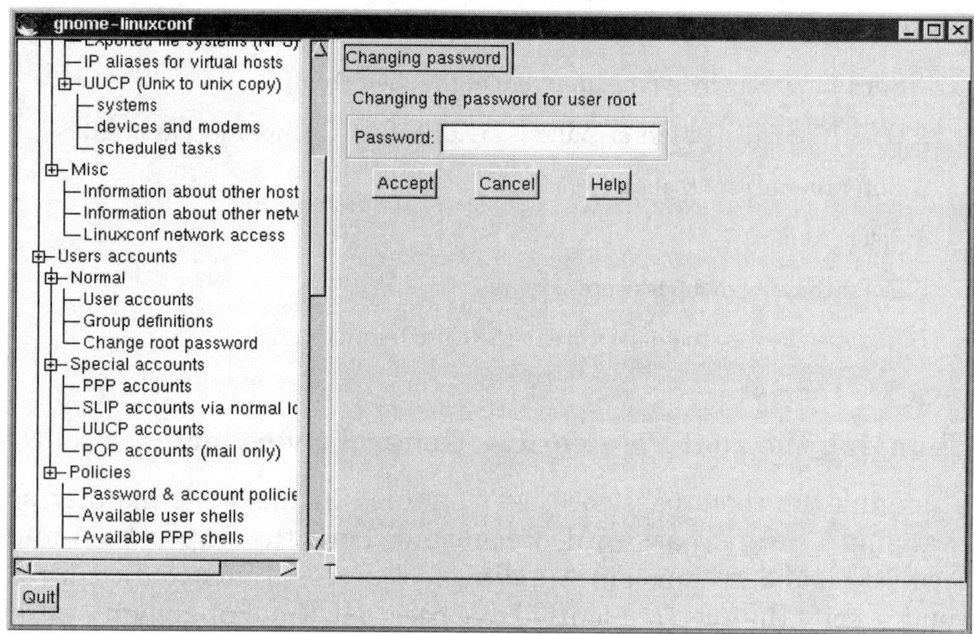

Figure 8-7: Root Password Verification Screen

The screen is a little confusing because neither the title, nor the description really explains the screen's purpose. Linuxconf seems to be asking for the new password, which isn't actually the case. Instead, Linuxconf wants the current root password to verify access to the root account. Linuxconf does require root access to run, but once running there's nothing to keep anyone from sitting down at the computer if the person using Linuxconf steps out for a minute. The potential pitfalls are extensive! If the person who was originally using Linuxconf logs out of root, they won't be able to get back into it. A lack of validation would also give free reign over the computer to whoever had changed root's password. Once you have entered root's current password, it will prompt you for a new password. There is also a field called **Confirmation** where you will need to type the password again (see figure 8-5). This is to prevent you from mistyping the password. Passwords must be at least 6 characters in length. They may contain numbers as well as a mix of lowercase and uppercase letters. If you decide against changing the root password, just hit **Cancel**. Once you have entered the new password select **Accept**. The change takes place immediately and is effective not only for logging in as root, but also for becoming root using the `su` command.

Disabling a User Account — Quick Reference

1 Start Linuxconf by typing linuxconf at the shell prompt.

2 Open [Config] -> [Users accounts] -> [Normal] -> [User accounts].

3 Select the account.

4 De-select **the account is enabled** check box.

5 Select **Accept**.

Disabling a User Account — General Overview

Why disable an account? Good question! There's no single answer, but we can provide some reasons why this option is available. The biggest reason is security. For example, you may have created a special account to be used by clients, co-workers, or friends to access specific files on your system. This account gets used from time to time, but should only be used when you know there's a need. Leaving an unused account around is a target for people who'd want to break into your system. Deleting it requires you to recreate it every time you want to use it. Disabling an account solves both problems by allowing you to simply select or de-select a check-box. To disable an account:

1 Start Linuxconf by typing linuxconf at the shell prompt.

2 Open [Config] -> [Users accounts] -> [Normal] -> [User accounts].

3 De-select the check-box that states that **The account is enabled**. Select the **Accept** button at the bottom of the window and you're all set.

The account is disabled and can be enabled later using a similar method.

Enabling a User Account

By default, all newly created user accounts are enabled. If you need to enable an account, you can use Linuxconf to do it.

Start Linuxconf by typing linuxconf at the shell prompt.

Open [Config] -> [Users accounts] -> [Normal] -> [User accounts].

Select the account you want to enable.

Select the The account is enabled check-box and then select Accept at the bottom of the screen.

Deleting a User Account — Quick Reference

Start Linuxconf by typing linuxconf at the shell prompt.

Open [Config] -> [Users accounts] -> [User accounts].

Select the account you wish to delete.

On the User information screen select Del.

On the Deleting account... screen, choose the appropriate option for the account's data.

Select Accept.

Deleting a User Account — General Overview

> **Please Note:** While there are a couple options that let you retain files associated with an account, any information or files deleted are gone and effectively unrecoverable. Take care when using this option! To delete an account:

- Start Linuxconf by typing linuxconf at the shell prompt.
- Open [Config] -> [Users accounts] -> [User accounts].
- On the **User accounts** screen (see figure 8-3) select the account you wish to delete.
- At the bottom of the **User information** screen (see figure 8-6) select **Del** to delete the account.

Linuxconf will then prompt you with a list of options.

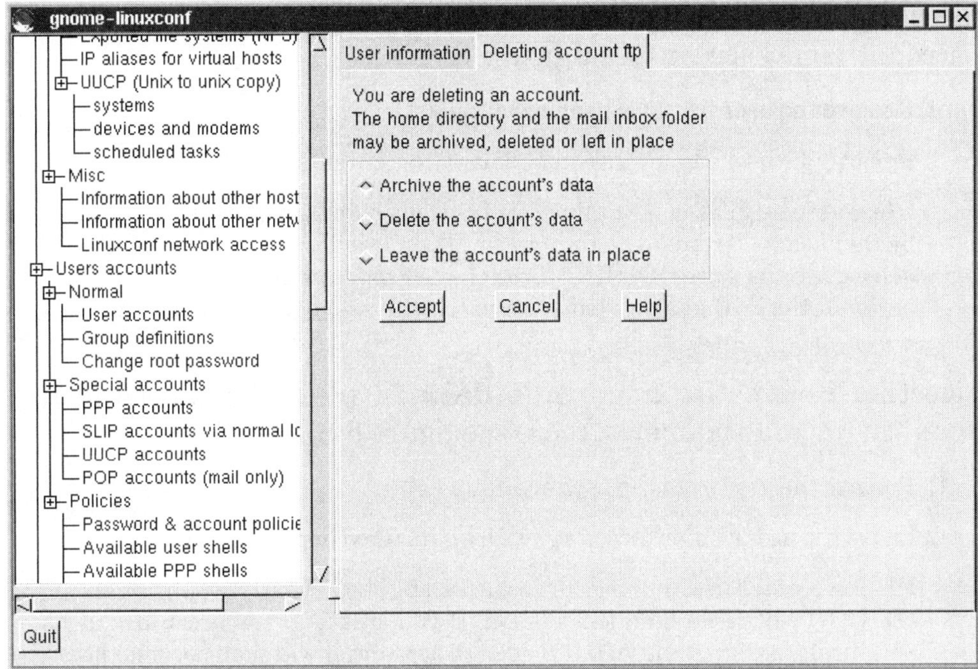

Figure 8-8: Deleting Account Screen

The default option is to archive the account's data. The archive option has the following effects:

1 Removes the user from the user accounts list;

2 Takes everything contained in the user's home directory and archives it (using tar and gzip compression), storing the resulting file in a directory called oldaccounts. For an account named useraccount the file name would be similar to:`useraccount-1999-10-10-497.tar.gz` The date indicates when the account was deleted, and the number following it is the ID of the process that actually performed the deletion. The oldaccounts directory is created in the same place as all of your user directories, and is created automatically the first time you remove a user account using this option.

3 Files not contained in the user's home directory, but owned by that user remain. The file is owned by the deleted account's user ID (UID). If you create a new account and specifically assign it the UID of a deleted account, it will then become the owner of any remaining files.

Selecting **Delete the account's data** on the **Deleting account** <accountname> screen (see figure 8-8) will:

1 Remove the user from the user accounts list;

2 Remove the user's home directory and all its contents.

Please Note: Files not contained in the user's home directory, but owned by that user will remain on the system. The file will still be owned by the deleted account's user ID (UID). If you create a new account and specifically assign it the UID of a deleted account, it will then become the owner of any such "orphaned" files.

Selecting **Leave the account's data in place** on the **Deleting account** <accountname> screen (see figure 8-8) will:

1 Remove the user from the user accounts list;

2 Leave the user's home directory (with all its files) in place.

Please Note: Files and directories owned by the deleted account's user ID (UID) will remain on the system. If you create a new account and specifically assign it the UID of a deleted account, it will then become the owner of these "orphaned" files.

Groups

All users belong to one or more groups. Just as each file has a specific owner, each file belongs to a particular group as well. The group might be specific to the owner of the file, or may be a group shared by all users. The ability to read, write or execute a file can be assigned to a group; this is separate from the owner's rights. For example, the owner of a file will be able to write to a document, while other group members may only be able to read it.

Creating a Group — Quick Reference

1 Start Linuxconf by typing linuxconf at the shell prompt.

2 Open [Config] -> [Users accounts] -> [Normal] -> [Group definition].

3 Select **Add**.

4 Enter the Group name, and optionally alternate members.

5 Select **Accept**.

Creating a Group — General Overview

To create a new group:

- Start Linuxconf by typing linuxconf at the shell prompt.
- Open [Config] -> [Users accounts] -> [Normal] -> [Group definition].

If you have more than 15 groups, you will be given the option to select the groups by providing a prefix.

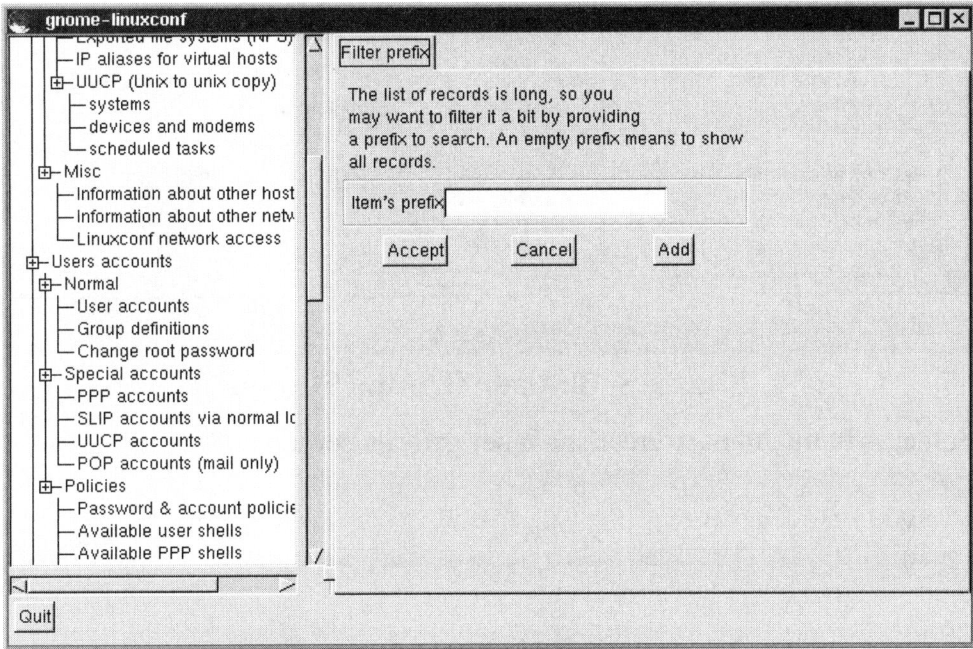

Figure 8-9: Group Filter Screen

You may add a group directly from this screen, or move on to the **User groups** screen. To move on select choice Accept with or without a prefix, to add a new group, hit choice **Add**.

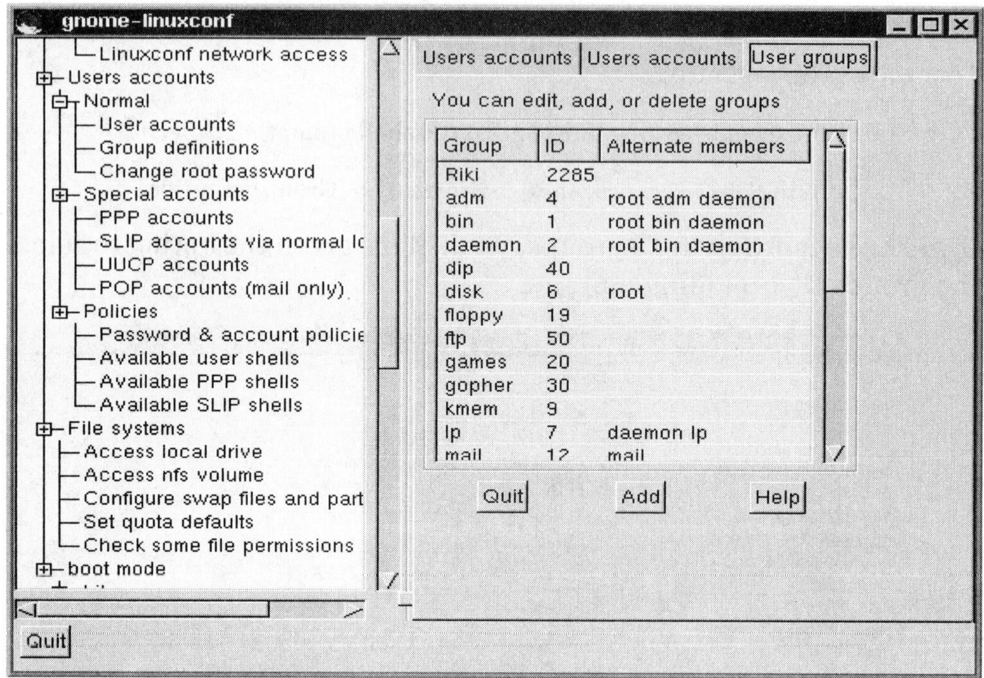

Figure 8-10: User Groups Screen

Select Add at the bottom of the User groups screen.

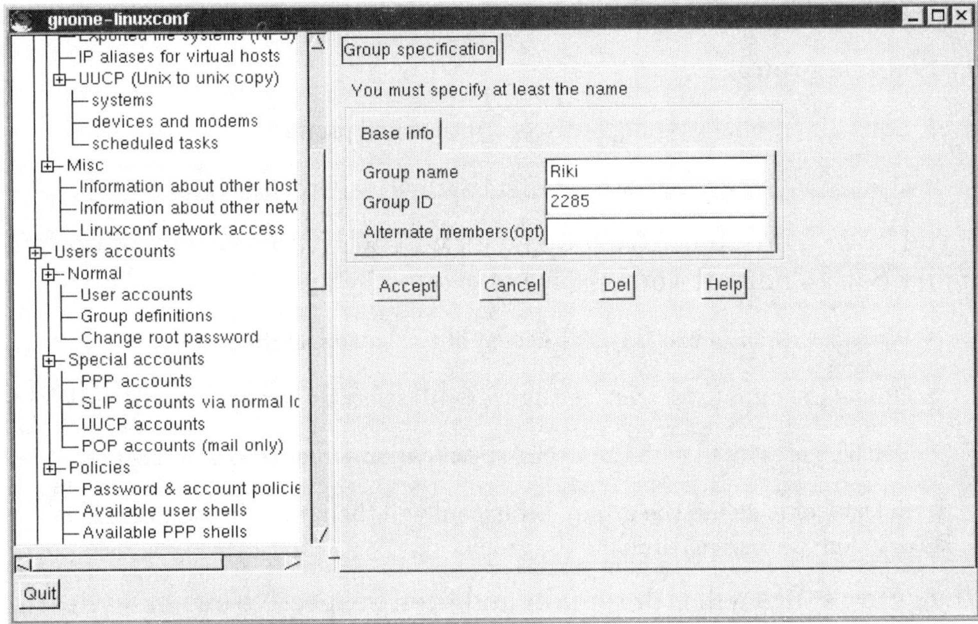

Figure 8-11: Group Specification Screen

Enter a group name. You may also wish to specify members of the group and can do so in the Alternate members field. The list of users should be space delimited, meaning that each username must have a space between it and the next one. When you're finished, select Accept and the group will be created.

Deleting a Group – Quick Reference

1 Start Linuxconf by typing linuxconf at the shell prompt.

2 Open [Config] -> [Users accounts] -> [Normal] -> [Group definitions].

3 Select the group you wish to delete.

4 Select Del.

5 Confirm deletion.

Deleting a Group — General Overview

To delete a group:

- Start Linuxconf by typing linuxconf at the shell prompt.
- Open [Config] -> [Users accounts] -> [Normal] -> [Group definitions].

If you have more than 15 groups, you will be given a filter screen (see figure 8-9) to narrow your choice of groups by specifying a prefix.

- With or without a prefix select Accept at the bottom of the screen.
- On the User groups screen (see figure 8-10) select the group you wish to delete.
- You'll be presented with the Group specification screen (see figure 8-11).
- Select Del to delete the group. Linuxconf will then prompt you to confirm the deletion. Choose yes to delete the group.

The group's files will still remain and their respective owners will still have sole control over them. The group name will be replaced with the deleted group's ID. The files may be assigned to a new group by using the chgrp command. More information on chgrp can be found by typing the command info chgrp or man chgrp at the shell prompt. If a new group is created and the deleted group's ID is specified then the new group will have access to the deleted group's files. Don't worry, Linuxconf doesn't recycle old group numbers any more than it does old user IDs, so it won't happen by accident.

Modifying Group Membership

There are two ways to modify the list of users that belong to a group. You can either update each user account itself, or you can update the group definitions. In general, the fastest way is to update each of the group definitions. If you're planning on changing more information for each user than just the group information, then updating each user account may prove easier.

Modifying Group Membership — Quick Reference

Under Groups

1 Start Linuxconf by typing linuxconf at the shell prompt.

2 Open [Config] -> [Users accounts] -> [Normal] -> [Group definitions].

3 Select the group to which you wish to add or remove users.

4 Add or remove new users to the **Alternate members(opt)** field; make sure all user names are separated with a space " " character.

5 Select Accept.

Modifying Group Membership — Quick Reference

Under Users

1 Start Linuxconf by typing linuxconf at the shell prompt.

2 Open [Config] -> [Users accounts] -> [Normal] -> [User accounts].

3 Select a user to which you wish to add or remove groups. Adjust the Supplementary groups field accordingly; make sure all the group names are separated with a space " " character.

4 Select **Accept**.

5 Repeat steps 3 through 5 for each additional user to be added.

Modifying Group Membership — General Overview

We'll start by detailing the group definitions method.

- Start Linuxconf by typing linuxconf at the shell prompt.
- Open [Config] -> [Users accounts] -> [Normal] -> [Group definitions].

If you have more than 15 groups, you will be given a filter screen (see figure 8-9) to narrow your choice of groups by specifying a prefix.

- With or without a prefix, select **Accept** at the bottom of the screen.
- Select the group you wish to modify. This will open the **Group specification** screen (see figure 8-11).

- Add or remove each user from the **Alternate members** field. Make sure that all of the user names are separated by a space " " character.
- Once you've done this select **Accept** which can be found at the bottom of the screen.

This will automatically update each user account with the group showing up in the **Supplementary groups** field if added or absent if removed. Adding and removing groups can also be done by modifying each individual user account.

- Start Linuxconf by typing linuxconf at the shell prompt.
- Open [Config] -> [Users accounts] -> [Normal] -> [User accounts].

If you have more than 15 accounts on the system, Linuxconf will provide you with a filter screen (see figure 8-2).

- On the User accounts screen (see figure 8-3), select a user that you wish to update. You will be presented with the User information screen (see figure 8-6).
- Add or remove the desired groups from the, Supplementary groups field. Each group should be separated by a space " " character.
- Once you've made all the changes you'd like, select Accept at the bottom of the screen.

This will automatically update the group definitions. Repeat the process for each user.

CD-ROMs, Diskettes, Hard Drives and Filesystems – the Inside Track

A filesystem is composed of files and directories, all starting from a single root directory. The root directory may contain any number of files and other directories, with each directory in turn following suit. The average filesystem often looks like an inverted tree with the directories as branches and the files as leaves. Filesystems reside on mass storage devices such as diskette drives, hard drives, and CD-ROMs.

For example, a diskette drive on DOS and Windows machines is typically referenced by `A:\`. This describes both the device (`A:`), and the root directory on that device (`\`). The primary hard drive on the same systems is typically referred to as the "C" drive because the device specification for the first hard drive is `C:`. To specify the root directory on the C drive, you would use `C:\`.

Under this arrangement, there are two filesystems — the one on `A:`, and the one on `C:`. In order to specify any file on a DOS/Windows filesystem, you must either explicitly specify the device on which the file resides, or it must be on the system's default drive (which is where DOS' infamous C prompt comes from — that's the default drive in a system with a single hard drive).

Under Linux, it is possible to link the filesystems on several mass storage devices together into a single, larger, filesystem. This is done by placing one device's filesystem "under" a directory on another device's filesystem. So while the root directory of a diskette drive on a DOS machine may be referred to as `A:\`, the same drive on a Linux system may be accessible as `/mnt/floppy`.

The process of merging filesystems in this way is known as mounting. When a device is mounted, it is then accessible to the system's users. The directory "under" which a mounted device's filesystem becomes accessible is known as the mount point. In the previous paragraph's example, `/mnt/floppy` was the diskette drive's mount point. Note that there are no restrictions (other than common conventions) as to the naming of mount points. We could have just as easily mounted the floppy to `/long/path/to/the/floppy/drive`.

One thing to keep in mind is that all of a device's files and directories are relative to its mount point. Consider the following example:

- A Linux System
  - √ / — system root directory
  - √ /foo — mount point for the CD-ROM
- A CD-ROM
  - √ / — CD-ROM's root directory
  - √ /images — a directory of images on the CD-ROM
  - √ /images/old — a directory of old images

So, if the above describes the individual filesystems, and you mount the CD-ROM at `/foo`, the new operating system directory structure would be:

- A Linux System (with the CD-ROM mounted)
  - √ / — system root directory
  - √ /foo — CD-ROM root directory
  - √ /foo/images — a directory of images on the CD-ROM
  - √ /foo/images/old — a directory of old images

To mount a filesystem make sure to be logged in as root, or become root using the su command. For the latter, type su at the shell prompt and then enter the root password. Once you are root, type mount followed by the device and then the mount point. For example, to mount the first diskette drive on `/mnt/floppy`, you would type the command `mount /dev/fd0 /mnt/floppy`.

At installation, Red Hat Linux will create `/etc/fstab`. This file contains information on devices and associated mount points. The advantage to this file is that it allows you to shorten your mount commands.

Using the information in `/etc/fstab`, you can type mount and then either the mount point or the device. The mount command will look for the rest of the information in `/etc/fstab`. It's possible to modify this file by hand, or by using Linuxconf. To use Linuxconf, please see Section **Reviewing Your Current Filesystem** immediately following.

Reviewing Your Current Filesystem — Quick Reference

1 Start Linuxconf by typing linuxconf at the shell prompt.

2 Open [Config] -> [File systems] -> [Access local drive]

or to look at your network environment:

Open [Config] -> [File systems] -> [Access nfs volume].

Reviewing Your Current Filesystem — General Overview

We'll start by looking at your current directory structure.

- Start Linuxconf by typing linuxconf at the shell prompt.
- Open [Config] -> [File systems] -> [Access local drive].

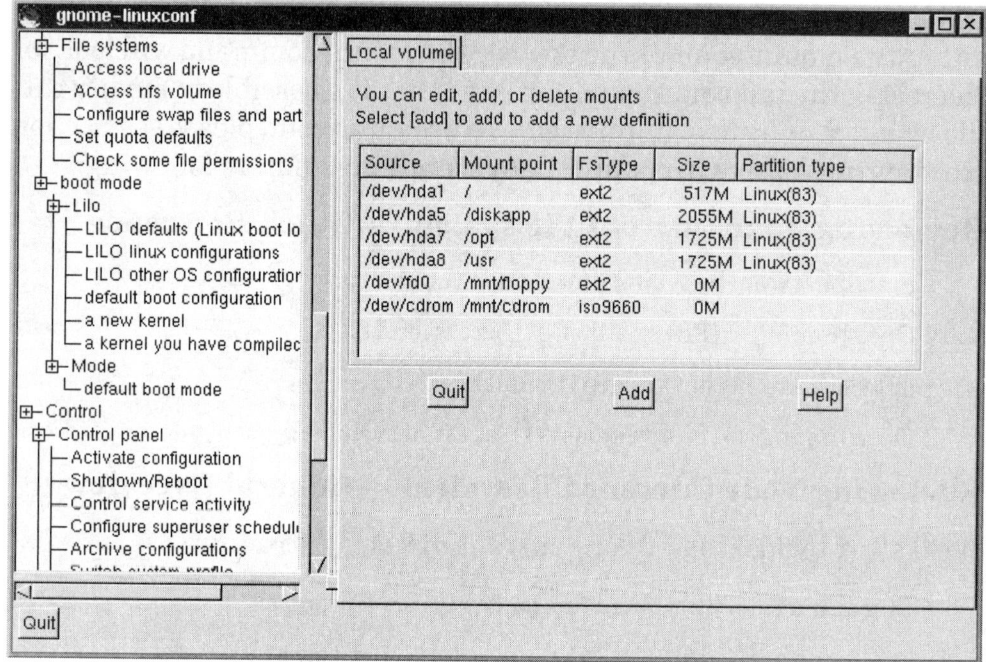

Figure 8-12: Local Volume Screen

The fields are:

- **Source** — The physical hardware; hd indicates an IDE hard drive, fd indicates a diskette drive, and cdrom typically indicates a CD-ROM drive. If your system has a SCSI drive, you will see an sd instead. More than one drive of a type are listed by letters, so hda represents the first IDE drive, while hdb would be the second. In some cases, you'll see numbers following these letters; on hard drives, the numbers represent the partitions on that drive, while for diskette drives, this number refers to the actual unit.

- **Mount point** — This is where in the system the drive is to be mapped when mounted.

- **FsType** — This is where the type of filesystem is indicated. A standard Linux partition uses the ext2 filesystem type. A filesystem type of vfat indicates a DOS filesystem with long filename support, while a fat filesystem type is for DOS filesystems supporting traditional 8.3 filenames. The iso9660 filesystem type indicates a CD-ROM drive, as seen in figure 8-12. **Please Note:** Red Hat Linux 6.0 can access FAT32 filesystems using the vfat filesystem type.

- **Size** — Size indicates the size of the filesystem in megabytes (M). For removable media devices such as diskette and CD-ROM drives the stated size is listed as zero.
- **Partition type** — A description of the filesystem used on that partition.

Filesystems from other machines on a network may also be available. These can range from single small directories to entire volumes. No information on Size or Partition type is available for these partitions, either. Additional information on these filesystems (should you have any available) will be contained under: `[Config] -> [File systems] -> [Access nfs volume]`

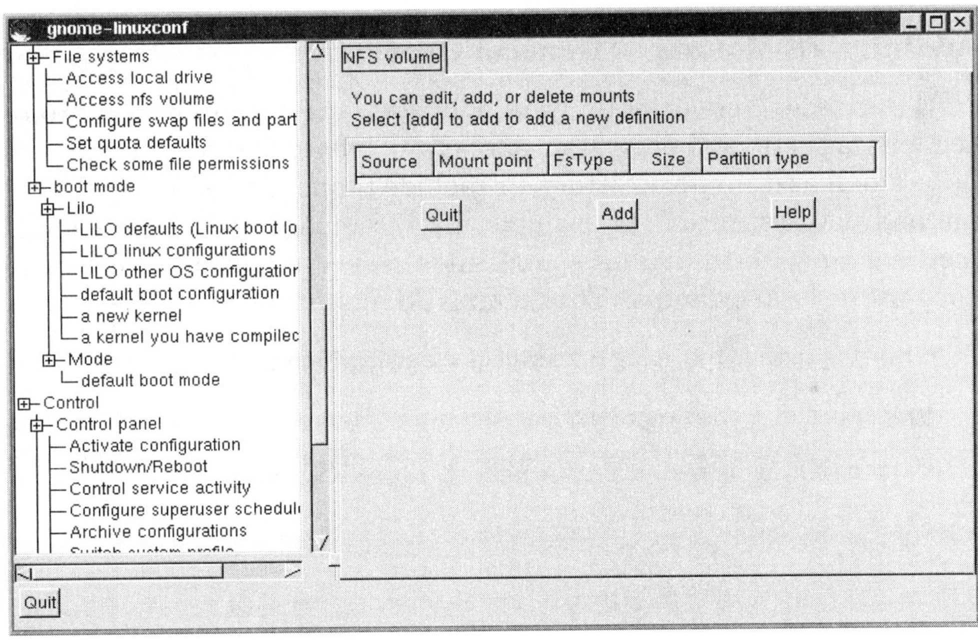

Figure 8-13: NFS Volume Screen

The screen is similar to the **Local volume** screen (see figure 8-12), with some notable differences in the information provided for each entry:

- **Source** — This will be the name of the machine serving the filesystem, followed by the remote directory. For example: foo:/var/spool/mail where foo is the machine serving the directory, and /var/spool/mail is the directory being served.

- **FsType** — This will always be "nfs."

Adding NFS Mounts – Quick Reference

1 Start Linuxconf by typing linuxconf at the shell prompt.

2 Open [Config] -> [File systems] -> [Access nfs volume].

3 Select **Add**.

4 Enter the host name where the filesystem resides.

5 Enter the path to the remote filesystem in the Volume field. For example, `/var/spool/mail`.

6 Specify the mount point on your system. For example, `/mnt/foo`. Select **Accept**.

Adding NFS Mounts – General Overview

NFS stands for Network FileSystem. It is a way for computers to share sections of their local filesystem across a network. These sections may be as small as a single directory, or include thousands of files in a vast hierarchy of directories. For example, many companies will have a single mail server with individuals' mail files served as an NFS mount to each users' local systems. To add an NFS mount:

- Start Linuxconf by typing linuxconf at the shell prompt.
- Open [Config] -> [File systems] -> [Access nfs volume].
- On the **NFS volume** screen (see figure 8-13), select **Add**.

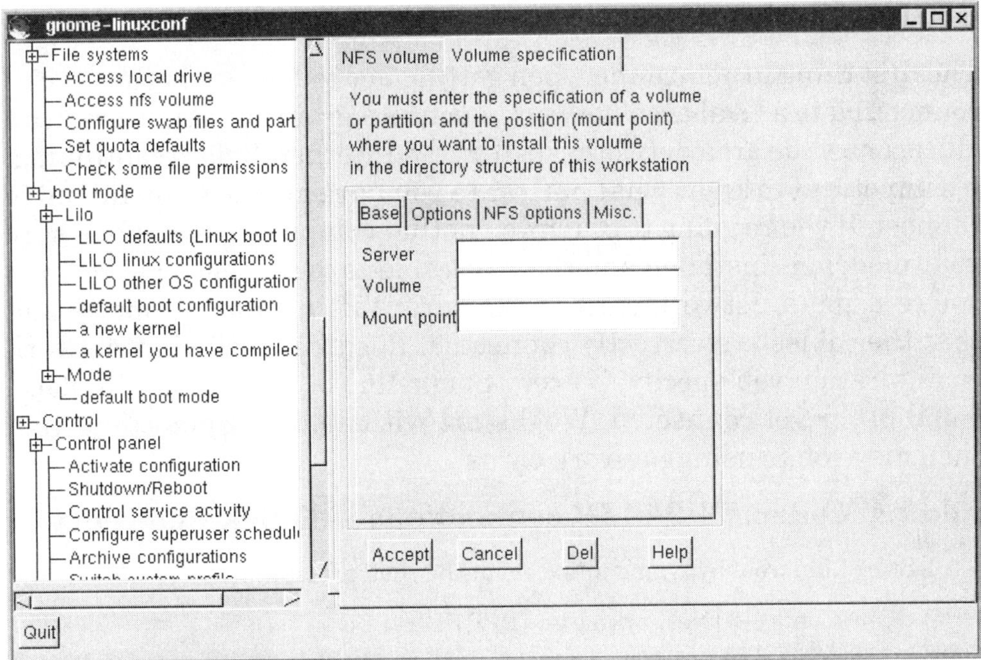

Figure 8-14: Volume Specification Screen

The three fields on the Base tab are what you'll need to concern yourself with.

- **Server** — The host name of the machine the desired filesystem resides on. For example, foo.bar.com.
- **Volume** — The filesystem you wish to add. For example, `/var/spool/mail`.
- **Mount point** — Where in your system you want the remote file system accessible from. For example, `/mnt/mail`.

This is all you need to get the mount created. Linuxconf will update your `/etc/fstab` file accordingly. If you are aware of additional requirements, please read the help file on the **Volume specification** screen and see the mount man page for more information. Once you have entered the information, select **Accept**.

Getting Connected (Network Configuration)

The first thing to determine when getting hooked up is whether you're connecting to a local area network, such as a group of computers in an office, or a wide area network, such as the Internet. Before continuing, it's important to know what hardware you have and how you intend to connect. If you're going to dial into another computer, then make sure your modem is installed and that the cables are arranged properly. If you're using a network card, make sure it is installed properly and that the cables are correctly connected. Regardless of what network configuration you specify, if every phone line or cable is not in place, you'll never get connected. We'll start with modem connections and then move on to using network cards.

Adding Modem/PPP/SLIP connections — Quick Reference

1 Start Linuxconf by typing linuxconf at the shell prompt.

2 Open [Config] -> [Networking] -> [PPP/SLIP/PLIP].

3 Select Add.

4 Select the type of connection.

5 Enter the Phone number, login name and password.

6 Select Use PAP authentication only if necessary (only available for PPP accounts).

7 Select Accept.

Adding Modem/PPP/SLIP connections — General Overview

There are several pieces of information you will need to get from your ISP (Internet Service Provider) or systems administrator before getting your PPP or SLIP account working. In the case of some providers, you may have to sort through directions on how to set up a PPP connection on a Linux system. Some ISPs are ill-equipped to handle individuals using Linux. Don't worry, you can still get connected; you just need some additional information from your ISP. The following is what you need for a connection with Red Hat Linux. The ISP representatives may respond that you don't need this information, or may suggest that you need more than this. Red Hat has streamlined the information needed using intelligent defaults and tools such as Linuxconf to simplify this process for you. Unless they have a document specifically for Red Hat Linux, just request the information below and go from there. Specifically, you'll need:

- the IP address for a domain nameserver (DNS);
- the telephone number to dial;
- your login and password;
- an IP address for your machine if the network you are connecting to isn't going to provide you with a dynamic one;
- whether or not your ISP uses an authentication method such as PAP, CHAP or MS-CHAP. If so, you will need a "secret" to enable authentication. The secret will be a word or sequence of characters. CHAP and MS-CHAP are not currently supported using Linuxconf, and are rarely used.

Additional information which may be helpful, but isn't necessary includes a secondary nameserver address, and a search domain. Once you have all this information, you're ready to get connected.

- Start Linuxconf by typing linuxconf at the shell prompt.
- Open [Config] -> [Networking] -> [PPP/SLIP/PLIP].
- Select **Add**.

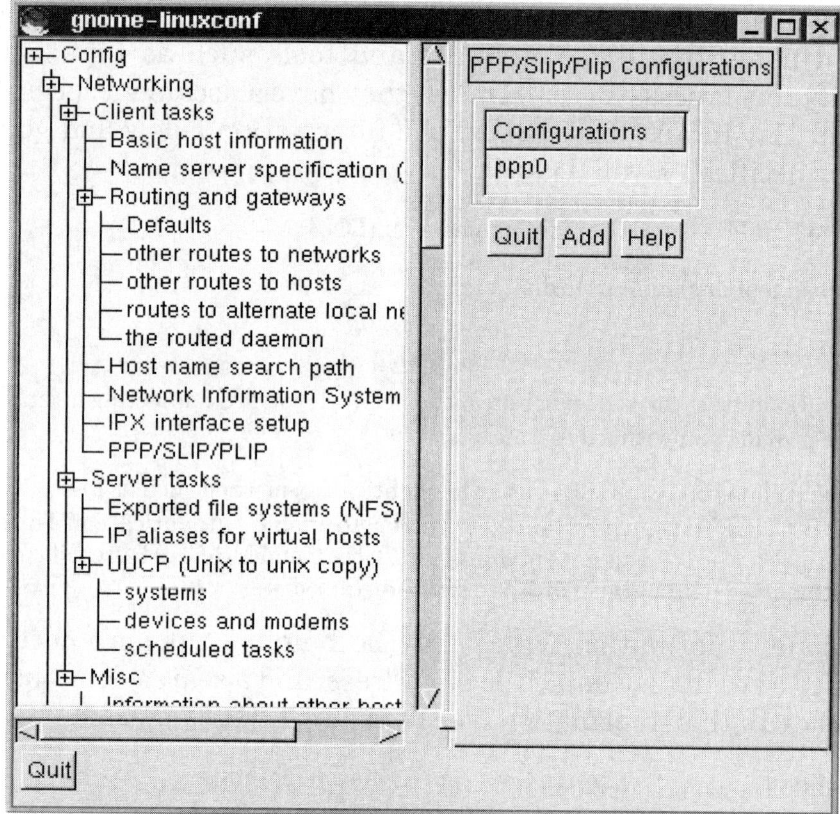

Figure 8-15: PPP/SLIP/PLIP Configurations Screen

Initially there won't be any configurations specified. When you select **Add** you will be given a choice between PPP, SLIP and PLIP.

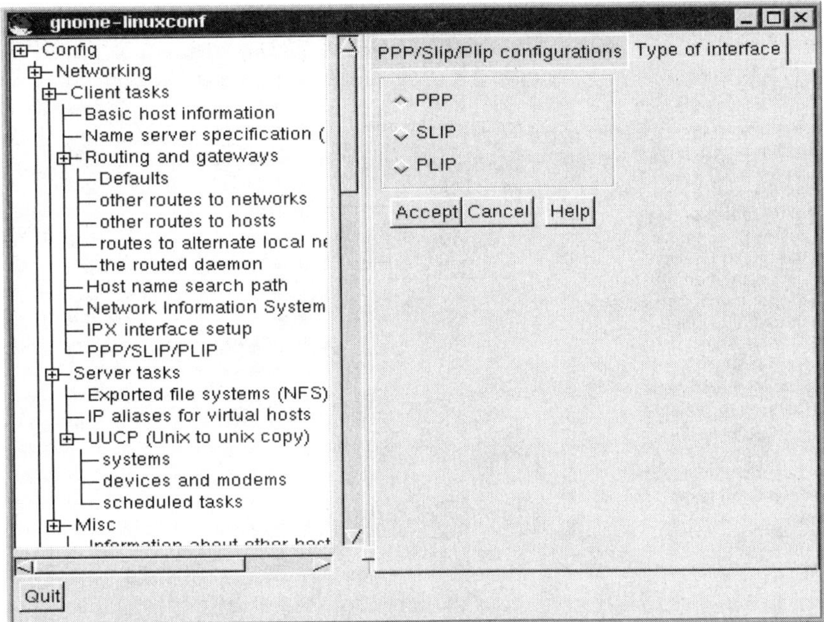

Figure 8-16: Type of Interface Screen

PPP is the most commonly used interface and is the default. To set up a PPP connection select PPP and hit Accept.

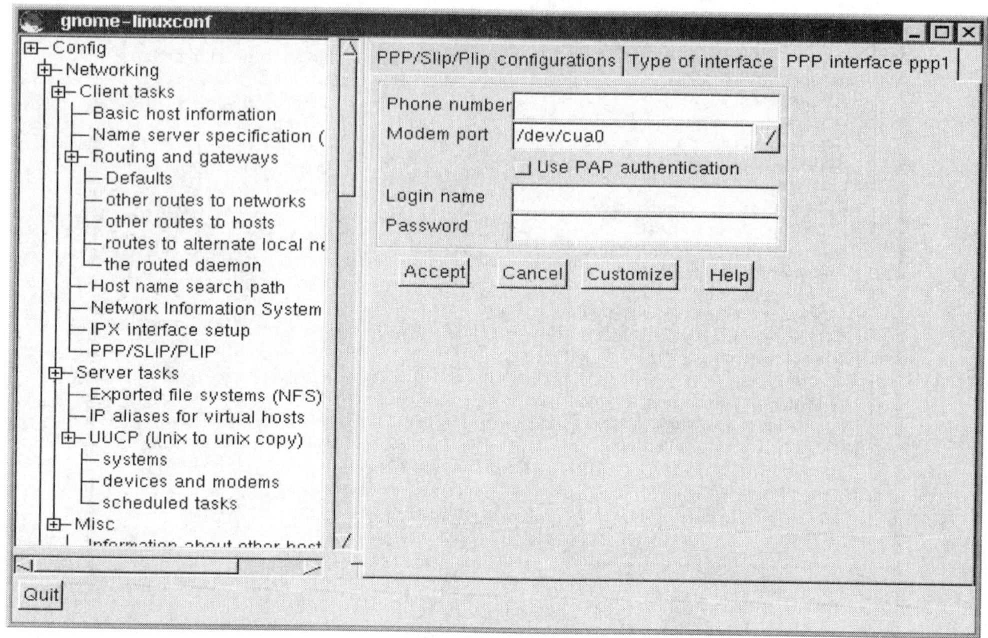

Figure 8-17: PPP Interface Screen

You'll see the following fields:

- Phone number - number used to access to remote system;
- Modem port - indicates where your modem is. Should already be set.
- Use PAP authentication (check box) - check if you know that the system you are dialing into requires this;
- Login name - your login name for the PPP account;
- Password - your password for the PPP account.

Notice that the title bar is **PPP interface ppp0**. ppp0 is the first PPP interface, ppp1 would be the second and so on. It's important to keep track of which interface you're using if you have more than one. SLIP connections use sl instead of ppp for their interface prefix. With the exception of a PAP authentication option, the entry screens for adding a PPP or a SLIP account are identical.

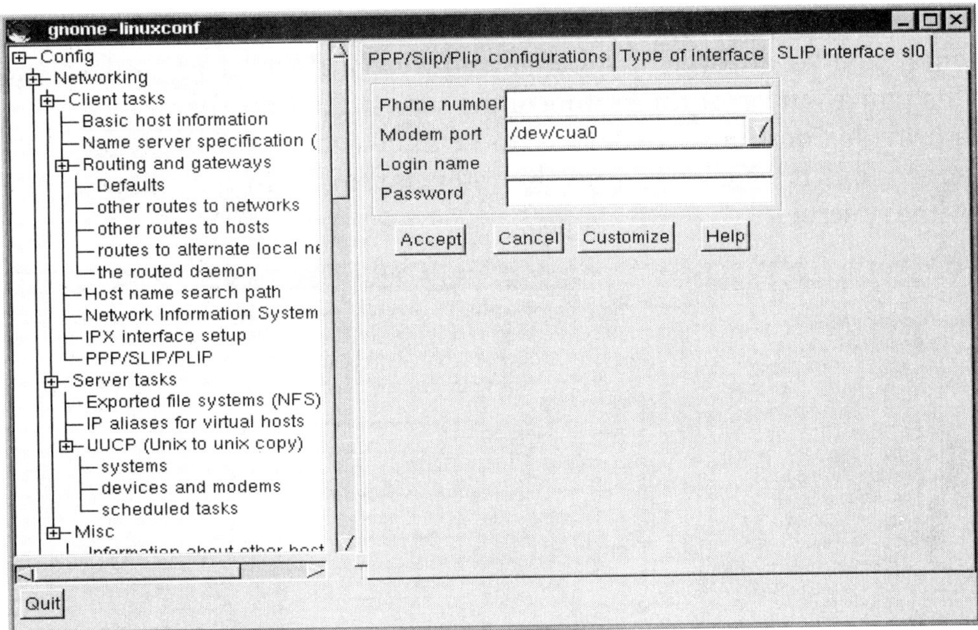

Figure 8-18: SLIP Interface Screen

Enter the complete phone number for the remote machine, and make sure to include any numbers required to access outside lines. For example, if you need to dial "9" and then the number, and the computer you're connecting to has a telephone number of "555-0111", then you'd enter "95550111". The next thing it asks you for is the modem port. This is a drop down box of available ports. If you're using a dual-boot Linux/Windows system and you know the COM port your modem is on, the following map may be of use: Map to Windows COM ports are as follows:

- cua0 – COM1: under MS-DOS;
- cua1 – COM2: under MS-DOS;
- cua2 – COM3: under MS-DOS;
- cua3 – COM4: under MS-DOS.

The login name is the one for the PPP account. The password you enter will be shown in plain text, so be careful who you have around when you enter it! If you will be using PAP authentication, check the box; when you've entered the other required information, select the Customize button at the bottom of the screen. All the other information is provided on the various tabs and can be set within the Customize screen, but it's easier to find the information all in one place on the primary screen.

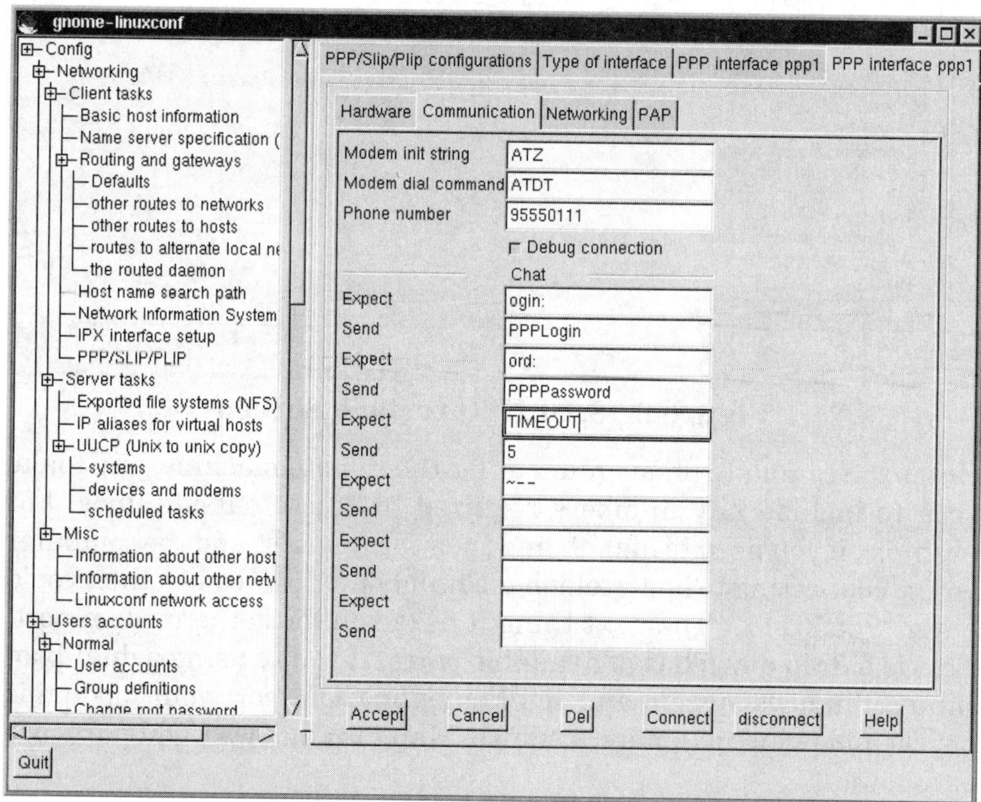

Figure 8-19: PPP Interface Customization Screen

Select the **PAP** tab and enter your username and then the secret the ISP has provided you in the **Secret** field. The other defaults should be sufficient, but if you need to, you can edit the initial settings using the **Customize** option.

Modifying a PPP or SLIP Configuration – Quick Reference

1 Start Linuxconf by typing linuxconf at the shell prompt.

2 Open [Config] -> [Networking] -> [PPP/SLIP/PLIP].

3 Select the configuration to modify.

4 Change the desired settings; most are on the Communications tab.

5 Select Accept.

Modifying a PPP or SLIP Configuration – General Overview

You can edit an existing configuration as well as delete it by selecting it from the list on the **PPP/SLIP/PLIP configurations** screen.

- Start Linuxconf by typing linuxconf at the shell prompt.
- Open [Config] -> [Networking] -> [PPP/SLIP/PLIP].
- You will then be presented with the **PPP/SLIP/PLIP configurations** screen (see figure 8-15). Select the configuration you would like to modify or delete.

This will open the appropriate interface screen for your configuration. If you wish to delete the configuration, the handy **Del** button is there at the bottom of the screen. The Modem port is on the **Hardware** tab and is a drop down menu. If you want to change the other settings you entered when you originally created the configuration, select the **Communication** tab. The first **Send** field contains your login, and the next **Send** field contains your password. The **Expect** fields correspond to the login: and password: prompts, which explains the ogin: and ord: entries.

> **Please Note:** The ogin: and ord: entries may not be the same for your system. Different **ISP/PPP** servers may use different text and should be changed to fit the needs of whatever server type you are logging in to. Instead, you may see such prompts as User ID and authentification.

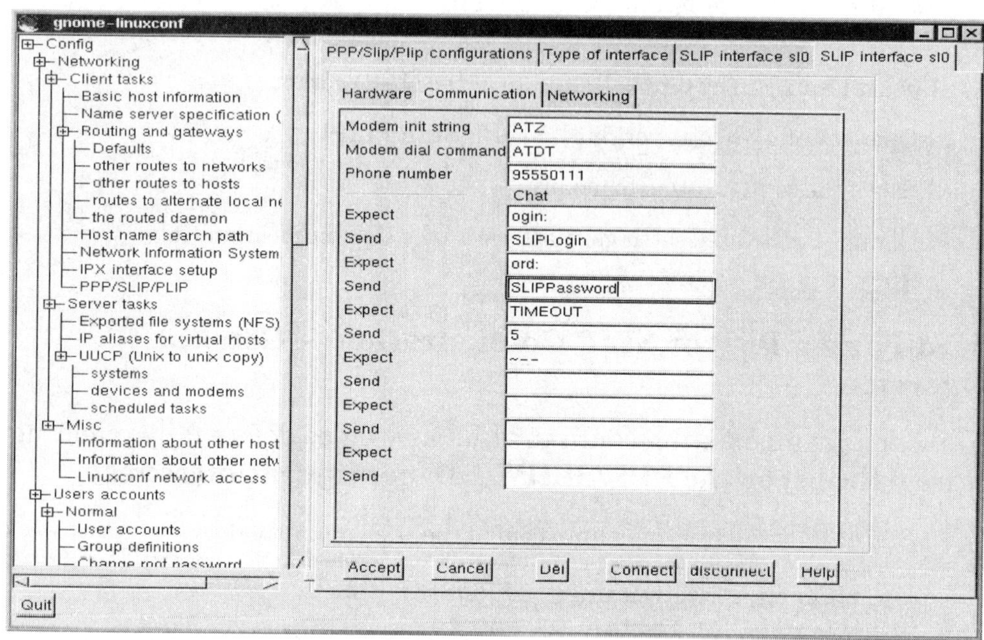

Figure 8-20: SLIP Interface Customization Screen

Once you have made your changes, you can test to see if your configuration is working. Select **Connect** from the bottom of the screen. This will attempt to connect you to the remote system using the information you've entered. Once you've finished configuring and testing your setup, we recommend using the usernet utility to control your dial-up networking connection on a daily basis. See the usernet man page for more information.

Other Network Connections — Quick Reference

Due to the number of possible choices and sub-choices, no quick reference is available for this section.

Other Network Connections — General Overview

Setting up a network connection over ethernet requires an entirely different type of setup. Network connections to token ring or arcnet networks follow a similar procedure, but will not be discussed here.

- First you will need to have an Ethernet card installed.
- Start Linuxconf by typing linuxconf at the shell prompt.
- Open [Config] -> [Networking] -> [Client tasks] -> [Basic host information]. The Host name tab will request a host name, which should be specified by default unless you did not setup your networking during the installation process. If it is not already specified, please take the time now to configure it. Skip this tab. Select the tab for **Adaptor 1**.

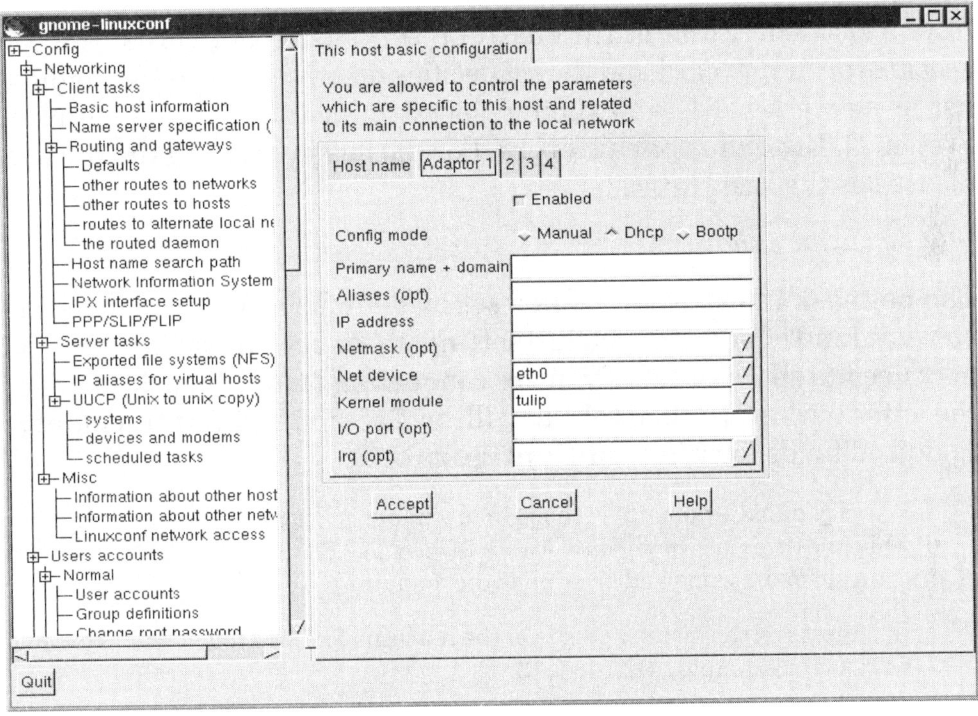

Figure 8-21: Adapter 1

The first item on this screen is a check box to indicate whether this adapter is enabled or not. It should be checked if this is the one you intend to use. Below that is a choice of Config modes. **Manual** means that you will be providing all the information and entering it yourself. **DHCP** and **bootp** retrieve their information from a remote server of the corresponding kind. If you're not sure what option to choose, talk to your systems administrator.

DHCP and bootp Required fields:

- Net device - The type of network card you are using; for example, eth0 would be the appropriate entry to use the first Ethernet card.
- Kernel module - The correct module based on your network card; for further information see the list below.

For DHCP and bootp configurations you only need to specify the **Net device** and the **Kernel module**. For the **Net device**, you will choose from a list where the eth prefix represents ethernet cards, the arc specifies an arcnet card and the tr specifies token ring cards. A complete list of network cards and their respective modules can be found in Section D, **Ethernet parameters**. For the most recent up-to-date list, please see the Red Hat website at

http://www.redhat.com

The netmask information will be set by default, although depending on what kind of network you are setting up, or becoming a part of, you may need to specify this. If you are connecting to an ISP, ask them for the information. Most likely it will be 255.255.255.0 (the default). Required fields for **Manual Configuration**:

- Primary name + domain — the primary name is the name of your computer, while the domain is how your network is specified. For example, foo.bar.com; foo is the primary name and bar.com is the domain.
- IP address — this is the address of the machine and will follow the pattern of x.x.x.x. For example, 192.168.0.13.
- Net device — type of network card you are using; eth0 would be the appropriate entry to use the first ethernet card.
- Kernel module — the correct module based on your network card.

Information on net devices and kernel modules is described above. The appropriate primary name + domain and IP address will depend on whether you are adding the computer to an existing network or creating a new network. For connecting to an existing network, contact your systems administrator for the information. Getting a network connected to the Internet is beyond the scope of this book, and we recommend the following starting point:

TCP/IP Network Administration, 2nd Edition, by Craig Hunt (O'Reilly and Associates).

If you're setting up a private network that won't ever be connected to the Internet, then you can choose any primary name + domain name you would like and have several choices for IP addresses (See Figure 8-22).

Addresses available	Examples
10.0.0.0 - 10.255.255.255	10.5.12.14
172.16.0.0 - 172.31.255.255	172.16.9.1, 172.28.2.5
192.168.0.0 - 192.168.255.255	192.168.0.13

Figure 8-22: Private Address Ranges

The three sets of numbers above correspond to class a, b, and c networks respectively. The classes are used to describe the number of IP addresses available as well as the range of numbers used to described each. The numbers above have been set aside for private networks.

> **Please Note:** You should not use these IP addresses if you connect to the Internet since 192.168.0.* and 192.168.255.* are not reliably considered private. If you want your network to be connected to the Internet, or think you might want to at some point in the future, do yourself a favor and get yourself non-private addresses now.

Nameserver Specification

A nameserver and default domain are also needed to establish a network connection. The nameserver is used to translate host names such as private.network.com to their corresponding IP address such as 192.168.7.3. The default domain tells the computer where to look if a fully qualified hostname isn't specified. Fully qualified means that the full address is given, so `foo.redhat.com` is the fully qualified hostname, while the hostname is simply `foo`. If you specified your default domain as `redhat.com`, then you could use just the hostname to connect successfully. For example `ftp foo` would be sufficient if your search domain is `redhat.com`, while `ftp foo.redhat.com` would be required if it wasn't. To specify the nameserver, open `[Config] -> [Networking] -> [Name server specification (DNS)]`.

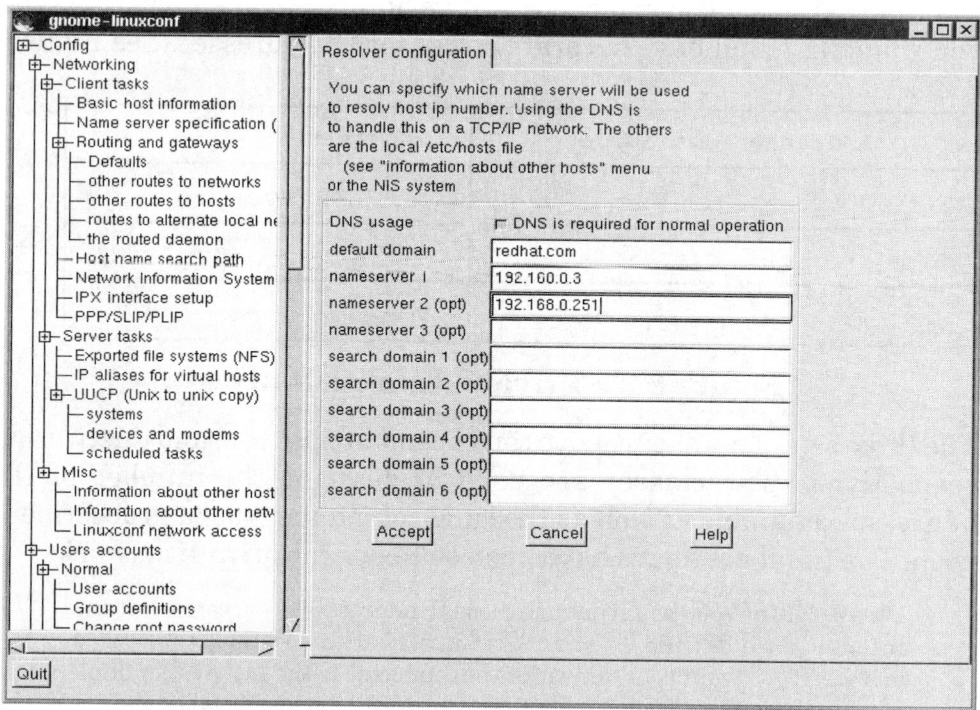

Figure 8-23: Resolver Configuration Screen

Nameservers are ranked according to the order in which they are accessed, so it's not unusual to see nameservers referred to as primary, secondary, tertiary and so on down the list if more than one is specified. Each of these must be an IP address and not a name. The computer has no way to resolve the name until it connects to a nameserver. Screamingly obvious when stated, but occasionally overlooked when people are simply asked to supply an address for a computer. In addition to a default domain, you can also specify search domains. Search domains work differently; they progress from one to six in a similar manner to the nameserver. However, they all take precedence over the default domain! Keep this in mind when specifying search domains. Search domains are not commonly used. The one item not yet covered is the check box for DNS usage. If you are running a small private network with no Internet connection, then using /etc/hosts files and keeping them all synchronized will work. As you add more and more machines, the complexity increases until it is easier to have a single machine run a DNS than to continue to sync /etc/hosts files. There is another reason for not using DNS, and that is if your network is going to use NIS instead. Note that NIS can be used in conjunction with DNS. So to sum it all up, unless you know why using /etc/hosts or NIS would be best for your situation, DNS is probably going to be your best choice. You can add, modify, or delete entries from the /etc/hosts file using Linuxconf. Open [Config] -> [Networking] -> [Misc] -> [Information about other hosts].

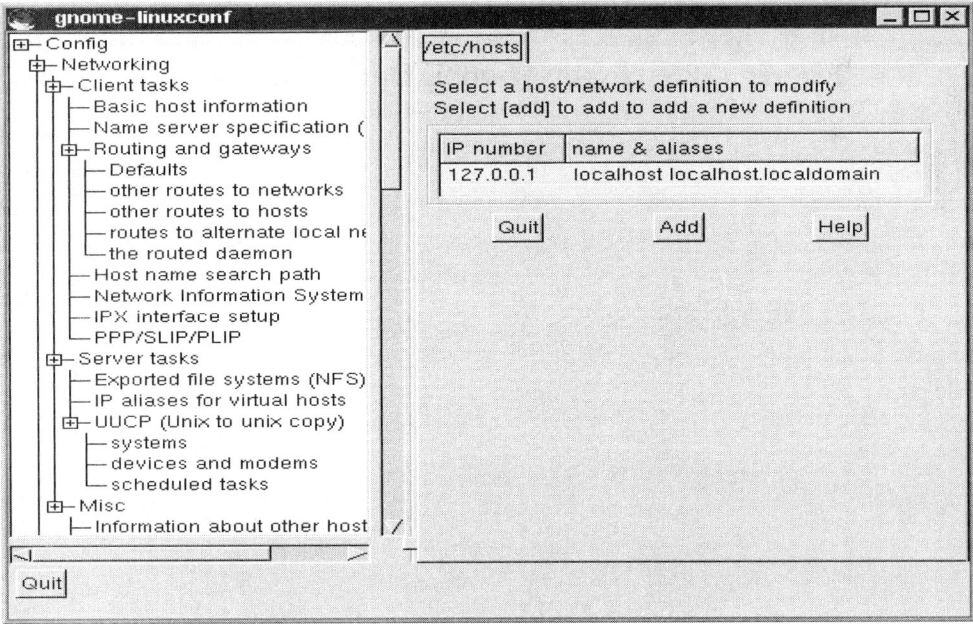

Figure 8-24: /etc/hosts Screen

To modify or delete an entry select it. To delete the entry, select **Del** at the bottom of the **host/network definition** screen.

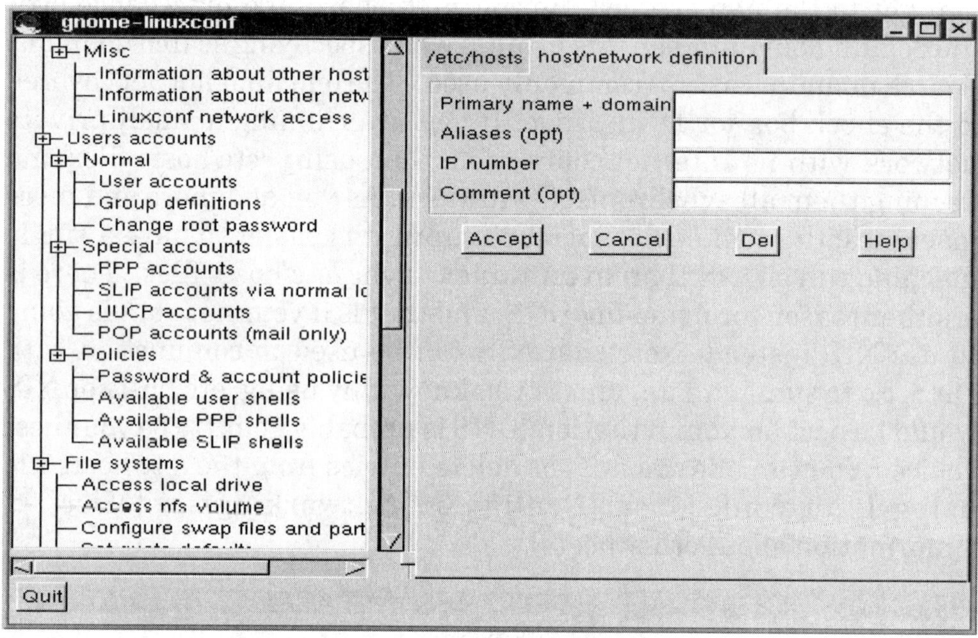

Figure 8-25: Host/Network Definition Screen

To modify it, change the information as necessary. To add a new entry, select **Add** at the bottom of the `/etc/hosts` screen. This will also open the **host/network definition** screen. Required Fields:

- **Primary name + domain** — the primary name is the name of the computer, while the domain is how the network it is attached to is specified. For example, given foo.bar.com, foo is the primary name and bar.com is the domain.
- **IP number** — also referred to as IP address; this is the address of the machine and will follow the pattern of x.x.x.x. For example, 192.168.0.13

Optional Fields:

- **Alias** — A shorthand for the fully qualified domain name. This is often the same as the primary name. So, for example, if the fully qualified domain name is foo.bar.com, you could select foo as the alias.
- **Comment** — a comment on the machine. For example, "The remote nameserver." You will need to specify both the primary name + domain and the IP number. The other fields are optional. Once finished, select Accept.

Date and Time

To get to the **date & time** control panel:

- Start Linuxconf by typing linuxconf at the shell prompt.
- Enter root's password when prompted (if not already root).
- Open `[Control] -> [Date & Time].`

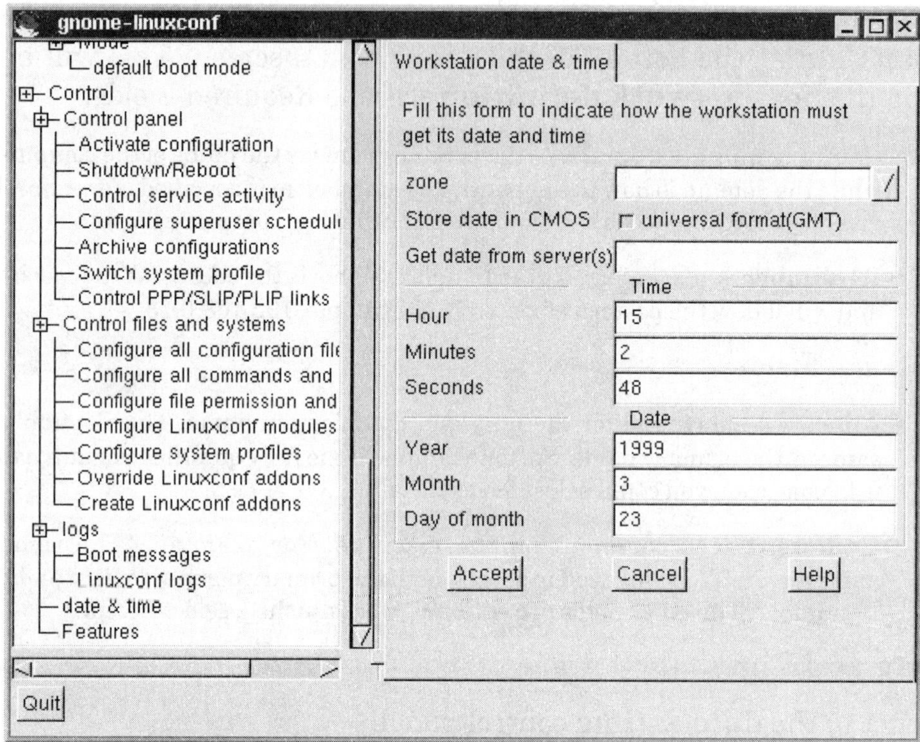

Figure 8-26: Workstation Date & Time

The **zone** field is a pull-down list that is long and extensive. It is often designated by a large region and then a city or zone within it. Examples include Europe/Vienna and US/Eastern. There is a check box to **Store date in CMOS in GMT format**. Hours are specified from 0 (midnight) to 23 (11 PM). Months are specified by number as well. For the year, please specify all four digits. All other fields should be self-explanatory.

System Configuration with the Control Panel

Please Note: Most of what can be done with the control panel applications can also be done using Linuxconf. In addition, Linuxconf supports both character-cell and graphical user interfaces. Please refer to **System Configuration With Linuxconf** for an introduction to Linuxconf.

The control panel is a launching pad for a number of different system administration tools (see Figure 8-27). These tools make your life easier by letting you configure things without remembering configuration file formats and awkward command line options.

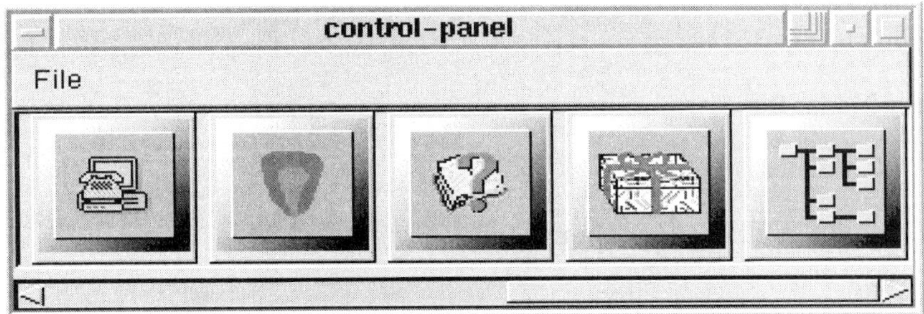

Figure 8-27: The Control Panel

To start the control-panel, start the X Window System as root with `startx` and type `control-panel` in an xterm. You will need to be root to run the control-panel tools successfully. You can do this as well if you already have X running as a normal user. Just type `su -c control-panel` and then type the root password when prompted. If you plan to do other tasks as root, you could type `su` followed by the root password when prompted.

Please Note: If you are not running X as root, you may need to give root access to your system's X server. To do this, enter the following command on a *non-root* terminal window:

```
xhost +localhost
```

After starting the control panel, simply clicking on an icon starts up a tool. Please note that you are not prevented from starting two instances of any tool, but doing so is a very bad idea because you may try to edit the same files in two places and end up overwriting your own changes. If you do accidentally start a second copy of a tool, you should quit it immediately. Also, do not manually edit any files managed by the control-panel tools while the tools are running. Similarly, do not run any other programs (such as Linuxconf) that may change those files while the tools are running.

Printer Configuration

The printer configuration tool (printtool) maintains the `/etc/printcap` file, print spool directories, and print filters. The filters allow you to print many different types of files, including:

- plain text (ASCII) files
- PostScript files
- TeX .dvi files
- GIF, JPEG, TIFF, and other graphics formats
- RPMs

In other words, simply printing a GIF or RPM file using the lpr command will result in the printer doing "the right thing."

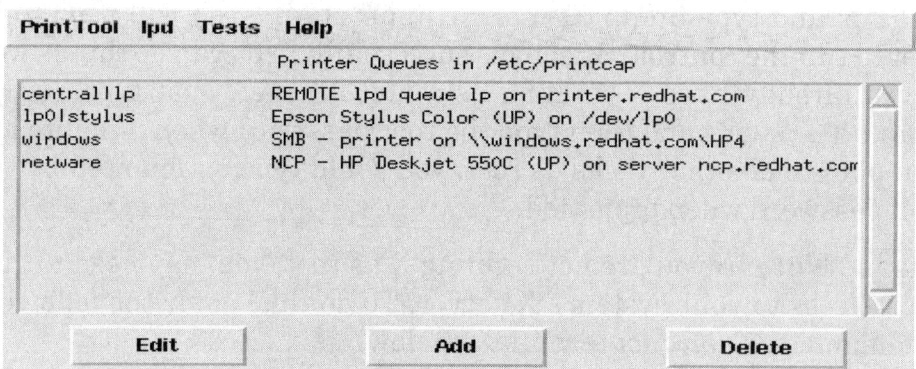

Figure 8-28: Print Tool

In order to create a new print queue, choose **Add**. Then, select what type of printer is being added. There are four types of print queues which can be configured with printtool:

- **Local** print queues are for printers attached to a printer or serial port on your Red Hat Linux system.
- **Remote** print queues are attached to a different system which you can access over a TCP/IP network.

- **SMB** print queues are attached to a different system which uses LAN-Manager-type (SMB) networking.
- **NCP** print queues are attached to a different system which uses Novell's NetWare network technology.

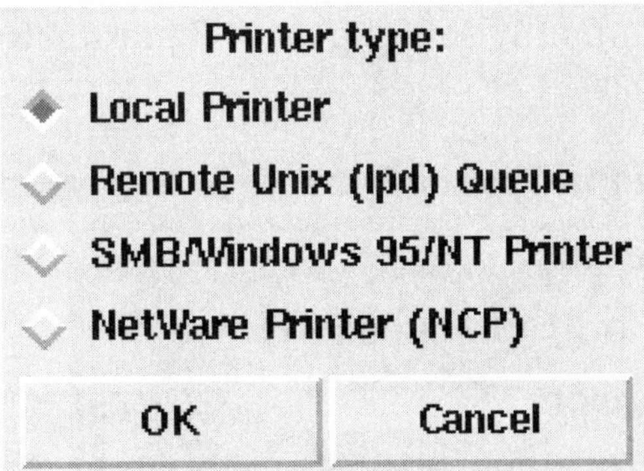

Figure 8-29: Selecting a Printer Type

After choosing the printer type, a dialog box requests further information about the print queue (see Figure 8-30). All types of print queues require the following information:

- **Queue Name:** What the queue will be called. Multiple names can be specifed with the | (pipe) character separating entries.
- **Spool Directory:** This is the directory on the local machine where files are stored before printing occurs. Be careful to not have more than one printer queue use a given spool directory.
- **File Limit:** Maximum size print job accepted, in kilobytes (1 kb = 1024 bytes). A size of 0 indicates no limit should be imposed.
- **Input Filter:** Filters convert printed files into a format the printer can handle. Press **Select** to choose the filter which best matches your printer (see Figure 8-31)

  In addition to configuring print queues able to print graphical and PostScript output, you can configure a text-only printer, which will only print plain ASCII text. Most printer drivers are also able to print ASCII text without converting it to PostScript first; simply choose **Fast text printing** when you configure the filter. **Please Note:** This only works for non-PostScript printers.

- **Suppress Headers:** Check this if you don't want a header page printed at the beginning of each print job.

For local printers, the following information is also required:

Printer Device: Usually /dev/lp1; the name of the port which the printer is attached to. Serial printers are usually on /dev/ttyS? ports. Note that you will need to manually configure serial parameters.

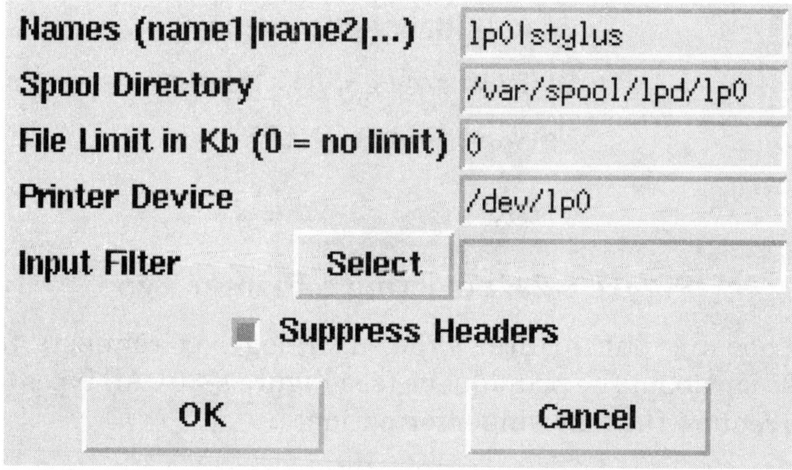

Figure 8-30: Adding a Local Printer

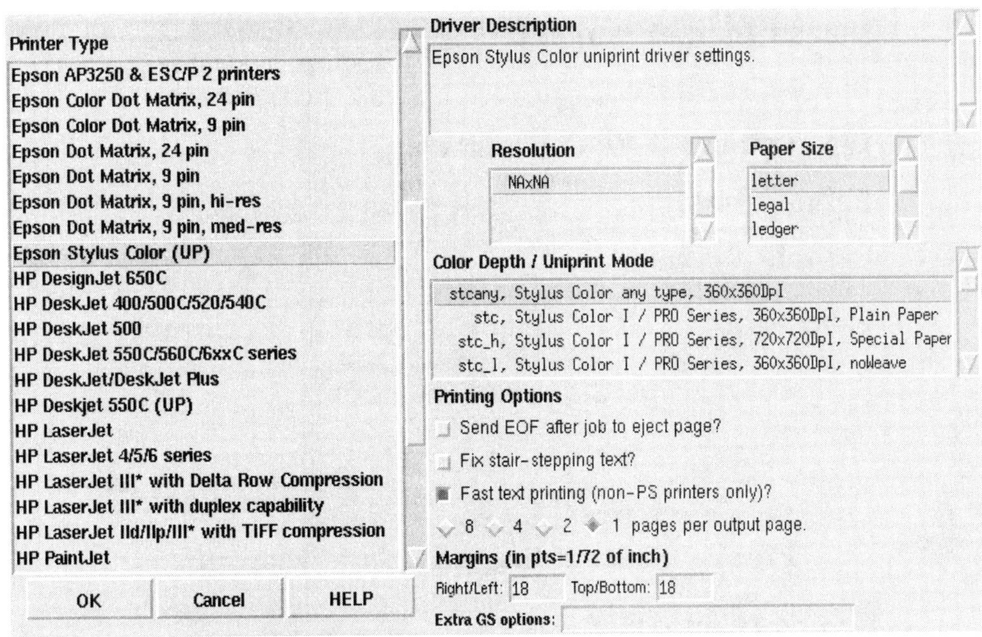

Figure 8-31: Configuring a Print Filter

For remote printers, the dialog box contains additional fields; fill in the following information:

- **Remote Host:** Hostname of the remote machine hosting the printer.
- **Remote Queue**: Name of the queue to print to on the remote machine.

The remote machine must be configured to allow the local machine to print on the desired queue. Typically `/etc/hosts.lpd` controls this.

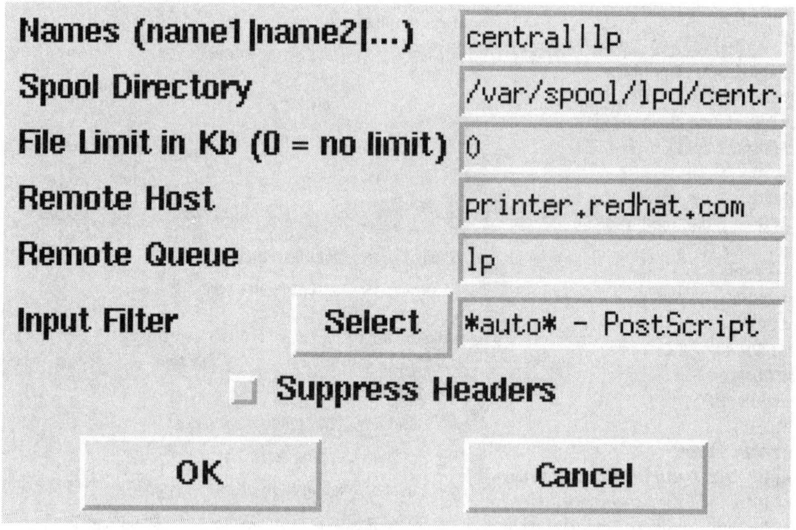

Names (name1|name2|...)	central|lp
Spool Directory	/var/spool/lpd/centr
File Limit in Kb (0 = no limit)	0
Remote Host	printer.redhat.com
Remote Queue	lp
Input Filter [Select]	*auto* - PostScript

Suppress Headers

OK Cancel

Figure 8-32: Adding a Remote Printer

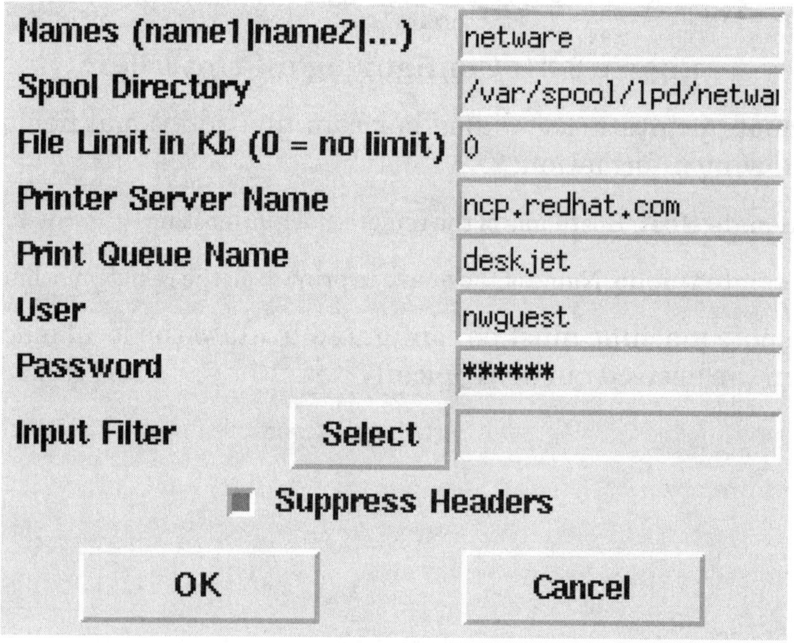

Names (name1|name2|...)	netware
Spool Directory	/var/spool/lpd/netwa
File Limit in Kb (0 = no limit)	0
Printer Server Name	ncp.redhat.com
Print Queue Name	deskjet
User	nwguest
Password	******
Input Filter [Select]	

Suppress Headers

OK Cancel

Figure 8-33: Adding an NCP Printer

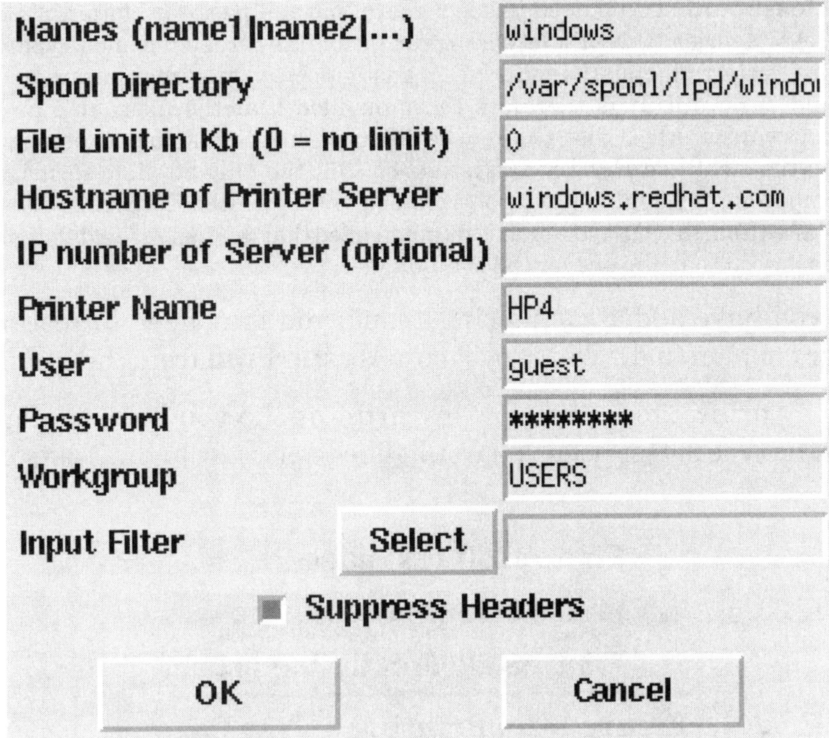

Figure 8-34: Adding an SMB Printer

For SMB and NCP printers, fill in the following information:

- **Hostname of Printer Server:** Name of the machine to which the printer you want to use is attached.
- **IP number of Server:** The IP address of the machine to which the printer you want to use is attached; this is optional and only relevant for SMB printers.
- **Printer Name:** Name of the printer on which you want to print.
- **User:** Name of user you must login as to access the printer (typically guest for Windows servers, or nobody for Samba servers).
- **Password:** Password (if required) to use the printer (typically blank). Someone should be able to tell you this if you do not already know it.

Please Note: If you need to use a username and password for an SMB (LAN Manager) or NCP (NetWare) print queue, they are stored unencrypted in a local script. Thus, it is possible for another person to learn the username and password. It is therefore recommended that the username and password for use of the printer to be different than that for a user account on the local Red Hat Linux system, so that the only possible security compromise would be unauthorized use of the printer. If there are file shares from the SMB server, it is recommended that they also use a different password than the one for the print queue.

After you have added your print queue, you may need to restart the printer daemon (lpd). To do so, choose **Restart lpd** from the **lpd** menu.

You may print a test page for any print queue you have configured. Select the type of test page you would like to print from the **Tests** menu.

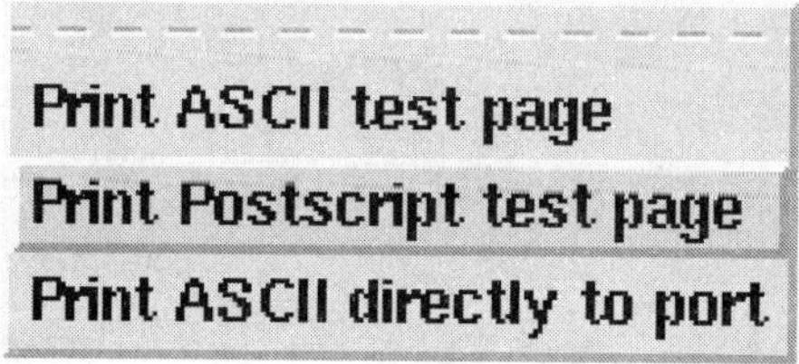

Figure 8-35: Printing a Test Page

Kernel Daemon Configuration

Red Hat Linux includes kerneld, the Kernel Daemon, which automatically loads some software and hardware support into memory as it is needed, and unloads it when it is no longer being used. The tool shown in Figure 8-36 manages the configuration file for kerneld. While kerneld can load some things, such as filesystems, without explicit configuration, it needs to be told what hardware support to load when it is presented with a generic hardware request.

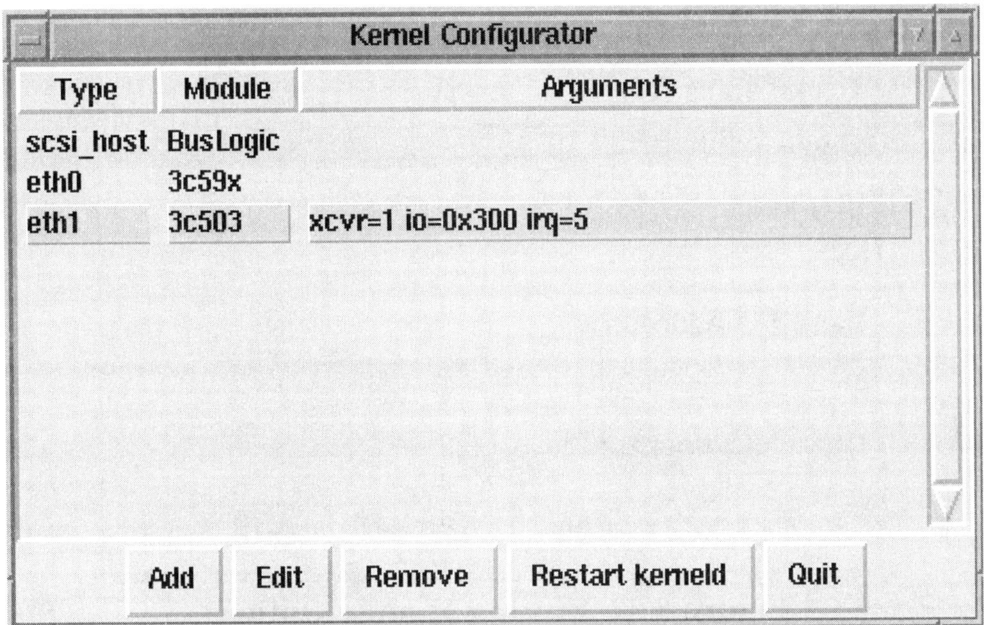

Figure 8-36: Kernel Module Management

For instance, when the kernel wants to load support for ethernet, kerneld needs to know which ethernet card you have, and if your ethernet card requires special configuration, it needs to know about that, too.

Changing Module Options

To change the options being given to a module when it is loaded, click on the line to select it, then click the Edit button. kernelcfg will bring up a window which looks like Figure 8-37. The options kernelcfg knows about (normally all available options) will each have their own field. Normally, you will want to ignore the Other arguments field. Some modules normally take no arguments; just in case, they have an Arguments field which allows you to enter configuration information.

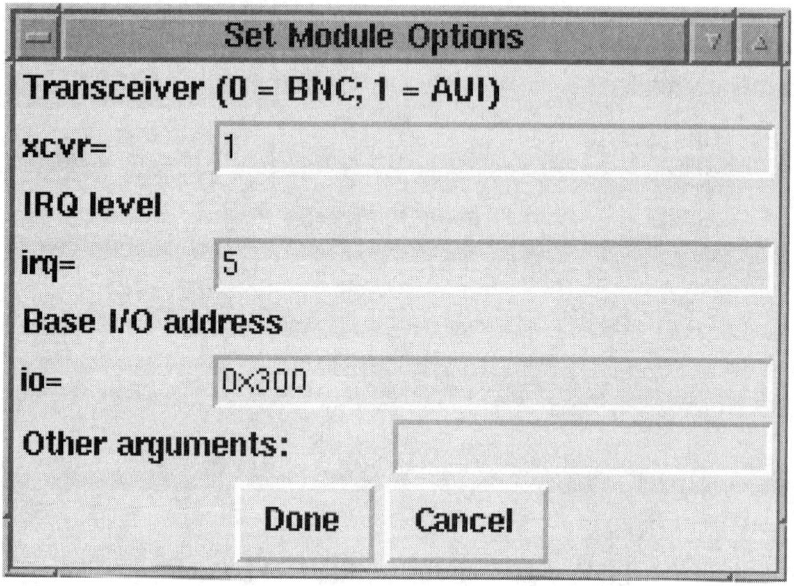

Figure 8-37: Editing Module Options

Changing Modules

To change which module gets invoked to provide a generic service, such as an ethernet card or SCSI host adapter module, you need to delete the old one and add a new one. To delete a module, select it by clicking on it, then click on **Remove**. Then click on **Add** to add the new module, as explained in the following section. If you have changed your SCSI controller (scsi_hostadapter), remember to make a new initial ramdisk with the `/sbin/mkinitrd` command as documented in **Making an initrd image** in Chapter 11.

Adding Modules

To add a module of any type, click on the **Add** button. You will be presented with a dialog box (Figure 8-38) asking you to choose a module type. Ethernet is eth, Token Ring is tr, SCSI controllers are scsi_hostadapter, and so on. Click **Ok** to continue to the next dialog box.

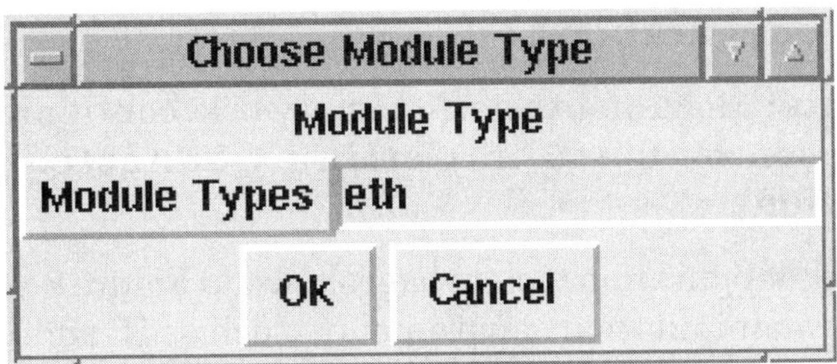

Figure 8-38: Adding a module

If there is more than one module which can be used for the module type you have chosen, you will be presented with a dialog box (Figure 8-39) which asks which module you want to use, and may also ask for specifics about the type of module; for ethernet, for example, you need to choose from eth0, eth1, etc. When you are done, click **Ok** again to continue to specify any module options in the next dialog box (Figure 8-39), which is the same as the dialog for editing a module.

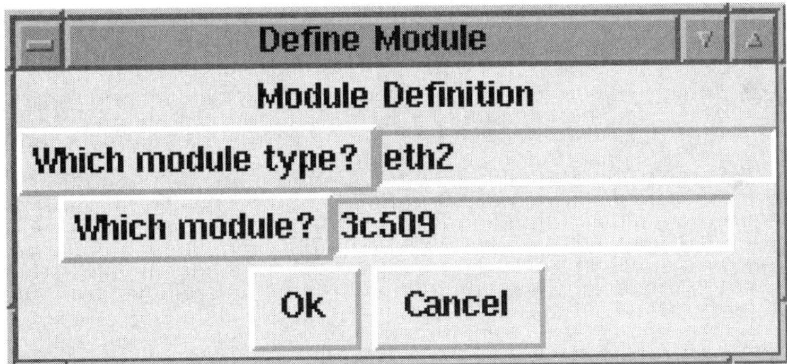

Figure 8-39: Selecting From Available Modules

Restarting Kerneld

The changes that you make with the Kernel Daemon Configuration tool will be made in the `/etc/conf.modules` file, which kerneld reads whenever it is started. Once you have made changes, you can restart kerneld by clicking on the **Restart kerneld** button. This will **not** cause any modules which are currently in use to be reloaded, it will only notify kerneld to use the configuration when it loads more modules in the future.

Network Configuration

Please Note: Documentation on network configuration using Linuxconf can be found in **Getting Connected (Network Configuration)**.

The network configuration tool (netcfg) shown in Figure 8-40 is designed to allow easy manipulation of parameters such as IP address, gateway address, and network address, as well as name servers and `/etc/hosts`.

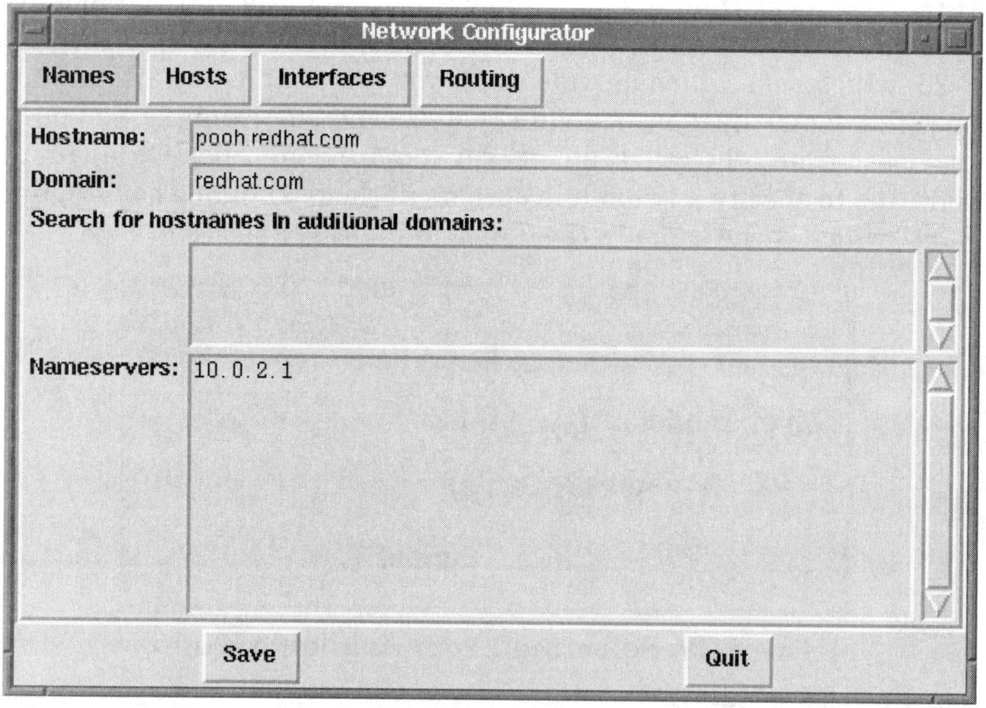

Figure 8-40: Network Configuration Panel

Network devices can be added, removed, configured, activated, deactivated and aliased. Ethernet, arcnet, token ring, pocket (ATP), PPP, SLIP, PLIP and loopback devices are supported. PPP/SLIP/PLIP support works well on most hardware, but some hardware setups may exhibit unpredictable behavior. When using the Network Configuration Tool click **Save** to write your changes to disk, to quit without making any changes select **Quit**.

Managing Names

The **Names** panel of the Network Configuration tool serves two primary purposes: setting the hostname and domain of the computer, and determining which name server will be used to look up other hosts on the network. The Network tool is not capable of configuring a machine as a nameserver. To edit a field or add information to a field simply click on the field with the left mouse button and type the new information.

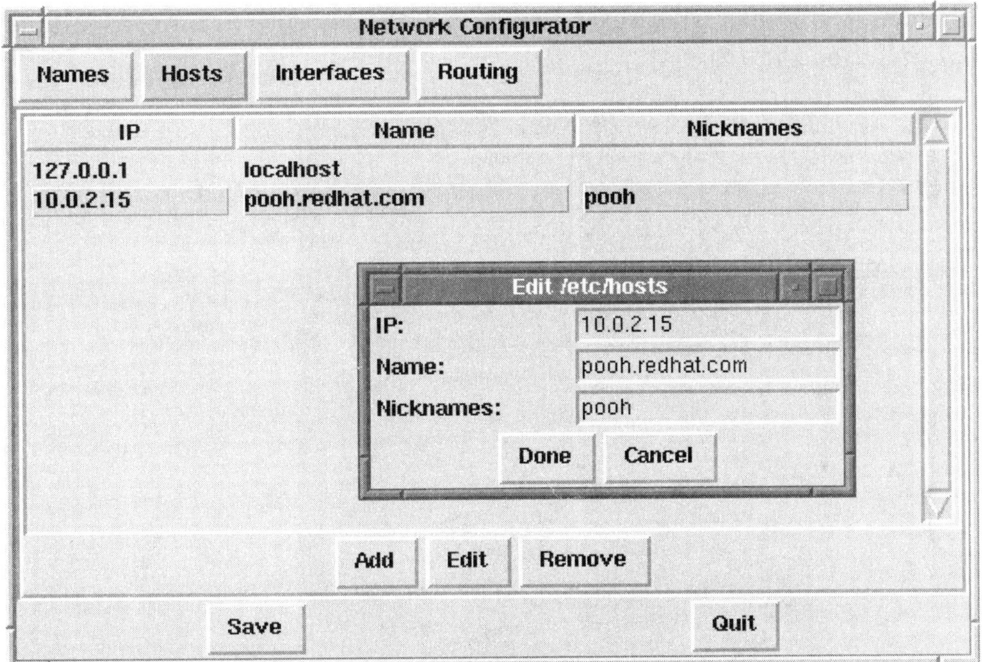

Figure 8-41: Adding/Editing Hosts

Managing Hosts

In the **Hosts** management panel you have the ability to add, edit, or remove hosts from the `/etc/hosts` file. Adding or editing an entry involves identical actions. An edit dialog box will appear, simply type the new information and click **Done** when you are finished. See Figure 8-41 for an example.

Adding a Networking Interface

If you have added a networking interface to your machine since installing Red Hat Linux, or you didn't configure your ethernet card at install time, you can configure it with a few clicks of a mouse. **Please Note:** You may need to configure kerneld to load a driver for the network interface you are adding (e.g., eth0); see **Kernel Daemon Configuration** for more information.

Begin adding an interface by clicking on Interfaces in the main panel. This will bring up a window of configured devices with a row of available options. See Figure 8-42.

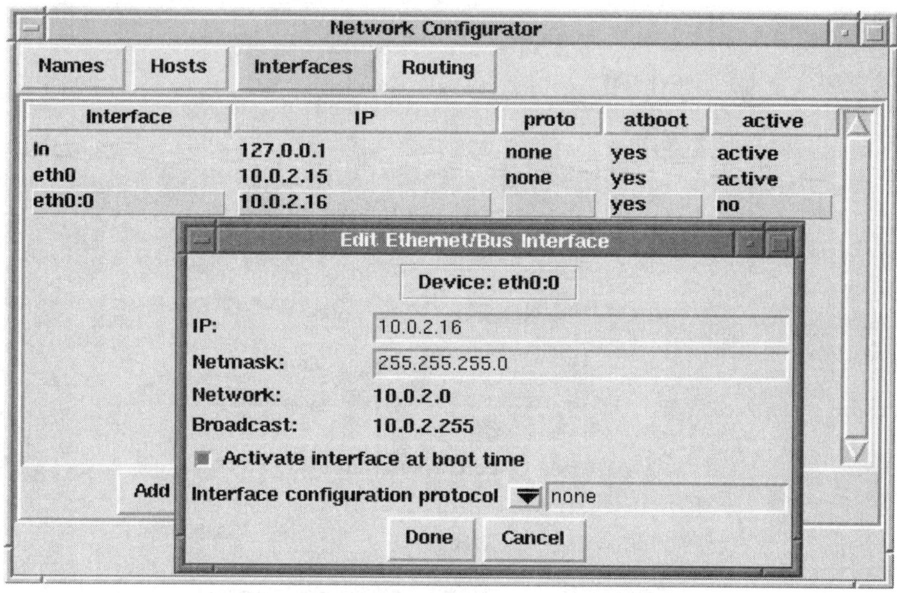

Figure 8-42: Configured Interfaces

To add a device, first click the **Add** button then select the type of interface you want to configure from the box that appears (See Figure 8-43).

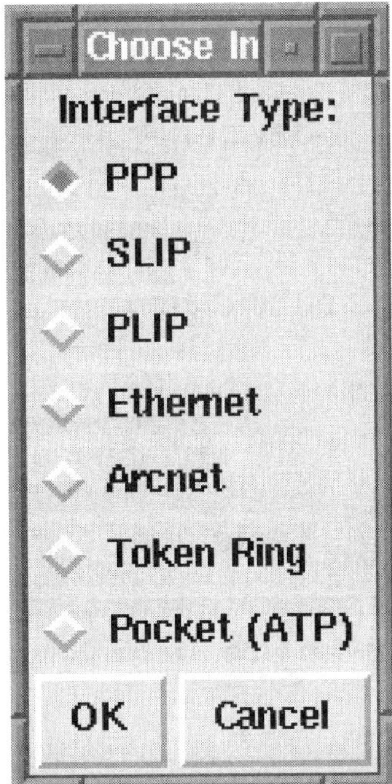

Figure 8-43: Choose Interface Type

Please Note: There is now a **clone** button available in netcfg. This button can be used to create a "clone" of an already-existing interface. By using clone interfaces, it is possible for a laptop to have one Ethernet interface defined for a work LAN, and a clone Ethernet device defined for a home LAN.

PPP Interface

— Adding a PPP interface can be as simple as supplying the phone number, login name and password in the **Create PPP Interface** dialog shown in Figure 8-44. If you need to use PAP authentication for your PPP connection, choose **Use PAP authentication**. In many cases some degree of customization will be needed to establish a PPP connection. Choosing the **Customize** button will allow you to make changes to the hardware, communication, and networking settings for the PPP interface.

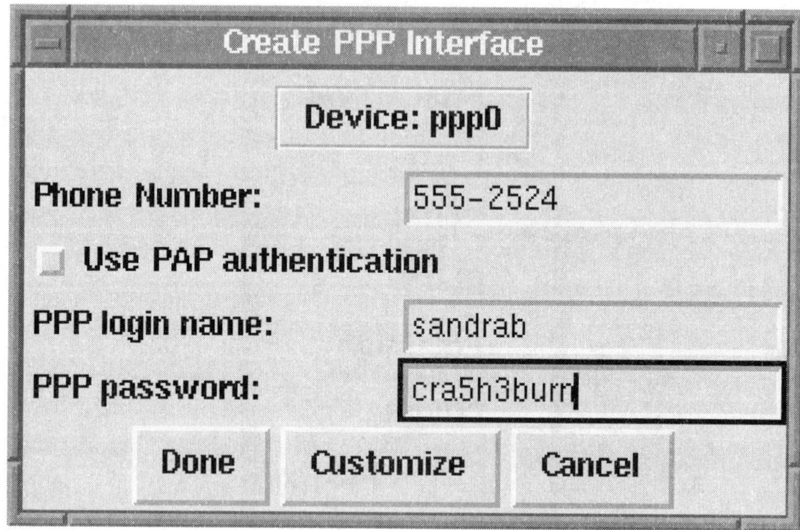

Figure 8-44: Create PPP Interface

SLIP Interface

In order to configure a SLIP interface you must first supply a phone number, login name, and password. This will supply the initial parameters for the chat script needed to establish a SLIP connection. When you choose **Done**, a dialog titled **Edit SLIP Interface** appears that enables you to further customize the hardware, communication and networking parameters for your SLIP interface.

PLIP Interface

To add a PLIP interface to your system you only have to supply the IP address, the remote IP address, and the Netmask. You can also select if you want to activate the interface at boot time.

Ethernet, Arcnet, Token Ring and Pocket Adapter Interfaces

If you are adding an ethernet, arcnet, token ring or pocket adapter to your computer you will need to supply the following information:

- **Device:** This is determined by netconfig based on the devices already configured.
- **IP Address:** Enter an IP address for your network device.
- **Netmask:** Enter the network mask for your network device. The network and broadcast addresses are calculated automatically based on the IP address and netmask you enter.
- **Activate interface at boot time:** If you want the device to be configured automatically when your machine boots select this by clicking on the box.
- **Allow any user to (de)activate interface:** Check this if you want any user to be able to activate or deactivate the interface.
- **Interface configuration protocol:** If you have a BOOTP or DHCP server on your network and would like to use it to configure the interface, choose the appropriate option; otherwise, choose **none**.

After providing the configuration information for your new device, click **Done**. The device should appear in your **Interfaces** list as an inactive device. (The active column should have a label of **no**.) To activate the new device, first select it with a mouse click and then choose on the **Activate** button. If it does not come up properly, you may need to reconfigure it by choosing on **Edit**.

Managing Routes

In the Routes management screen you have the ability to add, edit, or remove static networking routes. Adding or editing an entry involves identical actions, just like the Hosts panel. An edit dialog box will appear; simply type the new information and click Done when you are finished. See Figure 8-45 for an example.

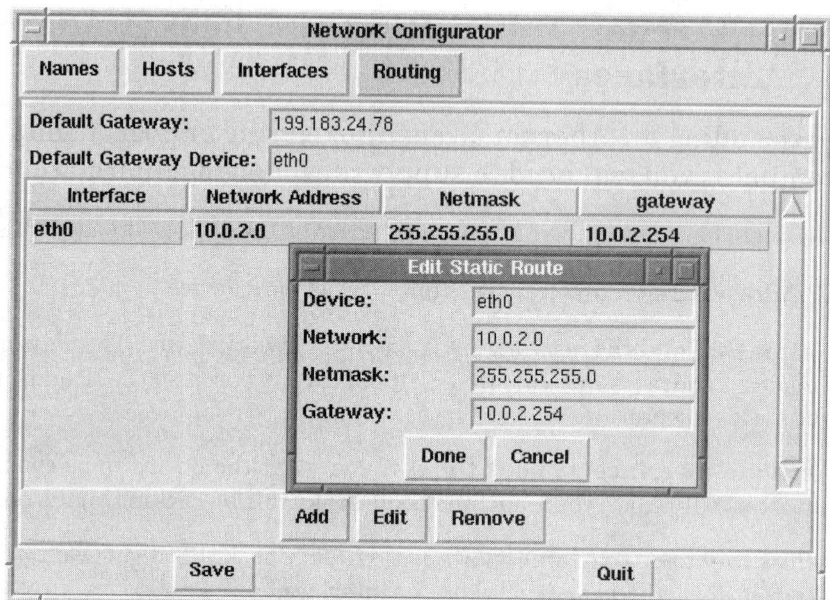

Figure 8-45: Adding/Editing Routes

Time and Date

> **Please Note:** Documentation on setting your system's time and date using Linuxconf can be found in the **Time and Date** section of **System Configuration with the Control Panel**.

The time machine allows you to change the time and date by clicking on the appropriate part of the time and date display and clicking on the arrows to change the value.

The system clock is not changed until you click on the **Set System Clock** button.

Click on **Reset Time** to set the time machine time back to that of the system.

> **Please Note:** Changing the time can seriously confuse programs that depend on the normal progression of time, and could possibly cause problems. Try to quit as many applications and processes as possible before changing the time or date.

9 Package Management with RPM

The **R**ed Hat **P**ackage **M**anager (RPM), is an open packaging system available for anyone to use, and works on Red Hat Linux as well as other Linux and UNIX systems. Red Hat Software encourages other vendors to take the time to look at RPM and use it for their own products. RPM is distributable under the terms of the GPL. For the end user, RPM provides many features that make maintaining a system far easier than it has ever been. Installing, uninstalling, and upgrading RPM packages are all one line commands, and all the messy details have been taken care of for you. RPM maintains a database of installed packages and their files, which allows you to perform powerful queries and verification of your system. During upgrades RPM handles configuration files specially, so that you never lose your customizations – a feature that is impossible with straight .tar.gz files. For the developer, RPM allows you to take source code for software and package it into source and binary packages for end users. This process is quite simple and is driven from a single file and optional patches that you create. This clear delineation of “pristine” sources and your patches and build instructions eases the maintenance of the package as new versions of the software are released.

Please Note: Although it does not hurt to understand the concepts behind RPM, there is an alternative for installing, uninstalling and upgrading packages. For those of you that prefer a graphical interface to the command line, we suggest you use GnoRPM. Please see Chapter 10 for more information.

RPM Design Goal

Before trying to understand how to use RPM, it helps to have an idea of what the design goals are.

Upgradability

With RPM you can upgrade individual components of your system without completely reinstalling. When you get a new release of an operating system based on RPM (such as Red Hat Linux), you don't need to reinstall on your machine (as you do with operating systems based on other packaging systems). RPM allows intelligent, fully-automated, in-place upgrades of your system. Configuration files in packages are preserved across upgrades, so you won't lose your customizations.

Powerful Querying

RPM is also designed to have powerful querying options. You can do searches through your entire database for packages or just certain files. You can also easily find out what package a file belongs to and where it came from. The files an RPM package contains are in a compressed archive, with a custom binary header containing useful information about the package and its contents, allowing you to query individual packages quickly and easily.

System Verification

Another powerful feature is the ability to verify packages. If you are worried that you deleted an important file for some package, simply verify the package. You will be notified of any anomalies. At that point, you can reinstall the package if necessary. Any configuration files that you modified are preserved during reinstallation.

Pristine Sources

A crucial design goal was to allow the use of "pristine" software sources, as distributed by the original authors of the software. With RPM, you have the pristine sources along with any patches that were used, plus complete build instructions. This is a big advantage for several reasons. For instance, if a new version of a program comes out, you don't necessarily have to start from scratch to get it to compile. You can look at the patch to see what you might need to do. All the compiled-in defaults, and all of the changes that were made to get the software to build properly are easily visible this way. This goal may only seem important for developers, but it results in higher quality software for end users too. We would like to thank the folks from the BOGUS distribution for originating the pristine source concept.

Using RPM

RPM has five basic modes of operation (not counting package building): installing, uninstalling, upgrading, querying, and verifying. This section contains an overview of each mode. For complete details and options try rpm —help, or turn to **Other RPM Resources** for more information on RPM.

Installing

RPM packages typically have file names like foo-1.0-1.i386.rpm, which includes the package name (foo), version (1.0), release (1), and architecture (i386). Installing a package is as simple as:

```
# rpm -ivh foo-1.0-1.i386.rpm
foo ####################################
```

As you can see, RPM prints out the name of the package (which is not necessarily the same as the file name, which could have been 1.rpm), and then prints a succession of hash marks as the package is installed, as a sort of progress meter. Installing packages is designed to be simple, but you can get a few errors:

Package Already Installed

If the package is already installed, you will see:

```
# rpm -ivh foo-1.0-1.i386.rpm
foo package fpackagesoo-1.0-1 is already
installed
error: foo-1.0-1.i386.rpm cannot be installed
#
```

If you really want to install the package anyway, you can use `--replacepkgs` on the command line, which tells RPM to ignore the error:

```
# rpm -ivh —replacepkgs foo-1.0-1.i386.rpm
foo ####################################
```

Conflicting Files

If you attempt to install a package that contains a file that has already been installed by another package, you'll see:

```
# rpm -ivh foo-1.0-1.i386.rpm
foo /usr/bin/foo conflicts with file from bar-
1.0-1
error: foo-1.0-1.i386.rpm cannot be installed
#
```

To cause RPM to ignore that error, use `--replacefiles` on the command line:

```
# rpm -ivh —replacefiles foo-1.0-1.i386.rpm
foo ####################################
```

Unresolved Dependency

RPM packages can "depend" on other packages, which means that they require other packages to be installed in order to run properly. If you try to install a package for which there is such an unresolved dependency, you'll see:

```
# rpm -ivh bar-1.0-1.i386.rpm
failed dependencies: foo is needed by bar-1.0-1
#
```

To handle this error you should install the requested packages. If you want to force the installation anyway (a bad idea since the package probably will not run correctly), use —nodeps on the command line.

Uninstalling

Uninstalling a package is just as simple as installing:

```
# rpm -e foo
#
```

Notice that we used the package name "foo," not the name of the original package *file* "`foo-1.0-1.i386.rpm`". You can encounter a dependency error when uninstalling a package if some other installed package depends on the one you are trying to remove. For example:

```
# rpm -e foo
removing these packages would break dependencies:
    foo is needed by bar-1.0-1
#
```

To cause RPM to ignore that error and uninstall the package anyway (which is also a bad idea since the package that depends on it will probably fail to work properly), use `--nodeps` on the command line.

Upgrading

Upgrading a package is almost just like installing.

```
# rpm -Uvh foo-2.0-1.i386.rpm
foo ########################################
```

What you don't see above is that RPM automatically uninstalled any old versions of the foo package. In fact you may want to always use -U to install packages, since it works fine even when there are no previous versions of the package installed. Since RPM performs intelligent upgrading of packages with configuration files, you may see a message like:

```
saving /etc/foo.conf as /etc/foo.conf.rpmsave
```

This means that your changes to the configuration file may not be "forward compatible" with the new configuration file in the package, so RPM saved your original file, and installed a new one. You should investigate and resolve the differences between the two files as soon as possible to ensure that your system continues to function properly. Since upgrading is really a combination of uninstalling and installing, you can encounter any errors from those modes, plus one more: If RPM thinks you are trying to upgrade to a package with an older version number, you will see:

```
# rpm -Uvh foo-1.0-1.i386.rpm
foo package foo-2.0-1 (which is newer) is already
installed
error: foo-1.0-1.i386.rpm cannot be installed
#
```

To cause RPM to "upgrade" anyway, use —oldpackage on the command line:

```
# rpm -Uvh —oldpackage foo-1.0-1.i386.rpm
foo ########################################
```

Freshening

Freshening a package is similar to upgrading:

```
# rpm -Fvh foo-1.2-1.i386.rpm
foo ########################################
```

RPM's freshen option checks the versions of the packages specified on the command line against the versions of packages that have already been installed on your system. When a newer version of an already-installed package is processed by RPM's freshen option, it will be upgraded to the newer version. However, RPM's freshen option will not install a package if no previously-installed package of the same name exists. This differs from RPM's upgrade option, as an upgrade will install packages, whether or not an older version of the package was already installed. RPM's freshen option works well with single packages or with a group of packages. It's especially handy if you've just downloaded a large number of different packages, and you only want to upgrade those packages that are already installed on your system. Using the freshen option means that you won't have to pick through the downloaded packages, deleting any unwanted ones before using RPM. In this case, you can simply issue the following command:

```
# rpm -Fvh *.rpm
```

RPM will automatically upgrade only those packages that have already been installed.

Querying

Querying the database of installed packages is accomplished with rpm -q. A simple use is rpm -q foo which will print the package name, version, and release number of the installed package foo:

```
# rpm -q foofoo-2.0-1
#
```

Instead of specifying the package name, you can use the following options with -q to specify what package(s) you want to query. These are called *Package Specification Options*.

- -a queries all currently installed packages.
- -f <file> will query the package owning <file>.
- -p <packagefile> queries the package <packagefile>.

There are a number of ways to specify what information to display about queried packages. The following options are used to select the information you are interested in. These are called *Information Selection Options*.

- -i displays package information such as name, description, release, size, build date, install date, vendor, and other miscellaneous information.
- -l displays the list of files that the package "owns".
- -s displays the state of all the files in the package.
- -d displays a list of files marked as documentation (man pages, info pages, README's, etc).
- -c displays a list of files marked as configuration files. These are the files you change after installation to adapt the package to your system (sendmail.cf, passwd, inittab, etc).

For those options that display file lists, you can add -v to your command line to get the lists in a familiar ls -l format.

Verifying

Verifying a package compares information about files installed from a package with the same information from the original package. Among other things, verifying compares the size, MD5 sum, permissions, type, owner and group of each file. `rpm -V` *verifies* a package. You can use any of the *Package Selection Options* listed for querying to specify the packages you wish to verify. A simple use is `rpm -V foo` which verifies that all the files in the `foo` package are as they were when they were originally installed. For example:

- To verify a package containing particular file

  ```
  rpm -Vf /bin/vi
  ```

- To verify ALL installed packages

  ```
  rpm -Va
  ```

- To verify an installed package against an RPM package file:

  ```
  rpm -Vp foo-1.0-1.i386.rpm
  ```

This can be useful if you suspect that your RPM databases are corrupt.

If everything verified properly there will be no output. If there are any discrepancies they will be displayed. The format of the output is a string of 8 characters, a possible "c" denoting a configuration file, and then the file name. Each of the 8 characters denotes the result of a comparison of one attribute of the file to the value of that attribute recorded in the RPM database. A single "." (period) means the test passed. The following characters denote failure of certain tests:

5

MD5 checksum

S

File size

L
: Symbolic link

T
: File modification time

D
: Device

U
: User

G
: Group

M
: Mode (includes permissions and file type)

If you see any output, use your best judgment to determine if you should remove or reinstall the package, or somehow fix the problem.

Impressing Your Friends with RPM

RPM is a very useful tool for both managing your system and diagnosing and fixing problems. The best way to make sense of all the options is to look at some examples.

- Let's say you delete some files by accident, but you aren't sure what you deleted. If you want to verify your entire system and see what might be missing, you would enter:

  ```
  rpm -Va
  ```

  If some files are missing, or appear to have been corrupted, you should probably either re-install the package or uninstall, then re-install the package.

- Let's say you run across a file that you don't recognize. To find out which package owns it, you would enter:

  ```
  rpm -qf /usr/X11R6/bin/xjewel
  ```

  The output would look like:

  ```
  xjewel-1.6-1
  ```

- We can combine the above two examples in the following scenario. Say you are having problems with /usr/bin/paste. You would like to verify the package that owns that program but you don't know which package that is. Simply enter:

  ```
  rpm -Vf /usr/bin/paste
  ```

  and the appropriate package will be verified.

- If you are using a program and want to find out more information about it, you can enter the following to find out what documentation came with the package that "owns" that program (in this case ispell):

  ```
  rpm -qdf /usr/bin/ispell
  ```

  The output would be:

  ```
  /usr/man/man4/ispell.4
  /usr/man/man4/english.4
  /usr/man/man1/unsq.1
  /usr/man/man1/tryaffix.1
  /usr/man/man1/sq.1
  /usr/man/man1/munchlist.1
  /usr/man/man1/ispell.1
  /usr/man/man1/findaffix.1
  /usr/man/man1/buildhash.1
  /usr/info/ispell.info.gz
  /usr/doc/ispell-3.1.18-1/README
  ```

- You find a new koules RPM, but you don't know what it is. To find out some information on it, enter:

  ```
  rpm -qip koules-1.2-2.i386.rpm.
  ```

The output would be:

```
Name          : koules Distribution:Red Hat Linux Colgate
Version       : 1.2          Vendor:Red Hat Software
Release       : 2        Build Date:Mon Sep 02 11:59:12 1996
Install date  : (none)    Build Host:porky.redhat.com
Group         : Games     Source RPM:koules-1.2-2.src.rpm
Size          : 614939
Summary       : SVGAlib action game;multiplayer, network
Description   :
This arcade-style game is novel in conception and excellent
in execution.  No shooting, no blood, no guts,no gore.  The
play is simple, but you still must develop skill to play.
This version uses SVGAlib to run on a graphics console.
```

- Now you want to see what files the koules RPM installs. You would enter:

  ```
  rpm -qlp koules-1.2-2.i386.rpm
  ```

  The output is:

  ```
  usr/man/man6/koules.6
  /usr/lib/games/kouleslib/start.raw
  /usr/lib/games/kouleslib/end.raw/
  usr/lib/games/kouleslib/destroy2.raw
  /usr/lib/games/kouleslib/destroy1.raw
  /usr/lib/games/kouleslib/creator2.raw
  /usr/lib/games/kouleslib/creator1.raw
  /usr/lib/games/kouleslib/colize.raw
  /usr/lib/games/kouleslib
  /usr/games/koules
  ```

These are just several examples. As you use the system you will find many more uses for RPM.

Other RPM Resources

For more information on RPM, check out the man page, the help screen (rpm —help), and the RPM documents available at

http://www.rpm.org/

There is also an RPM book available. It's called *Maximum RPM* , and it is available from Red Hat Software and your local bookstore. It contains a wealth of information about RPM for both the end-user and the package builder. An on-line version of the book is available at *http://www.rpm.org/*. There is also a mailing list for discussion of RPM related issues, called `rpm-list@redhat.com`. The list is archived on *http://www.redhat.com/support/mailing-lists/*. To subscribe, send mail to `rpm-list-request@redhat.com` with the word `subscribe` in the subject line.

10 GnoRPM

New to Red Hat Linux 6.0 is GnoRPM, a graphical tool which runs under the X Window System. Written by James Henstridge (james@daa.com.au), GnoRPM replaces GLINT. Although GnoRPM shares some similarities with GLINT, it is faster, more powerful and holds a more user-friendly interface. GnoRPM is "GNOME-compliant," meaning that it seamlessly integrates into GNOME, the X Window System desktop environment. With GnoRPM, you can easily.

- install RPM packages
- uninstall RPM packages
- upgrade RPM packages
- find new RPM packages
- query RPM packages
- verify RPM packages

The interface features a menu, a toolbar, a tree and a display window of currently installed packages. Operations are performed in GnoRPM by finding and selecting packages, then choosing the type of operation to perform via push-button on the toolbar or through the menu.

- Installing a package places all of the components of that package on your system in the correct locations.
- Uninstalling one removes all traces of the package except for configuration files you have modified.
- Upgrading a package installs the newly available version and uninstalls all other versions that were previously installed. This allows quick upgrading to the latest releases of packages. Refer to **Package Manipulation** for information about how to alter the default settings for installing and uninstalling packages.

You can also use the **Web find** option to search the Internet for newly released packages. You can direct GnoRPM to search for particular distributions when you want to look for new packages. (If you have a slow connection, this option can take some time to fully execute.) See **Package Manipulation** for more information about this feature.

Please Note: Exercise caution if you choose to use the **Web find** option, since there is no way to verify the integrity of the many packages which are available at numerous repositories. Before installing packages, you should perform a query on that package to help you determine whether it can be trusted. Packages not produced by Red Hat Software are not supported in any way by Red Hat Software.

Using GnoRPM to perform all of these and many other operations is the same as using rpm from the shell prompt. However, the graphical nature of GnoRPM often makes these operations easier to perform.

The normal way to handle GnoRPM is to display the available packages, select the package(s) you want to operate on, and then select an option from the toolbar or menu which performs the operation.

For instance, you can install, upgrade or uninstall several packages with a few button clicks. Similarly, you can query and verify more than one package at a time.

Starting GnoRPM

You can start GnoRPM from either an X terminal window or from the GNOME desktop panel, under System. To start GnoRPM from an X terminal window, at the shell prompt, simply type

```
gnorpm
```

That will bring up the main GnoRPM window (as shown in Figure 10-1).

> **Please Note:** If you would like to install, upgrade or uninstall packages, you must be in root. The easiest way to do this is to type su root and then the root password at a shell prompt. However, you do not need to be in root to query and verify packages.

There are several parts to the GnoRPM interface.

- **Package Panel** - On the left; allows you to browse and select packages on your system.
- **Display window** - To the right of the package panel; shows you contents from folders in the panel.
- **Toolbar** - Above the display and panel; a graphical display of package tools.
- **Menu** - Above the toolbar; contains text-based commands, as well as help info, preferences and other settings.
- **Status bar** - Beneath the panel and display windows; shows the total number of selected packages.

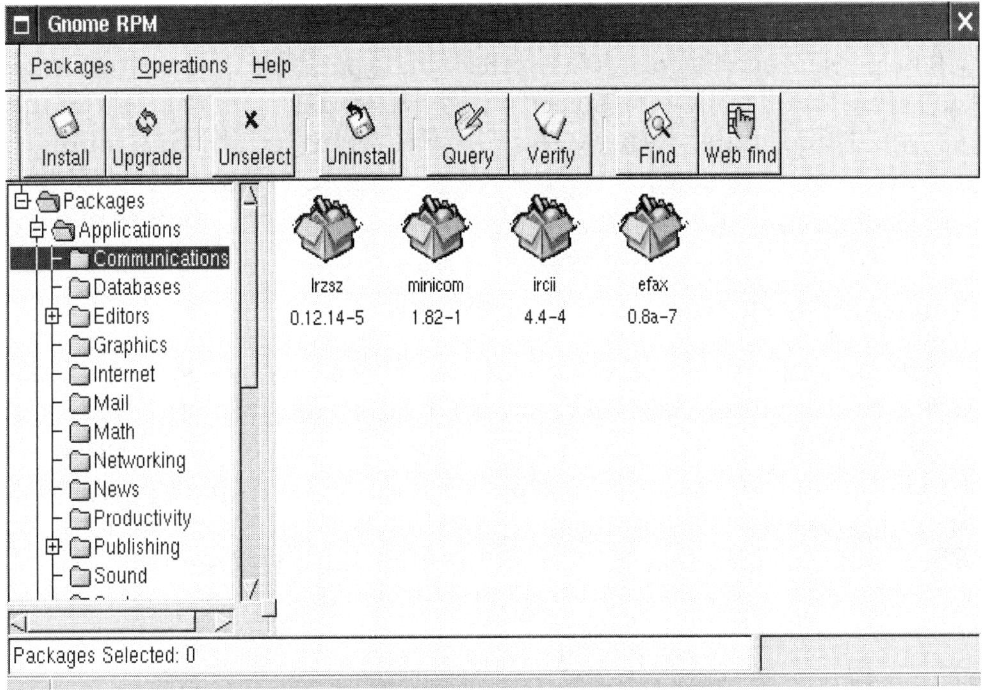

Figure 10-1: Main GnoRPM Window

The Package Display

Each folder icon in the tree view at left represents a group of packages. Each group can contain subgroups. Groups are used to place packages that perform similar functions in similar locations. For example, the folder Editors contains text editors such as ed, vim and GXedit. From the tree view on the left, you might find another folder beneath Editors called Emacs, which would contain both emacs and emacs-X11. The tree view is also arranged in an expandable and collapsible manner, which helps you to easily navigate through the packages. A folder which appears with a + next to it indicates that there are subfolders within that category. To view the packages and subgroups within a group, click once on a folder or a + with your left mouse button. The display window will then show you the contents of that folder. By default, you will be presented with icons to represent the packages. You can change that view to a list view by selecting **View as list** from the **Interface** tab you'll find under **Operations -> Preferences**. In this manner, you can move about the tree view, opening and expanding folders containing applications, games, tools and more. The contents of each folder will be displayed at the right.

Selecting Packages

To select a single package, click on it with the left mouse button. You'll notice that highlighting will appear around the package's title (as shown in Figure 10-2) which shows that it's currently selected. To unselect it, either click on an empty space in the display panel with the left mouse button, or click on the Unselect button on the toolbar. When you unselect a package, the highlighting will disappear.

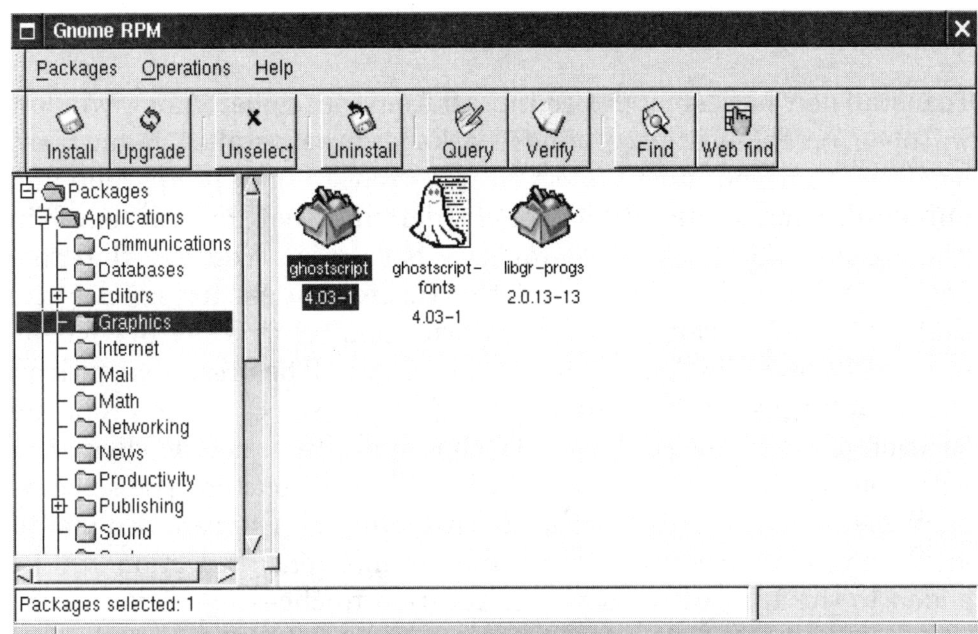

Figure 10-2: Selecting Packages in GnoRPM

You can select and unselect more than one package at a time, in more than one folder in the tree panel. To select more than one package incrementally, left-click with your mouse button, while holding down the Control key; you'll see highlighting around each additional selection.

To select more than one package "globally," that is, make larger selections within a folder, left-click one package, then, while holding down the Shift key, left-click on the final package you wish to select. By doing so, you'll notice that individual packages between your starting and ending selections will also be highlighted for selection. Using this option makes selecting groups of packages much quicker than selecting each package individually.

The status bar at the bottom of GnoRPM will display the total number of packages you have selected.

Installing New Packages

To install new packages, choose **Install** from the toolbar. A new window will open, revealing a space for new packages to be installed. Remember, however, that you must be logged in as root to install, upgrade and uninstall. Choose the **Add** button. By default, GnoRPM will search in `/mnt/cdrom/RedHat/RPMS` for new packages. (You can find this option in the **Interface** tab of the **Preferences** dialog. See the Configuration section for more information on this feature.) If no packages are available in the default path, you'll be presented with an **Add Packages** window from which you can select the appropriate location of your new package. To choose an item, double-click on it with your left mouse button, or click on the **Add** button. The selected package(s) will be added to the **Install** window. You can also install more than one package in the same manner; each selection will be added to the **Install** window. In addition to choosing to install the packages from within the **Install** window, you can install after performing a query on the selected package. Click on **Query**, which will open the **Package Info** window. Here, you can find a variety of details about the file(s) you've selected to install. Information will include the origination of the package, the date it was built, its size and more. Within this **Package Info** window, you have the option of installing or upgrading packages: If the package has not been installed on your system, you'll find an **Install** button at the bottom of the window. If the package already exists on your system and you're querying a newer release, the **Package Info** window provides an **Upgrade** button, which will perform an upgrade to newer releases. You can also "drag and drop" packages from GNOME Midnight Commander File Manager and place them into the **Install** window. To accomplish this, open the file manager (for example, by going to the GNOME Panel, clicking on the GNOME footprint and opening the **File Manager** menu). Locate the directory in which your packages can be found, click on the directory in the tree menu on the left. In the display window to the right, left-click on the package name and, when it's highlighted, "drag" the file by keeping your finger pressed on the mouse button, releasing the pressure (and the package) once you're over the **Install** window. You'll see a progress indicator when your package is being installed.

Configuration

GnoRPM offers a wide selection of choices for installing and uninstalling packages, documentation and other features. You can customize GnoRPM through the **Preferences** dialog, which you can access from **Operations -> Preferences** on the menu. To make selections in the **Preferences** dialog, select the check boxes next to the options. Under the **Behavior** tab, you'll find a number of options for configuring the way GnoRPM installs, uninstalls and upgrades packages. The Behavior tab is split into five sections: Install, Upgrade, Other, Database and Architecture. Note that by default these boxes are not checked. Under **Install Options**, you have the following choices:

- **No dependency checks** - When selected, this will install or upgrade a package without checking for other types of files on which the program may be dependent in order to work. However, unless you know what you're doing we strongly suggest you not use this option as some packages may depend on other packages for files, libraries or programs to function correctly.
- **No reordering** - This option is useful if RPM is unable to change the installation order of some packages to satisfy dependencies.
- **Don't run scripts** - Pre- and post-install scripts are sequences of commands that are sometimes included in packages to assist with installation. This check box is similar to the —noscripts option when installing from the shell prompt.

Under **Upgrade Options**, you can select the following:

- **Allow replacement of packages** - Replaces a package with a new copy of itself. Similar to the —replacepkgs option from the shell prompt. This option can be useful if an already-installed package has become damaged or may require other repair to function correctly.
- **Allow replacement of files** - Allows the replacement of files which are owned by another package. The shell prompt equivalent for this RPM option is —

replacefiles. This option can sometimes be useful when there are two packages with the same file name but different contents.

- **Allow upgrade to old version** - Like the shell prompt RPM option equivalent —oldpackage, this option allows you to "upgrade" to an earlier package. It can sometimes be useful if the latest version of a package doesn't function correctly for your system.

- **Keep packages made obsolete** - Prevents packages listed in an Obsoletes header from being removed.

In **Other Options**, you can select:

- **Don't install documentation** - Like —excludedocs, this option can save on disk space by excluding documentation such as man pages or other information related to the package.

- **Install all files** - Installs all files in the package.

The choices available in **Database Options** and **Architecture Options** allow you to decide, among other things, whether you want to perform a "test" installation (which will check for file conflicts without actually performing an install), or whether you want to exclude packages for other operating systems or system architectures. In the **Interface** tab, you'll find a choice of displays for your packages: either as icons, which will be graphically-based, or as a list, which is not graphical but can provide more information about the packages. Beneath these choices, you can specify the path through which GnoRPM can find new RPMs on your system. When you're using your Red Hat Linux CD-ROM, this will probably be

```
/mnt/cdrom/RedHat/RPMS
```

which is set as the default path for GnoRPM. If you download new RPMs from the Internet or want to install RPMs via a NFS mounted CD-ROM this path will be different for you.

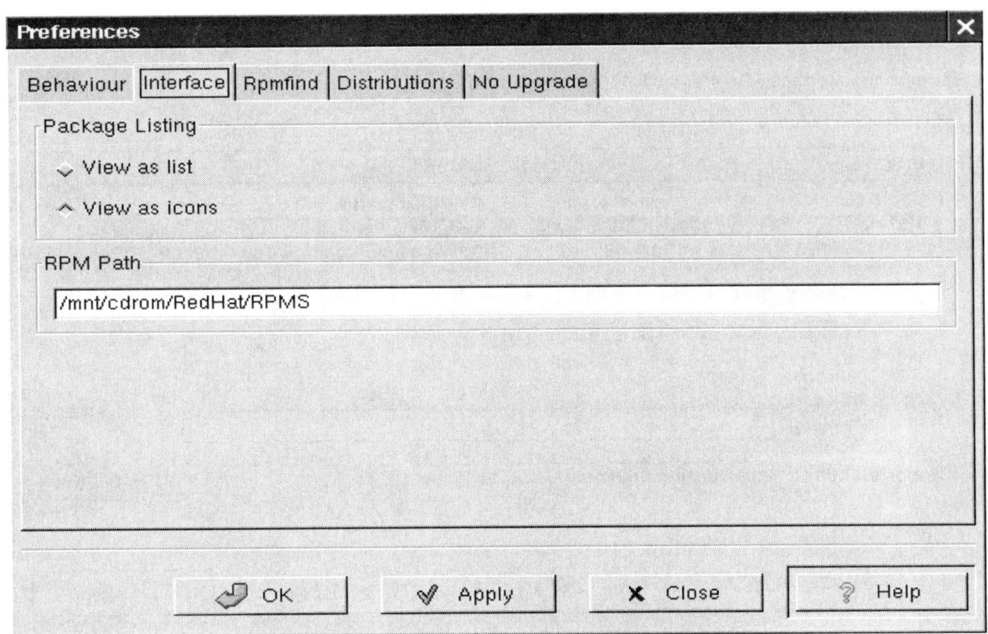

Figure 10-3: Interface Window

To change this path, type the full path to the RPMs you'd like to work with. Choosing the **Apply** or **OK** buttons will save this path, making it the default for future sessions. After changing this path and closing the dialog box, you can use the **Install** button to view the packages available in the new location. Optionally, if the path for your RPMs doesn't match the default path in your preferences, you'll be presented with a browser window, which will allow you to select the correct path for your new RPMs. In addition to using the file dialog to add files to your install list, you can "drag" files from the GNOME Midnight Commander File Manager to add them to the list. In the **Rpmfind** tab, you'll find settings and options which correspond to the **Web find** feature. The **Metadata server** sets the server to be used for searches. The **Download dir:** entry allows you to specify where you want the files to be stored. The **Local Hostname:** entry allows you to set your hostname (so that **Rpmfind** can guess the closest mirror). Additionally, you can specify the vendor, distribution name and whether to find sources and/or the latest files.

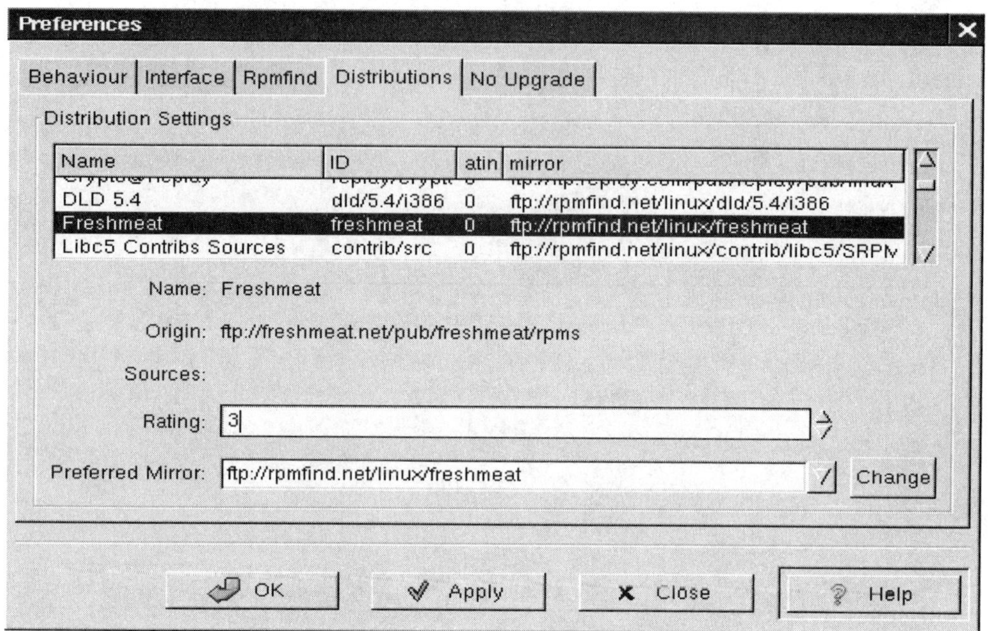

Figure 10-4: Distribution Settings in Preferences

In the **Distribution Settings** tab, you can set the options for choosing the most appropriate package out of the selections **Rpmfind** returns, as well as which mirror you would like to use. The higher the rating you indicate for your selection (as shown in Figure 10-4) the higher the priority it will receive; a lower rating, such as `-1`, will specify that packages not be recommended.

Package Manipulation

Querying Packages

The easiest way to query packages is to use the **Query** option from the menu at the top. If you want to query more than one package, make all your selections then press the **Query** button on the menu. You'll be presented with a window like the one shown in Figure 10-5. The more packages you've queried, the more "tabs" you'll find within the **Query** box, each tab representing a **Query** window for a package.

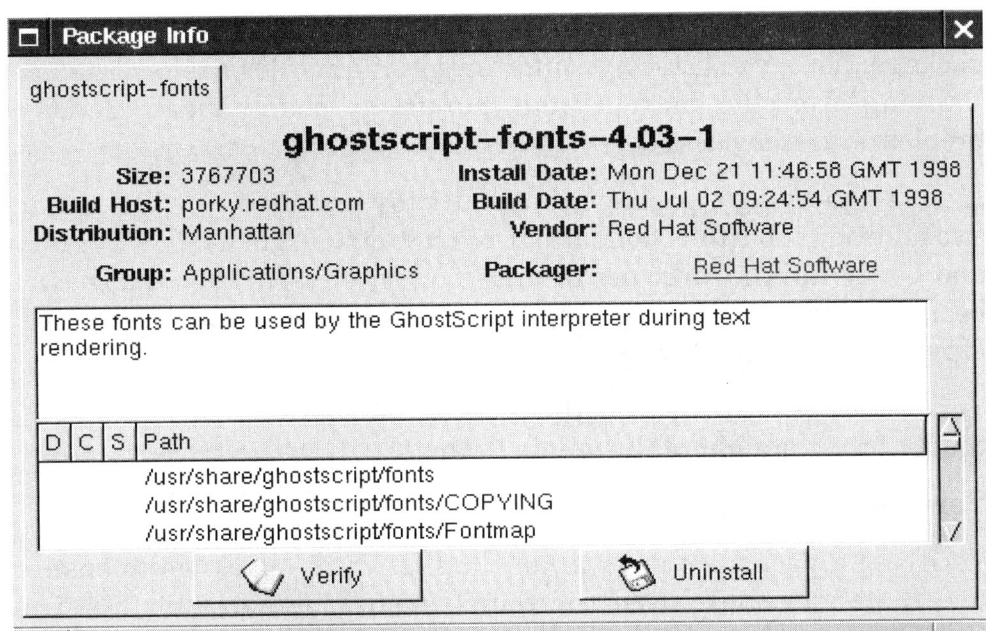

Figure 10-5: Query Window

The name of the package is centered at the top of the box. Below, the box is divided into two columns of listed information; below this information, you'll see a display area showing package files.

In the left column in the information list, you'll find the size of the file, the machine on which the file is found, the name of the package distribution and the group to which its function belongs.

In the right column, you'll find the date of the package's installation on your machine, the date the package was built, the name of the vendor and the name of the group who packaged the software. If the package has not been installed on your machine, that space will simply read, "not installed."

Below the description is a list of the files contained in the package. If a D appears in its related column to the left of the path, that file is a documentation file and would be a good thing to read for help on using the application. If a C appears in its respective column, the file is a configuration file. Under the S column, you can view the "state" of the package; here, you'll receive information if any files are reported as "missing" from the package (and therefore probably mean there's a problem with the package).

If you're querying a package that's already installed, you'll also find two additional buttons beneath at the bottom of this window: **Verify** and **Uninstall**. If you're performing a query on a package that hasn't been installed yet, the buttons on the bottom will be labeled **Install**, **Upgrade** and **Check Sig**.

To close the query window without performing any action, left-click on the **X** at the top right of the window bar.

Verifying Packages

Verifying a package checks all of the files in the package to ensure they match the ones present on your system. The checksum, file size, permissions, and owner attributes are all checked against the database. This check can be used when you suspect that one of the program's files has become corrupted for some reason. Choosing the packages to verify is like choosing the packages to query. Select the packages in the display window and use the Verify button on the toolbar or from Packages -> Verify on the menu. A window opens like the one in Figure 10-6.

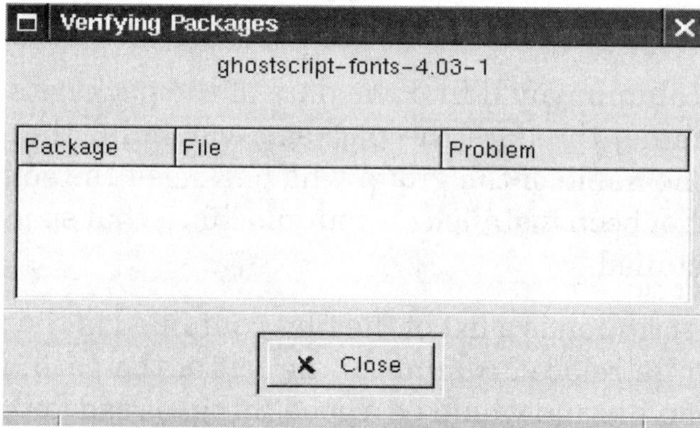

Figure 10-6: Verify Window

As the package is being checked, you'll see the progress in the **Verify** window. If there are any problems discovered during the verify process, they'll be described in the main display area.

Uninstalling Packages

Uninstalling a package removes the application and associated files from your machine. When a package is uninstalled, any files it uses that are not needed by other packages on your system are also removed. Changed configuration files are copied to `<filename>.rpmsave` so you can reuse them later. **Please Note:** Remember that you must be root to uninstall packages. If uninstalling a package would break "dependencies" (which could hobble other applications that require one or more of the removed files in the package), a dialog will pop up, asking you to confirm the deletion. This will occur if you haven't selected the "No dependency checks" box from the **Preferences** menu (as shown in Figure 10-7).

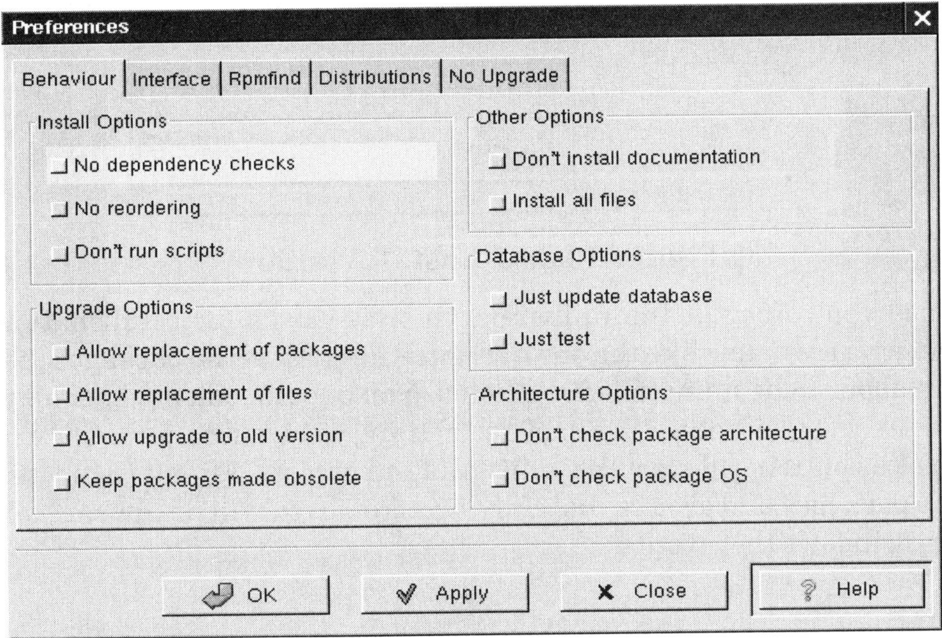

Figure 10-7: The Behavior Tab in Preferences

There are a variety of methods through which you can remove a selected package: from the menu, under **Packages**; from the toolbar and from the **Query** function. If you decide to remove more than one package at a time, you can choose either an incremental or global selection in the same way as you would when installing, querying or verifying. The total of your selections will be reflected in the status bar on the bottom of the main window. Because you can remove more than one package at a time, use caution to select only those which you wish to remove.

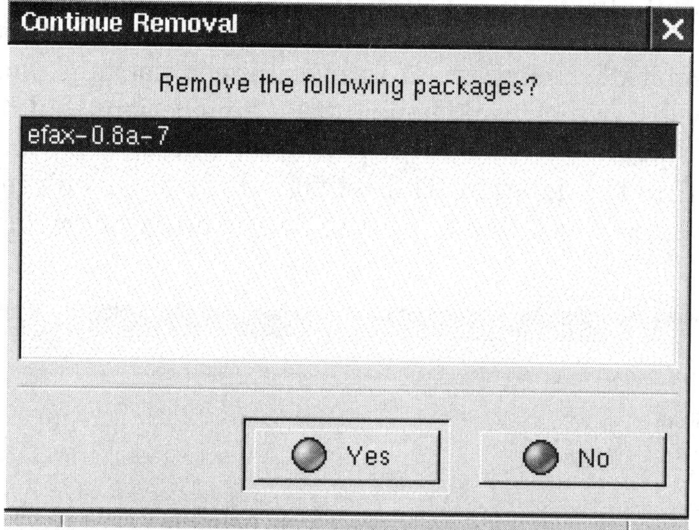

Figure 10-8: Uninstall Window

Once you've begun the uninstall, GnoRPM asks for confirmation, showing a window like the one in Figure 10-8. All of the packages that are about to be uninstalled are listed. You should look at them all to ensure you're not about to remove something you want to keep. Clicking the **Yes** button will start the uninstallation process. After it completes, the packages and groups that have been removed will disappear from any windows they were in.

Upgrading Packages

When a new version of a package has been released, it is easy to install it on your system. Select the packages from the window of available packages in the same way you select packages for installation. Both the **Upgrade** button on the toolbar and, from the menu, under **Operations -> Upgrade** will begin the process. You simply Add packages in the same manner as you would a new package installation. During the upgrade, you'll see a progress indicator like the one for installing packages. When it's finished, any old versions of the packages will be removed, unless you specify otherwise (refer to **Package Manipulation** for more information).

It is much better to use the upgrade option than to uninstall the old versions of a package and then install the new one. Using upgrade ensures that any changes you made to package configuration files are preserved properly, while uninstalling and then reinstalling a new package could cause those changes to be lost.

If you run out of disk space during an installation, the install will fail. However, the package which was being installed when the error occurred may leave some files around. To clean this up, reinstall the package after you've made more disk space available.

11 System Administration

This chapter is an overview of the Red Hat Linux system. It will illustrate things that you may not know about the system and things that are somewhat different from other UNIX systems.

Filesystem Structure

Red Hat Software is committed to the Linux File System Standard, a collaborative document that defines the names and locations of many files and directories. We will continue to track the standard to keep Red Hat compliant. While compliance with the standard means many things, the two most important are compatibility with other compliant systems, and the ability to mount the `/usr` partition read-only. The `/usr` partition contains common executables and is not meant to be changed by users. Because of this, the `/usr` partition can be mounted from the CD-ROM or from another machine via read-only NFS. The current Linux Filesystem Standard (FSSTND) document is the authoritative reference to any FSSTND compliant filesystem, but the standard leaves many areas undefined or extensible. In this section we provide an overview of the standard and a description of the parts of the filesystem not covered by the standard. The complete standard can be viewed at:

http://www.pathname.com/fhs/

Overview of the FSSTND

The directories and files noted here are a small subset of those specified by the FSSTND document. Check the latest FSSTND document for the most up-to-date and complete information.

The `/dev` Directory

The `/dev` directory contains file system entries that represent devices that are attached to the system. These files are essential for the system to function properly.

The /etc Directory

The /etc directory is reserved for configuration files that are local to your machine. No binaries are to be put in /etc. Binaries that were in the past put in /etc should now go into /sbin or possibly /bin. The X11 and skel directories should be subdirectories of /etc:

```
/etc |- X11 +- skel
```

The X11 directory is for X11 configuration files such as XF86Config. The skel directory is for "skeleton" user files, which are files used to populate a home directory when a user is first created.

The /lib Directory

The /lib directory should contain only those libraries that are needed to execute the binaries in /bin and /sbin.

The /proc Directory

The /proc directory contains special files that either extract information or send information to the kernel. It is an easy method of accessing information about the operating system using the cat command.

The /sbin Directory

The /sbin directory is for executables used only by the root user, and only those executables needed to boot and mount /usr and perform system recovery operations. The FSSTND says:

"/sbin typically contains files essential for booting the system in addition to the binaries in /bin. Anything executed after /usr is known to be mounted (when there are no problems) should be placed in /usr/sbin. Local-only system administration binaries should be placed into /usr/local/sbin."

At a minimum, the following programs should be in /sbin:

```
clock, getty, init, update, mkswap, swapon, swapoff, halt,
reboot, shutdown, fdisk, fsck.*, mkfs.*, lilo, arp, ifconfig,
route
```

The /usr Directory

The /usr directory is for files that are shareable across a whole site. The /usr directory usually has its own partition, and it should be mountable read only. The following directories should be subdirectories of /usr:

```
/usr
   |- X11R6
   |- bin
   |- dict
   |- doc
   |- etc
   |- games
   |- include
   |- info
   |- lib
   |- local
   |- man
   |- sbin
   |- share
   +- src
```

The X11R6 directory is for the X Window System (XFree86 on Red Hat Linux), bin is for executables, doc is for random non-man-page documentation, etc is for site-wide configuration files, include is for C header files, info is for GNU info files, lib is for libraries, man is for man pages, sbin is for system administration binaries (those that do not belong in `/sbin`), and src is for source code.

The `/usr/local` Directory

The FSSTND says:

> "The /usr/local hierarchy is for use by the system administrator when installing software locally. It needs to be safe from being overwritten when the system software is updated. It may be used for programs and data that are shareable amongst a group of machines, but not found in /usr."

The `/usr/local` directory is similar in structure to the `/usr` directory. It has the following subdirectories, which are similar in purpose to those in the `/usr` directory:

```
/usr/local
        |- bin
        |- doc
        |- etc
        |- games
        |- include
```

```
        |- info
        |- lib
        |- man
        |- sbin
        +- src
```

The /var Directory

Since the FSSTND requires that you be able to mount /usr read-only, any programs that write log files or need spool or lock directories probably should write them to the /var directory. The FSSTND states /var is for "... variable data files. This includes spool directories and files, administrative and logging data, and transient and temporary files." The following directories should be subdirectories of /var:

```
/var
   |- log
   |- catman
   |- lib
   |- local
   |- named
   |- nis
   |- preserve
   |- run
   |- lock
   |- tmp
   +- spool
         |- at
         |- cron
         |- lpd
         |- mail
         |- mqueue
         |- rwho
         |- smail
         |- uucp
         +- news
```

System log files such as wtmp and lastlog go in /var/log. The /var/lib directory also contains the RPM system databases. Formatted man pages go in /var/catman, and lock files go in /var/lock. The /var/spool directory has subdirectories for various systems that need to store data files.

/usr/local in Red Hat Linux

In Red Hat Linux, the intended use for `/usr/local` is slightly different from that specified by the FSSTND. The FSSTND says that /usr/local should be where you store software that is to remain safe from system software upgrades. Since system upgrades from Red Hat Software are done safely with the RPM system and GnoRPM, you don't need to protect files by putting them in `/usr/local`. Instead, we recommend you use `/usr/local` for software that is local to your machine. For instance, let's say you have mounted /usr via read-only NFS from beavis. If there is a package or program you would like to install, but you are not allowed to write to beavis, you should install it under `/usr/local`. Later perhaps, if you've managed to convince the system administrator of beavis to install the program on `/usr`, you can uninstall it from `/usr/local`.

Special Red Hat File Locations

In addition to the files pertaining to the RPM system that reside in `/var/lib/rpm` (see Chapter 9), there are two other special locations that are reserved for Red Hat Linux configuration and operation.

The control-panel and related tools put lots of stuff in `/usr/lib/rhs`. There is probably nothing here that you would want to edit. It is mostly small scripts, bitmaps and text files.

The other location, `/etc/sysconfig`, stores configuration information. The major users of the files in this directory are the scripts that run at boot time. It is possible to edit these by hand, but it would be better to use the proper control-panel tool.

Users, Groups and User-Private Groups

Managing users and groups has traditionally been tedious. Red Hat Linux has a few tools and conventions that make users and groups easier to manage, and more useful. The easiest way to manage users and groups is through Linuxconf (see Chapter 8). However, you can also use adduser to create a new user from the command line.

Standard Users

Table 133 lists the standard users set up by the installation process (this is essentially the `/etc/passwd` file). The group id (GID) in this table is the primary group for the user. See **User Private Groups** for details on how groups are used.

User	UID	GID	Home Directory	Shell
root	0	0	/root	/bin/bash
bin	1	1	/bin	
daemon	2	2	/sbin	
adm	3	4	/var/adm	
lp	4	7	/var/spool/lpd	
sync	5	0	/sbin	/bin/sync
shutdown	6	0	/sbin	/sbin/shutdown
halt	7	0	/sbin	/sbin/halt
mail	8	12	/var/spool/mail	
news	9	13	/var/spool/news	
uucp	10	14	/var/spool/uucp	
operator	11	0	/root	
games	12	100	/usr/games	
gopher	13	30	/usr/lib/gopher-data	
ftp	14	50	/home/ftp	
nobody	99	99	/	

Figure 11-1: Standard Users

Standard Groups

Table 134 lists the standard groups as set up by the installation process (this is essentially the `/etc/group` file).

Group	GID	Members
root	0	root
bin	1	root,bin,daemon
daemon	2	root,bin,daemon
sys	3	root,bin,adm
adm	4	root,adm,daemon
tty	5	
disk	6	root
lp	7	daemon,lp
mem	8	
kmem	9	
wheel	10	root
mail	12	mail
news	13	news
uucp	14	uucp
man	15	
games	20	
gopher	30	
dip	40	
ftp	50	
nobody	99	
users	100	
floppy	19	

Figure 11-2: Standard Groups

User Private Groups

Red Hat Linux uses a user private group (UPG) scheme, which makes UNIX groups much easier to use. The UPG scheme does not add or change anything in the standard UNIX way of handling groups. It simply offers a new convention for handling groups. Whenever you create a new user, by default, he or she has a unique group. The scheme works as follows:

User Private Group
: Each user has its own primary group, of which only it is a member.

umask = 002
: The traditional UNIX umask is 022, which prevents other users and other members of a user's primary group from modifying a user's files. Since every user has their own private group in the UPG scheme, this "group protection" is not needed. A umask of 002 will prevent users from modifying other users' private files. The umask is set in `/etc/profile`.

setgid bit on Directories
: If you set the setgid bit on a directory (with chmod g+s directory), files created in that directory will have their group set to the directory's group.

Most computing sites like to create a group for each major project and assign people to the groups they need to be in. Managing files traditionally has been difficult, though, because when someone creates a file it is owned by the primary group he or she belongs to. When a single person works on multiple projects, it becomes hard to make the files owned by the group that is associated with that project. In the UPG scheme, groups are automatically assigned to files on a project-by-project basis, which makes managing group projects very simple. Let's say you have a big project called devel, with many people editing the devel files in a devel directory. Make a group called devel, chgrp the devel directory to devel, and add the all the devel users to the devel group. Now, all devel users will be able to edit the devel files and create new files in the devel directory, and these files will always retain their devel group. Thus, they will always be editable by other devel users. If you have multiple projects like devel, and users who are working on multiple projects, these users will never have to change their umask or group when they move from project to project. The setgid bit on each project's main directory "selects" the proper group. Since each user's HOME directory is owned by the user and their private group, it is safe to set the setgid bit on the HOME directory. However, by default, files are created with the primary group of the user, so the setgid bit would be redundant.

User Private Group Rationale

Although UPG is not new to Red Hat Linux 6.0, many people still have questions about it, such as why UPG is necessary. The following is the rationale for the scheme.

- You'd like to have a group of people work on a set of files in say, the

  ```
  /usr/lib/emacs/site-lisp
  ```

  directory. You trust a few people to mess around in there, but certainly not everyone.

- So you enter:

  ```
  chown -R root.emacs /usr/lib/emacs/site-lisp
  ```

  and you add the proper users to the group.

- To allow the users to actually create files in the directory you enter:

  ```
  chmod 775 /usr/lib/emacs/site-lisp
  ```

- But when a user creates a new file it is assigned the group of the user's default group (usually users). To prevent this you enter

  ```
  chmod 2775 /usr/lib/emacs/site-lisp
  ```

  which causes everything in the directory to be created with the "emacs" group.

- But the new file needs to be mode 664 for another user in the emacs group to be able to edit it. To do this you make the default umask 002.

- Well, this all works fine, except that if your default group is "users," every file you create in your home directory will be writable by everybody in "users" (usually everyone).

- To fix this, you make each user have a "private group" as their default group.

At this point, by making the default umask 002 and giving everyone a private default group, you can easily set up groups that users can take advantage of without doing any magic. Just create the group, add the users, and do the above chown and chmod on the group's directories.

Configuring Console Access

When normal (non-root) users log in to a computer locally, they are given two types of special permission; they can run certain programs that they would not otherwise be able to run, and they can access certain files (normally special device files used to access diskettes, CD-ROMS, etc.) that they would not otherwise be able to access. Since there are multiple consoles on a single computer, and multiple users can be logged into the computer locally at the same time, one of the users has to "win" the fight to access the files. The first user to log in at the console owns those files. Once the first user logs out, the next user who logs in will own the files. In contrast, every user who logs in on the console will be allowed to run programs normally restricted to the root user. By default, those programs will ask for the user's password. This will be done graphically if X is running which makes it possible to make these actions menu items from within a graphical user interface. As shipped, the console-accessible programs are `shutdown`, `halt`, and `reboot`.

Disabling Console Program Access

In environments where the console is otherwise secured (BIOS and LILO passwords are set, control-alt-delete is disabled, the power and reset switches are disabled, etc.), it may not be desirable to allow arbitrary users at the console to run shutdown, halt, and reboot. In order to disable all access by console users to console programs, you should run the command:

```
rm -f /etc/security/console.apps/*
```

Disabling All Console Access

In order to disable all console access, including program and file access, in the /etc/pam.d/ directory, comment out all lines that refer to pam_console.so. The following script will do the trick:

```
cd /etc/pam.d
for i in * ; do
  sed '/[#].*pamconsole.so/s//#/' < i > foo mv foo i
done
```

Defining the Console

The /etc/security/console.perms file defines the console group. The syntax of that file is very flexible, so it's possible to edit that file so that these instructions no longer apply. However, the default file has a line that looks like this:

```
<console>=tty[0-9][0-9]* :[0-9].[0-9] :[0-9]
```

When users log in, they are attached to some sort of named terminal, either an X server with a name like :0 or mymachine.example.com:1.0; or a device like /dev/tty0 or /dev/pts/2. The default is to define that local virtual consoles and local X servers are considered local, but if you want to consider the serial terminal next to you on port /dev/ttyS1 to also be local, you can change that line to read:

```
<console>=tty[0-9][0-9]* :[0-9].[0-9] :[0-9] /dev/ttyS1
```

Making Files Console-Accessible

In /etc/security/console.perms, there is a section with lines like:

```
<cdrom>=/dev/cdrom
```

You can also add your own lines:

```
<scanner>=/dev/sga
```

(of course, make sure that /dev/sga is really your scanner and not, say, your hard drive). That's the first part. The second part is to define what is done with those files. Look in the last section of /etc/security/console.perms for lines similar to

```
<console> 0600 <cdrom> 0600 root
```

and add a line like

```
<console> 0600 <scanner> 0600 root
```

Then when you log in at the console, you will be given ownership of the /dev/sga device and the permissions will be 0600 (readable and writable by you only). When you log out, the device will be owned by root and still have 0600 (now: readable and writable by root only) permissions.

Enabling Console Access for Other Applications

If you wish to make other applications besides shutdown, reboot, and halt accessible to console users, you will have to do just a little bit more work. First of all, console access only works for applications which reside in /sbin or /usr/sbin, so the application that you wish to run must be there. Create a link from the name of your application to the /usr/bin/consolehelper application:

```
cd /usr/bin
ln -s consolehelper foo
```

Create the file /etc/security/console.apps/foo touch /etc/security/console.apps/foo Create a PAM configuration file for the foo service in /etc/pam.d/. We suggest that you start with a copy of the shutdown service, then change it if you want to change the behavior:

```
cp /etc/pam.d/shutdown /etc/pam.d/foo
```

Now, when you run /usr/bin/foo, it will call consolehelper, which with the help of /usr/sbin/userhelper will authenticate the user (asking for the users password if /etc/pam.d/foo is a copy of /etc/pam.d/shutdown; otherwise, it will do precisely what is specified in /etc/pam.d/foo) and then run /usr/sbin/foo with root permissions.

The floppy Group

If, for whatever reason, console access is not appropriate for you, and you need to give non-root users access to your system's diskette drive, this can be done using the floppy group. Simply add the user(s) to the floppy group using the tool of your choice. Here's an example showing how gpasswd can be used to add user fred to the floppy group:

```
[root@bigdog root]# gpasswd -a fred floppy
Adding user fred to group floppy
[root@bigdog root]#
```

User fred will now be able to access the system's diskette drive (using the mtools utility programs, for instance).

User Authentication with PAM

Programs which give users access to privileges of any sort need to be able to authenticate the users. When you log into a system, you provide your name and password, and the login process uses those to authenticate the login — to verify that you are who you say you are. Other forms of authentication than passwords are possible, and it is possible for the passwords to be stored in different ways. PAM, which stands for "Pluggable Authentication Modules," is a way of allowing the system administrator to set authentication policy without having to recompile programs which do authentication. With PAM, you control how the modules are plugged into the programs by editing a configuration file. Most Red Hat Linux users will never need to touch this configuration file. When you use RPM to install programs that need to do authentication, they automatically make the changes that are needed to do normal password authentication. However, you may want to customize your configuration, in which case you need to understand the configuration file.

PAM Modules

There are four types of modules defined by the PAM standard. auth modules provide the actual authentication, perhaps asking for and checking a password, and set "credentials" such as group membership or kerberos "tickets." account modules check to make sure that the authentication is allowed (the account has not expired, the user is allowed to log in at this time of day, etc.). password modules are used to set passwords. session modules are used once a user has been authenticated to make it possible for them to use their account, perhaps mounting the user's home directory or making their mailbox available. These modules may be stacked, so that multiple modules are used. For instance, rlogin normally makes use of at least two authentication methods: if "rhosts" authentication succeeds, it is sufficient to allow the connection; if it fails, then standard password authentication is done. New modules can be added at any time, and PAM-aware applications can then be made to use them. For instance, if you have a one-time-password calculator system, and you can write a module to support it (documentation on writing modules is included with the system), PAM-aware programs can use the new module and work with the new one-time-password calculators without being recompiled or otherwise modified in any way.

Services

Each program using PAM defines its own "service" name. The login program defines the service type login, ftpd defines the service type ftp, etc. In general, the service type is the name of the program used to access the service, not (if there is a difference) the program used to provide the service.

The Configuration Files

The directory /etc/pam.d is used to configure all PAM applications. (This used to be /etc/pam.conf in earlier PAM versions; while the pam.conf file is still read if no /etc/pam.d/ entry is found, its use is deprecated.) Each application (really, each service) has its own file. A file looks like this:

```
#
auth required /lib/security/pamsecuretty.so
auth required /lib/security/pampwdb.so shadow
nullok
auth required /lib/security/pamnologin.so
account required /lib/security/pampwdb.so
password required /lib/security/pamcracklib.so
password required /lib/security/pampwdb.so shadow
¬ nullok useauthtok
session required /lib/security/pampwdb.so
```

The first line is a comment. Any line that starts with a # character is a comment. Lines two through four stack up three modules to use for login authorization. Line two makes sure that if the user is trying to log in as root, the tty on which they are logging in is listed in the `/etc/`

securetty file if that file exists. Line three causes the user to be asked for a password and the password checked. Line four checks to see if the file /etc/nologin exists, and if it does, displays the contents of the file, and if the user is not root, does not let him or her log in. Note that all three modules are checked, *even if the first module fails*. This is a security decision—it is designed to not let the user know why their authentication was disallowed, because knowing why it was disallowed might allow them to break the authentication more easily. You can change this behavior by changing required to requisite; if any requisite module returns failure, PAM fails immediately without calling any other modules. The fifth line causes any necessary accounting to be done. For example, if shadow passwords have been enabled, the pam_pwdb.so module will check to see if the account has expired, or if the user has not changed his or her password and the grace period for changing the password has expired. The sixth line subjects a newly changed password to a series of tests to ensure that it cannot, for example, be easily determined by a dictionary-based password cracking program. The seventh line (which we've had to wrap) specifies that if the login program changes the user's password, it should use the pam_pwdb.so module to do so. (It will do so only if an auth module has determined that the password needs to be changed—ie, if a shadow password has expired.) The eighth and final line specifies that the pam_pwdb.so module should be used to manage the session. Currently, that module doesn't do anything; it could be replaced (or supplemented by stacking) by any necessary module. Note that the order of the lines within each file matters. While it doesn't really matter much in which order required modules are called, there are other *control flags* available. While optional is rarely used, and never used by default on a Red Hat Linux system, sufficient and requisite cause order to become important. Let's look at the auth configuration for rlogin:

```
auth required /lib/security/pamsecuretty.so
auth sufficient /lib/security/pamrhostsauth.so
auth required /lib/security/pampwdb.so shadow nullok
auth required /lib/security/pamnologin.so
```

That looks *almost* like the `login` entry, but there's an extra line specifying an extra module, and the modules are specified in a different order. First, `pam_securetty.so` keeps root logins from happening on insecure terminals. This effectively disallows all root rlogin attempts. If you wish to allow them (in which case we recommend that you either not be Internet-connected or be behind a good firewall), you can simply remove that line. Second, `pam_nologin.so` checks `/etc/nologin`, as specified above. Third, if `pam_rhosts_auth.so` authenticates the user, PAM immediately returns success to rlogin without any password checking being done. If pam_rhosts_auth.so fails to authenticate the user, that failed authentication is ignored. Finally (if `pam_rhosts_auth.so` has failed to authenticate the user), the `pam_pwdb.so` module performs normal password authentication. Note that if you do not want to prompt for a password if the securetty check fails, you can change the `pam_securetty.so` module from `required` to `requisite`.

Shadow Passwords

The `pam_pwdb.so` module will automatically detect that you are using shadow passwords and make all necessary adjustments. Please refer to **Shadow Utilities** for more information.

Rexec and PAM

For security reasons, rexec is not enabled in Red Hat Linux 6.0. Should you wish to enable it, you will need to comment out one line in the file /etc/pam.d/rexec. Here is a sample of the file (note that your file may differ slightly):

```
#
auth required /lib/security/pampwdb.so shadow
nullok
auth required /lib/security/pamnologin.so
account required /lib/security/pampwdb.so
```

To enable rexec, the line referring to the pam_nologin.so module must be commented out:

```
#
auth required /lib/security/pampwdb.so shadow
nullok
#auth required /lib/security/pamnologin.so
account required /lib/security/pampwdb.so
```

After this file is modified, rexec will be enabled.

Please Note: If your /etc/pam.d/rexec file contains a line referring to the pam_securetty.so module, you will not be able to rexec as root. To do so, you must also comment out the line referring to the pam_securetty.so module.

More Information

This is just an introduction to PAM. More information is included in the `/usr/doc/pam*` directory, including a *System Administrators' Guide*, a *Module Writers' Manual*, an *Application Developers' Manual*, and the PAM standard, DCE-RFC 86.0. In addition, documentation is available from the Red Hat website, at *http://www.redhat.com/linux-info/pam/*.

Shadow Utilities

Support for shadow passwords has been enhanced significantly for Red Hat Linux 6.0. Shadow passwords are a method of improving system security by moving the encrypted passwords (normally found in /etc/passwd) to another file with more restrictive file access permissions. During the installation, you were given the option of setting up shadow password protection on your system. The shadow-utils package contains a number of utilities that support:

- Conversion from normal to shadowed passwords and back (pwconv, pwunconv).
- Verification of the password, group, and associated shadow files (pwck, grpck).
- Industry-standard methods of adding, deleting and modifying user accounts (useradd, usermod, and userdel).

- Industry-standard methods of adding, deleting, and modifying user groups (groupadd, groupmod, and groupdel).
- Industry-standard method of administering the /etc/group file (gpasswd).

Please Note: There are a few additional points of interest concerning these utilities:

- The utilities will work properly whether shadowing is enabled or not.
- The utilities have been slightly modified to support Red Hat Software's user private group scheme. For a description of the modifications, please see the useradd man page. For more information on user private groups, please turn to **User Private Groups**.
- The adduser script has been replaced with a symlink to `/usr/sbin/useradd`.

Building a Custom Kernel

With the introduction of modularization in the Linux 2.2.x kernel there have been some significant changes in building customized kernels. In the past you were required to compile support into your kernel if you wanted to access a particular hardware or filesystem component. For some hardware configurations the size of the kernel could quickly reach a critical level. To require ready support for items that were only occasionally used was an inefficient use of system resources. With the capabilities of the 2.2.x kernel, if there are certain hardware components or filesystems that are used infrequently, driver modules for them can be loaded on demand. For information on handling kernel modules see Chapter 8, the **Kernel Daemon Configuration** subsection of the **System Configuration with the Control Panel** section.

Many people new to Linux often ask, "why should I build my own kernel?" Given the advances that have been made in the use of kernel modules, the most accurate response to that question is, "unless you know why you need to build your own kernel, you probably don't." So unless you have a specific reason to build a customized kernel (or you're just the curious sort), you may skip ahead to **Sendmail**.

Building a modularized kernel

These instructions provide you with the knowledge needed to take advantage of the power and flexibility available through kernel modularization. If you do not wish to take advantage of modularization, please see **Changing Module Options** for an explanation of the different aspects of building and installing a monolithic kernel. It's assumed that you've already installed the kernel-headers and kernel-source packages and that you issue all commands from the `/usr/src/linux` directory.

It is important to begin a kernel build with the source tree in a known condition. Therefore, it is recommended that you begin with the command `make mrproper`. This will remove any configuration files along with the remains of any previous builds that may be scattered around the source tree. Now you must create a configuration file that will determine which components to include in your new kernel. Depending upon your hardware and personal preferences there are three methods available to configure the kernel.

- make config — An interactive text program. Components are presented and you answer with Y (yes), N (no), or M (module).
- make menuconfig — A graphic, menu driven program. Components are presented in a menu of categories, you select the desired components in the same manner used in the Red Hat Linux installation program. Toggle the tag corresponding to the item you want included; **Y** (yes), **N** (no), or **M** (module).
- make xconfig — An X Windows program. Components are listed in different levels of menus, components are selected using a mouse. Again, select **Y** (yes), **N** (no), or **M** (module).

Please Note: In order to use kerneld (see **Kernel Daemon Configuration** for details) and kernel modules you must answer **Yes** to **kerneld support** and **module version (CONFIG_MODVERSIONS)** support in the configuration.

Please Note: If you are building a Linux/Intel kernel on (or for) a machine that uses a "clone" processor (for example, one made by Cyrix or AMD), it is recommended to choose a **Processor type** of **386**.

If you wish to build a kernel with a configuration file (/usr/src/linux/.config) that you have already created with one of the above methods, you can omit the make mrproper and make config commands and use the command make dep followed by make clean to prepare the source tree for the build.

The next step consists of the actual compilation of the source code components into a working program that your machine can use to boot. The method described here is the easiest to recover from in the event of a mishap. If you are interested in other possibilities, details can be found in the Kernel-HOWTO or in the Makefile in `/usr/src/linux` on your Linux system.

- Build the kernel with make boot.
- Build any modules you configured with make modules.
- Move the old set of modules out of the way with:

  ```
  rm -rf /lib/modules/2.0.36-old
  mv /lib/modules/2.0.36 /lib/modules/2.0.36-old
  ```

  Of course, if you have upgraded your kernel, replace 2.0.36 with the version you are using.
- Install the new modules (even if you didn't build any) with make modules_install.

If you have a SCSI adapter and made your SCSI driver modular, build a new initrd image (see **Making an initrd image**; note that there are few practical reasons to make the SCSI driver modular in a custom kernel).

In order to provide a redundant boot source to protect from a possible error in a new kernel you should keep the original kernel available. Adding a kernel to the LILO menu is as simple as renaming the original kernel in /boot, copying the new kernel to `/boot`, adding a few lines in `/etc/lilo.conf` and running `/sbin/lilo`. Here is an example of the default /etc/lilo.conf file shipped with Red Hat Linux:

```
boot=/dev/hda
map=/boot/map
```

```
install=/boot/boot.b
prompt
timeout=100
image=/boot/vmlinuz
    label=linux
    root=/dev/hda1
    read-only
```

Now you must update /etc/lilo.conf. If you built a new initrd image you must tell LILO to use it. In this example of /etc/lilo.conf we have added four lines in the middle of the file to indicate another kernel to boot from. We have renamed /boot/vmlinuz to /boot/vmlinuz.old and changed its label to old. We have also added an initrd line for the new kernel:

```
boot=/dev/hda
map=/boot/map
install=/boot/boot.b
prompt
timeout=100
image=/boot/vmlinuz
    label=linux
    initrd=/boot/initrd
    root=/dev/hda1
    read-only
image=/boot/vmlinuz.old
    label=old
    root=/dev/hda1
    read-only
```

Now when the system boots and you press [Tab] at the LILO boot: prompt two choices will be shown;

```
LILO boot:
linux old
```

To boot the new kernel (linux) simply press [Enter], or wait for LILO to time out. If you want to boot the old kernel (old), type old and press [Enter]. Here is a summary of the steps:

- mv /boot/vmlinuz /boot/vmlinuz.old
- cp /usr/src/linux/arch/i386/boot/zImage /boot/vmlinuz
- edit /etc/lilo.conf
- run /sbin/lilo

You can begin testing your new kernel by rebooting your computer and watching the messages to ensure your hardware is detected properly.

Making an initrd image

An initrd image is needed for loading your SCSI module at boot time. The shell script /sbin/mkinitrd can build a proper initrd image for your machine if the following conditions are met:

- The loopback block device is available.
- The /etc/conf.modules file has a line for your SCSI adapter; for example:

  ```
  alias scsihostadapter BusLogic
  ```

To build the new initrd image, run `/sbin/mkinitrd` with parameters such as this:

```
/sbin/mkinitrd /boot/newinitrd-image 2.0.36
```

where `/boot/newinitrd-image` is the file to use for your new image, and `2.0.36` is the kernel whose modules (from `/lib/modules`) should be used in the initrd image (not necessarily the same as the version number of the currently running kernel).

Building a monolithic kernel

To build a monolithic kernel you follow the same steps as building a modularized kernel with a few exceptions.

- When configuring the kernel only answer **Yes** and **No** to the questions (don't make anything modular).
- Omit the steps:

```
make modules
make modules_install
```

- Edit the file /etc/rc.d/rc.sysinit and comment out the line depmod -a by inserting a "#" at the beginning of the line.

Sendmail

A default `sendmail.cf` file will be installed in `/etc`. The default configuration should work for most SMTP-only sites. It will not work for UUCP sites; you will need to generate a new sendmail.cf if you must use UUCP mail transfers. To generate a new sendmail.cf, you will need to install m4 and the sendmail source package. Read the README file in the sendmail sources for more details on creating sendmail configuration files. Also, O'Reilly & Associates publishes a good sendmail reference entitled *sendmail*, by Bryan Costales. One common sendmail configuration is to have a single machine act as a mail gateway for all the machines on your network. For instance, at Red Hat Software there is the machine mail.redhat.com that does all their mail. On that machine we simply need to add the names of machines for which mail.redhat.com will handle mail to `/etc/sendmail.cw`. Here is an example:

```
# sendmail.cw - include all aliases for your
machine
# here.
torgo.redhat.com
poodle.redhat.com
devel.redhat.com
```

Then on the other machines, `torgo`, `poodle`, and `devel`, we need to edit `/etc/sendmail.cf` to "masquerade" as `mail.redhat.com` when sending mail, and to forward any local mail processing to `redhat.com`.

Find the DH and DM lines in /etc/sendmail.cf and edit them thusly:

```
# who I send unqualified names to
# (null means deliver locally)
DRmail.redhat.com
# who gets all local email
trafficDHmail.redhat.com
# who I masquerade as (null for no masquerading)
DMredhat.com
```

With this type of configuration, all mail sent will appear as if it were sent from redhat.com, and any mail sent to torgo.redhat.com or the other hosts will be delivered to mail.redhat.com. Please be aware that if you configure your system to masquerade as another, any e-mail sent from your system to your system will be sent to the machine you are masquerading as. For example, in the above illustration, log files that are periodically sent to root@poodle.redhat.com by the cron daemon would be sent to root@mail.redhat.com.

Controlling Access to Services

As a security measure, most network services are managed by a protective program called a *TCP wrapper*. The protected services are those listed in /etc/inetd.conf that specify /usr/sbin/tcpd. tcpd can allow or deny access to a service based on the origin of the request, and the configuration in /etc/hosts.allow and /etc/hosts.deny.

By default Red Hat Linux allows all service requests. To disable or limit services you can edit /etc/hosts.allow. Here is an example /etc/hosts.allow file:

```
ALL: redhat.com .redhat.com
in.talkd: ALL
in.ntalkd: ALL
in.fingerd: ALL
in.ftpd: ALL
```

This configuration allows all connections from `redhat.com` and `*.redhat.com` machines. It also allows talk, finger, and ftp requests from all machines. `tcpd` allows much more sophisticated access control, using a combination of `/etc/hosts.allow` and `/etc/hosts.deny`. Read the `tcpd(8)` and `hosts_access(5)` man pages for complete details.

Anonymous FTP

Setting up anonymous FTP is simple. All you need to do is install the anon-ftp rpm package (which you may have already done at install time). Once it is installed, anonymous FTP will be up and running. There are a few files you might wish to edit to configure your FTP server.

`/etc/ftpaccess`
— This file defines most of the access control for your ftp server. Some of the things that you can do are: set up logical "groups" to control access from different sites, limit the number of simultaneous FTP connections, configure transfer logging, and much more. Read the ftpaccess man page for complete details.

`/etc/ftphosts`
— The ftphosts file is used to allow or deny access to certain accounts from various hosts. Read the ftphosts man page for details.

`/etc/ftpusers`
— This file lists all the users that are not allowed to ftp into your machine. For example, root is listed in /etc/ftpusers by default. That means that you cannot ftp to your machine and log in as root. This is a good security measure, but some administrators prefer to remove root from this file.

NFS Configuration

NFS stands for Network File System, and is a way to share files between machines as if they were on your local hard drive. Linux can be both an NFS server and an NFS client, which means that it can export filesystems to other systems, and mount filesystems exported from other machines.

Mounting NFS Filesystems

Use the mount command to mount an NFS filesystem from another machine:

```
mkdir /mnt/local
```

Only required if `/mnt/local` doesn't exist

```
mount bigdog:/mnt/export /mnt/local
```

In this command, `bigdog` is the hostname of the NFS fileserver, `/mnt/export` is the filesystem that `bigdog` is exporting, and `/mnt/local` is a directory on my local machine where we want to mount the filesystem. After the mount command runs (and if we have the proper permissions from bigdog) we can enter `ls /mnt/local` and get a listing of the files in `/mnt/export` on `bigdog`.

Exporting NFS Filesystems

The file that controls what filesystems you wish to export is `/etc/exports`. Its format is

```
directory hostname(options)
```

the (options) are optional. For example:

```
/mnt/export speedy.redhat.com
```

would allow `speedy.redhat.com` to mount `/mnt/export`, but:

```
/mnt/export speedy.redhat.com(ro)
```

would just allow speedy to mount `/mnt/export` read-only. Each time you change `/etc/exports`, you must tell the NFS daemons to examine it for new information. One simple way to accomplish this is to just stop and start the daemons:

```
/etc/rc.d/init.d/nfs stop
/etc/rc.d/init.d/nfs start
```

The following will also work:

```
killall -HUP rpc.nfsd rpc.mountd
```

See the following man pages for more details: nfsd(8), mountd(8), and exports(5). Another good reference is *Managing NFS and NIS Services*, by Hal Stern, published by O'Reilly & Associates.

The Boot Process, Init, and Shutdown

This section contains information on what happens when a Red Hat Linux system is booted and shut down. Let's start with information on the files in `/etc/sysconfig`.

Sysconfig Information

The following information outlines the various files in /etc/sysconfig, their function, and their contents.

Files in /etc/sysconfig

The following files are normally found in `/etc/sysconfig`:

- /etc/sysconfig/clock
- /etc/sysconfig/keyboard
- /etc/sysconfig/mouse
- /etc/sysconfig/network
- /etc/sysconfig/pcmcia
- /etc/sysconfig/amd
- /etc/sysconfig/tape

Let's take a look at each one.

`/etc/sysconfig/clock`

— The `/etc/sysconfig/clock` file controls the interpretation of values read from the system clock. Earlier releases of Red Hat Linux used the following values (which is deprecated):

- **CLOCKMODE**=*mode*, where *mode* is one of the following:

  √ **GMT** — indicates that the clock is set to UTC.

  Currently, the correct values are:

- **UTC**=*boolean*, where *boolean* is one of the following:

  √ true — indicates that the clock is set to UTC. Any other value indicates that it is set to local time.

`/etc/sysconfig/keyboard`

— The /etc/sysconfig/keyboard file controls the behavior of the keyboard. The following values may be used:

- **KEYTABLE**=*file*, where *file* is the name of a keytable file. For example:

```
KEYTABLE="/usr/lib/kbd/keytables/us.map"
```

`/etc/sysconfig/mouse`

— The `/etc/sysconfig/mouse` file is used to specify information about the available mouse. The following values may be used:

- **MOUSETYPE**=*type*, where *type* is one of the following:

  √ **microsoft** — A Microsoft mouse.

  √ **mouseman** — A MouseMan mouse.

  √ **mousesystems** — A Mouse Systems mouse.

  √ **ps/2** — A PS/2 mouse.

  √ **msbm** — A Microsoft bus mouse.

  √ **ogibm** — A Logitech bus mouse.

  √ **atibm** — An ATI bus mouse.

  √ **logitech** — A Logitech mouse.

  √ **mmseries** — An older MouseMan mouse.

  √ **mmhittab** — An mmhittab mouse.

- **XEMU3**=*emulation*, where *emulation* is one of the following:

  √ **yes** — Three mouse buttons should be emulated.

  √ **no** — The mouse already has three buttons.

  In addition, /dev/mouse is a symlink that points to the actual mouse device.

/etc/sysconfig/network

— The `/etc/sysconfig/network` file is used to specify information about the desired network configuration. The following values may be used:

- **NETWORKING**=*answer*, where *answer* is one of the following:

  √ **yes** — Networking should be configured.

  √ **no** — Networking should not be configured.

- **HOSTNAME**=*hostname*, where *hostname* should be the FQDN (Fully Qualified Domain Name), but can be whatever hostname you want.

  Please Note: For compatibility with older software that people might install (such as trn), the `/etc/HOSTNAME` file should contain the same value as here.

- **FORWARD_IPV4**=*answer*, where *answer* is one of the following:

  √ **yes** — Perform IP forwarding.

  √ **no** — Do not perform IP forwarding.

  (The current Red Hat Linux installation sets this to "no" by default (for RFC compliance), but if FORWARD_IPV4 is not set at all, forwarding is enabled for compatibility with the configuration files used on Red Hat Linux versions 4.2 and earlier.)

- **GATEWAY**=*gw-ip*, where *gw-ip* is the IP address of the network's gateway.

- **GATEWAYDEV**=*gw-dev*, where *gw-dev* is the gateway device (e.g. eth0).

- **NISDOMAIN**=*dom-name*, where *dom-name* is the NIS domain name.

`/etc/sysconfig/pcmcia`
— The `/etc/sysconfig/pcmcia` file is used to specify PCMCIA configuration information. The following values may be used:

- **PCMCIA**=answer, where answer is one of the following:

  √ **yes** — PCMCIA support should be enabled.

  √ **no** — PCMCIA support should not be enabled.

- **PCIC**=pcic-type, where pcic-type is one of the following:

  √ **i82365** — The computer has an i82365-style PCMCIA socket chipset.

  √ **tcic** — The computer has a tcic-style PCMCIA socket chipset.

- **PCIC_OPTS**=*option*, where *option* is the socket driver (i82365 or tcic) timing parameters.

- **CORE_OPTS**=*option*, where *option* is the list of pcmcia_core options.
- **CARDMGR_OPTS**=*option*, where *option* is the list of options for the PCMCIA cardmgr.

`/etc/sysconfig/amd`

— The `/etc/sysconfig/amd` file is used to specify operational parameters for amd. The following values may be used:

- **ADIR**=*path*, where *path* is the amd directory. It should be "/.automount." and is normally never changed.
- **MOUNTPTS**=*mountpts*, where *mountpts* is, for example, "/net /etc/amd.conf"
- **AMDOPTS**=*options*, where *options* are any extra options for AMD.

`/etc/sysconfig/tape`

— The `/etc/sysconfig/tape` file is used to specify tape-related configuration information. The following values may be used:

- **DEV**=*devnam*, where *devnam* is the tape device (for example, "`/dev/nst0`)." Use the non-rewinding device for these scripts. For SCSI tapes this is "`/dev/nst#`," where "#" is the number of the tape drive you want to use. If you only have one, then use "`/dev/nst0`." For IDE tapes you use "`/dev/ht#`," where "#" is the number of the tape drive you want to use. If you only have one, then use "`/dev/ht0`." For floppy tape drives use "`/dev/ftape`."
- **ADMIN**=*account*, where *account* is the user account to send mail to if the backup fails for any reason. Normally set to "root."
- **SLEEP**=*time*, where *time* is the time to sleep between tape operations. Some drives need a bit more than others, but "5" seems to work for 8mm, 4mm, and DLT.
- **BLOCKSIZE**=*size*, where *size* is the tape drive's optimal block size. A value of "32768" worked fine for 8mm, then 4mm, and now DLT. An optimal setting is probably however much data your drive writes at one time.
- **SHORTDATE**=*date*, where *date* is a string that evaluates to a short date string, to be used in backup log filenames. The default setting is: "$(date +%y:%m:%d:%H:%M)."
- **DAY**=*date*, where *date* is a string that evaluates to a date string, to be used for the log file directory. The default setting is: "$(date +log-%y:%m:%d)."

- **DATE**=*date*, where *date* is a string that evaluates to a regular date string, to be used in log files. The default setting is: "$(date)."
- **LOGROOT**=*path*, where *path* is the root of the logging directory.
- **LIST**=*file*, where *file* is the file name the incremental backup will use to store the incremental list. It will be followed by a sequence number.
- **DOTCOUNT**=*count*, where *count* is the name of a file used for counting as you go, to know which incremental list to use.
- **COUNTER**=*count-file*, where *count-file* is used for rewinding when done.
- **BACKUPTAB**=*file*, where *file* is the name of the file in which we keep our list of backup(s) we want to make.

Files in /etc/sysconfig/network-scripts/

The following files are normally found in `/etc/sysconfig/network-scripts`:

- `/etc/sysconfig/network-scripts/ifup`
- `/etc/sysconfig/network-scripts/ifdown`
- `/etc/sysconfig/network-scripts/network-functions`
- `/etc/sysconfig/network-scripts/ifcfg-`*<interface-name>*
- `/etc/sysconfig/network-scripts/ifcfg-`*<interface-name>-<clone-name>*
- `/etc/sysconfig/network-scripts/chat-`*<interface-name>*
- `/etc/sysconfig/network-scripts/dip-`*<interface-name>*
- `/etc/sysconfig/network-scripts/ifup-post`
- `/etc/sysconfig/network-scripts/ifdhcpc-done`

Let's take a look at each one.

/etc/sysconfig/network-scripts/ifup, /etc/sysconfig/network-scripts/ifdown
— Symlinks to `/sbin/ifup` and `/sbin/ifdown`, respectively. These are the only two scripts in this directory that should be called directly; these two scripts call all the other scripts as needed. These symlinks are here for legacy purposes only — they will probably be removed in future versions, so only `/sbin/ifup` and `/sbin/ifdown` should currently be used. These scripts take one argument normally: the name of the device (e.g. "`eth0`"). They are called with a second argument of "`boot`" during the boot sequence so that

devices that are not meant to be brought up on boot (ONBOOT=no, [see below]) can be ignored at that time.

/etc/sysconfig/network-scripts/network-functions
— Not really a public file. Contains functions which the scripts use for bringing interfaces up and down. In particular, it contains most of the code for handling alternative interface configurations and interface change notification through netreport.

/etc/sysconfig/network-scripts/ifcfg-<interface-name>, /etc/sysconfig/network-scripts/ifcfg-<interface-name>-<clone-name>
— The first file defines an interface, while the second file contains only the parts of the definition that are different in a "clone" (or alternative) interface. For example, the network numbers might be different, but everything else might be the same, so only the network numbers would be in the clone file, while all the device information would be in the base `ifcfg` file. The items that can be defined in an `ifcfg` file depend on the interface type. The following values are common to all base files:

- **DEVICE**=*name*, where *name* is the name of the physical device (except dynamically-allocated PPP devices where it is the "logical name").
- **IPADDR**=*addr*, where *addr* is the IP address.
- **NETMASK**=*mask*, where *mask* is the netmask value.
- **NETWORK**=*addr*, where *addr* is the network address.
- **BROADCAST**=*addr*, where *addr* is the broadcast address.
- **GATEWAY**=*addr*, where *addr* is the gateway address.
- **ONBOOT**=*answer*, where *answer* is one of the following:
  - √ **yes** — This device should be activated at boot-time.
  - √ **no** — This device should not be activated at boot-time.
- **USERCTL**=*answer*, where *answer* is one of the following:
  - √ **yes** — Non-root users are allowed to control this device.
  - √ **no** — Non-root users are not allowed to control this device.
- **BOOTPROTO**=*proto*, where *proto* is one of the following:

√ **none** — No boot-time protocol should be used.

√ **bootp** — The bootp protocol should be used.

√ **dhcp** — The dhcp protocol should be used.

The following values are common to all PPP and SLIP files:

- **PERSIST**=*answer*, where *answer* is one of the following:

  √ **yes** — This device should be kept active at all times, even if deactivated after a modem hangup.

  √ **no** — This device should not be kept active at all times.

- **MODEMPORT**=*port*, where *port* is the modem port's device name (for example, "`/dev/modem`").

- **LINESPEED**=*baud*, where *baud* is the modem's linespeed (for example, "115200").

- **DEFABORT**=*answer*, where *answer* is one of the following:

  √ **yes** — Insert default abort strings when creating/editing the script for this interface.

  √ **no** — Do not insert default abort strings when creating/editing the script for this interface.

The following values are common to all PPP files:

- **DEFROUTE**=*answer*, where *answer* is one of the following:

  √ **yes** — Set this interface as the default route.

  √ **no** — Do not set this interface as the default route.

- **ESCAPECHARS**=*answer*, where *answer* is one of the following:

  √ **yes** — Use the pre-defined asyncmap.

  √ **no** — Do not use the pre-defined asyncmap

(This represents a simplified interface; it doesn't let people specify which characters to escape. However, almost everyone can use an asyncmap of 00000000 anyway, and it's possible to set PPPOPTIONS to use an arbitrary asyncmap if so desired.)

- **HARDFLOWCTL**=*answer*, where *answer* is one of the following:

  √ **yes** — Use hardware flow control.

  √ **no** — Do not use hardware flow control.

- **PPPOPTIONS**=*options*, where *options* is an arbitrary option string. It is placed last on the command line so it can override other options (such as asyncmap) that were specified previously.

- **PAPNAME**=*name*, where *name* is used as part of "name $PAPNAME" on the pppd command line. Note that the "remotename" option is always specified as the logical PPP device name, like "`ppp0`" (which might perhaps be the physical device ppp1 if some other PPP device was brought up earlier...), which makes it easy to manage pap/chap files — name/password pairs are associated with the logical PPP device name so that they can be managed together. In principle, there shouldn't anything that would keep the logical PPP device names from being "worldnet" or "myISP" instead of "`ppp0`" — "`pppN`."

- **REMIP**=*addr*, where *addr* is the remote IP address (which is normally unspecified).

- **MTU**=*value*, where *value* is the value to be used as MTU.

- **MRU**=*value*, where *value* is the value to be used as MRU.

- **DISCONNECTTIMEOUT**=*value*, where *value* represents the number of seconds to wait before re-establishing the connection after a successfully-connected session terminated.

- **RETRYTIMEOUT**=*value*, where *value* represents the number of seconds to wait before re-attempting to establish a connection after a previous attempt has failed.

`/etc/sysconfig/network-scripts/chat-`*`<interface-name>`*
: — This file is a chat script for PPP or SLIP connections, and is intended to establish the connection. For SLIP devices, a DIP script is written from the chat script; for PPP devices, the chat script is used directly.

`/etc/sysconfig/network-scripts/dip-`*`<interface-name>`*
: — This write-only script is created from the chat script by `netcfg`. Do not modify this file. In the future, this file may disappear and instead will be created on-the-fly from the chat script.

`/etc/sysconfig/network-scripts/ifup-post`

— This file is called when any network device (except a SLIP device) comes up. Calls /etc/sysconfig/network-scripts/ifup-routes to bring up static routes that depend on that device. Brings up aliases for that device. Sets the hostname if it is not already set and a hostname can be found for the IP for that device. Sends SIGIO to any programs that have requested notification of network events. Could be extended to fix up nameservice configuration, call arbitrary scripts, and more, as needed.

`/etc/sysconfig/network-scripts/ifdhcpc-done`

— This file is called by dhcpcd once dhcp configuration is complete; sets up `/etc/resolv.conf` from the version dhcpcd dropped in `/etc/dhcpc/resolv.conf`.

System V Init

This section is a brief description of the internals of the boot process. It covers in detail how the machine boots using SysV init, as well as the differences between the init used in older Linux releases, and SysV init. Init is the program that gets run by the kernel at boot time. It is in charge of starting all the normal processes that need to run at boot time. These include the getty processes that allow you to log in, NFS daemons, FTP daemons, and anything else you want to run when your machine boots. SysV init is fast becoming the standard in the Linux world to control the startup of software at boot time. This is because it is easier to use and more powerful and flexible than the traditional BSD init. SysV init also differs from BSD init in that the config files are in a subdirectory of `/etc` instead of residing directly in `/etc`. This directory is called `rc.d`. In there you will find `rc.sysinit` and the following directories:

```
init.d
rc0.d
rc1.d
rc2.d
rc3.d
rc4.d
rc5.d
rc6.d
```

`init.d` contains a bunch of scripts. Basically, you reqire one script for each service you may need to start at boot time or when entering another runlevel. Services include things like networking, nfs, sendmail, httpd, etc. Services do not include things like setserial that must only be run once and then exited. Things like that should go in `rc.local` or `rc.serial`. If you want `rc.local`, it should be in `/etc/rc.d`. Most systems include one even though it doesn't do much. You can also include an rc.serial in `/etc/rc.d` if you need to do serial port specific things at boot time. The chain of events is as follows:

- The kernel looks in several places for init and runs the first one it finds
- init runs /etc/rc.d/rc.sysinit
- rc.sysinit does a bunch of necessary things and then runs rc.serial (if it exists)
- init runs all the scripts for the default runlevel.
- init runs rc.local

The default runlevel is decided in `/etc/inittab`. You should have a line close to the top like:

```
id:3:initdefault:
```

From this, you'd look in the second column and see that the default runlevel is 3, as should be the case for most systems. If you want to change it, you can edit `/etc/inittab` by hand and change the 3. Be very careful when you are messing with the inittab. If you do mess up, you can fix it by rebooting and doing:

```
LILO boot: linux single
```

This *should* allow you to boot into single user mode so you can fix inittab. Now, how does it run all the right scripts? If you enter `ls -l` on `rc3.d`, you might see something like:

```
lrwxrwxrwx 1 root root 17 3:11 S10network -> ../init.d/network
lrwxrwxrwx 1 root root 16 3:11 S30syslog -> ../init.d/syslog
lrwxrwxrwx 1 root root 14 3:32 S40cron -> ../init.d/cron
lrwxrwxrwx 1 root root 14 3:11 S50inet -> ../init.d/inet
lrwxrwxrwx 1 root root 13 3:11 S60nfs -> ../init.d/nfs
lrwxrwxrwx 1 root root 15 3:11 S70nfsfs -> ../init.d/nfsfs
lrwxrwxrwx 1 root root 18 3:11 S90lpd -> ../init.d/lpd.init
lrwxrwxrwx 1 root root 11 3:11 S99local -> ../rc.local
```

What you'll notice is that there are no real "files" in the directory. Everything there is a link to one of the scripts in the init.d directory. The links also have an "S" and a number at the beginning. The "S" means to start this particular script and a "K" would mean to stop it. The number is there just for ordering purposes. Init will start all the services based on the order in which they appear. You can duplicate numbers, but it will only confuse you somewhat. You only need to use a two digit number, along with an upper case "S" or "K" to start or stop the services you require to. How does init start and stop services? Simple. Each of the scripts is written to accept an argument which can be "start" and "stop." You can execute those scripts by hand, in fact, with a command like:

```
/etc/rc.d/init.d/httpd.init stop
```

to stop the httpd server. Init just reads the name and if it has a "K," it calls the script with the "stop" argument. If it has an "S" it calls the script with a "start" argument. Why all these runlevels? Some people want an easy way to set up machines to be multipurpose. You could have a "server" runlevel that just runs httpd, sendmail, networking, etc. Then you could have a "user" runlevel that runs xdm, networking, etc.

Init Runlevels

Generally, Red Hat Linux operates in run level 3—full multiuser mode. The following runlevels are defined in Red Hat Linux:

0
: Halt

1
: Single user mode

2
: Multiuser mode, without NFS

3
: Full multiuser mode

4
: Not used

5
: Full multiuser mode (with an X-based login screen)

6
: Reboot

If your machine gets into a state where it will not boot due to a bad `/etc/inittab`, or will not let you log in because you have a corrupted /etc/passwd or have simply forgotten your password, boot into single user mode by typing linux 1 at the LILO boot prompt. A very bare system will come up and you will be given a shell from which you can fix things.

Initscript Utilities

The `chkconfig` utility provides a simple command-line tool for maintaining the `/etc/rc.d` directory hierarchy. It relieves system administrators from having to directly manipulate the numerous symlinks in `/etc/rc.d`. In addition, there is the ntsysv utility, that provides a screen-oriented interface, versus chkconfig's command-line interface. Please see the chkconfig and ntsysv man pages for more information.

Running Programs at Boot Time

The file `/etc/rc.d/rc.local` is executed at boot time, after all other initialization is complete, and whenever you change runlevels. You can add additional initialization commands here. For instance, you may want to start up additional daemons, or initialize a printer. In addition, if you require serial port setup, you can edit `/etc/rc.d/rc.serial`, and it will be executed automatically at boot time. The default `/etc/rc.d/rc.local` simply creates a nice login banner with your kernel version and machine type.

Shutting Down

To shut down Red Hat Linux, issue the shutdown command. You can read the shutdown man page for complete details, but the two most common usages are:

```
shutdown -h now
```

```
shutdown -r now
```

Each will cleanly shutdown the system. After shutting everything down, the first will halt the machine, and the second will reboot. Although the `reboot` and `halt` commands are now "smart" enough to invoke `shutdown` if run while the system is in runlevels 1-5, it is a bad habit to get into, as not all Linux-like operating systems have this feature.

Rescue Modes

When things go wrong, there are several ways to work on fixing them. However, they require that you understand the system well. This manual can't teach you what to do, but we will present the ways that you can use our products to get into rescue modes where you can use your own knowledge to rescue the system.

Through LILO

If your system boots, but does not allow you to log in when it has completed booting, you can use the single or emergency boot option. At the LILO boot: prompt, type linux single in order to boot in single-user mode. In single-user mode, your local filesystems will be mounted, but your network will not be activated. In emergency mode, almost nothing will be set up. Only the root filesystem will be mounted, and it will be mounted read-only.

Emergency Boot Diskettes
: The boot diskette created during installation of Red Hat Linux 6.0 may be used as part of a rescue diskette set. For more information, please read the file rescue.txt in the `/doc` on your Red Hat Linux 6.0 CD-ROM or refer to the Red Hat Linux Getting Started Guide.

A Handy Trick

Have you ever rebuilt a kernel and, eager to try out your new handiwork, rebooted before running LILO? And you didn't have an entry for an older kernel in lilo.conf? Read on... Here's a handy trick. In many cases, it's possible to boot your Red Hat Linux/Intel from the Red Hat Linux boot diskette with your root filesystem mounted and ready to go. Here's how: Enter the following command at the boot diskette's boot:

```
prompt: linux single root=/dev/hdXX initrd=
```

(Replace the XX in /dev/hdXX with the appropriate letter and number for your root partition.) What does this do? First, it starts the boot in single-user mode, with the root partition set to your root partition. The empty initrd specification bypasses the installation-related image on the boot diskette, which will cause you to enter single-user mode immediately. Is there a downside to this trick? Unfortunately, yes. Because the kernel on the Red Hat Linux boot diskette only has support for IDE built-in, those of you with SCSI-based systems won't be able to use this trick. In that case, you'll have to use the boot/rescue diskette combination mentioned above.

Appendix A
Making Installation Diskettes

It is sometimes necessary to create a diskette from an image file (for example, you might need to use updated diskette images obtained from the Red Hat Linux Errata). As the name implies, an image file is a file that contains an exact copy (or image) of a diskette's contents. Since a diskette contains filesystem information in addition to the data contained in files, the image file is not usable until it has been written to a diskette. To start, you'll need a blank, formatted, high-density (1.44 MB), 3.5-inch diskette. You'll need access to a computer with a 3.5-inch diskette drive, and capable of running a DOS program, or the dd utility program found on most Linux-like operating systems. The image files are found in the following directories on your Red Hat Linux CD:

- **images** – Contains the boot and PCMCIA support images for Red Hat Linux.

Once you've selected the proper image, it's time to transfer the image file onto a diskette. As mentioned previously, this can be done on a DOS-capable system, or on a system running a Linux-like operating system.

Making a Diskette Under MS-DOS

To make a diskette under MS-DOS, use the rawrite utility included on the Red Hat Linux CD in the dosutils directory. First, label a blank, formatted 3.5-inch diskette appropriately (eg. "Boot Diskette," "Supplemental Diskette," etc). Insert it into the diskette drive. Then, use the following commands (assuming your CD is drive d:):

```
C:\> d:
D:\> cd \dosutils
D:\dosutils> rawrite
Enter disk image source file name:
..\images\boot.img
Enter target diskette drive: a:
Please insert a formatted diskette into drive A:
and
press -ENTER- : [Enter]
D:\dosutils>
```

`rawrite` first asks you for the filename of a diskette image; enter the directory and name of the image you wish to write (for example, `..\images\boot.img`). Then rawrite asks for a diskette drive to write the image to; enter a:. Finally, rawrite asks for confirmation that a formatted diskette is in the drive you've selected. After pressing [Enter] to confirm, `rawrite` copies the image file onto the diskette. If you need to make another diskette, label another diskette, and run `rawrite` again, specifying the appropriate image file.

Making a Diskette Under a Linux-like O/S

To make a diskette under Linux (or any other Linux-like operating system), you must have permission to write to the device representing a 3.5-inch diskette drive (known as `/dev/fd0` under Linux). First, label a blank, formatted diskette appropriately (eg. "Boot Diskette," "Supplemental Diskette," etc.). Insert it into the diskette drive (but don't issue a mount command). After mounting the Red Hat Linux CD, change directory to the directory containing the desired image file, and use the following command (changing the name of the image file and diskette device as appropriate):

```
# dd if=boot.img of=/dev/fd0 bs=1440k
```

If you need to make another diskette, label another diskette, and run `dd` again, specifying the appropriate image file.

Appendix B
An Introduction to Disk Partitions

Disk partitions are a standard part of the personal computer landscape, and have been for quite some time. However, with so many people purchasing computers featuring preinstalled operating systems, relatively few people understand how partitions work. This chapter attempts to explain how disk partitions work so you'll find your Red Hat Linux installation is as simple as possible.

Hard Disk Basic Concepts

Hard disks perform a very simple function — they store data and reliably retrieve it on command. When discussing issues such as disk partitioning, it's important to know a bit about the underlying hardware; unfortunately, it's easy to become bogged down in details. Therefore, let's use a simplified diagram of a disk drive to help us explain what goes on "under the hood." Figure B-1 shows a brand-new, unused disk drive.

Figure B-1: An Unused Disk Drive

Not much to look at, is it? But if we're talking about disk drives on a basic level, it will do. Let's say that we'd like to store some data on this drive. As things stand now, it won't work. There's something we need to do first...

It's Not What You Write, it's How You Write It

The old-timers in the audience probably got this one on the first try. We need to format the drive. Formatting (usually known as "making a filesystem" in Linux parlance) writes information to the drive, creating order out of the empty space in an unformatted drive.

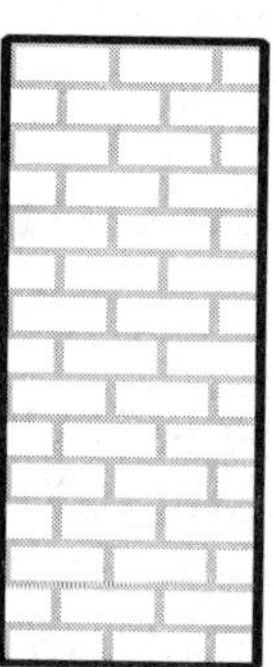

Figure B-2: Disk Drive with a Filesystem

As Figure B-2 implies, the order imposed by a filesystem involves some tradeoffs:

- A small percentage of the drive's available space is used to store filesystem-related data, and can be considered as overhead.
- A filesystem splits the remaining space into small, consistently-sized segments. In the Linux world, these segments are known as *inodes*[1].

Given that filesystems make things like directories and files possible, these tradeoffs are usually seen as a small price to pay. It's also worth

1 Inodes really *are* consistently-sized, unlike our illutstrations. Also, keep in mind that an average disk drive contains thousands of indoes. But for the purposes of this dicsussion, please ignore these minor discrepancies.

noting that there is no single, universal filesystem; as Figure B-3 shows, a disk drive may have one of many different filesystems written on it. As you might guess, different filesystems tend to be incompatible; that is, an operating system that supports one filesystem (or a handful of related filesystem types) may not support another. This last statement is not a hard-and-fast rule, however. For example, Red Hat Linux supports a wide variety of filesystems (including many commonly used by other operating systems), making data interchange easy.

Figure B-3: Disk Drive with a Different Filesystem

Of course, writing a filesystem to disk is only the beginning. The goal of this process is to actually store and retrieve data. Let's take a look at our drive after some files have been written to it.

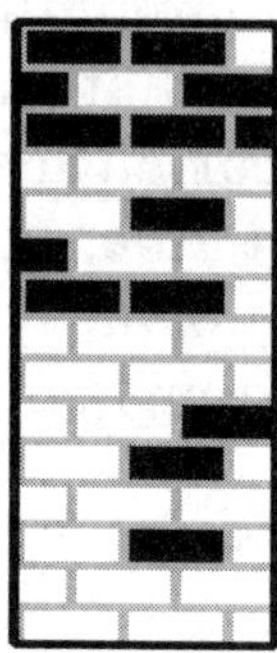

Figure B-4: Disk Drive with Data Written to It

As Figure B-4 shows, 14 of the previously-empty inodes are now holding data. We cannot determine how many files reside on this drive; it may be as few as one or as many as 14, as all files use as least one inode. Another important point to note is that the used inodes do not have to form a contiguous region; used and unused inodes may be interspersed. This is known as fragmentation. Fragmentation can play a part when attempting to resize an existing partition.

As with most computer-related technologies, disk drives continued to change over time. In particular, they changed in one specific way — they got bigger. Not bigger in size, but bigger in capacity. And it was this additional capacity that drove a change in the way disk drives were used.

Partitions – Turning One Drive Into Many

As disk drive capacities soared, some people started wondering if having all that space in one big chunk wasn't such a great idea. This line of thinking was driven by several issues, some philosophical, some technical. On the philosophical side, above a certain size, it just seemed that the additional space provided by a larger drive made for more clutter. On the technical side, some filesystems were never designed to support larger drives. Or the filesystems could support larger drives, but the overhead imposed by the filesystem became excessive. The solution to this problem was to divide disks into partitions. Each partition can be accessed as if it was a separate disk. This is done through the addition of a partition table.

> **Please Note:** While the diagrams in this chapter show the partition table as being separate from the actual disk drive, this is not entirely accurate. In reality, the partition table is stored at the very start of the disk, before any filesystem or user data. But for clarity, we'll keep it separate in our diagrams.

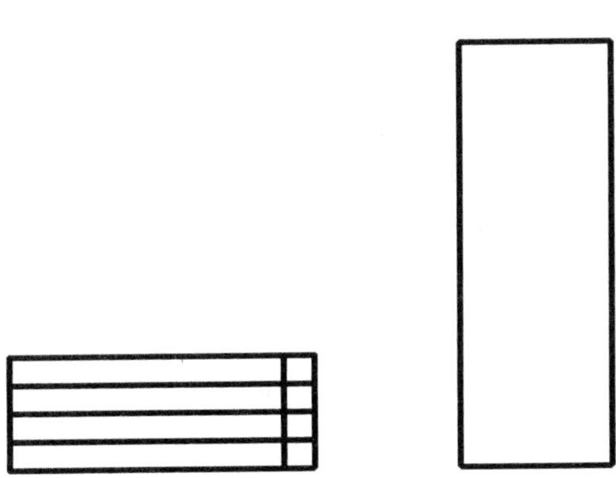

Figure B-5: Disk Drive with Partition Table

As Figure B-5 shows, the partition table is divided into four sections. Each section can hold the information necessary to define a single partition, meaning that the partition table can define no more than four partitions.

Each partition table entry contains several important characteristics of the partition:

- The points on the disk where the partition starts and ends;
- Whether the partition is "active";
- The partition's type.

Let's take a closer look at each of these characteristics. The starting and ending points actually define the partition's size and location on the disk. The "active" flag is used by some operating systems' boot loaders. In other words, the operating system in the partition that is marked "active" will be booted.

The partition's type can be a bit confusing. The type is a number that identifies the partition's anticipated usage. If that statement sounds a bit vague, that's because the meaning of the partition type is a bit vague. Some operating systems use the partition type to denote a specific filesystem type, to flag the partition as being associated with a particular operating system, to indicate that the partition contains a bootable operating system, or some combination of the three.

Figure B-6 contains a listing of some popular (and obscure) partition types, along with their numeric values.

Partition Type	Value	Partition Type	Value
Empty	00	Novell Netware 386	65
DOS 12-bit FAT	01	PC/IX	75
XENIX root	02	Old MINIX	80
XENIX usr	03	Linux/MINIX	81
DOS 16-bit <=32M	04	Linux swap	82
Extended	05	Linux native	83
DOS 16-bit >=32M	06	Linux extended	85
OS/2 HPFS	07	Amoeba	93
AIX	08	Amoeba BBT	94
AIX bootable	09	BSD/386	a5
OS/2 Boot Manager	0a	OpenBSD	a6
Win95 FAT32	0b	NEXTSTEP	a7
Win95 FAT32 (LBA)	0c	BSDI fs	b7
Win95 FAT16 (LBA)	0e	BSDI swap	b8
Win95 Extended (LBA)	0f	Syrinx	c7
Venix 80286	40	CP/M	db
Novell?	51	DOS access	e1
Microport	52	DOS R/O	e3
GNU HURD	63	DOS secondary	f2
Novell Netware 286	64	BBT	ff

Figure B-6: Partition Types

Now you might be wondering how all this additional complexity is normally used. See Figure B-7 for an example.

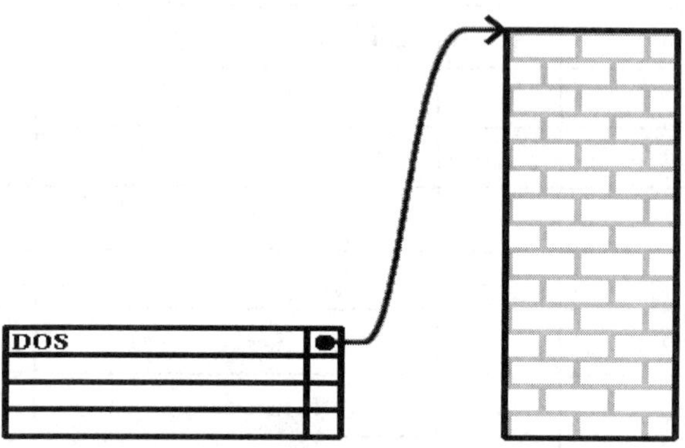

Figure B-7: Disk Drive With Single Partition

That's right — in many cases there is but a single partition spanning the entire disk, essentially duplicating the pre-partitioned days of yore. The partition table has only one entry used, and it points to the start of the partition. We've labeled this partition as being of type "DOS," although as you can see from Figure B-6, that's a bit simplistic, but adequate for the purposes of this discussion. This is a typical partition layout for most newly purchased computers with some version of Windows pre-installed.

Partitions within Partitions — An Overview of Extended Partitions

Of course, in time it became obvious that four partitions would not be enough. As disk drives continued to grow, it became more and more likely that a person could configure four reasonably-sized partitions and still have disk space left over. There needed to be some way of creating more partitions. Enter the extended partition. As you may have noticed in Figure B-6, there is an "Extended" partition type; it is this partition type that is at the heart of extended partitions. Here's how it works.

When a partition is created and its type is set to "Extended," an extended partition table is created. In essence, the extended partition is like a disk drive in its own right — it has a partition table that points to one or more partitions (now called logical partitions, as opposed to the four primary partitions) contained entirely within the extended partition itself. Figure B-8 shows a disk drive with one primary partition, and one extended partition containing two logical partitions (along with some unpartitioned free space).

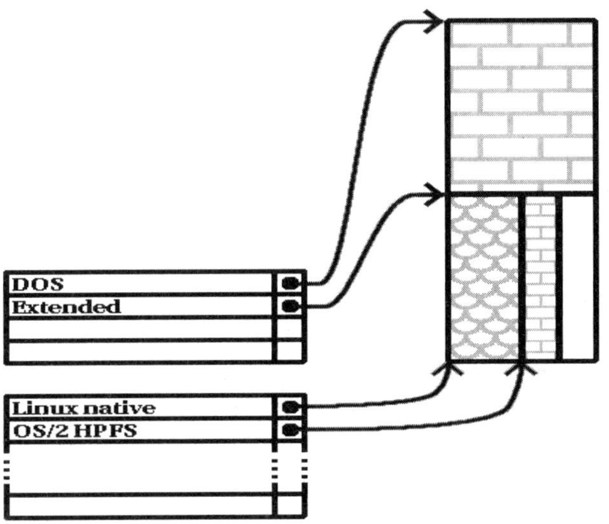

Figure B-8: Disk Drive With Extended Partition

As this figure implies, there is a difference between primary and logical partitions — there can only be four primary partitions, but there is no fixed limit to the number of logical partitions that can exist. (However, in reality it is probably not a good idea to try to define and use more than 12 logical partitions on a single disk drive.)

Appendix C
Package List

This appendix lists the packages that make up Red Hat Linux. In each entry, you'll find the following information:

- The name of the package
- The packaged software's version number
- The size of the packaged software, in kilobytes
- A short description of the software

In addition, some packages will have one or more of the following icons alongside the package name:

- [B] This package is part of the Red Hat Linux base, meaning that it is always installed.
- W] Workstation-class installations include this package.
- [S] Server-class installations include this package.

Please Note: This package list was automatically generated right before Red Hat Linux 6.0 went into production. Because of the short timeframes involved, you might find minor typesetting problems in the package lists. However, we felt that an up-to-date package list was more important than a picture-perfect package list. We hope you'll agree... You may also notice that some packages have different versions, and that packages listed here are not mentioned in the installation program (and vice versa). Any differences in package versions are normally due to the normal bug fixing process. It's possible that "missing" or "extra" packages are the result of last-minute changes prior to pressing CD-ROMs. Also note that all the packages in the "Base" group (and subgroups) are always installed, therefore you will not see them mentioned explicitly during the installation process.

Using the Package List After Installation

This list can come in handy even after you've installed Red Hat Linux. You can use it to search for documentation. Here's how:

1 Find the package in this list.

2 Note the package name (The very first thing listed in bold at the start of each package description).

3 Enter the following command, taking care to enter the package name exactly as it is shown in the list (the package name is case-sensitive):

```
rpm -qd package-name
```

(Replacing package-name with the actual name of the package, of course.)

If you installed the package, you should get a list of filenames. Each file contains documentation relating to the package you specified. Here are some of the types of filenames you'll see:

- **/usr/man... something.n** – This is a man page. You can view it by using the man command (for example, man something. You might also need to include the file's ending number in the man command (as in man n something.
- **/usr/X11R6/man...** something.nx – This is a man page for part of the X Window System. View these files the same way as a regular man page.
- **/usr/doc/something...** – Files under /usr/doc can be in any number of different formats. Sometimes the end of the filename can provide a clue as to how it should be viewed:
  - √ **.html** – An HTML file. View with the web browser of your choice.
  - √ **.txt** – A text file. View with cat or less.
  - √ **.ps** – A PostScript file. You can print it to a Postscript printer, or you can view it with gv.
  - √ **.gz** – A file compressed with gzip. If you make a copy of the original file, you can use gunzip to decompress it (you'll probably want to keep the original file compressed to save space). You can then view the file as you would normally. The zless command combines gunzip and less, and makes it possible to read compressed text files without making interim copies. There are other, more elegant ways to work with compressed files, but this approach will work for those just starting to use Linux.

In general, most of the documentation files you'll find will be one of those listed above. If in doubt, it's a good bet that the file is text. You can always try the file command to see if the file's contents can be identified.

- **/usr/info...** — Files in /usr/info are meant to be viewed using the info (or Emacs' Info mode). If you use Emacs, press [Ctrl]-[I], followed by [I] to view the main Info screen.

Amusements

This section lists the packages that provide fun and entertainment to Red Hat Linux system owners the world over.

Games

This section lists packages that contain a variety of games.

cxhextris — (Version 1.0, 39K)
CXHextris is a color version of the popular xhextris game, which is a Tetris-like game that uses hexagon shapes instead of square shapes. CXHextris runs within the X Window System. Install cxhextris if you enjoy playing Tetris or Tetris-like games and you'd like to play one on your system. You'll need to have X installed in order to play CXHextris.

fortune-mod — (Version 1.0, 2,342K)
Fortune-mod contains the ever-popular fortune program. Want a little bit of random wisdom revealed to you when you log in? Fortune's your program. Fun-loving system administrators can add fortune to users' .login files, so that the users get their dose of wisdom each time they log in. Install fortune if you want a program which will bestow these random bits o' wit.

gnome-games — (Version 1.0.2, 3,356K)
[W] GNOME is the GNU Network Object Model Environment. That's a fancy name, but really GNOME is a nice GUI desktop environment. Its powerful, friendly and easy-to-configure interface makes using your computer easy. This package installs some GNOME games on your system, such as gnothello, solitaire, tetris and others.

gnuchess — (Version 4.0.pl79, 1,428K)
The gnuchess package contains the GNU chess program. By default, GNUchess uses a curses text-based interface. Alternatively, GNUchess can be used in conjunction with the xboard user interface and the X Window System for a graphical chessboard. You should install the gnuchess package if you would like to play chess on your computer. You'll also need to install the curses package.

If you'd like to use a graphical interface with GNUchess, you'll also need to install the xboard package and the X Window System.

kdegames – (Version 1.1, 5,289K)
Games for the K Desktop Environment. Included with this package are: kabalone, kasteroids, kblackbox, kmahjongg, kmines, konquest, kpat, kpoker, kreversi, ksame, kshisen, ksokoban, ksmiletris, ksnake, ksirtet.

trojka – (Version 1.1, 16K)
The game of Trojka involves a set of falling blocks. The point is to move the blocks around as they fall, so that three of the same blocks end up next to each other, either horizontally or diagonally. Once the blocks fill up the entire game area, the game is over. Install the trojka package if you want to play a non-X game of falling blocks.

xbill – (Version 2.0, 183K)
The xbill game tests your reflexes as you seek out and destroy all forms of Bill, establish new operating systems and boldly go where no geek has gone before. Xbill has become an increasingly attractive option as the Linux Age progresses, and it is very popular at Red Hat.

xboard – (Version 4.0.0, 601K)
Xboard is an X Window System based graphical chessboard which can be used with the GNUchess and Crafty chess programs, with Internet Chess Servers (ICSs), with chess via email, or with your own saved games. Install the xboard package if you need a graphical chessboard.

xboing – (Version 2.4, 1,043K)
Xboing is an X Window System based game like the Breakout arcade game. The object of the game is to keep a ball bouncing on the bricks until you've broken through all of them.

xgammon – (Version 0.98, 3,282K)
Xgammon is an X Window System based backgammon game. Xgammon allows you to play against the computer, or you can play against another person. Xgammon also supports playing a game against another person on a remote X terminal, and will display a second board there for their use.

xjewel – (Version 1.6, 52K)
Xjewel is an X Window System game much like Domain/Jewelbox, Sega's Columns and/or Tetris. The point of the game is to move or rotate the blocks as they fall, to get jewels in patterns of three when they come to rest.

xpat2 — (Version 1.04, 456K)

Xpat2 is a generic patience or Solitaire game for the X Window System. Xpat2 can be used with different rules sets, so it can be used to play Spider, Klondike, and other card games.

xpilot — (Version 3.6.2, 1,617K)

Xpilot is an X Window System based multiplayer game of aerial combat. The object of the game is to shoot each other down, or you can use the race mode to just fly around. Xpilot resembles the Commodore 64 Thrust game, which is similar to Atari's Gravitar and Asteriods (note: this is not misspelled). Unless you already have an xpilot server on your network, you'll need to set up the server on one machine, and then set up xpilot clients on all of the players' machines.

xpuzzles — (Version 5.4.1, 469K)

A set of geometric puzzles and toys for the X Window System. Xpuzzles includes a version of Rubik's cube and various other geometric Rubik's cube style puzzles.

xtrojka — (Version 1.2.3, 216K)

The xtrojka game is an X Window System game of falling blocks, like Xjewel or Tetris.

Graphics

This section lists packages that provide graphics that are fun to look at.

mxp — (Version 1.0, 55K)

The mxp (Mandelbrot explorer) program is an X Window System application for computing and exploring Mandelbrot sets. Mxp supports zoom/un-zoom, dynamic resizing of drawing windows, setup save/load, asynchronous image generation, GIF outputs, animation, nine color schemes, color rotation, color change options, and detailed statistics. Install the mxp package if you need a Mandelbrot set generator for the X Window System.

xbanner — (Version 1.31, 505K)

[W] [S]

The XBanner program allows the display of text, patterns and images in the root window, so users can customize the XDM style login screen and/or the normal X background. Install XBanner if you'd like to change the look of your X login screen and/or X background.

xdaliclock – (Version 2.14, 80K)

The xdaliclock program displays a digital clock, with digits that merge into the new digits as the time changes. Xdaliclock can display the time in 12 or 24 hour modes and will display the date if you hold your mouse button down over it. Xdaliclock has two large fonts built in, but is capable of animating other fonts. Install the xdaliclock package if you want a fairly large clock, with a melting special effect, for your system.

xearth – (Version 1.0, 192K)

Xearth is an X Window System based graphic that shows a globe of the Earth, including markers for major cities and Red Hat Software. The Earth is correctly shaded for the current position of the sun, and the displayed image is updated every five minutes.

xfishtank – (Version 2.0, 388K)

The xfishtank program displays an animated aquarium background on your screen. Xfishtank works with the X Window System.

xloadimage – (Version 4.1, 255K)

The xloadimage utility displays images in an X Window System window, loads images into the root window, or writes images into a file. Xloadimage supports many images types (GIF, TIFF, JPEG, XPM, XBM, etc.). Install the xloadimage package if you need a utility for displaying images or loading images into the root window.

xlockmore – (Version 4.13, 759K)

The xlockmore utility is an enhanced version of the standard xlock program, which allows you to lock an X session so that other users can't access it. Xlockmore runs a provided screensaver until you type in your password. Install the xlockmore package if you need a locking program to secure X sessions.

xmorph – (Version 1996.07.12, 127K)

[W]

Xmorph is a digital image warping (aka morphing) program. Xmorph provides the tools needed and comprehensible instructions for you to create morphs: changing one image into another. Xmorph runs under the X Window System. Install the xmorph package if you need a program that will create morphed images.

xscreensaver — (Version 3.08, 3,172K)
[W]

The xscreensaver package contains a variety of screensavers for your mind-numbing, ambition-eroding, time-wasting, hypnotized viewing pleasure. Install the xscreensaver package if you need screensavers for use with the X Window System.

xwpick — (Version 2.20, 50K)
The xwpick program allows you to choose an image or a rectangular piece of an image from an X Window System window and then write the image to a file in a variety of formats, incuding PostScript(TM), GIF, and PICT. Install the xwpick program if you need to take screenshots from X Window System screens and write them to files.

Applications

This section contains packages that contain various applications for Red Hat Linux.

Archiving

This section contains packages that are associated with the efficient storing and/or copying of files.

cpio — (Version 2.4.2, 70K)
[B]

GNU cpio copies files into or out of a cpio or tar archive. Archives are files which contain a collection of other files plus information about them, such as their file name, owner, timestamps, and access permissions. The archive can be another file on the disk, a magnetic tape, or a pipe. GNU cpio supports the following archive formats: binary, old ASCII, new ASCII, crc, HPUX binary, HPUX old ASCII, old tar and POSIX.1 tar. By default, cpio creates binary format archives, so that they are compatible with older cpio programs. When it is extracting files from archives, cpio automatically recognizes which kind of archive it is reading and can read archives created on machines with a different byte-order. Install cpio if you need a program to manage file archives.

dump — (Version 0.4b4, 153K)
The dump package contains both dump and restore. Dump examines files in a filesystem, determines which ones need to be backed up, and copies those files to a specified disk, tape or other storage medium. The restore command performs the inverse function of dump; it can restore a full backup of a filesystem.

Subsequent incremental backups can then be layered on top of the full backup. Single files and directory subtrees may also be restored from full or partial backups. Install dump if you need a system for both backing up filesystems and restoring filesystems after backups.

lha – (Version 1.00, 56K)
[W]

LHA is an archiving and compression utility for LHarc format archives. LHA is mostly used in the DOS world, but can be used under Linux to extract DOS files from LHA archives. Install the lha package if you need to extract DOS files from LHA archives.

ncompress – (Version 4.2.4, 31K)
[B]

The ncompress package contains the compress and uncompress file compression and decompression utilities, which are compatible with the original UNIX compress utility (.Z file extensions). These utilities can't handle gzipped (.gz file extensions) files, but gzip can handle compressed files.

rmt – (Version 0.4b4, 12K)
[B]

The rmt utility provides remote access to tape devices for programs like dump (a filesystem backup program), restore (a program for restoring files from a backup) and tar (an archiving program).

sharutils – (Version 4.2, 221K)
[W] [S]

The sharutils package contains the GNU shar utilities, a set of tools for encoding and decoding packages of files (in binary or text format) in a special plain text format called shell archives (shar). This format can be sent through email (which can be problematic for regular binary files). The shar utility supports a wide range of capabilities (compressing, uuencoding, splitting long files for multi-part mailings, providing checksums), which make it very flexible at creating shar files. After the files have been sent, the unshar tool scans mail messages looking for shar files. Unshar automatically strips off mail headers and introductory text and then unpacks the shar files. Install sharutils if you send binary files through email very often.

taper – (Version 6.9, 847K)
Taper is a backup and restoration program with a user friendly interface. Files may be backed up to a tape drive or to a hard disk. The interface for selecting files to be backed up/restored is very similar to the Midnight Commander interface,

and allows easy traversal of directories. Taper supports recursive selection of directories. Taper also supports backing up SCSI, ftape, zftape and removable drives. By default, taper is set for incremental backups and automatic most recent restore. Install the taper package if you need a user friendly file backup and restoration program.

tar — (Version 1.12, 474K)
[B]

The GNU tar program saves many files together into one archive and can restore individual files (or all of the files) from the archive. Tar can also be used to add supplemental files to an archive and to update or list files in the archive. Tar includes multivolume support, automatic archive compression/ decompression, the ability to perform remote archives and the ability to perform incremental and full backups. If you want to use Tar for remote backups, you'll also need to install the rmt package. You should install the tar package, because you'll find its compression and decompression utilities essential for working with files.

unarj — (Version 2.41a, 26K)
The UNARJ program is used to uncompress .arj format archives. The .arj format archive was mostly used on DOS machines. Install the unarj package if you need to uncompress .arj format archives.

unzip — (Version 5.31, 370K)
[W]

The unzip utility is used to list, test, or extract files from a zip archive. Zip archives are commonly found on MS-DOS systems. The zip utility, included in the zip package, creates zip archives. Zip and unzip are both compatible with archives created by PKWARE(R)'s PKZIP for MS-DOS, but the programs' options and default behaviors do differ in some respects. Install the unzip package if you need to list, test or extract files from a zip archive.

zip — (Version 2.1, 217K)
[W]

The zip program is a compression and file packaging utility. Zip is analogous to a combination of the UNIX tar and compress commands and is compatible with PKZIP (a compression and file packaging utility for MS-DOS systems). Install the zip package if you need to compress files using the zip program.

Communications

This section contains packages that are associated with communications.

dip – (Version 3.3.7o, 88K)
[W] [S]

Dip is a modem dialer. Dip handles the connections needed for dialup IP links like SLIP or PPP. Dip can handle both incoming and outgoing connections, using password security for incoming connections. Dip is useful for setting up PPP and SLIP connections, but isn't required for either. Netcfg uses dip for setting up SLIP connections. Install dip if you need a utility which will handle dialup IP connections.

efax – (Version 0.8a, 205K)
Efax is a small ANSI C/POSIX program that sends and receives faxes using any Class 1, 2 or 2.0 fax modem. You need to install efax if you want to send faxes and you have a Class 1, 2 or 2.0 fax modem.

getty_ps – (Version 2.0.7j, 127K)
[B]

The getty_ps package contains the getty and uugetty programs, basic programs for accomplishing the login process on a Red Hat Linux system. Getty and uugetty are used to accept logins on the console or a terminal. Getty is invoked by the init process to open tty lines and set their modes, to print the login prompt and get the user's name, and to initiate a login process for the user. Uugetty works just like getty, except that uugetty creates and uses lock files to prevent two or more processes from conflicting in their use of a tty line. Getty and uugetty can also handle answer a modem for dialup connections, but mgetty is recommended for that purpose.

kpilot – (Version 3.1b8, 876K)
KPilot allows you to synchronize your PalmPilot with your desktop. It allows you to backup and restore the various databases (Addressbook, ToDo List, Memos, etc.) as well as install applications to the pilot. Two "conduits" for the third party application KOrganizer are included which will let you sync your ToDo list and Calendar with that program.

lrzsz — (Version 0.12.20, 391K)
[W] [S]

Lrzsz (consisting of lrz and lsz) is a cosmetically modified zmodem/ymodem/xmodem package built from the public-domain version of the rzsz package. Lrzsz was created to provide a working GNU copylefted Zmodem solution for Linux systems. You should install lrzsz if you're also installing a Zmodem communications program that uses lrzsz. If you're installing minicom, you need to install lrzsz.

mgetty-sendfax — (Version 1.1.14, 272K)
Sendfax is a standalone backend program for sending fax files. The mgetty program (a getty replacement for handling logins over a serial line) plus sendfax will allow you to send faxes through a Class 2 modem. If you'd like to send faxes over a Class 2 modem, you'll need to install the mgetty-sendfax and the mgetty packages.

mgetty-viewfax — (Version 1.1.14, 94K)
Viewfax displays the fax files received using mgetty in an X11 window. Viewfax is capable of zooming in and out on the displayed fax. If you're installing the mgetty-viewfax package, you'll also need to install mgetty.

mgetty-voice — (Version 1.1.14, 651K)
The mgetty-voice package contains the vgetty system, which enables mgetty and your modem to support voice capabilities. In simple terms, vgetty lets your modem act as an answering machine. How well the system will work depends upon your modem, which may or may not be able to handle this kind of implementation. Install mgetty-voice along with mgetty if you'd like to try having your modem act as an answering machine.

minicom — (Version 1.82, 302K)
[W] [S]

Minicom is a simple text-based modem control and terminal emulation program somewhat similar to MSDOS Telix. Minicom includes a dialing directory, full ANSI and VT100 emulation, an (external) scripting language, and other features. Minicom should be installed if you need a simple modem control program or terminal emulator.

pilot-link — (Version 0.9.0, 2,222K)
This suite of tools allows you to upload and download programs and data files between a *nix machine and the USR Pilot. It has a few extra utils that will allow for things like syncing the Pilot's calendar app with Ical. Note that you might still need to consult the sources for pilot-link if you would like the Python, Tcl, or Perl bindings.

sliplogin – (Version 2.1.1, 54K)

The sliplogin utility turns the terminal line on standard input into a SLIP (Serial Line Internet Protocol) link to a remote host. Sliplogin is usually used to allow dial-in SLIP connections. Install the sliplogin package if you need to support dial-in SLIP connections.

uucp – (Version 1.06.1, 2,079K)

[W] [S]

The uucp command copies files between systems. Uucp is primarily used by remote machines downloading and uploading email and news files to local machines. Install the uucp package if you need to use uucp to transfer files between machines.

Databases

This section contains packages that are associated with databases.

postgresql – (Version 6.4.2, 6,918K)

[S]

Postgresql includes the programs needed to create and run a PostgreSQL server, which will in turn allow you to create and maintain PostgreSQL databases. PostgreSQL is an advanced Object-Relational database management system (DBMS) that supports almost all SQL constructs (including transactions, subselects and user-defined types and functions). You should install postgresql if you want to create and maintain your own PostgreSQL databases and/or your own PostgreSQL server. If you are installing postgresql, you should also install postgresql-data, which will help you get started with PostgreSQL.

postgresql-clients – (Version 6.4.2, 917K)

[S]

Postgresql-clients includes the client programs and client libraries that you'll need to access a PostgreSQL database management system server. This package contains the client libraries for C, C++ and PERL, as well as command-line utilities for managing PostgreSQL databases on a remote server. If you just want to connect to an existing remote PostgreSQL server, this package is all you need. You should install postgresql-clients if you're installing postgresql. You should also install postgresql-clients if you're not installing postgresql, but you want to access PostgreSQL databases on a remote PostgreSQL server.

Editors

This section contains packages that are associated with editing text files.

GXedit — (Version 1.23, 570K)

Here is a fast, easy-to-use editor which is both network- oriented and very secure. GXedit is a graphical text editor which features a toolbar, network bar and tooltips, spell checking, inline help, the ability to send text as e-mail, macros and more. GXedit was designed to balance these and many other features without becoming too bloated. You'll need GTK+ to use GXedit.

emacs — (Version 20.3, 17,340K)

[W] [S]

Emacs is a powerful, customizable, self-documenting, modeless text editor. Emacs contains special code editing features, a scripting language (elisp), and the capability to read mail, news and more without leaving the editor. This package includes the libraries you need to run the Emacs editor, so you need to install this package if you intend to use Emacs. You also need to install the actual Emacs program package (emacs-nox or emacs-X11). Install emacs-nox if you are not going to use the X Window System; install emacs-X11 if you will be using X.

emacs-X11 — (Version 20.3, 5,782K)

[W]

Emacs-X11 includes the Emacs text editor program for use with the X Window System (it provides support for the mouse and other GUI elements). Emacs-X11 will also run Emacs outside of X, but it has a larger memory footprint than the 'non-X' Emacs package (emacs-nox). Install emacs-X11 if you're going to use Emacs with the X Window System. You should also install emacs-X11 if you're going to run Emacs both with and without X (it will work fine both ways). You'll also need to install the emacs package in order to run Emacs.

emacs-el — (Version 20.3, 21,631K)

Emacs-el contains the emacs-elisp sources for many of the elisp programs included with the main Emacs text editor package. You need to install emacs-el only if you intend to modify any of the Emacs packages or see some elisp examples.

emacs-leim — (Version 20.3, 4,216K)

The Emacs Lisp code for input methods for various international character scripts.

emacs-nox — (Version 20.3, 2,434K)
[W] [S]

Emacs-nox is the Emacs text editor program without support for the X Window System. You need to install this package only if you plan on exclusively using Emacs without the X Window System (emacs-X11 will work both in X and out of X, but emacs-nox will only work outside of X). You'll also need to install the emacs package in order to run Emacs.

gedit — (Version 0.5.1, 340K)
[W]

gEdit is a small but powerful text editor designed expressly for GNOME. It includes such features as split-screen mode, a plugin API, which allows gEdit to be extended to support many features while remaining small at its core, multiple document editing through the use of a 'tabbed' notebook and many more functions. GNOME is required to use gEdit (Gnome-Libs and Gtk+).

gnotepad+ — (Version 1.1.3, 189K)
[W]

gnotepad+ is an easy-to-use, yet fairly feature-rich, simple text editor for systems running X11 and using GTK+. It is designed for as little bloat as possible, while still providing many of the common features found in a modern GUI-based text editor.

jed — (Version 0.98.7, 140K)
Jed is a fast, compact editor based on the slang screen library. Jed features include emulation of the Emacs, EDT, WordStar and Brief editors; support for extensive customization with slang macros, colors, keybindings, etc.; and a variety of programming modes with syntax highlighting. You should install jed if you've used it before and you like it, or if you haven't used any text editors before and you're still deciding what you'd like to use. You'll also need to have slang installed.

jed-common — (Version 0.98.7, 1,502K)
The jed-common package contains files (such as .sl files) that are needed by any jed binary in order to run.

jed-xjed — (Version 0.98.7, 166K)
Xjed is a version of the Jed text editor that will work with the X Window System. You should install xjed if you like Jed and you'd like to use it with X. You'll also need to have the X Window System installed.

joe — (Version 2.8, 282K)

Joe is an easy to use, modeless text editor which would be very appropriate for novices. Joe uses the same WordStar keybindings used in Borland's development environment You should install joe if you've used it before and you liked it, or if you're still deciding what text editor you'd like to use, or if you have a fondness for WordStar. If you're just starting out, you should probably install joe because it is very easy to use.

vim-X11 — (Version 5.3, 1,395K)

VIM (VIsual editor iMproved) is an updated and improved version of the vi editor. Vi was the first real screen-based editor for UNIX, and is still very popular. VIM improves on vi by adding new features: multiple windows, multi-level undo, block highlighting and more. VIM-X11 is a version of the VIM editor which will run within the X Window System. If you install this package, you can run VIM as an X application with a full GUI interface and mouse support. Install the vim-X11 package if you'd like to try out a version of vi with graphics and mouse capabilities. You'll also need to install the vim-common package.

vim-common — (Version 5.3, 4,355K)

[B]

VIM (VIsual editor iMproved) is an updated and improved version of the vi editor. Vi was the first real screen-based editor for UNIX, and is still very popular. VIM improves on vi by adding new features: multiple windows, multi-level undo, block highlighting and more. The vim-common package contains files which every VIM binary will need in order to run. If you are installing any version of the VIM editor, you'll also need to the vim-common package installed.

vim-enhanced — (Version 5.3, 1,297K)

VIM (VIsual editor iMproved) is an updated and improved version of the vi editor. Vi was the first real screen-based editor for UNIX, and is still very popular. VIM improves on vi by adding new features: multiple windows, multi-level undo, block highlighting and more. The vim-enhanced package contains a version of VIM with extra, recently introduced features like Python and Perl interpreters. Install the vim-enhanced package if you'd like to use a version of the VIM editor which includes recently added enhancements like interpreters for the Python and Perl scripting languages. You'll also need to install the vim-common package.

vim-minimal — (Version 5.3, 445K)
[B]

VIM (VIsual editor iMproved) is an updated and improved version of the vi editor. Vi was the first real screen-based editor for UNIX, and is still very popular. VIM improves on vi by adding new features: multiple windows, multi-level undo, block highlighting and more. The vim-minimal package includes a minimal version of VIM, which is installed into /bin/vi for use when only the root partition is present.

Emulators

This section contains packages associated with the emulation of other operating systems.

dosemu — (Version 0.99.10, 1,812K)
[W]

Dosemu is a DOS emulator. Once you've installed dosemu, start the DOS emulator by typing in the dos command. You need to install dosemu if you use DOS programs and you want to be able to run them on your Red Hat Linux system. You may also need to install the dosemu-freedos package.

dosemu-freedos — (Version 0.99.10, 8,194K)
Generally, the dosemu DOS emulator requires either that your system have some version of DOS available or that your system's partitions were formatted and installed with DOS. If your system does not meet either of the previous requirements, you can instead use the dosemu-freedos package, which contains an hdimage file which will be installed in the `/var/lib/dosemu` directory. The hdimage file is already bootable with FreeDOS. You will need to edit your `/etc/dosemu.conf` file to add the image to the list of disk 'drives' used by dosemu. Install dosemu-freedos if you are installing the dosemu package and you don't have a version of DOS available on your system, and your system's partitions were not formatted and installed with DOS.

xdosemu — (Version 0.99.10, 26K)
[W]

Xdosemu is a version of the dosemu DOS emulator that runs with the X Window System. Xdosemu provides VGA graphics and mouse support. Install xdosemu if you need to run DOS programs on your system, and you'd like to do so with the convenience of graphics support and mouse capabilities.

Engineering

This section contains packages that are associated with the engineering arts.

bc — (Version 1.05a, 128K)
[B]

The bc package includes bc and dc. Bc is an arbitrary precision numeric processing arithmetic language. Dc is an interactive arbitrary precision stack based calculator, which can be used as a text mode calculator. Install the bc package if you need its number handling capabilities or if you would like to use its text mode calculator.

gnuplot — (Version 3.7, 918K)
Gnuplot is a command-line driven, interactive function plotting program especially suited for scientific data representation. Gnuplot can be used to plot functions and data points in both two and three dimensions and in many different formats. Install gnuplot if you need a graphics package for scientific data representation.

units — (Version 1.0, 25K)
Units converts an amount from one unit to another, or tells you what mathematical operation you need to perform to convert from one unit to another. Units can only handle multiplicative scale changes (i.e., it can't tell you how to convert from Celsius to Fahrenheit, which requires an additive step in addition to the multiplicative conversion). Units is a handy little program which contains a large number of conversions, from au's to parsecs and tablespoons to cups. You probably don't need to install it, but it comes in handy sometimes.

xlispstat — (Version 3.52.9, 2,871K)
The xlispstat package contains XLISP-PLUS, an implementation of the Lisp programming language for the X Window System. XLISP-PLUS also includes extensions for performing advanced statistical computations. Install the xlispstat package if you need a version of the Lisp programming language for X with statistics extensions.

File

This section contains packages that are associated with file manipulation.

bzip2 – (Version 0.9.0b, 233K)

Bzip2 is a freely available, patent-free, high quality data compressor. Bzip2 compresses files to within 10 to 15 percent of the capabilities of the best techniques available. However, bzip2 has the added benefit of being approximately two times faster at compression and six times faster at decompression than those techniques. Bzip2 is not the fastest compression utility, but it does strike a balance between speed and compression capability. Install bzip2 if you need a high quality compression utility.

file – (Version 3.26, 206K)

[B]

The file command is used to identify a particular file according to the type of data contained by the file. File can identify many different file types, including ELF binaries, system libraries, RPM packages, and different graphics formats. You should install the file package, since the file command is such a useful utility.

fileutils – (Version 4.0, 1,283K)

[B]

The fileutils package includes a number of GNU versions of common and popular file management utilities. Fileutils includes the following tools: chgrp (changes a file's group ownership), chown (changes a file's ownership), chmod (changes a file's permissions), cp (copies files), dd (copies and converts files), df (shows a filesystem's disk usage), dir (gives a brief directory listing), dircolors (the setup program for the color version of the ls command), du (shows disk usage), install (copies files and sets permissions), ln (creates file links), ls (lists directory contents in color), mkdir (creates directories), mkfifo (creates FIFOs, which are named pipes), mknod (creates special files), mv (renames files), rm (removes/ deletes files), rmdir (removes empty directories), sync (synchronizes memory and disk), touch (changes file timestamps), and vdir (provides long directory listings). You should install the fileutils package, because it includes many file management utilities that you'll use frequently.

findutils – (Version 4.1, 118K)
[B]

The findutils package contains programs which will help you locate files on your system. The find utility searches through a hierarchy of directories looking for files which match a certain set of criteria (such as a filename pattern). The locate utility searches a database (create by updatedb) to quickly find a file matching a given pattern. The xargs utility builds and executes command lines from standard input arguments (usually lists of file names generated by the find command). You should install findutils because it includes tools that are very useful for finding things on your system.

git – (Version 4.3.17, 715K)
[W]

GIT (GNU Interactive Tools) provides an extensible file system browser, an ASCII/hexadecimal file viewer, a process viewer/killer and other related utilities and shell scripts. GIT can be used to increase the speed and efficiency of copying and moving files and directories, invoking editors, compressing and uncompressing files, creating and expanding archives, compiling programs, sending mail and more. GIT uses standard ANSI color sequences, if they are available. You should install the git package if you are interested in using its file management capabilities.

gzip – (Version 1.2.4, 242K)
[B]

The gzip package contains the popular GNU gzip data compression program. Gzipped files have a .gz extension. Gzip should be installed on your Red Hat Linux system, because it is a very commonly used data compression program.

slocate – (Version 1.4, 19K)
[B]

slocate searches through a central database (updated nightly) for files which match a given glob pattern. This allows you to quickly find files anywhere on your system.

stat – (Version 1.5, 6K)
[B]

The stat utility prints out filesystem level information about a specified file, including size, permissions, link count, inode, etc.

tree — (Version 1.2, 19K)

The tree utility recursively displays the contents of directories in a tree-like format. Tree is basically a UNIX port of the tree DOS utility. Install tree if you think it would be useful to view the contents of specified directories in a tree-like format.

Internet

This section contains packages that are associated with the Internet.

elm — (Version 2.5.0, 616K)

[W] [S]

Elm is a popular terminal mode email user agent. Elm includes all standard mailhandling features, including MIME support via metamail. Elm is still used by some people, but is no longer in development. If you've used Elm before and you're devoted to it, you should install the elm package. If you would like to use metamail's MIME support, you'll also need to install the metamail package.

exmh — (Version 2.0.2, 1,814K)

[W] [S]

Exmh provides an X interface for MH/nmh mail, a feature-rich email handling system. Exmh supports almost all (but not all) of MH's features: viewing the messages in a folder, reading/deleting/refiling messages, and sorting arriving mail into different folders before the messages are read. Exmh highlights which folders have new mail, and indicates which messages have not been read (so you don't lose the sorted, unread mail). If you like MH/nmh mail, you should install exmh, because it makes the MH/nmh mail system much more user friendly. You may also want to use exmh if you prefer a graphical user interface for your mail client. Note that you will also have to install the nmh package.

faces — (Version 1.6.1, 144K)

Faces is a program for visually monitoring a list (typically a list of incoming mail messages, a list of jobs in a print queue or a list of system users). Faces operates in five different modes: monitoring for new mail, monitoring an entire mail file, monitoring a specified print queue, monitoring users on a machine and custom monitoring. Faces also includes a utility for including a face image (a compressed, scanned image) with mail messages. The image has to be compressed in a certain way, which can then be uncompressed and displayed on-the-fly in the mail program. This feature of faces is typically used with the exmh mail handling system. Install faces if you'd like to use its list monitoring capability or its face image inclusion capability. If you would like to include face images in email, you'll also need to install the faces-xface package. If you would like to develop xface applications, you'll need to also install faces-devel.

faces-xface — (Version 1.6.1, 21K)

Faces-xface includes the utilities that mail user agent programs need to handle X-Face mail headers. When an email program reads the X-face header line in an email message, it calls these utilities to display the face image included in the message. You'll need to install faces-xface if you want your mail program to display Faces' X-face images.

fetchmail — (Version 4.7.0, 538K)

[W] [S]

Fetchmail is a remote mail retrieval and forwarding utility intended for use over on-demand TCP/IP links, like SLIP or PPP connections. Fetchmail supports every remote-mail protocol currently in use on the Internet (POP2, POP3, RPOP, APOP, KPOP, all IMAPs, ESMTP ETRN) for retrieval. Then Fetchmail forwards the mail through SMTP, so you can read it through your normal mail client. Install fetchmail if you need to retrieve mail over SLIP or PPP connections.

fetchmailconf — (Version 4.7.0, 55K)

Fetchmailconf is a tcl/tk application for graphically configuring your .fetchmailrc preferences file. Fetchmail has many options which can be daunting to the new user. This utility takes some of the guesswork and hassle out of setting up fetchmail.

finger — (Version 0.10, 32K)

[W] [S]

Finger is a utility which allows users to see information about system users (login name, home directory, name, how long they've been logged in to the system, etc.). The finger package includes a standard finger client and server. The server daemon (fingerd) runs from `/etc/inetd.conf`, which must be modified to disable finger requests. You should install finger if your system is used by multiple users and you'd like finger information to be available.

ftp — (Version 0.10, 89K)

[W] [S

The ftp package provides the standard UNIX command-line FTP client. FTP is the file transfer protocol, which is a widely used Internet protocol for transferring files and for archiving files. If your system is on a network, you should install ftp in order to do file transfers.

fwhois – (Version 1.00, 8K)
[W] [S]

The fwhois program is a different style of the whois program. Both fwhois and whois query Internet whois databases to find information about system users. Fwhois is smaller and more compact than whois, and runs in a different manner. Install fwhois if you or your system's users need a program for querying whois databases. You may also want to install whois, and then decide for yourself which program you prefer.

gftp – (Version 1.13, 553K)
[W]

gFTP is a multithreaded FTP client for X Windows written using Gtk. It allows simultaneous downloads, resumtion of interrupted file transfers, file transfer queues, has a very nice connection manager and many more features.

ircii – (Version 4.4, 997K)
IrcII is a popular Internet Relay Chat (IRC) client. IRC clients communicate with IRC servers, enabling users to "chat" via the Internet. Install ircii if you want to participate in chat rooms.

kdenetwork – (Version 1.1, 7,317K)
Network applications for the K Desktop Environment. Includes: karchie (ftp archive searcher); kbiff (mail delivery notification) kfinger ("finger" utility); kmail (mail client); knu (network utilities); korn (mailbox monitor tool); kppp (easy PPP connection configuration); krn (news reader); ktalkd (talk daemon); ksirc (irc client).

kppload – (Version 1.04, 88K)
Monitors the load on your PPP connection. Looks a lot like xload.

lynx – (Version 2.8.1, 2,011K)
[W] [S]

Lynx is a text-based Web browser. Lynx does not display any images, but it does support frames, tables and most other HTML tags. Lynx's advantage over graphical browsers is its speed: Lynx starts and exits quickly and swiftly displays Web pages. Install lynx if you would like to try this fast, non-graphical browser (you may come to appreciate its strengths).

mailx — (Version 8.1.1, 89K)
[B]

The mailx package installs the /bin/mail program, which is used to send quick email messages (i.e., without opening up a full-featured mail user agent). Mail is often used in shell scripts. You should install mailx because of its quick email sending ability, which is especially useful if you're planning on writing any shell scripts.

metamail — (Version 2.7, 341K)
[W] [S]

Metamail is a system for handling multimedia mail, using the mailcap file. Metamail reads the mailcap file, which tells Metamail what helper program to call in order to handle a particular type of non-text mail. Note that metamail can also add multimedia support to certain non-mail programs. Metamail should be installed if you need to add multimedia support to mail programs and some other programs, using the mailcap file.

mutt — (Version 0.95.4us, 1,369K)
[W] [S]

Mutt is a text mode mail user agent. Mutt supports color, threading, arbitrary key remapping, and a lot of customization. You should install mutt if you've used mutt in the past and you prefer it, or if you're new to mail programs and you haven't decided which one you're going to use.

nc — (Version 1.10, 105K)
The nc package contains Netcat (the program is actually nc), a simple utility for reading and writing data across network connections, using the TCP or UDP protocols. Netcat is intended to be a reliable back-end tool which can be used directly or easily driven by other programs and scripts. Netcat is also a feature-rich network debugging and exploration tool, since it can create many different connections and has many built-in capabilities. You may want to install the netcat package if you are administering a network and you'd like to use its debugging and network exploration capabilities.

ncftp — (Version 3.0beta18, 725K)
[W] [S]

Ncftp is an improved FTP client. Ncftp's improvements include support for command line editing, command histories, recursive gets, automatic anonymous logins and more. Install ncftp if you use FTP to transfer files and you'd like to try some of ncftp's additional features.

netscape-common – (Version 4.51, 7,128K)
[W] [S]

This package contains the files that are shared between the Netscape Navigator Web browser and the Netscape Communicator suite of tools (the Navigator Web browser, an e-mail client, a news reader and Web page editor). Install the netscape-common package if you're installing the netscape-navigator and/or the netscape-communicator program.

netscape-communicator – (Version 4.51, 13,522K)
[W] [S]

Netscape Communicator is the industry-leading Web browser. It supports the latest HTML standards, Java, JavaScript and some style sheets. It also includes a full-featured Usenet news reader as well as a complete e-mail client. Information on the Netscape Communicator license may be found in the file `/usr/doc/netscape-common-4.51/LICENSE`

netscape-navigator – (Version 4.51, 7,242K)
Netscape Navigator is the industry-leading Web browser. It supports the latest HTML standards, Java, JavaScript and some style sheets. Information on the Netscape Navigator license may be found in the file `/usr/doc/netscape-common-4.51/LICENSE`. This will install the basic Netscape Navigator Web browser. If you want additional features, such as the Usenet news reader and HTML editor, you should install the netscape-communicator package.

nmh – (Version 0.27, 4,646K)
[W] [S]

Nmh is an email system based on the MH email system and is intended to be a (mostly) compatible drop-in replacement for MH. Nmh isn't a single comprehensive program. Instead, it consists of a number of fairly simple single-purpose programs for sending, receiving, saving, retrieving and otherwise manipulating email messages. You can freely intersperse nmh commands with other shell commands or write custom scripts which utilize nmh commands. If you want to use nmh as a true email user agent, you'll want to also install exmh to provide a user interface for it—nmh only has a command line interface. If you'd like to use nmh commands in shell scripts, or if you'd like to use nmh and exmh together as your email user agent, you should install nmh.

pine – (Version 4.10, 3,427K)
[W] [S]

Pine is a very popular, easy to use, full-featured email user agent which includes a simple text editor called pico. Pine supports MIME extensions and can also be used to read news. Pine also supports IMAP, mail and MH style folders. Pine should be installed because Pine is a very commonly used email user agent and it is currently in development.

rsh — (Version 0.10, 127K)
[W] [S]

The rsh package contains a set of programs which allow users to run commands on remote machines, login to other machines and copy files between machines (rsh, rlogin and rcp). All three of these commands use rhosts style authentication. This package contains the clients and servers needed for all of these services. It also contains a server for rexec, an alternate method of executing remote commands. All of these servers are run by inetd and configured using `/etc/inetd.conf` and PAM. The rexecd server is disabled by default, but the other servers are enabled. The rsh package should be installed to enable remote access to other machines.

rsync — (Version 2.3.0, 223K)
Rsync uses a quick and reliable algorithm to very quickly bring remote and host files into sync. Rsync is fast because it just sends the differences in the files over the network (instead of sending the complete files). Rsync is often used as a very powerful mirroring process or just as a more capable replacement for the rcp command. A technical report which describes the rsync algorithm is included in this package. Install rsync if you need a powerful mirroring program.

slrn — (Version 0.9.5.4, 425K)
[W] [S]

SLRN is a powerful, easy to use, threaded Internet news reader. SLRN is highly customizable and allows you to design complex filters to sort or kill news articles. SLRN works well over slow network connections, and includes a utility for reading news off-line. Install slrn if you need a full-featured news reader, if you have a slow network connection, or if you'd like to save on-line time by reading your news off-line.

slrn-pull — (Version 0.9.5.4, 66K)
This package provides slrnpull, which allows set up of a small news spool for offline news reading.

talk — (Version 0.10, 33K)
[W] [S]

The ntalk package provides client and daemon programs for the Internet talk protocol, which allows you to chat with other users on different systems. Talk is a communication program which copies lines from one terminal to the terminal of another user. Install ntalk if you'd like to use talk for chatting with users on different systems.

tcpdump – (Version 3.4, 214K)
[W] [S]

Tcpdump is a command-line tool for monitoring network traffic. Tcpdump can capture and display the packet headers on a particular network interface or on all interfaces. Tcpdump can display all of the packet headers, or just the ones that match particular criteria. Install tcpdump if you need a program to monitor network traffic.

telnet – (Version 0.10, 180K)
[W] [S]

Telnet is a popular protocol for logging into remote systems over the Internet. The telnet package provides a command line telnet client as well as a telnet daemon, which will support remote logins into the host machine. The telnet daemon is enabled by default. You may disable the telnet daemon by editing `/etc/inetd.conf`. Install the telnet package if you want to telnet to remote machines and/or support remote logins to your own machine.

tin – (Version 1.4_990216, 1,193K)
[W] [S]

Tin is a basic, easy to use Internet news reader. Tin can read news locally or remotely via an NNTP (Network News Transport Protocol) server. Install tin if you need a basic news reader.

traceroute – (Version 1.4a5, 27K)
[W] [S]

The traceroute utility displays the route used by IP packets on their way to a specified network (or Internet) host. Traceroute displays the IP number and host name (if possible) of the machines along the route taken by the packets. Traceroute is used as a network debugging tool. If you're having network connectivity problems, traceroute will show you where the trouble is coming from along the route. Install traceroute if you need a tool for diagnosing network connectivity problems.

trn – (Version 3.6, 446K)
[W] [S]

Trn is a basic news reader that supports threading. This version is configured to read news from an NNTP news server. Install trn if you need a basic news reader that shows you newsgroup postings in threaded format.

urlview – (Version 0.7, 37K)
urlview extracts URLs from a given text file, and presents a menu of URLs to view using a user specified command.

wget – (Version 1.5.3, 335K)
GNU Wget is a file retrieval utility which can use either the HTTP or FTP protocols. Wget features include the ability to work in the background while you're logged out, recursive retrieval of directories, file name wildcard matching, remote file timestamp storage and comparison, use of Rest with FTP servers and Range with HTTP servers to retrieve files over slow or unstable connections, support for Proxy servers, and configurability. Install wget if you need to retrieve large numbers of files with HTTP or FTP, or if you need a utility for mirroring web sites or FTP directories.

xchat – (Version 0.9.4, 205K)
[W]

X-Chat is yet another IRC client for the X Window System, using the Gtk+ toolkit. It is pretty easy to use compared to the other Gtk+ IRC clients and the interface is quite nicely designed.

xmailbox – (Version 2.5, 33K)
[W] [S]

The xmailbox program is an X Window System program which notifies you when mail arrives. Xmailbox is similar to the xbiff program, but it offers more features and notification options. Install the xmailbox package if you'd like a graphical program for X which will notify you when new mail arrives.

xrn – (Version 9.01, 253K)
[W] [S]

A simple Usenet News reader for the X Window System. Xrn allows you to point and click your way through reading, replying and posting news messages. Install the xrn package if you need a simple news reader for X.

ytalk – (Version 3.1, 68K)
The YTalk program is essentially a chat program for multiple users. YTalk works just like the UNIX talk program and even communicates with the same talk daemon(s), but YTalk allows for multiple connections (unlike UNIX talk). YTalk also supports redirection of program output to other users as well as an easy-to-use menu of commands. Install the ytalk package if you need a chat program for multiple users.

Multimedia

This section contains packages that are associated with multimedia.

ImageMagick – (Version 4.2.2, 3,150K)
[W] [S]

ImageMagick is a powerful image display, conversion and manipulation tool. It runs in an X session. With this tool, you can view, edit and display a variety of image formats. This package installs the necessary files to run ImageMagick.

aktion – (Version 0.3.3, 314K)
Movie player for the K Desktop Environment. Requires 'xanim' to function.

aumix – (Version 1.18.2, 65K)
[W]

Aumix is a tty based, interactive method of controlling a sound card mixer. It lets you adjust the input levels from the CD, microphone, and onboard synthesizers, as well as the output volume. Aumix can adjust audio mixers from the command line, from a script, or interactively at the console or terminal with a full-screen ncurses-based interface. Install aumix if you need to control an audio mixer. If you install aumix, you will also need to install ncurses (since aumix's interface is based on ncurses) and gpm (for mouse support).

awesfx – (Version 0.4.3a, 299K)
[W]

The awesfx package contains necessary utilities for the AWE32 sound driver. If you must use an AWE32 sound driver, you should install this package.

cdp – (Version 0.33, 39K)
[W]

The cdp program plays audio CDs in your computer's CD-ROM drive. Cdp includes a full-screen interface version and a command line version. Install cdp to play audio CDs on your system.

desktop-backgrounds – (Version 1.0.0, 5,451K)
[W]

If you use a desktop environment like GNOME you can use these images to spruce up your background.

ee – (Version 0.3.8, 450K)
[W]

The ee package contains the Electric Eyes image viewer for the GNOME desktop environment. Electric Eyes is primarily an image viewer, but it also allows many types of image manipulations. Electric Eyes can handle almost any type of image. Install the ee package if you need an image viewer.

giftrans – (Version 1.12.2, 22K)
Giftrans will convert an existing GIF87 file to GIF89 format. In other words, Giftrans can make one color in a .gif image (normally the background) transparent. Install the giftrans package if you need a quick, small, one-purpose graphics program to make transparent .gifs out of existing .gifs.

gimp – (Version 1.0.4, 8,060K)
[W]

The GIMP is an image manipulation program suitable for photo retouching, image composition and image authoring. Many people find it extremely useful in creating logos and other graphics for web pages. The GIMP has many of the tools and filters you would expect to find in similar commercial offerings, and some interesting extras as well. The GIMP provides a large image manipulation toolbox, including channel operations and layers, effects, sub-pixel imaging and anti-aliasing, and conversions, all with multi-level undo. This version of The GIMP includes a scripting facility, but many of the included scripts rely on fonts that we cannot distribute. The GIMP ftp site has a package of fonts that you can install by yourself, which includes all the fonts needed to run the included scripts. Some of the fonts have unusual licensing requirements; all the licenses are documented in the package. Get ftp://ftp.gimp.org/pub/gimp/fonts/freefonts-0.10.tar.gz and ftp://ftp.gimp.org/pub/gimp/fonts/sharefonts-0.10.tar.gz if you are so inclined. Alternatively, choose fonts which exist on your system before running the scripts.

gimp-data-extras – (Version 1.0.0, 7,825K)
Patterns, gradients etc. for gimp. This package isn't required, but contains lots of goodies for gimp.

gnome-audio – (Version 1.0.0, 828K)
[W] [S]

If you use the GNOME desktop environment, you may want to install this package of complementary sounds.

gnome-media – (Version 1.0.1, 291K)
[W]

GNOME (GNU Network Object Model Environment) is a user-friendly set of applications and desktop tools to be used in conjunction with a window manager for the X Window System. GNOME is similar in purpose and scope to CDE and KDE, but GNOME is based completely on Open Source software. GNOME's powerful environment is pleasing to the eye, easy to configure and use. This package will install such media features as the GNOME CD player.

kdegraphics – (Version 1.1, 2,685K)
Graphics applications for the K Desktop Environment. Includes: kdvi (displays TeX .dvi files); kfax (displays fax files); kfract (a fractal generator); kghostview (displays PostScript files); kiconedit (icon editor); kpaint (a simple drawing program); ksnapshot (screen capture utility); kview (image viewer for GIF, JPEG, TIFF, etc.).

kdemultimedia – (Version 1.1, 2,277K)
Multimedia applications for the K Desktop Environment. Included: kmedia (media player); kmid (MIDI/karaoke player); kmidi (MIDI-to-WAV player/converter); kmix (mixer); kscd (CD audio player)

libgr-progs – (Version 2.0.13, 1,580K)
[W] [S]

The libgr-progs package contains a group of scripts for manipulating the graphics files in formats which are supported by the libgr library. For example, libgr-progs includes the rasttopnm script, which will convert a Sun rasterfile into a portable anymap. Libgr-progs contains many other scripts for converting from one graphics file format to another. If you need to use these conversion scripts, you should install libgr-progs. You'll also need to install the libgr package.

libungif-progs – (Version 4.1.0, 336K)
The libungif-progs package contains various programs for manipulating GIF format image files. Install this package if you need to manipulate GIF format image files. You'll also need to install the libungif package.

mikmod – (Version 3.1.5, 784K)
[W]

MikMod is one of the best and most well known MOD music file players for UNIX-like systems. This particular distribution is intended to compile fairly painlessly in a Linux environment. MikMod uses the OSS `/dev/dsp` driver including all recent kernels for output, and will also write .wav files. Supported file formats include MOD, STM, S3M, MTM, XM, ULT, and IT. The player uses ncurses for console output and supports transparent loading from gzip/ pkzip/ zoo archives and the loading/saving of playlists. Install the mikmod package if you need a MOD music file player.

mpg123 – (Version 0.59q, 207K)
[W]

Mpg123 is a fast, free and portable MPEG audio player for Unix. It supports MPEG 1.0/2.0 layers 1, 2 and 3 ("mp3" files). For full CD quality playback (44 kHz, 16 bit, stereo) a Pentium CPU is required. Mono and/or reduced quality playback (22 kHz or 11 kHz) is possible on 486 CPUs. For information on the MP3 License, please visit: *http://www.mpeg.org/*

multimedia – (Version 2.1, 344K)
[W]

The multimedia package contains several X Window System utilities for handling multimedia files: xplaycd, xmixer and xgetfile. Xplaycd is a CD player for playing audio CDs on your machine's CD-ROM drive. Xmixer controls the volume settings on your machine's sound card. Xgetfile is a versatile file browser, intended for use in shell scripts. Install the multimedia package if you need an audio CD player, a sound card volume controller, or a file browser for use in shell scripts.

playmidi – (Version 2.4, 133K)
[W]

Playmidi plays MIDI (Musicial Instrument Digital Interface) sound files through a sound card synthesizer. This package includes basic drum samples for use with simple FM synthesizers. Install playmidi if you want to play MIDI files using your computer's sound card.

playmidi-X11 – (Version 2.4, 39K)
[W]

Playmidi-X11 provides an X Window System interface for playing MIDI (Musical Instrument Digital Interface) sound files through a sound card synthesizer. This package includes basic drum samples for use with simple FM synthesizers. Install playmidi-X11 if you want to use an X interface to play MIDI sound files using your computer's sound card.

rhsound – (Version 1.8, 11K)
[W]

The rhsound package provides a script which can save and restore the mixer settings and volume level of the standard kernel sound drivers. These mixer settings are preserved through shutdowns and restarts. Install the rhsound package if you need to preserve the kernel sound driver module's mixer settings through shutdowns and reboots.

sndconfig – (Version 0.31, 221K)
[W]

Sndconfig is a text based tool which sets up the configuration files you'll need to use a sound card with a Red Hat Linux system. Sndconfig can be used to set the proper sound type for programs which use the `/dev/dsp`, `/dev/audio` and `/dev/mixer` devices. The sound settings are saved by the aumix and sysV runlevel scripts. Install sndconfig if you need to configure your sound card.

sox – (Version 12.15, 233K)
[W]

SoX (Sound eXchange) is a sound file format converter for Linux, UNIX and DOS PCs. The self-described 'Swiss Army knife of sound tools,' SoX can convert between many different digitized sound formats and perform simple sound manipulation functions, including sound effects. Install the sox package if you'd like to convert sound file formats or manipulate some sounds.

transfig – (Version 3.2.1, 292K)
The transfig utility creates a makefile which translates FIG (created by xfig) or PIC figures into a specified LaTeX graphics language (for example, PostScript(TM)). Transfig is used to create TeX documents which are portable (i.e., they can be printed in a wide variety of environments).

x11amp – (Version 0.9_alpha3, 1,341K)
[W]

X11amp is a X Windows based mp3 player with a nice interface borrowed from WinAMP. For information on the MP3 License, please visit: *http://www.mpeg.org/*

xanim – (Version 27070, 847K)
[W]

The XAnim program is an animation/video/audio viewer for the X Window System. XAnim can display a large variety of animation, audio and video formats. Install the xanim package if you need a viewer for an animation, video or audio file.

xfig — (Version 3.2.2, 2,545K)

Xfig is an X Window System tool for creating basic vector graphics, including bezier curves, lines, rulers and more. The resulting graphics can be saved, printed on PostScript printers or converted to a variety of other formats (e.g., X11 bitmaps, Encapsulated PostScript, LaTeX). You should install xfig if you need a simple program to create vector graphics.

xpaint — (Version 2.4.9, 448K)

[W]

XPaint is an X Window System color image editing program which supports most standard paint program options. XPaint also supports advanced features like image processing algorithms. XPaint allows you to edit multiple images simultaneously and supports a variety of image formats, including PPM, XBM, TIFF, JPEG, etc. Install the xpaint package if you need a paint program for X.

zgv — (Version 3.0, 175K)

Zgv is an image viewer which can display graphics in GIF, JPEG/JFIF, PNG, PBM/PGM/PPM, BMP, TGA, PCX and MRF formats on VGA and SVGA displays. Zgv can also display thumbnails of the images. Zgv is based on svgalib, which you will need to have on your system in order to use zgv. Install zgv if you need an image viewer.

Productivity

This section contains packages that are associated with increasing productivity.

gnome-pim — (Version 1.0.3, 673K)

[W]

The GNOME Personal Information Manager consists of applications to make keeping up with your busy life easier. Currently these apps are present: - gnomecal : personal calendar and todo list - gnomecard: contact list of friends and business associates.

gnumeric — (Version 0.21, 5,008K)

[W]

GNOME is the GNU Network Object Model Environment. This powerful environment is both easy to use and easy to configure. This package will install Gnumeric the GNOME spreadsheet program. This program is intended to be a replacement for a commercial spreadsheet, so quite a bit of work has gone into the program. Install this package if you want to use the GNOME spreadsheet Gnumeric.

ical – (Version 2.2, 790K)
[W] [S]

Ical is an X Window System based calendar program. Ical will easily create `/edit/delete` entries, create repeating entries, remind you about upcoming appointments, print and list item occurrences, and allow shared calendars between different users. Install ical if you need a calendar program to track your schedule. You'll need to have the X Window System installed in order to use ical.

korganizer – (Version 1.1, 1,220K)
KOrganizer is a complete calendar and scheduling program for KDE. It allows interchange with other calendar applications through the industry standard vCalendar file format.

Publishing

This section contains packages that are associated with publishing.

enscript – (Version 1.6.1, 1,515K)
Enscript is a print filter. It can take ASCII input and format it into PostScript output. At the same time, it can also do nice transformations like putting two ASCII pages on one physical page (side by side) or changing fonts.

ghostscript – (Version 5.10, 3,330K)
[W] [S]

Ghostscript is a software set that provides a PostScript(TM) interpreter, a set of C procedures (the Ghostscript library, which implements the graphics capabilities in the PostScript language) and an interpreter for Portable Document Format (PDF) files. Ghostscript translates PostScript code into many common, bitmapped formats, like those understood by your printer or screen. Ghostscript is normally used to display PostScript files and to print PostScript files to non-PostScript printers. If you need to display PostScript files or print them to non-PostScript printers, you should install ghostscript. If you install ghostscript, you also need to install the ghostscript-fonts package.

ghostscript-fonts – (Version 5.10, 1,490K)
[W] [S]

These fonts can be used by the GhostScript interpreter during text rendering. They are in addition to the shared fonts between GhostScript and X11.

groff – (Version 1.11a, 2,842K)
[B]

Groff is a document formatting system. Groff takes standard text and formatting commands as input and produces formatted output. The created documents can be shown on a display or printed on a printer. Groff's formatting commands allow you to specify font type and size, bold type, italic type, the number and size of columns on a page, and more. You should install groff if you want to use it as a document formatting system. Groff can also be used to format man pages. If you are going to use groff with the X Window System, you'll also need to install the groff-gxditview package.

groff-gxditview – (Version 1.11a, 73K)
Gxditview displays the groff text processor's output on an X Window System display. If you are going to use groff as a text processor, you should install gxditview so that you preview your processed text files in X. You'll also need to install the groff package and the X Window System.

gv – (Version 3.5.8, 424K)
[W] [S]

Gv provides a user interface for the ghostscript PostScript(TM) interpreter. Derived from the ghostview program, gv can display PostScript and PDF documents using the X Window System. Install the gv package if you'd like to view PostScript and PDF documents on your system. You'll also need to have the ghostscript package installed, as well as the X Window System.

lout – (Version 3.08, 3,452K)
Lout is a high-level language for document formatting. Lout reads a high-level description of a document (similar in style to LaTeX) and can produce a PostScript(TM) file for printing or produce plain text. Lout supports the typesetting of documents which contain floating figures, tables, diagrams, rotated and scaled text or graphics, footnotes, running headers, footers, an index, a table of contents and bibliography, cross-references, mathematical equations and statistical graphs. Lout can be extended with definitions that should be easier to write than other languages, since Lout is a high-level language. Lout supports (with hyphenation) a variety of languages: Czech, Danish, Dutch, English, Finnish, French, German, Norwegian, Russian, Slovenian, Spanish and Swedish. Install the lout package if you'd like to try the Lout document formatting system. Unless you're already a Lout expert, you'll probably want to also install the lout-doc package, which contains the documentation for Lout.

lout-doc – (Version 3.08, 2,069K)

The lout-doc package includes all of the documentation for the Lout document formatting language. The documentation includes manuals for regular users and for experts, written in Lout and available as PostScript(TM) files. The documentation provides good examples for how to write large documents with Lout. If you're installing the lout package, you should install the lout-doc package.

mpage – (Version 2.4, 90K)

[W] [S]

The mpage utility takes plain text files or PostScript(TM) documents as input, reduces the size of the text, and prints the files on a PostScript printer with several pages on each sheet of paper. Mpage is very useful for viewing large printouts without using up tons of paper. Mpage supports many different layout options for the printed pages. Mpage should be installed if you need a useful utility for viewing long text documents without wasting paper.

printtool – (Version 3.40, 113K)

[W] [S]

The printtool is a printer configuration tool with a graphical user interface. Printtool can manage both local and remote printers, including Windows (SMB) and NetWare (NCP) printers. Printtool should be installed so that you can manage local and remote printers.

rhs-printfilters – (Version 1.51, 101K)

[W] [S]

The rhs-printfilters package contains a set of print filters which are primarily meant to be used with the Red Hat printtool. These print filters provide an easy way for users to handle printing numerous file formats.

sgml-tools – (Version 1.0.9, 1,877K)

SGMLtools is a text formatting package based on SGML (Standard Generalized Markup Language). SGMLtools allows you to produce LaTeX, HTML, GNU info, LyX, RTF, plain text (via groff), and other format outputs from a single source. SGMLtools is intended for writing technical software documentation. Install SGMLTools if you need a text formatting program that can produce a variety of different formats from a single source file. You should probably also install and try SGMLTtools if you're going to write technical software documentation.

tetex — (Version 0.9, 39,613K)
[W]

TeTeX is an implementation of TeX for Linux or UNIX systems. TeX takes a text file and a set of formatting commands as input and creates a typesetter independent .dvi (DeVice Independent) file as output. Usually, TeX is used in conjunction with a higher level formatting package like LaTeX or PlainTeX, since TeX by itself is not very user-friendly. Install tetex if you want to use the TeX text formatting system. If you are installing tetex, you will also need to install tetex-afm (a PostScript(TM) font converter for TeX), tetex-dvilj (for converting .dvi files to HP PCL format for printing on HP and HP compatible printers), tetex-dvips (for converting .dvi files to PostScript format for printing on PostScript printers), tetex-latex (a higher level formatting package which provides an easier-to-use interface for TeX) and tetex-xdvi (for previewing .dvi files in X). Unless you're an expert at using TeX, you'll also want to install the tetex-doc package, which includes the documentation for TeX.

tetex-afm — (Version 0.9, 3,030K)
[W]

Tetex-afm provides afm2tfm, a converter for PostScript font metric files. PostScript fonts are accompanied by .afm font metric files which describe the characteristics of each font. To use PostScript fonts with TeX, TeX needs .tfm files that contain similar information. Afm2tfm will convert .afm files to .tfm files. If you are installing tetex in order to use the TeX text formatting system, you will need to install tetex-afm. You will also need to install tetex-dvilj (for converting .dvi files to HP PCL format for printing on HP and HP compatible printers), tetex-dvips (for converting .dvi files to PostScript format for printing on PostScript printers), tetex-latex (a higher level formatting package which provides an easier-to-use interface for TeX) and tetex-xdvi (for previewing .dvi files in X). Unless you're an expert at using TeX, you'll probably also want to install the tetex-doc package, which includes documentation for TeX.

tetex-doc — (Version 0.9, 29,426K)
The tetex-doc package contains documentation for the TeX text formatting system. If you want to use TeX and you're not an expert at it, you should install the tetex-doc package. You'll also need to install the tetex package, tetex-afm (a PostScript font converter for TeX), tetex-dvilj (for converting .dvi files to HP PCL format for printing on HP and HP compatible printers), tetex-dvips (for converting .dvi files to PostScript format for printing on PostScript printers), tetex-latex (a higher level formatting package which provides an easier-to-use interface for TeX) and tetex-xdvi (for previewing .dvi files).

tetex-dvilj – (Version 0.9, 351K)
[W]

Dvilj and dvilj's siblings (included in this package) will convert TeX text formatting system output .dvi files to HP PCL (HP Printer Control Language) commands. Using dvilj, you can print TeX files to HP LaserJet+ and fully compatible printers. With dvilj2p, you can print to HP LaserJet IIP and fully compatible printers. And with dvilj4, you can print to HP LaserJet4 and fully compatible printers. If you are installing tetex, so that you can use the TeX text formatting system, you will also need to install tetex-dvilj. In addition, you will need to install tetex-afm (for converting PostScript font description files), tetex-dvips (for converting .dvi files to PostScript format for printing on PostScript printers), tetex-latex (a higher level formatting package which provides an easier-to-use interface for TeX) and tetex-xdvi (for previewing .dvi files in X). If you're installing TeX and you're not a TeX expert, you'll also want to install the tetex-doc package, which contains documentation for TeX.

tetex-dvips – (Version 0.9, 856K)
[W]

Dvips converts .dvi files produced by the TeX text formatting system (or by another processor like GFtoDVI) to PostScript(TM) format. Normally the PostScript file is sent directly to your printer. If you are installing tetex, so that you can use the TeX text formatting system, you will also need to install tetex-dvips. In addition, you will need to install tetex-afm (for converting PostScript font description files), tetex-dvilj (for converting .dvi files to HP PCL format for printing on HP and HP compatible printers), tetex-latex (a higher level formatting package which provides an easier-to-use interface for TeX) and tetex-xdvi (for previewing .dvi files in X). If you're installing TeX and you're not an expert at it, you'll also want to install the tetex-doc package, which contains documentation for the TeX system.

tetex-latex – (Version 0.9, 7,898K)
[W]

LaTeX is a front end for the TeX text formatting system. Easier to use than TeX, LaTeX is essentially a set of TeX macros which provide convenient, predefined document formats for users. If you are installing tetex, so that you can use the TeX text formatting system, you will also need to install tetex-latex. In addition, you will need to install tetex-afm (for converting PostScript font description files), tetex-dvilj (for converting .dvi files to HP PCL format for printing on HP and HP compatible printers), tetex-dvips (for converting .dvi files to PostScript format for printing on PostScript printers) and tetex-xdvi (for previewing .dvi files in X). If you're not an expert at TeX you'll probably also want to install the tetex-doc package, which contains documentation for TeX.

tetex-xdvi — (Version 0.9, 1,030K)
[W] [S]

Xdvi allows you to preview the TeX text formatting system's output .dvi files on an X Window System. If you are installing tetex, so that you can use the TeX text formatting system, you will also need to install tetex-xdvi. In addition, you will need to install tetex-afm (a PostScript font converter for TeX), tetex-dvilj (for converting .dvi files to HP PCL format for printing on HP and HP compatible printers), tetex-dvips (for converting .dvi files to PostScript format for printing on PostScript printers), and tetex-latex (a higher level formatting package which provides an easier-to-use interface for TeX). If you're not a TeX expert, you'll probably also want to install the tetex-doc package, which contains documentation for the TeX text formatting system.

texinfo — (Version 3.12f, 799K)
[W] [S]

Texinfo is a documentation system that can produce both online information and printed output from a single source file. Normally, you'd have to write two separate documents: one for online help or other online information and the other for a typeset manual or other printed work. Using Texinfo, you only need to write one source document. Then when the work needs revision, you only have to revise one source document. The GNU Project uses the Texinfo file format for most of its documentation. Install texinfo if you want a documentation system for producing both online and print documentation from the same source file and/or if you are going to write documentation for the GNU Project.

xpdf — (Version 0.80, 1,351K)
Xpdf is an X Window System based viewer for Portable Document Format (PDF) files. PDF files are sometimes called Acrobat files, after Adobe Acrobat (Adobe's PDF viewer). Xpdf is a small and efficient program which uses standard X fonts. Install the xpdf package if you need a viewer for PDF files.

System

This section contains packages that are associated with system-level operations.

SVGATextMode – (Version 1.8, 852K)
SVGATextMode is a utility for reprogramming (S)VGA hardware, which can improve the appearance of text consoles. You should install SVGATextMode if you want to alter the appearance of your text consoles. The utility uses a configuration file (Xconfig or XF86Config) to set up textmodes with higher resolution, larger fonts, higher display refresh rates, etc. Although SVGATextMode can be used to program any text mode size, your results will depend on your VGA card.

arpwatch – (Version 2.1a4, 104K)
The arpwatch package contains arpwatch and arpsnmp. Arpwatch and arpsnmp are both network monitoring tools. Both utilities monitor Ethernet or FDDI network traffic and build databases of Ethernet/IP address pairs, and can report certain changes via email. Install the arpwatch package if you need networking monitoring devices which will automatically keep traffic of the IP addresses on your network.

bind-utils – (Version 8.2, 1,320K)
[W] [S]

Bind-utils contains a collection of utilities for querying DNS (Domain Name Service) name servers to find out information about Internet hosts. These tools will provide you with the IP addresses for given host names, as well as other information about registered domains and network addresses. You should install bind-utils if you need to get information from DNS name servers.

comanche – (Version 990330, 372K)
Comanche (COnfiguration MANager for apaCHE) is a front-end for the Apache Web server, the most popular Web server used on the Internet. Comanche aims to make it easier to manage and configure Apache. Install the comanche package if you need a configuration manager for the Apache Web server. You'll also need to install the apache package.

console-tools – (Version 19990302, 1,393K)
[B]

This package contains utilities to load console fonts and keyboard maps. It also includes a number of different fonts and keyboard maps.

control-panel — (Version 3.11, 186K)
[W] [S]

The Red Hat control panel is a configuration program launcher for the X Window System. Both convenient and pleasing, the Red Hat control panel allows you easy access to numerous X-based system administration tools included in your Red Hat Linux system. Eventually, you'll want to work with many of your system administration tools; this package helps you locate and launch many of them.

dialog — (Version 0.6, 88K)
[W]

Dialog is a utility that allows you to show dialog boxes (containing questions or messages) in TTY (text mode) interfaces. Dialog is called from within a shell script. The following dialog boxes are implemented: yes/no, menu, input, message, text, info, checklist, radiolist, and gauge. Install dialog if you would like to create TTY dialog boxes.

ext2ed — (Version 0.1, 288K)
Ext2ed is a program which provides a text and window interface for examining and editing an ext2 filesystem. Ext2ed is supposed to be easier to use than debugfs, but debugfs is more powerful. Note that this program should only be used by someone who is very experienced at hacking filesystems. Install ext2ed if you want to examine and/or edit your ext2 filesystem, and you know what you're doing.

fbset — (Version 2.0.19990118, 34K)
fbset is a utility for querying and changing video modes of fbcon consoles.

gnome-linuxconf — (Version 0.21, 320K)
[W] [S]

GNOME (GNU Network Object Model Environment) is a user-friendly set of applications and desktop tools to be used in conjunction with a window manager for the X Window System. The gnome-linuxconf package includes GNOME's front end for the Linuxconf system configuration utility.

gnome-utils — (Version 1.0.1, 774K)
[W]

GNOME is the GNU Network Object Model Environment. This powerful environment is both easy to use and easy to configure. This package will install some GNOME utilities, such as the calendar and calculator.

gnorpm – (Version 0.7, 374K)
[W] [S]

Gnome RPM is a graphical front end to RPM, similar to Glint, but written with the GTK widget set and the GNOME libraries. It is currently under development, so there are some features missing, but you can currently query packages in the filesystem and database, install upgrade, uninstall and verify packages.

gtop – (Version 1.0.1, 267K)
[W]

GNOME is the GNU Network Object Model Environment. This powerful environment is both easy to use and easy to configure. This package will install the GNOME system monitor gtop, which shows memory graphs and processes.

hdparm – (Version 3.3, 37K)
[B]

Hdparm is a useful system utility for setting (E)IDE hard drive parameters. For example, hdparm can be used to tweak hard drive performance and to spin down hard drives for power conservation.

ipxutils – (Version 1.0, 53K)
[S]

The ipxutils package includes utilities (ipx_configure, ipx_internal_net, ipx_interface, ipx_route) necessary for configuring and debugging IPX interfaces and networks under Linux. IPX is the low-level protocol used by Novell's NetWare file server system to transfer data. Install ipxutils if you need to configure IPX networking on your network.

isicom – (Version 1.0, 38K)
Binary images and loader for Multitech IntelligentSerialInternal (ISI) data files.

kdeadmin – (Version 1.1, 1,378K)
System Administration tools for the K Desktop Environment. Included with this package are: kdat (tape backup); ksysv (sysV init editor); kuser (user administration tool)

kdeutils – (Version 1.1, 2,977K)
Utilities for the K Desktop Environment. Includes: ark (tar/gzip archive manager); kab (address book); karm (personal time tracker); kcalc (scientific calculator); kedit (simple text editor); kfloppy (floppy formatting tool); khexedit (hex editor); kjots (note taker); klipper (clipboard tool); kljettool(HP printer

configuration tool); klpq (print queue manager) knotes (post-it notes for the desktop); kpm (process manager similar to 'top', but more advanced); kwrite (improved text editor).

kernelcfg — (Version 0.5, 58K)
[W] [S]

The kernelcfg package contains an X Window System based graphical user interface tool for configuring the kernel daemon (kerneld). Kerneld automatically loads some hardware and software support into memory as needed and unloads the support when it is no longer being used. The kernel configurator tool can be used to tell kerneld what hardware support to load when it is presented with a generic hardware request. Kernelcfg should be installed because it is a useful utility for managing the kernel daemon.

knfsd-clients — (Version 1.2, 10K)
The nfs-server-clients package contains the showmount program. Showmount queries the mount daemon on a remote host for information about the NFS (Network File System) server on the remote host. For example, showmount can display the clients which are mounted on that host. This package is not needed to mount NFS volumes. Install nfs-server-clients if you'd like to use the showmount tool for querying NFS servers.

linuxconf — (Version 1.14r2, 11,322K)
[B]

Linuxconf is an extremely capable system configuration tool. Linuxconf provides four different interfaces for you to choose from: command line, character-cell (like the installation program), an X Window System based GUI and a web-based interface. Linuxconf can manage a large proportion of your system's operations, including networking, user accounts, file systems, boot parameters, and more. Linuxconf will simplify the process of configuring your system. Unless you are completely happy with configuring your system manually, you should install the Linuxconf package and use Linuxconf instead.

macutils — (Version 2.0b3, 218K)
The macutils package includes a set of utilities for manipulating files that are commonly used by Macintosh machines. Macutils includes utilities like binhex, hexbin, macunpack, etc. Install macutils if you need to manipulate files that are commonly used by Macintosh machines.

mkdosfs-ygg — (Version 0.3b, 17K)
[W]

The mkdosfs program is used to create an MS-DOS FAT file system on a Linux system device, usually a disk partition. The mkdosfs package should be installed if your machine needs to support MS-DOS style file systems.

mkisofs — (Version 1.12b5, 153K)
The mkisofs program is used as a pre-mastering program; i.e., it generates the ISO9660 filesystem. Mkisofs takes a snapshot of a given directory tree and generates a binary image of the tree which will correspond to an ISO9660 filesystem when written to a block device. Mkisofs is used for writing CD-ROMs, and includes support for creating bootable El Torito CD-ROMs. Install the mkisofs package if you need a program for writing CD-ROMs.

mkxauth — (Version 1.7, 15K)
[W] [S]

The mkxauth utility helps create and maintain X authentication databases (.Xauthority files). Mkxauth is used to create an .Xauthority file or to merge keys from another local or remote .Xauthority file .Xauthority files are used by the xauth user-oriented access control program, which grants or denies access to X servers based on the contents of the .Xauthority file. The mkxauth package should be installed if you're going to use user-oriented access control to provide security for your X Window System (a good idea).

modemtool — (Version 1.21, 15K)
[W] [S]

The modemtool is a simple graphical configuration tool for selecting the serial port to which your modem is connected. Install modemtool if you use a modem.

mt-st — (Version 0.5b, 67K)
[B]

The mt-st package contains the mt and st tape drive management programs. Mt (for magnetic tape drives) and st (for SCSI tape devices) can control rewinding, ejecting, skipping files and blocks and more. This package can help you manage tape drives.

mtools — (Version 3.9.1, 486K)
[W]

Mtools is a collection of utilities for accessing MS-DOS files. Mtools allow you to read, write and move around MS-DOS filesystem files (normally on MS-DOS floppy disks). Mtools supports Windows95 style long file names, OS/2 Xdf disks, and 2m disks. Mtools should be installed if you need to use MS-DOS disks.

ncpfs — (Version 2.2.0.12, 553K)
[S]

Ncpfs is a filesystem which understands the Novell NetWare(TM) NCP protocol. Functionally, NCP is used for NetWare the way NFS is used in the TCP/IP world. For a Linux system to mount a NetWare filesystem, it needs a special mount program. The ncpfs package contains such a mount program plus other tools for configuring and using the ncpfs filesystem. Install the ncpfs package if you need to use the ncpfs filesystem to use Novell NetWare files or services.

netcfg — (Version 2.20, 165K)
[W] [S]

A Red Hat Linux tool which provides a graphical user interface for setting up and configuring networking for your machine.

open — (Version 1.4, 13K)
The open command starts a specified command with the first available virtual console, or on a virtual console that you specify. Install the open package if you regularly use virtual consoles to run programs.

pciutils — (Version 1.99.4, 120K)
This package contains various utilities for inspecting and setting devices connected to the PCI bus. It requires kernel version 2.1.82 or newer (supporting the `/proc/bus/pci` interface).

procinfo — (Version 16, 54K)

The procinfo command gets system data from the `/proc` directory (the kernel filesystem), formats it and displays it on standard output. You can use procinfo to acquire information about your system from the kernel as it is running. Install procinfo if you'd like to use it to gather and display system data.

procps — (Version 2.0.2, 298K)
[B]

The procps package contains a set of system utilities which provide system information. Procps includes ps, free, skill, snice, tload, top, uptime, vmstat, w, and watch. The ps command displays a snapshot of running processes. The top command provides a repetitive update of the statuses of running processes. The free command displays the amounts of free and used memory on your system. The skill command sends a terminate command (or another specified signal) to a specified set of processes. The snice command is used to change the scheduling priority of specified processes. The tload command prints a graph of the current system load average to a specified tty. The uptime command displays the current time, how long the system has been running, how many users are logged on and system load averages for the past one, five and fifteen minutes. The w command displays a list of the users who are currently logged on and what they're running. The watch program watches a running program. The vmstat command displays virtual memory statistics about processes, memory, paging, block I/O, traps and CPU activity.

procps-X11 – (Version 2.0.2, 0K)
The procps-X11 package contains the XConsole shell script, a backwards compatibility wrapper for the xconsole program.

psacct – (Version 6.3, 87K)
The psacct package contains several utilities for monitoring process activities, including ac, lastcomm, accton and sa. The ac command displays statistics about how long users have been logged on. The lastcomm command displays information about previous executed commands. The accton command turns process accounting on or off. The sa command summarizes information about previously executed commmands. Install the psacct package if you'd like to use its utilities for monitoring process activities on your system.

psmisc – (Version 18, 46K)
[B]

The psmisc package contains utilities for managing processes on your system: pstree, killall and fuser. The pstree command displays a tree structure of all of the running processes on your system. The killall command sends a specified signal (SIGTERM if nothing is specified) to processes identified by name. The fuser command identifies the PIDs of processes that are using specified files or filesystems.

rdate – (Version 0.960923, 5K)
[W] [S]

The rdate utility retrieves the date and time from another machine on your network, using the protocol described in RFC 868. If you run rdate as root, it will set your machine's local time to the time of the machine that you queried. Note that rdate isn't scrupulously accurate. If you are worried about milliseconds, get the xntpd program instead.

rdist — (Version 6.1.5, 141K)
[W] [S]

The rdist program maintains identical copies of files on multiple hosts. If possible, rdist will preserve the owner, group, mode and mtime of files and it can update programs that are executing.

rhmask — (Version 1.0, 8K)
The rhmask utility creates mask files from original and updated files. The mask files, which may be the latest new versions of software, can then be freely distributed on public Internet servers. The mask files are only useful for people who who already have a copy of the original package. The rhmask utility uses a simple XOR scheme for creating the file mask and uses file size and md5 sums to ensure the integrity of the result. Install the rhmask package if you need a utility for creating file masks.

rhs-hwdiag — (Version 0.35, 75K)
[B]

The rhs-hwdiag package contains the Red Hat Hardware Discovery Tools. These tools probe the serial and parallel ports on your system, and are useful for finding and reporting hardware errors to Red Hat support if you're having problems. These tools could cause adverse side-effects in some situations, so you should use them carefully.

screen — (Version 3.7.6, 368K)
The screen utility allows you to have multiple logins on just one terminal. Screen is useful for users who telnet into a machine or are connected via a dumb terminal, but want to use more than just one login. Install the screen package if you need a screen manager that can support multiple logins on one terminal.

setconsole — (Version 1.0, 3K)
[B]

Setconsole is a basic system utility for setting up the `/etc/inittab`, `/dev/systty` and `/dev/console` files to handle a new console. The console can be either the local terminal (i.e., directly attached to the system via a video card) or a serial console.

setserial — (Version 2.15, 37K)
[B]

Setserial is a basic system utility for displaying or setting serial port information. Setserial can reveal and allow you to alter the I/O port and IRQ that a particular serial device is using, and more. You should install setserial because you may find it useful for detecting and/or altering device information.

setuptool – (Version 1.2, 17K)
[B]

Setuptool is a user-friendly text mode menu utility which allows you to access all of the text mode configuration programs included in the Red Hat Linux operating system. You should install the setuptool package because you will find yourself using its features for essential system administration.

statserial – (Version 1.1, 289K)
[W] [S]

The statserial utility displays a table of the signals on a standard 9-pin or 25-pin serial port and indicates the status of the handshaking lines. Statserial is useful for debugging serial port and/or modem problems. Install the statserial package if you need a tool to help debug serial port or modem problems.

swatch – (Version 2.2, 129K)
The Swatch utility monitors system log files, filters out unwanted data and takes specified actions (i.e., sending email, executing a script, etc.) based upon what it finds in the log files. Install the swatch package if you need a program that will monitor log files and alert you in certain situations.

symlinks – (Version 1.2, 212K)
The symlinks utility performs maintenance on symbolic links. Symlinks checks for symlink problems, including dangling symlinks which point to nonexistent files. Symlinks can also automatically convert absolute symlinks to relative symlinks. Install the symlinks package if you need a program for maintaining symlinks on your system.

time – (Version 1.7, 18K)
[B]

The GNU time utility runs another program, collects information about the resources used by that program while it is running and displays the results. Time can help developers optimize their programs.

timeconfig – (Version 2.6, 107K)
[B]

The timeconfig package contains two utilities: timeconfig and setclock. Timeconfig provides a simple text mode tool for configuring the time parameters in `/etc/sysconfig/clock` and `/etc/localtime`. The setclock tool sets the hardware clock on the system to the current time stored in the system clock.

timetool – (Version 2.5, 22K)
[W] [S]

The timetool utility provides a graphical user interface for setting the current date and time on your system.

tksysv – (Version 1.0, 35K)
[W] [S]

Tksysv is an X Window System based graphical interface for editing the services provided by different runlevels. Tksysv is used to set which services are stopped and which services are started in the different runlevels on your system. Install the tksysv package if you'd like to use a graphical tool for editing runlevel services.

tunelp – (Version 1.3, 9K)
The tunelp utility sets various parameters for lp devices (`/dev/lp0`, /dev/lp1, `/dev/lp2`). Tunelp can set parameters like the lp device's interrupt usage, polling rate, etc. Install the tunelp package if you need a utility for setting lp device parameters.

ucd-snmp-utils – (Version 3.6.1, 253K)
[W] [S]

The ucd-snmp package contains various utilities for use with the UCD-SNMP network management project. Install this package if you need utilities for managing your network using the SNMP protocol. You'll also need to install the ucd-snmp package.

usermode – (Version 1.6, 94K)
[W] [S]

The usermode package contains several graphical tools for users: userinfo, usermount and userpasswd. Userinfo allows users to change their finger information. Usermount lets users mount, unmount, and format filesystems. Userpasswd allows users to change their passwords. Install the usermode package if you would like to provide users with graphical tools for certain account management tasks.

usernet – (Version 1.0.9, 24K)
[W] [S]

The usernet utility provides a graphical interface for manipulating network interfaces (bringing them up or down and viewing their status). Users can only manipulate interfaces that are user-controllable. The superuser can control all interfaces. Install the usernet package if you'd like to provide a graphical utility for manipulating network interfaces.

vlock – (Version 1.3, 9K)
The vlock program locks one or more sessions on the console. Vlock can lock the current terminal (local or remote) or the entire virtual console system, which completely disables all console access. The vlock program unlocks when either the password of the user who started vlock or the root password is typed. Install vlock if you need to disable access to one console or to all virtual consoles.

which – (Version 1.0, 7K)
[B]

The which command shows the full pathname of a specified program, if the specified program is in your PATH.

xcpustate – (Version 2.5, 33K)
The xcpustate utility is an X Window System based monitor which shows the amount of time that the CPU is spending in different states. On a Linux system, xcpustate displays a bar that indicates the amounts of idle, user, nice and system time (from left to right) used by the CPU. Install the xcpustate package if you'd like to use a horizontal bar style CPU state monitor.

xosview – (Version 1.7.1, 109K)
The xosview utility displays a set of bar graphs which show the current system state, including memory usage, CPU usage, system load, etc. Xosview runs under the X Window System. Install the xosview package if you need a graphical tool for monitoring your system's performance.

xsysinfo – (Version 1.6, 22K)
Xsysinfo is a graphic kernel monitoring tool for the X Window System. Xsysinfo displays vertical bars for certain kernel parameters: CPU load average, CPU load, memory and swap sizes. Install the xsysinfo package if you'd like to use a graphical kernel monitoring tool.

xtoolwait – (Version 1.2, 10K)
Xtoolwait is a utility which starts an X client in the background, waits for a window to be mapped on the root window, and then exits. Xtoolwait can improve performance for users who start a bunch of X clients automatically (for example, xterm, xlock, xconsole, whatever) when the X session starts. Install xtoolwait if you'd like to try to speed up the startup time for X sessions.

Text

This section contains packages that are associated with the manipulation of text.

diffutils – (Version 2.7, 152K)
[B]

Diffutils includes four utilities: diff, cmp, diff3 and sdiff. Diff compares two files and shows the differences, line by line. The cmp command shows the offset and line numbers where two files differ, or cmp can show the characters that differ between the two files. The diff3 command shows the differences between three files. Diff3 can be used when two people have made independent changes to a common original; diff3 can produce a merged file that contains both persons' changes and warnings about conflicts. The sdiff command can be used to merge two files interactively. Install diffutils if you need to compare text files.

ed – (Version 0.2, 102K)
[B]

Ed is a line-oriented text editor, used to create, display, and modify text files (both interactively and via shell scripts). For most purposes, ed has been replaced in normal usage by full-screen editors (emacs and vi, for example). Ed was the original UNIX editor, and may be used by some programs. In general, however, you probably don't need to install it and you probably won't use it much.

gawk – (Version 3.0.3, 2,303K)
[B]

The gawk packages contains the GNU version of awk, a text processing utility. Awk interprets a special-purpose programming language to do quick and easy text pattern matching and reformatting jobs. Gawk should be upwardly compatible with the Bell Labs research version of awk and is almost completely compliant with the 1993 POSIX 1003.2 standard for awk. Install the gawk package if you need a text processing utility. Gawk is considered to be a standard Linux tool for processing text.

grep – (Version 2.3, 287K)
[B]

The GNU versions of commonly used grep utilities. Grep searches one or more input files for lines which contain a match to a specified pattern and then prints the matching lines. GNU's grep utilities include grep, egrep and fgrep. You should install grep on your system, because it is a very useful utility for searching through text files, for system administration tasks, etc.

indent — (Version 1.9.1, 81K)

Indent is a GNU program for beautifying C code, so that it is easier to read. Indent can also convert from one C writing style to a different one. Indent understands correct C syntax and tries to handle incorrect C syntax. Install the indent package if you are developing applications in C and you'd like to format your code automatically.

ispell — (Version 3.1.20, 4,049K)

[W] [S]

Ispell is the GNU interactive spelling checker. Ispell will check a text file for spelling and typographical errors. When it finds a word that is not in the dictionary, it will suggest correctly spelled words for the misspelled word. You should install ispell if you need a program for spell checking (and who doesn't...).

less — (Version 332, 142K)

[B]

The less utility is a text file browser that resembles more, but has more capabilities. Less allows you to move backwards in the file as well as forwards. Since less doesn't have to read the entire input file before it starts, less starts up more quickly than text editors (for example, vi). You should install less because it is a basic utility for viewing text files, and you'll use it frequently.

m4 — (Version 1.4, 120K)

[W] [S]

A GNU implementation of the traditional UNIX macro processor. M4 is useful for writing text files which can be logically parsed, and is used by many programs as part of their build process. M4 has built-in functions for including files, running shell commands, doing arithmetic, etc. The autoconf program needs m4 for generating configure scripts, but not for running configure scripts. Install m4 if you need a macro processor.

mawk — (Version 1.2.2, 131K)

Mawk is a version of the awk programming language. Awk interprets a special-purpose programming language to do quick text pattern matching and reformatting. Mawk improves on awk in certain ways and can sometimes outperform gawk, the standard awk program for Linux. Mawk conforms to the POSIX 1003.2 (draft 11.3) definition of awk. You should install mawk if you use awk.

rgrep — (Version 0.98.7, 17K)

The rgrep utility can recursively descend through directories as it greps for the specified pattern. Note that this ability does take a toll on rgrep's performance, which is somewhat slow. Rgrep will also highlight the matching expression. Install the rgrep package if you need a recursive grep which can highlight the matching expression.

sed — (Version 3.02, 68K)

[B]

The sed (Stream EDitor) editor is a stream or batch (non-interactive) editor. Sed takes text as input, performs an operation or set of operations on the text and outputs the modified text. The operations that sed performs (substitutions, deletions, insertions, etc.) can be specified in a script file or from the command line.

textutils — (Version 1.22, 694K)

[B]

A set of GNU utilities for modifying the contents of files, including programs for splitting, joining, comparing and modifying files.

Base

This section contains packages that are associated with the part of Red Hat Linux that is common to all installations of the operating system.

redhat-logos — (Version 1.0.2, 239K)

[B]

redhat-logos (the "Package") contains files of the Red Hat "Shadow Man" logo and the RPM logo (the "Logos"). Red Hat, the Red Hat "Shadow Man" logo, RPM, and the RPM logo are trademarks or registered trademarks of Red Hat Software, Inc. in the United States and other countries.

Red Hat Software, Inc. grants you the right to use the Package during the normal operation of other software programs that call upon the Package. Red Hat Software, Inc. grants to you the right and license to copy and redistribute the Package, but only in conjunction with copying or redistributing additional software packages that call upon the Package during the normal course of operation. Such rights are granted to you without fee, provided that:

1. The above copyright notice and this license are included with each copy you make, and they remain intact and are not altered, deleted, or modified in any way; 2. You do not modify the Package, or the appearance of any or all of the Logos in any manner; and 3. You do not use any or all of the Logos as, or as part of, a trademark, trade name, or trade identifier; or in any other fashion except as set forth in this license.

NO WARRANTY. THIS PACKAGE IS PROVIDED "AS IS" AND ANY EXPRESS OR IMPLIED WARRANTIES, INCLUDING, BUT NOT LIMITED TO, THE IMPLIED WARRANTIES OF MERCHANTABILITY AND FITNESS FOR A PARTICULAR PURPOSE ARE DISCLAIMED. IN NO EVENT SHALL RED HAT SOFTWARE, INC. BE LIABLE FOR ANY DIRECT, INDIRECT, INCIDENTAL, SPECIAL, EXEMPLARY, OR CONSEQUENTIAL DAMAGES (INCLUDING, BUT NOT LIMITED TO, PROCUREMENT OF SUBSTITUTE GOODS OR SERVICES; LOSS OF USE, DATA OR PROFITS; OR BUSINESS INTERRUPTION) HOWEVER CAUSED AND ON ANY THEORY OF LIABILITY, WHETHER IN CONTRACT, STRICT LIABILITY, OR TORT (INCLUDING NEGLIGENCE OR OTHERWISE) ARISING IN ANY WAY OUT OF THE USE OF THIS PACKAGE, EVEN IF ADVISED OF THE POSSIBILITY OF SUCH DAMAGE.

redhat-release — (Version 5.9.5.2, 0K)
[B]

Red Hat Linux release file

Development

This section contains packages that are associated with the development of software under Red Hat Linux.

Debuggers

This section contains packages that are associated with debugging programs under Red Hat Linux.

gdb – (Version 4.17.0.11, 1,171K)
[W] [S]

Gdb is a full featured, command driven debugger. Gdb allows you to trace the execution of programs and examine their internal state at any time. Gdb works for C and C++ compiled with the GNU C compiler gcc.

If you are going to develop C and/or C++ programs and use the GNU gcc compiler, you may want to install gdb to help you debug your programs.

lslk – (Version 1.19, 35K)
Lslk is a lock file lister. Lslk attempts to list all of the locks on the executing system's local files (i.e., on the active inodes). Install lslk if you need a utility for listing file locks.

lsof – (Version 4.40, 547K)
Lsof's name stands for LiSt Open Files, and it does just that. It lists information about files that are open by the processes running on a UNIX system.

ltrace – (Version 0.3.6, 75K)
Ltrace is a debugging program which runs a specified command until the command exits. While the command is executing, ltrace intercepts and records both the dynamic library calls called by the executed process and the signals received by the executed process. Ltrace can also intercept and print system calls executed by the process. You should install ltrace if you need a sysadmin tool for tracking the execution of processes.

strace – (Version 3.1, 123K)
[W] [S]

The strace program intercepts and records the system calls called and received by a running process. Strace can print a record of each system call, its arguments and its return value. Strace is useful for diagnosing problems and debugging, as well as for instructional purposes. Install strace if you need a tool to track the system calls made and received by a process.

xxgdb — (Version 1.12, 103K)
[W]

Xxgdb is an X Window System graphical interface to the GNU gdb debugger. Xxgdb provides visual feedback and supports a mouse interface for the user who wants to perform debugging tasks like the following: controlling program execution through breakpoints, examining and traversing the function call stack, displaying values of variables and data structures, and browsing source files and functions. Install the xxgdb package if you'd like to use a graphical interface with the GNU gdb debugger. You'll also need to have the gdb package installed.

Languages

This section contains packages that are associated with the programming languages available under Red Hat Linux.

cpp — (Version 1.1.2, 135K)
[W] [S]

The C preprocessor is a 'macro processor' which is used automatically by the C compiler to transform your program before actual compilation. It is called a macro processor because it allows you to define 'macros,' which are abbreviations for longer constructs. The C preprocessor provides four separate facilities that you can use as you see fit: * Inclusion of header files. These are files of declarations that can be substituted into your program. * Macro expansion. You can define 'macros,' which are abbreviations for arbitrary fragments of C code, and then the C preprocessor will replace the macros with their definitions throughout the program. * Conditional compilation. Using special preprocessing directives, you can include or exclude parts of the program according to various conditions. * Line control. If you use a program to combine or rearrange source files into an intermediate file which is then compiled, you can use line control to inform the compiler about where each source line originated. You should install this package if you are a programmer who is searching for such a macro processor.

egcs — (Version 1.1.2, 3,525K)
[W] [S]

EGCS is a free software project that intends to further the development of GNU compilers using an open development environment. The egcs package contains the egcs compiler, a compiler aimed at integrating all the optimizations and features necessary for a high-performance and stable development environment. Install egcs if you'd like to use an experimental GNU compiler.

egcs-c++ — (Version 1.1.2, 5,912K)
[W]

This package adds C++ support to the GNU C compiler. It includes support for most of the current C++ specification, including templates and exception handling. It does include the static standard C++ library and C++ header files; the library for dynamically linking programs is available separately.

egcs-g77 — (Version 1.1.2, 4,631K)
The egcs-g77 package provides support for compiling Fortran 77 programs with the GNU gcc compiler. You should install egcs-g77 if you are going to do Fortran development and you would like to use the gcc compiler. You will also need to install the gcc package.

egcs-objc — (Version 1.1.2, 1,969K)
Egcs-objc provides Objective C support for the GNU C compiler (gcc). Mainly used on systems running NeXTSTEP, Objective C is an object-oriented derivative of the C language. Install egcs-objc if you are going to do Objective C development and you would like to use the gcc compiler. You will also need to install the gcc package.

expect — (Version 5.28, 748K)
[W] [S]

Expect is a tcl extension for automating interactive applications such as telnet, ftp, passwd, fsck, rlogin, tip, etc. Expect is also useful for testing the named applications. Expect makes it easy for a script to control another program and interact with it. Install the expect package if you'd like to develop scripts which interact with interactive applications. You'll also need to install the tcl package.

gnome-objc — (Version 1.0.1, 497K)
This package installs basic libraries you must have to use GNOME programs that are built with Objective C. GNOME is the GNU Network Object Model Environment. It's a powerful, pleasing, easy to use and configure environment for your computer.

guavac — (Version 1.2, 2,157K)
The guavac package includes guavac and guavad. Guavac is a stand-alone compiler for the Java programming language. Guavac was written entirely in C++ and it should be portable to any platform supporting GNU's C++ (gcc) or a similar compiler. Guavad is guavac's disassembler. Install guavac if you need a Java compiler on your system.

guile – (Version 1.3, 1,029K)
[W]

GUILE (GNU's Ubiquitous Intelligent Language for Extension) is a library implementation of the Scheme programming language, written in C. GUILE provides a machine-independent execution platform that can be linked in as a library during the building of extensible programs. Install the guile package if you'd like to add extensibility to programs that you are developing. You'll also need to install the guile-devel package.

itcl – (Version 3.0.1, 4,251K)
[incr Tcl]

is an object-oriented extension of the Tcl language. It was created to support more structured programming in Tcl. Tcl scripts that grow beyond a few thousand lines become extremely difficult to maintain. This is because the building blocks of vanilla Tcl are procedures and global variables, and all of these building blocks must reside in a single global namespace. There is no support for protection or encapsulation. [incr Tcl] introduces the notion of objects. Each object is a bag of data with a set of procedures or "methods" that are used to manipulate it. Objects are organized into "classes" with identical characteristics, and classes can inherit functionality from one another. This object-oriented paradigm adds another level of organization on top of the basic variable/procedure elements, and the resulting code is easier to understand and maintain.

kaffe – (Version 1.0.b3, 1,671K)
Kaffe is a free virtual machine designed to execute Java(TM) bytecode. Kaffe can be configured in two modes. In the first mode, it operates as a pure bytecode interpreter (not unlike Javasoft's machine). In the second mode, it performs "just-in-time" code conversion from the abstract code to the host machine's native code. The second mode will ultimately allow execution of Java code at the same speed as standard compiled code, while also maintaining the advantages and flexibility of code independence. Install the kaffe package if you need a Java virtual machine.

p2c-devel – (Version 1.22, 26K)
The p2c-devel package contains the files necessary for development of the p2c Pascal to C translation system. Install the p2c-devel package if you want to do p2c development.

perl – (Version 5.00502, 15,224K)
[B]

Perl is a high-level programming language with roots in C, sed, awk and shell scripting. Perl is good at handling processes and files, and is especially good at handling text. Perl's hallmarks are practicality and efficiency. While it is used to do a lot of different things, Perl's most common applications (and what it excels at) are probably system administration utilities and web programming. A large proportion of the CGI scripts on the web are written in Perl. You need the perl package installed on your system so that your system can handle Perl scripts.

perl-MD5 – (Version 1.7, 30K)
[S]

The perl-MD5 package provides the MD5 module for the Perl programming language. MD5 is a Perl interface to the RSA Data Security Inc. Message Digest Algorithm, which allows Perl programs to use the algorithm. The perl-MD5 package should be installed if any Perl programs on your system are going to use RSA's Message Digest Algorithm.

pygnome – (Version 1.0.1, 1,650K)
PyGNOME is an extension module for python that gives you access to the base GNOME libraries. This means you have access to more widgets, simple configuration interface, metadata support and many other features.

pygtk – (Version 0.5.12, 2,259K)
PyGTK is an extension module for python that gives you access to the GTK+ widget set. Just about anything you can write in C with GTK+ you can write in python with PyGTK (within reason), but with all of python's benefits.

python – (Version 1.5.1, 5,829K)
[W] [S]

Python is an interpreted, interactive, object-oriented programming language often compared to Tcl, Perl, Scheme or Java. Python includes modules, classes, exceptions, very high level dynamic data types and dynamic typing. Python supports interfaces to many system calls and libraries, as well as to various windowing systems (X11, Motif, Tk, Mac and MFC). Programmers can write new built-in modules for Python in C or C++. Python can be used as an extension language for applications that need a programmable interface. This package contains most of the standard Python modules, as well as modules for interfacing to the Tix widget set for Tk and RPM. Note that documentation for Python is provided in the python-docs package.

tcl – (Version 8.0.4, 5,516K)
[W] [S]

Tcl is a simple scripting language designed to be embedded into other applications. Tcl is designed to be used with Tk, a widget set, which is provided in the tk package. This package also includes tclsh, a simple example of a Tcl application. If you're installing the tcl package and you want to use Tcl for development, you should also install the tk and tclx packages.

tclx – (Version 8.0.4, 1,964K)
[W] [S]

TclX is a set of extensions which make it easier to use the Tcl scripting language for common UNIX/Linux programming tasks. TclX enhances Tcl support for files, network access, debugging, math, lists, and message catalogs. TclX can be used with both Tcl and Tcl/Tk applications. Install TclX if you are developing applications with Tcl/Tk. You'll also need to install the tcl and tk packages.

tix – (Version 4.1.0.6, 2,732K)
[W] [S]

Tix (Tk Interface Extension), an add-on for the Tk widget set, is an extensive set of over 40 widgets. In general, Tix widgets are more complex and more capable than the widgets provided in Tk. Tix widgets include a ComboBox, a Motif-style FileSelectBox, an MS Windows-style FileSelectBox, a PanedWindow, a NoteBook, a hierarchical list, a directory tree and a file manager. Install the tix package if you want to try out more complicated widgets for Tk. You'll also need to have the tcl and tk packages installed.

tk – (Version 8.0.4, 5,289K)
[W] [S]

Tk is a X Windows widget set designed to work closely with the tcl scripting language. It allows you to write simple programs with full featured GUI's in only a little more time then it takes to write a text based interface. Tcl/Tk applications can also be run on Windows and Macintosh platforms.

tkinter – (Version 1.5.1, 643K)
[W] [S]

The Tkinter (Tk interface) program is an graphical user interface for the Python scripting language. You should install the tkinter package if you'd like to use a graphical user interface for Python programming.

umb-scheme – (Version 3.2, 1,211K)
[W]

UMB Scheme is a public domain implementation of the Scheme programming language. Scheme is a statically scoped and properly tail-recursive dialect of the Lisp programming language, designed with clear and simple semantics and a minimal number of ways to form expressions. Install the umb-scheme package if you need an implementation of the Scheme programming language.

Libraries

This section contains packages that are associated with the libraries used during the development of software under Red Hat Linux.

ImageMagick-devel – (Version 4.2.2, 1,594K)
If you want to create applications that will use ImageMagick code or APIs, you'll need to install these packages as well as ImageMagick. These additional packages aren't necessary if you simply want to use ImageMagick, however. ImageMagick-devel is an addition to ImageMagick which includes static libraries and header files necessary to develop applications.

ORBit-devel – (Version 0.4.2, 1,471K)
ORBit is a high-performance CORBA ORB (object request broker) with support for the C language. It allows programs to send requests and receive replies from other programs, regardless of the locations of the two programs. This package contains the header files, libraries and utilities necessary to write programs that use CORBA technology.

XFree86-devel – (Version 3.3.3.1, 7,875K)
[W]

XFree86-devel includes the libraries, header files and documentation you'll need to develop programs which run in X clients. XFree86 includes the base Xlib library as well as the Xt and Xaw widget sets. For guidance on programming with these libraries, O'Reilly & Associates produces a series on X programming which you might find useful. Install XFree86-devel if you are going to develop programs which will run as X clients.

Xaw3d-devel — (Version 1.3, 657K)
[W]

Xaw3d is an enhanced version of the MIT Athena widget set for the X Window System. Xaw3d adds a three-dimensional look to those applications with minimal or no source code changes. Xaw3d-devel includes the header files and static libraries for developing programs that take full advantage of Xaw3d's features. You should install Xaw3d-devel if you are going to develop applications using the Xaw3d widget set. You'll also need to install the Xaw3d package.

apache-devel — (Version 1.3.6, 269K)
The apache-devel package contains the source code for the Apache 1.3.1 Web server and the APXS binary you'll need to build Dynamic Shared Objects (DSOs) for Apache. If you are installing the Apache Web server version 1.3.1, and you want to be able to compile or develop additional modules for Apache, you'll need to install this package.

audiofile-devel — (Version 0.1.6, 100K)
Libraries, include files and other resources you can use to develop audiofile applications.

bind-devel — (Version 8.2, 1,294K)
The bind-devel package contains all the include files and the library required for DNS (Domain Name Service) development for bind versions 8.x.x. You should install bind-devel if you want to develop bind DNS applications. If you install bind-devel, you'll need to install bind, as well.

control-center-devel — (Version 1.0.5, 38K)
If you're interested in developing panels for the GNOME control center, you'll want to install this package. Control-center-devel helps you create the 'capplets' which are used in the control center.

e2fsprogs-devel — (Version 1.14, 260K)
E2fsprogs-devel contains the libraries and header files needed to develop second extended (ext2) filesystem-specific programs. You should install e2fsprogs-devel if you want to develop ext2 filesystem-specific programs. If you install e2fsprogs-devel, you'll also want to install e2fsprogs.

esound-devel — (Version 0.2.9, 45K)
Libraries, include files and other resources you can use to develoop EsounD applications.

faces-devel — (Version 1.6.1, 22K)
[W]

Faces-devel contains the faces program development environment, (i.e., the static libraries and header files). If you want to develop Faces applications, you'll need to install faces-devel. You'll also need to install the faces package.

fnlib-devel — (Version 0.4, 34K)
Headers, static libraries and documentation for Fnlib.

freetype-devel — (Version 1.2, 511K)
This package is only needed if you intend to develop or compile applications which rely on the FreeType library. If you simply want to run existing applications, you won't need this package.

gd-devel — (Version 1.3, 7K)
[W]

These are the development libraries and header files for gd, the .gif graphics library. If you're installing the gd graphics library, you must install gd-devel.

gdbm-devel — (Version 1.7.3, 72K)
[W]

Gdbm-devel contains the development libraries and header files for gdbm, the GNU database system. These libraries and header files are necessary if you plan to do development using the gdbm database. Install gdbm-devel if you are developing C programs which will use the gdbm database library. You'll also need to install the gdbm package.

gedit-devel — (Version 0.5.1, 8K)
gEdit is a small but powerful text editor for GTK+ and/or GNOME. This package allows you to develop plugins that work within gEdit. Plugins can create new documents and manipulate documents in arbitrary ways.

gimp-devel — (Version 1.0.4, 258K)
Static libraries and header files for writing GIMP plugins and extensions.

glib-devel — (Version 1.2.1, 309K)
[W]

Static libraries and header files for the support library for the GIMP's X libraries, which are available as public libraries. GLIB includes generally useful data structures.

glibc-devel – (Version 2.1.1, 32,857K)
[W] [S]

To develop programs which use the standard C libraries (which nearly all programs do), the system needs to have these standard header files and object files available for creating the executables.

glibc-profile – (Version 2.1.1, 30,448K)
When programs are being profiled using gprof, they must use these libraries instead of the standard C libraries for gprof to be able to profile them correctly.

gmp-devel – (Version 2.0.2, 319K)
The static libraries, header files and documentation for using the GNU MP arbitrary precision library in applications. If you want to develop applications which will use the GNU MP library, you'll need to install the gmp-devel package. You'll also need to install the gmp package.

gnome-core-devel – (Version 1.0.4, 122K)
Panel libraries and header files for creating GNOME panels.

gnome-games-devel – (Version 1.0.2, 42K)
This packages installs the libraries and files needed to develop some GNOME games.

gnome-libs-devel – (Version 1.0.5, 7,329K)
GNOME (GNU Network Object Model Environment) is a user-friendly set of applications and desktop tools to be used in conjunction with a window manager for the X Window System. GNOME is similar in purpose and scope to CDE and KDE, but GNOME is based completely on Open Source software. The gnome-libs-devel package includes the libraries and include files that you will need to develop GNOME applications. You should install the gnome-libs-devel package if you would like to develop GNOME applications. You don't need to install gnome-libs-devel if you just want to use the GNOME desktop environment. If you are going to develop GNOME applications and/or you're going to use the GNOME desktop environment, you'll also need to install the gnome-core and gnome-libs packages. If you want to use Linuxconf with a GNOME front end, you'll also need to install the gnome-linuxconf package.

gnome-objc-devel – (Version 1.0.1, 694K)
Libraries, include files and other files you can use to develop Objective C GNOME applications. If you're interested in developing GNOME applications, you should install this package.

gnome-pim-devel – (Version 1.0.3, 38K)
Files needed to develop apps which interact with gnome-pim applications via CORBA.

gpm-devel — (Version 1.17.5, 27K)
[W]

The gpm-devel program contains the libraries and header files needed for development of mouse driven programs. This package allows you to develop text-mode programs which use the mouse. Install gpm-devel if you need to develop text-mode programs which will use the mouse. You'll also need to install the gpm package.

gtk+-devel — (Version 1.2.1, 2,461K)
[W]

The gtk+-devel package contains the static libraries and header files needed for developing GTK+ (GIMP ToolKit) applications. The gtk+-devel package contains glib (a collection of routines for simplifying the development of GTK+ applications), GDK (the General Drawing Kit, which simplifies the interface for writing GTK+ widgets and using GTK+ widgets in applications), and GTK+ (the widget set). Install gtk+-devel if you need to develop GTK+ applications. You'll also need to install the gtk+ package.

guile-devel — (Version 1.3, 963K)
The guile-devel package includes the libraries, header files, etc., that you'll need to develop applications that are linked with the GUILE extensibility library. You need to install the guile-devel package if you want to develop applications that will be linked to GUILE. You'll also need to install the guile package.

imlib-devel — (Version 1.9.4, 547K)
The header files, static libraries and documentation needed for developing Imlib applications. Imlib is an image loading and rendering library for X11R6. Install the imlib-devel package if you want to develop Imlib applications. You'll also need to install the imlib and imlib_cfgeditor packages.

inn-devel — (Version 2.2, 1,737K)
The inn-devel package contains the INN (InterNetNews) library, which several programs that interface with INN need in order to work (for example, newsgate and tin). If you are installing a program which must interface with the INN news system, you should install inn-devel.

libghttp-devel — (Version 1.0.2, 42K)
Libraries and includes files you can use for libghttp development

libgr-devel — (Version 2.0.13, 320K)
[W]

The libgr-devel package contains the header files and static libraries, etc., for developing programs which can handle the various graphics file formats supported by the libgr library. Install libgr-devel if you want to develop programs for handling the graphics file formats supported by the libgr library. You'll also need to have the libgr package installed.

libgtop-devel — (Version 1.0.1, 326K)
GNOME (GNU Network Object Model Environment) is a user-friendly set of applications and desktop tools to be used in conjunction with a window manager for the X Window System. GNOME is similar in purpose and scope to CDE and KDE, but GNOME is based completely on Open Source software. The gnome-libs-devel package includes the libraries and include files that you will need to develop GNOME applications. You should install the gnome-libs-devel package if you would like to develop GNOME applications. You don't need to install gnome-libs-devel if you just want to use the GNOME desktop environment. If you are going to develop GNOME applications and/or you're going to use the GNOME desktop environment, you'll also need to install the gnome-core and gnome-libs packages. If you want to use Linuxconf with a GNOME front end, you'll also need to install the gnome-linuxconf package.

libjpeg-devel — (Version 6b, 233K)
[W]

The libjpeg-devel package includes the header files and static libraries necessary for developing programs which will manipulate JPEG files using the libjpeg library. If you are going to develop programs which will manipulate JPEG images, you should install libjpeg-devel. You'll also need to have the libjpeg package installed.

libpcap — (Version 0.4, 121K)
Libpcap provides a portable framework for low-level network monitoring. Libpcap can provide network statistics collection, security monitoring and network debugging. Since almost every system vendor provides a different interface for packet capture, the libpcap authors created this system-independent API to ease in porting and to alleviate the need for several system-dependent packet capture modules in each application. Install libpcap if you need to do low-level network traffic monitoring on your network.

libpng-devel — (Version 1.0.3, 485K)
[W]

The libpng-devel package contains the header files and static libraries necessary for developing programs using the PNG (Portable Network Graphics) library. If you want to develop programs which will manipulate PNG image format files, you should install libpng-devel. You'll also need to install the libpng package.

libtermcap-devel — (Version 2.0.8, 12K)
[W]

This package includes the libraries and header files necessary for developing programs which will access the termcap database. If you need to develop programs which will access the termcap database, you'll need to install this package. You'll also need to install the libtermcap package.

libtiff-devel — (Version 3.4, 1,614K)
[W]

This package contains the header files and static libraries for developing programs which will manipulate TIFF format image files using the libtiff library. If you need to develop programs which will manipulate TIFF format image files, you should install this package. You'll also need to install the libtiff package.

libungif-devel — (Version 4.1.0, 271K)
This package contains the static libraries, header files and documentation necessary for development of programs that will use the libungif library to load and save GIF format image files. You should install this package if you need to develop programs which will use the libungif library functions for loading and saving GIF format image files. You'll also need to install the libungif package.

libxml-devel — (Version 1.0.0, 127K)
This packages contains the libraries, include and other files you can use to develop libxml applications.

linuxconf-devel — (Version 1.14r2, 3,742K)
[W]

Linuxconf is an extremely capable system configuration tool. It provides a variety of interfaces through which you can configure your Linux system and manage a large proportion of the system's operations. This package provides the components necessary for developing Linuxconf modules outside of the Linuxconf source tree and/or developing stand-alone utilities using the Linuxconf interface toolkit. Install linuxconf-devel if you want to develop Linuxconf modules. You must also have Linuxconf installed.

ncurses-devel – (Version 4.2, 7,149K)
[W]

The header files and libraries for developing applications that use the ncurses CRT screen handling and optimization package. Install the ncurses-devel package if you want to develop applications which will use ncurses.

newt-devel – (Version 0.40, 120K)
[W]

The newt-devel package contains the header files and libraries necessary for developing applications which use newt. Newt is a development library for text mode user interfaces. Newt is based on the slang library. Install newt-devel if you want to develop applications which will use newt.

pilot-link-devel – (Version 0.9.0, 1,635K)
This package contains the development headers that are used to build the pilot-link package. It also includes the static libraries necessary to build static pilot apps.

popt – (Version 1.2.3, 54K)
Popt is a C library for parsing command line parameters. Popt was heavily influenced by the getopt() and getopt_long() functions, but it improves on them by allowing more powerful argument expansion. Popt can parse arbitrary argv[] style arrays and automatically set variables based on command line arguments. Popt allows command line arguments to be aliased via configuration files and includes utility functions for parsing arbitrary strings into argv[] arrays using shell-like rules. Install popt if you're a C programmer and you'd like to use its capabilities.

postgresql-devel – (Version 6.4.2, 662K)
[S]

This package contains the header files and libraries needed to compile applications which will directly interact with a PostgreSQL server. Install this package if you want to develop applications which will interact with a PostgreSQL server.

python-devel – (Version 1.5.1, 3,499K)
The Python programming language's interpreter can be extended with dynamically loaded extensions and can be embedded in other programs. This package contains the header files and libraries needed to do these types of tasks. Install python-devel if you want to develop Python extensions. The python package will also need to be installed. You'll probably also want to install the python-docs package, which contains Python documentation.

qt-devel — (Version 1.44, 9,809K)

Contains the files necessary to develop applications using Qt: header files, the Qt meta object compiler, man pages, HTML documentation and example programs. See http://www.troll.no for more information about Qt, or file:/usr/lib/qt/html/index.html for Qt documentation in HTML.

readline-devel — (Version 2.2.1, 261K)

[W]

The readline library will read a line from the terminal and return it. Use of the readline library allows programmers to provide an easy to use and more intuitive interface for users. If you want to develop programs which will use the readline library, you'll need to have the readline-devel package installed. You'll also need to have the readline package installed.

rpm-devel — (Version 2.93, 338K)

[W]

This package contains the RPM C library and header files. These development files will simplify the process of writing programs which manipulate RPM packages and databases and are intended to make it easier to create graphical package managers or any other tools that need an intimate knowledge of RPM packages in order to function. This package should be installed if you want to develop programs that will manipulate RPM packages and databases.

slang-devel — (Version 1.2.2, 1,192K)

[W]

This package contains the S-Lang extension language static libraries and header files which you'll need if you want to develop S-Lang based applications. Documentation which may help you write S-Lang based applications is also included. Install the slang-devel package if you want to develop applications based on the S-Lang extension language.

sox-devel — (Version 12.15, 855K)

This package contains the library needed for compiling applications which will use the SoX sound file format converter. Install sox-devel if you want to develop applications which will use SoX.

svgalib-devel — (Version 1.3.1, 505K)

[W]

The svgalib-devel package contains the libraries and header files needed to build programs which will use the SVGAlib low-level graphics library. Install the svgalib-devel package if you want to develop applications which will use the SVGAlib library.

ucd-snmp-devel – (Version 3.6.1, 275K)
The ucd-snmp-devel package contains the development libraries and header files for use with the UCD-SNMP project's network management tools. Install the ucd-snmp-devel package if you would like to develop applications for use with the UCD-SNMP project's network management tools. You'll also need to have the ucd-snmp and ucd-snmp-utils packages installed.

w3c-libwww-devel – (Version 5.2.6, 1,512K)
Static libraries and header files for programs that use w3c-libwww.

x11amp-devel – (Version 0.9_alpha3, 13K)
Static libraries and header files for building x11amp plugins.

xpm-devel – (Version 3.4j, 221K)
[W]

The xpm-devel package contains the development libraries and header files necessary for developing applications which will use the XPM library. The XPM library is used by many programs for displaying pixmaps in the X Window System. Install the xpm-devel package if you want to develop applications using the XPM pixmap library. You'll also need to install the xpm package.

– (Version 1.1.3, 165K)
[W]

The zlib-devel package contains the header files and libraries needed to develop programs that use the zlib compression and decompression library. Install the zlib-devel package if you want to develop applications that will use the zlib library.

System

This section contains packages that are associated with building system-level software under Red Hat Linux.

kernel-headers – (Version 2.2.5, 2,692K)
[W] [S]

Kernel-headers includes the C header files for the Linux kernel. The header files define structures and constants that are needed for building most standard programs. The header files are also needed for rebuilding the kernel.

kernel-source – (Version 2.2.5, 46,139K)
The kernel-source package contains the source code files for the Linux kernel. These source files are needed to build most C programs, since they depend on the constants defined in the source code. The source files can also be used to build a custom kernel that is better tuned to your particular hardware, if you are so inclined (and you know what you're doing).

Tools

This section contains packages that are associated with the various tools needed to develop software under Red Hat Linux.

ElectricFence – (Version 2.0.5, 44K)
[W] [S]

If you know what malloc() violations are, you'll be interested in ElectricFence. ElectricFence is a tool which can be used for C programming and debugging. It uses the virtual memory hardware of your system to detect when software overruns malloc() buffer boundaries, and/or to detect any accesses of memory released by free(). ElectricFence will then stop the program on the first instruction that caused a bounds violation and you can use your favorite debugger to display the offending statement. This package will install ElectricFence, which you can use if you're searching for a debugger to find malloc() violations.

autoconf – (Version 2.13, 580K)
[W] [S]

NU's Autoconf is a tool for configuring source code and Makefiles. Using Autoconf, programmers can create portable and configurable packages, since the person building the package is allowed to specify various configuration options. You should install Autoconf if you are developing software and you'd like to use it to create shell scripts which will configure your source code packages. If you are installing Autoconf, you will also need to install the GNU m4 package. Note that the Autoconf package is not required for the end user who may be configuring software with an Autoconf-generated script; Autoconf is only required for the generation of the scripts, not their use.

automake – (Version 1.4, 867K)
[W] [S]

Automake is an experimental Makefile generator. Automake was inspired by the 4.4BSD make and include files, but aims to be portable and to conform to the GNU standards for Makefile variables and targets. You should install Automake if you are developing software and would like to use its capabilities of automatically generating GNU standard Makefiles. if you install Automake, you will also need to install GNU's Autoconf package.

bin86 – (Version 0.4, 73K)
[W] [S]

The bin86 package provides an assembler and linker for real mode 80x86 instructions. You'll need to have this package installed in order to build programs that run in real mode, including LILO and the kernel's bootstrapping code, from their sources. You should install bin86 if you intend to build programs that run in real mode from their source code.

binutils – (Version 2.9.1.0.22b, 5,165K)
[B] [W] [S]

Binutils is a collection of binary utilities, including ar (for creating, modifying and extracting from archives), nm (for listing symbols from object files), objcopy (for copying and translating object files), objdump (for displaying information from object files), ranlib (for generating an index for the contents of an archive), size (for listing the section sizes of an object or archive file), strings (for listing printable strings from files), strip (for discarding symbols), c++filt (a filter for demangling encoded C++ symbols), addr2line (for converting addresses to file and line), and nbnconv (for converting object code into an NLM). Install binutils if you need to perform any of these types of actions on binary files. Most programmers will want to install binutils.

bison – (Version 1.27, 153K)
[W] [S]

Bison is a general purpose parser generator which converts a grammar description for an LALR context-free grammar into a C program to parse that grammar. Bison can be used to develop a wide range of language parsers, from ones used in simple desk calculators to complex programming languages. Bison is upwardly compatible with Yacc, so any correctly written Yacc grammar should work with Bison without any changes. If you know Yacc, you shouldn't have any trouble using Bison (but you do need to be very proficient in C programming to be able to use Bison). Many programs use Bison as part of their build process. Bison is only needed on systems that are used for development. If your system will be used for C development, you should install Bison since it is used to build many C programs.

blt – (Version 2.4g, 4,007K)
BLT is an extension to the Tk toolkit. BLT's most useful feature is the provision of more widgets for Tk, but it also provides more geometry managers and miscellaneous other commands. Note that you won't need to do any patching of the Tcl or Tk source files to use BLT, but you will need to have Tcl/Tk installed in order to use BLT. If you are programming with the Tk toolkit, you should install BLT. You will need to have Tcl/Tk installed.

byacc – (Version 1.9, 54K)
[W] [S]

Byacc (Berkeley Yacc) is a public domain LALR parser generator which is used by many programs during their build process. If you are going to do development on your system, you will want to install this package.

cdecl – (Version 2.5, 80K)
[W] [S]

The cdecl package includes the cdecl and c++decl utilities, which are used to translate English to C or C++ function declarations and vice versa. You should install the cdecl package if you intend to do C and/or C++ programming.

cproto – (Version 4.6, 85K)
[W] [S]

Cproto generates function prototypes and variable declarations from C source code. Cproto can also convert function definitions between the old style and the ANSI C style. This conversion will overwrite the original files, however, so be sure to make a backup copy of your original files in case something goes wrong. Since cproto uses a Yacc generated parser, it shouldn't be confused by complex function definitions (as much as other prototype generators) because it uses a Yacc generated parser. Cproto will be useful for C programmers, so install cproto if you are going to do any C programming.

ctags – (Version 3.2, 146K)
[W] [S]

Ctags generates an index (or tag) file of C language objects found in C source and header files. The index makes it easy for text editors or other utilities to locate the indexed items. Ctags can also generate a cross reference file which lists information about the various objects found in a set of C language files in human readable form. Exuberant Ctags improves on ctags because it can find all types of C language tags, including macro definitions, enumerated values (values inside enum...), function and method definitions, enum/struct/union tags, external function prototypes, typedef names and variable declarations. Exuberant Ctags is far less likely to be fooled by code containing #if preprocessor conditional constructs than ctags. Exuberant ctags supports output of emacs style TAGS files and can be used to print out a list of selected objects found in source files. Install ctags if you are going to use your system for C programming.

cvs – (Version 1.10.5, 3,088K) [W] [S]

CVS means Concurrent Version System; it is a version control system which can record the history of your files (usually, but not always, source code). CVS only stores the differences between versions, instead of every version of every file you've ever created. CVS also keeps a log of who, when and why changes occurred, among other aspects. CVS is very helpful for managing releases and controlling the concurrent editing of source files among multiple authors. Instead of providing version control for a collection of files in a single directory, CVS provides version control for a hierarchical collection of directories consisting of revision controlled files. These directories and files can then be combined together to form a software release. Install the cvs package if you need to use a version control system.

diffstat – (Version 1.25, 11K)

The diff command compares files line by line. Diffstat reads the output of the diff command and displays a histogram of the insertions, deletions and modifications in each file. Diffstat is commonly used to provide a summary of the changes in large, complex patch files. Install diffstat if you need a program which provides a summary of the diff command's output. You'll need to also install diffutils.

flex – (Version 2.5.4a, 302K)

[W] [S]

The flex program generates scanners. Scanners are programs which can recognize lexical patterns in text. Flex takes pairs of regular expressions and C code as input and generates a C source file as output. The output file is compiled and linked with a library to produce an executable. The executable searches through its input for occurrences of the regular expressions. When a match is found, it executes the corresponding C code. Flex was designed to work with both Yacc and Bison, and is used by many programs as part of their build process. You should install flex if you are going to use your system for application development.

gettext – (Version 0.10.35, 889K)

[W] [S]

The GNU gettext package provides a set of tools and documentation for producing multi-lingual messages in programs. Tools include a set of conventions about how programs should be written to support message catalogs, a directory and file naming organization for the message catalogs, a runtime library which supports the retrieval of translated messages, and stand-alone programs for handling the translatable and the already translated strings. Gettext provides an easy to use library and tools for creating, using, and modifying natural language catalogs and is a powerful and simple method for internationalizing programs. If you would like to internationalize or incorporate multi-lingual messages into programs that you're developing, you should install gettext.

gperf – (Version 2.7, 122K)

Gperf is a perfect hash function generator written in C++. Simply stated, a perfect hash function is a hash function and a data structure that allows recognition of a key word in a set of words using exactly one probe into the data structure. Install gperf if you need a program that generates perfect hash functions.

libtool – (Version 1.2f, 973K)

The libtool package contains the GNU libtool, a set of shell scripts which automatically configure UNIX and UNIX-like architectures to generically build shared libraries. Libtool provides a consistent, portable interface which simplifies the process of using shared libraries. If you are developing programs which will use shared libraries, you should install libtool.

make – (Version 3.77, 265K)

[W] [S]

A GNU tool for controlling the generation of executables and other non-source files of a program from the program's source files. Make allows users to build and install packages without any significant knowledge about the details of the build process. The details about how the program should be built are provided for make in the program's makefile. The GNU make tool should be installed on your system because it is commonly used to simplify the process of installing programs.

patch – (Version 2.5, 99K)

[W] [S]

The patch program applies diff files to originals. The diff command is used to compare an original to a changed file. Diff lists the changes made to the file. A person who has the original file can then use the patch command with the diff file to add the changes to their original file (patching the file). Patch should be installed because it is a common way of upgrading applications.

pmake – (Version 2.1.33, 1,031K)

[W] [S]

Make is a GNU tool which allows users to build and install programs without any significant knowledge of the build process. Details about how the program should be built are included in the program's Makefile. Pmake is a particular version (BSD 4.4) of make. Pmake supports some additional syntax which is not in the standard make program. Some Berkeley programs have Makefiles written for pmake. Pmake should be installed on your system so that you will be able to build programs which require using pmake instead of make.

pmake-customs — (Version 2.1.33, 982K)
Customs is a remote execution facility for PMake. Customs is designed to run on a network of machines with a consistent, shared filesystem. Customs requires Sun RPC in order to use XDR (eXternal Data Representation) routines for logging functions. A single server is designated as the master agent and is additionally responsible for noting when a machine goes down, from which machines any given machine will accept jobs and parcelling out available machines to requesting clients. The job of master is not given to any one machine but, rather, is decided among the active agents whenever the previous master dies. Clients are provided to: - alter the availability criteria for the local machine (importquota) - find the status of all registered hosts on the net (reginfo). - abort, restart or ping any customs agent on the network (cctrl). - export a command from the shell (export). - accept log information from all hosts on the net (logd).

rcs — (Version 5.7, 536K) [W] [S]
The Revision Control System (RCS) is a system for managing multiple versions of files. RCS automates the storage, retrieval, logging, identification and merging of file revisions. RCS is useful for text files that are revised frequently (for example, programs, documentation, graphics, papers and form letters). The rcs package should be installed if you need a system for managing different versions of files.

Documentation

This section contains packages that are associated with documentation for Linux in general and Red Hat Linux in particular.

bash2-doc — (Version 2.03, 2,275K)
This is a separate documentation package for the GNU Bourne Again shell.

faq — (Version 5.2, 891K)
The faq package includes the text of the Frequently Asked Questions (FAQ) about Linux from the SunSITE website (*http://sunsite.unc.edu/pub/Linux/docs/faqs/linux-faq/Linux-FAQ*). The Linux FAQ is a great source of information about Linux. Install faq if you'd like to read the Linux FAQ off your own machine.

gimp-manual — (Version 1.0.0, 17,979K)
The gimp-manual package contains the GIMP (GNU Image Manipulation Program) User Manual (GUM) in HTML format. Please note that the HTML version of the GUM is not as good a quality as the other versions, which can be obtained from the GUM website at *http://manual.gimp.org/pub/manual*. On the GUM website, the manual is provided in HTML (for viewing the GUM online), in PostScript(TM) and PDF formats (for printing) as well as in FM

(FrameMaker) source code. The FrameMaker source code is provided for people who would like to contribute to the Graphic Documentation Project. Submissions to the GUM are covered by the manual's license agreement and terms, included in the file COPYING. The GUM is a complete guide for using the GIMP. This version of the GUM includes improvements over previous versions. Be sure to check out the new Gallery chapter, which provides a good overview of what the GIMP can do. The Gallery displays cool images and give you hints on how to create them with the GIMP. For more information about the GUM, check the GUM website at *http://manual.gimp.org/*.

gnome-users-guide — (Version 1.0.5, 3,564K)
[W]

This package will install the users' guide for the GNOME Desktop Environment on your computer. You should install this package if you are going to use GNOME and you want a quick, handy reference.

helptool — (Version 2.4, 23K)
[W] [S]

The helptool provides a unified graphical user interface for searching through many of the help sources available (including man pages and GNU texinfo documents). Install helptool if you'd like to use it to search for help files. You'll need to have the X Window System installed to use the helptool.

howto — (Version 6.0, 11,103K)
Linux HOWTOs are detailed documents which describe a specific aspect of configuring or using Linux. Linux HOWTOs are a great source of practical information about your system. The latest versions of these documents are located at http://sunsite.unc.edu/linux. Install the howto package if you'd like to be able to access the Linux HOWTO documentation from your own system.

howto-chinese — (Version 6.0, 13,445K)
The howto-chinese package contains the Linux HOWTO documents that have been translated into Chinese. Linux HOWTOs are detailed documents describing a specific aspect of configuring or using Linux. Install the howto-chinese package if you'd like to use the Linux HOWTO documentation in Chinese. Please note that not all of the HOWTOs have been translated. If you need to have a complete set of HOWTOs, you'll need to install the English version (the howto package).

howto-croatian — (Version 6.0, 1,897K)
The howto-chinese package contains the Linux HOWTO documents that have been translated into Croatian. Linux HOWTOs are detailed documents which describe a specific aspect of configuring or using Linux. Install the howto-croatian package if you'd like to use the Linux HOWTO documentation in Croatian.

Please note that not all of the HOWTOs have been translated. If you need to have a complete set of HOWTOs, you'll need to install the English version (the howto package).

howto-french — (Version 6.0, 29,195K)
This package contains the Linux HOWTO documents that have been translated into French. Linux HOWTOs are detailed documents which describe a specific aspect of configuring or using Linux. Install the howto-french package if you'd like to use the Linux HOWTOs in French. Please note that not all of the HOWTOs have been translated. If you need to have a complete set of HOWTOs, you'll need to install the English version (the howto package).

howto-german — (Version 6.0, 22,361K)
This package contains the Linux HOWTO documents that have been translated into German. Linux HOWTOs are detailed documents which describe a specific aspect of configuring or using Linux. Install the howto-german package if you'd like to use the Linux HOWTOs in German. Please note that not all of the HOWTOs have been translated. If you need to have a complete set of HOWTOs, you'll need to install the English version (the howto package).

howto-greek — (Version 6.0, 7,712K)
This package contains the Linux HOWTO documents that have been translated into Greek. Linux HOWTOs are detailed documents which describe a specific aspect of configuring or using Linux. Install the howto-greek package if you'd like to use the Linux HOWTOs in Greek. Please note that not all of the HOWTOs have been translated. If you need to have a complete set of HOWTOs, you'll need to install the English version (the howto package).

howto-html — (Version 6.0, 12,824K)
This package contains the Linux HOWTO documents in HTML format, so they can be viewed with a Web browser. Linux HOWTOs are detailed documents which describe a specific aspect of configuring or using Linux. Install the howto-html package if you'd like to view the Linux HOWTOs with your Web browser off your own machine, or if you'd like to provide the HTML HOWTOs from your Web server.

howto-indonesian — (Version 6.0, 8,491K)
This package contains the Linux HOWTO documents that have been translated into Indonesian. Linux HOWTOs are detailed documents which describe a specific aspect of configuring or using Linux. Install the howto-indonesian package if you'd like to use the Linux HOWTOs in Indonesian. Please note that not all of the HOWTOs have been translated. If you need to have a complete set of HOWTOs, you'll need to install the English version (the howto package).

howto-italian — (Version 6.0, 21,596K)
This package contains the Linux HOWTO documents that have been translated into Italian. Linux HOWTOs are detailed documents which describe a specific aspect of configuring or using Linux. Install the howto-italian package if you'd like to use the Linux HOWTOs in Italian. Please note that not all of the HOWTOs have been translated. If you need to have a complete set of HOWTOs, you'll need to install the English version (the howto package).

howto-japanese — (Version 6.0, 11,888K)
This package contains the Linux HOWTO documents that have been translated into Japanese. Linux HOWTOs are detailed documents which describe a specific aspect of configuring or using Linux. Install the howto-japanese package if you'd like to use the Linux HOWTOs in Japanese. Please note that not all of the HOWTOs have been translated. If you need to have a complete set of HOWTOs, you'll need to install the English version (the howto package).

howto-korean — (Version 6.0, 19,242K)
This package contains the Linux HOWTO documents that have been translated into Korean. Linux HOWTOs are detailed documents which describe a specific aspect of configuring or using Linux. Install the howto-korean package if you'd like to use the Linux HOWTOs in Korean. Please note that not all of the HOWTOs have been translated. If you need to have a complete set of HOWTOs, you'll need to install the English version (the howto package).

howto-polish — (Version 6.0, 9,474K)
This package contains the Linux HOWTO documents that have been translated into Polish. Linux HOWTOs are detailed documents which describe a specific aspect of configuring or using Linux. Install the howto-polish package if you'd like to use the Linux HOWTOs in Polish. Please note that not all of the HOWTOs have been translated. If you need to have a complete set of HOWTOs, you'll need to install the English version (the howto package).

howto-serbian — (Version 6.0, 37K)
This package contains the Linux HOWTO documents that have been translated into Serbian. Linux HOWTOs are detailed documents which describe a specific aspect of configuring or using Linux. Install the howto-serbian package if you'd like to use the Linux HOWTOs in Serbian. Please note that not all of the HOWTOs have been translated. If you need to have a complete set of HOWTOs, you'll need to install the English version (the howto package).

howto-sgml — (Version 6.0, 9,767K)
The howto-sgml package contains the Linux HOWTO documents in SGML format. The SGML format documents are the "source" files. Other file formats (text, PostScript(TM), DVI, HTML) are translated from the SGML documents.

Linux HOWTOs are detailed documents which describe a specific aspect of configuring or using Linux. Install the howto-sgml package if you'd like to use the Linux HOWTO documents in SGML format.

howto-slovenian – (Version 6.0, 3,791K)
This package contains the Linux HOWTO documents that have been translated into Slovenian. Linux HOWTOs are detailed documents which describe a specific aspect of configuring or using Linux. Install the howto-slovenian package if you'd like to use the Linux HOWTOs in Slovenian. Please note that not all of the HOWTOs have been translated. If you need to have a complete set of HOWTOs, you'll need to install the English version (the howto package).

howto-spanish – (Version 6.0, 7,739K)
This package contains the Linux HOWTO documents that have been translated into Spanish. Linux HOWTOs are detailed documents which describe a specific aspect of configuring or using Linux. Install the howto-spanish package if you'd like to use the Linux HOWTOs in Spanish. Please note that not all of the HOWTOs have been translated. If you need to have a complete set of HOWTOs, you'll need to install the English version (the howto package).

howto-swedish – (Version 6.0, 4,009K)
This package contains the Linux HOWTO documents that have been translated into Swedish. Linux HOWTOs are detailed documents which describe a specific aspect of configuring or using Linux. Install the howto-swedish package if you'd like to use the Linux HOWTOs in Swedish. Please note that not all of the HOWTOs have been translated. If you need to have a complete set of HOWTOs, you'll need to install the English version (the howto package).

howto-turkish – (Version 6.0, 816K)
This package contains the Linux HOWTO documents that have been translated into Turkish. Linux HOWTOs are detailed documents which describe a specific aspect of configuring or using Linux. Install the howto-turkish package if you'd like to use the Linux HOWTOs in Turkish. Please note that not all of the HOWTOs have been translated. If you need to have a complete set of HOWTOs, you'll need to install the English version (the howto package).

indexhtml – (Version 5.8, 6K)
[W] [S]

The indexhtml package contains the HTML page and graphics for a welcome page shown by your Web browser, which you'll see after you've successfully installed Red Hat Linux. The Web page provided by indexhtml tells you how to register your Red Hat software and how to get any support that you might need.

install-guide — (Version 3.2, 1,373K)

The install-guide contains the Linux Documentation Project (LDP) Getting Started Guide in HTML format. The LDP Getting Started Guide is intended to be an installation manual and an entry-level guide to Linux. If you're installing the Red Hat Linux operating system, you should ignore the installation instructions included here and instead use Red Hat's Installation Guide. You should install the install-guide package if you'd like to use the LDP's Getting Started Guide in HTML format using your Web browser off your own machine, or if you'd like to provide the LDP's Getting Started Guide on your Web server.

kernel-doc — (Version 2.2.5, 2,306K)

This package contains documentation files form the kernel source. Various bits of information about the Linux kernel and the device drivers shipped with it are documented in these files. You also might want install this package if you need a reference to the options that can be passed to Linux kernel modules at load time.

lpg — (Version 0.4, 1,739K)

The lpg package includes a generic guide for programming on Linux systems, in HTML format. You may want to check the Linux Documentation Project's website at http://sunsite.unc.edu/LDP/ for more information and possible updates to the programming guide. If you'd like to view the Linux programming guide using your Web browser from files on your own machine, or if you'd like to provide it from your Web server, you should install the lpg package.

man-pages — (Version 1.23, 1,795K)

[W] [S]

A large collection of man pages (reference material) from the Linux Documentation Project (LDP). The man pages are organized into the following sections: Section 1: User commands (intro only) Section 2: System calls Section 3: Libc calls Section 4: Devices (e.g., hd, sd) Section 5: File formats and protocols (e.g., wtmp, /etc/passwd, nfs) Section 6: Games (intro only) Section 7: Conventions, macro packages, etc. (e.g., nroff, ascii) Section 8: System administration (intro only)

nag — (Version 1.0, 1,217K)

The nag package contains the Linux Documentation Project's Network Administrators' Guide. The NAG covers the wide world of Linux networking, including TCP/IP, UUCP, SLIP, DNS, mail systems, NNTP and news systems, and NFS. Be sure to check the LDP's website at http://sunsite.unc.edu/linux/ldp.html for possible updates to the NAG. Install the nag package if you'd like to use the LDP's Network Administrators' Guide off your own machine.

python-docs – (Version 1.5.1, 2,611K)

The python-docs package contains documentation on the Python programming language and interpreter. The documentation is provided in ASCII text files and in LaTeX source files. Install the python-docs package if you'd like to use the documentation for the Python language.

rhl-alpha-install-addend-en – (Version 5.2, 200K)

The rhl-alpha-install-addend-en package contains the Red Hat Linux 5.2 Alpha Installation Addendum document in HTML format. Install the rhl-alpha-install-addend-en package if you'd like to use an HTML version of the Alpha Installation Addendum loaded on your own machine.

rhl-install-guide-en – (Version 5.2, 2,245K)

The rhl-install-guide-en package contains the Red Hat Linux 5.2 Installation Guide in HTML format. An online copy of the Red Hat Linux 5.2 Installation Guide is available from the Red Hat Software Web page at *http://www.redhat.com*. Install the rhl-install-guide-en package if you would like to use an HTML version of the Installation Guide from your own machine.

sag – (Version 0.6, 644K)

The Linux Documentation Project's System Administrators' Guide, provided in HTML format. This document provides a generic guide to Linux system administration. Check the Linux Documentation Project's website at *http://sunsite.unc.edu/LDP/ldp.html* for other formats of this document or for any updates. Install the sag package if you'd like to use the HTML version of the LDP's System Administrators' Guide on your own machine.

sendmail-doc – (Version 8.9.3, 1,360K)

The sendmail-doc package contains documentation about the Sendmail Mail Transport Agent (MTA) program, including release notes, the Sendmail FAQ and a few papers written about Sendmail. The papers are provided in PostScript(TM) and troff formats. Install the sendmail-doc package if you need documentation about Sendmail.

specspo – (Version 6.0, 850K)

The specspo package contains the portable object catalogues used to internationalize Red Hat packages.

System Environment

This section contains packages that are required to provide the Red Hat Linux system environment.

Base

This section contains packages that are required for the basic system environment.

MAKEDEV – (Version 2.4, 25K)

[B]

The `/dev` directory contains important files which correspond to the hardware on your system, such as sound cards, serial or printer ports, tape and CD-ROM drives and more. MAKEDEV is a script which helps you create and maintain the files in your /dev directory. These are the files needed to install MAKEDEV.

SysVinit – (Version 2.74, 151K)

[B]

The SysVinit package contains a group of processes that control the very basic functions of your system. SysVinit is the first program started by the Linux kernel when the system boots, controlling the startup, running and shutdown of all other programs.

adjtimex – (Version 1.3, 23K)

Adjtimex is a kernel clock management program, which the superuser may use to correct any drift in the system's clock. Users can use adjtimex to view the time variables.

authconfig – (Version 1.7, 27K)

[B]

Authconfig is a terminal mode program for setting up Network Information Service (NIS) and shadow (more secure) passwords on your system. Authconfig also configures the system to automatically turn on NIS at system startup.

basesystem – (Version 6.0, 0K)

[B]

Basesystem defines the components of a basic Red Hat Linux system (for example, the package installation order to use during bootstrapping). Basesystem should be the first package installed on a system, and it should never be removed.

chkconfig – (Version 1.0.4, 69K)

[B]

Chkconfig is a basic system utility. It updates and queries runlevel information for system services. Chkconfig manipulates the numerous symbolic links in /etc/rc.d, so system administrators don't have to manually edit the symbolic links as often.

chkfontpath – (Version 1.3, 18K)
[W] [S]

This is a simple terminal mode program for adding, removing and listing the directories contained in the X font server's path. It is mostly intended to be used 'internally' by RPM when packages with fonts are added or removed, but it may be useful as a stand-alone utility in some instances.

crontabs – (Version 1.7, 4K)
[B]

The crontabs package contains root crontab files. Crontab is the program used to install, uninstall or list the tables used to drive the cron daemon. The cron daemon checks the crontab files to see when particular commands are scheduled to be executed. If commands are scheduled, it executes them. Crontabs handles a basic system function, so it should be installed on your system.

dev – (Version 2.7.3, 7K)
[B]

The Red Hat Linux operating system uses file system entries to represent devices (CD-ROMs, floppy drives, etc.) attached to the machine. All of these entries are in the `/dev` tree (although they don't have to be). This package contains the most commonly used `/dev` entries. The dev package is a basic part of your Red Hat Linux system and it needs to be installed.

e2fsprogs – (Version 1.14, 1,134K)
[B]

The e2fsprogs package contains a number of utilities for creating, checking, modifying and correcting any inconsistencies in second extended (ext2) filesystems. E2fsprogs contains e2fsck (used to repair filesystem inconsistencies after an unclean shutdown), mke2fs (used to initialize a partition to contain an empty ext2 filesystem), debugfs (used to examine the internal structure of a filesystem, to manually repair a corrupted filesystem or to create test cases for e2fsck), tune2fs (used to modify filesystem parameters) and most of the other core ext2fs filesystem utilities. You should install the e2fsprogs package if you need to manage the performance of an ext2 filesystem.

eject – (Version 2.0.2, 46K)
[B]

The eject program allows the user to eject removable media (typically CD-ROMs, floppy disks or Iomega Jaz or Zip disks) using software control. Eject can also control some multi- disk CD changers and even some devices' auto-eject features. Install eject if you'd like to eject removable media using software control.

etcskel — (Version 1.6, 2K)
[B]

The etcskel package is part of the basic Red Hat system. Etcskel provides the /etc/skel directory's files. These files (.Xdefaults, .bash_logout, .bash_profile, .bashrc) are then placed in every new user's home directory when new accounts are created.

filesystem — (Version 1.3.4, 80K)
[B]

The filesystem package is one of the basic packages that is installed on a Red Hat Linux system. Filesystem contains the basic directory layout for a Linux operating system, including the correct permissions for the directories.

genromfs — (Version 0.3, 12K)
Genromfs is a tool for creating romfs filesystems, which are lightweight, read-only filesystems supported by the Linux kernel.

info — (Version 3.12f, 245K)
[B]

The GNU project uses the texinfo file format for much of its documentation. The info package provides a standalone TTY-based browser program for viewing texinfo files. You should install info, because GNU's texinfo documentation is a valuable source of information about the software on your system.

initscripts — (Version 3.98, 148K)
[B]

The initscripts package contains the basic system scripts used to boot your Red Hat system, change run levels, and shut the system down cleanly. Initscripts also contains the scripts that activate and deactivate most network interfaces.

ipchains — (Version 1.3.8, 316K)
[W] [S]

Linux IP Firewalling Chains is an update to (and hopefully an improvement upon) the normal Linux Firewalling code, for 2.0 and 2.1 kernels. It lets you do things like firewalls, IP masquerading, etc.

isapnptools — (Version 1.18, 237K)
[B]

The isapnptools package contains utilities for configuring ISA Plug-and-Play (PnP) cards/boards which are in compliance with the PnP ISA Specification Version 1.0a. ISA PnP cards use registers instead of jumpers for setting the board address and interrupt assignments. The cards also contain descriptions of the resources which need to be allocated. The BIOS on your system, or isapnptools, uses a protocol described in the specification to find all of the PnP boards and allocate the resources so that none of them conflict. Note that the BIOS doesn't do a very good job of allocating resources. So isapnptools is suitable for all systems, whether or not they include a PnP BIOS. In fact, a PnP BIOS adds some complications. A PnP BIOS may already activate some cards so that the drivers can find them. Then these tools can unconfigure them or change their settings, causing all sorts of nasty effects. If you have PnP network cards that already work, you should read through the documentation files very carefully before you use isapnptools. Install isapnptools if you need utilities for configuring ISA PnP cards.

kbdconfig – (Version 1.9, 40K)
[B]

The kbdconfig utility is a terminal mode program for setting the keyboard map for your system. Keyboard maps are necessary for using any keyboard besides the US default keyboard. Kbdconfig will load the selected keymap before exiting and configure your machine to use that keymap automatically after rebooting. You should install kbdconfig if you need a utility for changing your keyboard map.

ld.so – (Version 1.9.5, 247K)
[B]

This package contains the shared library configuration tool, ldconfig, which is required by many packages. It also includes the shared library loader and dynamic loader for Linux libc 5.

ldconfig – (Version 1.9.5, 223K)
[B]

Ldconfig is a basic system program which determines run-time link bindings between ld.so and shared libraries. Ldconfig scans a running system and sets up the symbolic links that are used to load shared libraries properly. It also creates a cache (/etc/ld.so.cache) which speeds the loading of programs which use shared libraries.

lilo – (Version 0.21, 1,095K)
[B]

LILO (LInux LOader) is a basic system program which boots your Linux system. LILO loads the Linux kernel from a floppy or a hard drive, boots the kernel and passes control of the system to the kernel. LILO can also boot other operating systems.

logrotate — (Version 3.1, 52K)
[B]

The logrotate utility is designed to simplify the administration of log files on a system which generates a lot of log files. Logrotate allows for the automatic rotation compression, removal and mailing of log files. Logrotate can be set to handle a log file daily, weekly, monthly or when the log file gets to a certain size. Normally, logrotate runs as a daily cron job. Install the logrotate package if you need a utility to deal with the log files on your system.

losetup — (Version 2.9, 8K)
[B]

Linux supports a special block device called the loop device, which maps a normal file onto a virtual block device. This allows for the file to be used as a "virtual file system" inside another file. Losetup is used to associate loop devices with regular files or block devices, to detach loop devices and to query the status of a loop device.

mailcap — (Version 2.0.1, 34K)
[B]

The mailcap file is used by the metamail program. Metamail reads the mailcap file to determine how it should display non-text or multimedia material. Basically, mailcap associates a particular type of file with a particular program that a mail agent or other program can call in order to handle the file. Mailcap should be installed to allow certain programs to be able to handle non-text files.

man — (Version 1.5f, 217K)
[B]

The man package includes three tools for finding information and/or documentation about your Linux system: man, apropos and whatis. The man system formats and displays on-line manual pages about commands or functions on your system. Apropos searches the whatis database (containing short descriptions of system commands) for a string. Whatis searches its own database for a complete word. The man package should be installed on your system because it is the primary way for finding documentation.

mgetty — (Version 1.1.14, 845K)
The mgetty package contains a "smart" getty which allows logins over a serial line (i.e., through a modem). If you're using a Class 2 or 2.0 modem, mgetty can receive faxes. If you also need to send faxes, you'll need to install the sendfax program. If you'll be dialing in to your system using a modem, you should install the mgetty package. If you'd like to send faxes using mgetty and your modem, you'll need to install the mgetty-sendfax program. If you need a viewer for faxes, you'll also need to install the mgetty-viewfax package.

mingetty – (Version 0.9.4, 32K)
[B]

The mingetty program is a lightweight, minimalist getty program for use only on virtual consoles. Mingetty is not suitable for serial lines (you should use the mgetty program instead for that purpose).

mkbootdisk – (Version 1.1, 5K)
[B]

The mkbootdisk program creates a standalone boot floppy disk for booting the running system. The created boot disk will look for the root filesystem on the device mentioned in /etc/fstab and includes an initial ramdisk image which will load any necessary SCSI modules for the system.

mkinitrd – (Version 2.0, 7K)
[B]

Mkinitrd creates filesystem images for use as initial ramdisk (initrd) images. These ramdisk images are often used to preload the block device modules (SCSI or RAID) needed to access the root filesystem. In other words, generic kernels can be built without drivers for any SCSI adapters which load the SCSI driver as a module. Since the kernel needs to read those modules, but in this case it isn't able to address the SCSI adapter, an initial ramdisk is used. The initial ramdisk is loaded by the operating system loader (normally LILO) and is available to the kernel as soon as the ramdisk is loaded. The ramdisk image loads the proper SCSI adapter and allows the kernel to mount the root filesystem. The mkinitrd program creates such a ramdisk using information found in the /etc/conf.modules file.

mkkickstart – (Version 1.1, 4K)
The mkkickstart program writes a kickstart description from the host machine. The kickstart description can then be used, during a CD-ROM or NFS installation, to automatically build that machine's configuration of Red Hat Linux on one or more other machines. Install mkkickstart if you want to use the kickstart method to automatically install Red Hat Linux.

mktemp – (Version 1.5, 8K)
[B]

The mktemp utility takes a given file name template and overwrites a portion of it to create a unique file name. This allows shell scripts and other programs to safely create and use /tmp files. Install the mktemp package if you need to use shell scripts or other programs which will create and use unique /tmp files.

mount — (Version 2.9, 115K)
[B]

The mount package contains the mount, umount, swapon and swapoff programs. Accessible files on your system are arranged in one big tree or hierarchy. These files can be spread out over several devices. The mount command attaches a filesystem on some device to your system's file tree. The umount command detaches a filesystem from the tree. Swapon and swapoff, respectively, specify and disable devices and files for paging and swapping.

mouseconfig — (Version 3.7, 136K)

[B]

Mouseconfig is a text-based mouse configuration tool. Mouseconfig sets up the files and links needed for configuring and using a mouse on a Red Hat Linux system. The mouseconfig tool can be used to set the correct mouse type for programs like gpm, and can be used with Xconfigurator to set up the mouse for the X Window System.

net-tools — (Version 1.51, 395K)
[B]

The net-tools package contains the basic tools needed for setting up networking: arp, rarp, ifconfig, netstat, ethers and route.

ntsysv — (Version 1.0.4, 23K)
[B]

ntsysv updates and queries runlevel information for system services. ntsysv relieves system administrators of having to directly manipulate the numerous symbolic links in `/etc/rc.d`.

pam — (Version 0.66, 1,850K)
[B]

PAM (Pluggable Authentication Modules) is a system security tool which allows system administrators to set authentication policy without having to recompile programs which do authentication.

passwd — (Version 0.50, 28K)
[B]

The passwd package contains a system utility (passwd) which sets and/or changes passwords, using PAM (Pluggable Authentication Modules). To use passwd, you should have PAM installed on your system.

pwdb – (Version 0.56, 417K)
[B]

The pwdb package contains libpwdb, the password database library. Libpwdb is a library which implements a generic user information database. Libpwdb was specifically designed to work with Linux's PAM (Pluggable Authentication Modules). Libpwdb allows configurable access to and management of security tools like `/etc/passwd`, `/etc/shadow` and network authentication systems including NIS and Radius.

quota – (Version 1.66, 79K)
[B]

The quota package contains system administration tools for monitoring and limiting users' and or groups' disk usage, per filesystem.

raidtools – (Version 0.90, 151K)
This package includes the tools you need to set up and maintain a software RAID device under Linux. It only works with Linux 2.2 kernels and later, or 2.0 kernel specifically patched with newer raid support.

rootfiles – (Version 5.2, 1K)
[B]

The rootfiles package contains basic required files that are placed in the root user's account. These files are basically the same as the files found in the etcskel package, which are placed in regular users' home directories.

rpm – (Version 2.93, 1,599K)
[B]

The Red Hat Package Manager (RPM) is a powerful command line driven package management system capable of installing, uninstalling, verifying, querying, and updating software packages. Each software package consists of an archive of files along with information about the package like its version, a description, etc.

setup – (Version 2.0.1, 15K)
[B]

The setup package contains a set of very important system configuration and setup files, such as passwd, group, profile and more. You should install the setup package because you will find yourself using its many features for system administration.

shadow-utils — (Version 980403, 604K)
[B]

The shadow-utils package includes the necessary programs for converting UNIX password files to the shadow password format, plus programs for managing user and group accounts. The pwconv command converts passwords to the shadow password format. The pwunconv command unconverts shadow passwords and generates an npasswd file (a standard UNIX password file). The pwck command checks the integrity of password and shadow files. The lastlog command prints out the last login times for all users. The useradd, userdel and usermod commands are used for managing user accounts. The groupadd, groupdel and groupmod commands are used for managing group accounts.

shapecfg — (Version 2.0.36, 6K)
The Shapecfg program configures and adjusts traffic shaper bandwidth limiters. Traffic shaping means setting parameters to which traffic should conform - setting the standards for bandwidth consumption. To use Shapecfg, you must have also installed the kernel which supports the shaper module (kernel versions 2.0.36 or later and late 2.1.x kernels). Install the shapecfg package if you want to set traffic bandwidth parameters, and if you have the appropriate kernel.

termcap — (Version 9.12.6, 424K)
[B]

The termcap package provides the /etc/termcap file. /etc/termcap is a database which defines the capabilities of various terminals and terminal emulators. Certain programs use the /etc/termcap file to access various features of terminals (the bell, colors, and graphics, etc.).

tmpwatch — (Version 1.5.1, 9K)
[B]

The tmpwatch utility recursively searches through specified directories and removes files which have not been accessed in a specified period of time. Tmpwatch is normally used to clean up directories which are used for temporarily holding files (for example, /tmp). Tmpwatch ignores symlinks, won't switch filesystems and only removes empty directories and regular files.

utempter — (Version 0.3, 21K)
[B]

Utempter is a utility which allows programs to log information to a privledged file (`/var/run/utmp`), without compromising system security. It accomplishes this task by acting as a buffer between root and the programs.

util-linux — (Version 2.9o, 960K)
[B]

The util-linux package contains a large variety of low-level system utilities that are necessary for a Linux system to function. Among many features, Util-linux contains the fdisk configuration tool and login program. You should install util-linux for its essential system tools.

vixie-cron — (Version 3.0.1, 57K)
[B]

The vixie-cron package contains the Vixie version of cron. Cron is a standard UNIX daemon that runs specified programs at scheduled times. Vixie cron adds better security and more powerful configuration options to the standard version of cron.

yp-tools — (Version 2.1, 161K)
[W] [S]

The Network Information Service (NIS) is a system which provides network information (login names, passwords, home directories, group information) to all of the machines on a network. NIS can enable users to login on any machine on the network, as long as the machine has the NIS client programs running and the user's password is recorded in the NIS passwd database. NIS was formerly known as Sun Yellow Pages (YP). This package's NIS implementation is based on FreeBSD's YP and is a special port for glibc 2.x and libc versions 5.4.21 and later. This package only provides the NIS client programs. In order to use the clients, you'll need to already have an NIS server running on your network. An NIS server is provided in the ypserv package. Install the yp-tools package if you need NIS client programs for machines on your network. You will also need to install the ypbind package on every machine running NIS client programs. If you need an NIS server, you'll need to install the ypserv package on one machine on the network.

Daemons

This section contains packages associated with the daemon processes that run under Red Hat Linux.

ORBit — (Version 0.4.2, 1,273K)
[W] [S]

ORBit is a high-performance CORBA ORB (object request broker). It allows programs to send requests and receive replies from other programs, regardless of the locations of the two programs. You will need to install this package and the related header files, libraries and utilities if you want to write programs that use CORBA technology.

XFree86-xfs — (Version 3.3.3.1, 505K)
[W] [S]

This is a font server for XFree86. You can serve fonts to other X servers remotely with this package, and the remote system will be able to use all fonts installed on the font server, even if they are not installed on the remote computer.

am-utils — (Version 6.0, 1,954K)
Am-utils includes an updated version of Amd, the popular BSD automounter. An automounter is a program which maintains a cache of mounted filesystems. Filesystems are mounted when they are first referenced by the user and unmounted after a certain period of inactivity. Amd supports a variety of filesystems, including NFS, UFS, CD-ROMS and local drives. You should install am-utils if you need a program for automatically mounting and unmounting filesystems.

anonftp — (Version 2.8, 1,540K)
[S]

The anonftp package contains the files you need in order to allow anonymous FTP access to your machine. Anonymous FTP access allows anyone to download files from your machine without having a user account. Anonymous FTP is a popular way of making programs available via the Internet. You should install anonftp if you would like to enable anonymous FTP downloads from your machine.

apache — (Version 1.3.6, 2,111K)
[S]

Apache is a powerful, full-featured, efficient and freely-available Web server. Apache is also the most popular Web server on the Internet. This package will install the Apache Web server on your machine.

apmd — (Version 3.0beta5, 70K)
This is a Advanced Power Management daemon and utilities. It can watch your notebook's battery and warn all users when the battery is low. Patches to Rik Faith's original version have been added for shutting down the PCMCIA sockets before a suspend.

at — (Version 3.1.7, 64K)
[B]

At and batch read commands from standard input or from a specified file. At allows you to specify that a command will be run at a particular time (now or a specified time in the future). Batch will execute commands when the system load levels drop to a particular level. Both commands use /bin/sh to run the commands. You should install the at package if you need a utility that will do time-oriented job control. Note: you should use crontab instead, if it is a recurring job that will need to be repeated at the same time every day/week/etc.

autofs – (Version 3.1.3, 126K)
Autofs controls the operation of the automount daemons. The automount daemons automatically mount filesystems when you use them and unmount them after a period of inactivity. Filesystems can include network filesystems, CD-ROMs, floppies and others. Install this package if you want a program for automatically mounting and unmounting filesystems. If your Red Hat Linux machine is on a network, you should install autofs.

bdflush – (Version 1.5, 10K)

[B]

The bdflush process starts the kernel daemon which flushes dirty buffers back to disk (i.e., writes all unwritten data to disk). This helps to prevent the buffers from growing too stale. Bdflush is a basic system process that must run for your system to operate properly.

bind – (Version 8.2, 4,370K)
[S]

Bind includes the named name server, which resolves host names to IP addresses (and vice versa), and a resolver library (a set of routines in a system library that provide the interface for programs to use when accessing domain name services). A name server is a network service which enables clients to name resources or objects and share this information with other network machines. The named name server can be used on workstations as a caching name server, but is generally only needed on one machine for an entire network. Note that the configuration files for making bind act as a simple caching nameserver are included in the caching-nameserver package. Install the bind package if you need a name server for your network. If you want bind to act a caching name server, you will also need to install the caching-nameserver package.

bootparamd – (Version 0.10, 18K)
The bootparamd process provides bootparamd, a server process which provides the information needed by diskless clients in order for them to successfully boot. Bootparamd looks first in /etc/bootparams for an entry for that particular client; if a local bootparams file doesn't exist, it looks at the appropriate Network Information Service (NIS) map. Some network boot loaders (notably Sun's) rely

on special boot server code on the server, in addition to the rarp and tftp servers. This bootparamd server process is compatible with SunOS bootparam clients and servers which need that boot server code. You should install bootparamd if you need to provide boot information to diskless clients on your network.

caching-nameserver — (Version 6.0, 3K)
[S]

The caching-nameserver package includes the configuration files which will make bind, the DNS name server, act as a simple caching nameserver. Many users on dialup connections use this package along with bind for such a purpose. If you would like to set up a caching name server, you'll need to install the caching-nameserver package; you'll also need to install bind.

cleanfeed — (Version 0.95.7b, 107K)
[S]

Cleanfeed is an automatic spam filter for Usenet news servers and routers (INN, Cyclone, Typhoon, Breeze and NNTPRelay). Cleanfeed is highly configurable, easily modified and very fast. It can be configured to block binary posts to non-binary newsgroups, to cancel already-rejected articles, and to reject some spamming from local users. Install the cleanfeed package if you need a spam filter for a Usenet news server.

comsat — (Version 0.10, 17K)
The biff client and comsat server are an antiquated method of asynchronous mail notification. Although they are still supported, most users use their shell's MAIL variable (or csh shell's mail variable) to check for mail, or a dedicated application like xbiff or xmailbox. If the comsat service is not enabled, biff won't work and you'll need to use either the MAIL or mail variable. You may want to install biff if you'd like to be notified when mail arrives. However, you should probably check out the more modern methodologies of mail notification (xbiff or xmailbox) instead.

dhcp — (Version 2.0b1pl6, 257K)
DHCP (Dynamic Host Configuration Protocol) is a protocol which allows individual devices on an IP network to get their own network configuration information (IP address, subnetmask, broadcast address, etc.) from a DHCP server. The overall purpose of DHCP is to make it easier to administer a large network. The dhcp package includes the DHCP server and a DHCP relay agent. You should install dhcp if you want to set up a DHCP server on your network. You will also need to install the dhcpcd package, which provides the DHCP client daemon, on client machines.

esound – (Version 0.2.9, 178K)
[W] [S]

EsounD – the Enlightened Sound Daemon – is a server process that allows multiple applications to share a single sound card. For example, when you're listening to music from your CD and you receive a sound-related event from ICQ, your applications won't have to jockey for the attention of your sound card. EsounD mixes several audio streams for playback by a single audio device. Install esound if you'd like to allow for such event sharing by your audio device.

gated – (Version 3.5.10, 2,434K)
GateD is a modular software program consisting of core services, a routing database, and protocol modules which support multiple routing protocols (RIP versions 1 and 2, DCN HELLO, OSPF version 2, EGP version 2, BGP versions 2 through 4). GateD is designed to handle dynamic routing with a routing database built from the information exchanged by routing protocols. Install gated if you need a routing daemon.

gpm – (Version 1.17.5, 258K)
[B]

Gpm provides mouse support to text-based Linux applications like the emacs editor, the Midnight Commander file management system, and other programs. Gpm also provides console cut-and-paste operations using the mouse and includes a program to allow pop-up menus to appear at the click of a mouse button. Gpm should be installed if you intend to use a mouse with your Red Hat Linux system.

imap – (Version 4.5, 1,485K)
The imap package provides server daemons for both the IMAP (Internet Message Access Protocol) and POP (Post Office Protocol) mail access protocols. The POP protocol uses a "post office" machine to collect mail for users and allows users to download their mail to their local machine for reading. The IMAP protocol provides the functionality of POP, but allows a user to read mail on a remote machine without downloading it to their local machine. Install the imap package if you need a server to support the IMAP or the POP mail access protocols.

inews – (Version 2.2, 74K)
The inews program is used by some news programs (for example, inn and trn) to post Usenet news articles to local news servers. Inews reads an article from a file or standard input, adds headers, performs some consistency checks and then sends the article to the local news server specified in the inn.conf file. Install inews if you need a program for posting Usenet articles to local news servers.

inn – (Version 2.2, 6,246K)
[S]

INN (InterNetNews) is a complete system for serving Usenet news and/or private newsfeeds. INN includes innd, an NNTP (NetNews Transport Protocol) server, and nnrpd, a newsreader that is spawned for each client. Both innd and nnrpd vary slightly from the NNTP protocol, but not in ways that are easily noticed. Install the inn package if you need a complete system for serving and reading Usenet news. You may also need to install inn-devel, if you are going to use a separate program which interfaces to INN, like newsgate or tin.

intimed – (Version 1.10, 210K)
The intimed package contains a server (in.timed), which keeps networked machines' clocks correctly synchronized to the server's time. Install intimed if you need a network time server.

knfsd – (Version 1.2, 163K)
[W] [S]

This is the *new* kernel NFS server and related tools. It provides a much higher level of performance than the traditional Linux user-land NFS server.

lpr – (Version 0.35, 180K)
[W] [S]

The lpr package provides the basic system utility for managing printing services. Lpr manages print queues, sends print jobs to local and remote printers and accepts print jobs from remote clients. If you will be printing from your system, you'll need to install the lpr package.

mars-nwe – (Version 0.99pl15, 657K)
[S]

The mars_nwe (MARtin Stover's NetWare Emulator) package enables Linux to provide both file and print services for NetWare clients (i.e., providing the services of a Novell NetWare file server). Mars_nwe allows the sharing of files between Linux machines and Novell NetWare clients, using NetWare's native IPX protocol suite. Install the mars_nwe package if you need a Novell NetWare file server on your Red Hat Linux system.

mcserv – (Version 4.5.29, 122K)
The Midnight Commander file management system will allow you to manipulate the files on a remote machine as if they were local. This is only possible if the remote machine is running the mcserv server program. Mcserv provides clients

running Midnight Commander with access to the host's file systems. Install mcserv on machines if you want to access their file systems remotely using the Midnight Commander file management system.

mod_perl – (Version 1.18, 1,261K)
Mod_perl incorporates a Perl interpreter into the Apache web server, so that the Apache web server can directly execute Perl code. Mod_perl links the Perl runtime library into the Apache web server and provides an object-oriented Perl interface for Apache's C language API. The end result is a quicker CGI script turnaround process, since no external Perl interpreter has to be started. Install mod_perl if you're installing the Apache web server and you'd like for it to directly incorporate a Perl interpreter.

mod_php – (Version 2.0.1, 676K)
PHP is an HTML-embedded scripting language. PHP attempts to make it easy for developers to write dynamically generated web pages. PHP also offers built-in database integration for several commercial and non-commercial database management systems, so writing a database-enabled web page with PHP is fairly simple. The most common use of PHP coding is probably as a replacement for CGI scripts. The mod_php module enables the Apache web server to understand and process the embedded PHP language in web pages. This package contains PHP/FI, or PHP version 2.01. Unless you use applications which specifically rely on PHP/FI, you should instead install the mod_php3 package, which contains PHP3. PHP3 is an improved and more capable update to PHP/FI.

mod_php3 – (Version 3.0.7, 3,892K)
PHP is an HTML-embedded scripting language. PHP attempts to make it easy for developers to write dynamically generated web pages. PHP also offers built-in database integration for several commercial and non-commercial database management systems, so writing a database-enabled web page with PHP is fairly simple. The most common use of PHP coding is probably as a replacement for CGI scripts. The mod_php module enables the Apache web server to understand and process the embedded PHP language in web pages. This package contains PHP3, or PHP version 3.05. If you use applications which specifically rely on PHP/FI, you should instead install the PHP/FI module contained in the mod_php package. If you're just starting with PHP, you should install this package. You'll also need to install the Apache web server.

netkit-base – (Version 0.10, 61K)
[W] [S]

The netkit-base package contains the basic networking tools ping and inetd. The ping command sends a series of ICMP protocol ECHO_REQUEST packets to a specified network host and can tell you if that machine is alive and receiving network traffic. Inetd listens on certain Internet sockets for connection requests, decides what program should receive each request, and starts up that program. The netkit-base package should be installed on any machine that is on a network.

nscd – (Version 2.1.1, 33K)

nscd caches name service lookups; it can dramatically improve performance with NIS+, and may help with DNS as well. You cannot use nscd with 2.0 kernels, due to bugs in the kernel-side thread support. nscd happens to hit these bugs particularly hard.

pidentd – (Version 2.8.5, 129K)

[W] [S]

The pidentd package contains identd, which implements the RFC1413 identification server. Identd looks up specific TCP/IP connections and returns either the user name or other information about the process that owns the connection.

portmap – (Version 4.0, 49K)

[W] [S]

The portmapper program is a security tool which prevents theft of NIS (YP), NFS and other sensitive information via the portmapper. A portmapper manages RPC connections, which are used by protocols like NFS and NIS. The portmap package should be installed on any machine which acts as a server for protocols using RPC.

ppp – (Version 2.3.7, 301K)

[W] [S]

The ppp package contains the PPP (Point-to-Point Protocol) daemon and documentation for PPP support. The PPP protocol provides a method for transmitting datagrams over serial point-to-point links. The ppp package should be installed if your machine need to support the PPP protocol.

procmail – (Version 3.13, 207K)

[B]

The procmail program is used by Red Hat Linux for all local mail delivery. In addition to just delivering mail, procmail can be used for automatic filtering, presorting and other mail handling jobs. Procmail is also the basis for the SmartList mailing list processor.

pump — (Version 0.4, 30K)
[B]

DHCP (Dynamic Host Configuration Protocol) and BOOTP (Boot Protocol) are protocols which allow individual devices on an IP network to get their own network configuration information (IP address, subnetmask, broadcast address, etc.) from network servers. The overall purpose of DHCP and BOOTP is to make it easier to administer a large network. Pump is a combined BOOTP and DHCP client daemon, which allows your machine to retrieve configuration information from a server. You should install this package if you are on a network which uses BOOTP or DHCP.

routed — (Version 0.10, 39K)
[W] [S]

The routed routing daemon handles incoming RIP traffic and broadcasts outgoing RIP traffic about network traffic routes, in order to maintain current routing tables. These routing tables are essential for a networked computer, so that it knows where packets need to be sent. The routed package should be installed on any networked machine.

rusers — (Version 0.10, 36K)
[W] [S]

The rusers program allows users to find out who is logged into various machines on the local network. The rusers command produces output similar to who, but for the specified list of hosts or for all machines on the local network. Install rusers if you need to keep track of who is logged into your local network.

rwall — (Version 0.10, 18K)
The rwall command sends a message to all of the users logged into a specified host. Actually, your machine's rwall client sends the message to the rwall daemon running on the specified host, and the rwall daemon relays the message to all of the users logged in to that host. The rwall daemon is run from /etc/inetd.conf and is disabled by default on Red Hat Linux systems (it can be very annoying to keep getting all those messages when you're trying to play Quake—I mean trying to get some work done). Install rwall if you'd like the ability to send messages to users logged in to a specified host machine.

rwho – (Version 0.10, 25K)
[W] [S]

The rwho command displays output similar to the output of the who command (it shows who is logged in) for all machines on the local network running the rwho daemon. Install the rwho command if you need to keep track of the users who are logged in to your local network.

samba – (Version 2.0.3, 6,498K)
[S]

Samba provides an SMB server which can be used to provide network services to SMB (sometimes called "Lan Manager") clients, including various versions of MS Windows, OS/2, and other Linux machines. Samba also provides some SMB clients, which complement the built-in SMB filesystem in Linux. Samba uses NetBIOS over TCP/IP (NetBT) protocols and does NOT need NetBEUI (Microsoft Raw NetBIOS frame) protocol. Samba-2 features an almost working NT Domain Control capability and includes the new SWAT (Samba Web Administration Tool) that allows samba's smb.conf file to be remotely managed using your favourite web browser. For the time being this is being enabled on TCP port 901 via inetd. Please refer to the WHATSNEW.txt document for fixup information. This binary release includes encrypted password support. Please read the smb.conf file and ENCRYPTION.txt in the docs directory for implementation details. NOTE: Red Hat Linux 5.X Uses PAM which has integrated support for Shadow passwords. Do NOT recompile with the SHADOW_PWD option enabled. Red Hat Linux has built in support for quotas in PAM.

sendmail – (Version 8.9.3, 526K)
[B]

The Sendmail program is a very widely used Mail Transport Agent (MTA). MTAs send mail from one machine to another. Sendmail is not a client program, which you use to read your email. Sendmail is a behind-the-scenes program which actually moves your email over networks or the Internet to where you want it to go. If you ever need to reconfigure Sendmail, you'll also need to have the sendmail.cf package installed. If you need documentation on Sendmail, you can install the sendmail-doc package.

sendmail-cf – (Version 8.9.3, 503K)
This package includes the configuration files which you'd need to generate the sendmail.cf file distributed with the sendmail package. You'll need the sendmail-cf package if you ever need to reconfigure and rebuild your sendmail.cf file. For example, the default sendmail.cf file is not configured for UUCP. If someday you needed to send and receive mail over UUCP, you'd need to install the sendmail-cf package to help you reconfigure Sendmail. Install the sendmail-cf package if you need to reconfigure your sendmail.cf file.

squid – (Version 2.2.DEVEL3, 1,861K)

Squid is a high-performance proxy caching server for web clients, supporting FTP, gopher, and HTTP data objects. Unlike traditional caching software, Squid handles all requests in a single, non-blocking, I/O-driven process. Squid keeps meta data and especially hot objects cached in RAM, caches DNS lookups, supports non-blocking DNS lookups, and implements negative caching of failed requests. Squid supports SSL, extensive access controls, and full request logging. By using the lightweight Internet Cache Protocol, Squid caches can be arranged in a hierarchy or mesh for additional bandwidth savings. Squid consists of a main server program squid, a Domain Name System lookup program dnsserver, a program for retrieving FTP data ftpget, and some management and client tools. When squid starts up, it spawns a configurable number of dnsserver processes, each of which can perform a single, blocking Domain Name System (DNS) lookup. This reduces the amount of time the cache waits for DNS lookups. Squid is derived from the ARPA-funded Harvest project.

sysklogd – (Version 1.3.31, 112K)

[B]

The sysklogd package contains two system utilities (syslogd and klogd) which provide support for system logging. Syslogd and klogd run as daemons (background processes) and log system messages to different places, like sendmail logs, security logs, error logs, etc.

tcp_wrappers – (Version 7.6, 270K)

[W] [S]

The tcp_wrappers package provides small daemon programs which can monitor and filter incoming requests for systat, finger, ftp, telnet, rlogin, rsh, exec, tftp, talk and other network services. Install the tcp_wrappers program if you need a security tool for filtering incoming network services requests.

tftp – (Version 0.10, 34K)

[W] [S]

The Trivial File Transfer Protocol (TFTP) is normally used only for booting diskless workstations. The tftp package provides the user interface for TFTP, which allows users to transfer files to and from a remote machine. This program, and TFTP, provide very little security, and should not be enabled unless it is expressly needed. The TFTP server is run from /etc/inetd.conf, and is disabled by default on Red Hat Linux systems.

timed — (Version 0.10, 74K)
[W] [S]

The timed package contains the timed daemon and the timedc program for controlling the timed program. Timed synchronizes its host machine's time with the time on other local network machines. The timedc program is used to control and configure the operation of timed. Install the timed package if you need a system for keeping networked machines' times in synchronization.

ucd-snmp — (Version 3.6.1, 1,504K)
[W] [S]

SNMP (Simple Network Management Protocol) is a protocol used for network management (hence the name). The UCD-SNMP project includes various SNMP tools: an extensible agent, an SNMP library, tools for requesting or setting information from SNMP agents, tools for generating and handling SNMP traps, a version of the netstat command which uses SNMP, and a Tk/Perl mib browser. This package contains the snmpd and snmptrapd daemons, documentation, etc. Install the ucd-snmp package if you need network management tools. You will probably also want to install the ucd-snmp-utils package, which contains UCD-SNMP utilities.

wu-ftpd — (Version 2.4.2b18, 398K)
[S]

The wu-ftpd package contains the wu-ftpd FTP (File Transfer Protocol) server daemon. The FTP protocol is a method of transferring files between machines on a network and/or over the Internet. Wu-ftpd's features include logging of transfers, logging of commands, on the fly compression and archiving, classification of users' type and location, per class limits, per directory upload permissions, restricted guest accounts, system wide and per directory messages, directory alias, cdpath, filename filter and virtual host support. Install the wu-ftpd package if you need to provide FTP service to remote users.

xntp3 — (Version 5.93, 968K)
The Network Time Protocol (NTP) is used to synchronize a computer's time with another reference time source. The xntp3 package contains utilities and daemons which will synchronize your computer's time to Coordinated Universal Time (UTC) via the NTP protocol and NTP servers. Xntp3 includes ntpdate (a program for retrieving the date and time from remote machines via a network) and xntpd (a daemon which continuously adjusts system time). Install the xntp3 package if you need tools for keeping your system's time synchronized via the NTP protocol.

ypbind – (Version 3.3, 48K)
[W] [S]

The Network Information Service (NIS) is a system which provides network information (login names, passwords, home directories, group information) to all of the machines on a network. NIS can enable users to login on any machine on the network, as long as the machine has the NIS client programs running and the user's password is recorded in the NIS passwd database. NIS was formerly known as Sun Yellow Pages (YP). This package provides the ypbind daemon. The ypbind daemon binds NIS clients to an NIS domain. Ypbind must be running on any machines which are running NIS client programs. Install the ypbind package on any machines which are running NIS client programs (included in the yp-tools package). If you need an NIS server, you'll also need to install the ypserv package to a machine on your network.

ypserv – (Version 1.3.6.91, 289K)
The Network Information Service (NIS) is a system which provides network information (login names, passwords, home directories, group information) to all of the machines on a network. NIS can enable users to login on any machine on the network, as long as the machine has the NIS client programs running and the user's password is recorded in the NIS passwd database. NIS was formerly known as Sun Yellow Pages (YP). This package provides the NIS server, which will need to be running on your network. NIS clients do not need to be running the server. Install ypserv if you need an NIS server for your network. You'll also need to install the yp-tools and ypbind packages onto any NIS client machines.

Kernel

This section contains packages that are related to the Linux kernel on which Red Hat Linux is based.

kernel – (Version 2.2.5, 9,812K)
[B]

The kernel package contains the Linux kernel (vmlinuz), the core of your Red Hat Linux operating system. The kernel handles the basic functions of the operating system: memory allocation, process allocation, device input and output, etc.

kernel-BOOT – (Version 2.2.5, 5,881K)
This package includes a trimmed down version of the Linux 2.2.5 kernel. This kernel is used on the installation boot disks only and should not be used for an installed system, as many features in this kernel are turned off because of the size constraints.

kernel-pcmcia-cs — (Version 2.2.5, 561K)
[B]

Many laptop machines (and some non-laptops) support PCMCIA cards for expansion. Also known as "credit card adapters," PCMCIA cards are small cards for everything from SCSI support to modems. PCMCIA cards are hot swappable (i.e., they can be exchanged without rebooting the system) and quite convenient to use. The kernel-pcmcia-cs package contains a set of loadable kernel modules that implement an applications program interface, a set of client drivers for specific cards and a card manager daemon that can respond to card insertion and removal events by loading and unloading drivers on demand. The daemon also supports hot swapping, so that the cards can be safely inserted and ejected at any time. Install the kernel-pcmcia-cs package if your system uses PCMCIA cards.

kernel-smp — (Version 2.2.5, 9,494K)
This package includes a SMP version of the Linux 2.2.5 kernel. It is required only on machines with two or more CPUs, although it should work fine on single-CPU boxes.

modutils — (Version 2.1.121, 841K)
[B]

The modutils packages includes the kerneld program for automatic loading of modules under 2.0 kernels and unloading of modules under 2.0 and 2.2 kernels, as well as other module management programs. Loaded and unloaded modules are device drivers and filesystems, as well as other things.

Libraries

This section contains the packages associated with the libraries that are required to run programs under Red Hat Linux.

XFree86-libs — (Version 3.3.3.1, 2,060K)
[W] [S]

XFree86-libs contains the shared libraries that most X programs need to run properly. These shared libraries are in a separate package in order to reduce the disk space needed to run X applications on a machine without an X server (i.e, over a network). If you are installing the X Window System on your machine, you will need to install XFree86-libs. You will also need to install the XFree86 package, the XFree86-75dpi-fonts package or the XFree86-100dpi-fonts package (depending upon your monitor's resolution), the Xconfigurator package and the X11R6-contrib package. And, finally, if you are going to be developing applications that run as X clients, you will also need to install XFree86-devel.

Xaw3d – (Version 1.3, 292K)
[W] [S]

Xaw3d is an enhanced version of the MIT Athena Widget set for the X Window System. Xaw3d adds a three-dimensional look to applications with minimal or no source code changes. You should install Xaw3d if you are using applications which incorporate the MIT Athena widget set and you'd like to incorporate a 3D look into those applications.

audiofile – (Version 0.1.6, 183K)
[W] [S]

Library to handle various audio file formats. Used by the esound daemon.

cracklib – (Version 2.7, 75K)
[B]

CrackLib tests passwords to determine whether they match certain security-oriented characteristics. You can use CrackLib to stop users from choosing passwords which would be easy to guess. CrackLib performs certain tests: * It tries to generate words from a username and gecos entry and checks those words against the password; * It checks for simplistic patterns in passwords; * It checks for the password in a dictionary. CrackLib is actually a library containing a particular C function which is used to check the password, as well as other C functions. CrackLib is not a replacement for a passwd program; it must be used in conjunction with an existing passwd program. Install the cracklib package if you need a program to check users' passwords to see if they are at least minimally secure. If you install CrackLib, you'll also want to install the cracklib-dicts package.

cracklib-dicts – (Version 2.7, 235K)
[B]

The cracklib-dicts package includes the CrackLib dictionaries. CrackLib will need to use the dictionary appropriate to your system, which is normally put in /usr/dict/words. Cracklib-dicts also contains the utilities necessary for the creation of new dictionaries. If you are installing CrackLib, you should also install cracklib-dicts.

fnlib – (Version 0.4, 352K)
[W]

Fnlib is a library that provides full, scalable 24-bit color font rendering abilities for X.

freetype — (Version 1.2, 937K)
[W] [S]

The FreeType engine is a free and portable TrueType font rendering engine. It has been developed to provide TT support to a great variety of platforms and environments. Note that FreeType is a library, not a stand-alone application, though some utility applications are included.

gd — (Version 1.3, 314K)
[B]

Gd is a graphics library for drawing .gif files. Gd allows your code to quickly draw images (lines, arcs, text, multiple colors, cutting and pasting from other images, flood fills) and write out the result as a .gif file. Gd is particularly useful in web applications, where .gifs are commonly used as inline images. Note, however, that gd is not a paint program. Install gd if you are developing applications which need to draw .gif files. If you install gd, you'll also need to install the gd-devel package.

gdbm — (Version 1.7.3, 28K)
[B]

Gdbm is a GNU database indexing library, including routines which use extensible hashing. Gdbm works in a similar way to standard UNIX dbm routines. Gdbm is useful for developers who write C applications and need access to a simple and efficient database or who are building C applications which will use such a database. If you're a C developer and your programs need access to simple database routines, you should install gdbm. You'll also need to install gdbm-devel.

gimp-libgimp — (Version 1.0.4, 173K)
[W]

Libraries used to communicate between The GIMP and other programs which may function as "GIMP plugins".

glib — (Version 1.2.1, 317K)
[B] [W]

Glib is a handy library of utility functions. This C library is designed to solve some portability problems and provide other useful functionality which most programs require. Glib is used by GDK, GTK+ and many applications. You should install Glib because many of your applications will depend on this library.

glib10 — (Version 1.0.6, 54K)
[W] [S]

The glib package contains a useful library of utility functions, which are necessary for the successful operation of many different programs on your Red Hat Linux system.

glibc — (Version 2.1.1, 25,792K)
[B]

Contains the standard libraries that are used by multiple programs on the system. In order to save disk space and memory, as well as to ease upgrades, common system code is kept in one place and shared between programs. This package contains the most important sets of shared libraries, the standard C library and the standard math library. Without these, a Linux system will not function. It also contains national language (locale) support and timezone databases.

gmp — (Version 2.0.2, 117K)
[B]

The gmp package contains GNU MP, a library for arbitrary precision arithmetic, signed integers operations, rational numbers and floating point numbers. GNU MP is designed for speed, for both small and very large operands. GNU MP is fast for several reasons: It uses fullwords as the basic arithmetic type, it uses fast algorithms, it carefully optimizes assembly code for many CPUs' most common inner loops and it generally emphasizes speed over simplicity/elegance in its operations. Install the gmp package if you need a fast arbitrary precision library.

gnome-audio-extra — (Version 1.0.0, 2,659K)
[W]

This package contains extra sound files useful for customizing the sounds that the GNOME desktop environment makes.

gnome-libs — (Version 1.0.5, 2,210K)
[W] [S]

GNOME (GNU Network Object Model Environment) is a user-friendly set of applications and desktop tools to be used in conjunction with a window manager for the X Window System. GNOME is similar in purpose and scope to CDE and KDE, but GNOME is based completely on Open Source software. The gnome-libs package includes libraries that are needed by GNOME. You should install the gnome-libs package if you would like to use the GNOME desktop environment. You'll also need to install the gnome-core package. If you would like to develop GNOME applications, you'll also need to install gnome-libs-devel. If you want to use Linuxconf with a GNOME front end, you'll also need to install the gnome-linuxconf package.

gsl — (Version 0.3f, 868K)

The gsl package includes the GNU Scientific Library (GSL). The GSL is a collection of routines for numerical analysis, written in C. The GSL is in alpha development. It now includes a random number suite, an FFT package, simulated annealing and root finding. In the future, it will include numerical and Monte Carlo integration and special functions. Linking against the GSL allows programs to access functions which can handle many of the problems encountered in scientific computing. Install the gsl package if you need a library for high-level scientific numerical analysis.

gtk+ — (Version 1.2.1, 1,981K)

[W] [S]

The gtk+ package contains the GIMP ToolKit (GTK+), a library for creating graphical user interfaces for the X Window System. GTK+ was originally written for the GIMP (GNU Image Manipulation Program) image processing program, but is now used by several other programs as well. If you are planning on using the GIMP or another program that uses GTK+, you'll need to have the gtk+ package installed.

gtk+10 — (Version 1.0.6, 1,139K)

[W] [S]

The X libraries originally written for the GIMP, which are now used by several other programs as well. This RPM is a set of compatibility libraries needed to run applications linked against the 1.0 series of gtk+ and glib.

gtk-engines — (Version 0.5, 2,387K)

[W]

These are the graphical engines for the various GTK+ toolkit themes. Included themes are: - Notif - Redmond95 - Pixmap - Metal (swing-like)

imlib — (Version 1.9.4, 423K)

[W] [S]

Imlib is a display depth independent image loading and rendering library. Imlib is designed to simplify and speed up the process of loading images and obtaining

X Window System drawables. Imlib provides many simple manipulation routines which can be used for common operations. Install imlib if you need an image loading and rendering library for X11R6. You may also want to install the imlib-cfgeditor package, which will help you configure Imlib.

imlib-cfgeditor – (Version 1.9.4, 333K)
[W]

The imlib-cfgeditor package contains the imlib_config program, which you can use to configure the Imlib image loading and rendering library. Imlib_config can be used to control how Imlib uses color and handles gamma corrections, etc. If you're installing the imlib package, you should also install imlib_cfgeditor.

kdelibs – (Version 1.1, 5,771K)
Libraries for the K Desktop Environment: KDE Libraries included: kdecore (KDE core library), kdeui (user interface), kfm (file manager), khtmlw (HTML widget), kfile (file access), kspell (spelling checker), jscript (javascript), kab (addressbook), kimgio (image manipulation), mediatool (sound, mixing and animation).

kdesupport – (Version 1.1, 2,138K)
Support Libraries for the K Desktop Environment, but not part of it. Libraries included: QwSpriteField, js (javascript), uulib, mimelib, rdb; depending on the Red Hat release, libraries gdbm jpeg and gif are either also included, or the versions supplied by Red Hat are required. This package also provides extra KDE support for Red Hat Linux: a script "usekde" that users can run to set up KDE as their default desktop (which is also done automatically when a new user is created), and scripts for activating the KDE X Display Manager "kdm" to replace "xdm".

libPropList – (Version 0.8.3, 111K)
The purpose of PL is to closely mimic the behavior of the property lists used in the GNUstep/OPENSTEP (they're formed with the NSString, NSData, NSArray and NSDictionary classes) and to be duly compatible. PL enables programs that use configuration or preference3 files to make these compatible with GNUstep/OPENSTEP's user defaults handling mechanism, without needing to use Objective-C or GNUstep/ OPENSTEP themselves.

libc – (Version 5.3.12, 5,259K
[B]

Older Linux systems (including all Red Hat Linux releases between 2.0 and 4.2, inclusive) were based on libc version 5. The libc package includes the libc5 libraries and other libraries based on libc5. With these libraries installed, old applications which need them will be able to run on your glibc (libc version 6) based system. The libc package should be installed so that you can run older applications which need libc version 5.

libelf — (Version 0.6.4, 76K)
The libelf package contains a library for accessing ELF object files. Libelf allows you to access the internals of the ELF object file format, so you can see the different sections of an ELF file. Libelf should be installed if you need access to ELF object file internals.

libghttp — (Version 1.0.2, 85K)
[W] [S]

Library for making HTTP 1.1 requests.

libgr — (Version 2.0.13, 235K)
[W] [S]

The libgr package contains a library of functions which support programs for handling various graphics file formats, including .pbm (portable pitmaps), .pgm (portable graymaps), .pnm (portable anymaps), .ppm (portable pixmaps) and others.

libgtop — (Version 1.0.1, 431K)
[W]

A library that fetches information about the running system such as CPU and memory useage, active processes and more. On Linux systems, this information is taken directly from the /proc filesystem while on other systems a server is used to read that information from other /dev/kmem, among others.

libgtop-examples — (Version 1.0.1, 937K)
These are examples for LibGTop, a library which retrieves information about your system, such as CPU and memory usage.

libjpeg — (Version 6b, 239K)
[W] [S]

The libjpeg package contains a library of functions for manipulating JPEG images, as well as simple client programs for accessing the libjpeg functions. Libjpeg client programs include cjpeg, djpeg, jpegtran, rdjpgcom and wrjpgcom. Cjpeg compresses an image file into JPEG format. Djpeg decompresses a JPEG file into a regular image file. Jpegtran can perform various useful transformations on JPEG files. Rdjpgcom displays any text comments included in a JPEG file. Wrjpgcom inserts text comments into a JPEG file.

libjpeg6a – (Version 6a, 137K)

This package is a library of functions that manipulate jpeg images, along with simple clients for manipulating jpeg images. This version of the package includes only a library that is needed for preserving the backwards compatibility with previous releases of Red Hat Linux.

libpng – (Version 1.0.3, 270K)

[W] [S]

The libpng package contains a library of functions for creating and manipulating PNG (Portable Network Graphics) image format files. PNG is a bit-mapped graphics format similar to the GIF format. PNG was created to replace the GIF format, since GIF uses a patented data compression algorithm. Libpng should be installed if you need to manipulate PNG format image files.

libstdc++ – (Version 2.9.0, 3,421K)

[B]

EGCS is a free software project that intends to further the development of GNU compilers using an open development environment. The egcs package contains the egcs compiler, a compiler aimed at integrating all the optimizations and features necessary for a high-performance and stable development environment. EGCS includes the shared libraries necessary for running C++ appplications, along with additional GNU tools. Install egcs if you'd like to use an experimental GNU compiler.

libtermcap – (Version 2.0.8, 58K)

[B]

The libtermcap package contains a basic system library needed to access the termcap database. The termcap library supports easy access to the termcap database, so that programs can output character-based displays in a terminal-independent manner.

libtiff – (Version 3.4, 568K)

[W] [S]

The libtiff package contains a library of functions for manipulating TIFF (Tagged Image File Format) image format files. TIFF is a widely used file format for bitmapped images. TIFF files usually end in the .tif extension and they are often quite large. The libtiff package should be installed if you need to manipulate TIFF format image files.

libungif – (Version 4.1.0, 80K)
[W] [S]

The libungif package contains a shared library of functions for loading and saving GIF format image files. The libungif library can load any GIF file, but it will save GIFs only in uncompressed format (i.e., it won't use the patented LZW compression used to save "normal" compressed GIF files). Install the libungif package if you need to manipulate GIF files. You should also install the libungif-progs package.

libxml – (Version 1.0.0, 154K)
[W] [S]

This library allows you to manipulate XML files.

ncurses – (Version 4.2, 2,627K)
[B]

The curses library routines are a terminal-independent method of updating character screens with reasonable optimization. The ncurses (new curses) library is a freely distributable replacement for the discontinued 4.4BSD classic curses library.

ncurses3 – (Version 1.9.9e, 330K)
The curses library routines are a terminal-independent method of updating character screens with reasonable optimization. The ncurses (new curses) library is a freely distributable replacement for the discontinued 4.4BSD classic curses library.

newt – (Version 0.40, 128K)
[B]

Newt is a programming library for color text mode, widget based user interfaces. Newt can be used to add stacked windows, entry widgets, checkboxes, radio buttons, labels, plain text fields, scrollbars, etc., to text mode user interfaces. This package also contains the shared library needed by programs built with newt, as well as a /usr/bin/dialog replacement called whiptail. Newt is based on the slang library.

p2c – (Version 1.22, 723K)
P2c is a system for translating Pascal programs into the C language. P2c accepts input source files in certain Pascal dialects: HP Pascal, Turbo/UCSD Pascal, DEC VAX Pascal, Oregon Software Pascal/2, Macintosh Programmer's Workshop Pascal and Sun/Berkeley Pascal. P2c outputs a set of .c and .h files which make up a C program equivalent to the original Pascal program. The C program can then be compiled using a standard C compiler, such as gcc. Install the p2c package if you need a program for translating Pascal code into C code.

pythonlib – (Version 1.22, 236K)
[W] [S]

The pythonlib package contains Python code used by a variety of Red Hat Linux programs. Pythonlib includes code needed for multifield listboxes and entry widgets with non-standard keybindings, among other things.

qt – (Version 1.44, 2,093K)
Qt is a GUI software toolkit. Qt simplifies the task of writing and maintaining GUI (graphical user interface) applications for X Windows. Qt is written in C++ and is fully object-oriented. It has everything you need to create professional GUI applications. And it enables you to create them quickly. Qt is a multi-platform toolkit. When developing software with Qt, you can run it on the X Window System (Unix/X11) or Microsoft Windows NT and Windows 95/98. Simply recompile your source code on the platform you want. This package contains the shared library needed to run Qt applications, as well as the README files for Qt.

readline – (Version 2.2.1, 262K)
[B]

The readline library reads a line from the terminal and returns it, allowing the user to edit the line with standard emacs editing keys. The readline library allows programmers to provide an easy to use and more intuitive interface for users. If you want to develop programs that will use the readline library, you'll also need to install the readline-devel package.

slang – (Version 1.2.2, 250K)
[B]

S-Lang is an interpreted language and a programming library. The S-Lang language was designed so that it can be easily embedded into a program to provide the program with a powerful extension language. The S-Lang library, provided in this package, provides the S-Lang extension language. S-Lang's syntax resembles C, which makes it easy to recode S-Lang procedures in C if you need to.

svgalib – (Version 1.3.1, 489K)
[W]

The svgalib package provides the SVGAlib low-level graphics library for Linux. SVGAlib is a library which allows applications to use full screen graphics on a variety of hardware platforms. Many games and utilities use SVGAlib for their graphics. You'll need to have the svgalib package installed if you use any of the programs which rely on SVGAlib for their graphics support.

w3c-libwww — (Version 5.2.6, 2,097K)

Libwww is a general-purpose Web API written in C for Unix and Windows (Win32). With a highly extensible and layered API, it can accommodate many different types of applications including clients, robots, etc. The purpose of libwww is to provide a highly optimized HTTP sample implementation as well as other Internet protocols and to serve as a testbed for protocol experiments.

words — (Version 2, 411K

[B]

The words file is a dictionary of English words for the /usr/dict directory. Programs like ispell use this database of words to check spelling.

xpm — (Version 3.4j, 60K)

[W] [S]

The xpm package contains the XPM pixmap library for the X Window System. The XPM library allows applications to display color, pixmapped images, and is used by many popular X programs.

zlib — (Version 1.1.3, 61K)

[B]

The zlib compression library provides in-memory compression and decompression functions, including integrity checks of the uncompressed data. This version of the library supports only one compression method (deflation), but other algorithms may be added later, which will have the same stream interface. The zlib library is used by many different system programs.

Shells

This section contains packages that are associated with the shells that provide the command-line user interface on Red Hat Linux.

ash — (Version 0.2, 361K)

[B]

The ash shell is a clone of Berkeley's Bourne shell. Ash supports all of the standard sh shell commands, but is considerably smaller than bash. The ash shell lacks some features (for example, command-line histories), but needs a lot less memory. You should install ash if you need a lightweight shell with many of the same capabilities as the bash shell.

bash — (Version 1.14.7, 1,218K)
[B]

Bash is a GNU project sh-compatible shell or command language interpreter. Bash (Bourne Again shell) incorporates useful features from the Korn shell (ksh) and the C shell (csh). Most sh scripts can be run by bash without modification. Bash offers several improvements over sh, including command line editing, unlimited size command history, job control, shell functions and aliases, indexed arrays of unlimited size and integer arithmetic in any base from two to 64. Bash is ultimately intended to conform to the IEEE POSIX P1003.2/ISO 9945.2 Shell and Tools standard. Bash is the default shell for Red Hat Linux. You should install bash because of its popularity and power. You'll probably end up using it.

bash2 — (Version 2.03, 1,168K)
Bash is a GNU project sh-compatible shell or command language interpreter. Bash (Bourne Again shell) incorporates useful features from the Korn shell (ksh) and the C shell (csh). Most sh scripts can be run by bash without modification. Bash offers several improvements over sh, including command line editing, unlimited size command history, job control, shell functions and aliases, indexed arrays of unlimited size and integer arithmetic in any base from two to 64. Bash is ultimately intended to conform to the IEEE POSIX P1003.2/ISO 9945.2 Shell and Tools standard.

mc — (Version 4.5.29, 2,449K)
[W]

Midnight Commander is a visual shell much like a file manager, only with way more features. It is text mode, but also includes mouse support if you are running GPM. Its coolest feature is the ability to ftp, view tar, zip files, and poke into RPMs for specific files. :-)

pdksh — (Version 5.2.13, 402K)
The pdksh package contains PD-ksh, a clone of the Korn shell (ksh). The ksh shell is a command interpreter intended for both interactive and shell script use. Ksh's command language is a superset of the sh shell language. Install the pdksh package if you want to use a version of the ksh shell.

sash — (Version 2.1, 402K)
[B]

Sash is a simple, standalone, statically linked shell which includes simplified versions of built-in commands like ls, dd and gzip. Sash is statically linked so that it can work without shared libraries, so it is particularly useful for recovering from certain types of system failures. Sash can also be used to safely upgrade to new versions of shared libraries.

sh-utils — (Version 1.16, 355K)
[B]

The GNU shell utilities are a set of useful system utilities which are often used in shell scripts. The sh-utils package includes basename (to remove the path prefix from a specified pathname), chroot (to change the root directory), date (to print/set the system time and date), dirname (to remove the last level or the filename from a given path), echo (to print a line of text), env (to display/modify the environment), expr (to evaluate expressions), factor (to print prime factors), false (to return an unsuccessful exit status), groups (to print the groups a specified user is a member of), id (to print the real/effective uid/gid), logname (to print the current login name), nice (to modify a scheduling priority), nohup (to allow a command to continue running after logging out), pathchk (to check a file name's portability), printenv (to print environment variables), printf (to format and print data), pwd (to print the current directory), seq (to print numeric sequences), sleep (to suspend execution for a specified time), stty (to print/change terminal settings), su (to become another user or the superuser), tee (to send output to multiple files), test (to evaluate an expression), true (to return a successful exit status), tty (to print the terminal name), uname (to print system information), users (to print current users' names), who (to print a list of the users who are currently logged in), whoami (to print the effective user id), and yes (to print a string indefinitely).

tcsh — (Version 6.08tcsh package.00, 488K)
[B]

Tcsh is an enhanced but completely compatible version of csh, the C shell. Tcsh is a command language interpreter which can be used both as an interactive login shell and as a shell script command processor. Tcsh includes a command line editor, programmable word completion, spelling correction, a history mechanism, job control and a C language like syntax.

zsh — (Version 3.0.5, 956K)
The zsh shell is a command interpreter usable as an interactive login shell and as a shell script command processor. Zsh resembles the ksh shell (the Korn shell), but includes many enhancements. Zsh supports command line editing, built-in spelling correction, programmable command completion, shell functions (with autoloading), a history mechanism and more. Install the zsh package if you'd like to try out a different shell.

User Interface

This section contains packages that are associated with providing a user interface on Red Hat Linux.

Desktops

This section contains packages that are associated with the desktop environments available on Red Hat Linux.

AfterStep – (Version 1.7.75, 3,870K)
[W] [S]

AfterStep is a continuation of the BowMan window manager which was originally put together by Bo Yang. BowMan was based on the fvwm window manager, written by Robert Nation. Fvwm was based on code from twm. And so on... It was originally designed to emulate some of the look and feel of the NEXTSTEP user interface, but has since taken steps towards adding more useful, requested, and neat features especially in 1.4 version! The changes which comprise AfterStep's personality were originally part of bowman development, but due to a desire to move past simple emulation and into a niche as its own valuable window manager, AfterStep designers decided to change the project name and move on. Important features of AfterStep include:

1 Wharf: a free-floating application loader which can "Swallow" running programs and also can contain "Folders" of more applications.

2 Gradient filled TitleBars with 5 button : help/zap, action/tasks, iconize/maximise, shade/stick & close/destroy buttons

3 Gradient filled root window PopUp menus which can be configured to accomodate different tastes and styles of management

4 NEXTSTEP style icons which give a consistent look to the entire desktop

5 Pixmapped Pager with desktop pixmmaping

6 Easy to use look files, to share you desktop appearance with your friends

7 Start menu entries in a hierarchy of directories

8 WinList : a tasklist which can be horizontal or vertical

9 Many modules & asapps to give a good look to your X window station

AfterStep-APPS — (Version 990329, 1,119K)
[W] [S]

What's a cool window manager without some cool applets? Well... it's still cool, but these applets which can be used in the Wharf module for AfterStep or Window Maker can add both spice and productivity to your preferred window manager, such as a handy clock and information about system resources. If you've installed the AfterStep packages, you should also install these packages. Enjoy!

AnotherLevel — (Version 0.8, 302K)
[W] [S]

AnotherLevel is a custom configuration of the popular fvwm2 window manager. Fvwm stands for (?) virtual window manager. You can fill in the blank for the 'f': fast, flexible, friendly and fabulous all could apply. This window manager is based on TheNextLevel desktop configuration, created by Greg J. Badros, which won the 1996 Red Hat Desktop Contest. AnotherLevel is designed to be easily configured by the user.

WindowMaker — (Version 0.51.2, 3,933K)
Window Maker is an X11 window manager which emulates the look and feel of the NeXTSTEP (TM) graphical user interface. It is relatively fast, feature rich and easy to configure and use. Window Maker is part of the official GNU project, which means that Window Maker can interoperate with other GNU projects, such as GNOME. Window Maker allows users to switch themes 'on the fly,' to place favorite applications on either an application dock, similar to AfterStep's Wharf or on a workspace dock, a 'clip' which extends the application dock's usefulness. You should install the WindowMaker package if you use Window Maker as your window manager or if you'd like to try using it. If you do install the WindowMaker package, you may also want to install the AfterStep-APPS package, which includes applets that will work with both AfterStep and Window Maker window managers.

control-center — (Version 1.0.5, 981K)
[W]

Control-center is a configuration tool for easily setting up your GNOME environment. GNOME is the GNU Network Object Model Environment. That's a fancy name, but really GNOME is a nice GUI desktop environment. It's a powerful, easy to configure environment which helps to make your computer easy to use.

enlightenment – (Version 0.15.5, 3,703K)
[W]

Enlightenment is a window manager for the X Window System that is designed to be powerful, extensible, configurable and pretty darned good looking! It is one of the more graphically intense window managers. Enlightenment goes beyond managing windows by providing a useful and appealing graphical shell from which to work. It is open in design and instead of dictating a policy, allows the user to define their own policy, down to every last detail. This package will install the Enlightenment window manager.

enlightenment-conf – (Version 0.15, 386K)
[W]

A Configuration tool for easily setting up Enlightenment

fvwm – (Version 1.24r, 573K)
[W] [S]

FVWM (the F stands for whatever you want, but the VWM stands for Virtual Window Manager) is a window manager for the X Window System. FVWM was derived from the twm window manager. FVWM is designed to minimize memory consumption, to provide window frames with a 3D look, and to provide a simple virtual desktop. FVWM can be configured to look like Motif. Install the fvwm package if you'd like to use the FVWM window manager. If you install fvwm, you'll also need to install fvwm2-icons.

fvwm2 – (Version 2.2, 1,730K)
[W] [S]

FVWM2 (the F stands for whatever you want, but the VWM stands for Virtual Window Manager) is an improved version of the FVWM window manager for the X Window System and shares the same characteristics as FVWM. Install the fvwm2 package if you'd like to use the FVWM2 window manager. If you install fvwm2, you'll also need to install fvwm2-icons.

fvwm2-icons – (Version 2.2, 408K)
[W] [S]

The fvwm2-icons package contains icons, bitmaps and pixmaps used by the FVWM and FVWM2 X Window System window managers. You'll need to install fvwm2-icons if you are installing fvwm and/or fvwm2.

gmc — (Version 4.5.29, 7,078K)
[W]

Midnight Commander is a visual shell much like a file manager, only with way more features. This is the GNOME version. It's coolest feature is the ability to ftp, view tar, zip files and poke into RPMs for specific files. The GNOME version of Midnight Commander is not yet finished though. :-(

gnome-core — (Version 1.0.4, 3,253K)
[W]

GNOME (GNU Network Object Model Environment) is a user-friendly set of applications and desktop tools to be used in conjunction with a window manager for the X Window System. GNOME is similar in purpose and scope to CDE and KDE, but GNOME is based completely on Open Source software. The gnome-core package includes the basic programs and libraries that are needed to install GNOME. You should install the gnome-core package if you would like to use the GNOME desktop environment. You'll also need to install the gnome-libs package. If you want to use Linuxconf with a GNOME front end, you'll also need to install the gnome-linuxconf package.

kdebase — (Version 1.1, 11,806K)
Core applications for the K Desktop Environment. Included are: kdm (replacement for xdm), kwm (window manager), kfm (filemanager, web browser, ftp client, ...), konsole (xterm replacement), kpanel (application starter and desktop pager), kaudio (audio server), kdehelp (viewer for kde help files, info and man pages), plus other KDE components (kcheckpass, kikbd, kvt, kscreensaver, kcontrol, kfind, kfontmanager, kmenuedit, kappfinder) PAM password authentication is supported via PAM service: kde.

switchdesk — (Version 1.5, 90K)
[W]

The Desktop Switcher is a tool which enables users to easily switch between various desktop environments that they have installed. The tool includes support for GNOME, KDE, and AnotherLevel. Support for different environments on different computers is available, as well as setting a "global default."

switchdesk-gnome — (Version 1.5, 10K)
[W]

Provides the desktop switching tool with a GNOME look and feel.

switchdesk-kde — (Version 1.5, 22K)
Provides the desktop switching Tool with a KDE look and feel.

wmakerconf – (Version 1.7, 569K)

Wmakerconf is a GTK+ based graphical user interface configuration tool for the Window Maker window manager. Wmakerconf supports all Window Maker attributes. Wmakerconf provides a font selection browser, a pixmap preview browser, a color selection dialog, a shortcut dialog, and a file selection dialog. Wmakerconf also provides tooltips in multiple languages. If you use the Window Maker window manager, you should probably install the wmakerconf package, because it will make configuration a little easier.

wmconfig – (Version 0.9.3, 53K)

[W] [S]

The wmconfig program is a helper program which provides output for use in configuring window managers. Wmconfig will produce a list of menu definitions for a specified X window manager (currently, FVWM2, FVWM95, AfterStep, MWM, IceWM and KDE are supported). Wmconfig's output can be placed into your .rc file or you can use the output for other configuration purposes.

xfm – (Version 1.3.2, 706K)

[W]

Xfm is a file manager for the X Window System. Xfm supports moving around the directory tree, multiple windows, moving/copying/deleting files, and launching programs. Install xfm if you would like to use a graphical file manager program.

X Hardware Support

This section contains packages that are associated with providing hardware support for specific video cards under Red Hat Linux.

XFree86-3DLabs – (Version 3.3.3.1, 2,211K)

X server for cards built around 3D Labs GLINT and Permedia chipsets, including GLINT 500TX with IBM RGB526 RAMDAC, GLINT MX with IBM RGB526 and IBM RGB640 RAMDAC, Permedia with IBM RGB526 RAMDAC and the Permedia 2 (classic, 2a, 2v).

XFree86-8514 – (Version 3.3.3.1, 1,743K)

If you are installing the X Window System and the video card in your system is an older IBM 8514 or a compatible from a company such as ATI, you should install XFree86-8514. To install the X Window System, you will need to install the XFree86 package, one or more of the XFree86 fonts packages, the X11R6-contrib package, the Xconfigurator package and the XFree86-libs package. If you are going to develop applications that run as X clients, you will also need to install the XFree86-devel package.

XFree86-AGX – (Version 3.3.3.1, 1,925K)
This is the X server for AGX-based cards, such as the Boca Vortex, Orchid Celsius, Spider Black Widow and Hercules Graphite. If you are installing the X Window System and the video card in your system is an AGX, you'll need to install XFree86-AGX. To install the X Window System, you will need to install the XFree86 package, one or more of the XFree86 fonts packages, the X11R6-contrib package, the Xconfigurator package and the XFree86-libs package. Finally, if you are going to develop applications that run as X clients, you will also need to install the XFree86-devel package.

XFree86-FBDev – (Version 3.3.3.1, 2,001K)
This is the X server for the generic frame buffer device used on Amiga, Atari and Macintosh/m68k machines. Support for Intel and Alpha architectures is included in the Linux 2.2 kernel, as well.

XFree86-I128 – (Version 3.3.3.1, 2,182K)
This is the X server for the #9 Imagine 128 and similar video boards.

XFree86-Mach32 – (Version 3.3.3.1, 1,886K)
XFree86-Mach32 is the X server package for video cards built around ATI's Mach32 chip, including the ATI Graphics Ultra Pro and Ultra Plus. If you are installing the X Window System and the video card in your system is based on the Mach32 chip, you need to install XFree86-Mach32. You will also need to install the XFree86 package, one or more of the XFree86 fonts packages, the X11R6-contrib package, the Xconfigurator package and the XFree86-libs package. And, finally, if you are going to develop applications that run as X clients, you will also need to install XFree86-devel.

XFree86-Mach64 – (Version 3.3.3.1, 2,008K)
XFree86-Mach64 is the server package for cards based on ATI's Mach64 chip, such as the Graphics Xpression, GUP Turbo, and WinTurbo cards. Note that this server is known to have problems with some Mach64 cards. Check *http://www.xfree86.org* for current information on updating this server. If you are installing the X Window System and the video card in your system is based on the Mach64 chip, you need to install XFree86-Mach64. You will also need to install the XFree86 package, one or more of the XFree86 fonts packages, the X11R6-contrib package, the Xconfigurator package and the XFree86-libs package. And, finally, if you are going to be developing applications that run as X clients, you will also need to install XFree86-devel.

XFree86-Mach8 – (Version 3.3.3.1, 1,755K)
XFree86-Mach 8 is the X server for video cards built around ATI's Mach8 chip, including the ATI 8514 Ultra and Graphics Ultra. If you are installing the X Window System and the video card in your system is based on the Mach8 chip,

you need to install XFree86-Mach8. You will also need to install the XFree86 package, one or more of the XFree86 fonts packages, the X11R6-contrib package, the Xconfigurator package and the XFree86-libs package. And, finally, if you are going to be developing applications that run as X clients, you will also need to install XFree86-devel.

XFree86-Mono – (Version 3.3.3.1, 2,052K)
XFree86-Mono is a generic monochrome (2 color) server for VGA cards. XFree86-Mono will work for nearly all VGA compatible cards, but will only support a monochrome display. If you are installing the X Window System and your VGA card is not currently supported, you should install and try either XFree86-Mono or XFree86-VGA16, depending upon the capabilities of your display. You will also need to install the XFree86 package, one or more of the XFree86 fonts packages, the X11R6-contrib package, the Xconfigurator package and the XFree86-libs package. And, finally, if you are going to develop applications that run as X clients, you will also need to install XFree86-devel.

XFree86-P9000 – (Version 3.3.3.1, 1,945K)
XFree86-P9000 is the X server for video cards built around the Weitek P9000 chip, such as most Diamond Viper cards and the Orchid P9000 card. If you are installing the X Window System and you have a Weitek P9000 based video card, you should install XFree86-P9000. You will also need to install the XFree86 package, one or more of the XFree86 fonts packages, the X11R6-contrib package, the Xconfigurator package and the XFree86-libs package. And, finally, if you are going to develop applications that run as X clients, you will also need to install XFree86-devel.

XFree86-S3 – (Version 3.3.3.1, 2,431K)
XFree86-S3 is the X server for video cards based on S3 chips, including most #9 cards, many Diamond Stealth cards, Orchid Farenheits, Mirco Crystal 8S, most STB cards, and some motherboards with built-in graphics accelerators (such as the IBM ValuePoint line). Note that if you have an S3 ViRGE based video card, you'll need XFree86-S3V instead of XFree86-S3. If you are installing the X Window System and you have a video card based on an S3 chip, you should install XFree86-S3. You will also need to install the XFree86 package, one or more XFree86 fonts packages, the X11R6-contrib package, the Xconfigurator package and the XFree86-libs package. And, finally, if you are going to develop applications that run as X clients, you will also need to install XFree86-devel.

XFree86-S3V – (Version 3.3.3.1, 2,160K)
XFree86-S3V is the X server for video cards based on the S3 ViRGE chipset. If you are installing the X Window System and you have a video card based on an S3 ViRGE chip, you should install XFree86-S3V. You will also need to install the

XFree86 package, one or more of the XFree86 fonts packages, the X11R6-contrib package, the Xconfigurator package and the XFree86-libs package. And, finally, if you are going to develop applications that run as X clients, you will also need to install XFree86-devel.

XFree86-SVGA – (Version 3.3.3.1, 3,097K)
X server for most simple framebuffer SVGA devices, including cards built from ET4000 chips, Cirrus Logic chips, Chips and Technologies laptop chips, Trident 8900 and 9000 chips, and Matrox chips. It works for Diamond Speedstar, Orchid Kelvins, STB Nitros and Horizons, Genoa 8500VL, most Actix boards, the Spider VLB Plus, etc. It also works for many other chips and cards, so try this server if you are having problems.

XFree86-VGA16 – (Version 3.3.3.1, 1,944K)
XFree86-VGA16 is a generic 16 color server for VGA boards. XFree86-VGA16 will work on nearly all VGA style graphics boards, but will only support a low resolution, 16 color display. If you are installing the X Window System and your VGA video card is not specifically supported by another X server package, you should install either XFree86-Mono or XFree86-VGA16, depending upon the capabilities of your display. You will also need to install the XFree86 package, one or more of the XFree86 fonts packages, the X11R6-contrib package, the Xconfigurator package and the XFree86-libs package. And, finally, if you are going to be develop applications that run as X clients, you will also need to install XFree86-devel.

XFree86-W32 – (Version 3.3.3.1, 1,793K)
XFree86-W32 is the X server for cards built around ET4000/W32 chips, including the Genoa 8900 Phantom 32i, the Hercules Dynamite, the LeadTek WinFast S200, the Sigma Concorde, the STB LightSpeed, the TechWorks Thunderbolt, and the ViewTop PCI. If you are installing the X Window System and your VGA video card is based on the ET4000/W32 chipset, you should install XFree86-W32. You will also need to install the XFree86 package, one or more of the XFree86 fonts packages, the X11R6-contrib package, the Xconfigurator package and the XFree86-libs package. And, finally, if you are going to develop applications that run as X clients, you will also need to install XFree86-devel.

XFree86-XF86Setup – (Version 3.3.3.1, 596K)
XF86Setup is a graphical user interface configuration tool for setting up and configuring XFree86 servers. XF86Setup can configure video settings, keyboard layouts, mouse types, etc. XF86Setup can't be used with non-VGA compatible video cards, with fixed-frequency monitors, or with OS/2. Install XF86Setup if you have used it before and prefer to keep using it to configure your X server. If you do not have a preference for XF86Setup, you should instead install and use Xconfigurator, Red Hat's graphical user interface configuration tool for the X Window System.

XFree86-Xnest — (Version 3.3.3.1, 2,242K)

Xnest is an X Window System server which runs in an X window. Xnest is a 'nested' window server, actually a client of the real X server, which manages windows and graphics requests for Xnest, while Xnest manages the windows and graphics requests for its own clients. You will need to install Xnest if you require an X server which will run as a client of your real X server (perhaps for testing purposes).

XFree86-Xvfb — (Version 3.3.3.1, 2,707K)

Xvfb (X Virtual Frame Buffer) is an X Windows System server that is capable of running on machines with no display hardware and no physical input devices. Xvfb emulates a dumb framebuffer using virtual memory. Xvfb doesn't open any devices, but behaves otherwise as an X display. Xvfb is normally used for testing servers. Using Xvfb, the mfb or cfb code for any depth can be exercised without using real hardware that supports the desired depths. Xvfb has also been used to test X clients against unusual depths and screen configurations, to do batch processing with Xvfb as a background rendering engine, to do oad testing, to help with porting an X server to a new platform, and to provide an unobtrusive way of running applications which really don't need an X server but insist on having one. If you need to test your X server or your X clients, you may want to install Xvfb for that purpose.

Xconfigurator — (Version 4.1.3, 433K)

[W] [S]

Xconfigurator is a full-screen, menu-driven program which walks you through setting up your X server. Xconfigurator is based on the sources for xf86config, a utility from XFree86. You should install Xconfigurator if you are installing the X Window System.

X

This section contains packages associated with the X Window System graphical user interface.

X11R6-contrib — (Version 3.3.2, 474K)

[W] [S]

If you want to use the X Window System, you should install X11R6-contrib. This package holds many useful programs from the X Window System, version 11, release 6 contrib tape. The programs, contributed by various users, include listres, xbiff, xedit, xeyes, xcalc, xload and xman, among others. You will also need to install the XFree86 package, the XFree86 package which corresponds to your video card, one or more of the XFree86 fonts packages, the Xconfigurator package and the XFree86-libs package. Finally, if you are going to develop applications that run as X clients, you will also need to install XFree86-devel.

XFree86-100dpi-fonts – (Version 3.3.3.1, 1,228K)

If you're going to use the X Window System and you have a high resolution monitor capable of 100 dpi, you should install XFree86-100dpi-fonts. This package contains a set of 100 dpi fonts used on most Linux systems. If you are installing the X Window System, you will also need to install the XFree86 package, the XFree86 package corresponding to your video card, the X11R6- contrib package, the Xconfigurator package and the XFree86-libs package. If you need to display certain fonts, you may also need to install other XFree86 fonts packages. And finally, if you are going to develop applications that run as X clients, you will also need to install the XFree86-devel package.

XFree86 – (Version 3.3.3.1, 14,458K)

[W] [S]

If you want to install the X Window System (TM) on your machine, you'll need to install XFree86. The X Window System provides the base technology for developing graphical user interfaces. Simply stated, X draws the elements of the GUI on the user's screen and builds methods for sending user interactions back to the application. X also supports remote application deployment–running an application on another computer while viewing the input/output on your machine. X is a powerful environment which supports many different applications, such as games, programming tools, graphics programs, text editors, etc. XFree86 is the version of X which runs on Linux, as well as other platforms. This package contains the basic fonts, programs and documentation for an X workstation. However, this package doesn't provide the program which you will need to drive your video hardware. To control your video card, you'll need the particular X server package which corresponds to your computer's video card. In addition to installing this package, you will need to install the XFree86 package which corresponds to your video card, the X11R6-contrib package, the Xconfigurator package and the XFree86-libs package. You may also need to install one of the XFree86 fonts packages. And finally, if you are going to develop applications that run as X clients, you will also need to install XFree86-devel.

XFree86-75dpi-fonts – (Version 3.3.3.1, 1,060K)

[W] [S]

XFree86-75dpi-fonts contains the 75 dpi fonts used on most X Window Systems. If you're going to use the X Window System, you should install this package, unless you have a monitor which can support 100 dpi resolution. In that case, you may prefer the 100dpi fonts available in the XFree86-100dpi-fonts package. You may also need to install other XFree86 font packages. To install the X Window System, you will need to install the XFree86 package, the XFree86 package corresponding to your video card, the X11R6-contrib package, the

Xconfigurator package and the XFree86-libs package. Finally, if you are going to develop applications that run as X clients, you will also need to install the XFree86-devel package.

XFree86-ISO8859-2 — (Version 1.0, 77K)
If you use the X Window System and you want to display Central European fonts, you should install the XFree86-ISO8859-2 package. This package contains a full set of Central European fonts, in compliance with the ISO 8859-2 standard. The fonts included in this package are distributed free of charge and can be used freely, subject to the accompanying copyright: Copyright (c) 1996, 1997 BIZNET Poland, Inc. All Rights Reserved. BIZNET is a registered trademark of BIZNET Poland, Inc. You may also need to install one or more other XFree86 fonts packages. To install the X Window System, you will need to install the XFree86 package, the XFree86 package which corresponds to your video card, the X11R6-contrib package, the Xconfigurator package and the XFree86-libs package. Finally, if you are going to develop applications that run as X clients, you will also need to install XFree86-devel.

XFree86-ISO8859-2-100dpi-fonts — (Version 1.0, 1,003K)
The XFree86-ISO8859-2-100dpi-fonts package includes Central European (ISO 8859-2) fonts, in 100 dpi resolution, for the X Window System. If you need to display the special characters used by Central European languages on your X Window System, and your monitor can support 100 dpi resolution, you should install the XFree86-ISO8859-2-100dpi-fonts package. You may need to install one or more of the other XFree86 fonts packages, as well. To install the X Window System, you will need to install the XFree86 package, the XFree86 video card package which corresponds to your video card, the X11R6-contrib package, the Xconfigurator package and the XFree86-libs package. If you're going to develop applications which run as X clients, you'll also need to install XFree86-devel.

XFree86-ISO8859-2-75dpi-fonts — (Version 1.0, 877K)
The XFree86-ISO8859-2-75dpi-fonts package contains a set of Central European language fonts in 75 dpi resolution for the X Window System. If you have a high resolution monitor capable of supporting 100 dpi, you should install the 100 dpi version of this package instead. If you are installing the X Window System and you need to display Central European language characters in 75 dpi resolution, you should install this package. You may also need to install one or more of the other XFree86 fonts packages as well. To install the X Window System, you will need to install the XFree86 package, the XFree86 video card package that corresponds to your video card, the X11R6-contrib package, the Xconfigurator package and the XFree86-libs package. If you are going to develop applications that will run as X clients, you will also need to install XFree86-devel.

XFree86-ISO8859-2-Type1-fonts — (Version 1.0, 1,905K)

The XFree86-ISO8859-2-Type1-fonts package contains Central European Type 1 fonts for the X Window System. This set of fonts is known as the ulT1mo (or ultimo) collection. All of the included fonts are copyrighted to their authors and freeware. Original fonts were taken from the Internet or CDs. If you need to display Central European language fonts on your X Window System, you should install the XFree86-ISO8859-2-Type1-fonts package. You may need to also install one or more of the other XFree86 fonts packages. To install the X Window System, you will need to install the XFree86 package, the XFree86 video card package which corresponds to your video card, the X11R6-contrib package, the Xconfigurator package and the XFree86-libs package. Finally, if you are going to develop applications that will run as X clients, you'll need to install XFree86-devel.

XFree86-ISO8859-9-100dpi-fonts — (Version 2.1.2, 1,142K)

The XFree86-ISO8859-9-100dpi-fonts package contains a set of Turkish language fonts in 100 dpi resolution and in accordance with the ISO8859-9 standard for the X Window System. If you need to display Turkish language fonts for the X Window System, and your monitor is capable of supporting 100 dpi resolution, you should install this package. You may also need to install one or more of the other XFree86 fonts packages. To install the X Window System, you will need to install the XFree86 package, the XFree86 video card package which corresponds to your video card, the X11R6-contrib package, the Xconfigurator package and the XFree86-libs package. If you are going to develop applications that will run as X clients, you will also need to install XFree86-devel.

XFree86-ISO8859-9 — (Version 2.1.2, 85K)

The XFree86-ISO8859-9 package contains Turkish language (ISO8859-9) terminal fonts, modmaps for the Q and F style of Turkish keyboard mappings and a simple utility for changing the modmap. If you need to display Turkish language fonts on your X Window System, or if you need a to use the Q and F style keyboard mappings, you should install the XFree86-ISO8859-9 package. You may also need to install other XFree86 font packages. If you're installing the X Window System, you'll need to install the XFree86 package, the XFree86 video card package which corresponds to your video card, the X11R6-contrib package, the Xconfigurator package and the XFree86-libs package. If you're going to develop applications that run as X clients, you will also need to install XFree86-devel.

XFree86-ISO8859-9-75dpi-fonts — (Version 2.1.2, 1,032K)

The XFree86-ISO8859-9-75dpi-fonts package contains a set of Turkish language (ISO8859-9) fonts in 75 dpi resolution for the X Window System. If you need to display Turkish language fonts on your X Window System, you should install this package. If your monitor is capable of supporting 100 dpi resolution, you should instead install the 100 dpi font package. You may also need to install one or more of the other XFree86 fonts packages. If you're installing the X Window System, you need to install the XFree86 package, the XFree86 video card package which corresponds to your video card, the X11R6-contrib package, the Xconfigurator package and the XFree86-libs package. Finally, if you are going to develop applications that will run as X clients, you will also need to install XFree86-devel.

XFree86-cyrillic-fonts – (Version 3.3.3.1, 301K)
The Cyrillic fonts included with XFree86 3.3.2 and higher. Those who use a language requiring the Cyrillic character set should install this package.

gdm – (Version 1.0.0, 246K)
[W]

GNOME Display Manager allows you to log into your system with the X Window System running. It is highly configurable, allowing you to run several different X sessions at once on your local machine, and can manage login connections from remote machines as well.

gqview – (Version 0.6.0, 186K)
[W]

GQview is a browser for graphics files. Offering single click viewing of your graphics files. Includes thumbnail view, zoom and filtering features. And external editor support.

kterm – (Version 6.2.0, 154K)
The kterm package provides a terminal emulator for the Kanji Japanese character set. Install kterm if you need a Kanji character set terminal emulator. You'll also need to have the X Window System installed.

rxvt – (Version 2.6.PRE2, 490K)
[W] [S]

Rxvt is a color VT102 terminal emulator for the X Window System. Rxvt is intended to be an xterm replacement for users who don't need the more esoteric features of xterm, like Tektronix 4014 emulation, session logging and toolkit style configurability. Since it doesn't support those features, rxvt uses much less swap space than xterm uses. This is a significant advantage on a machine which is serving a large number of X sessions. The rxvt package should be installed on any machine which serves a large number of X sessions, if you'd like to improve that machine's performance.

urw-fonts — (Version 1.1, 2,160K)
[W] [S]

Free versions of the 35 standard PostScript fonts. With newer releases of ghostscript quality versions of the standard 35 Type 1 PostScript fonts are shipped. They were donated and licenced under the GPL by URW. The fonts.dir was specially made to match the original Adobe names of the fonts, e.g. Times, Helvetica etc. With X, LaTeX, or Ghostscript, these fonts are a must to have!

x3270 — (Version 3.1.1.6, 561K)
The x3270 program opens a window in the X Window System which emulates the actual look of an IBM 3278/3279 terminal, commonly used with mainframe applications. x3270 also allows you to telnet to an IBM host from the x3270 window. Install the x3270 package if you need to access IBM hosts using an IBM 3278/3279 terminal emulator.

xinitrc — (Version 2.1, 8K)
[W] [S]

The xinitrc package contains the xinitrc file, a script which is used to configure your X Window System session or to start a window manager. The xinitrc package should be installed if you use the X Window System.

Appendix D
General Parameters and Modules

This appendix is provided to illustrate some of the possible parameters that may be needed by certain drivers. It should be noted that, in most cases, these additional parameters are unnecessary. Also included is a list of network hardware and the associated modules required by that hardware. Please keep in mind that if a device you are attempting to use requires one of these parameters, and support for that device is not compiled into the kernel, the traditional method of adding the parameter to the LILO boot command will not work. Drivers loaded as modules require that these parameters are specified when the module is loaded. The Red Hat Linux installation program gives you the option to specify module parameters when a driver is loaded. For more information concerning the device support compiled into the kernel used by the Red Hat Linux installation program, please refer to Section 2.9.

Please Note: Not all of the cards that are listed are supported. Please check the hardware compatibility list on Red Hat Software's World Wide Web site at *http://www.redhat.com/support/docs/hardware.html* to make sure your card is supported.

One of the more commonly used parameters, the `hdX=cdrom` parameter, can be entered at the boot prompt, as it deals with support for IDE/ATAPI CD-ROMs, which is part of the kernel.

In the tables below, most modules without any parameters listed are either able to auto-probe to find the hardware, or require you to manually change settings in the module source code, and recompile.

CD-ROM parameters

Hardware	Module	Parameters
ATAPI/IDE CD-ROM Drives		hdX=cdrom
Aztech CD268-01A, Orchid CD-3110,	aztcd.o	aztcd=io_port
Okano/Wearnes CDD110,		
Conrad TXC, CyCDROM CR520		
CyCDROM CR540 (non-IDE)		
Sony CDU 31A or 33A CD-ROM	cdu31a.o	cdu31a=io_port,IRQ[,PAS]
		cdu31a_port=base_addr
		cdu31a_irq=irq
Philips/LMS CDROM drive 206	cm206.o	cm206=io_port,IRQ
with cm260 host adapter card		
Goldstar R420 CD-ROM	gscd.o	gscd=io_port
ISP16, MAD16, or Mozart sound card	isp16.o	isp16=io_port,IRQ,dma,drive_type
CD-ROM interface (OPTi 82C928 and		isp16_cdrom_base=io_port
OPTi 82C929) with Sanyo/Panasonic,		isp16_cdrom_irq=IRQ
Sony, or Mitsumi drives		isp16_cdrom_dma=dma
		isp16_cdrom_type=drive_type
Mitsumi CD-ROM, Standard	mcd.o	mcd=io_port,IRQ
Mitsumi CD-ROM, Experimental	mcdx.o	mcdx=io_port_1,IRQ_1,io_port_n,IRQ_n
Optics storage 8000 AT CD-ROM	optcd.o	optcd =io_port
"Dolphin" drive; Lasermate CR328A		
SB Pro 16 compatible	sbpcd.o	sbpcd=io_port,sb_pro_Setting
Sanyo CDR-H94A	sjcd.o	sjcd=io_port sjcd_base=io_port
Sony CDU-535 & 531	sonycd535.o	sonycd535=io_port
(some Procomm drives)		

Here are some examples of these modules in use:

Configuration	Example
ATAPI CD-ROM, jumpered as master on	hdc=cdrom
2nd IDE channel	
non-IDE Mitsumi CD-ROM on port 340, IRQ 1	mcd=0x340,11
Three non-IDE Mitsumi CD-ROM drives using the	mcdx=0x300,5,0x304,10,0x320,11
experimental driver, io ports 300, 304, and 320 with	
IRQs 5, 10 and 11	
Sony CDU 31 or 33 at port 340, no IRQ	cdu31=0x340,0
(module arguments for above)	cdu31_port=0x340 cdu31a_irq=0
Aztech CD-ROM at port 220	aztcd=0x220
Panasonic-type CD-ROM on a SoundBlaster	sbpcd=0x230,1
interface at port 220	
Phillips/LMS cm206 and cm260 at IO 340	cm206=0x340,11
and IRQ 11	
Goldstar R420 at IO 300	gscd=0x300
Mitsumi drive on a MAD16 soundcard at IO Addr 330	isp16=0x330,11,0,Mitsumi
and IRQ 1, probing DMA	
Sony CDU 531 at IO address 320	sonycd535=0x320

Please Note: Most newer Sound Blaster cards come with IDE interfaces. For these cards, you do not need to use sbpcd parameters, only use hdx parameters

SCSI parameters

Hardware	Module	Parameters
NCR53c810/820/720	53c7,8xx.o	
NCR53c700/710/700-66	53c7,8xx.o	
AM53/79C974 PC-SCSI Driver	AM53C974.o	AM53C974=host-scsi-id,
Qlogic PCI-Basic		target-scsi-id,max-rate, max-offset
Most Buslogic (now Mylex)	BusLogic.o	BusLogic_Options=option,option,...
cards with "BT" part number		(See /usr/src/linux/drivers/scsi/README.BusLogic)
	NCR53c406a.o	ncr53c406a=io_port[,IRQ[,FASTPIO]]
		ncr53c406a io=io_port irq=IRQ fastpio=FASTPIO
Advansys SCSI Cards	advansys.o	
Adaptec AHA 152x	aha152x.o	aha152x=io_base,IRQ,scsi_id,reconnect,parity
Adaptec AHA 1542	aha1542.o	aha1542=io_base,buson,busoff,dmaspeed
Adaptec AHA 1740	aha1740.o	
Adaptec AHA-274x, AHA-284x,	aic7xxx.o	aic7xxx=string
AHA-29xx, AHA-394x, AHA-398x,		
AHA-274x, AHA-274xT, AHA-2842,		
AHA-2910B, AHA-2920C,		
AHA-2930/U/U2,		
AHA-2940/W/U/UW/AU/U2W/U2/U2B/,		
U2BOEM, AHA-2944D/WD/UD/UWD,		
AHA-2950U2/W/B,		
AHA-3940/U/W/UW/,		
AUW/U2W/U2B, AHA-3950U2D,		
AHA-3985/U/W/UW, AIC-777x,		
AIC-785x, AIC-786x, AIC-787x,		
AIC-788x , AIC-789x, AIC-3860		
Data Technology Corp DTC3180/3280	dtc.o	
DTP SCSI host adapters (EATA/DMA)	eata.o	eata=port0,port1,port2,...options
PM2011B/9X ISA, PM2021A/9X ISA,		
PM2012A,		eata io_port=port0,port1,port2,...option=value
PM2012B, PM2022A/9X EISA,		
PM2122A/9X, PM2322A/9X,		

SmartRAID PM3021, PM3222,		
PM3224		
DTP SCSI Adapters PM2011,		
PM2021, PM2041,	eata_dma.o	
PM3021, PM2012B, PM2022, PM2122,		
PM2322, PM2042, PM3122, PM3222,		
PM3332, PM2024, PM2124, PM2044,		
PM2144, PM3224, PM3334		
DTP EATA-PIO boards	eata_pio.o	
Future Domain TMC-16x0- based cards	fdomain.o	fdomain=io_base,IRQ[,ADAPTER_ID]
TMC-1800, TMC-18C50,		
TMC-18C30, TMC-36C70,		
Future Domain TMC-1650,		
TMC-1660, TMC-1670, TMC-1680,		
TMC-1610M/MER/MEX,		
TMC-3260 (PCI),		
Quantum ISA-200S, ISA-250MG		
Adaptec AHA-2920A (PCI)		
(NOT AHA-2920C)		
NCR5380 and NCR53c400 cards	g_NCR5380.o	ncr5380=io_port,IRQ,dma
		ncr53c400=io_port,IRQ
		ncr5380 io=io_port irq=IRQ dma=dma
		ncr53c400 io=io_port irq=IRQ
GDT ISA/EISA/PCI Disk Array Controller	gdth.o	gdth=IRQ0,IRQ1,IRQ2,...options:values
IOMEGA MatchMaker parallel port		
SCSI adapter	imm.o	
Always IN2000 ISA SCSI card	in2000.o	in2000=setup_string:value
		in2000 setup_string=value
Initio INI-9X00U/UW SCSI host adapters	initio.o	
AMI MegaRAID 418, 428, 438, 466, 762	megaraid.o	
NCR SCSI controllers with 810/810A/815/	ncr53c8xx.o	ncr53c8xx=option1:value1,option2:value2,...
825/825A/860/875/876/895 chipsets		ncr53c8xx="option1:value1 option2:value2..."
Pro Audio Spectrum/Studio 16	pas16.o	pas16=port,irq
IOMEGA PPA3 parallel port		

SCSI host adapter	ppa.o	
Perceptive Solutions PSI-240I EIDE	psi240i.o	
QLogic Fast SCSI FASXXX		
ISA/VLB/PCMCIA	qlogicfas.o	
QLogic ISP2100 SCSI-FCP	qlogicfc.o	
QLogic ISP1020 Intelligent SCSI cards	qlogicisp.o	
IQ-PCI, IQ-PCI-10, IQ-PCI-D		
Seagate ST01/ST02	seagate.o	controller_type=1 base_address=base_addr irq=irq
Future Domain TMC-885, TMC-950	seagate.o	controller_type=2 base_address=base_addr irq=irq
Cards with the sym53c416 chipset	sym53c416.o	sym53c416=PORTBASE[,IRQ]
		sym53c416 io=PORTBASE irq=IRQ
Trantor T128/T128F/T228		
SCSI Host Adapter	t128.o	
Tekram DC390 and other AMD53C974A	tmscsim.o	tmscsim=ID,SPEED
based PCI SCSI adapters		
UltraStor 14F/34F SCSI host adapters	u14-34f.o	u14-34f=io_port1,io_port2,...io_port10
(14F, 24F, 34F)		u14-34f io_port=io_port1,io_port2,...io_port10
UltraStor 14F, 24F, and 34F	ultrastor.o	
WD7000-FASST2,WD7000-ASC,	wd7000.o	wd7000=IRQ,dma,io_port
WD7000-AX/MX/EX		wd7000 io=io_port irq=IRQ dma=dma

Here are some examples of these modules in use:

Configuration	Example
Adaptec AHA1522 at port 330, IRQ 11, SCSI ID 7	aha152x=0x330,11,7
Adaptec AHA1542 at port 330	bases=0x330
Future Domain TMC-800 at CA000, IRQ 10	controller_type=2 base_address=0xca000 irq=10

When a parameter has commas, make sure you do not put a space after a comma.

Ethernet parameters

Hardware	Module	Parameters
3Com 3c501	3c501.o	3c501=io_port,IRQ
3Com 3c503 and 3c503/16	3c503.o	3c503=io_port,IRQ
		3c503 io=io_port_1,io_port_n irq=IRQ_1,IRQ_n
3Com EtherLink Plus (3c505)	3c505.o	3c505=io_port,IRQ,DMA
		3c505 io=io_port_1,io_port_n irq=IRQ_1,IRQ_2
		dma=dma_1,dma_n
3Com EtherLink 16	3c507.o	3c507=io_port,IRQ 3c507 io=io_port irq=IRQ
3Com EtherLink III	3c509.o	3c509=IRQ
3Com ISA EtherLink XL	3c515.o	
"Corkscrew" 3Com EtherLink PCI III/XL	3c59x.o	
Vortex (3c590, 3c592, 3c595, 3c597)		
Boomerang (3c900, 3c905, 3c595)		
Apricot 680x0 VME, 82596 chipset	82596.o	82596=IRQ 82596 irq=IRQ
Ansel Communications AC3200 EISA	ac3200.o	ac3200=io_port,IRQ
		ac3200 io=io_port_1,io_port_n irq=IRQ_1,IRQ_n
Alteon AceNIC	acenic.o	acenic=trace,link
Gigabit Ethernet driver		acenic trace=trace link=val
Allied Telesis AT1700	at1700.o	at1700=io_port,IRQ
		at1700 io=io_port irq=IRQ
Tangent ATB-II, Novel NL-10000,	cops.o	cops=io_port,IRQ
Daystar Digital LT-200, Dayna DL2000,		cops io=io_port irq=IRQ
DaynaTalk PC (HL), COPS LT-95,		
Farallon PhoneNET PC II, III		
Modular driver for the COSA or	cosa.o	cosa=io_port,IRQ,dma
SRP synchronous serial card		
Crystal LAN CS8900/CS8920	cs89x0.o	cs89x0=io_port,IRQ,MEDIA_TYPE
		cs89x0 io=io_port irq=IRQ media=TYPE
EtherWORKS DE425 TP/COAX EISA,	de4x5.o	de4x5=io_port
DE434 TP PCI,		
DE435/450 TP/COAX/AUI PCI		de4x5 io=io_port
DE500 10/100 PCI		de4x5 args='ethX[fdx] autosense=MEDIA_STRING'

Kingston, LinkSys, SMC8432, SMC9332,		
Znyx31[45], and Znyx346 10/100 cards		
with DC21040 (no SROM), DC21041[A],		
DC21140[A], DC21142, DC21143 chipsets		
D-Link DE-600 Ethernet Pocket Adapter	de600.o	
D-Link DE-620 Ethernet Pocket Adapter	de620.o	
		de620 io=io_port irq=IRQ bnc=1 utp=1
DIGITAL DEPCA & EtherWORKS	depca.o	depca=io_port,IRQ
DEPCA, DE100, DE101,		
DE200 Turbo, DE201Turbo		depca io=io_port irq=IRQ
DE202 Turbo TP/BNC, DE210, DE422 EISA		
Digi Intl. RightSwitch SE-X EISA and PCI	dgrs.o	
Cabletron E2100 series ethercards	e2100.o	e2100=io_port,IRQ
		e2100 io=io_port irq=IRQ
Intel i82595 ISA	eepro.o	eepro=io_port,IRQ,mem
EtherExpressPro10/10+ driver		eepro io=io_port irq=IRQ mem=mem
Intel i82557/i82558 PCI	eepro100.o	
EtherExpressPro driver		
Intel EtherExpress 16 (i82586)	eexpress.o	eexpress=io_port,IRQ
		eexpress io=io_port irq=IRQ
SMC EtherPower II 9432 PCI	epic100.o	
(83c170/175 EPIC series)		
Racal-Interlan ES3210 EISA Network Adapter	es3210.o	es3210=io_port,IRQ,mem
		es3210 io=io_port irq=IRQ mem=mem
ICL EtherTeam 16i/32	eth16i.o	eth16i=io_port,mediatype
		eth16i ioaddr=io_port mediatype=type
EtherWORKS 3 (DE203, DE204 and DE205)	ewrk3.o	ewrk=io_port,IRQ
		ewrk io=io_port irq=IRQ
Fujitsu FMV-181/182/183/184	fmv18x.o	fmv18x=io_port,IRQ
		fmv18x io=io_port irq=IRQ
Modular driver for the Comtrol	hostess_sv11.o	hostess_sv11=io_port,IRQ,DMABIT
Hostess SV11		hostess_sv11 io=io_port irq=IRQ dma=DMABIT
HP PCLAN/plus	hp-plus.o	hp-plus=io_port,IRQ hp-plus io=io_port irq=IRQ

HP LAN Ethernet	hp.o	hp=io_port,IRQ
		hp io=io_port irq=IRQ
100VG-AnyLan Network Adapters	hp100.o	hp100=io_port,name
HP J2585B, J2585A, J2970, J2973, J2573		hp100 hp100_port=io_port hp100_name=name
Compex ReadyLink ENET100-VG4,		
FreedomLine 100/VG		
IBM Token Ring 16/4	ibmtr.o	ibmtr=io_port,IRQ,mem
		ibmtr io=io_port irq=IRQ mem=mem
AMD LANCE/PCnet	lance.o	lance=io_port,IRQ,dma
Allied Telesis AT1500, HP J2405A,		
NE2100, NE2500		lance io=io_port_1,io_port_n irq=IRQ_1,IRQ_2
		dma=dma_1,dma_n
Mylex LNE390 EISA cards (LNE390A, LNE390B)	lne390.o	lne390=io_port,IRQ,mem
		lne390 io=io_port irq=IRQ mem=mem
	ltpc.o	ltpc=io_port,IRQ
		ltpc io=io_port irq=IRQ
NE1000 / NE2000 (non-pci)	ne.o	ne=io_port,IRQ
		ne io=io_port irq=IRQ
PCI NE2000 cards	ne2k-pci.o	
RealTEk RTL-8029, Winbond 89C940,		
Compex RL2000, KTI ET32P2, NetVin,		
NV5000SC, Via 82C926, SureCom NE34,		
Novell NE3210 EISA Network Adapter	ne3210.o	ne3210=io_port,IRQ,mem
		ne3210 io=io_port irq=IRQ mem=mem
MiCom-Interlan NI5010 ethercard	ni5010.o	ni5010=io_port,IRQ
		ni5010 io=io_port irq=IRQ
NI5210 card (i82586 Ethernet chip)	ni52.o	ni52=io_port,IRQ
		ni52 io=io_port irq=IRQ
NI6510, ni6510 EtherBlaster	ni65.o	ni65=io_port,IRQ,dma
		ni65 io=io_port irq=IRQ dma=dma
AMD PCnet32 and AMD PCnetPCI	pcnet32.o	
RedCreek Communications PCI	rcpci.o	
RealTek cards using RTL8129	rtl8139.o	
or RTL8139 Fast Ethernet chipsets		

Sangoma S502/S508 multi-protocol FR	sdla.o	
Sangoma S502A, ES502A, S502E, S503,	sdladrv.o	
S507, S508, S509		
SysKonnect Token Ring ISA/PCI Adapter,	sktr.o	sktr=io_port,IRQ,mem
TR4/16(+) ISA or PCI, TR4/16 PCI, and		sktr io=io_port irq=IRQ mem=mem
older SK NET TR4/16 ISA cards		
SMC Ultra and SMC EtherEZ ISA ethercard	smc-ultra.o	smc-ultra=io_port,IRQ
(8K, 83c790)		smc-ultra io=io_port irq=IRQ
SMC Ultra32 EISA Ethernet card (32K)	smc-ultra32.o	
SMC 9000 series of Ethernet cards	smc9194.o s	mc9194=io_port,IRQ
		smc9194 io=io_port irq=IRQ ifport=[0,1,2]
Compaq Netelligent 10/100 TX PCI UTP	tlan.o	tlan=io_port,IRQ,aui,debug
Compaq Netelligent 10 T PCI UTP		tlan io=io_port irq=IRQ
Compaq Integrated NetFlex 3/P		Other Module Options:
Compaq Netelligent Dual 10/100 TX PCI UTP		speed=10Mbs,100Mbs
Compaq Netelligent Integrated 10/100 TX UTP		debug=0x0[1,2,4,8]
Compaq Netelligent 10/100 TX Embedded UTP		aui=1
Compaq Netelligent 10 T/2 PCI UTP/Coax		duplex=[1,2]
Compaq Netelligent 10/100 TX UTP		
Compaq NetFlex 3/P		
Olicom OC-2325, OC-2183, OC-2326		
Digital 21x4x Tulip PCI Ethernet cards	tulip.o	
SMC EtherPower 10 PCI(8432T/8432BT)		
SMC EtherPower 10/100 PCI(9332DST)		
DEC EtherWorks 100/10 PCI(DE500-XA)		
DEC EtherWorks 10 PCI(DE450)		
DEC QSILVER's, Znyx 312 etherarray		
Allied Telesis LA100PCI-T		
Danpex EN-9400, Cogent EM110		
VIA Rhine PCI Fast Ethernet cards with either	via-rhine.o	
the VIA VT86c100A Rhine-II PCI or		
3043 Rhine-I D-Link DFE-930-TX PCI 10/100		
AT&T GIS (nee NCR) WaveLan ISA Card	wavelan.o	wavelan=[IRQ,0],io_port,NWID

WD8003 and WD8013 "compatible" cards	wd.o	wd=io_port,IRQ,mem,mem_end
		wd io=io_port irq=IRQ mem=mem mem_end=end
Packet Engines Yellowfin	yellowfin.o	
G-NIC PCI Gigabit Ethernet adapter		
Z8530 based HDLC cards for AX.25	z85230.o	

Here are some examples of these modules in use:

Configuration	Example
NE2000 ISA card at IO address 300 and IRQ 11	ne=0x300,11
	ether=0x300,11,eth0
Wavelan card at IO 390, autoprobe for IRQ, and use the	wavelan=0,0x390,0x4321
NWID to 0x4321	ether=0,0x390,0x4321,eth0

Using Multiple Ethernet Cards

You can use multiple Ethernet cards in one machine. If each card uses a different driver (e.g., a 3c509 and a DE425), you simply need to add alias (and possibly options) lines for each card to `/etc/conf.modules`. See Section 8.2.2 for more information. If any two Ethernet cards use the same driver (e.g., two 3c509's or a 3c595 and a 3c905), you will need to either give the two card addresses on the driver's options line (in the case of ISA cards), or (for PCI cards) simply add one alias line for each card. For more information about using more than one Ethernet card, see the Linux Ethernet-HOWTO. If you installed the howto package when you installed Red Hat Linux, you can find it in the file `/usr/doc/HOWTO/Ethernet-HOWTO`.

Appendix E
Glossary

Alpha

A RISC (Reduced Instruction Set Computer) architecture developed by Digital Equipment Corporation.

ATAPI

An abbreviation for AT Attachment Packet Interface. ATAPI is the protocol by which CD-ROM drives communicate with a computer system over an IDE interface.

Binary

Although the base two-numbering system used by computers is known as binary, the word often refers to the executable form of a program. Contrast with "source code."

BIOS

An abbreviation for Basic Input/Output System. On PC-compatible systems, the BIOS is used to perform all necessary functions to properly initialize the system's hardware when power is first applied. The BIOS also controls the boot process, provides low-level input/output routines (hence its name) and (usually) allows the user to modify details of the system's hardware configuration.

Boot

Short for "bootstrap." The process by which a computer starts running an operating system when power is applied.

Boot Diskette

A diskette used to start many Red Hat Linux installations.

Bootstrap

See "Boot."

CISC

An abbreviation for Complex Instruction Set Computer. A design philosophy for computers whereby the processor is designed to execute a relatively large number of different instructions, each taking a different amount of time to execute (depending on the complexity of the instruction). Contrast with RISC.

CMOS

Originally an abbreviation for Complementary Metal Oxide Semiconductor — a semiconductor technology used in many integrated circuits. Now often used to describe the low-level hardware that contains a personal computer's BIOS setting, and the computer's hardware clock.

Cylinder

When referring to disk drives, the number of different positions the disk drive's read/write heads can take over the unit's disk platters. When viewed from above the platters, each head position describes an imaginary circle of different diameters on the platter's surface, but when viewed from the side, these circles can be thought of as a series of cylinders nested within each other, hence the term. See also Geometry.

Daemon

A daemon is a program that runs, without human intervention, to accomplish a given task. For example, lpd is a daemon that controls the flow of print jobs to a printer.

Dependencies

When referring to packages, dependencies are requirements that exist between packages. For example, package foo may require files that are installed by package bar. In this example, bar must be installed, or else foo will have unresolved dependencies. RPM will not normally allow packages with unresolved dependencies to be installed.

Device Driver

Software that controls a device that is connected to, or part of, a computer.

Disk Drive

See Hard Disk.

Disk Druid

Disk Druid is a component of the Red Hat Linux installation program that is used to partition disk drives during the installation process.

Diskette

A small mass storage device in a removable cartridge, meant to be read/written to, in a compatible drive.

Distribution

An operating system (usually Linux) that has been packaged so as to be easily installed.

Domain Name

A domain name is used to identify computers as belonging to a particular organization. Domain names are hierarchical in nature, with each level in the hierarchy being separated from other levels with a period (pronounced "dot"). For example, Foo Incorporated's Finance department might use the domain name "finance.foo.com."

Driver

See Device Driver.

Dual Boot

The act of configuring a computer system to boot more than one operating system. The name is something of a misnomer, as it is possible to boot more than the two operating systems the word "dual" implies.

EIDE

An abbreviation for Enhanced Integrated Drive Electronics, which is a newer version of the IDE interface standard and another term for a particular implementation for IDE interfaces. EIDE makes larger and faster disk drives possible; most systems sold today use EIDE.

Errata

Errata is Latin for "Ooops." When software is found to have bugs, quite often the software is fixed, and released as errata. Red Hat Linux is no exception to the rule; we have an Errata web page at http://www.redhat.com/errata.

Extended Partition

A segment of a disk drive that contains other partitions. See Partition.

FAQ

An abbreviation for Frequently Asked Questions. Linux information is often presented in the form of lists of questions and answers called FAQs.

fdisk

fdisk is a utility program that is used to create, delete or modify partitions on a disk drive.

Filesystem

A filesystem is the method by which information is stored on disk drives. Different operating systems normally use different filesystems, making it difficult to share the contents of a disk drive between two operating systems. However, Linux supports multiple filesystems, making it possible, for example, to read/write a partition dedicated to Windows.

Floppy

A somewhat historical term for a small mass storage device in a removable cartridge, meant to be read/written to in a compatible drive. See "diskette."

Formatting

The act of writing a filesystem on a disk drive.

FQDN

An abbreviation for Fully Qualified Domain Name. An FQDN is the human-readable name that includes a computer's hostname and associated domain name. For example, given a hostname of "foo," and a domain name of "bar.com," the FQDN would be "foo.bar.com."

FTP

An abbreviation for File Transfer Protocol. Also the name of a program that, as the name implies, permits the copying of files from one system on a network to another.

Gateway

In networking terms, refers to a device that connects one or more computers on a network to other networks. The device may be specialized hardware (such as a router), or may be a general-purpose computer system configured to act as a gateway.

Geometry

When referring to disk drives, the physical characteristics of the disk drive's internal organization. Note that a disk drive may report a "logical geometry" that is different from its "physical geometry," normally to get around BIOS-related limitations. See also Cylinder, Head and Sector.

GID

Short for Group ID. The means by which a user's membership in a group is identified to various parts of Red Hat Linux. GIDs are numeric, although human-readable names are stored in the /etc/group file.

Group

Groups are a way of assigning specific access rights to certain classes of users. For example, all users working on Project X could be added to group xproj. System resources (such as disk space) devoted to Project X could then be configured to permit only members of xproj full access.

Hard Disk

A hard disk contains rotating magnetic media (in the shape of disks) that spin rapidly. Small heads float over the surface of each disk, and are used to write to and read from the disk as it rotates. Head When referring to disk drives, the number of read/write heads within a disk drive. For each platter in a disk drive, there are normally two heads for each platter — one for each surface — although one surface may go unused. See also Geometry.

Hostname

A hostname is a human-readable string of characters used to identify a particular computer system.

I18n

See Internationalization.

IDE

An abbreviation for Integrated Drive Electronics, which is the name of a standard interface used to connect primarily disk and CD-ROM drives to a computer system. See also "EIDE" and "ATAPI."

Intel

Company responsible for producing the microprocessors that most commonly appear in PC-compatible personal computers. These processors include the 80386, 80486, Pentium, Pentium Pro, and Pentium II.

Internationalization

The practice of designing and writing programs that can be easily configured to interact with the user in more than one language. Often referred to as "i18n," due to the number of letters between the starting "i" and the ending "n."

IP Address

IP addresses are the method by which individual computer systems (or from a more strictly accurate interpretation, the network interfaces on those computer systems) are identified on a TCP/IP network. All IP addresses consist of four number blocks, each ranging from 0 to 255, and separated by periods.

Kernel

The central part of an operating system upon which the rest of the operating system is based.

Library

When speaking of computers, refers to a collection of routines that perform operations which are commonly required by programs. Libraries may be shared, meaning that the library routines reside in a file separate from the programs that use them. Library routines may also be "statically linked" to a program, meaning that copies of the library routines required by that program are physically added to the program. Such statically linked binaries do not require the existence of any library files in order to execute. Programs linked against shared libraries will not execute unless the required libraries have been installed.

LILO

A commonly-used bootstrap loader for Linux systems based on an Intel-compatible processor.

Linus Torvalds

Created Linux in 1991 while a university student.

Linuxconf

A versatile system configuration program written by Jacques Gelinas. Linuxconf provides a menu-based approach to system configuration via several different user interfaces.

Linux

A full-featured, robust, freely-available operating system originally developed by Linus Torvalds.

Logical Partition

A partition that exists within an extended partition. See also "partition" and "extended partition."

Master Boot Record

The master boot record (or MBR) is a section of a disk drive's storage space that is set aside for the purpose of saving information necessary to begin the bootstrap process on a personal computer.

MBR

See "Master Boot Record."

Memory

When referring to computers, memory (in general) is any hardware that can store data for later retrieval. In this context, memory usually specifically refers to RAM.

MILO

A commonly-used bootstrap loader for Linux systems based on the Alpha processor.

Module

In Linux, a module is a collection of routines that perform a system-level function, and may be dynamically loaded and unloaded from the running kernel as required. Often containing device drivers, modules are tightly bound to the version of the kernel; most modules built from one version of a kernel will not load properly on a system running another kernel version.

Mount Point
The directory under which a filesystem is accessible after being mounted.

Mount
The act of making a filesystem accessible to a system's users.

Nameserver
In TCP/IP networking terms, a nameserver is a computer that can translate a human-readable name (such as "foo.bar.com") into a numeric address (such as "10.0.2.14").

Netmask
A netmask is a set of four number blocks separated by periods. Each number is normally represented as the decimal equivalent of an eight-bit binary number, which means that each number may take any value between 0 (all eight bits cleared) and 255 (all eight bits set). Every IP address consist of two parts (the network address and the host number). The netmask is used to determine the size of these two parts. The positions of the bits that are set in the netmask are considered to represent the space reserved for the network address, while the bits that are cleared are considered to represent the space set aside for the host number.

NFS
An abbreviation for Network File System, NFS is a method of making the filesystem on a remote system accessible on the local system. From a user's perspective, an NFS-mounted filesystem is indistinguishable from a filesystem on a directly-attached disk drive.

Operating System
A collection of software that controls various resources of a computer.

Packages
Files that contain software, and written in a particular format that enables the software to be easily installed and removed.

PAM
An acronym for Pluggable Authentication Modules. PAM is an authentication system that controls access to Red Hat Linux.

Partition
A segment of a disk drive's storage space that can be accessed as if it was a complete disk drive.

Partition Table
The partition table is a section of a disk drive's storage space set aside to define the partitions that exist on that disk drive.

Partition Type

Partitions contain a field that is used to define the type of filesystem the partition is expected to contain. The partition type is actually a number, although many times the partition type is referred to by name. For example, the "Linux Native" partition type is 82. Note that this number is hexadecimal. PC Card See PCMCIA.

PCMCIA

Acronym for Personal Computer Memory Card International Association. This organization produced a series of standards that define the physical, electrical and software characteristics of small, credit card-sized devices that can contain memory, modems, network adapters and more. Also known as PC Cards, these devices are mainly used in laptop computers (although some desktop systems can use PCMCIA cards, too).

PCMCIA Support Diskette

A diskette required for Red Hat Linux installations that require the use of a PCMCIA device during the install.

Permissions

The set of identifiers that control access to files. Permissions consist of three fields: user, group, and world. The user field controls access by the user owning the file, while the group field controls access by anyone matching the file's group specification. As the name implies, the world field controls access by everyone else. Each field contains the same set of bits that specify operations that may or may not be performed, such as reading, writing and executing.

PLIP

An abbreviation for Parallel Line Internet Protocol. PLIP is a protocol that permits TCP/IP communication over a computer's parallel port using a specially-designed cable.

POSIX

A somewhat mangled abbreviation for Portable Operating System Interface. A set of standards that grew out of the UNIX operating system.

Process

A process (in somewhat simplistic terms) is one instance of a running program on a Linux system.

PS/2 Mouse

A PS/2 mouse gets its name from the original computer in which this type of mouse was first used — the IBM PS/2. A PS/2 mouse can be easily identified by the small, round connector at the end of its cable.

RAM

An acronym for Random Access Memory. RAM is used to hold programs while they are being executed, and data while it is being processed. RAM is also volatile, meaning that information written to RAM will disappear when the computer's power is turned off.

Reboot

To restart the boot process. See also "Boot."

Red Hat Software

A North Carolina software company. Produces and markets software for the Linux operating system, including Red Hat Linux.

Rescue Diskette

A diskette containing a rudimentary system environment. As the name implies, a rescue diskette is normally used in an attempt to "rescue" an ailing system from the necessity of reinstalling the entire operating system.

RISC

An abbreviation for Reduced Instruction Set Computer. A design philosophy for computers whereby the processor is optimized to execute a relatively small number of different instructions in a predictably small amount of time. Contrast with CISC.

ROM

An abbreviation for Read Only Memory. ROM is used to hold programs and data that must survive when the computer is turned off. Because ROM is nonvolatile; data in ROM will remain unchanged the next time the computer is turned back on. As the name implies, data cannot be easily written to ROM; depending on the technology used in the ROM, writing may require special hardware, or may be impossible. A computer's BIOS may be stored in ROM.

Root

The name of the login account given full and complete access to all system resources. Also used to describe the directory named "/"as in, "the root directory."

RPM

An abbreviation that stands for Red Hat Package Manager. RPM is also the name of a program that enables the installation, upgrading and removal of packages.

SCSI

An abbreviation for Small Computer System Interface, SCSI is a standard interface for connecting a wide variety of devices to a computer. Although the most popular SCSI devices are disk drives, SCSI tape drives and scanners are also common.

Sector
When referring to disk drives, the number of fixed-size (normally 512 byte) areas that can be accessed by one of the disk drive's read/write heads, in one rotation of the disk, without that head changing position. See Also Geometry.

Serial Mouse
A serial mouse is a mouse that is designed to be connected to a computer's serial port. A serial mouse can be easily identified by the rectangular-shaped connector at the end of its cable.

setgid
A system call that can be used to set the GID of a process. Programs can be written using setgid such that they can assume the group ID of any group on the system.

setuid
A system call that can be used to set the UID of a process. Programs can be written using setuid such that they can assume the user ID of any process on the system. This is considered a possible security problem if a program is "setuid root."

Shadow Password
Normally, each user's password is stored, encrypted, in the file /etc/passwd. This file must be readable by all users so that certain system functions will operate correctly. However, this means that copies of user's encrypted passwords are easily obtained, making it possible to run an automated password-guessing program against them. Shadow passwords, on the other hand, store the encrypted passwords in a separate highly-protected file, making it much more difficult to crack passwords.

SILO
A commonly-used bootstrap loader for Linux systems based on the SPARC processor.

SLIP

An acronym for Serial Line Internet Protocol. SLIP is a protocol that permits TCP/IP communication over serial line (typically over a dial-up modem connection).

source code
The human-readable form of instructions that comprise a program. Also known as "sources." Without a program's source code, it is very difficult to modify the program.

SPARC

A RISC (Reduced Instruction Set Computer) architecture developed by Sun Microsystems.

Swap

Also known as "swap space." When a program requires more memory than is physically available in the computer, currently-unused information can be written to a temporary buffer on the hard disk, called swap, thereby freeing memory. Some operating systems support swapping to a specific file, but Linux normally swaps to a dedicated swap partition. A misnomer, the term swap in Linux is used to define demand paging.

System Call

A system call is a routine that accomplishes a system-level function on behalf of a process.

TCP/IP

An abbreviation for Transmission Control Protocol/Internet Protocol, TCP/IP is the name given to the networking standard commonly used on the Internet today.

Torvalds, Linus

See Linus Torvalds.

UID

Short for User ID. The means by which a user is identified to various parts of Red Hat Linux. UIDs are numeric, although human-readable names are stored in the /etc/passwd file.

UNIX

A set of Linux-like operating systems that grew out of an original version written by some guys at a phone company.

Unmount

The act of revoking access to a file system (Note that the program that unmounts filesystems is called umount.)

Virtual Console

Virtual consoles provide multiple "screens" on which a user may log in and run programs. One screen is displayed on the computer's monitor at a given time; a key sequence is used to switch between virtual consoles.

Widget

A standardized on-screen representation of a control that may be manipulated by the user. Scroll bars, buttons, and text boxes are all examples of widgets.

X Window System

Also known as "X", this graphical user interface provides the well-known "windows on a desktop" metaphor common to most computer systems today. Under X, applications programs act as clients, accessing the X server, which manages all screen activity. In addition, client applications may be on a different system than the X server, permitting the remote display of the applications graphical user interface.

XFree86

A free implementation of the X Window System.

Appendix F
Kickstart Installations

Due to the need for automated installation, Red Hat Software has created the kickstart installation method. With this method, a system administrator can create a single file containing the answers to all the questions that would normally be asked during a typical Red Hat Linux installation. The kickstart installation method is powerful enough that often a single kickstart file can be used to install Red Hat Linux on multiple machines.

Please Note: Kickstart installations can only be performed using the CD-ROM and NFS installation methods. FTP, HTTP, SMB, or local hard disk installations cannot be automated using kickstart mode.

Where to Put A Kickstart File

To use kickstart mode, you must first create a kickstart file, and make it available to the Red Hat Linux installation program. Normally this is done by copying the kickstart file to the boot diskette, or making it available on the network. The network-based approach is most commonly used, as most kickstart installations tend to be performed on networked computers. This also makes it easier to install Red Hat Linux on many computers, as the kickstart files can be kept on single server system, and read by the individual computers during the installation. Let's take a more in-depth look at the locations where the kickstart file may be placed.

On Diskette

To perform a diskette-based kickstart installation, the kickstart file must be named ks.cfg, and reside in the boot diskette's top-level directory. Note that the Red Hat Linux boot diskettes are in MS-DOS format, making it easy to copy the kickstart file under Linux using the mcopy command (or, if you insist, you can also use Windows). Although there's no technological requirement for it, most diskette-based kickstart installations install Red Hat Linux from CD-ROM.

On the Network

Network installations using kickstart are quite common, because system administrators can easily automate the installation of many networked computers quickly and painlessly. In general, the approach most commonly used is for the administrator to have both a BOOTP/DHCP server and an NFS server on the local network. The BOOTP/DHCP server is used to give the client system its networking information, while the NFS server serves the actual files used during the installation. Often these two servers run on the same physical machine, but there is no requirement for this. To do a network-based kickstart installation, you must have a BOOTP/DHCP server on your network, and it must include configuration information for the machine you are attempting to install. The BOOTP/DHCP server will be used to give the client its networking information as well as the location of the kickstart file. If a kickstart file is specified by the BOOTP/DHCP server, the client system will attempt an NFS mount of the file's path, and will copy the specified file to the client, using it as the kickstart file. The exact settings required vary depending on the BOOTP/DHCP server you use. Here's an example for the DHCP server shipped with Red Hat Linux

```
filename "/usr/new-machine/kickstart/";
next-server blarg.redhat.com;
```

Note that you should use filename for the kickstart file's name (or the directory in which the kicstart file resides) and next-server to set the NFS server name. If the filename returned by the BOOTP/DHCP server ends with a slash (``/"), then it is interpreted as a path only. In this case, the client system mounts that path using NFS, and searches for a specially-named file. The filename the client searches for is:

```
<ip-addr>-kickstart
```

The <ip-addr> section of the filename should be replaced with the client's IP address in dotted decimal notation. For example, the filename for a computer with an IP address of 10.10.0.1 would be

10.10.0.1-kickstart. Note that if you don't specify a server name, then the client system will attempt to use the server that answered the BOOTP/DHCP request as its NFS server. If you don't specify a path or filename, the client system will try to mount /kickstart from the BOOTP/ DHCP server, and will try to find the kickstart file using the same <ip-addr>-kickstart filename as described above.

Starting a Kickstart Installation

To begin a kickstart installation, you must boot the system from a Red Hat Linux boot diskette, and enter a special boot command at the boot prompt. If the kickstart file resides on the boot diskette, the proper boot command would be:

```
boot: linux ks=floppy
```

If, on the other hand, the kickstart file resides on a server, the appropriate boot command would be:

```
boot: linux ks
```

The Kickstart File

Now that you have some background information on kickstart installations, let's take a look at the kickstart file itself. The kickstart file is a simple text file, containing a list of items, each identified by a keyword. You can create it by editing a copy of the README.ks file found in the docs/ directory of a Red Hat Linux CD-ROM, or you can create it from scratch. You should be able to edit it with any text editor or word processor that can save files as ASCII text. First, some ground rules to keep in mind while creating your kickstart file:

- Items must be specified in order. It is not a good idea to try to change the order of the required items.
- Items that aren't required can be omitted.
- For kickstart upgrades, the following items are required:

√ language

√ installation method

√ device specification

√ keyboard setup

√ the upgrade keyword

√ LILO configuration If any other items are specified for an upgrade, those items will be ignored (note that this includes package selection).

- Omitting any required item will result in the installation process prompting the user for an answer to that question, just as during a normal installation. If this happens, once the answer is given the installation will continue unattended (unless it comes across another missing item).
- Lines starting with a pound sign ("#") are treated as comments, and are ignored.

Let's take a look at each item in order.

lang – Language Setting

The first item that must appear is the language setting. The language you specify will be used during the installation as well as to configure any language-specific aspect of the installed system. The language specification must be a two letter ISO language code, such as en for English, de for German, fr for French, and so on. For example, to set the language to English, the kickstart file should contain the following line:

```
lang en
```

network – Networking Configuration

The next item is the network configuration information. This line is used to tell the system how it should configure networking for itself. It is optional, and if omitted, the system will be configured for stand-alone operation. There are three different methods of network configuration:

- DHCP
- BOOTP
- static

The DHCP method uses a DHCP server system to obtain its networking configuration. As you might guess, the BOOTP method is similar, requiring a BOOTP server to supply the networking configuration. The static method requires that you enter all the required networking information in the kickstart file. As the name implies, this information is static, and will be used during the installation, and after the installation as well. To direct a system to use DHCP to obtain its networking configuration, use the following line:

```
network —bootproto dhcp
```

To direct a machine to use BOOTP to obtain its networking configuration, use the following line in the kickstart file:

```
network —bootproto bootp
```

The line for static networking is more complex, as you must include all network configuration information on one line. You'll need to specify:

- IP address
- netmask
- gateway IP address
- nameserver IP address

Here's an example static line:

```
network —bootproto static ¬
—ip 10.0.2.15 ¬
—netmask 255.255.255.0 ¬
```

```
–gateway 10.0.2.254 ¬
–nameserver 10.0.2.1
```

Please Note: The entire network configuration must appear on one line! We've wrapped it here to make it easier to read.

There are two restrictions you must keep in mind should you use the static method:

All static networking configuration information must be specified on one line; you cannot wrap lines using a backslash, for example.

You can only specify one nameserver here. However, you can use the kickstart file's %post section (described in Section H.3.22) to add more nameservers, if needed.

Installation Methods

The next required item is the installation method. This item directs the installation program for the rest of the files required to install Red Hat Linux. There are two choices: NFS or CD-ROM. Let's look at both, starting with NFS.

nfs – The NFS Installation Method

For the NFS installation method, you must include the NFS server's name and the directory to be mounted. Here's an example:

```
nfs –server hostname.of.server –dir
/path/to/RH/CD/image
```

cdrom – The CD-ROM Installation Method

For a CD-ROM-based kickstart installation, simply use the following line:

```
cdrom
```

device — Optional Hardware Information

The next set of items in the kickstart file is used to specify optional hardware information. For most PCI-based hardware you can omit this step, as this information can be obtained directly from the hardware. Note that IDE hard disks and common PCI cards fall into this category. Any other hardware may need to be specified here. To specify a device, start with the device keyword, followed by the type of device:

- ethernet (for Ethernet cards)
- scsi (for SCSI cards)
- cdrom (for non-SCSI, non-IDE CD-ROM drives; usually sound cards with proprietary CD-ROM interfaces)

If a kernel module is required to support the device, the module name follows the device type. Finally, if there are any parameters that are required by a device, they can be specified by using the —opts option. Enclose the parameters in quotes after —opts. We'll show you some examples below. Note that you can specify more than one type of device in a given kickstart file. For example, if you know the machines you'll be kickstart-installing have either an Adaptec 1542 or a Buslogic SCSI card, you can enter both in the kickstart file. But be aware that the installation program uses only the first card found, so order the device entries appropriately. An example for an ISA 3com Ethernet card would be:

```
device ethernet 3c509 —opts "io=0x330, irq=7
```

" Here's an example line for an Adaptec 1542 SCSI card:

```
device scsi aha154x
```

An example of a SoundBlaster CD-ROM might look like this:

```
device cdrom —opts "io=0x240"
```

keyboard – Keyboard Type

The next item you'll need to specify is the correct code for your keyboard type. For US keyboards, the type is us. For the others, please run the /usr/sbin/kbdconfig program on an already-installed Red Hat Linux system. (An alternative approach would be to set the keyboard type to us and run kbdconfig on the installed system to set it properly after the installation completes.) An example of this would be:

```
keyboard us
```

noprobe

If you do not want your system device controllers to be automatically probed then you can issue the command:

```
noprobe
```

By configuring this command, your system will not probe for any device controllers, SCSI or otherwise. This is to be used only if you wish to manually specify the devices that are on your system.

Please Note: You will not be prompted to enter devices at any point. You will have to manually enter them into the kickstart configuration file or else you will not be able to continue with the installation.

device –continue

Your system is normally set up to take or find one device of a type. Without changes, the kickstart configuration will load the modules for one type of device, such as loading the module for one SCSI adapter type. Beyond that, the program will not load further modules for that type of device. In order to load modules for more than 1 adapter type, (for example, two different SCSI adapters) you will need to add the command:

```
device —continue
```

So, if you need to have modules for a Adaptec and a BusLogic adapter, then you will need to have both of these specified in the configuration file and you will need to have `—continue` after the first one in the configuration file:

```
device scsi aic7xxx —continue
device scsi
BusLogic
```

However, if you have multiple adapters of the same type, then you will not need to be concerned with this line, as the single module insertion is enough to control all adapters of that type. For example, if you have three Adaptec adapters, then the single line

```
device scsi aic7xxx
```

will load and allow all three adapters to function.

Partitioning

The hard drive in the machine must be partitioned before Red Hat Linux can be installed. In this section, we will describe how to specify disk partitioning in the kickstart file.

zerombr – Partition table initialization

First, if you are installing Red Hat Linux on a new machine, you should use the zerombr keyword to clear the current partition information. This is a good idea, because the partition table on new hard drives is usually bogus. Here's an example of `zerombr` on a new system:

```
zerombr yes
```

On the other hand, if you are installing machines that have a valid partition table, even if you want to change part (or all) of it, you should use zerombr this way:

```
zerombr no
```

clearpart – Removing partitions based on partition type

The next command is optional, but can come in handy. If you'd like to remove all partitions, or just any Linux-related partitions, you can use clearpart. For example, to clear all partitions of type "Linux native" and "Linux swap," you could add this line:

```
clearpart —linux
```

To clear all partitions from a disk, this line would do the trick:

```
clearpart —all
```

The only options clearpart supports are `—linux` and `—all`.

part – Partition definition

The next step is to specify the partitions you want to create. These will only be created using the system's unpartitioned free space. (In other words, if the machine had Windows-related partitions, and you had done `clearpart —linux` those Windows partitions would remain untouched.) You must enter one partition per line using the following format:

```
part <mntpt> —size <size in megs> [—grow] ¬
[—maxsize <size in megs>]
```

(This part line was broken to make it more readable.) `<mntpt>` is the location you are going to mount that partition in your installed system (for example, the root partition would have a mount point of /, while you may decide that another partition should have a mount point of `/home`). `<size in megs>` is the size of the partition in megabytes. You can optionally specify that the partition is growable by adding the `—grow` option. Note that making a partition growable does not mean that you can later increase its size. Instead, a growable partition will be automatically resized to use all available unpartitioned free space (after all fixed-size partitions have been created). Since the amount of unpartitioned free space can vary, and you probably want to use it all, by tagging partitions as growable you can easily make sure no space is wasted. If you have multiple partitions tagged as growable, the free space is split evenly among them. Note that you can also limit the size of growable partitions with the optional —maxsize argument. Here's an example of kickstart partitioning in action. Let's say you know the smallest disk out of a set of machines you plan to kickstart-install is 1GB. You'd like to use the same kickstart file. You could use the following partitioning scheme:

```
zerombr no
clearpart —all
part / —size 250
part swap —size 50
part /usr —size 500 —grow —maxsize 800
part /tmp —size 100 —grow
```

When defined this way, the installation program will first clear all partitions. It will then set up a 250MB root filesystem, followed by a 50MB swap partition. Next the installation program will create a `/usr` partition of at least 500MB (remember, it's growable), but it cannot grow beyond 800MB. Finally, the last line will create a /tmp partition of at least 100MB (again, it's growable). So for that 1GB system, you would end up with a 250MB root, a 50MB swap, a 550MB /usr, and a 150MB /tmp partition. If another system has a 2GB drive, you would get a 250MB root, a 50MB swap, a 800MB `/usr`, and a 900MB `/tmp`.

install and upgrade — Install/Upgrade Selection

The next item to specify is whether you are doing a fresh install, or an upgrade of an already-installed system. For a fresh install, use:

```
install
```

For an upgrade of an existing system, use:

```
upgrade
```

Keep in mind that for upgrades, the only items that matter are:

- installation media (CD-ROM or NFS)
- device specification (if necessary)
- keyboard setup
- install/upgrade specification (which should be upgrade, of course!)
- LILO configuration

mouse — Mouse Configuration

To define the type of mouse your system has, you must use the mouse keyword. Run `mouseconfig —help` on an already-installed Red Hat Linux for a list of mouse types. Depending on the type of mouse, you may also need to specify the device to which the mouse is attached. The default device is correctly set for bus mice. For serial mice, the default device is `/dev/cua0`, but can be overridden with the `—device` option followed by the device name, such as cua1. For example, for a three-button PS/2 mouse, you would use:

```
mouse —kickstart generic3ps/2
```

For a two-button PS/2 mouse, use:

```
mouse —kickstart genericps/2
```

For a two-button Microsoft mouse on your second serial port, use:

```
mouse —kickstart microsoft —device cua1
```

timezone — Timezone Definition

Red Hat Linux is timezone-aware, so you'll need to specify the timezone in which the machine will operate. This is done using the timezone keyword. There are many different timezones; the best way to find yours is to run `/usr/sbin/timeconfig` on an already-installed Red Hat Linux system. If you would like to have your system's hardware clock set to use GMT/UTC, add the `—utc` option to your timezone line. Here's an example that defines the timezone as US Eastern with the system clock set to GMT:

```
timezone —utc
US/Eastern
```

xconfig – X Window Setup

The next item is the X Window setup line. The installation program will normally find common PCI video hardware and will know which X server to install. The keyword for X configuration is xconfig. If your video card isn't autoprobed properly, you can use the `--card` option to explicitly specify the card. You can use Xconfigurator `--help` on a running Red Hat Linux system to get a list of supported cards to choose from. If your card isn't in the list but is supported by one of the existing servers, you can simply install the proper server by using the `--server` option. Again, use Xconfigurator `--help` to get the list of server names. You also need to specify a monitor type. If you don't, the installation will assume a generic monitor capable of 640x480@60hz. Use the `--monitor` option to specify something other than the default. Again, Xconfigurator `--help` will list all valid monitor types. If your monitor isn't listed, you can enter the actual monitor specifications by using the `--hsync` and `--vsync` options for horizontal and vertical sync rates, respectively. The rates may be single numbers (representing kilohertz and megahertz, as appropriate), groups of numbers separated by commas, or two numbers separated by a dash (signifying a range). For example:

```
xconfig --hsync "31.5,35.5,50-65" --vsync "50-70"
```

An example for a machine where the video card can be autoprobed properly would be:

```
xconfig --monitor "tatung cm14uhe"
```

An example for a machine where nothing is probed and the monitor isn't in the list might be:

```
xconfig --server "Mach64" --hsync "31.5,35.5,50-
65" --vsync "50-70"
```

rootpw – Setting the Root Password

You can put the root passwd in a kickstart file in the clear (in which case it would go over the network in the clear on an NFS install) or you can specify that an encrypted password is to be used. To specify an unencrypted password in the kickstart file, use the rootpw keyword, followed by the cleartext password:

```
rootpw mypasswd
```

If you would rather use an encrypted password, grab it out of `/etc/passwd` (or wherever you have the encrypted version stored), and add the `--iscrypted` option:

```
rootpw —iscrypted
encryptedpasswdstring
```

authconfig – Setting up Authentication Configuration

After you have set the root password, you have the ability to set up different network password authentications:

- Enable NIS — allows you to run a group of computers in the same Network Information Service domain with a common password and group file. There are two options here to choose from:

  √ NIS Domain — this option allows you to specify which domain or group of computers your system will belong to.

  √ NIS Server — this option causes your computer to use a specific NIS server, rather than ``broadcasting" a message to the local area network asking for any available server to host your system.

- Enable Shadow Passwords — provides a very secure method of retaining passwords for you.

- MD5 Passwordallows a long password to be used up to 256 characters, instead of the standard eight letters or less.

The `authconfig` format for kickstart looks similiar to:

```
auth --enablenis --nisdomain foo.redhat.com
--nisserverserver.foo.redhat.com [—useshadow]
[—enablemd5]
```

Please Note: The commands in the square brackets are optional. If you choose to set them up, you do not need to use the brackets.

You are able to change authconfig using these commands to set up the different password options:

```
--enablenis              enable nis by default
--nisdomain <domain>     default NIS domain
--nisserver <server>     default NIS server
--useshadow              use shadow passwords
--enablemd5              enable MD5 passwords
```

lilo — LILO Configuration

For machines that use LILO (Intel-based systems), you can specify the LILO configuration using the lilo keyword. The default line can be as simple as this:

```
lilo
```

This will install LILO in the hard drive's master boot record (MBR), and automatically configure boot entries for your Linux installation as well as a DOS or Windows installation (if one is present). If you don't want LILO installed in the MBR, you can do so with by using the `--location` option. There are three possible places where LILO can be installed:

- mbr - put LILO on the master boot record (default)
- partition - put LILO on the beginning of the root partition

- none - don't install LILO at all (in which case you'll need your own method of booting the installed system)

You can also use the `--append` option to add an `append=` line to the Linux boot entry. This is handy if you need to do things like set memory sizes, etc. For example, to install LILO on the MBR on a machine with 128MB of RAM, you would add the following `lilo` line:

```
lilo --append "mem=128M" --location mbr
```

(Due to the new kernel in Red Hat Linux 6.0, the mem boot-time option shouldn't be necessary, but we needed an example.)

%packages — Package Selection

You can use the %packages keyword to start the beginning of a kickstart file section that lists the packages you'd like to install (note that this is for installs only, as package selection during upgrades is not supported). Packages can be specified by component or by individual package name. The installation program defines several components that group together related packages. See the RedHat/base/comps file on any Red Hat Linux CD-ROM for a list of components. The components are defined by the lines that begin with a number followed by a space, and then the component name. Each of the packages in that component are then listed, line-by-line, until the end keyword. Individual packages lack the leading number found in front of component lines. In most cases, it's only necessary to list the desired components and not individual packages. Note that the Base component is always selected by default, so it's not necessary to specify it in the %packages section. Here's an example %packages section:

```
@ Networked Workstation
@ C Development
@ Web Server
@ X Window System
bsd-games
```

As you can see, components are specified, one to a line, starting with an "@" symbol, a space, and then the full component name as given in the comps file. Specify individual packages with no additional characters (the bsd-games line in the example above is an individual package).

Please Note: You can also direct the kickstart install to use the `workstation-` and `server-class` intallation methods. To do this, simply add one of the following lines to the %packages section:

```
@ Workstation
@ Server
```

%post – Post-Installation Configuration Section

You have the option of adding commands to be run on the installed system after the installation is complete. This section must be at the end of the kickstart file and must start with the %post keyword. Note that you can access the network in the %post section; however, nameservice has not yet been configured at this point, so only IP addresses will work. Here's an example %post section:

```
# add comment to /etc/motd
echo "Kickstart-installed Red Hat Linux `/bin/
date`" > /etc/motd
# add another nameserverecho "nameserver
10.10.0.2" >> /etc/resolv.conf
```

This section creates a message-of-the-day file containing the date the kickstart installation took place, and gets around the network keyword's one-nameserver-only limitation by adding another nameserver to `/etc/resolv.conf`.

Index

Symbols

A

B

C

D

H

I

O

P

S

T

U

V

W

X

Y

Z

Notes

Notes

Notes

Notes

Notes

Notes

Notes

Notes

The Getting Started Guide
for
Red Hat Linux 6.0

Red Hat Software, Inc.
2600 Meridian Parkway
Durham, NC 27713
P. O. Box 13588
Research Triangle Park, NC 27709
(919) 547-0012
redhat@redhat.com
http://www.redhat.com

Table of Contents

Introduction

Welcome to Red Hat Linux 6.0!

At Red Hat Software, they believe they offer the best Linux distribution on the market. They hope you'll agree that the time and the money you spent for Red Hat Linux was well spent, indeed.

Recently, Linux has gained quite a bit of attention from the national and international media. What began as a "hacker's hobby" several years ago has been embraced as a powerful and economical computer operating system.

If you count yourself among the many Linux users who are discovering Red Hat Linux for the first time, this book is for you!

Inside, you'll find valuable tips which will help you get acquainted with your new desktop environment and with the way your Red Hat Linux system works. You'll be able to learn some basics and you'll find pointers to places where you can turn for more information.

This publication is divided into two parts:

- **The GNOME User's Guide;**
- **The Newbie's Guide to Red Hat Linux.**

The GNOME User's Guide

Written by David A. Wheeler and Red Hat Software, the GNOME User's Guide is an indispensable resource for navigating and customizing GNOME. You can find the GNOME User's Guide, among other places, both on the Web, at *www.gnome.org* and on an installed Red Hat Linux system, under /usr/share/gnome/help/users-guide/C/, beginning with the Index page.

GNOME stands for GNU Network Object Model Environment. That's a fancy acronym, but it translates into a pleasing environment which offers all the power of Linux. GNOME is the default X Window System environment for Red Hat Linux 6.0.

In the GNOME User's Guide you'll find ways to create, move and copy files, investigate your new system and much more — all within a pleasing graphical environment.

Here's a preview of what you'll find in these 14 chapters:

1 **An Introduction to GNOME** – Learn a little about the history and ideas which have helped create GNOME.

2 **GNOME Quick Start** – Get a "quick start" on familiarizing yourself with the GNOME desktop.

3 **Window Managers and GNOME** – Learn a little about window managers, and which window managers you can use that work well with GNOME.

4 **The Enlightenment Window Manager** – An in-depth look at Enlightenment, the default window manager for Red Hat Linux. Although GNOME isn't dependent on any single window manager, Enlightenment (or "E") has captured quite a few fans because of its stylish features. Here, you'll find out how you can configure E to your liking.

5 **Using the GNOME Panel** – Learn the ins and outs of GNOME Panel, from which you can find and start your system's applications. Highly flexible, the Panel allows you add favorite applications, change its location, add new panels and more.

6 **The GNOME Desktop** – Your GNOME desktop is more than just a pretty face. Here's where you can find out how to "drag and drop" applications, store files, create folders, switch desktops and more.

7 **The GNOME File Manager** – The GNOME File Manager adds form to the function and power of the Midnight Commander. Here, you'll learn how to view and manipulate files — both on your system and on the Internet.

8 **Configuring the Panel** – Once you become comfortable with using panels, here's where you can learn how to add further productivity and style to their usefulness.

9 **Editing the Main Menu** — Even though it gives you easy access to applications, you're not stuck with the main menu's default configuration. Here's where you can learn how to make the menu work the way you work.

10 **The GNOME Control Center** — As advertised, the GNOME Control Center allows you to control the way your environment looks, "feels" and behaves. You'll learn how to tweak your environment in many ways.

11 **A Word About Session Management** — Learn how you can automatically start favorite applications when you log in.

12 **Panel Applets** — From system monitors to multimedia enhancements, these small applications can add productivity and fun to your environment. You'll learn what applets can serve you best in this chapter.

13 **GNOME CD Player** — This chapter shows you how to access and get the most out of your pre-loaded GNOME CD player.

14 **The GNOME Calendar** — Keep track of more than the days of the week with this application.

You'll find quite a few translations of the GNOME User's Guide, as well as the latest GNOME documentation and software at the official website:

http://www.gnome.org.

Now, on to some of your Red Hat Linux system's details...

The Newbie's Guide to Red Hat Linux

Are you rattled by terms like root and user account? The following is for you!

The second part of the Red Hat Linux Getting Started Guide, this "newbie's guide" will help you gain a toehold on the basics of your new Linux system — from creating a new account to working with files in a non-graphical environment.

There's nothing wrong with a little hand-holding — and that's what you'll find in these remaining chapters. Here's a glimpse of what you can find:

15 **Welcome to Linux** — Learn how to create your own user account to maximize your system's safety. You'll also find out how to shut down your system, create rescue disks and more.

16 **You Are Here** — Learn how to navigate through your system at the shell prompt, how to combine commands and see how everything fits together.

17 **Managing Files and Directories** — Here, you'll learn more about the powerful shell you're using, how to save yourself time and frustration when you're typing in commands and how to rename, copy, delete and move files and directories.

18 **What Do I Do Now?** — Looking for pointers to more information about your Red Hat Linux system? Here, you'll find tips about where you can find plenty of documentation and help. You can also learn more about your X Window System and how to work with other system tasks.

More to Come

As Linux evolves, so does the support you'll find for Red Hat Linux. The Getting Started Guide for Red Hat Linux is part of that support — and evolution. In coming editions, expect to find more essential information to help you get the utmost from your Red Hat Linux system.

That's also where you come in.

A Thousand Thanks

This guide is the definition of a group project, since so many provided valuable assistance, from offering suggestions and sharing knowledge to proofreading.

Thank you to Edward C. Bailey, the documentation department's manager. Ed was there from concept to "when the rubber hit the road," offering his expert advice on style and substance.

Thank you also to Sandra A. Moore, in charge of the Official Red Hat Linux Installation Guide, for her patience and help in formatting and proofing. And to David Mason, RHAD Labs' technical writer, who worked like to a demon to put together the GNOME User's Guide.

Red Hat Software's support team — particularly Stephen Smoogen and Eric Rahn Nolen ("Thor") were more than generous in offering their time and advice.

And to the engineers, who build the best Linux distribution, a big "thank you"! It is their work which makes Red Hat Linux so worthwhile.

And, of course, thank you to Linus Torvalds and the thousands of Linux developers around the world. Ultimately, this is their operating system — and it is a wonder.

Paul Gallagher

1 An Introduction to GNOME

What is GNOME

GNOME is a user-friendly desktop environment that enables users to easily use and configure their computers. GNOME includes a panel (for starting applications and displaying status), a desktop (where data and applications can be placed), a set of standard desktop tools and applications, and a set of conventions that make it easy for applications to cooperate and be consistent with each other. Users of other operating systems or environments should feel right at home using the powerful graphics-driven environment GNOME provides.

GNOME is completely open source (free software), with freely available source code developed by hundreds of programmers around the world. If you would like to learn more about the GNOME project please visit the GNOME web site at http://www.gnome.org.

GNOME has a number of advantages for users. GNOME makes it easy to use and configure applications without using text-only interfaces.

GNOME is highly configurable, enabling you to set your desktop the way you want it to look and feel. GNOME's session manager remembers previous settings, so once you've set things the way you like they'll stay that way. GNOME supports many human languages, and you can add more without changing the software. GNOME even supports several Drag and Drop protocols for maximum interoperability with applications that aren't GNOME-compliant.

GNOME also has a number of advantages for developers which indirectly also help users. Developers don't need to purchase an expensive software license to make their commercial application GNOME compliant. In fact, GNOME is vendor neutral - no component of the interface is controlled solely by one company or restricted from modification and redistribution. GNOME applications can be developed in a variety of computer languages, so you're not stuck with a single language. GNOME uses the Common Object Request Broker

Architecture (CORBA) to allow software components to interoperate seamlessly, regardless of the computer language in which they are implemented, or even what machine they are running on. Finally, GNOME runs on a number of Unix-like operating systems, including Linux.

GNOME is an acronym for the GNU Network Object Model Environment, so GNOME is a part of the larger GNU project. The GNU Project started in 1984 to develop a completely free Unix-like operating system. If you'd like to learn more about the GNU project you can read about it at http://www.gnu.org.

About This Guide

This users guide is designed to help you find your way around GNOME with ease. Both new and experienced computer users can benefit from this guide. If you're new to GNOME, or even computers, you'll gain an idea of how to use your desktop. If you're an advanced user, you can work with expert tips which will help you to become familiar with GNOME.

Although this was written originally in English, there are many translations of the guide available now or in the near future. If you would like to have this guide in another language you should check your operating system distribution or visit the GNOME Web Site to find out more information on translation.

2 GNOME Quick Start

GNOME Quick Start

Figure 2-1 shows an example of GNOME running. GNOME is very configurable, so your screen may look quite different.

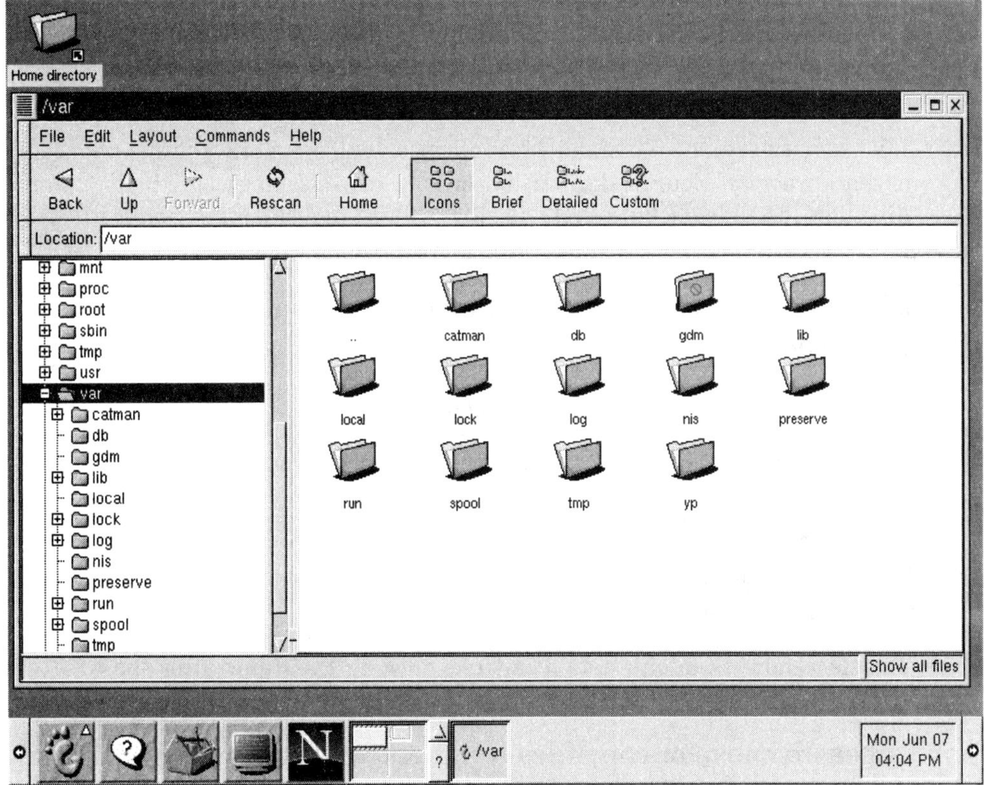

Figure 2-1: Sample GNOME Display.

The long bar at the bottom of *Figure 2-1* is a GNOME Panel, which contains a collection of useful panel applets and menus. Panel applets are tiny programs designed to be placed in a panel, for example, the clock applet on the far right shows the current time. The arrows on each side of the panel hide (and unhide) the panel.

The button in the panel containing a stylized foot is the Main Menu Button. Just click on the Main Menu Button and you'll see a menu of pre-loaded applications and actions, including a logout command.

The rest of the screen space is called the "Desktop." Just place on your desktop the items you use most often and you can double-click on an item (with the left mouse button) to use it:

- If the item is a program, that program will start.
- If it's data, the appropriate program will be start up with that data loaded.
- If it's a directory, the file manager application will start and show the contents of that directory. Your desktop will probably have a folder icon labelled "Home directory". Double-clicking on it will start a file manager at your home directory.

The file manager application lets you manipulate your files. The left side of its window shows directories, and the right side shows the selected directory's contents:

- To move the file or directory, just drag and drop it.
- To copy a file, hold down the **CTRL** key while dragging.
- To run a program or edit a data file, double-click it.
- To perform other operations on a file (such as rename or delete), select it using the right mouse button.
- To select more than one item at a time, click on the items after the first one while holding down the SHIFT key.

You can easily move or copy files between directories by starting two file manager applications, each one showing a different directory. If you want to put a file on your desktop, simply drag it from the file manager onto the desktop. In fact, dragging and dropping items onto other items generally "does the right thing" in GNOME, making it easy to get work done.

GNOME is very configurable; for example, you can have multiple panels (horizontal and vertical), choose what goes in them, and have them hide automatically. There are many panel applets you can include in your panel. You can also change how the screen looks; later portions of this document tell you how.

GNOME follows several UNIX conventions you should be aware of. The left mouse button is used to select and drag items. The right mouse button brings up a menu for the selected object (if a menu applies). Most UNIX mice have 3 buttons, and the middle button is used to paste text (if in a text area) or to move things. If you only have two buttons, press the left and right buttons simultaneously to simulate the middle button. To copy text, use the left button to drag across the text you want to copy, move to the place you want the text to be, and press the middle button.

When an application window is displayed, there will be some buttons in its borders for controlling the window. These include buttons to minimize, maximize, and close the window. Their appearance can be configured and is controlled by a component called a "window manager."

Two examples of border styles are the Clean style (*Figure 2-2*) and the ICE style (*Figure 2-3*):

- In the Clean border style, the underscore means minimize, the square means maximize (use the whole screen), and the X button means close the window.
- In the ICE style, the X button will close the window. Clicking the arrow with the left mouse button minimizes the window, while clicking with the right mouse button shows a menu of other options.

Figure 2-2: Clean Border Style

Figure 2-3: ICE Border Style

If you are using a default installation of GNOME you may notice that minimizing a window actually causes that window to disappear from your desktop. To regain that window you may use the GNOME Pager which is located on the Panel. The Pager will show you which tasks are running and where they are on your desktops. You will find the application you minimized in the task list on the right side of the GNOME Pager. Press the button for that application and it will return to your desktop.

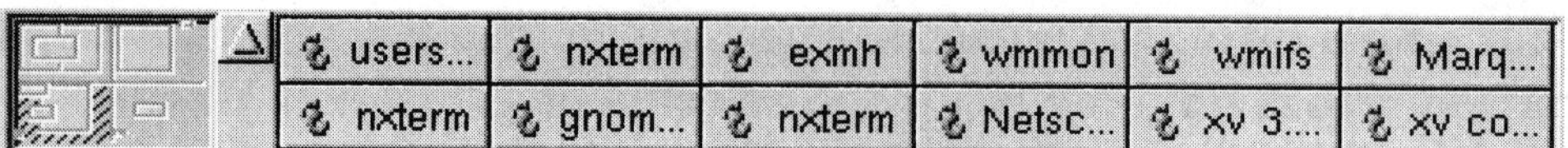

Figure 2-4: The GNOME Pager

You may read more about the GNOME Pager in the section called *GNOME Pager* in Chapter 12.

The following sections go into more detail, describing each component of the system.

3 Window Managers and GNOME

About Window Managers

The window manager is the piece of software that controls the windows in the X window environment. The placement, borders, and decorations of any window are managed by the window manager. This is very different from many other operating systems, and the way GNOME deals with window managers is different from other desktop environments.

As stated earlier in this guide, GNOME is not dependent on any one window manager. This means that major parts of your desktop environment will not change when you decide to switch window managers. GNOME works with the window manager to give you the easiest work environment you can have. GNOME does not worry about window placement but gets information from the window manager about their placement. The GNOME Pager will only work with a GNOME compliant window manager that will drag and drop on the desktop.

At the time of this version of the GNOME User's Guide the Enlightenment Window Manager is the only window manager that is 100% compliant. There are many other window managers that are partially compliant or are being worked on to meet compliance.

Some of the window managers that have partial to full compliance at the time of this version of the GNOME User's Guide are:

- **Enlightenment** - http://www.enlightenment.org
- **Icewm** - http://www.kiss.uni-lj.si/~k4fr0235/icewm/
- **Window Maker** - http://www.windowmaker.org
- **FVWM** - http://www.fvwm.org/

Changing Window Managers

At any time you may change the window manager you are using by utilizing the Window Manager Capplet in the GNOME Control Center. You may read more about this Capplet in the section called *Window Manager Capplet* in Chapter 10.

> **IMPORTANT:** Keep in mind that the window manager you choose to use may not be compliant with GNOME and you may not benefit from some of GNOME features if you use it.

4 The Enlightenment Window Manager

Introduction

GNOME is a desktop environment that is not dependent on any one window manager in order to control how applications and other features interact with each other. GNOME can work with a variety of window managers. The window manager is what controls the window borders, window decorations, and the functionality of those windows. Currently there are about three or four window managers that are considered GNOME compliant. Being GNOME compliant means much more than simply being able to run with GNOME; it also means being aware of GNOME and what GNOME offers. This includes session management, desktop settings, and interactivity with applications such as the GNOME Pager.

The Default Window Manager for this release of Red Hat Linux is a window manager called Enlightenment. Within Enlightenment there is a tool which will help you to configure the window manager to your specifications.

The Enlightenment Configuration Tool

There are two ways to launch the Enlightenment Configuration tool (E-conf). You may open the GNOME Control Center and select the *Window Manager Capplet* from the *Desktop* group. If you have Enlightenment as your current window manager you may run E-conf by pressing the **Run Configuration Tool for Enlightenment** button.

You may also launch E-conf by clicking your middle mouse button (or both right and left mouse buttons if you have emulation) on the desktop and selecting the **Enlightenment Configuration** item from the **pop-up** menu.

E-conf is divided into many sections that control various effects and functions within Enlightenment (E). You will find a list of these sections in the top left corner of the E-conf. The sections to choose from include: Basic Options, Desktops, Behavior, Audio, Special FX, Backgrounds, Themes, and Shortcuts.

Basic Options

The Basic Options section of E-conf lets you configure how E controls the movement and focus of windows on your desktop. Each method for controlling windows has a small image to show you what they look like, but perhaps the best way to get a feel is to select one, press the Apply button and move the window around. There are three areas to configure: Move Methods, Resize Methods, and Keyboard focus follows.

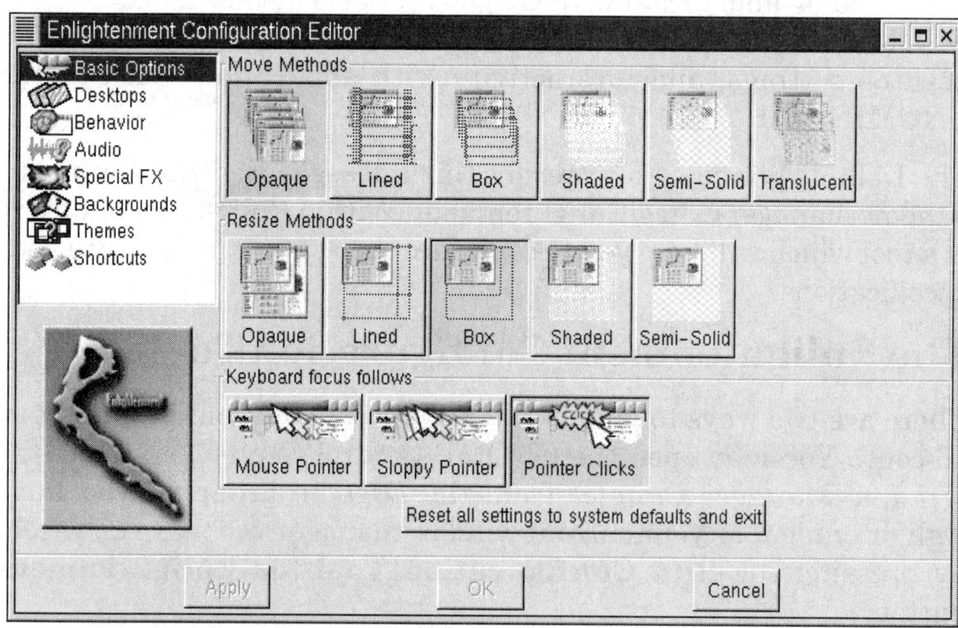

Figure 4-1: Enlightenment Basic Options

- **Move Methods** - This area controls the way windows look when you move them around your desktop with your mouse. You may choose from Opaque, Lined, Box, Shaded, Semi-Solid, and Translucent. Depending on your machine speed some of these move methods may work slower than others.
- **Resize Methods** - The Resize Methods option controls how the windows look

when you resize them. You may choose among Opaque, Lined, Box, Shaded, and Semi-Solid. Again, depending on your machine speed some of these methods may work slower than others.

- **Keyboard focus follows** – This area controls which window gets the focus. Getting the focus means that the keyboard can control the window and if there is a distinction in your enlightenment theme, the window will be highlighted. You may choose from Mouse Pointer, Sloppy Focus, and Pointer Clicks.

- **Mouse Pointer** - will focus the window whenever the mouse is over the window. **Sloppy Pointer** will do the same but will focus the window when the mouse is over it and keep the focus until the mouse is over another window. For example, you can put the mouse over a window and then over the desktop and the window will still have focus until it is over another window. **Pointer Clicks** means that you have to actually click on the window to give it focus.

At any time you may reset all of the Enlightenment configurations to the default settings by pressing the **Reset all settings to system defaults and exit** button.

Desktops

As you will read in the section called *Desktop Areas* in Chapter 7, GNOME supports the use of multiple desktop areas, and for the advanced user, multiple desktops. The control over these areas and desktops is actually handled by the window manager. The Enlightenment Configuration tool allows you to change the number of areas and desktops you have use of in your work environment.

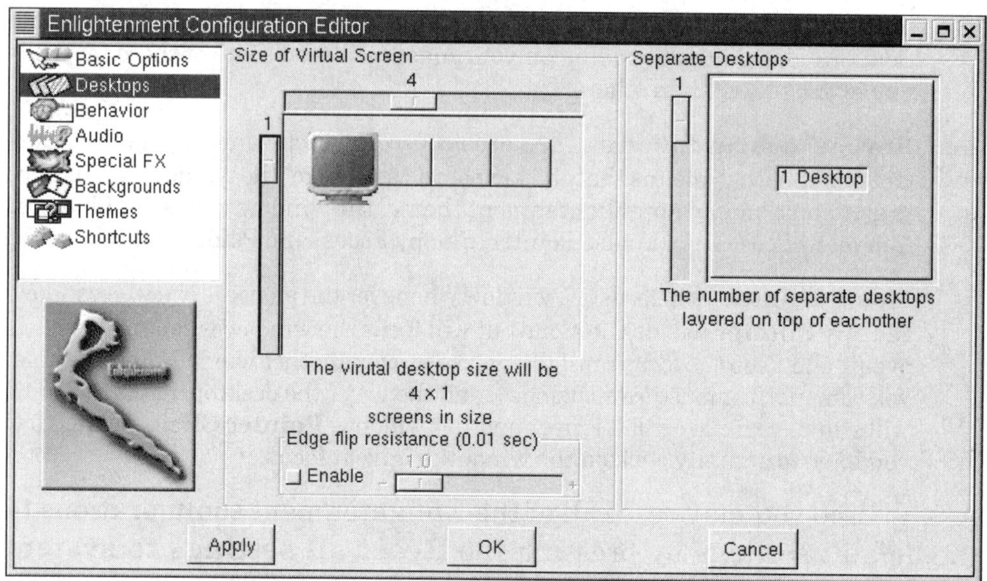

Figure 4-2: Enlightenment Desktops

The Desktops Section of E-conf has two main tools to let you change the number of areas and desktops you use. The first tool is the *Size of Virtual Screen* which controls the number of desktop areas. Desktop areas are really just one big screen broken into many "virtual areas". The advantage to using virtual areas over multiple desktops is that drag and drop on the desktop will work across areas as will work being done in applications such as the GNOME File Manager. To use this tool slide the two sliders until you have the number of virtual areas, across and down, that you wish to use.

The second tool is *Separate Desktops,* which allows you to set the number of desktops you wish to use. Unlike desktop areas, these are completely separate desktops. To use this tool move the slider up or down until you have the number of desktops you wish to use.

One good way to visualize your multiple areas/desktops situation is to make sure you have the GNOME Pager running. The GNOME Pager will show you how many areas and desktops you have and where your applications are within those spaces. You may also use the GNOME Pager to navigate from area to area and desktop to desktop. You can read more about the GNOME Pager in the section called *GNOME Pager* in Chapter 13.

Edge resistance factor for auto flip - If you are using desktop areas you may choose to have the areas switch when your mouse goes past the edge of the screen in the direction of another area. If you have this feature on you may change the resistance the mouse has when it is moving past the edge by moving the slider to the number of seconds it takes to change to the next desktop.

Behavior

The Behavior Section of E-conf allows you to control various focus and miscellaneous behaviors in E.

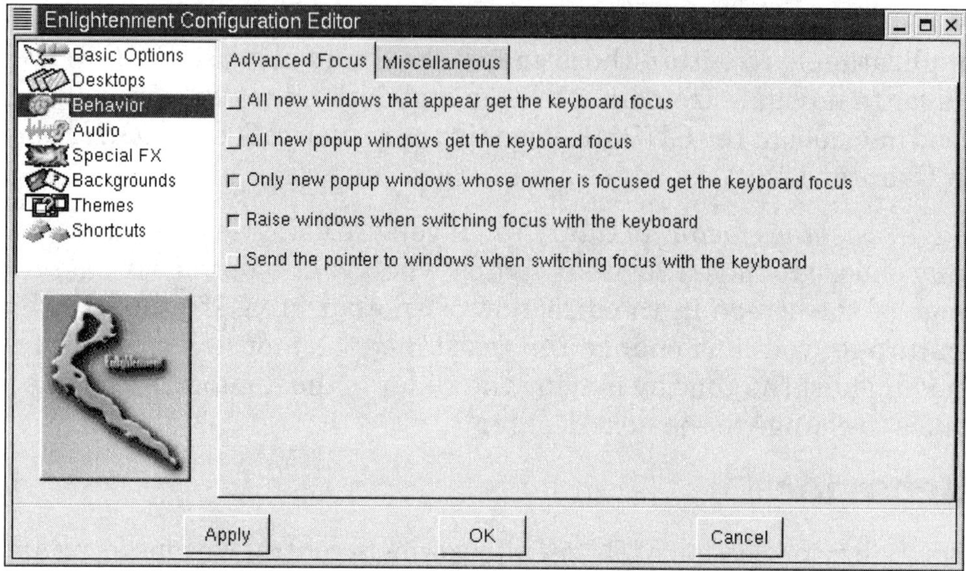

Figure 4-3: Enlightenment Behavior

- **Advanced Focus** - This tab allows you to change properties related to focusing windows.
- **All new windows that appear get the keyboard focus** - This ensures that when you start a new application you can start working on it when it appears without moving the mouse to get the focus of the window.
- **All new pop-up windows get the keyboard focus** - This will give the focus to new pop-up windows only. If you have this selected and the "All new windows that appear get the keyboard focus" not selected, your pop-ups will get the focus no matter where they appear, but new applications started will not. An example of a pop-up window is an error message you might get in an application.
- **Only new pop-up windows whose owner is focused get the keyboard focus** - This will give the focus to new pop-up windows only if the application that launched the window has the focus beforehand.
- **Raise windows when switching focus with the keyboard** - If you use keystrokes to change the focus of your windows this will bring the focused window to the foreground.

- **Send pointer to windows when switching focus with the keyboard** - If you use keystrokes to change the focus of your windows, this will send your mouse pointer to the focused window.
- **Miscellaneous** - This tab has miscellaneous Enlightenment behaviors.
- **Tooltips ON/OFF & timeout for tooltip pop-up** - This controls whether you would like tooltips to display on various parts of an Enlightenment-controlled window. A tooltip is a small information window which opens when your mouse pointer hovers over an element in an application or component. The time slide bar next to the button lets you change how long it takes for the tooltips to appear once your mouse is over a component controlled by E. The speed is measured in seconds.
- **Automatic raising of windows after X seconds** - This will focus a non-focused window after the seconds you specify when your mouse is over it.
- **Transient pop-up windows appear together with leader** - If your application brings up small pop-up windows as part of its normal function this will ensure that those pop-up windows stay with the main window. This can be helpful if your workflow is interrupted by the pop-up window showing up on the opposite side of your screen while you are working.
- **Switch to where pop-up window appears** - This will send the mouse cursor and keyboard control to any pop-up window that appears on the desktop.
- **Display icons when windows are iconified** - If you check this option and minimize your window, this will display available icons for the application running in the window onto a tile that is created. If you are using the GNOME Pager you do not need to enable this option as it will allow you to access minimized applications.
- **Place windows manually** - If you wish to place a new window yourself this will give the mouse the placement control of any new window.

Audio

You can turn on Enlightenment's own sound events in this section.

Special FX

The Special FX Section on E-conf controls various special effects that E can use to control windows. If you have a slower machine you might consider disabling these features in this section.

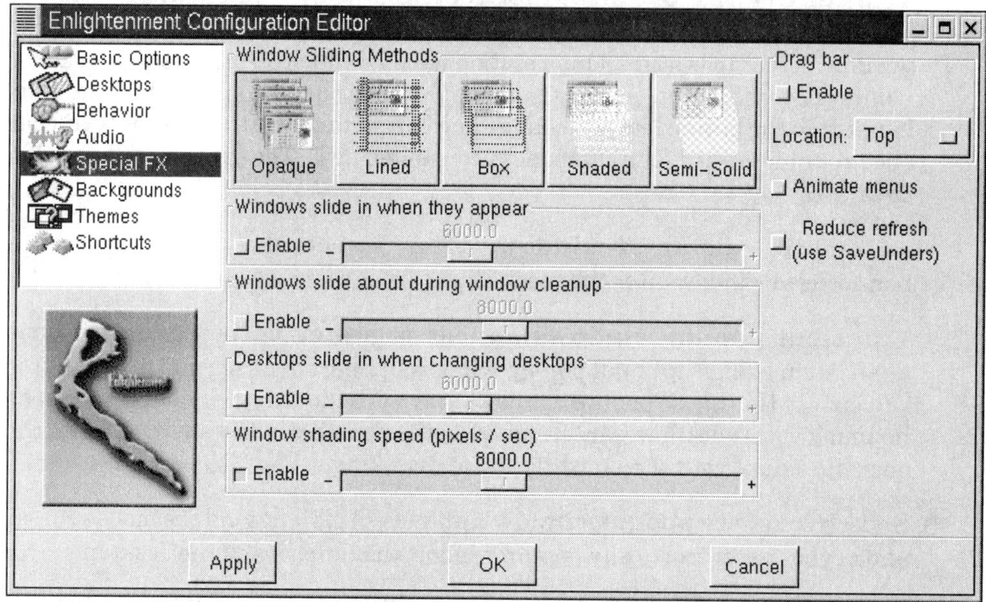

Figure 4-4: Enlightenment Special Effects

- **Windows Sliding Methods** - This area controls what windows look like when they slide in on first display. You must have the slide in feature enabled for these to work. You may choose from Opaque, Lined, Box, Shaded, and Semi-Solid.

- **Windows slide in when they appear** - This is where you can turn on or off the special effect of windows sliding in. To turn it on or off press the small button beside the speed slide bar. The speed slide bar controls how fast the windows slide and is based on pixels per second.

- **Windows slide about when cleanup in progress** - This controls the special effect of windows sliding in when you select the **Cleanup Windows** menu item from the Enlightenment menus. To turn it on or off press the small button beside the speed slide bar. The speed slide bar controls how fast the windows slide about and is based on pixels per second. For more information about the **Cleanup Window** function see the section called *Enlightenment Menus*.

- **Desktops slide in when changed** - If you use multiple desktops this will make the desktops slide in when you switch to a new one. To turn it on or off press the small button beside the speed slide bar. The speed slide bar controls how fast the desktop slides in and is based on pixels per second.

- **Window shading speed** - If you choose to have this option you can shade a window by double clicking on its title bar. Shading will draw the body of the window up into the title bar so that you only see the title bar on the screen. Another double click will return the window to its original state. The time slide bar next to the button controls how fast this behavior works. The speed is measured in pixels per second.

- **Drag bar** - Some Enlightenment themes will include a Drag bar which allows you to slide and peek into the next Desktop area or Desktop. If you wish not to have this on, make sure it is not selected. You may also decide where to place the Drag bar if you do have it enabled.

- **Animate Menus** - This will control the way Enlightenment menus are displayed. The menus will be animated if you enable this feature by pressing the small button.

- **Reduce refresh by using more memory** - This will place menus into memory to speed them up. Depending on your menus this can place a sizeable hit on your system memory.

Backgrounds

You may choose to let Enlightenment control your desktop background images. Setting the background is controlled in this area of the Enlightenment Configuration tool.

> **IMPORTANT**: If you do choose to have Enlightenment set the desktop background you will not be able to use the GNOME Control Center's Background Properties Capplet. If you are new to GNOME or Enlightenment it is recommended that you do not use this feature.

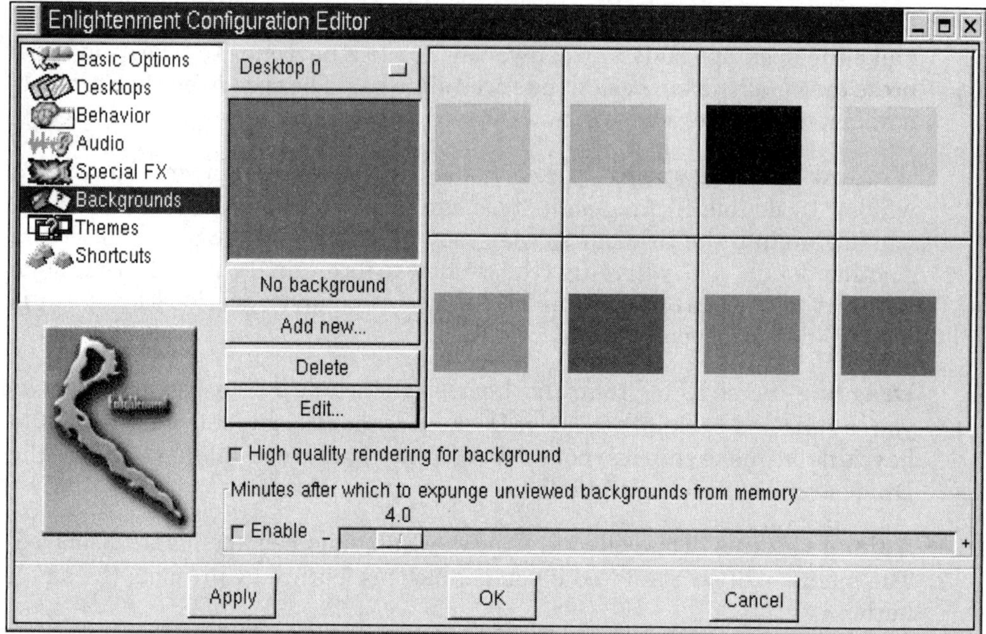

Figure 4-5: Enlightenment Backgrounds

Setting the Background

The Enlightenment background selector acts as much as a file viewer for your backgrounds as it does a creator of them. You will notice first that there is a large area to preview the backgrounds. This area is not only a good place to preview your backgrounds but it acts as an area for "bookmarking" them.

To set a background for your desktop you must first choose which desktop you want to set the background for. The top button which reads **Desktop 0** will show you which desktop you are setting the background for. If you want to set it for another desktop you can press the button and select the proper desktop.

> **NOTE**: Desktop 0 is the first desktop in any series of desktops. If you are using virtual areas on one desktop it is Desktop 0 as well.

Once you have chosen the desktop you wish to set a background for you may select a background for that desktop. To select one simply locate the image or color in the collection on the right of the preview area or select the **No background** button.

If you do not like the selections in your collection you may create a new one. You will find more information about making a new background in the next section.

> **NOTE:** If you select the No Background button for a desktop, another application or the GNOME Control Center's Background Properties Capplet can set the background for that particular desktop.

Creating a New Background

To create a new background you must first press the **Add new** button to start adding the new background to the current collection of backgrounds on the right. This will add a new box to the collection which will be blank at first.

You can start to edit the new image by selecting the new box you have just added and pressing the **Edit** button. This will bring up the *Edit Background* dialog which allows you to set the background image.

The *Edit Background* dialog contains three tabs which represent three different types of backgrounds you can have: *Solid Color, Gradient, Background Image,* and *Overlayed Logo.*

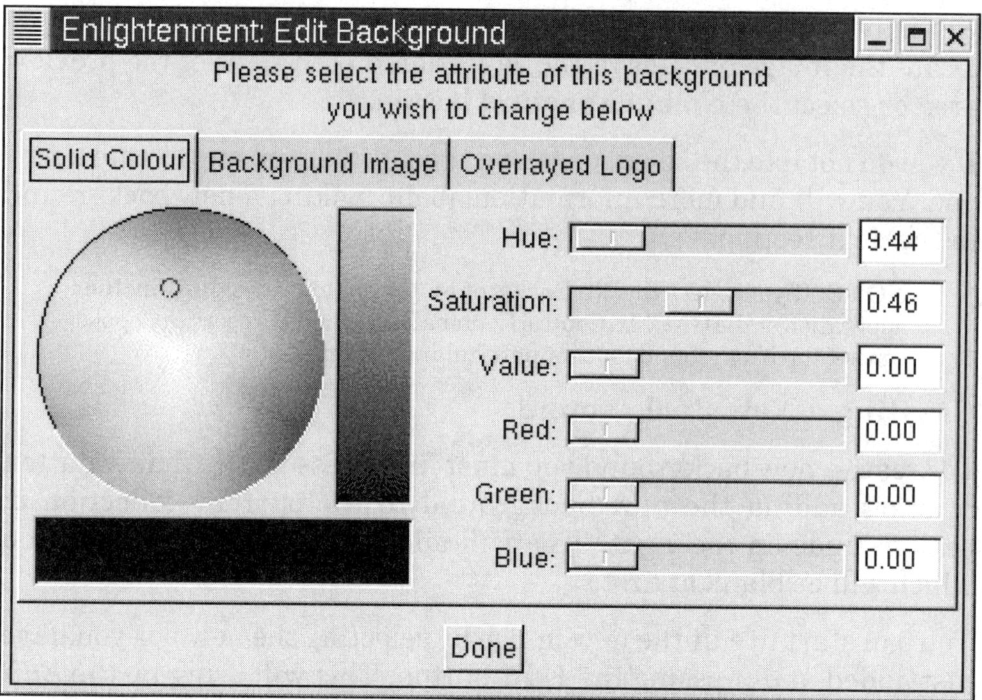

Figure 4-6: Solid Color Background

- **Solid Color** - This tab includes a color selector and color properties slidebars which allow you to choose the solid color you wish to use for your background.

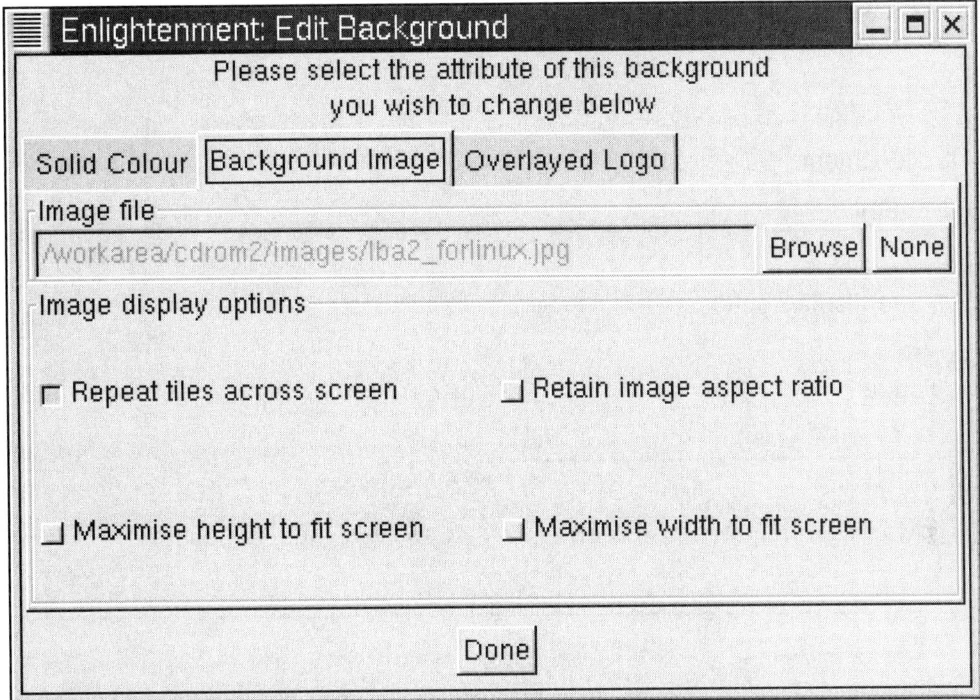

Figure 4-7: Background Image

- *Background Image* -This tab allows you to select an image on your system to display as your background. You may press the Browse button to find the image and the None button to clear any selected image.

Once you have found the image you want you may decide whether the image should repeat as tiles across the screen, retain its own aspect ratio, maximize its height to fit the screen, or maximize its width to fit the screen.

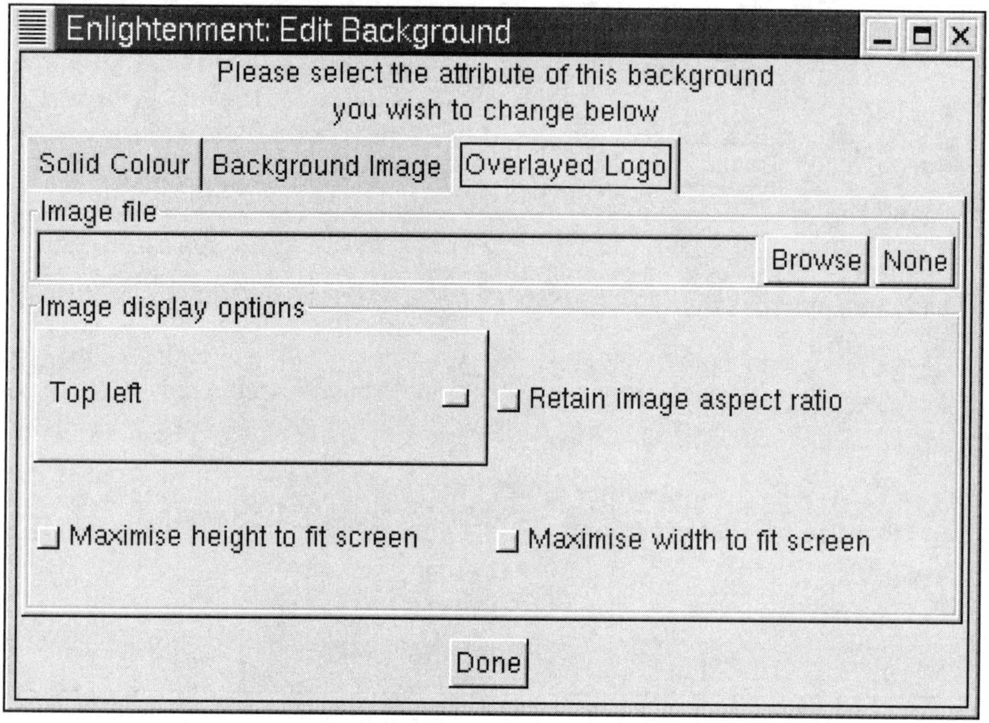

Figure 4-8: Overlayed Logo

- **Overlayed Logo** - This tab will allow you to overlay an image on the background you have already set in the other tabs. You may search for the correct image with the **Browse** button and clear any selection with the **None** button.

Once you have found the image you wish to overlay you can select where you would like the image to be displayed with the placement drop-down list. You may also decide if you want to maintain the image's original aspect ratio, maximize its height to fit the screen, or maximize its width to fit the screen.

When you have completed editing your image, press the **Done** button to return to E-conf.

Themes

Enlightenment is known for many things to the Linux community, not least of which is the sometimes fantastic and personalized look.

This can be attributed to the one of the most fun features of Enlightenment, support of themes. These themes have been created by Raster and many E users throughout the world. In fact, a Web site has been set up to be a repository of E themes, *http://e.themes.org*.

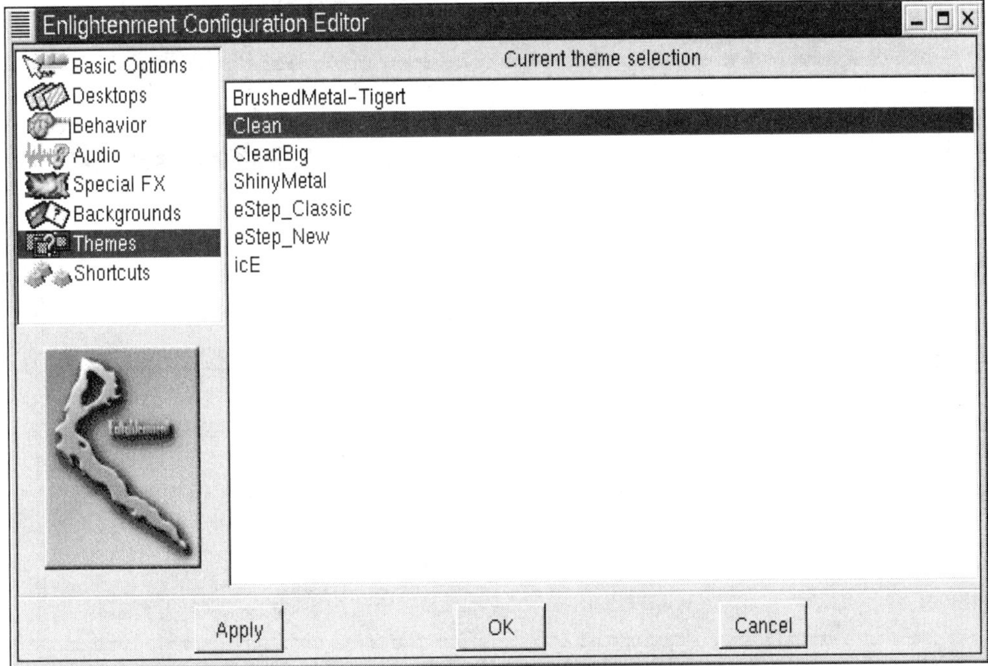

Figure 4-9: Enlightenment Themes

E themes must have an extension of *.etheme* to work. Some themes might be made for older version of Enlightenment and will not work with the newest release so make sure you are getting a compatible version.

Once you have found a theme you would like to have for E you must put it in your `~/.enlightenment/themes/` directory. All *.etheme* files in this directory will be available for selection in the *Themes* section of the Enlightenment Configuration tool.

To change themes select the theme you would like in the list of available themes and press the Apply button on the bottom of the E-conf.

Keyboard Shortcuts

The Keyboard Shortcuts section will allow you to change the keyboard shortcuts used for controlling windows, starting commands, and navigating between windows, areas, and desktops.

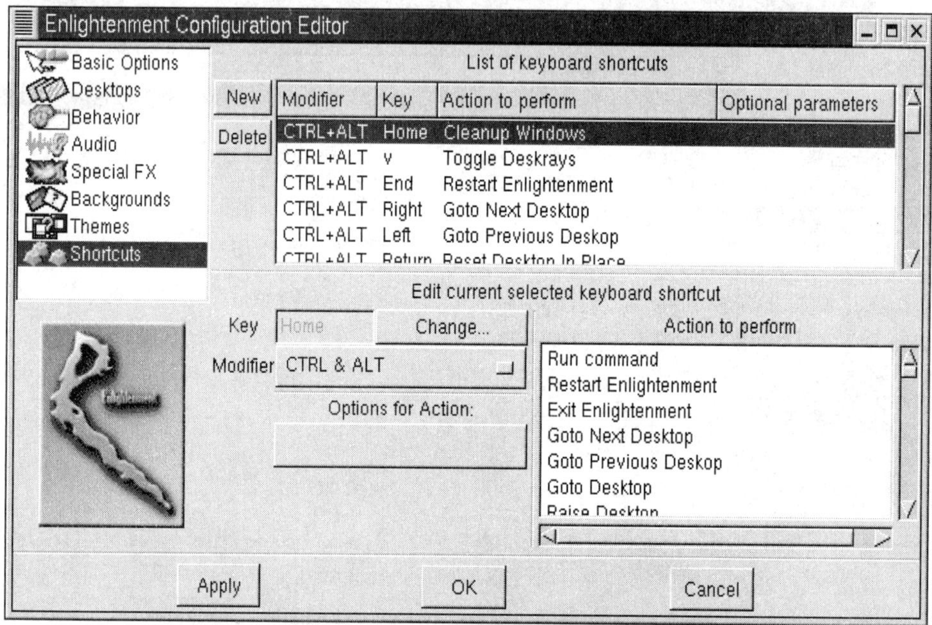

Figure 4-10: Enlightenment Keyboard Shortcuts

The Keyboard Shortcuts section is divided into two main areas, *List of keyboard shortcuts* and the *Edit current selected keyboard shortcut.*

In the *List of keyboard shortcuts* you can see which shortcuts have already been defined and select them to edit. You may also add new shortcuts by pressing the **New** button and delete them by pressing the **Delete** button.

The *Edit current selected keyboard shortcut* area is where you actually define what the keyboard shortcut will be. To use this area, you must select the shortcut you wish to edit, or select a newly added shortcut after you press the New button. Once a shortcut has been selected you can change the keys it uses or even the function it performs.

To change the keys used for a shortcut press the *Modifier* selection button and select which modifiers you wish to use. Modifiers are the keys **ALT, CTRL,** and **SHIFT.** You may select one modifier or a combination of modifiers to use with your shortcut.

At this point you will also need to change the key being used by pressing the **Change** button beside the *Key* definition box. Once you press the **Change** button you will receive a short message pop-up window which will tell you to press the desired key. Press the key and the definition will be changed.

To assign the new shortcut to an action simply scroll through the *Action to perform* list and select the action you wish to perform with this shortcut.

Some keystrokes you wish to use might have an action that needs defining. For example, if you wish to use a keyboard shortcut to change to a particular desktop you may select **Goto Desktop.** In the *Options for Action* you may define which desktop you want to go to by typing in the correct number.

Enlightenment Menus

Like all other window managers Enlightenment is designed to be used with or without a desktop environment like GNOME running on top of it. This means that there is some functionality in it which allows you to do things like start applications and move between desktops, etc.

To this end, Enlightenment provides you with menus to launch applications and perform tasks. These menus may be used in one of two places that provide different functionality: the desktop and any window border.

Enlightenment Desktop Menus

To access the desktop menus, click with your middle mouse button (or both right and left mouse buttons if you have emulation enabled) on the desktop. This will bring up the Enlightenment menus.

The desktop menus will provide you with various applications that you might have installed on your system. There are some applications in the menu that you may not have installed which the creator of Enlightenment chose to put in the menus.

The GNOME main menu items are mirrored in the Enlightenment menus as well. Plus you can launch the Enlightenment Configuration tool or change themes on the fly.

Guide to Enlightenment Desktop Menus

> **IMPORTANT:** These menus may be different if the creator of an Enlightenment theme changes them. If there are options not covered in this guide you should check the documentation associated with the theme you are using.

- **GNOME Apps** - This is a mirror of the GNOME Main Menu applications.
- **User Apps** - This is a mirror of any apps you have added to the User menu in the GNOME Main Menu.
- **Other Programs** - These are applications that the creator of Enlightenment or the creator of the theme you are using decides to include. You may or may not have these applications loaded on you machine.
- **Desktop** - This menu includes items that make changes to your desktops.
  - **Cleanup Desktop** - This will rearrange the windows on your desktop to a cleaner pattern by arranging them in a pre-determined order. This is very useful if you are having trouble finding an application due to the clutter on your desktop.
  - **Go to Next Desktop** - This will take you to either the next desktop or the next desktop area you have, depending on which is next.
  - **Go to Previous Desktop** - This will take you to either the previous desktop or area, depending on which is next.
  - **FX Ripples** - If you have time on your hands and perhaps a good sense of humor, select this item and keep a close eye on the bottom of your screen.
- **Themes** - This will search the themes directory for any themes you have installed on your machine. You may select any theme you have available and change the theme on the fly.

- **Enlightenment Configuration** - This will launch the Enlightenment Configuration tool.
- **About Enlightenment** - This will launch a small window to give you more information on Enlightenment.
- **Help** - This will launch Enlightenment's Help System
- **Restart Enlightenment** - This will restart Enlightenment completely. If you are using GNOME on top of Enlightenment this is not a recommended option, instead, you should use the GNOME Logout.

Enlightenment Window Menus

The menus that are provided on the window borders can be launched in one of two ways. If the creator of the theme you are using has included it you may use a menu button. You might find that this is not the case for certain themes, in which case you can use the second selection method.

The second way to get the window border menus is to press the **Alt** key and the right mouse button anywhere on the window border or in the window itself. This will work with the default keyboard shortcuts that ship with Enlightenment but you should check and make sure that you have not changed this keystroke in the Enlightenment Configuration Tool.

The Enlightenment window border menus allow you to do specific things to the window itself.

Guide to Enlightenment Window Menus

IMPORTANT: These menus may be different if the creator of an Enlightenment theme changes them. If there are options not covered in this guide you should check the documentation associated with the theme you are using.

- **Close** - This will close the window.
- **Annihilate** - This will kill the application if you are having trouble closing the window.
- **Iconify** - This will iconify your window. If you are using the GNOME Pager it will simply minimize the window to the task list on the GNOME Pager. If you are not running the GNOME Pager it will minimize it to an icon based on the application
- **Raise** - This will raise the window to the front of all other windows on your desktop.
- **Lower** - This will lower the window to the bottom of all of the windows on the desktop.
- **Shade/Unshade** - This will "shade" a window or unshade it if it has already been shaded. Shading a window will "draw" the window up into the window titlebar so that all you see is the titlebar itself.
- **Stick/Unstick** - This menu item allows you to make a window visible on all desktops and desktop areas.
- **Desktop** - The items in this menu allow you to move a window to another desktop area. The selections available are: **Move to Area Right; Move to Area Left; Move to Area Above; Move to Area Below.**
- **Window Size** - The items in this menu allow you to resize your window to certain ranges. The ranges are divided into Height, Width, and Size (both height and width). Within these ranges you can select how you wish to resize to the ranges.

5 Using the GNOME Panel

Introduction

The Panel is the heart of the GNOME interface and acts as a repository for all of your system applications, applets, and the Main Menu. The Panel is also designed to be highly configurable. The Panel gives you a place that always contains menus and applications as you want them to be.

The Basics

Using the GNOME Panel is very simple and will come easily to anyone who has used a graphical based operating system. You may add new panels, add applications to the panel, and add various applets. All of these functions and more will be described in this section.

Using the Main Menu

To start using any pre-loaded application press the Main Menu Button. The Main Menu has the picture of the stylized foot and on first use is on the bottom left of the screen. You should release the mouse button after pressing the Main Menu button so that you can take advantage of other features in the Main Menu such as right mouse clicks and drag and drop from the menu.

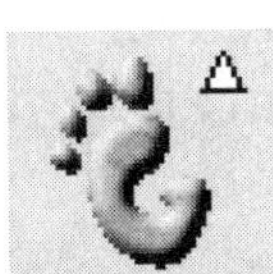

Figure 5-1: The Main Menu Button

The Main Menu is the starting point for all of the applications on your system. Later in this manual you will learn how to customize the Main Menu to suit your work environment, but for now you can use the menu that is established when you install GNOME. The Main Menu works like any other menu you might have used in other graphical desktop environments. Simply press the Main Menu Button and select from the menu that pops up from the button.

Hiding the Panel

At any time you may hide the GNOME Panel by pressing the Hide Button

Figure 5-2: The Hide Button

This will hide the GNOME Panel in the direction of the arrow on the Hide Button. There are hide buttons on both sides of a Panel so you can hide it in either direction.

You may decide that you want the Panel to hide on its own when you are not using it. This can be a helpful function if you are unable to run your system in a high resolution. You can find out how to autohide the Panel in Chapter 8.

Moving and Adding Panels

Any Panel you have on your desktop can be moved by using the middle mouse button, or by simultaneously pressing the left and right mouse buttons, to drag the panel to the desired edge of your screen. If you do not have a middle mouse button or did not configure your mouse to emulate a middle button you may also move a Panel by changing its location in the Panel Configuration dialog. You can read more in Chapter 8 of this documentation.

You may also add a new Panel to your desktop by selecting the Add New Panel from the Main Menu | Panel menu. You will be given a choice of Edge or Corner Panels. Both of these Panel types are described below.

- **Edge Panel** - An Edge Panel is exactly like the main Panel that starts up with GNOME. By selecting this type of panel you may add a new Panel to another edge of your screen to give yourself more functionality.

- **Corner Panel** - The Corner Panel is a small Panel that will not stretch to the extent of the edge of the screen it is on. The Corner Panel will, however, stretch to the extent of icons and applets it contains. The hide buttons work just a bit differently with Corner Panels. The hide button closest to the edge of your screen will hide the Panel as usual but the other hide button will send the whole panel to the opposite edge. When the latter move is made it will not hide the Panel since it is changing the side of the screen it resides on. If you want to hide it you will have to press the hide button once again.

At any time you can change the current panel to the opposite type by selecting either the **Convert to edge panel** or the **Convert to corner panel** from the pop-up menu. The selection that is available depends on which type of panel you right mouse click on. The selection displayed will be the opposite of the current panel.

Adding Applications and Applets to the Panel

Adding Application Launchers

If you would like to add an Application Launcher (an icon that starts a particular application) to the Panel, right mouse click the Panel and select **Add New Launcher** from the pop-up.

After selecting the **Add New Launcher** menu item you will see a dialog which will allow you to set the properties for the application launcher you wish to add.

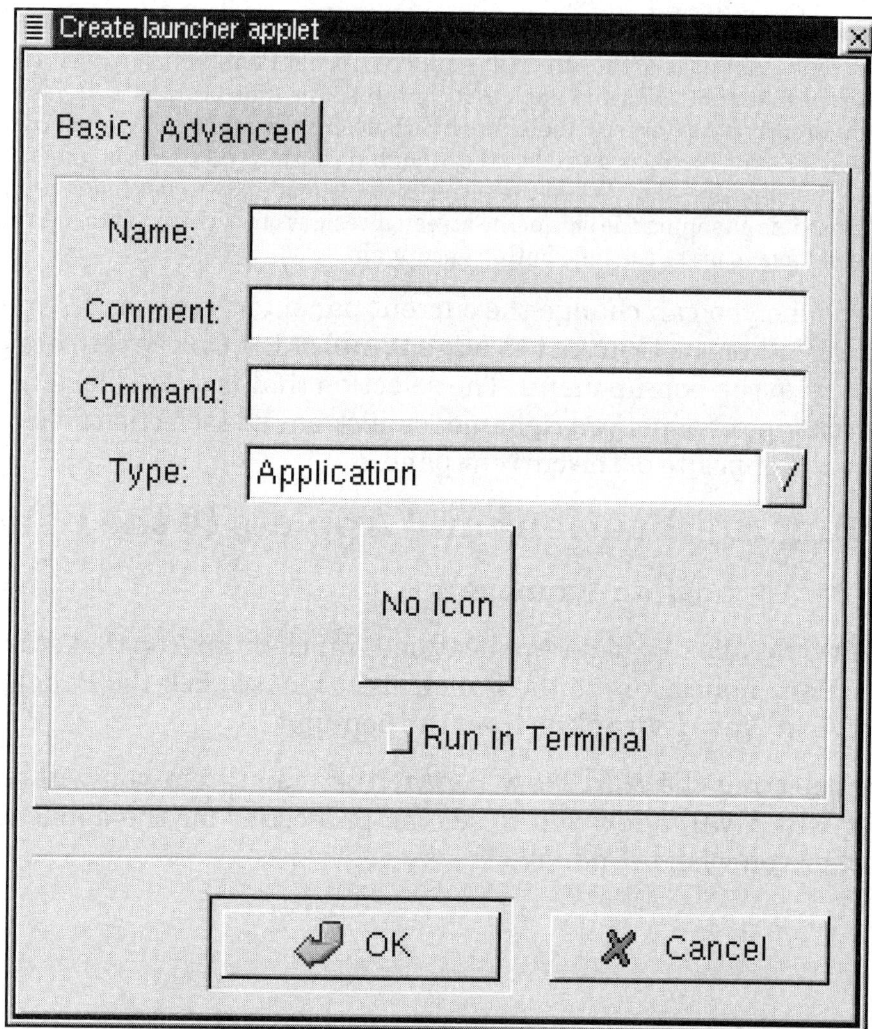

Figure 5-3: The Create Launcher Dialog

In the Create launcher applet dialog you may add a name for your launcher, a comment, the command line to launch the application, and define the application type. You may also press the icon button and choose an icon to represent the application from the icon picker. If no icon is chosen a default icon will be used.

Another, quicker method of adding an application launcher to the Panel is to go into the Main Menu and right mouse click on an application menu item. You will be given another menu selection which contains **Add this launcher to Panel**. If you select this menu item it will automatically add a launcher for that application to the Panel in which you invoked the Main Menu. At this point you may right mouse click on the launcher and select the Properties menu item to change any options for that launcher.

Grouping Items with Drawers

If you would like to group a subset of applications together you may use a Drawer. A Drawer is simply a small menu-like button that sits on your panel that groups application launchers together in one place. Once you have placed a Drawer on the Panel you may click on it to raise the menu of applications and click again to lower them.

Figure 5-4: A Drawer Running on the Panel

There are a couple of ways to place a Drawer on your Panel. First you may right mouse click on the Panel and select the **Add drawer** from the pop-up menu. Second, if you want a whole subset of menus from the Main Menu to become a drawer you may right mouse click on the title bar of that menu and select the **Add this as drawer to panel** from the pop-up menu.

You can add menus to your panel in the same way you add Drawers. Menus are very similar to Drawers except that they do not use large icons to represent application launchers, instead they use a style similar to the Main Menu, i.e. small icons and the application name. You may add a menu by right mouse clicking on the title bar of a menu and select the Add this as menu to panel from the pop-up menu. You may also add system directories to the Panel as menus by dragging a directory out of the GNOME File Manager and dropping it on the Panel.

Adding Applets

There are many applets which you can add to the Panel as well. Applets are small applications which can perform tasks within the Panel itself. There are many applets you can add to the Panel and these are covered in more detail in Chapter 12 of this manual. As an example of how to add an applet you can add another clock applet to your Panel. To add the clock applet to your Panel:

- Right mouse click on the Panel
- From the pop-up menu choose the Add new applet menu item.
- This will bring up more levels of pop-up menus.
- Choose the Utility | Clock menu item.
- The Clock will be added to your Panel.

Figure 5-5: The Clock Applet

To remove the clock applet you added you can right mouse click on the clock and select Remove from panel from the pop-up menu.

Running Applications

There are many ways to launch applications within GNOME. Remember that one of GNOME's strong points is that it allows you to start and control applications using only an easy-to-use graphical interface. There are many ways to start the applications you wish to use:

As you saw in the previous section you may use the Main Menu to find applications which have been pre-loaded or you provided using the Menu Editor. You can read more about the Menu Editor in the Chapter 9.

You may also add application launchers from the Panel which was covered in the section called *Adding Application Launchers*.

If you are using the GNOME File Manager you may double click on any executable file and it will run.

You may use the GNOME Run program to launch any application. To use it select the **Run program** menu item from the Main Menu. This will launch a simple dialog which allows you to type in the command for launching the application. For example, if you wish to start the Emacs editor and it is not in a menu or on your panel you may start the GNOME Run Program and type **emacs** in the text box on the dialog.

Logging Out of GNOME

GNOME has a couple of helpful methods for Logging out. You may either use the Logout menu item or the Logout button.

The Logout menu item is the first menu item you will find in the Main Menu. Simply select the Logout menu item and you will be prompted on whether you would like to log out or not. Select Yes and your GNOME session will end.

If you would like, you may add the Logout button to the Panel. This is just another method for logging out, it does not provide you any other functionality, other than a pretty button. To add the Logout button to the Panel right mouse click on the Panel and select the Add logout button menu item from the pop-up menu. Once the button is there you may press it to log out.

> **NOTE:** If you are running a window manager that is GNOME compliant the logout feature will quit the window manager as well as GNOME. If you are not running such a window manager you will have to end that window manager yourself.

The Logout dialog will display when you log out of GNOME. This dialog will ask you whether or not you really want to log out. It also provides you with different methods of quitting GNOME.

You have three choices on how to quit GNOME. You may Logout which will simply take you to a terminal, Halt which will shut down the whole system, or Reboot which will reboot the whole system.

If you do not want to log out you may press the No button and you will be returned to your GNOME session.

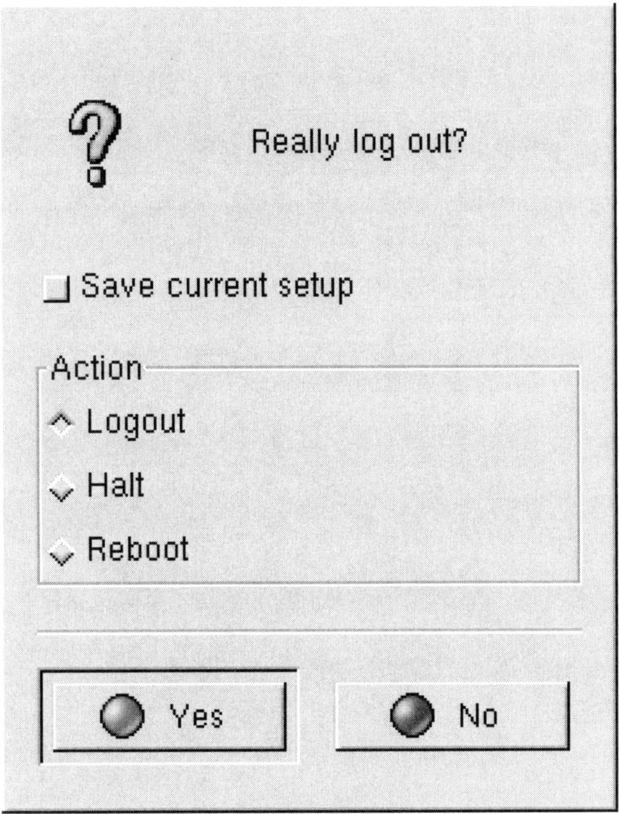

Figure 5-6: The Logout Dialog

Within the Logout Dialog there is one option you may choose before you leave GNOME.

If you would like to save your current setup you may select the Save current setup checkbox. This will save which programs you have open, and the configuration of your Panel.

6 The GNOME Desktop

Introduction

The GNOME Desktop provides you with all the functionality of any traditional operating system desktop. You can drag files, programs and directory folders to the desktop; you can also drag those items back into GNOME-compliant applications.

> **IMPORTANT:** The GNOME Desktop is actually provided by a backend process in the GNOME File Manager. If, for any reason, that backend process has stopped running you may start the GNOME File Manager again and your desktop will be restored. If you do have to do this you will not need to keep the GNOME File Manager window open to enable the desktop.

Using the Desktop

Using the Desktop is as simple as dragging items you wish to use routinely to the desktop. The default desktop will include a folder of your home directory (/home/[user name]). By default the GNOME File Manager window will also appear for you to access other areas of your system.

To utilize drag and drop you need to be using either a GNOME-compliant application or a Motif application. GNOME is compliant with Motif drag and drop so you will find it works with many applications you already have installed.

All items that are stored on your desktop are located in the following directory:

```
$/home/[user name]/.gnome-desktop/
```

This is helpful to remember when you want an item to appear on your desktop that you cannot utilize drag and drop with.

Once you have started GNOME you will notice that any drives you have connected to your system will be shown on your desktop with the appropriate icons. You may mount and access these drives utilizing these icons.

> **IMPORTANT:** You must have permission to mount the device shown on your desktop before you can utilize these icons. You must have the root password to accomplish this. If you do not have this password you should consult your system administrator.

Gaining mount access can be done quite easily if you have *linuxconf* installed on your machine. Just select the drive you want to access in the Access local drive section. In the Options tab select the User Mountable option. Your drive will now be mountable by users.

If you do not have *linuxconf* you must edit your */etc/fstab* to include user access. This is done by adding user access to the drive. For example:

If your fstab file looks like this:

```
/dev/cdrom /mnt/cdrom iso9660 exec,dev,ro,noauto 0 0
```

Add "user" to the fourth column:

```
/dev/cdrom /mnt/cdrom iso9660 user,exec,dev,ro,noauto 0 0
```

> **IMPORTANT:** There could be some security risks involved with this depending on your system and work environment. Please consult your system administrator before making any drive user-mountable.

Once you have permission to mount a drive you may right mouse click on the drive icon on your desktop. This will bring up a small pop-up menu.

You may select Mount device to mount it and Eject device to eject it. Once it is mounted you may either double-click it or choose Open from the pop-up menu to open and GNOME File Manager window to view the contents of the device.

If you are missing any drives that you might have added to your machine you may right mouse click on an empty space on the desktop and choose the Rescan Mountable Devices menu item from the pop-up menu.

Desktop Areas

Desktop areas allow you to keep a well organized system when you have many tasks to perform at one time. Just like adding a new desk when you have too much for one, desktop areas allow you to move to another area to launch more programs.

GNOME is aware of desktop areas even though they are controlled by another software program called the 'window manager'. You can set the number of desktop areas within the configuration of the window manager you are using. If you are using the default window manager or your window manager has a graphical configuration tool you may be able to launch it from the Window Manager Capplet. You may read more about this Capplet in the section called *Window Manager Capplet* in Chapter 10.

IMPORTANT: Most window managers will give you the option of having multiple desktops which are different from desktop areas. Desktop areas are virtual extensions of one desktop whereas multiple desktops are actually separate.

The default setup of GNOME is to use desktop areas with only one desktop. The reason for this is because in older applications, such as those which use Motif, users can experience problems with some drag and drop functionality across desktops.

Other Desktop Menus

There are a few desktop menus you may choose from in GNOME. These menus are accessed by making a right-button mouse click on any clean space on the desktop. This will bring up the pop-up menu which contains a few items:

- **New | Terminal** - This will launch a new GNOME Terminal window that will automatically navigate to the ~/.gnome-desktop directory.
- **New | Directory** - This allows you to create a new directory on your desktop. This can be a convenient tool to use if you wish to clean up your desktop by placing files in a new directory.

- **New | Launcher** - This allows you to place a new application launcher on the desktop. When you select this menu item it will launch an Application Launcher dialog that allows you to specify which application and its properties.
- **New | [application]** - Some applications may put items for you in the New menu. For example, the Gnumeric spreadsheet will put a New Gnumeric Spreadsheet menu item in the New menu so you can start up a new spreadsheet easily.
- **Arrange Icons** - This will automatically arrange your desktop icons.
- **Create New Window** - This will launch a new GNOME File Manager window displaying your Home directory.
- **Rescan Mountable Devices** - This will rescan the mountable devices on your machine and display an icon for any new device it might find.
- **Rescan Desktop** - This will rescan the files in your ~/.gnome-desktop directory.

7 The GNOME File Manager

Introduction

GNOME includes a file manager that allows you to manipulate the files on your system in a comfortable, powerful, graphical environment. This File Manager is known as GMC for GNU Midnight Commander. GMC is based on the Midnight Commander file manager which can be run in a terminal.

Midnight Commander has long been known for its power and ease of use. GMC has taken the power and ease of use from MC and added the GNOME graphical frontend.

As mentioned in the previous chapter, the GNOME File Manager provides the desktop functionality for GNOME. The GNOME File Manager also provides a place to manipulate files on your system by using the GNOME File Manager window.

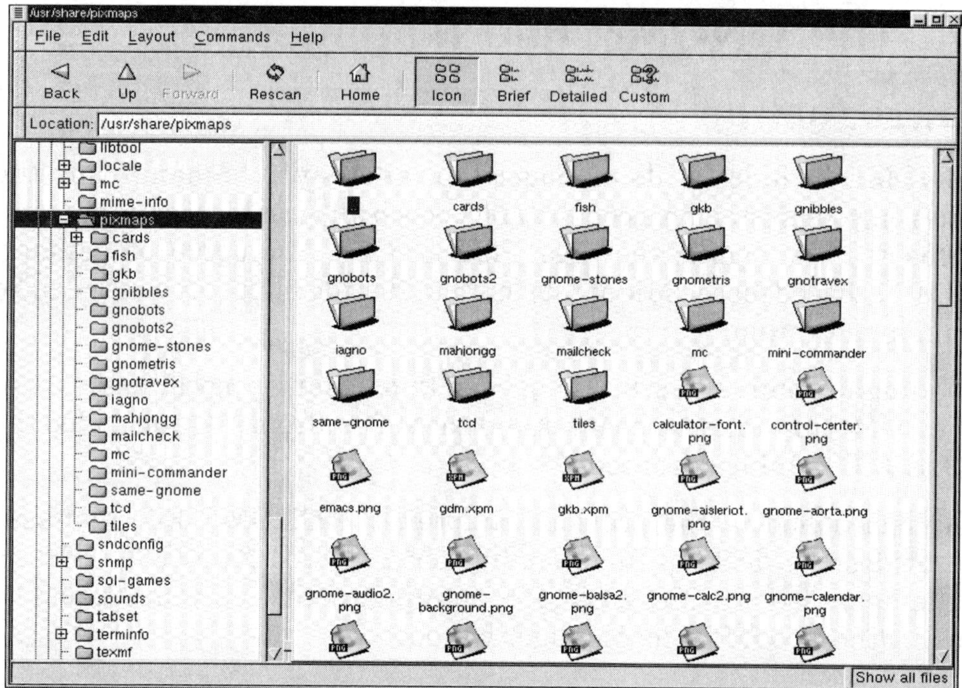

Figure 7-1: GNU Midnight Commander - The GNOME File Manager

There are two main windows within the GNOME File Manager. On the left is the tree view which represents all of the directories on your system by their hierarchical position. On the right is the directory window which will show you the contents of the directory which you have selected in the tree view.

To select a directory in the tree view simply use a single mouse click. This will change the main directory view, showing the files in the directory you have chosen. If there are directories contained within the directory, you may click on the plus sign in the tree view to expand the directory.

The main file view has a few viewing options you may wish to take advantage of: the icon view and detailed views.

The icon view is the default view and will display large icons for each file. The Brief view shows the files and directories in a list but without any extra information shown.The Detailed view will display a list view of the files in the directory and information about the files. The Custom view is a list view which allows you to select the information you want to view about files.

In the Brief, Detailed, and Custom views if you click on one of the information titles on the top of the window it will sort the files according to that information. For example, if you want to find the largest files in the directory you can click on the Size title and the files will be sorted by size from largest to smallest. One more click on the Size title will change the sorting from smallest to largest.

Moving Around the GNOME File Manager

Above the tree and main file windows in the GNOME File Manager there is a Location text box.

Within this text box you can type the path location of the file in which you would like to view in the main window.

The GNOME File Manager is also equipped to view FTP sites. To view an FTP site you will need to be connected to the Internet either through a dial up account or a network. Type the FTP address in Location text box using and the GNOME File Manager will attempt to connect to the site.

Make sure you type in FTP addresses in the following manner:

```
ftp://[site address]
```

Next to the Location text box are navigation buttons you might wish to use. These buttons with the arrow icons allow you to move within the directories adjacent to the one you are in. The left button will take you to the previous directory you were in, the middle button will take you up one level in the directory hierarchy, and the right button will take you to the next directory if you have just moved backwards.

TIP: You can open a secondary window by using your middle mouse button on any directory. Press the middle mouse button (or both left and right mouse buttons if you have emulation) on a directory in the main window and a new window will open showing the contents of the directory you clicked on.

Selecting Files

Selecting files is done with your mouse by clicking on the file or files in the GNOME File Manager. The file that is selected will then be highlighted to show you that it has been selected.

There are a couple of ways to select more than one file. One way is to use the "rubber band" select by clicking and dragging the mouse cursor around several files. This action will produce a small dotted line, the "rubber band", to show you the area in which files will be selected.

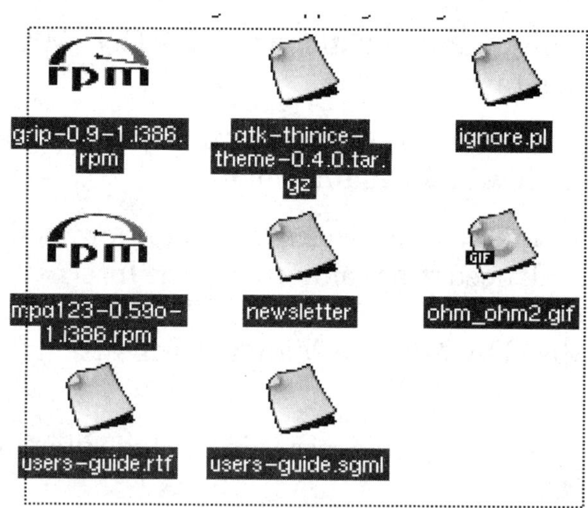

Figure 7-2: "Rubber Band Select"

If you wish to be more selective about the files you are choosing, or the files you need do not reside next to one another, you may use the **CTRL** key to keep the files you have selected while you are selecting more. This works by selecting a file, pressing and holding the **CTRL** key and selecting another file. While the **CTRL** key is pressed you will be able to add to the "list" of files that are selected. Once you have selected multiple files by either method you may copy or move the files.

You may also select all files in a directory by selecting the **Select All** menu item from the **Edit** menu.

You may also filter your selection by using the **Select Files** menu item in the Edit menu. Using Select Files will display a simple dialog which will allow you to type in criteria for your selection. In this field, the symbol * is interpreted as a wildcard, e.g., it matches any string. For example, if you would like to select all files in the directory that start with the letter **D**, you can type **D*** (note that filenames in Unix are case-sensitive).

Copying and Moving Files

The default action for drag and drop in the GNOME File Manager is to move files. But you can also use drag and drop to copy a file by pressing the **SHIFT** key while dragging the file(s). This will work the same for any files you drag to the desktop.

You may also toggle a menu which lets you decide what action to perform with a drag by using the middle mouse button to drag a file or pressing the **ALT** Key while dragging a file. Once you release the drag you will get a pop-up menu which contains the options Copy, Move, Link, and Cancel Drag.

Another way to copy or move files is to take advantage of the right mouse click pop-up menu. Right mouse click on the file you want to copy or move and select Move/rename or Copy from the pop-up menu. This will bring up a dialog in which to perform these tasks.

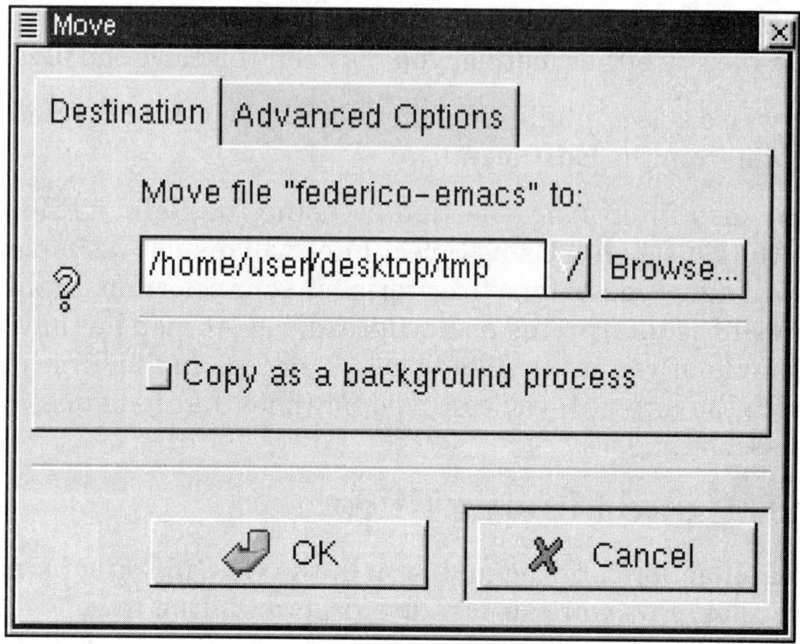

Figure 7-3: The Move Dialog

To use the move dialog you simply type in the path where you wish to move the file. If you want to rename the file you may type the new name of the file in the path string. The Copy dialog looks and works exactly the same way as the Move/rename dialog.

If the file you are moving has a symbolic link associated with it — that is, a virtual link to where the file actually resides — you may select the Advanced Options tab and select Preserve symlinks. Selecting this will make sure the link is preserved despite the move.

It is recommended that you use this method of moving a file if it has a symbolic link associated to it.

Renaming Files

Renaming files in the GNOME File Manager window or on the desktop can be achieved in two ways.

One method of renaming a file is to right mouse click on the file and choose the Properties menu item from the pop-up menu. In the Filename text box you may type in the new name as you wish it to appear.

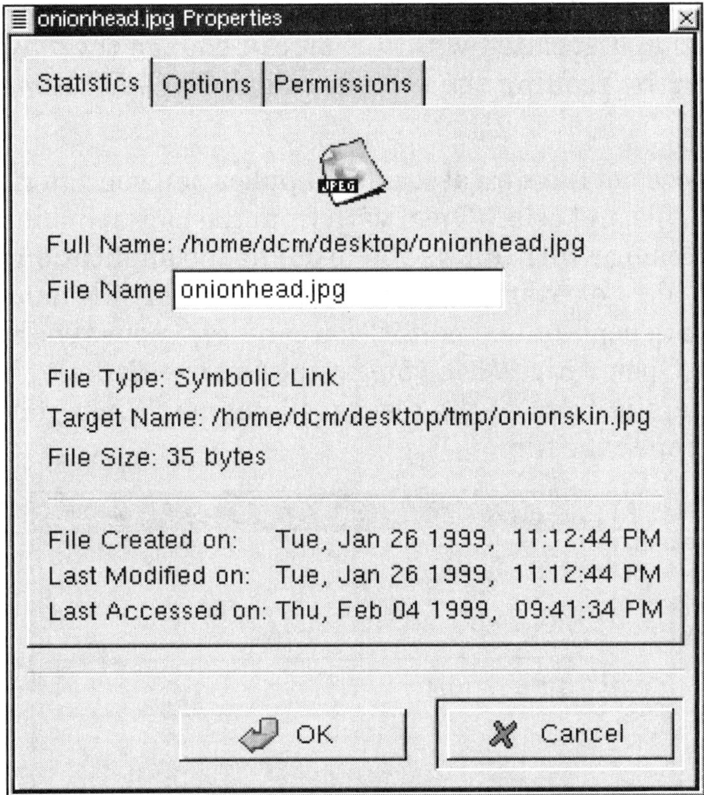

Figure 7-4: File Properties

A shortcut method to rename a file is to slowly double click on the file. Make sure this is slow so you do not launch the file but you simply highlight and then click again. At this point the name of the file will enter into the editing mode, your mouse cursor will change to an editing line, and you can type in the new name.

Launching Applications From the GNOME File Manager

The GNOME File Manager allows you to launch applications from the main window by simply double clicking your mouse on a file which has an application associated with it. You can change the way file types are handled by reading the section called *GNOME Mime Types* in Chapter 10.

If the file does not have an associated application you can right mouse click on the file and select Open with from the pop-up menu. This will bring up a dialog which allows you to define the application which will launch the file. For example, if you want to edit my file names test.txt with Emacs (a popular text editor) you can right mouse click on test.txt and choose Open with. When you get the Open with dialog box simply type in emacs in front of the test.txt file name. When you press OK Emacs will open the file.

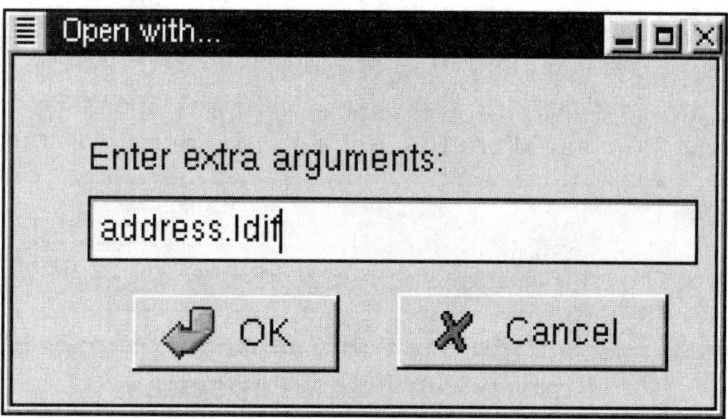

Figure 7-5: The Open With Dialog

File Properties and Actions

For any file in the main file display you may right mouse click on it and choose a variety of properties and actions for it from the pop-up menu:

- **Open** - This will open the file with the proper application associated with it. You may read more about editing these associations in the section called *GNOME Mime Types* in Chapter 10.
- **Open With** - You may open a file with any application using this menu item. You may read more about this in the section called *Launching Applications From the GNOME File Manager*.
- **View** - This will view the file with a basic text viewer.
- **Edit** - This will launch an editor to edit the file. The editor launched is determined by the application associated with that file type. You may read more about editing this association in the section called *GNOME Mime Types* in Chapter 10.
- **Copy** - This will copy the file to the clipboard so that it can be pasted elsewhere.
- **Delete** - This will delete the file.
- **Move** - This will bring up the Move dialog which will allow you to move the file. You can read more about this dialog and moving files in the section called *Copying and Moving Files*.
- **Properties** - The Properties menu item will launch the properties dialog. The Properties dialog allows you to edit and view the properties for the selected file.

The Properties dialog consists of three tabs, Statistics, Options, and Permissions.

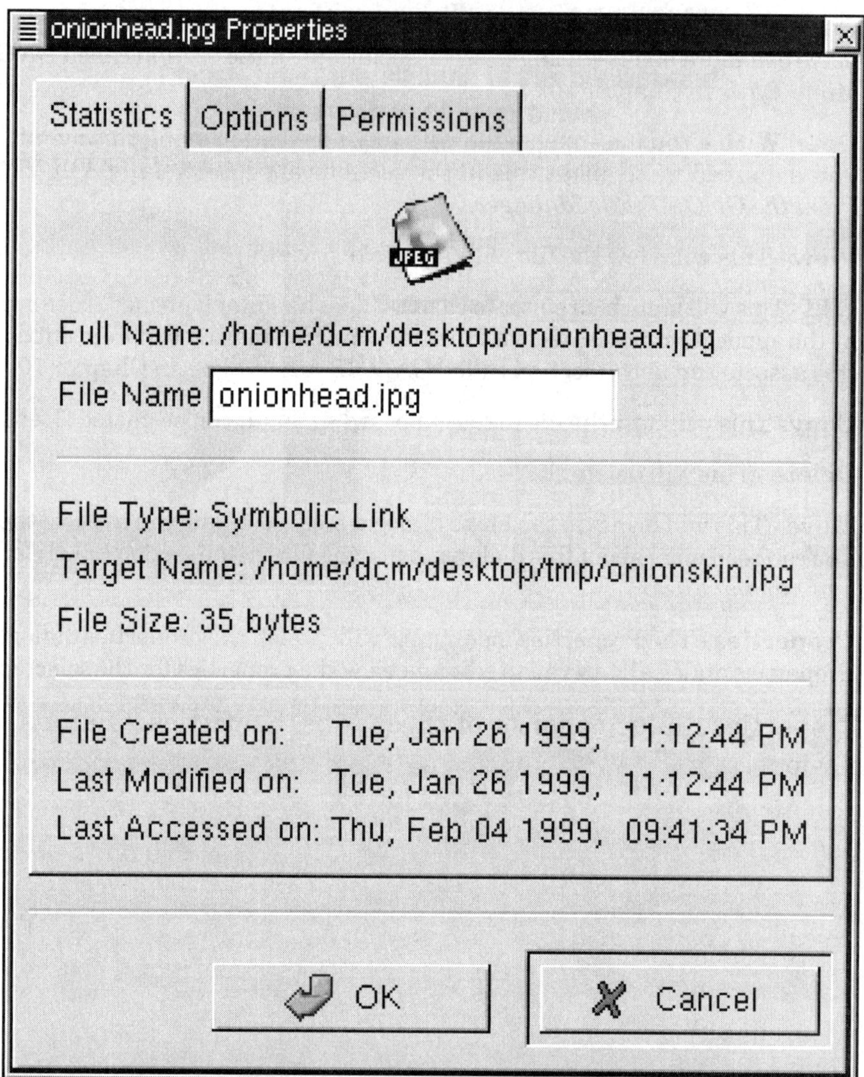

Figure 7-6: File Properties

- **Statistics** - This tab will show you the file information including the name, type, size, and history. You may change the name of the file in the File Name text box.
- **Options** - This tab will allow you to change the action options for the file. You can define how to open, view, and edit the file. If you need to open it in a terminal window you may select the Needs terminal to run checkbox.

  NOTE: If you bring up the Properties dialog from an icon on the desktop you will be able to change the icon for that file in the Options tab.

- **Permissions** - This tab allows you to change the permissions and ownership of a file if you have access to do so. You may select Read, Write, and Exec permissions for the User, Group, and Others. You may also set the UID, GID and Sticky as well as define who owns the file.

Changing Your Preferences in The File Manager

There are many settings you can configure for the GNOME File Manager.

These settings may be accessed from the GMC Preferences dialog. You may launch this dialog by selecting the Preferences menu item from the Edit menu.

The GMC Preferences dialog is divided into Five major sections: *File Display*, *Confirmation*, *Custom View*, *Caching Optimizations*, and *VFS*.

File Display

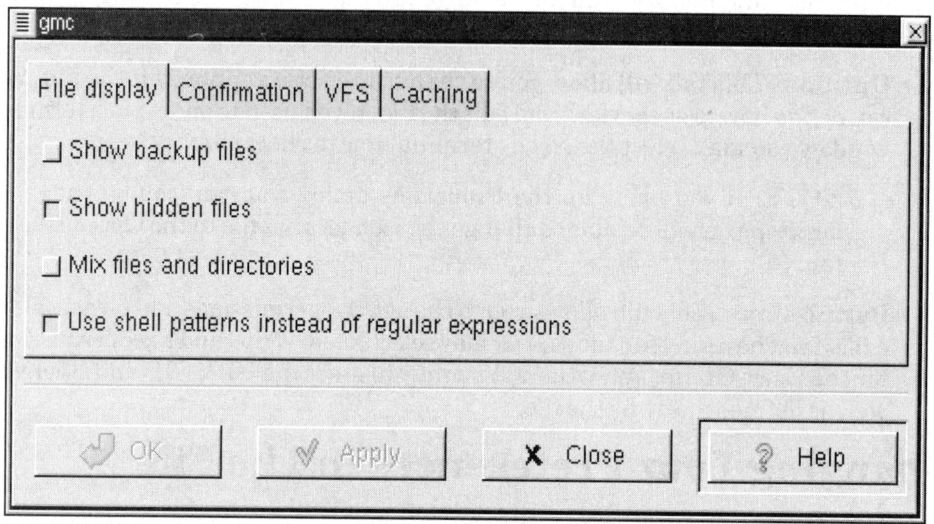

Figure 7-7: File Display Preferences

The File Display tab allows you to change the way files are displayed in GMC.

- **Show backup files** - This will show any backup file which might be on your system.
- **Show hidden files** - This will show all "dot files" or files that begin with a dot. This files typically include configuration files and directories.
- **Mix files and directories** - This option will display files and directories in the order you sort them instead of always having directories shown above files.
- **Use shell patterns instead of regular expressions** - This option is for advanced users only. If you are unfamiliar with Regular Expressions you should not use this option. If you are familiar with how to create regular expressions you may select this option to use them in your sorts and filters.

Confirmation

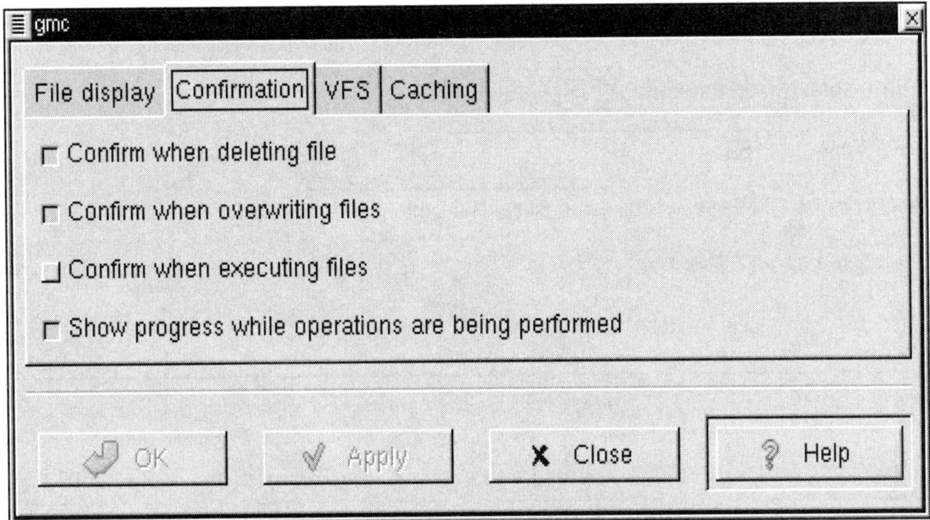

Figure 7-8: Confirmation Preferences

This tab allows you to change which functions ask for your confirmation before continuing.

- **Confirm when deleting file** - This will bring up a confirmation screen before deleting a file.
- **Confirm when overwriting files** - This will bring up a confirmation screen before overwriting a file.
- **Confirm when executing files** - This will bring up a confirmation screen before executing a file.
- **Show progress while operations are being performed** - This will bring up a progress bar while certain operations are being performed such as copying, moving, deleting, etc.

VFS

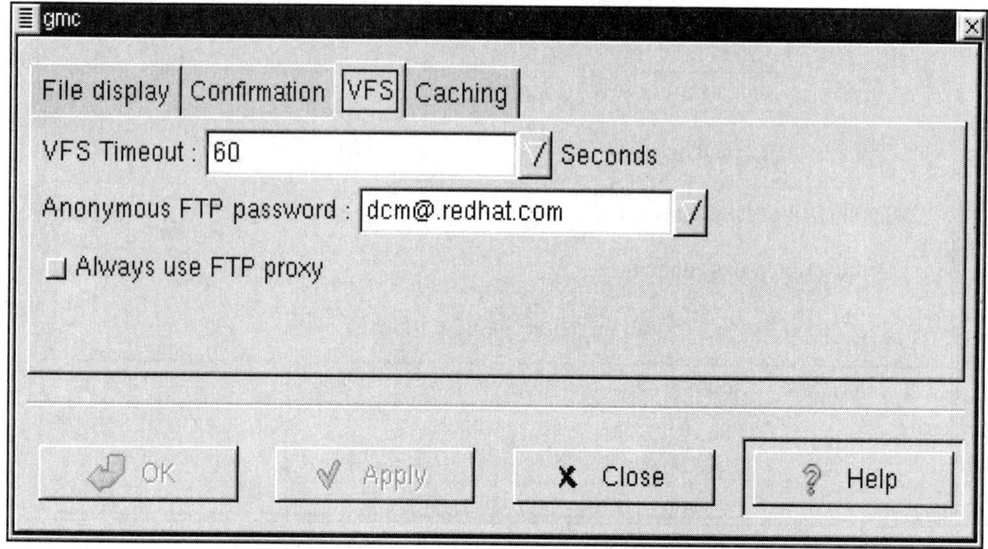

Figure 7-9: VFS Preferences

This tab allows you to configure the options for your Virtual File System.

The Virtual File System allows you to manipulate files that are not located on your local file system. There are different version of the VFS including ftpfs and tarfs. The ftpfs allows you to work on FTP sites while the tarfs gives you access inside .tar files.

> **NOTE:** The .tar file is the standard UNIX archive format

- **VFS Timeout** - This will determine how long you will be connected to any VFS without activity. The timeout is measured in seconds.
- **Anonymous FTP password** - This allows you to set a password for logging into anonymous FTP sites. Usually you will want to make this your email address.
- **Always use FTP proxy** - If you need to use a proxy to connect to FTP sites you will want to enable this.

Caching

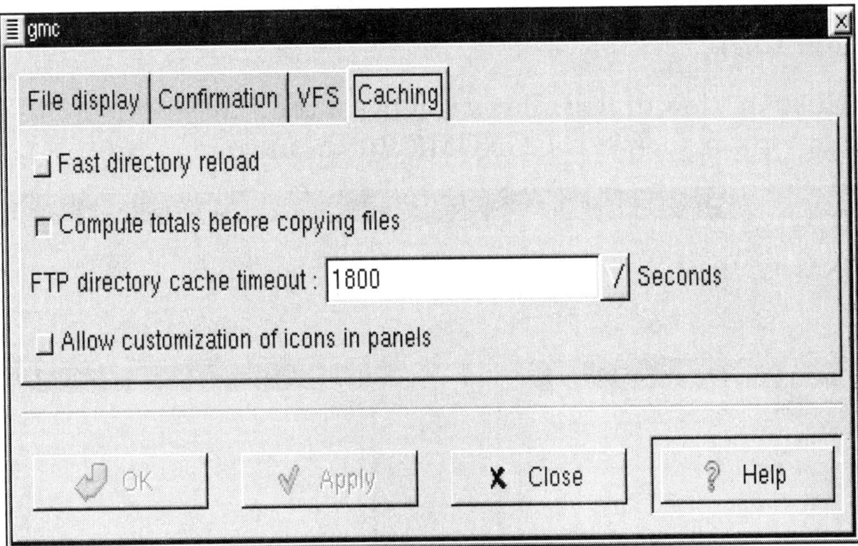

Figure 7-10: Caching Preferences

This tab allows you to configure items that will enhance the speed of GMC by using caching.

- **Fast directory reload** - This option will store directory information in cache so that it can load faster.

  IMPORTANT: If you enable the Fast directory reload you may experience problems with not seeing new files that have been added to directories.

- **Compute totals before copying files** - This will make GMC determine the number of files you are copying before it performs the task so that it can give you information about the process as its happening.

- **FTP directory cache timeout** - This option will keep recently visited FTP site information in cache for the amount of time you specify. The time is measured in seconds.

- **Allow customization of icons in icon view** - This will allow you to change the icons in the icon view by right mouse clicking on them and selecting the Properties menu item. You can always change the icons of items that are on your desktop but you can only change the icons in the icon view with this option turned on.

IMPORTANT: Turning on the Allow customization of icons in icon view function may result in a slower system.

Custom View

The Custom View dialog allows you to set the way you would like the Custom View to look in the GNOME File Manager.

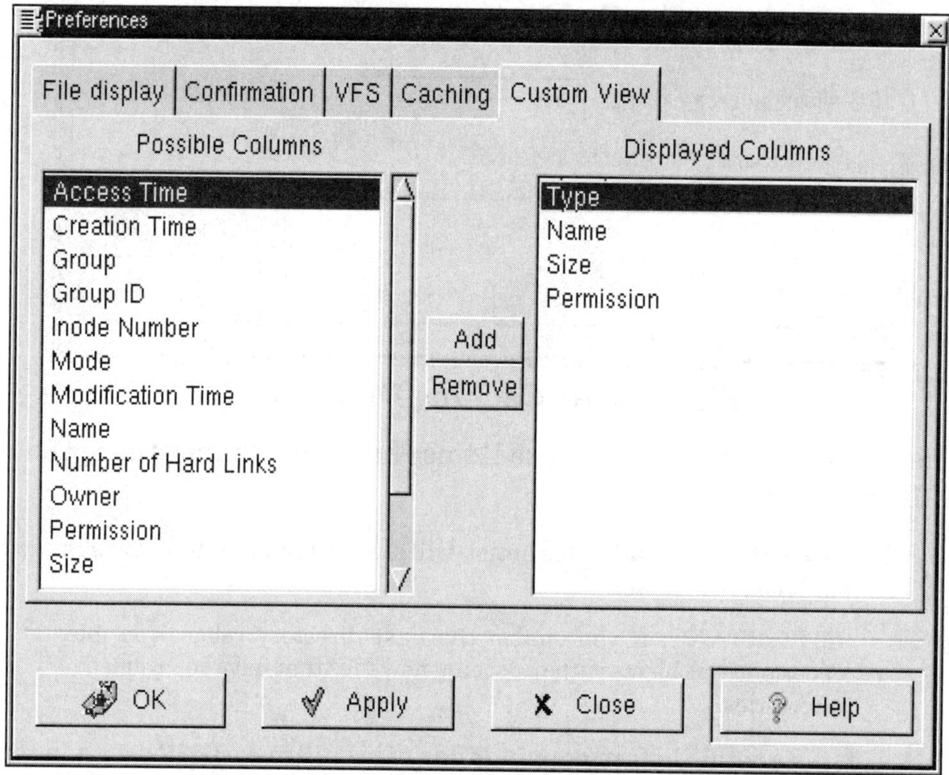

Figure 7-11: The Custom View Dialog

There are two main columns in the **Custom View**, the **Possible Columns** and the **Displayed Columns**.

The **Possible Columns** list includes all of the information types that can be displayed. If you would like to include on you may press the **Add button** and it will be added to the **Displayed Columns** list.

The **Displayed Columns** list shows you the current information types that will be included in your **Custom View**. If you wish to remove any you may press the **Remove** button.

If you would like to re-arrange the items in the **Displayed Columns** list you may drag them to the desired location with your mouse.

Menu Guide to the GNOME File Manager

In this section each menu item in the GNOME File Manager will be described.

> **Tip:** All menus in the GNOME File Manager are enabled with the tear-away feature. If you would like any menu to "float" on the desktop in its own window simply select the perforation line at the top of the menu.

- **File** - The File Menu contains items associated with files and higher level activity.
  - **New Window** - This will open a new File Manager Window.
  - **Open** - This will open the file you have selected with your mouse cursor.
  - **Copy** - This will launch the Copy dialog to enable you to copy the selected file to a destination you choose.
  - **Move** - This will launch the Move/rename dialog to enable you to move or rename the selected file to a destination you choose.
  - **Delete** - This will delete the file you have selected.
  - **Close** - This will close the GNOME File Manager
- **Edit** - The Edit menu contains items that are associated with editing and selecting files.
  - **Select All** - This will select all of the files in the directory you are currently in in the **GNOME File Manager**.
  - **Select Files** - This will launch a simple dialog box which will allow you to specify a file selection range. For example, if you wish to select all files beginning with the letter D you can simple type d* and press OK.
  - **Invert Selection** - This will invert the current selection. For example, if you have 7 files selected in a directory with 10 files, selecting Invert Selection will select the three remaining files and unselect the 7 files that were previously selected.

- **Rescan Directory** - This will rescan the current directory in case the files in the directory have changed.
- **Preferences** - This will launch the Preferences dialog so that you can customize the GNOME File Manager.

- **Layout** - This menu contains items that are associated with the layout in **GNOME File Manager**.
  - **Sort By** - This will launch a dialog box which will allow you to select how you wish the files to be sorted in the current directory. You may sort by one of the following:

    Name

    File Type

    Size

    Time Last Accessed

    Time Last Modified

    Time Last Changed
  - **Filter View** - This will bring up a simple dialog which allows you to only view files with certain attributes. For example, if you wish to only view files in the directory that start with the letter D you can type d* into the dialog and press OK. If you wish to see all files again you will need to launch the Filter View dialog again and clear the dialog or type in a *.
  - **Icon View** - Selecting this will display the files in the main view as large icons.
  - **Partial View** - Selecting this will display the files in the main view as a list with only file names.
  - **Full View** - Selecting this will display the files in the main view as a list with all file information.
  - **Custom View** - The Custom View main item switches your view to the Custom View which is a list view displaying the information about the files that you specify. To customize the Custom view you will need to use the Custom View Editor in the Preferences dialog. You may read more about the Preferences dialog in the section called *Changing Your Preferences in The File Manager*.
- **Commands** - The Command menu contains items that are commands to run

on files in the GNOME File Manager.

- **Find File** - Find File brings up a dialog which allows you to search for particular files on your system.
- **Edit mime types** - This option will launch the GNOME Control Center Capplet that allows you to edit Mime Types for GNOME. Mime types determine, among other things, what application will handle particular file types. You can read more about mime types in the section called *GNOME Mime Types* in Chapter 10.
- **Run Command** - This menu item allows you to run a command from GMC.
- **Run Command in panel** - This menu item lets you run preloaded commands or commands you specify within the directory that you are currently in. Such commands might be to find SUID or SGID programs, etc.
- **Exit** - This will allow you to exit out of the GNOME File Manager.

IMPORTANT: This will exit all GNOME File Manager processes which include the GNOME Desktop. If you exit you will lose all functionality on your desktop. This option is not recommended.

A Drag and Drop Tour of GNOME

There are many tips and tricks to the Desktop in GNOME. The Drag and Drop functionality extends to many areas of GNOME making it easy to interconnect GNOME in many interesting ways. Below is a series of tips and tricks to using GNOME Drag and Drop. This is a good tour of GNOME and will show you how to utilize GNOME to its fullest extent.

- **Drag a Color onto the Panel** - Whenever you have a color selector displayed you may drag a color from the selected color bar to the Panel and it will change the Panel to that color.
- **Drag a Pixmap to the Background Selector** - If you would like to change the background to an image, you can drag that image from your GNOME File Manager to the Monitor Image in the Background Capplet of the Control Center and it will change to that image.
- **Drag to an Application** - Many GNOME-compliant applications will accept

drag and drop. If you would like to open a file in Gnumeric, a GNOME compliant spreadsheet application, you may simply drag the file from the GNOME File Manager onto Gnumeric and it will open the file. The same is true for applications built using Motif. You may drag a saved URL onto Netscape 4x and it will open the URL. This can be very useful if you are working within the GNOME File Manager and wish to quickly open a file.

- **Adding an Application Launcher to the Panel** - If you would like to add an application launcher to the Panel you may drag and drop any executable file from the GNOME File Manager, or the Desktop, onto the Panel. This will display the Create Launcher applet dialog box which will allow you to select a name and an icon for that launcher.
- **Dragging Files** - There are many ways to use drag and drop to help you manage your system. You can open two GNOME File Manager windows to two different directories then drag files between the two windows to copy, move, or link files. You can drag files from the File Manager to the desktop to make it more accessible. Use the middle mouse button or the right and left mouse buttons together and Drag a directory folder to the desktop. Choose the link option from the pop-up menu to make a link to the desktop. This will give you a quick way to launch the File Manager to that directory.
- **Dragging Directories** - You can drag a directory out of the GNOME File Manager and place it on the Panel. This will create a new menu which allows you easy access to the files in that directory.

You may drag any sub menu from the Main Menu to the panel and a new menu launcher is added to the panel. This allows easier access to that subset of menus.

8 Configuring the Panel

Introduction

The GNOME Panel is highly configurable and comes equipped with many graphical tools to help you do the configuration. In this section you will learn how to configure any GNOME Panel the way you would like it.

Global Panel Properties

To start configuring the GNOME panel right click on the panel and select the Global Properties menu item. You may also press the Main Menu button and select the Panel | Global Properties menu item.

This will bring the Global Panel Configuration dialog up. With this dialog you can set the global properties for all panels you use now and any panels you add in the future.

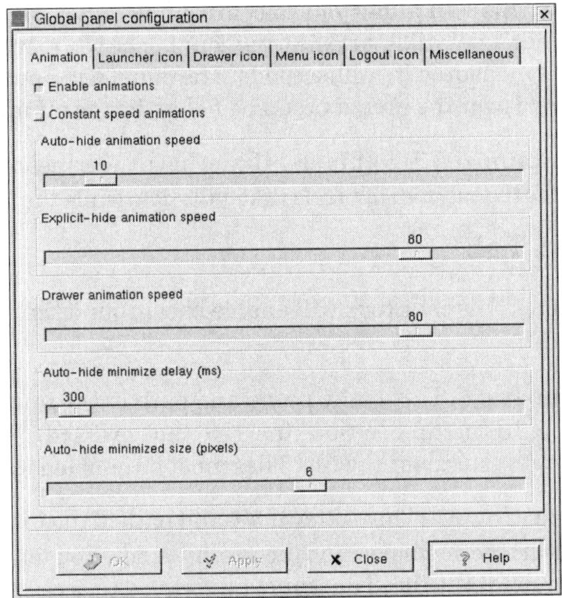

Figure 8-1: The Global Panel Configuration Dialog

The Global Panel Configuration Dialog contains six tabs which help you configure the global properties of the GNOME Panel: Animation, Launcher Icon, Drawer Icon, Menu Icon, and Miscellaneous. Each of these tabs is explained below.

Animation Tab

- **Enable animations** - This allows the animations configurable on this tab to be visible. The animations must be enabled to use the other features of this tab. The default position is on.
- **Auto-Hide Animation Speed** - If you have the panel hiding automatically this will control how fast it occurs.
- **Explicit-Hide Animation Speed** - This controls the hide speed when you press the Panel's Hide Button.
- **Drawer Animation Speed** - If you use a Drawer panel this will control how fast the drawer menu will raise.
- **Auto-Hide Minimize Delay(ms)** - If you have the Panel set to minimize automatically this will allow you to control how much time passes before it minimizes. The Panel will start the time count once the mouse is no longer over it. This time is measured in milliseconds. The panel will appear again when the mouse is passed over the area it occupied before it was minimized.
- **Auto-Hide Minimized Size(pixels)** - If you have the Panel hiding automatically this determines the number of pixels that will show while the Panel is minimized.

Launcher icon Tab

- **Tiles enabled** - This checkbox will enable background tiles for all icons on the Panel.
- **Tile filename (up)** - This is the name and path of the image file you wish to use for the tile in the up position (inactive, not pressed). You may press the Browse button to search for the file. Tiles must be enabled to access this option.
- **Tile filename (down)** - This is the name and path of the image file you wish to use for the tile in the down position (active, pressed). You may press the Browse button to search for the file. Tiles must be enabled to access this option.

- **Border width (tile only)** - This determines the width of the border around an icon. This is very useful if you have an icon that would normally cover up a tile. You can set the border to a smaller size and still be able to see your tile.

- **Depth (displacement when pressed)** - This determines the depth an icon will displace when pressed. Tiles must be enabled to access this option.

Drawer icon Tab

- **Tiles enabled** - This checkbox will enable background tiles for all drawers on the Panel.

- **Tile filename (up)** - This is the name and path of the image file you wish to use for the tile in the up position (inactive, not pressed) You may press the Browse button to search for the file. Drawer tiles must be enabled to access this option.

- **Tile filename (down)** - This is the name and path of the image file you wish to use for the tile in the down position (active, pressed). You may press the Browse button to search for the file. Drawer tiles must be enabled to access this option.

- **Border width (tile only)** - This determines the width of the border around a tile. Drawer tiles must be enabled to access this option.

- **Depth (displacement when pressed)** - This determines the depth a tile will displace when pressed. Drawer tiles must be enabled to access this option.

Menu icon Tab

- **Tiles enabled** - This checkbox will enable background tiles for the Main Menu button on the Panel.

- **Tile filename (up)** - This is the name and path of the image file you wish to use for the tile in the up position(inactive, not pressed) You may press the Browse button to search for the file. Menu tiles must be enabled to access this option.

- **Tile filename (down)** - This is the name and path of the image file you wish to use for the tile in the down position(active, pressed) You may press the Browse button to search for the file. Menu tiles must be enabled to access this option.

- **Border width (tile only)** - This determines the width of the border around a tile. Menu tiles must be enabled to access this option.

- **Depth (displacement when pressed)** - This determines the depth a tile will displace when pressed. Menu tiles must be enabled to access this option.

Logout Icon Tab

- **Tiles enabled** - This checkbox will enable background tiles for all Logout buttons on the Panel.
- **Tile filename (up)** - This is the name and path of the image file you wish to use for the tile in the up position (inactive, not pressed). You may press the Browse button to search for the file. Logout button tiles must be enabled to access this option.
- **Tile filename (down)** - This is the name and path of the image file you wish to use for the tile in the down position (active, pressed). You may press the Browse button to search for the file. Logout button tiles must be enabled to access this option.
- **Border width (tile only)** - This determines the width of the border around a tile. Logout button tiles must be enabled to access this option.
- **Depth (displacement when pressed)** - This determines the depth a tile will displace when pressed. Logout button tiles must be enabled to access this option.

Miscellaneous Tab

- **Tooltips enabled** - This enables tooltips for items on the panel. Tooltips are pop-up help dialogs that appear when you mouse is over an element on the panel.
- **Show Small Icons** - This will enable small icons in the Main Menu.
- **Show ... buttons** - This will enable three small dots to appear on Main Menu items that launch dialogs.
- **Show popup menus outside of panels** - This allows popup menus to appear away from the Panel when on. When toggle off the popups will appear over the Panel. This can be useful on smaller screens or cluttered desktops.
- **Keep menus in memory** - This will keep your menus in memory so that they do not rescan for added items. This can increase the speed of GNOME but may also result in you missing new items in your menu that are GNOME compliant.
- **Switched movement** - This allows launcher buttons on the panel to switch places with other icons when being moved.

- **Free Movement (doesn't disturb other applets)** - This feature locks the arrangement of your icons on the Panel. This is a good feature to use if you like the way your icons are arranged.
- **Prompt before logout** - This will bring up a yes/no dialog which asks you if you would really like to log out.
- **Raise panels on mouse-over** - If you are using a window manager that is not GNOME-compliant it will not understand its relationship with the Panel. This can cause your Panel to be covered by applications. If you enable this feature you can have the Panel automatically raise when your mouse is over it.
- **Keep panel below windows** - If you are using a GNOME-compliant window manager the window manager will understand its relationship with the Panel. If you choose this feature the window manager and GNOME will allow applications to appear over the Panel. This can be useful on smaller screens.
- **Close drawer if a launcher inside it is pressed** - By default drawers will remain open when you select an item within one. This can be annoying as the drawer will remain open until you close it with a mouse click. With this option selected drawers will close automatically when you select any item within one.
- **Applet padding** - This changes the amount of space (padding) between icons and applets.

This Panel Properties

Each Panel's properties can be configured individually. To change the configuration of the active Panel, right mouse click on the Panel and select the This panel properties menu item from the pop-up menu. You may also press the Main Menu button and select the Panel | This panel properties menu item.

This will bring up the Panel properties dialog box. In this box you can change the properties for the active Panel.

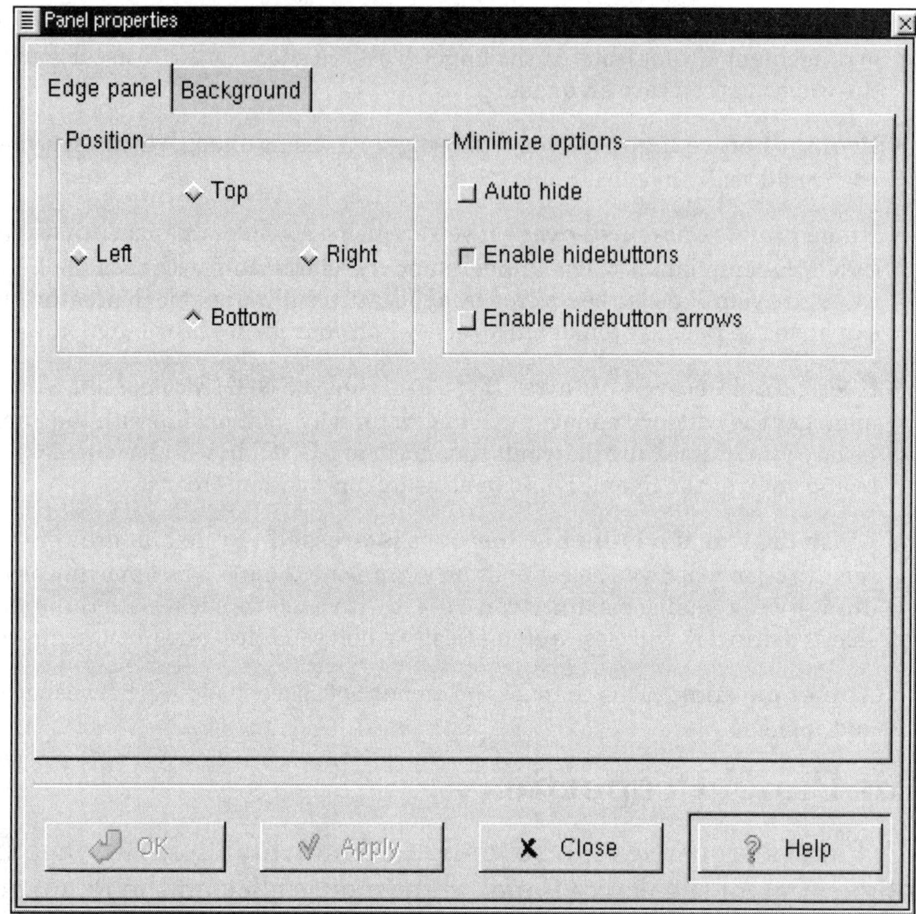

Figure 8-2: This Panel Properties Dialog

The Panel properties dialog contains two tabs to help you set the active Panel properties: Edge Panel and Background. Both of these tabs are explained below.

Edge Panel Tab

- **Position** - This changes the position of the Panel on the screen. You may select either Top, Right, Left or Bottom. The Panel will change position once you have pressed the Apply button.

- **Minimize Options** - The options here will enable you to either Explicitly hide the Panel yourself using the hide buttons or Auto Hide when the mouse is not over the Panel. If you choose to Auto Hide you might want to Disable the hide buttons here as well. You may also disable the hide button arrows graphics on the Panel as well.

Background Tab

- **Background** - These options allow you to change the background of the Panel itself. You may choose, if you wish, to have the standard, Pixmap, or Color background. The standard look for the Panel is determined by the GTK theme you are running at the time. The Pixmap option allows you to choose an image to tile or scale to the Panel. The Color option allows you to specify a particular color for the Panel.

  IMPORTANT: An easier way to change the background of your panel is to drag and drop an image file from the GNOME File Manager onto the Panel. This will automatically change the background of the panel to that image.

- **Image file** - If you choose to have a Pixmap for the background of your Panel this will allow you to choose which image to use. If you press the Browse button you can search for the file you want to use.

- **Scale image to fit panel** - This allows a background image to scale to the size of the panel. If not checked images will tile to the panel.

- **Background color** - If you choose to have your Panel one color this button will launch a dialog which allows you to specify which color to use.

9 Editing the Main Menu

Introduction

The Main Menu is a repository for your applications and can be found on the Panel. The Main Menu is preloaded with GNOME but it can be configured to fit your work habits. The Main Menu is broken up into two main subdirectories: the System menus and the User menus. The Menu Editor is available for you to add new applications to the Main Menu but you cannot add applications to the System menus if you are not the system administrator (root). In this section you will learn how to configure the Main Menu with applications you wish to use everyday.

Configuring the Main Menu

If you want to change properties of the Main Menu or any other menu you have on your Panel you may right click on the menu button and select Properties. This will launch the Menu properties dialog.

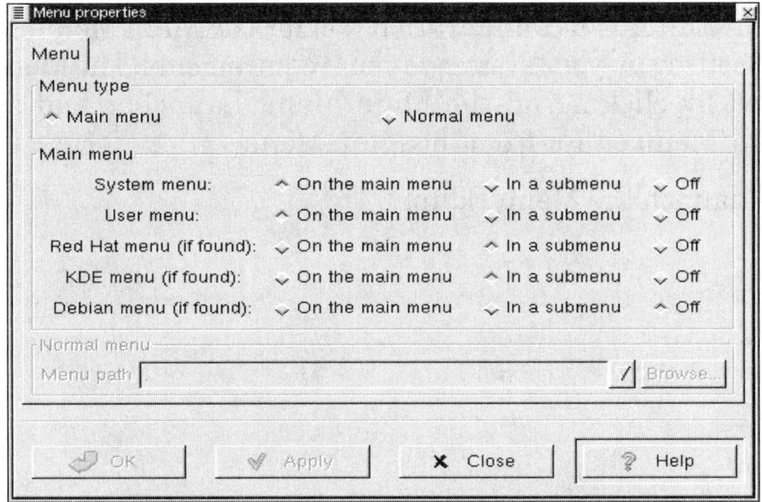

Figure 9-1: Menu Properties Dialog

The first selection item in the Menu properties dialog is the Menu type. This will allow you to change the menu from a Main Menu to a Normal Menu.

The other choices in the Menu properties dialog are sub-menu selections for Main Menus. These selections allow you to choose what is in your Main Menu which you can have in the Main Menu, in a submenu, or off:

- **System Menus** - This is the menu items that are the default applications that come with GNOME.
- **User Menu** - This contains any menu items you added using the Menu Editor for your user account.
- **Another Level Menu** - If you are using the Red Hat Linux build this is the set of applications that ship with it by default.
- **KDE Menu** - If you are a user of the Kool Desktop Environment you may choose to include the applications included in the KDE menus.
- **Debian Menu** - If you are using the Debian Linux build this is the set of applications that ship with it by default.

Using the Menu Editor

The Menu Editor is a configuration tool for the Main Menu. It is very useful in setting up your system to your requirements. The Menu Editor is started by clicking on the Main Menu Launcher and selecting Settings | Menu editor from the Main Menu.

This will launch the Menu Editor.

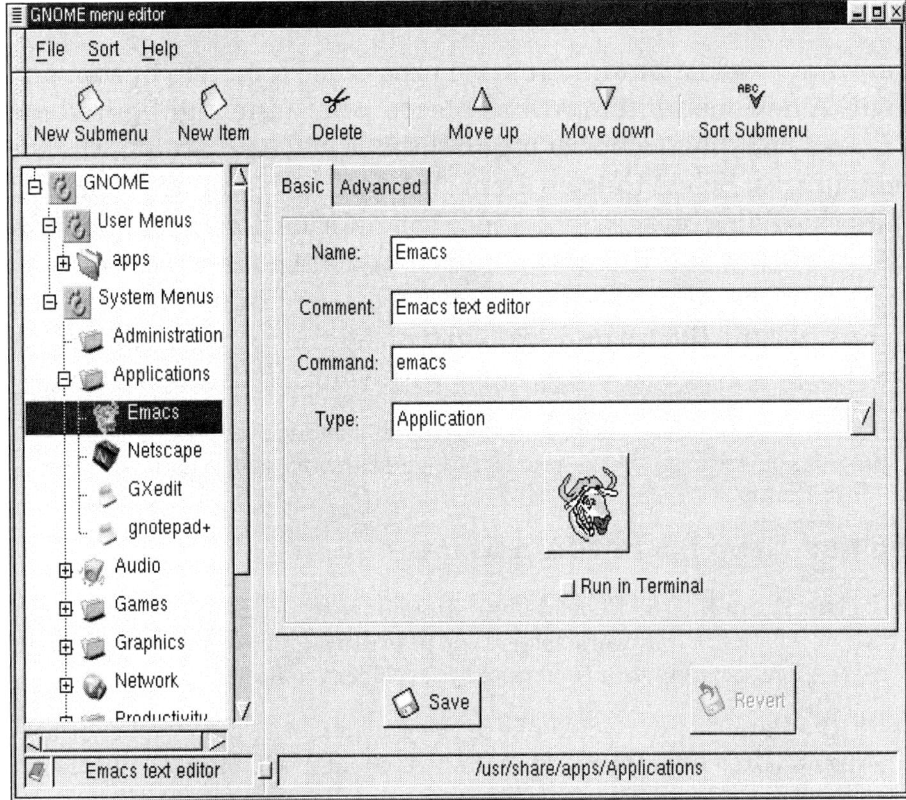

Figure 9-2: The Menu Editor

The Menu Editor is divided into two main panels. The left side contains the menu in its default state. The right side contains a tabbed dialog that allows you to add new applications to the menu.

On the left side in the menu tree you will notice that there are two main menu lists, one for User Menus and one for System Menus. The User Menus are for the current user and the System Menus are for all users on the system. The prepackaged applications are all located in the System Menus.

Within the menu list on the left side you may open and close folders and see what is in your current menu by clicking on the small plus signs beside the menus.

Adding a New Menu Item

If you want to add a new menu item press the New Item button on the toolbar. A new menu item will be placed where the highlighted menu is. If you do not have a menu highlighted it will be placed at the top of the menu tree. Select the new item and type in the information for the item in the dialog on the right. Once the information is complete press the Save button and the new menu item will be inserted where your cursor is on the right side menu tree. You may then move the menu item by pressing the up or down buttons on the toolbar. You may also move the menu item by dragging it with your left mouse button.

> **IMPORTANT:** Keep in mind that you cannot change the System menus unless you are logged in as root. If not, you can only add to, and edit, the User Menus.

Drag and Drop in the Main Menu

- **In the Menu Editor** - The Menu Editor supports drag and drop functionality which will make your work easier. You may drag applications to the folders you wish them to reside in or re-arrange your folders completely.

- **To the Panel** - If you would like to place a menu item onto the Panel you can drag and drop from the menu to the Panel and it will place a launcher there with all the appropriate properties set for you. If you prefer not to use drag and drop you may also right click on the menu item and choose the Add this launcher to panel from the pop-up menu.

10 The GNOME Control Center

Introduction

The GNOME Control Center allows you to configure various parts of your system using a collection of tools called "capplets". These capplets may be associated with the core set of GNOME applications or other applications for which the developers have written capplets.

Your Control Center may contain more capplets than are documented here depending on the applications installed on your system.

The Control Center is divided into two main sections, the menu of configurable capplets and the main work space.

Working with the Control Center simply requires you to select a capplet from the menu on the left and double click on it. Once this is done, the workspace will change, allowing you to configure the item.

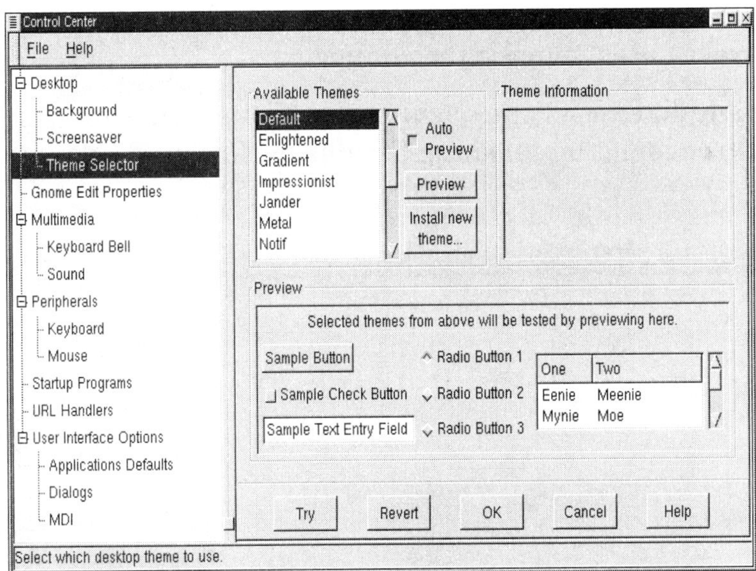

Figure 10-1: The GNOME Control Center

You may start the Control Center one of two ways. To launch the Control Center without any particular active capplet select the Control

Center menu item from the System menu.

If you know which capplet you would like to edit you may start that capplet by selecting the correct menu item in the Control Center menu.

Desktop Capplets

The Background Properties Capplet

The properties for your background image can be set here by either selecting a color or an image. If you select a color you have the option of having Solid or Gradient colors. If you choose to have Gradient colors you may choose between a Vertical or Horizontal gradient and choose the second color for the gradient to end on.

If you decide to have an image as wallpaper you may browse for the image you wish to use. Once you have found your image you need to decide whether you would like to have the image tiled, centered, scaled keeping aspect, or simply scaled. Once you have changed your background properties you may press the Try button at the bottom of the Control Center to make the change.

If you would like to set the background by any other means you may disable this capplet by selecting Disable background selection.

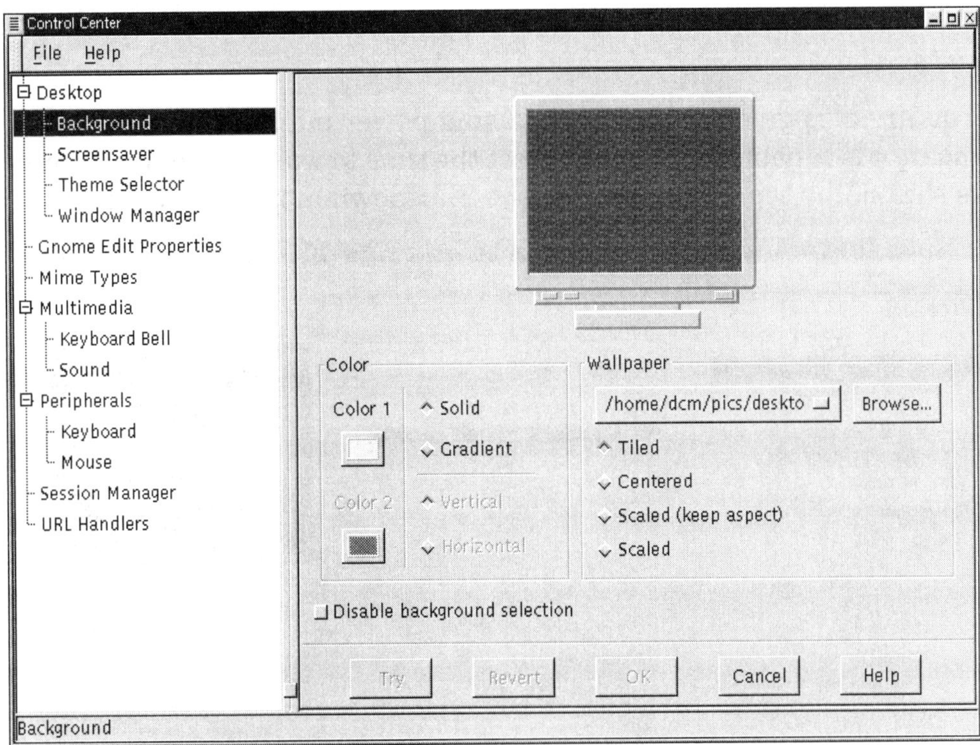

Figure 10-2: The Background Properties Capplet

The Screensaver Capplet

In this capplet you can change your xscreensaver properties. This capplet contains a list of available screen savers you may choose and a demo screen. Below these two dialogs you will see a set of tools that allow you to change the settings for the global screen saver properties. If the screen saver you choose has particular settings you can change those by pressing the Settings button that appears below the Screen Saver list.

Global Screen Saver settings - In this section of the capplet you can change the time, password, and power management properties. You can decide how long you would like the screen saver to wait before starting by typing the number of minutes in the Start After text box. If you would like a password to return to your desktop click the Require

Password button. Your account login password is the password set for the screen saver.

You are also given the option of using power management — if your monitor is capable of it. You may set the time to wait before the monitor is shut off by typing the time in the Shutdown monitor text box.

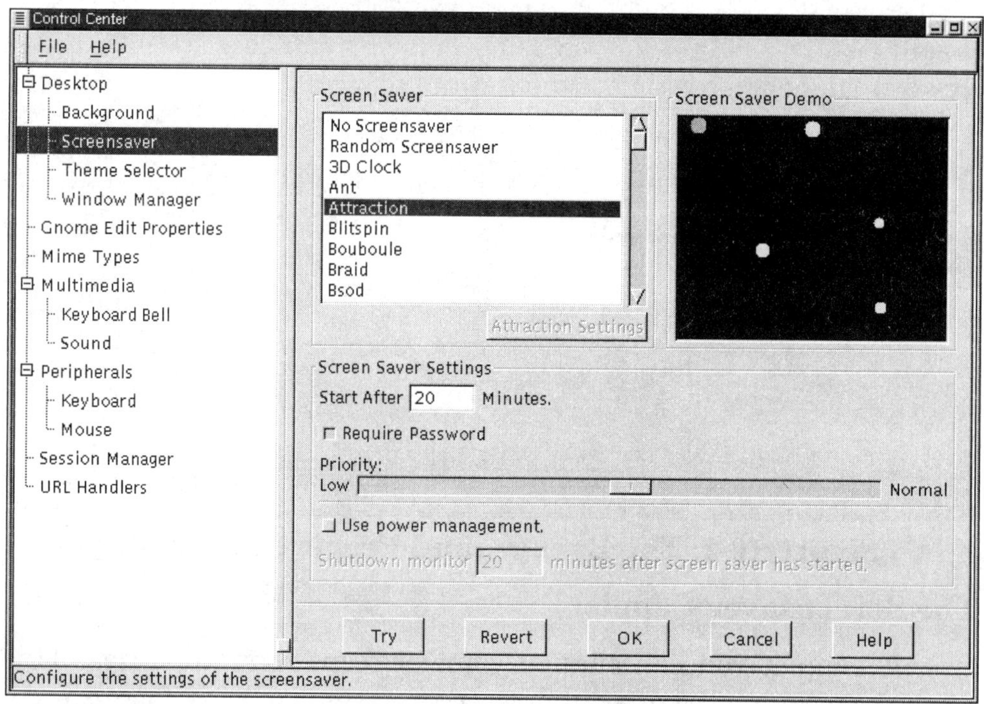

Figure 10-3: The Screensaver Properties Capplet

Theme Selector

The Appearances capplets contains the Theme Selector which allows you to select which GTK theme you would like to run.

GTK themes are themes which allow the GTK widget set to change look and feel. The widget set is the set of tools that provides buttons, scrollbars, checkboxes, etc. to applications. GNOME-compliant applications use the GTK tool set so most of your GNOME applications will change look and feel if you change the GTK theme.

To change your GTK theme select a theme from the Available Themes list on the left side of the main workspace. If you have Auto Preview selected you will be able to see what the theme looks like in the preview window below. If you like the theme press the Try button on the bottom of the GNOME Control Center to install it.

There are a few GTK themes that come loaded with GNOME when you install it. If you would like more themes you can check resources on the Internet like http://gtk.themes.org. Once you have found and downloaded a theme you like, press the Install new theme button. This will launch a file browser that allows you to find the theme you have just downloaded. The theme files should be in a **tar.gz** or **.tgz** format (otherwise known as a "tarball"). Once you have found the file press the OK and it will install the theme for you automatically. Now you can look in the Available Themes list for the theme you have installed.

Once the theme has been unpacked into the .themes directory it will be listed in the available themes window the next time you start the GNOME Control Center.

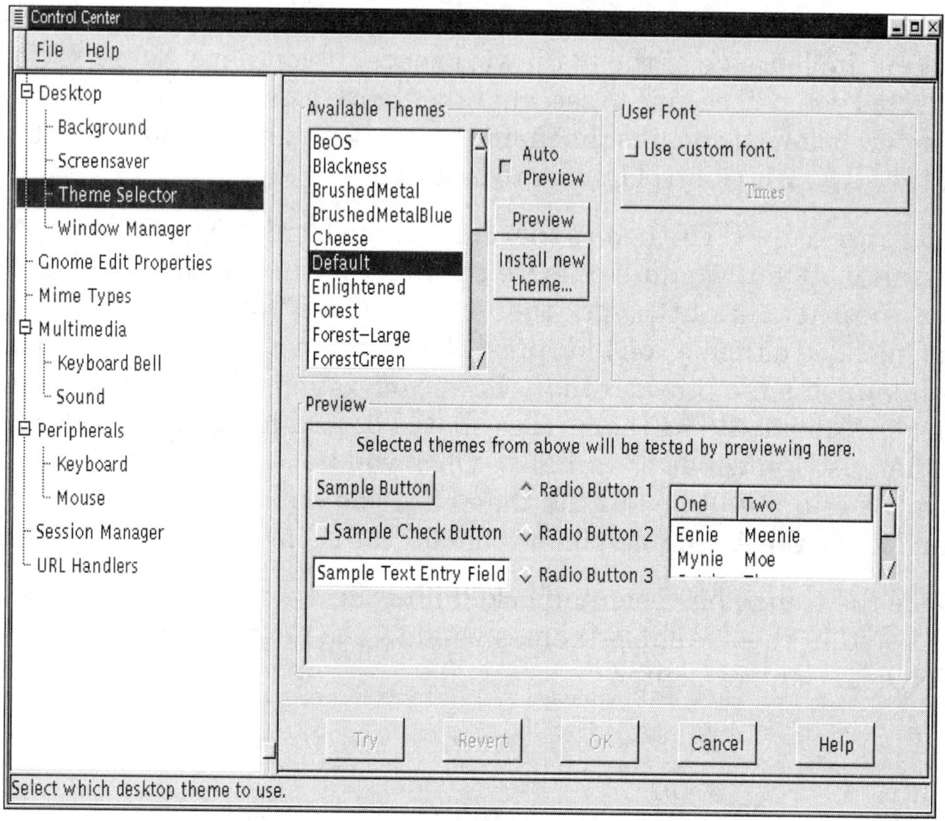

Figure 10-4: The Theme Selector Capplet

If you would like to change the font used in the current theme you may do so by selecting the Use custom font checkbox and selecting the font from the font button below it. This will bring up a font selection dialog which allows you to specify the font, its style, and size.

Window Manager Capplet

Because GNOME is not dependent on any one window manager this capplet allows you to select which window manager you wish to use. The Window Manager capplet does not determine which window managers you have available but allows you to define what, and where they are.

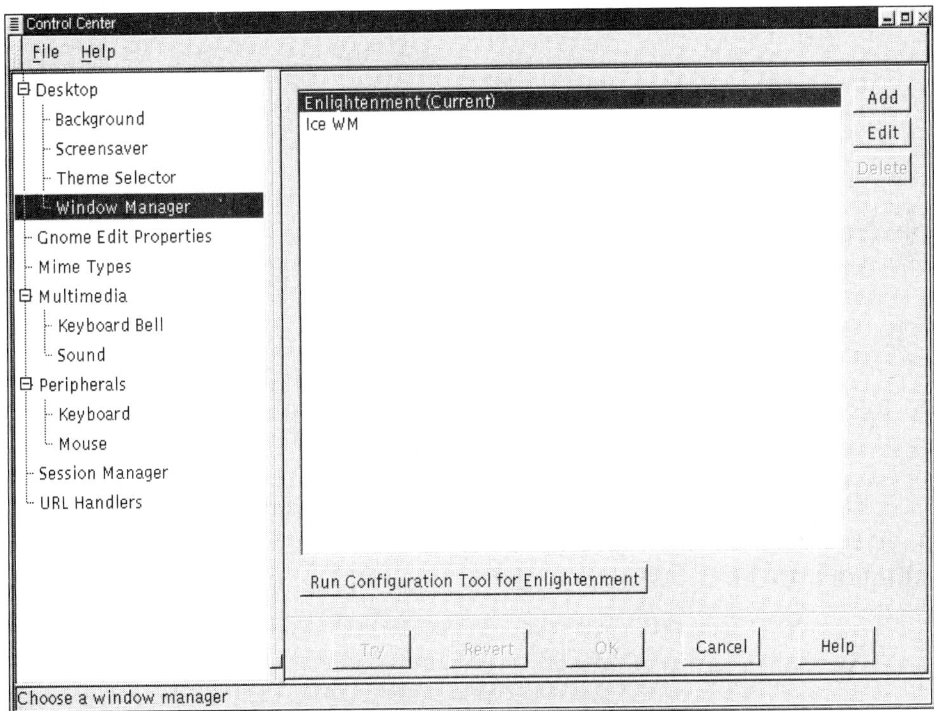

Figure 10-5: Window Manager Capplet

The Window Manager capplet has a main list of the window managers that you can currently select from. Whichever window manager is active is notated by the word "Current".

If you wish to add a new window manager to the main list you may press the Add button. This will launch the Add New Window Manager dialog.

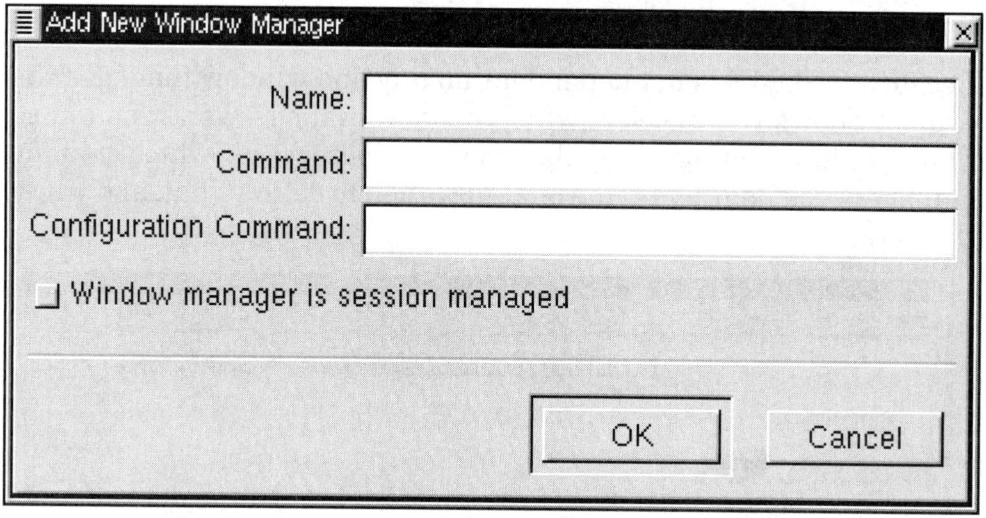

Figure 10-6: Add New Window Manager

In the Add New Window Manager you may specify the name you wish to give the window manager, the command to launch that window manager, and the command to launch any configuration tool that might be available for that window manager.

If you know that the window manager is fully GNOME-compliant and can be session managed you may select the Window manager is session managed button. If you are unsure you should check the documentation of your window manager.

Press OK when you are done.

Once you have finished adding your new window manager you will see it appear in the main list of window managers. If you need to change any of the properties you set in the Add New Window Manager dialog you may select the window manager from the main list with your mouse and press the Edit button.

You may also delete any window manager in the main list by selecting it with your mouse and pressing the Delete button.

If you are ready to switch the current window manager you may select the manager you wish to run from the main list and press the Try button. If you would like to run the configuration tool before or after you switch, make sure the manager you want to configure is selected and press the Run Configuration Tool for [window manager name] button.

GNOME Edit Properties

The GNOME Edit Properties Capplet allows you to select which editor will be your default editor while using GNOME. This will allow applications like the GNOME File Manager to launch the correct editor when you try to open files associated with editing. All popular editors available are included in the selection list. This Capplet is very similar to the Mime Type Capplet but is used in association with certain applications.

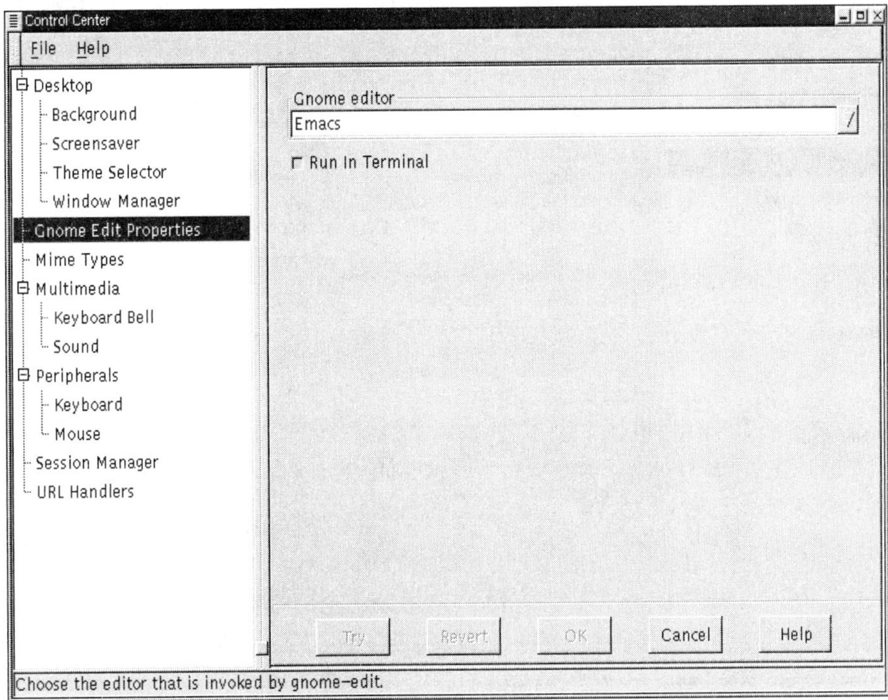

Figure 10-7: The GNOME Edit Properties

GNOME Mime Types

The GNOME Mime Types Capplet allows you to determine how you wish to handle certain file types, or Mime types. Mime stands for Multipurpose Internet Mail Extensions and was originally developed to allow e-mail to carry various forms of data. In GNOME you can define certain Mime types to be handled in any manner you wish. For example, if you use .sgml files frequently and you wish to always use Emacs to edit them you can configure the .sgml Mime type to always be handled by Emacs. This means that any program that wishes to launch the mime type for you will bring up Emacs. This includes double clicking on the file type in the GNOME File Manager.

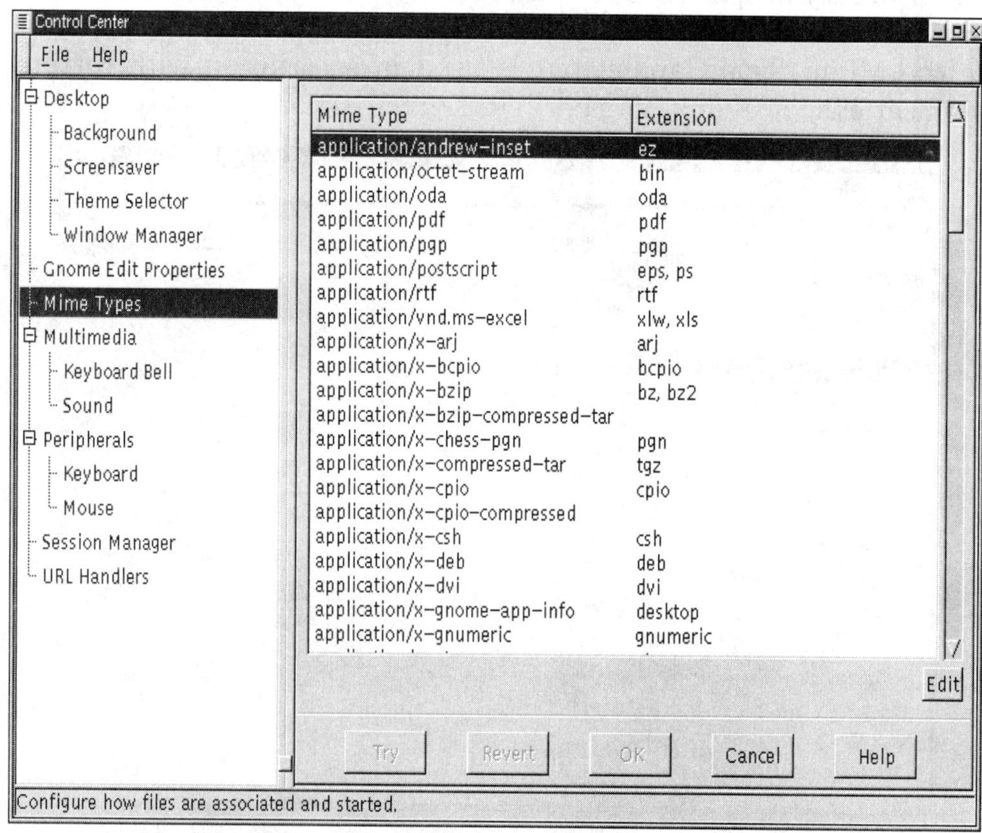

Figure 10-8: The GNOME Mime Types

To add a new mime type press the Add button. This will display the Add New Mime Type dialog in which you may define the new Mime type.

To edit an existing Mime type you may select the Mime type with your mouse cursor and press the Edit button. This will bring up the Set Actions for... dialog. You may define the icon used for the Mime type, the Open action, the View action and the Edit action.

Multimedia Capplets

Keyboard Bell

The Keyboard Bell capplet allows you to change the bell sound which is produced by your CPU speaker when a keyboard error or message is sent.

Volume changes the actual volume of the bell.

The pitch slider will change the pitch of the note that is played. By default it is set to 440Hz, or the A above middle C.

Duration changes the length of time the tone is played.

The Test button will allow you to hear the current settings of your keyboard bell.

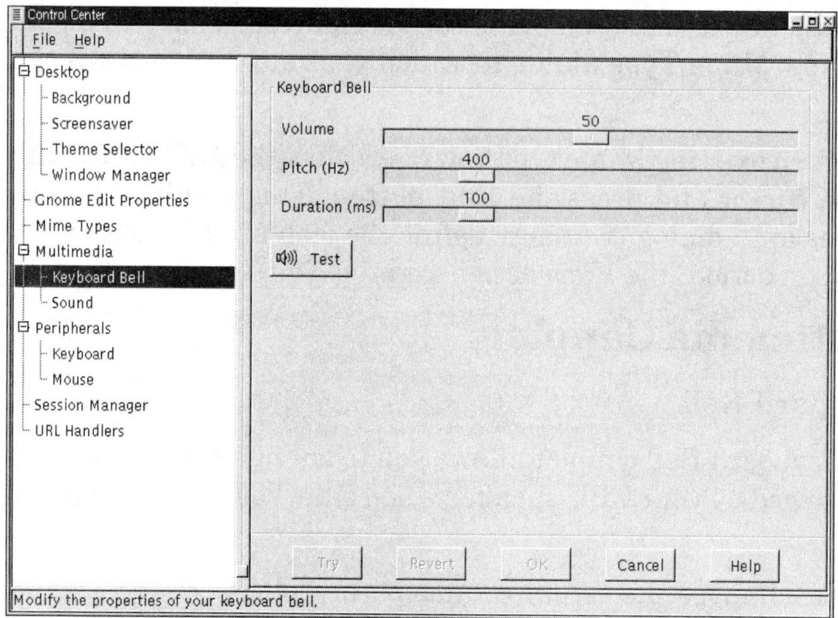

Figure 10-9: The Keyboard Bell Capplet

The Sound Capplet

The Sound capplet allows you to set the system sounds for your GNOME session. There are two tabs to select in the sound capplet: General and Sound Events.

- **General Tab** - At this point you have two options to choose from in the General tab, enabling sound for GNOME and for events. If you select **Enable Sound for GNOME** you will make sure that GNOME's sound engine (ESD) will be launched every session of GNOME you run. **Enable sound for events** will launch any sound files you have set in the **Sound Events** tab when those events occur. With these two items enabled you will utilize GNOME's session management which will remember your sound settings whenever you log in or out.

- **Sound Events Tab** - This tab allows you to navigate through the sound events in GNOME and change their sounds.

To change a sound associated with a GNOME event select the event in the hierarchical list on the left and press the Browse button to find a sound file on your system that you wish to associate with that event.

Once you have found a sound file you may press the Play button to test the sound and see if you like it enough to hear it every time the event occurs.

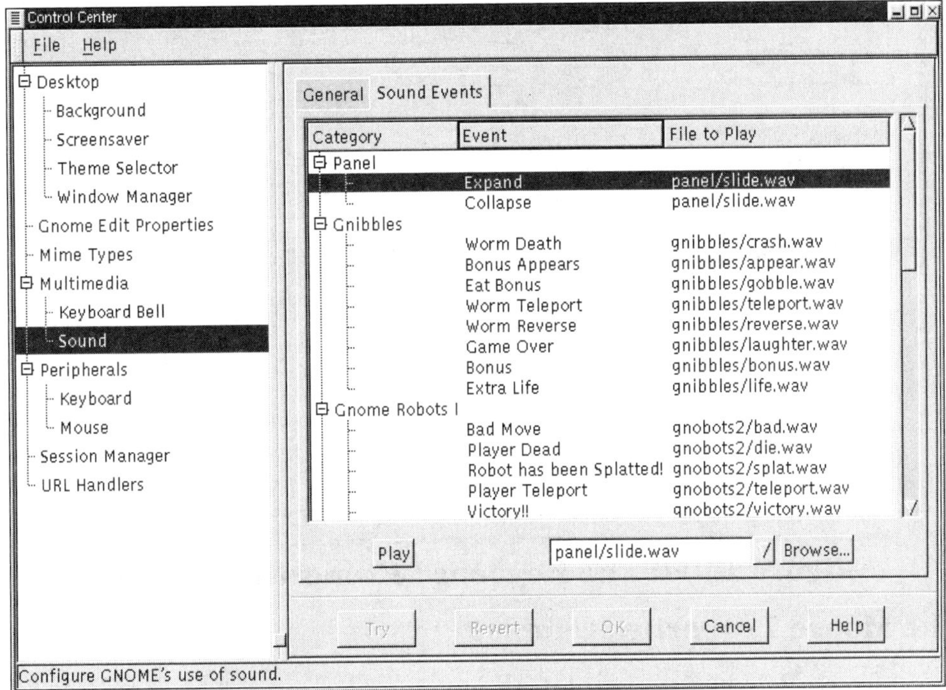

Figure 10-10: The Sound Properties Capplet

Peripherals

The capplets in this section of the Control Center will help you configure hardware input devices including keyboard, and mouse properties.

The Keyboard Properties Capplet

There are currently two settings for the keyboard in this capplet. You may change the properties of Auto-repeat and the Keyboard Click.

Auto-repeat enables you to hold a key down and have it repeat the character at the rate and delay you set in this capplet. Keyboard Click enables a small click sound to play at each key press.

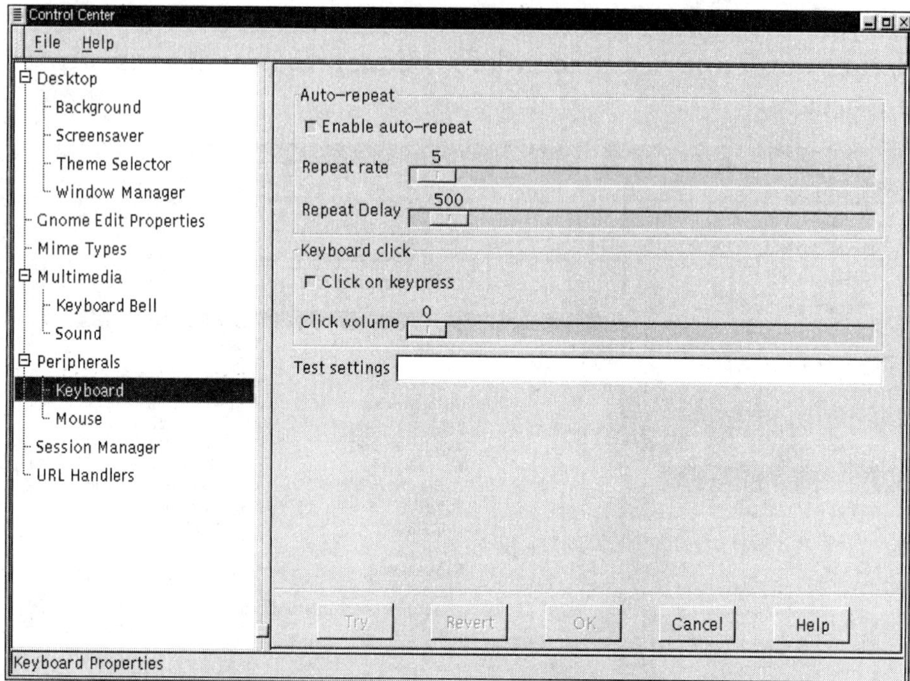

Figure 10-11: The Keyboard Properties Capplet

The Mouse Properties Capplet

The Mouse Properties capplet allows you to change between left and right handed mouse buttons and define the Accelerations and Threshold properties.

The Accelerations setting allows you to change the speed the mouse moves across the screen in relation to the movement of the mouse on your mouse pad. The Threshold setting allows you to set the speed at which you have to move your mouse before it starts the acceleration speed you have defined in the Acceleration setting.

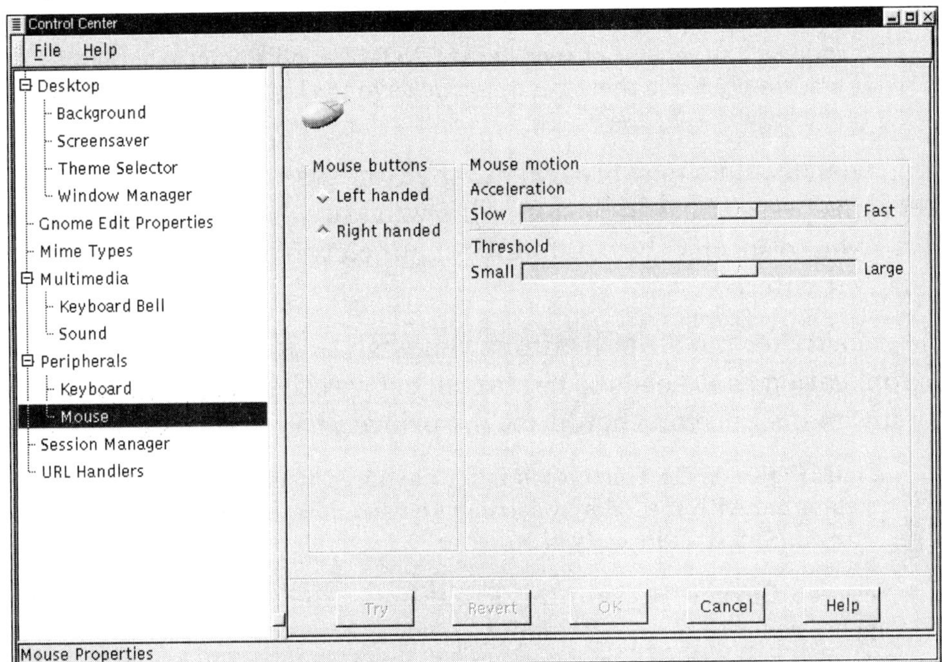

Figure 10-12: The Mouse Properties Capplet

Session Manager

The Session Manager Capplet allows you to control the GNOME Session Management. This includes which programs start up, how you save your GNOME configuration, and how you log out. You can find out more information about Session Management in Chapter 11.

- **Prompt on logout** - This first option allows you to disable the prompt when logging out.
- **Automatically save changes to session** - This will make the Session Management always save changes made to your GNOME session when you log out.
- **Non-session-managed Startup Programs** - This allows you to start non-session managed applications whenever you start a GNOME session.

> **NOTE:** Programs that are not GNOME-compliant are not session managed so you do not need to put GNOME applications in here, you can simply leave them running and save the current session when you log out.

If you wish to add a new program to the Non-session-managed Startup Programs press the Add button. This will launch a simple dialog that allows you to specify the command to launch the application and what priority it will receive.

The priority for most applications you wish to start is 50. If you have an application that needs to be started before other applications, like a window manager, you should set the priority to a lower number.

> **IMPORTANT:** This option is for advanced users. Unless you are familiar with the Priority settings you should keep you applications running with a Priority of 50.

- **Browse Currently Running Programs** - This allows you to see what applications are currently running. You may shut down those applications if you wish to and those applications will be removed from your GNOME session. The applications in this list are mostly higher level applications and should not be shut down. However, if there are parts of GNOME that you do not wish to have like the Panel, this is where you would shut it down for now and your next GNOME Session.

> **IMPORTANT:** This option is for advanced users only. You should not shut down applications you may wish to use the next time you log in to GNOME with this tool.

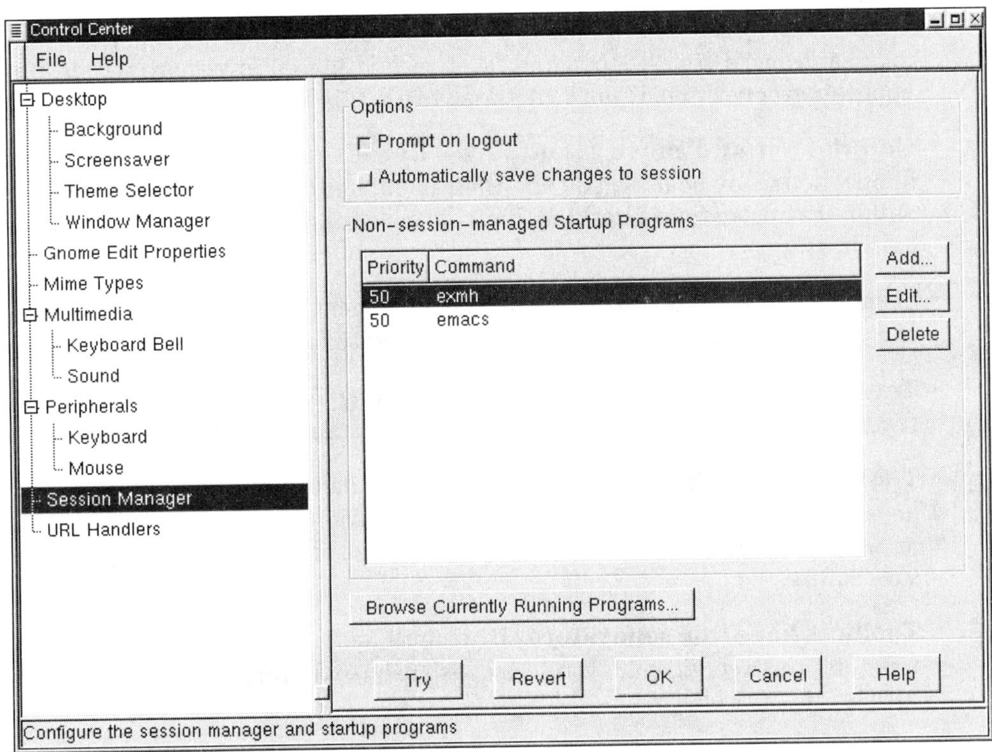

Figure 10-13: The Session Manager Capplet

User Interface Options

The User Interface Options allows you to change the appearance of applications that are GNOME-compliant. You may recognize these applications as ones that are pre-installed with GNOME or ones that say they are built with GTK (the GIMP Toolkit).

Application Defaults

The Application Defaults capplet allow you to change certain user interface aspects of your GNOME-compliant applications.

> **IMPORTANT:** Although this capplet gives you great control over the look and feel of your applications you should consider these tools for advanced use only.

- **Can detach and move toolbars** - By default toolbars in GNOME applications may be dragged from their usual location and placed anywhere within the application or desktop. If you do not wish to use this feature you may turn it off.
- **Can detach and move menubars** - By default menubars in GNOME applications may be dragged from their usual location and placed anywhere within the application or desktop. If you do not wish to use this feature you may turn it off.
- **Menubars have relieved borders** - By default menubars have relieved borders. If you do not like this look you may turn this feature off.
- **Toolbars have relieved borders** - By default toolbars have relieved borders. If you do not like this look you may turn this feature off.
- **Toolbar buttons have relieved borders** - By default toolbar buttons do not have relieved borders in their natural state. They do, however, change when the mouse is over them. If you wish them to be relieved at all times you may turn on this feature.
- **Toolbars have line separators** - By default toolbar buttons have small line separators between them. If you so not wish to have the line separators you may turn this feature off.
- **Toolbars have text labels** - By default toolbar buttons have images and text to identify them. If you are familiar with the buttons and do not need the text you may turn on this feature.
- **Statusbar in interactive when possible** - Some applications can have the status bar at the bottom become separated into its own window. If you would like to have those applications separate the status bar into another window you may turn on this option.
- **Statusbar progress meter on right** - Some applications have progress meters in their statusbars. By default these progress meters are on the right side of the statusbar. If you wish them to be on the left you may turn off this feature.
- **Dialog buttons have icons** - Some dialog buttons (for example "OK") can have icons on them. By default the applications which provide this have the icons turned on. If you wish not to see them you may turn off this feature.
- **Menu items have icons** - Some menu items in applications will have icons. If you wish not to see these icons in applications that use them you may turn off this feature.

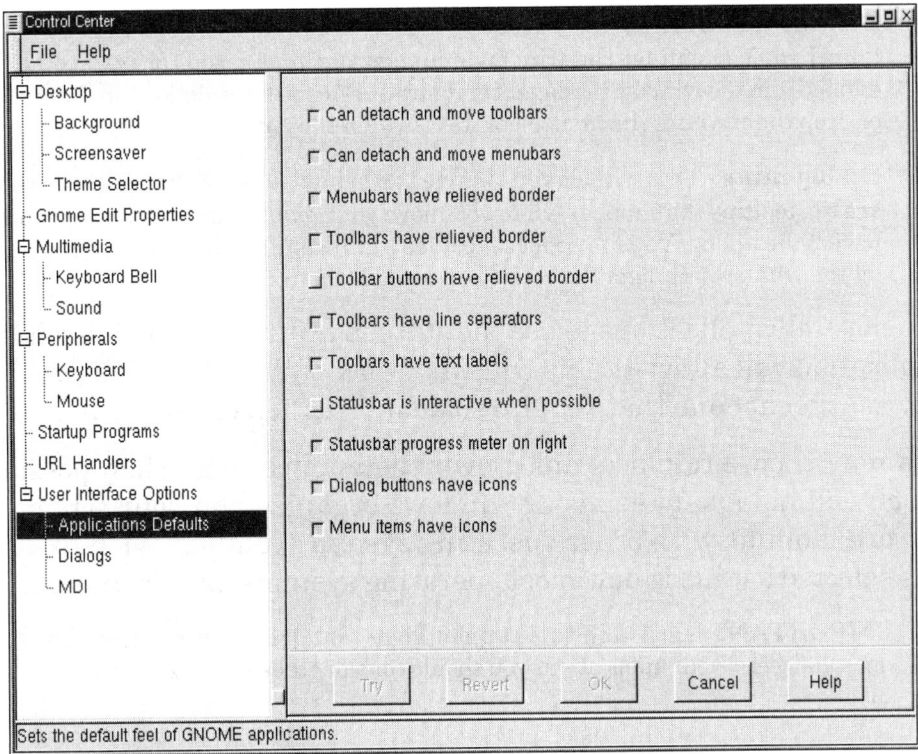

Figure 10-14: Applications Defaults Capplet

Dialogs

The Dialogs Capplet will allow you to change the default settings for dialog boxes in GNOME compliant applications. A dialog box is a window that is launched by an application to help perform a task needed by that application. An example of a dialog box is a Print dialog which appears when you press a print button. The dialog allows you to set print options and start the print process. The Dialogs capplet will allow you to change the following options:

- **Dialog buttons** - Choose to use the default buttons, buttons more spread out, put buttons on the edges, put the buttons on the left with left-justify, and put buttons on the right with right-justify.

- **Default position** - This will let you choose how the dialogs appear when launched. You can let the window manager decide for you (or how you have defined it in the window manager configuration), center the dialogs on the screen, or drop them where the mouse pointer is when they are launched.
- **Dialog hints** - This will let you change the behavior of the dialog hints which are the tooltips that appear when you move your mouse button over a button or part of the dialog. You may choose to have hints handled like other windows, or let the window manager decide how to display them.

You may tell applications to use the statusbar instead of a dialog if the application will allow it. This will only work with dialogs that provide information not one that require some interaction on your part.

You may choose to place dialog over the applications when possible which will help you keep your windows organized on your screen. If you are familiar with other operating systems you may wish to keep this selected as this is how most operating systems handle dialogs.

> **IMPORTANT:** Although this capplet gives you great control over the look and feel of your applications you should consider these tools for advanced use only.

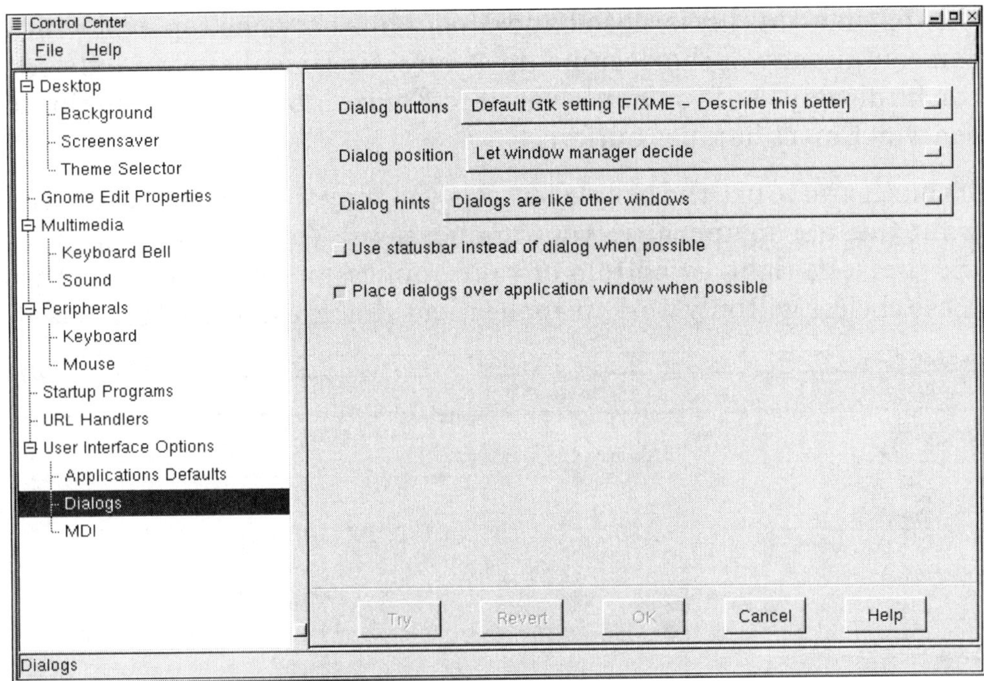

Figure 10-15: Dialog Capplet

MDI

The MDI capplet allows you to change the MDI mode for GNOME applications. MDI stands for Multiple Document Interface and refers to the how more than one document is displayed in GNOME applications.

> **IMPORTANT:** Although this capplet gives you great control over the look and feel of your applications you should consider these tools for advanced use only.

The default style in GNOME-compliant applications for MDI is usually tabs or "notebooks". If you do not like the tab look you may change it here.

In addition to Notebook, you will find, Toplevel and Modal. Notebook is the default tab look, Toplevel displays only the active document on the top view until it is closed and Modal has only one toplevel which can contain any of the documents at any one time, however only one can be displayed. If you have ever used Emacs Modal is very similar to the way Emacs handles buffers.

If you choose to use the Notebook style you may then decide where you want the tabs to appear in your applications. You may have them at the top, left, right, or bottom of your application. Keep in mind that these choices will only work in applications that are GNOME compliant.

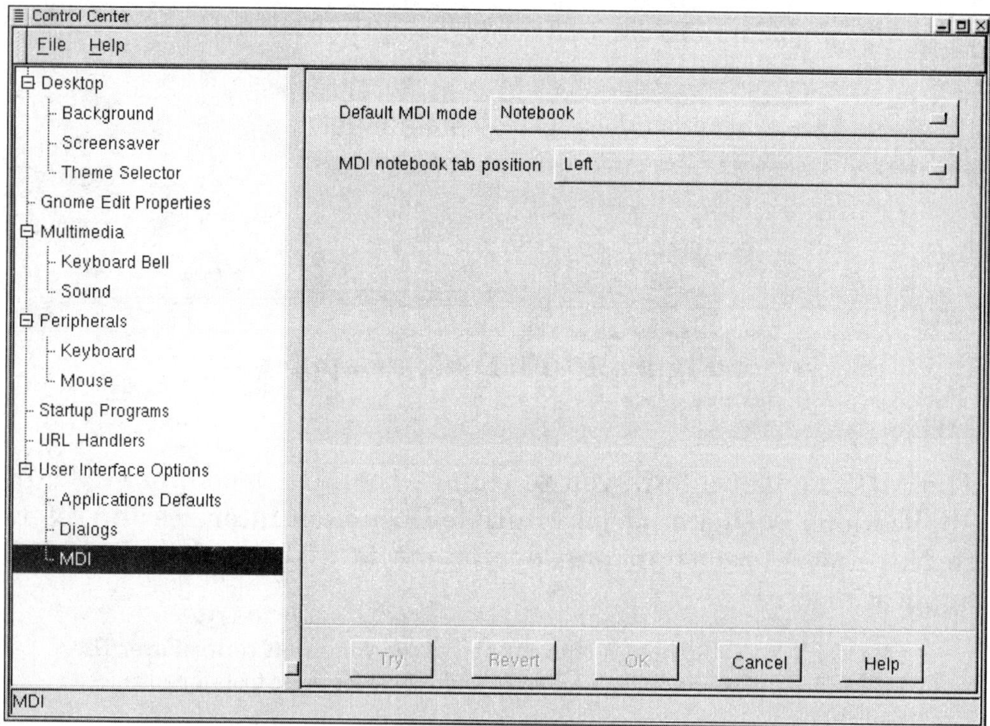

Figure 10-16: MDI Capplet

11 A Word About Session Management

Introduction

You might have seen a little bit about session management when you read about GNOME. Session management can be a very useful tool for you in your use of GNOME and GNOME applications.

The main idea of session management is that your work will be saved whenever you log out of GNOME. Your GNOME "Session" is currently saved when you log out, however you may not notice all that it can do.

Probably one of the most useful features of session management is the ability to start applications you had open when you logged out of GNOME. This is easily demonstrated as you exit GNOME and enter again. You will see your applications re-appear in the same location on your desktop as they were when you logged out.

If there are certain applications you wish to start up whenever you log in, even if they were not open the last time your session was saved, you may add them to the Session Manager Capplet which you can read about in the section called *Session Manager* in Chapter 10.

> **IMPORTANT:** If you have heard about application data being session managed you have heard about the future of GNOME. For application data to be saved correctly you must be using a fully compliant GNOME application. At the time of publication of this manual there were not any applications that offer full session management for your data, so until there are some and you are aware of its capabilities you should not rely on session management to save your application data.

Resetting the GNOME Session

One advanced feature of the GNOME Session Manager is the ability to recover a "clean session" if anything goes wrong for you. To do this you must hold down the **CTRL** and **SHIFT** keys together when you log in to GNOME.

This will bring up a dialog box which gives you two different options for restoring your GNOME Session.

The first option is to Start with default programs. This option will remove all of the session configuration setting in respect to applications. This will only erase the GNOME session data for applications you had running when you logged out last, it will not change any information you may have set in the Session Manager Capplet in the GNOME Control Center.

The second option is to Reset all user settings. This will reset all GNOME application and core configuration data. This option will destroy any configurations you have made to the Panel, the GNOME File Manager, the Session Manager Capplet, and any GNOME application. This option will not remove files on your desktop.

> **IMPORTANT:** These options are for advanced users and should only be used in case there is a problem with your GNOME Session. You can lose data for many applications if you utilize the functionality provided by these options.

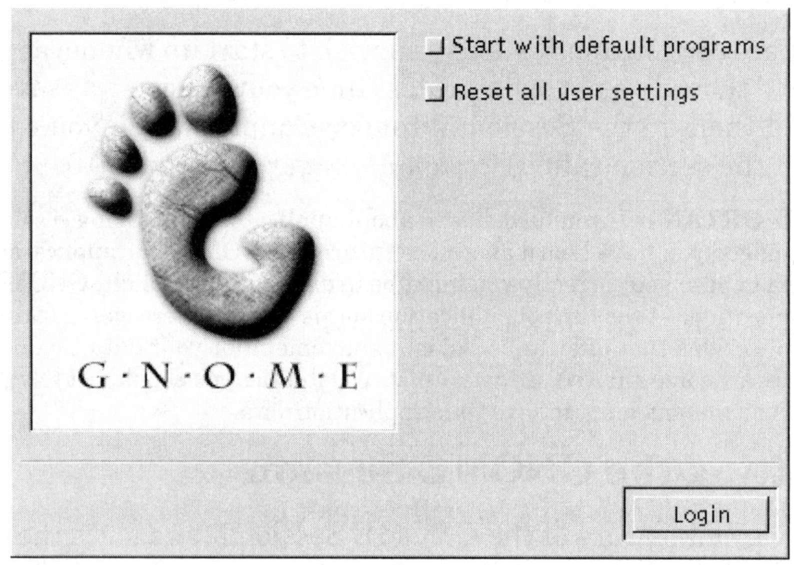

Figure 11-1: Login Screen for Resetting GNOME Session

12 Panel Applets

Introduction

This section describes the GNOME applets that are available to add to the GNOME Panel. To access these applets right mouse click on the Panel and select **Add new applet** from the pop-up menu.

Amusements

The Amusement applets are applets that are designed to make your life more enriched by providing you with a complete waste of time and resources purely for your entertainment. If you find that valuable space in your brain has been filled with something an Amusement applet has taught you then the authors of that applet have succeeded in their task.

Monitors

Monitor Applets are designed to be used to keep track of your system and its functions. You can monitor the resources left on your machine which allows you to keep close tabs on how things are working.

Battery Monitor

The Battery Monitor is a simple applet that allows you to see how much time you have remaining on your laptop monitor.

Battery Charge Monitor

The Battery Charge Monitor is used while you are charging the battery for you laptop. It will show you how much your battery has been charged and how much it has left to complete the task.

CPU/MEM Usage Monitor

The CPU/MEM Usage Monitor is an applet that will show you the current usage of CPU, Memory, and Swap Space. The applet consists of three bars that are shaded with colors to represent the usage. If you are running the applet on a horizontal panel the top bar is CPU, the middle bar is Memory, and the bottom bar is Swap Space. If you are running the applet on a vertical panel the CPU is the left bar, Memory is the middle bar, and Swap Space is the right bar.

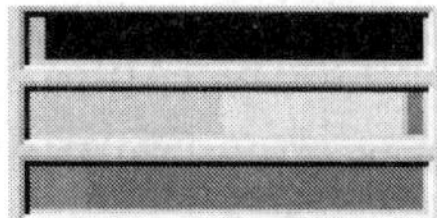

Figure 12-1: The CPU/MEM Applet

- **CPU** - The CPU bar will show the current CPU usage with one of three colors. The yellow shows the current hit by the current user. Grey shows the current hit by non-user specified system activity. Black show idle use.
- **MEMORY** - The Memory bar shows the current physical memory usage with one of four colors. The yellow shows the current shared memory usage. The grey-yellow shows other memory usage. The grey shows the buffers being used. The green shows free physical memory available on your system.
- **SWAP SPACE** - The Swap Space bar shows how much swap space is being used with a yellow bar. Any free swap space will be shown with a green bar.

CPULoad Applet

The CPULoad Applet is a simple graph that shows you the current CPU Usage using one of three colors:

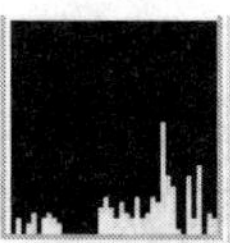

Figure 12-2: The CPULoad Applet

The yellow shows the current hit by the current user. Grey shows the current hit by non-user specified system activity. Black shows idle use.

MEMLoad Applet

The MEMLoad is a simple graph that shows you the current Memory usage using one of four colors:

Figure 12-3: The MEMLoad Applet

The yellow shows the current shared memory usage. The grey-yellow shows other memory usage. The grey shows the buffers being used. The green shows free physical memory available on your system.

SWAPLoad Applet

The SWAPLoad is a simple graph that shows you the current Swap Space usage using one of two colors:

Figure 12-4: The SWAPLoad Applet

The yellow bar shows how much swap space is currently being used. Any free swap space will be shown with a green bar.

Multimedia

The Multimedia Applets are a collection of applets that allow you to utilize multimedia on your system. You will find applets that control sound, video, and other multimedia.

CD Player Applet

The CD Player Applet is a simple CD player that resides in the panel.

When you have an audio CD in your CD-ROM drive you may use the Play/Pause, Stop, Forward, Backward and Eject buttons to control your CD for playback. Above the buttons is a small display that shows the time remaining on the track and in between the Forward and Backward buttons is the track number.

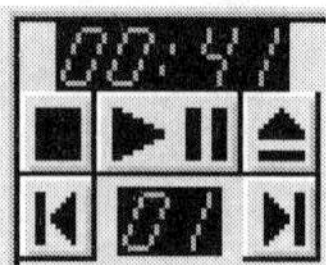

Figure 12-5: The CD Player Applet

IMPORTANT: You must have the correct access to your CD-ROM drive for this application to be successful. If you have the root password type the following in a terminal window:

```
$ su
$ Password: [type  in root password]
$ chmod a+r /dev/cdrom
$ exit
```

If your CDROM is located somewhere other than /dev/cdrom make sure you change it in the commands above.

If you want more control over your CD you may right mouse click on the CD Player Applet and select Run gtcd from the pop-up menu. This will launch the GNOME CD Player which you can read more about in Chapter 13.

IMPORTANT: When the CD Player Applet is running you will not have physical control over the eject button on your CD-ROM drive. If you wish to eject the CD you must use the Eject Button on the CD Player Applet.

Mixer Applet

The Mixer Applet is a simple applet that allows you to control the volume on your system. There are two main controls on the applet: the Volume Slidebar and the Mute button. To raise or lower the volume use the slide bar with your mouse. To mute your system press the small mute button on the bottom of the applet.

Figure 12-6: The Mixer Applet

If you want more control over your system volume you may right mouse click on the Mixer Applet and select the **Run gmix** menu item from the pop-up menu.

Network

Network applets are all applets that allow your work on a network or the internet to be monitored or enhanced. Network applets range from checking mail to monitoring the time you have spent on the internet.

MailCheck Applet

The Mailcheck applet will check mail on your system and let you know if there is some new mail waiting for you. At this point it will only check your local system mail. It will not query another server for your mail. To access the properties for the Mailcheck applet right mouse click on the applet and select the Properties menu item from the pop-up menu. The **Mail check properties** dialog box will appear and you may change the following properties. If you would like to execute a program before each update you may enter a command in the Execute text box. This can be useful if you want to run fetchmail to retrieve your mail from another server. You may also specify how often you check for mail and select which animation style you would like displayed in the applet.

PPP Dialer Applet

The PPP Dialer is an applet that will start your ppp connection. This is a simple applet that requires you to have a ppp connection set up properly on your system. Once you have your ppp connection configured properly you may press the On button (which displays play/ pause icons on it). This will launch your ppp connection.

WebControl Applet

The WebControl applet allows you to launch your web browser with the URL you indicate in the URL text box. If you would like to launch a new window instead of using the active one you may check the Launch new window checkbox. To clear the URL textbox, press the Clear button. To access the properties right mouse click on the WebControl applet and select the **Properties** menu item from the pop-up menu. The **Mail check properties** dialog box will appear and you can select whether you want to Display the URL text label and the launch new window options on your applet.

Utility

The Utility Applets are a set of general utilities to use in your work environment.

Clock Applet

The Clock applet is the only applet which is loaded by default when you install GNOME for the first time. To access the clock properties right mouse click on the clock and select the **Properties** menu item from the pop-up menu. The **Clock Properties** dialog box will appear allowing you to specify whether you would like 12 or 24 hour time to be displayed.

Printer Applet

The Printer Applet is represented by a small printer icon that lives on your Panel. If you drag a file to the Printer Applet it will print the file for you. To set up the Printer Applet right mouse click on it and select the **Properties** menu item from the pop-up menu. This will bring up the **Printer properties** dialog box. In this dialog you may specify a printer name and the Print Command. For most systems the Print Command will be **lpr**.

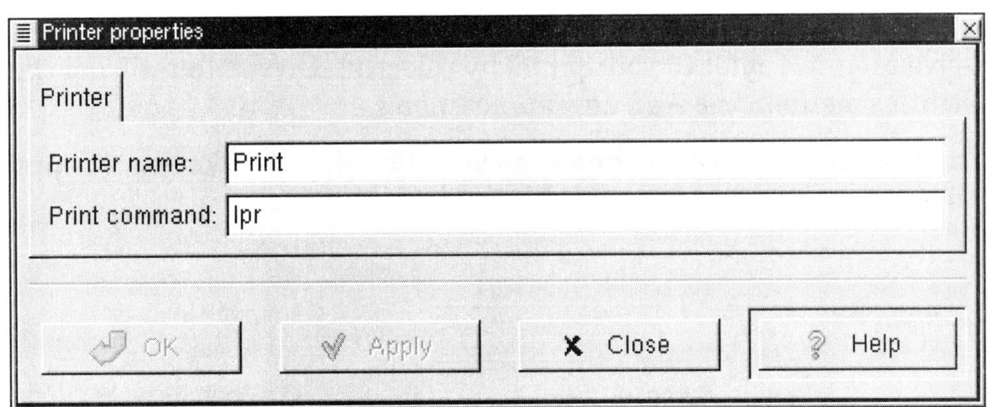

Figure 12-7: The Printer Applet Properties

Drive Mount Applet

On many Unix-like systems, after inserting a disk you must tell the computer to mount it in order to use that disk.

The Drive Mount Applet allows you or your systems administrator to mount a drive on your system by simply clicking the icon on your Panel. In order for this to work you will to have to set the drive you want to access as user mountable.

This can be done quite easily if you have *linuxconf* installed on your machine. Just select the drive you want to access in the Access local drive section. In the Options tab select the User Mountable option. Your drive will now be mountable by users.

If you do not have *linuxconf* you must edit your */etc/fstab* to include user access. This is done by adding user access to the drive. For example:

If your fstab file looks like this:

```
/dev/cdrom /mnt/cdrom iso9660 exec,dev,ro,noauto 0 0
```

Add "user" to the fourth column:

```
/dev/cdrom /mnt/cdrom iso9660 user,exec,dev,ro,noauto 0 0
```

Now that you can mount the drive without being root you may add the Drive Mount Applet to your panel by selecting Drive Mount from the Utilities menu in the Add new applet menu.

You will see a small drive image on your Panel that looks like a floppy drive.

Figure 12-8: The Drive Mount Applet

The Drive Mount applet will always default to access your floppy drive. You may change this by right mouse clicking on the applet and selecting the **Properties** item from the pop-up menu.

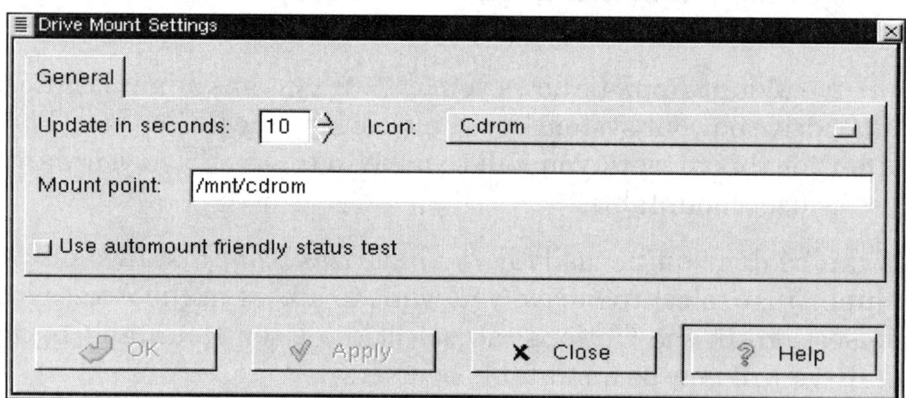

Figure 12-9: The Drive Mount Applet

The Drive Mount Settings dialog allows you to define which drive you want to mount and where it is located.

The first option is how many seconds you wish to have before the applet updates. This will check the drive to make sure it is still mounted (in case it was unmounted by other means) and will display the applet correctly.

The second option you have is which icon to be displayed. You have a choice of four icons, Floppy, CDROM, Zip Disk, and Hard Drive. After you have selected the icon you must put the correct mount point for the drive in the Mount point text box.

The last option to set in the Drive Mount Settings is whether or not you wish to Use automount friendly status test If you are using a system that utilizes autofs to auto-mount your drives the Drive Mount applet might interfere with autofs. If this is the case you should select this option. If you are not using autofs (which is most likely the case) do not select this option as it is taxing on your system and is much slower.

GNOME Pager

The GNOME Pager is an applet that will show you all of your virtual desktops and the applications within them. There are two main areas on the GNOME Pager, the Desktops view and the Applications view. In the Desktops view all of your desktops will be represented as a small rectangle. If there are any applications on the desktops, they will show up as small outlines according to their position on the desktop. The Applications view will show you the applications on your active desktop in a list view. If you press the button in the middle that contains the arrow it will show you a view of all desktops and list the applications that are currently on them.

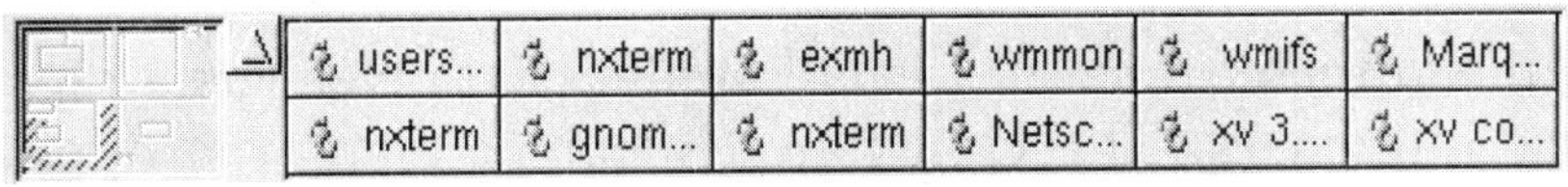

Figure 12-10: The GNOME Pager

> **NOTE:** If windows "disappear" from your screen when you iconify them, just add a GNOME Pager to your Panel.

You may access the GNOME Pager properties dialog with a right mouse click on the Pager and select the **Properties** menu item from the pop-up menu. On the left side of the GNOME Pager properties you may adjust: the maximum width of the task list, the number of rows in the task list, the number of columns in the task list and the number of rows in the pager. On the right side of the GNOME Pager properties you may turn on and off certain views on the Pager including: a view of all applications on all desktops, the tasks list, and the Pager view. You may also choose to use small pagers and include icons in the task list.

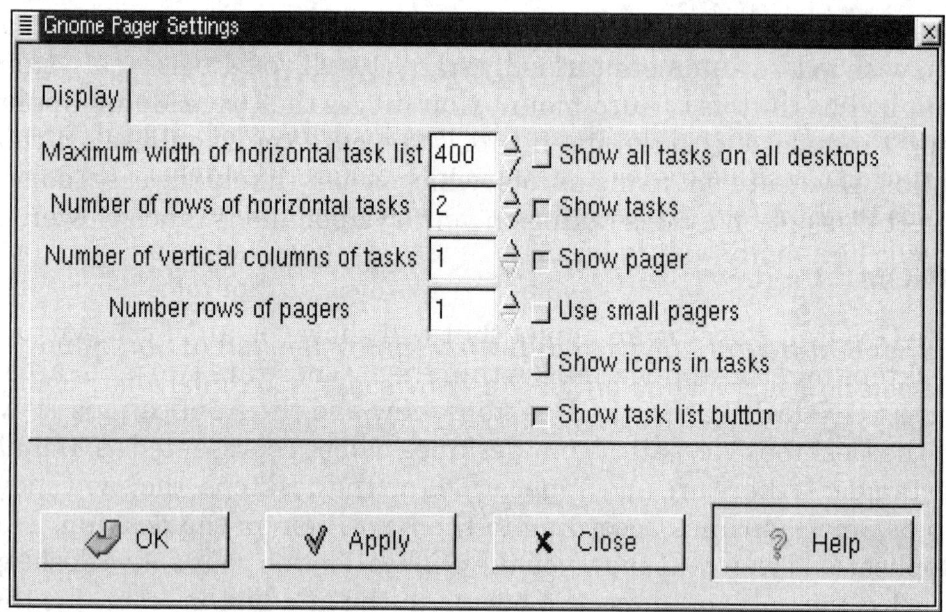

Figure 12-11: The GNOME Pager Properties

Quicklaunch Applet

The Quicklaunch Applet is a small applet that gives you a repository to place launchers. The Quicklaunch applet holds the application launchers you wish to have and allows you to click on them to launch the applications. Drag and drop functionality makes the setup of the Quicklaunch applet very easy and quick.

Figure 12-12: The Quicklaunch Applet

To add a launcher to the Quicklaunch applet you must already have the launcher set up in either the Main Menu or on your desktop. Once you have the launcher you may drag it onto the Quicklaunch applet to create a small launcher button. To launch the application simply press the launcher button.

To drag a launcher from you Main Menu click once on the menu to open it, and click once on the submenu to open it. With your left mouse button click and hold the application launcher and drag it to the Quicklaunch applet and release.

Once the launcher is in the Quicklaunch applet you may right mouse click on it and select **Properties** to change any properties associated with the launcher. The dialog that is launched is the standard GNOME launcher properties dialog which you can read more about in the section called *Adding Application Launchers* in Chapter 5.

13 GNOME CD Player

Introduction

The GNOME CD Player (gtcd) is a GNOME-enabled application which is preloaded with GNOME. This is a simple CD Player which allows you to listen to Compact Discs on your PC.

Using the GNOME CD Player

The GNOME CD Player will be available to you in the Main Menu in the Audio menu and can also be invoked in the command line with **$gtcd**.

Figure 13-1: The GNOME CD Player

IMPORTANT: You must have the correct access to your CD-ROM drive for this application to be successful. If you have the root password type the following in a terminal window:

```
$ su
$ Password: [type in root password]
$ chmod a+r /dev/cdrom
$ exit
```

If your CD-ROM is located somewhere other than **/dev/cdrom** make sure you change it in the commands above.

The GNOME CD Player works like any CD Player with common buttons such as Play, Stop, Pause, etc. Plus a track selector button which displays the track titles in a drop down menu. You have access to change various properties as well by pressing the Preferences button. This will bring up the GNOME CD Player Preferences dialog.

There are three tabs in the GNOME CD Player Preferences, Preferences, Keybindings, and CDDB Settings.

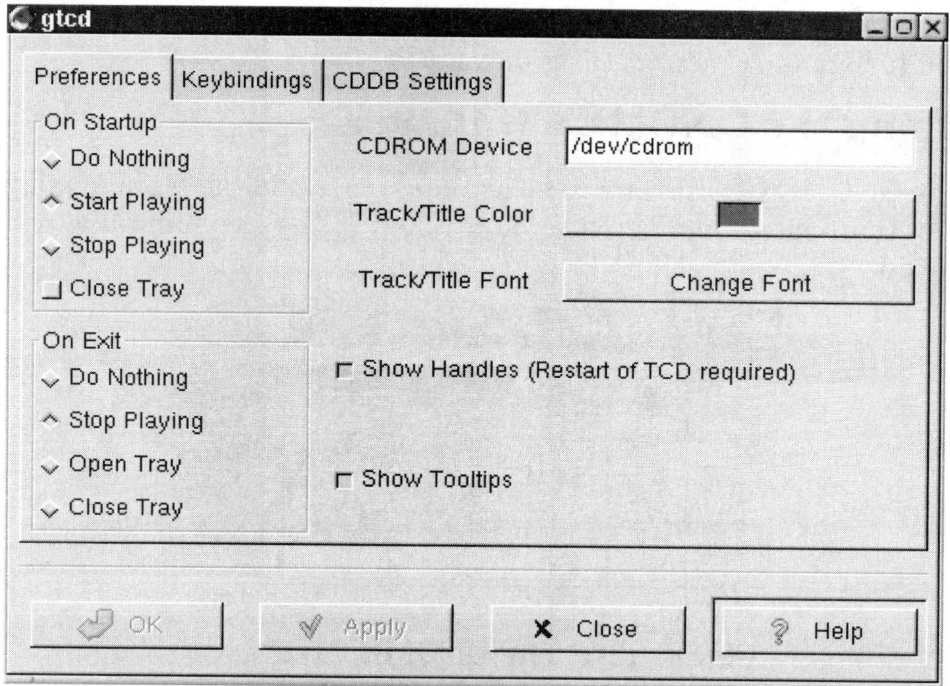

Figure 13-2: The GNOME CD Player Properties

- **Preferences Tab** - In this dialog you may specify:

  What you would like the GNOME CD Player to do when first started, and when exited.

  The location of your CD-ROM on your system. This is usually **/dev/cdrom**.

  The Color to display the Track and CD Title.

  The Font to display the Track and CD Title.

  Whether you would like handles on the title window which will allow you to drag the title window off the CD Player to float on the desktop.

Whether tooltips are enabled when your mouse is over the buttons.

- **Keybindings Tab** - In this tab you can change the keybindings associated with the GNOME CD Player. These keybindings allow you to use the Player without using your mouse. If you want to change one of the bindings select it with your mouse and type the new key in the **Click here to change** text box. Press Apply to save the changes
- **CDDB Settings Tab** - CDDB stands for CD Database and is a huge global database of CD information. Each CD has an identity which the CD Player can read. If you are connected to the Internet it will then search a CDDB server for that CD identity and return any information it has on it. This usually includes CD Title, Artist, and Track Titles. It can also include notes and lyric information. Once retrieved the GNOME CD Player will store the information on your hard drive for future access. In the CDDB Settings tab you can change the CDDB server and edit your local CDDB database. You can read more about CDDB by visiting the CDDB Website (*http://www.dccb.org*).

Another feature in the GNOME CD Player is the Track Editor. The track editor can be launched by the Track Editor button on the main GNOME CD Player window. The Track Editor allows you to edit the CD track information in case it is incorrect or there was no CDDB entry for your CD. You may also check the status of the CDDB information by pressing the CDDB Status button at the bottom of the Track Editor. This will show you what messages, if any, were returned from the CDDB server.

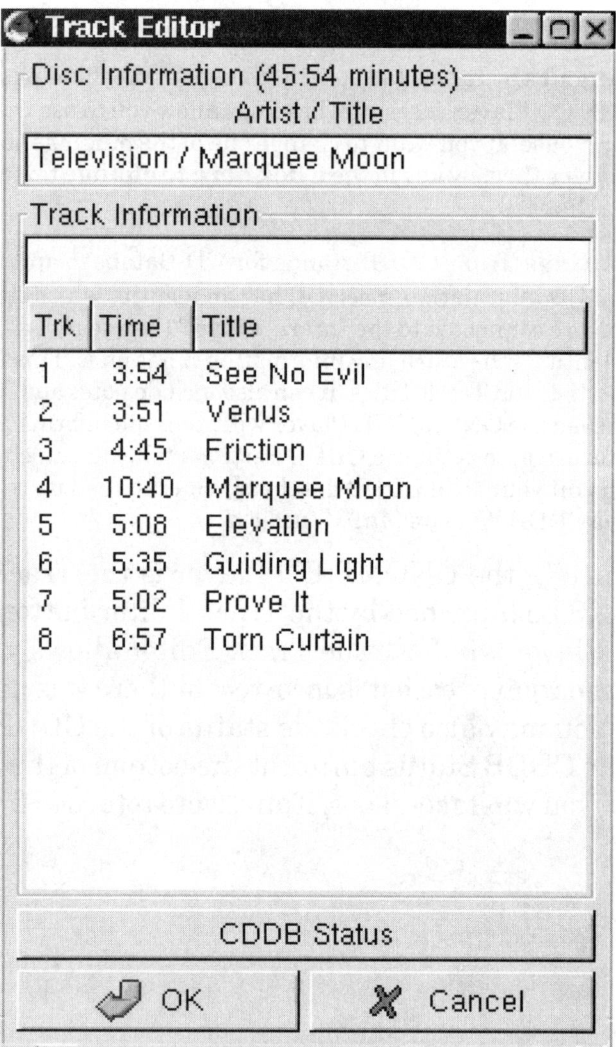

Figure 13-3: The GNOME CD Player Track Editor

14 The GNOME Calendar

Introduction

The GNOME Calendar is a simple calendar application which can be quite useful in your daily work. The Calendar, like the rest of GNOME, is in its infancy and while it is a very useful application, there will be some very impressive functionality that will come like network-shared calendar usage, and syncing capability with Palm Pilots and other hand held PDAs.

The Calendar is broken up into four main tabs: Day, Week, Month, and Year. Each view allows you to view the respective time period but will also allow you to schedule appointments from any one of the tabs.

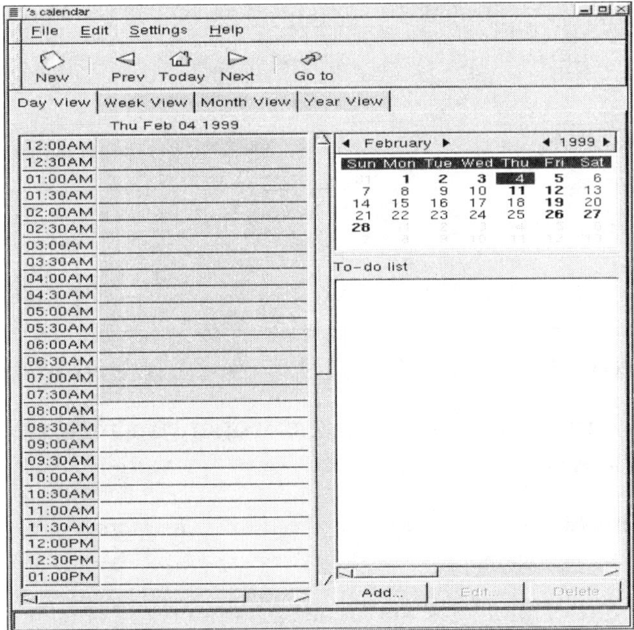

Figure 14-1: The GNOME Calendar

Setting Up the GNOME Calendar

The GNOME Calendar can be used in the state which it is shipped, but there are some tools available to make sure it is setup the way you would like it to be. The first place you should go is the GNOME Calendar Preferences. You can find the Preferences dialog by selecting the Preferences menu item from the File menu.

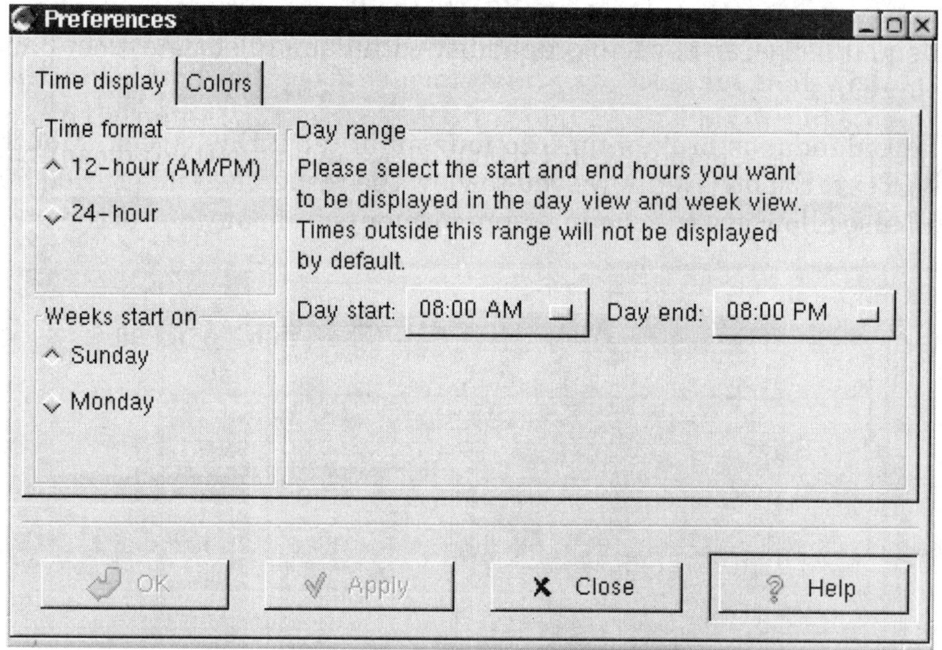

Figure 14-2: The GNOME Calendar Preferences

The Calendar Preferences dialog is broken up into two tabs, Time display and Colors.

- **Time** - This tab is broken up into three main sections: Time format, Weeks start on, and Day range.
- **Time format** - This allows you to choose between a 12 or 24 hour format clock.
- **Weeks start on** - This allows you to define what day your week will start on, Sunday or Monday. This will affect how the calendar is laid out in the Day and Week views.

- **Day range** - This section lets you choose what time your days will start and end. Any hours outside the range selected will not be displayed on your Day view.
- **Colors** - This tab allows you to change the default colors used in the Calendar. There are seven color choices you can customize: Outline, Headings, Empty days, Appointments, Highlighted day, Day numbers, and Current day's number. Each choice has a small color selector box next to it. When you press this box you will be given a color selector dialog in which you can choose the color you want. Once you have selected a color the small sample calendar on the right side of the tab will preview your choice.

Once you have made the changes to the Calendar Preferences you may press the Apply button to apply them.

Using the GNOME Calendar

Using the GNOME Calendar is quite simple and most tasks can be performed from any of the major views, Day, Week, Month or Year. Probably one of the most important features to remember is that at any time you may right mouse click on a particular day and add a new appointment. There are many other features which will be described below in each of the major views.

The Day View

The Day tab is probably the most useful view in the GNOME Calendar as it acts just as a day timer would. On the left of the tab is the hour listing for the current day. The light grey coloring in the hour list separates the work hours from the non-work hours. If you would like to change the work hours displayed in light grey you can do so in the section called *Setting Up the GNOME Calendar*.

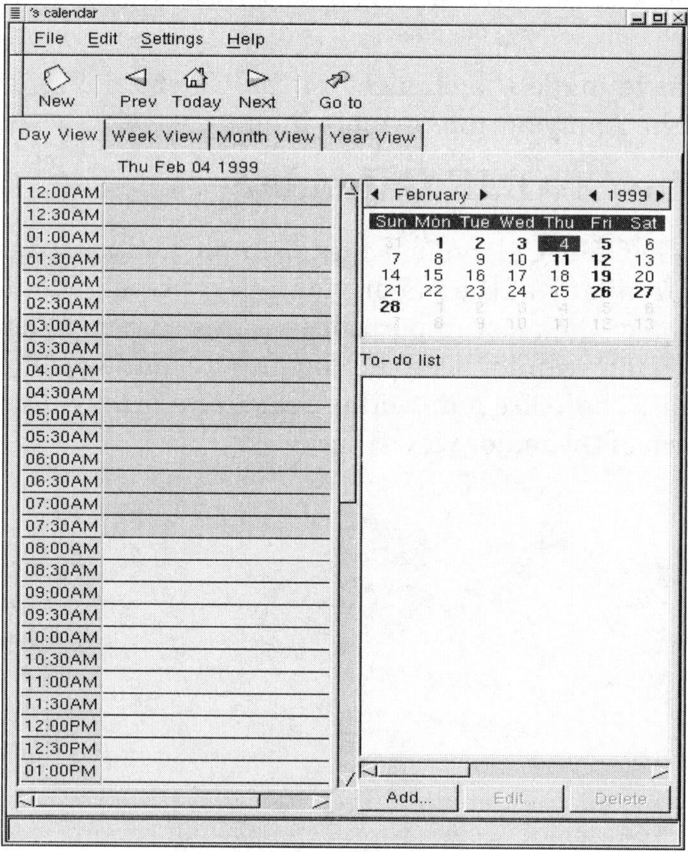

Figure 14-3: The Day View

> **TIP:** One tip for adding a new appointment in the Day View is to select a few hours in the hours list by clicking and dragging your mouse down the hours list. Once the correct range of time has been selected you may press Enter and type in the appointment. This will allow you to skip the Create New Appointment dialog.

Next to the hours listing in the right hand corner is a small full month calendar. You may change the month or year of the small month calendar by pressing the forward and backward arrows on the top. You may use the small month calendar to navigate the days as well. Double clicking on any day in the small month calendar will move the current day view to that particular day.

Below the small month calendar is your To-do list. The To-do list is a simple list where you can keep all your tasks on hand. To add an item to the To-do list press the Add button. This will launch a small editing box where you can type in the item. Once you have entered an item in the To-do list you may use the Edit and Delete to manage you items. The To-do items are available no matter which days are displayed in the Day View and can only be deleted with the Delete button.

The Week View

The Week View shows the current week with detailed descriptions of your appointments. If you would like to add an appointment any of the days in the week view you may right mouse click on the day and select the New appointment menu item from the pop-up menu. You may also use the week view to navigate to particular days in the Day View. Double-click on any day in the Week View and you will go to that day in the Day View.

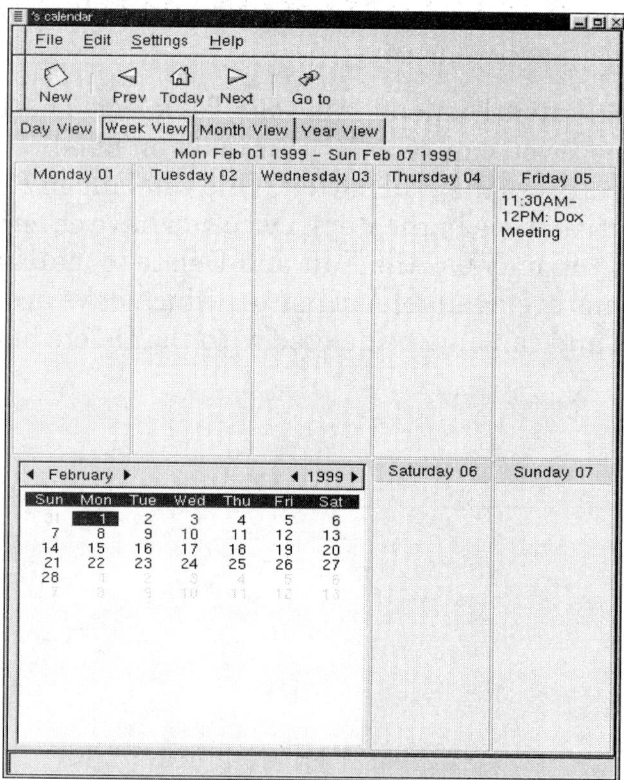

Figure 14-4: The Week View

In the lower left corner of the Week View there is a small month calendar. You may change the month or year of the small month calendar by pressing the forward and backward arrows on the top. You may use the small month calendar to navigate the days as well. Double clicking on any day in the small month calendar will move the current week view to that particular week.

The Month View

The Month View shows the entire month with brief detailed descriptions of your appointments. The Month View makes use of the customized colors available in the Calendar. You may read about how to set these colors in the section called *Setting Up the GNOME Calendar*. For any day with a brief description of an appointment you may click on the day to display a detailed description of the appointment in a pop-up window. If you would like to add an appointment to a day in the Month View you may right mouse click on any day and select the New Appointment in this day item from the pop-up menu. You may use the items in the pop-up menu to navigate in the Day, Week, and Year views by selecting either Jump to this day, Jump to this week, or Jump to this Year.

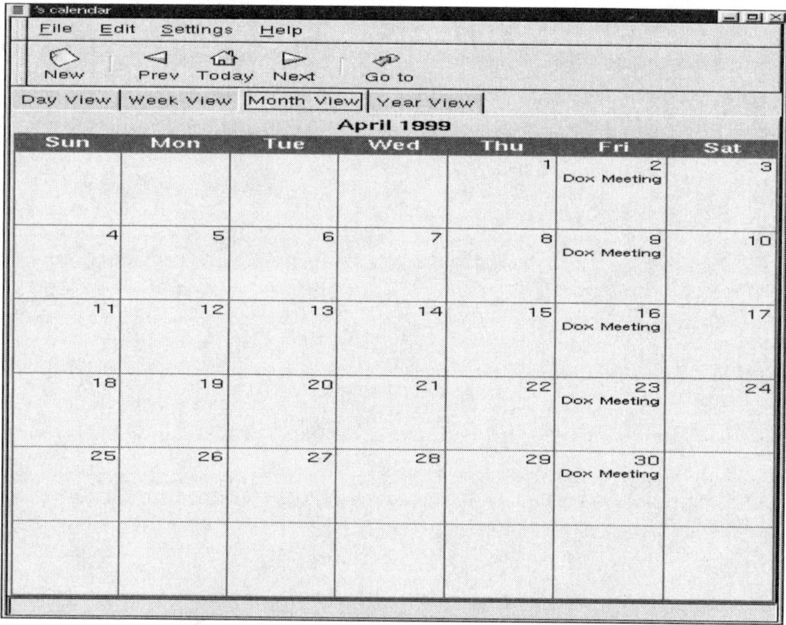

Figure 14-5: The Month View

The Year View

The Year View shows you the entire year with no descriptions of appointments. Like the Month View, the Year View makes use of the customized colors available in the Calendar. You may read about how to set these colors in the section called *Setting Up the GNOME Calendar*. If you have an appointment on a day you may click on that day and a description of the appointment will be displayed in the pop-up window. If you would like to add an appointment to a day in the Year View you may right mouse click on any day and select the New Appointment in this day item from the pop-up menu. You may use the items in the pop-up menu to navigate in the Day, Week, and Month views by selecting either Jump to this day, Jump to this week, or Jump to this Month.

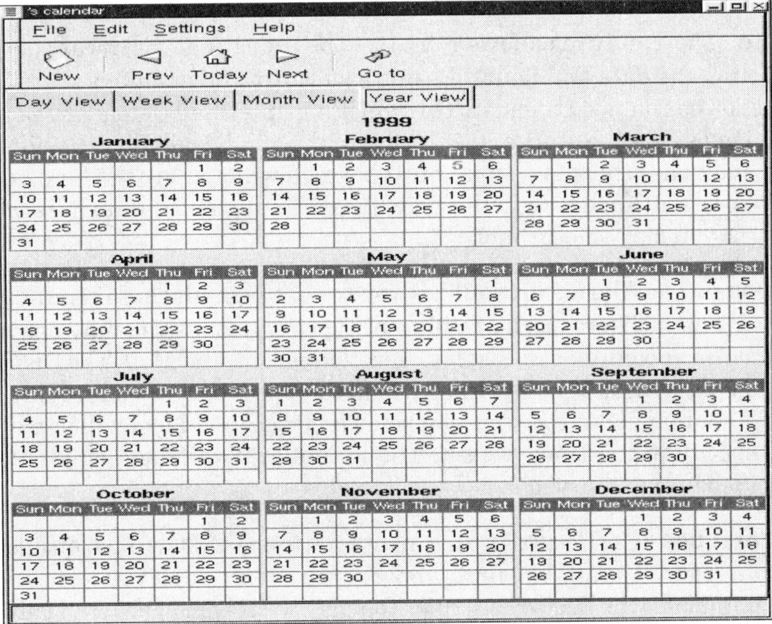

Figure 14-6: The Year View

Making a New Appointment

There are many methods for making a new appointment in the GNOME Calendar, the easiest by pressing the New button on the button bar. Whenever you make a new appointment you will launch the Create New Appointment dialog that allows you to set the properties of that appointment. The Create New Appointment dialog is broken into two different tabs, the General and the Recurrence tabs.

- **General** - The General tab is the area in which you define when the appointment is and set reminders for yourself. There are four different areas on the General tab: Summary, Time, Alarms, and Classification.
- **Summary** - The Summary box allows you to type a description of the appointment. Keep in mind that only a portion of this description will be available in the Week and Month Views.
- **Time** - The Time area allows you to set the time range for the appointment by selecting the date and hours. Beside each start and end days there is a small selection box named Calendar. This will bring up a small Calendar when pressed. You may select the start and end date in the small Calendar. Beside the start and end hours there is a small button which will display the hours of the day when pressed. Each hour in the list will have a submenu displaying each quarter hour so you may select them.
- **Alarms** - The Alarms area allows you to set up an alarm to remind you of an appointment. There are four different types of alarms you may use to remind yourself of appointments: Display, Audio, Program, and Mail. The Display alarm will display a message on your screen in the time you set. The Audio alarm will play an audio file in the time you set. The Program alarm will run a program you specify in the time you set. The Mail alarm will send email to the user specified in the time you set.
- **Recurrence** - The Recurrence tab allows you to specify how often an appointment should recur, if at all. The first property you should set if you want a recurring appointment is the Recurrence rule. You may choose among None, Daily, Weekly, Monthly, and Yearly. For each selection you may adjust the recurrence properties for your selection. In the Ending date area you may set a rule which will stop the recurrence of your appointment or allow it to repeat forever. In the Exceptions area you may make exceptions to the recurring appointment by selecting the date a pressing the Add button.

15 Welcome to Linux

Congratulations! As a new Red Hat Linux user, you've successfully installed one of today's most advanced computer operating systems. What began in 1991 as a hobby for a young Finnish student named Linus Torvalds has ballooned from a "hacker's darling" into an important tool for both home and business users. Just six years ago, there were an estimated 100,000 users. Today, about 12 million users worldwide depend on Linux to manage finances, use and control Internet services, create artwork and more. That number is rapidly growing; every day, new users are discovering the power and potential of Linux. This free, UNIX-like operating system is a multitasking, multi-user environment that has superior memory management, great security features, and more. In other words, power and, once you become more comfortable with Linux, ease of use.

- **Tip:** Linux is most frequently pronounced with the short "i" and the accent on the first syllable, as in "LIH-nucks".

What do you do next? Relax. In the chapters that follow, we hope to show you the basics of how to get the most out of your new system. If you're interested, we will also show you the roads to take which can lead you to becoming a Linux guru.

A Note About Conventions

At the time you installed your Red Hat Linux system, you were given the option of working entirely in a graphical environment, such as GNOME, or logging in from console mode, which is non-graphical.

If you're like many new Linux users, you're familiar with graphical environments such as Microsoft Windows, Apple Macintosh or IBM's OS/2.

So it's a fairly safe bet that you chose to work in a graphical environment when you installed Red Hat Linux 6.0.

You'll find plenty of opportunities to "point and click" on applications — either on your desktop or from the menu at the bottom of your desktop. But we're going to spend much of our time working from the "shell prompt."

Why? Because at the same time you accomplish tasks, you can learn a little more about how your Red Hat Linux system works.

- **Tip:** Unlike a graphical presentation, a "shell prompt" is the way you can type commands directly to the "shell." You need a shell to use Linux, because it's the tool you use to interact with your operating system. You'll find more information about your shell in Chapter 3.

Figure 15-1: The GNOME footprint on the panel

There are plenty of ways to get a shell prompt, depending on the kind of graphical environment you're using, such as GNOME. Depending on the environment chosen, just by right- or left-clicking in a blank space on your desktop, you'll see a reference to xterm.

By "dragging" your cursor over that item you will open a shell prompt window. Other times, you'll find you can get a shell prompt window through the menu on your desktop.

In addition to xterm, other references which will give you the shell prompt include:

- terminal emulator window
- GNOME terminal
- Color Xterm

We'll use GNOME as our example.

To begin, take your cursor to the GNOME footprint on the panel at the bottom of the desktop.

Now, left-click once on the footprint (see Figure 15-1), and a menu of "folders" will pop up. These folders represent categories of various software groups on our system. There are utilities, graphics programs, Internet applications and much more.

Once the menu pops up, "drag" the cursor to the **Utilities** section of the menu by holding down the mouse button while raising the mouse to the Utilities folder.

Once the cursor is over the folder, a new menu pops up to the right of the Utilities folder.

Here, in the first entries of this new submenu, there is a choice of terminal windows: `Regular xterm`, `Color xterm` and `GNOME terminal` (as shown in Figure 15-2). To get a shell prompt, position the cursor over the terminal window of your choice, and release the mouse button.

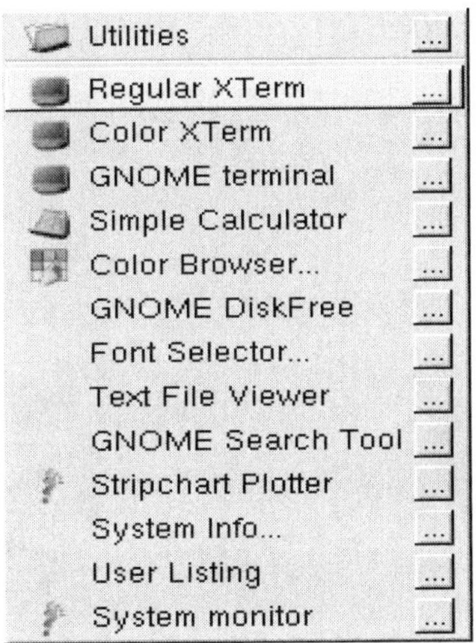

Figure 15-2: Shell prompt menus in Utilities

- **Tip:** Of the choices in the **Panel -> Utilities** menu, the GNOME terminal offers the ability to set background color and other preferences most easily.

Now, it's time to take your first steps.

The Root of the Matter

When your Red Hat Linux system starts, you'll see an array of messages speeding past you on the screen. Many of these messages simply tell you what services are starting on your computer.

- **Tip:** Want to read those startup messages more closely? At a shell prompt, type dmesg | more. You'll be able to read the file one screen at a time. To move forward, press the [Spacebar]; to quit, press [Q].

Finally, we'll come to "the login prompt" (as shown in Figure 15-3). You'll find:

```
Login:
Password:
```

At this point, some new users can easily feel rattled, but don't panic. Instead, think back: When you installed Red Hat Linux 6.0, you were asked for a *root password*.

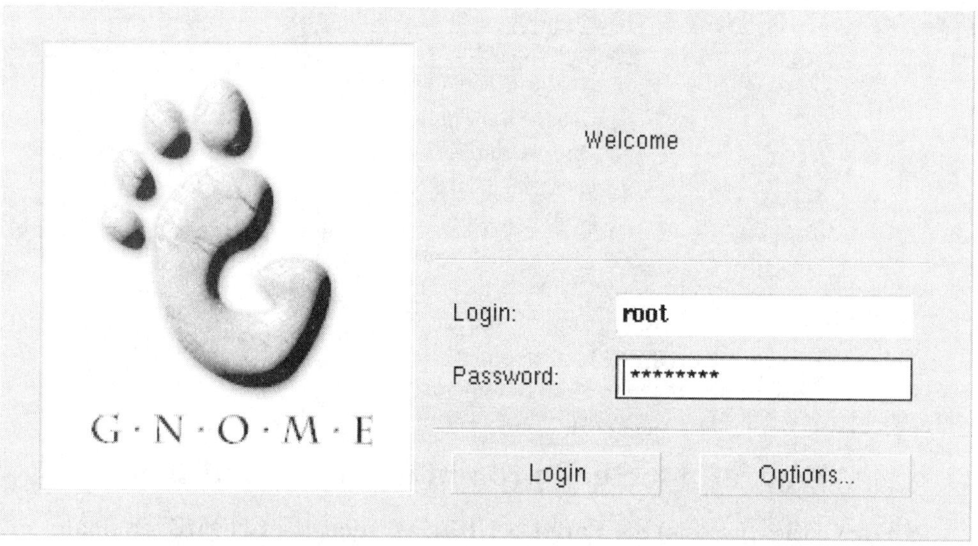

Figure 15-3: A sample screen of the graphical login prompt

In detail, that is the password you were asked to choose to log in to your root account. When you log in – either in the root account or other accounts – you're introducing yourself to the system. The root account, unlike all other accounts for your system, has access to everything. Also known as the superuser, the root account can control everything the system does. Go ahead and login; at the Login: prompt just type:

```
root
```

and press [Enter] or the [Tab] key.

- **Tip:** Case matters. Linux, like UNIX, makes a distinction between uppercase and lowercase letters. So root is not the same as Root. In fact, as far as Linux is concerned, they're two different accounts.

Don't worry about mistakes when you log in; you can always use the [Delete] key to start over. When you're asked, type in the password you chose when you installed Red Hat Linux. You won't see your password on the screen as you type; that's just one of the security features of your Linux system.

- **Tip:** Be sure to type commands exactly as you see them – spaces, dashes and all. To Linux, an extra space or letter can make all the difference in the world.

When you're finished typing in your password, press [Enter]. You'll be presented with your new desktop (similar to 4[7]). Once you become more comfortable with your new operating system and with GNOME, you'll probably be able to fill up that desktop quickly with applications.

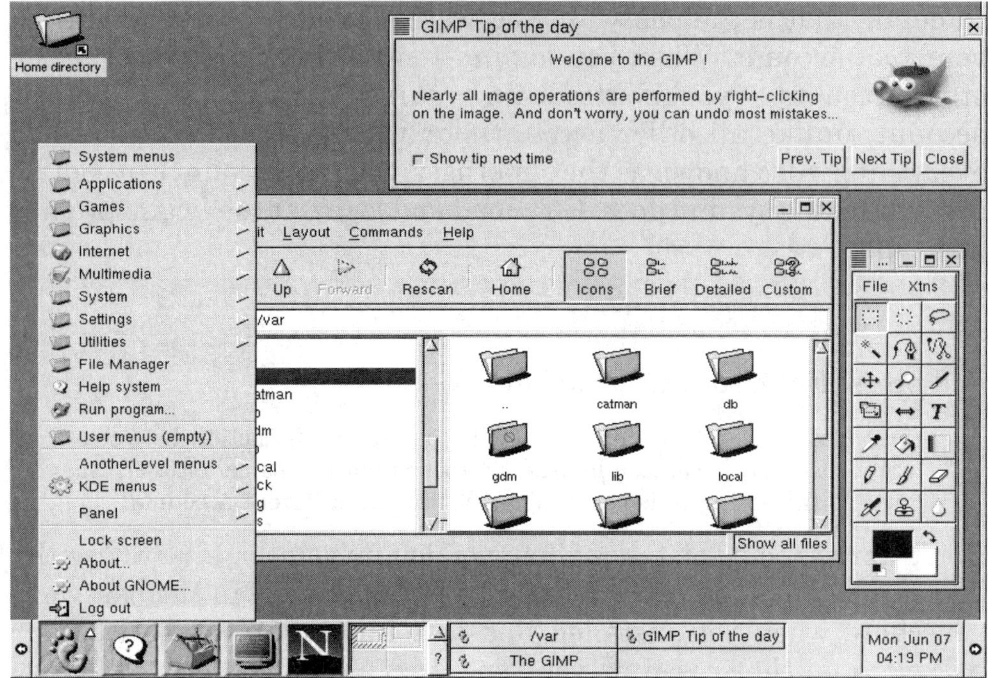

Figure 15-4: A sample GNOME desktop

There's plenty of space to fill up, not just on your current desktop but on numerous desktops — four by default.

- **Tip:** To learn specifics about GNOME, including applications and navigation, turn to the GNOME User's Guide section of this manual.

But for now, let's just concentrate on your current desktop. Go ahead and look around. You can begin by double-clicking with the left mouse button on the file folder called Home Directory on the desktop. Here, you'll find icons representing the various directories and files on your system. From the panel on the bottom, left-click once with your mouse, and you can begin to investigate some of the applications which have been included with your environment. From here, you can find ways to customize your workspace, search for files, write letters or other documents, start spreadsheets and more. But before you get too daring... While you're logged into the root account, avoid the temptation to make any changes to files or directories unless you know exactly what you're doing! Here's why: Whenever the system recognizes you as the root account you're allowed to do just about anything: change configuration files, make new directories, create and manage accounts for users who are allowed to use your computer and more. That kind of power comes with a price, and tinkering around with configuration files, accounts and directories can easily lead to disaster. So how are you supposed to operate safely? By creating a user account, which we'll cover shortly. With a user account, you can work and play with the assurance that you're not damaging your system.

How to Quit

When you're finished looking around for the first time, you can log out to quit your session (see Figure 15-5).

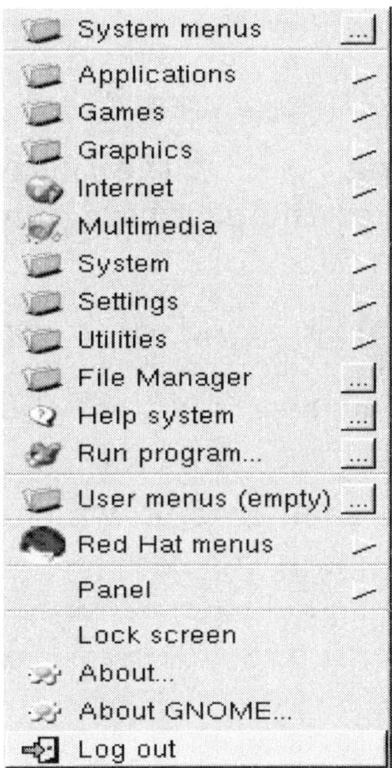

Figure 15-5: Locating the "Log out" selection

When you log out, you'll be returned to the opening screen you found when your system started. To log out, just go to the **GNOME footprint** on the panel, left- click once and click on **Log out**. You'll be presented with a box, asking you whether you want to log out. Click once on **Yes**. After a few moments, you'll be returned to the log in screen.

- **Summary:** At Login - type root At Password - type your-root-password To quit — Left-click on the GNOME footprint, then click on **Log out**, click **Yes**.

From Console Mode

When you were installing Red Hat Linux 6.0, you were given the option of starting from a graphical or console — non-graphical — screen. If you chose not to automatically start your computer in a graphical environment, you'll find a somewhat daunting, almost blank screen which will show you something like

```
Red Hat Linux release 6.0
Kernel 2.2 on an i686
login:
```

You can log in by typing `root` at the **Login:** prompt. Then, when **Password:** appears, type the password you chose at the time you installed Red Hat Linux 6.0.

- **Tip:** Just like the graphical login screen, don't expect to see your password "echoed" when you type in your password. Making sure that your password isn't seen is just one of Linux's many security features.

Now, you'll find a single shell prompt, which will appear similar to:

Figure 15-6: A sample shell prompt after your login

This tells you that you're logged in as root and in the directory called root (as shown in Figure 15-6).

You can exit at any time simply by typing logoff or exit.

- **Tip:** You can also press the [Ctrl] and [D] keys at the same time to return you to the login prompt.

X Marks the Spot

If you installed the X Window System (also known simply as X) at the time of your Red Hat Linux installation, you've got a pleasing, graphical environment in which to work. If you didn't install X at that time, and you wish to use the X Window System, your best bet is to return to the CD at this time and re-install Red Hat Linux 6.0. (Sigh...) Certainly, there are other ways of installing X, but if you're fairly new to Red Hat Linux, and if you're starting out with a brand new installation, you'll find it takes less time — and frustration — to simply redo the installation.

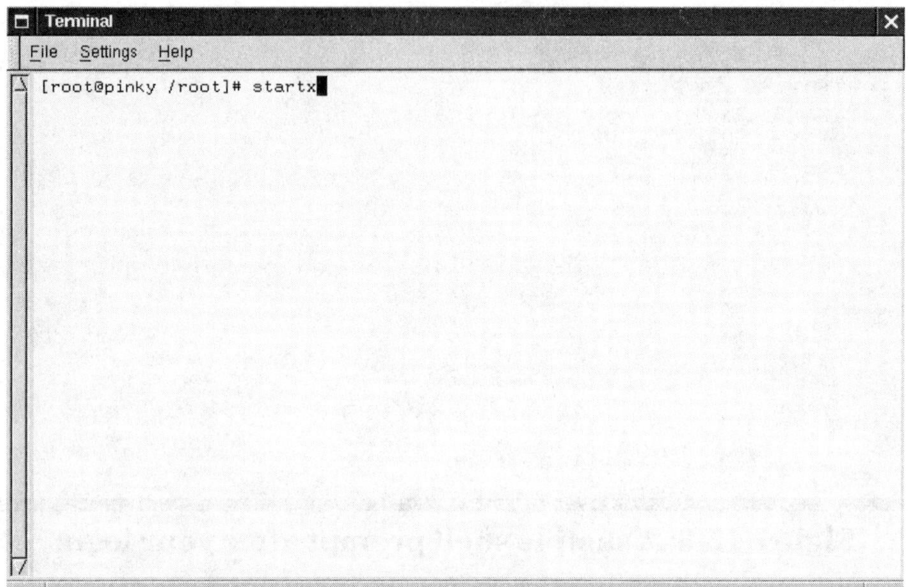

Figure 15-7: Starting the X Window System from the prompt

If you did install the X Window System — but didn't choose to start GNOME automatically you're still ready to go. At the shell prompt, type:

```
startx
```

and the X Window System will begin (refer to Figure 15-7).

Please Note: You're logged into the system as the root account, also known as superuser. There's a reason the root account is known as superuser: In this account, you can make changes to just about anything. Unless you know what you're doing, you can easily harm your system by mistakenly changing settings.

Although you may be tempted to modify files or directories, you should resist making any changes until you've created a user account.

To log out of X, bring your mouse cursor to the **GNOME panel**, then left-click on the **GNOME footprint**. A menu of applications, utilities, games and other programs will pop up.

"Drag" your cursor to the item labeled **Log out** (as shown in Figure 15-5).

- **Tip:** You can "drag" your cursor by keeping the mouse button depressed with your finger while moving the cursor to your selected item. Once the cursor is over the item on the menu, releasing the mouse button will start the program.

Now, a separate window will appear, asking you to confirm your decision to log out.

Click on **Yes**, and you'll be returned to the console.

You now will be back at your original shell prompt, so if you are done for the day, you should log out here too.

Whenever you want to start another X session, just type startx from the prompt.

- **Summary:** At the prompt, type startx; to exit — **GNOME panel -> Log out**

A Brand New You

Now, let's create a "user account." If you're familiar with MS-DOS or, to a lesser extent, Windows 98, you might be a little befuddled by the requirement of creating a user account. After all, if you can navigate the system and use programs in your root account, you might think that having two accounts on a single machine is excessive. Nothing could be further from the truth. Here's why: Linux is a multi-tasking, multi-user system, which means it can safely and securely accommodate many users at one time, performing plenty of tasks each user requires. But only one account can be root — capable of changing the way the operating system works. Because "rooting around" can easily lead to havoc, it's important to safeguard against accidents. That's why just about every Linux user — even if they're the system administrator — has their own user account. Once you're logged in as root, you have two ways to conveniently add a user to the system: from within X and from the shell prompt. Both methods are quick and painless. Let's say that the account you want to choose is called "billy." From X: One of the most powerful tools you can use for system administration is Linuxconf. You can use Linuxconf for adding and manipulating accounts, monitoring system activities and plenty of other system features.

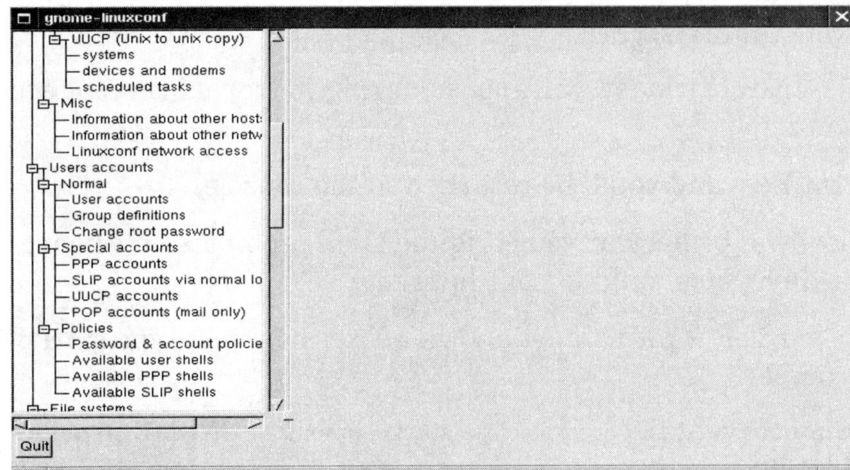

Figure 15-8: Finding the User accounts entry in Linuxconf

Completely documenting all the features of this utility would take much more space than we have here. For a more detailed look at the application's features — including greater depth on manipulating accounts — turn to the "System Configuration with Linuxconf" chapter in the Red Hat Linux Installation Guide.

- **Tip:** You can learn more about Linuxconf by visiting the official Linuxconf website: *http://www.solucorp.qc.ca/linuxconf/*.

One of the easiest ways to access Linuxconf is from the shell prompt. At the prompt, type:

```
linuxconf
```

We want to add an account, so let's scroll about a third of the way down the menu in the left panel, to the entry marked **Users accounts**. If the entry has a + next to it, go ahead and click on the "+". Now, the menu will expand to show entries in the **User accounts** listing (as shown in Figure 15-8).

The subentries will look like the following:

```
 |
-Users accounts
  | Normal
    |
        User accounts
    |
        Group definitions
    |
        Change root password
```

Left-click with your mouse button on the **User accounts** entry, under **Normal**.

In the right panel, you'll now see a box of the current user accounts (as shown in Figure 15-9).

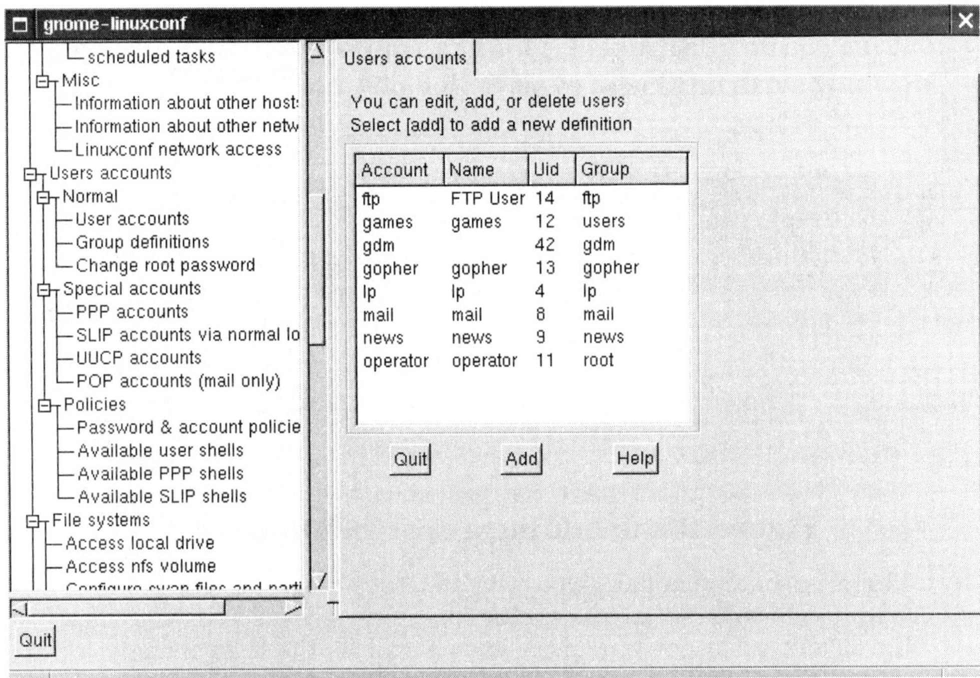

Figure 15-9: The Users accounts in Linuxconf

Toward the bottom of the right panel, click on the **Add** button, between the **Quit** and **Help** buttons.

Now, we'll see a dialog called **User account creation**. In here, we're going to fill in: **Login name**; **Full name** and **group**.

Make sure the button is indented next to the statement **The account is enabled**.

Now, let's type in a login name. It should be easy to remember (it's the password that should be complex, but more about that later...). Then, you can type in your full name.

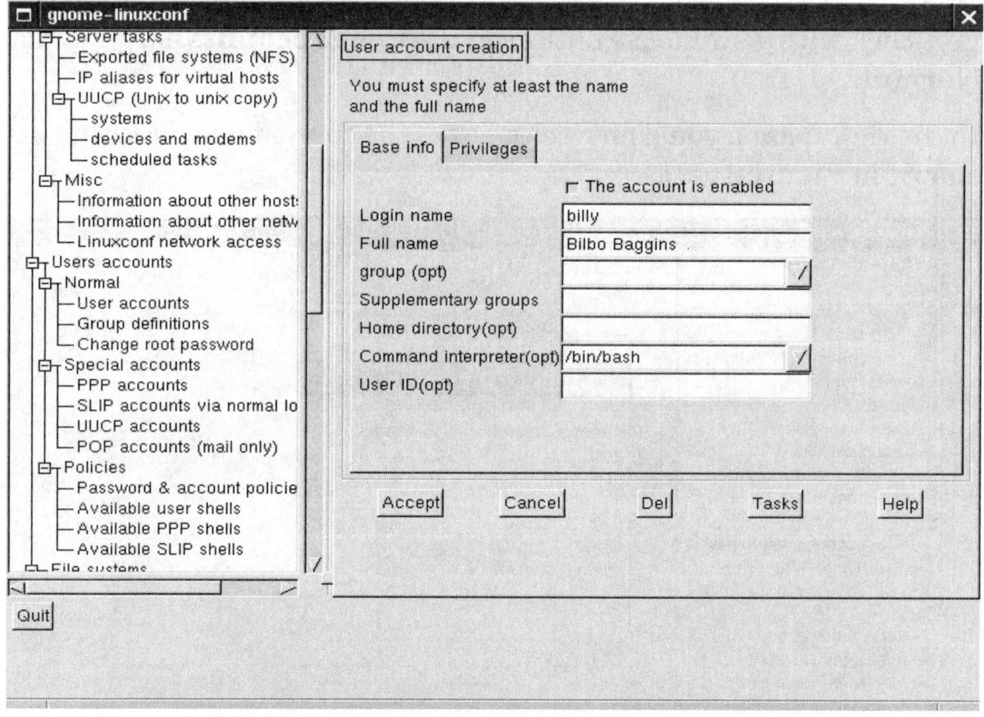

Figure 15-10: Adding a user in Linuxconf

- **Tip:** Everyone's account belongs to at least one group. Groups are used to determine file access permissions. Unless you specify a group, the default group for your user account will be the login name you choose (for example, a group called billy).

When you're finished, your entries should look like the following:

```
Login name.........billy
Full name..........Bilbo Baggins
group (opt)........billy
```

Now, just click on the button marked Accept.

We're almost finished. Next, we've got to come up with a password.

Passwords are one of the best methods to safeguard against prying eyes or malicious behavior. If you've got a secure password, which only you know, you've taken a big step in your system's security.

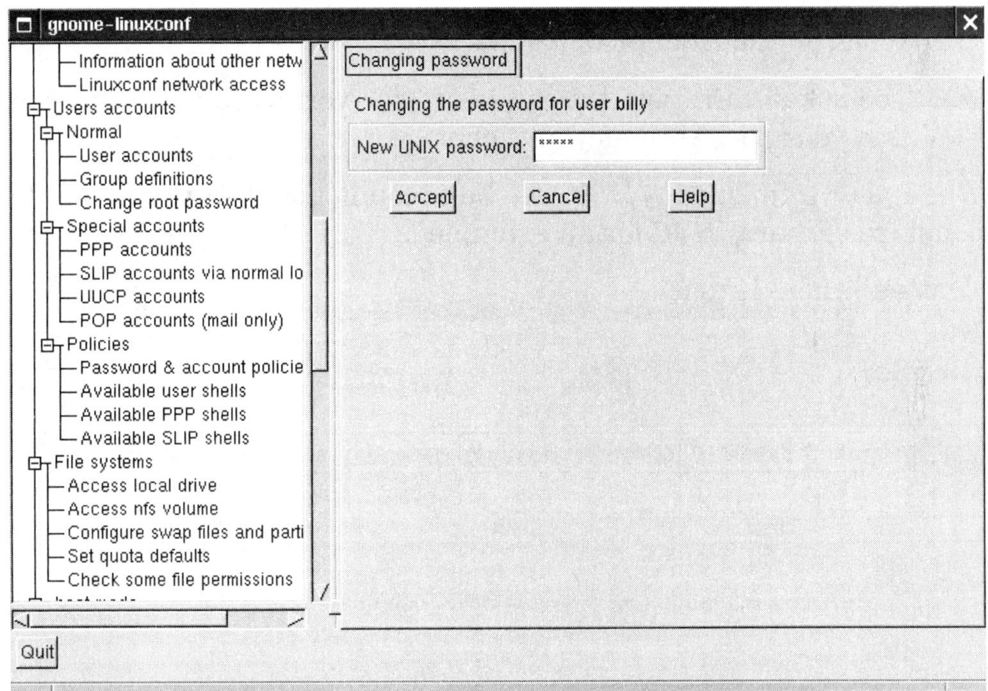

Figure 15-11: Creating a user account's password in Linuxconf

For both your root and user account, your passwords should be unique and easy enough for you to remember. (Passwords can't protect very well if they're jotted down on a piece of paper and taped to the monitor!)

What's both unique and easy to remember? Passwords which both numbers and letters. Here's an example:

- **Weak passwords**: airplane, icecream, california
- **Better passwords:** a!rpl8ne, !cec73am, c8Li70r&ia

One more thing: Passwords must be at least six characters — upper and lowercase letters and/or numbers — in length.

Once you decide on a password that you feel comfortable you'll remember, type it in the box provided. You won't see the password, except in a series of asterisks (as shown in Figure 15-11).

Then, click on the **Accept** button.

You'll be asked to retype the password for verification. Again, you won't see your password as you type it.

When you've finished, you'll see the account listed in the accounts panel (see Figure 15-12 for an example).

That's all there is to it.

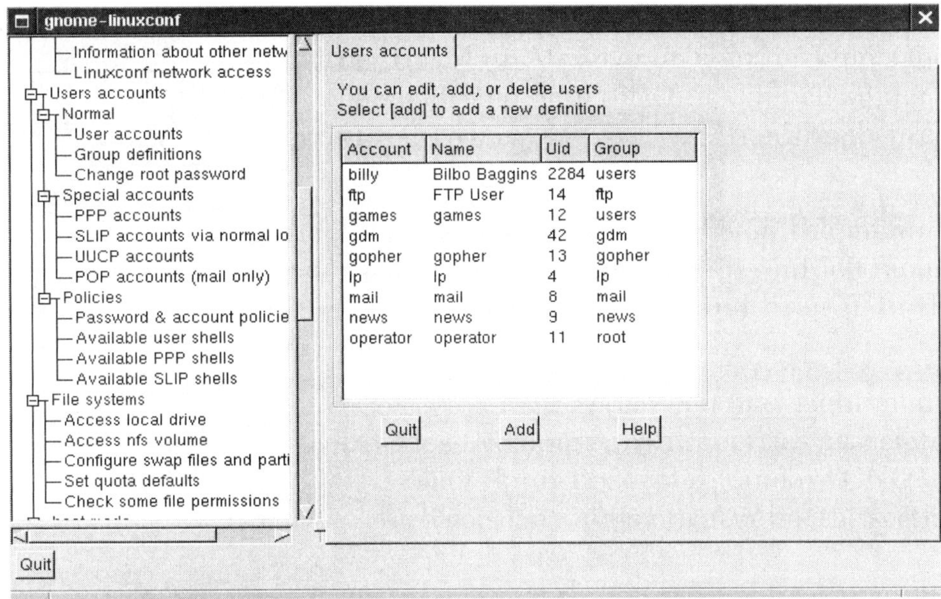

Figure 15-12: The new user account in Linuxconf

For additional security, you should change your passwords every now and then. From your user account, you can change your password by clicking on the account name, then clicking on the box marked **Passwd** at the bottom.

- **Tip:** Now that you've created your user account, you might want to reconsider whether your root account's password is secure enough. You can change this password easily, from within Linuxconf, by clicking on the Change root password item.

To learn more about how to modify your account or perform other account procedures, turn to the System Configuration chapter in the Red Hat Linux Installation Guide.

From the shell prompt type: `useradd billy`. It should look like this:

```
[root@localhost root]# useradd billy
[root@localhost root]#
```

(See Figure 15-13.)

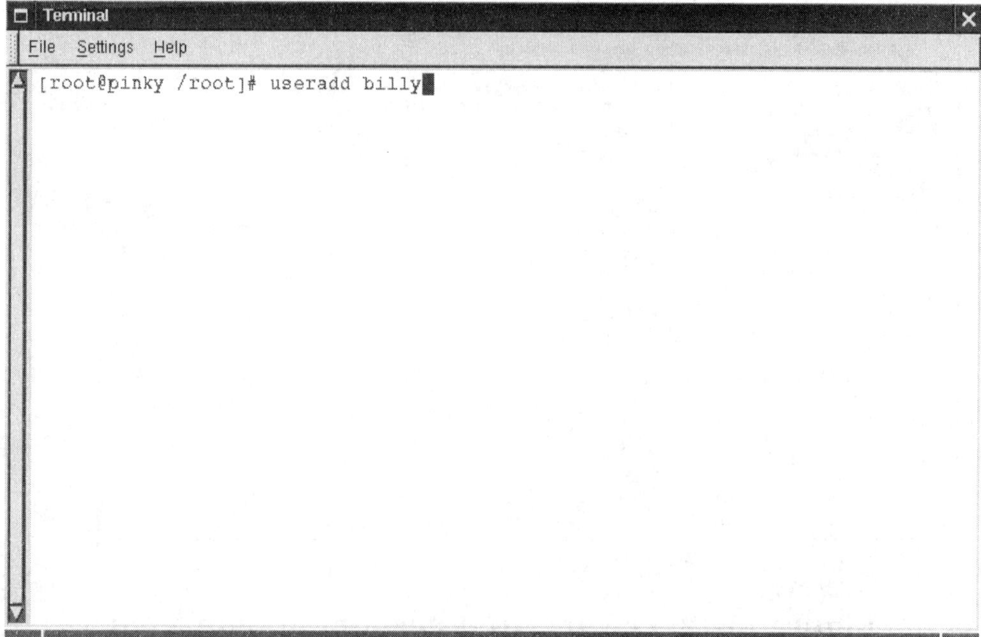

Figure 15-13: Adding a user at the shell prompt

Looks like nothing's changed, right? Wrong. Although you've got the same prompt, an entry has already been made for the new account. Now, it's time to specify a password.

At the prompt, type `passwd billy`. It should look like this:

```
[root@localhost root]# passwd billy
[root@localhost root]#
```

(See Figure 15-14.)

Remember that the password must be easy to recall and a unique mixture of letters, symbols and/or numbers.

That's it.

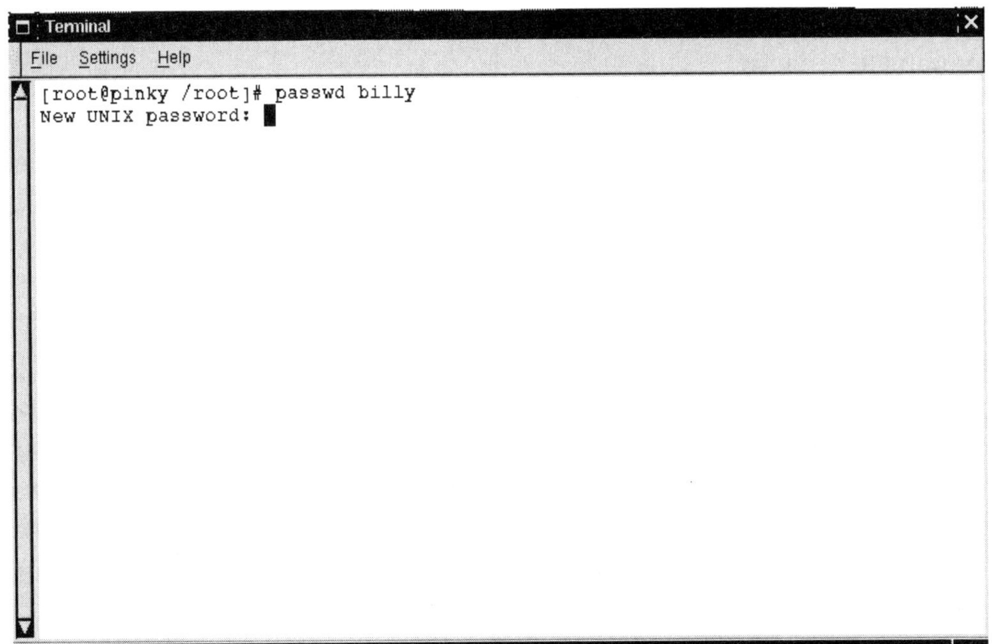

Figure 15-14: Adding a password at the shell prompt

From now on, whenever you want to add a user, change account information or change account passwords — including the root password — either useradd or linuxconf will fit the bill. Make sure you're logged in as the root user, however.

- **Tip:** If you find yourself switching around frequently between the root account and your user account, it can become confusing to know which account you're actually logged into. You can always tell you're in the root account when you see the word [root at the start of the shell prompt or the hash mark (#) at the end. If you see (for example) [billy, or the dollar sign ($), you're working in your user account.

Regardless of the method you choose — from the shell prompt or from Linuxconf — your new user account's "login directory" will be placed in a subdirectory of /home.

To finish up and try out your new account, log out from your root account.

You'll be taken back to the login screen. Now, you can log in to your new user account.

- **Summary: From X** — In a terminal emulation window, type linuxconf. Scroll to **User Accounts -> Normal -> User Accounts**. Click on **Add. From the shell prompt** — type useradd (accountname); at the shell prompt again, type passwd accountname. Type and re-type password.

Shutting Down

Some day, computers will probably be as easy to use as televisions are today (no, we're not there yet...). Maybe we'll have remote controls to navigate easily between features and to turn off the machine. At present, though, you can't simply turn off your computer when you're finished. You can always log out from your account, which will return you to your login screen, but if you want to completely shut off your machine, you've got a couple more steps to take.

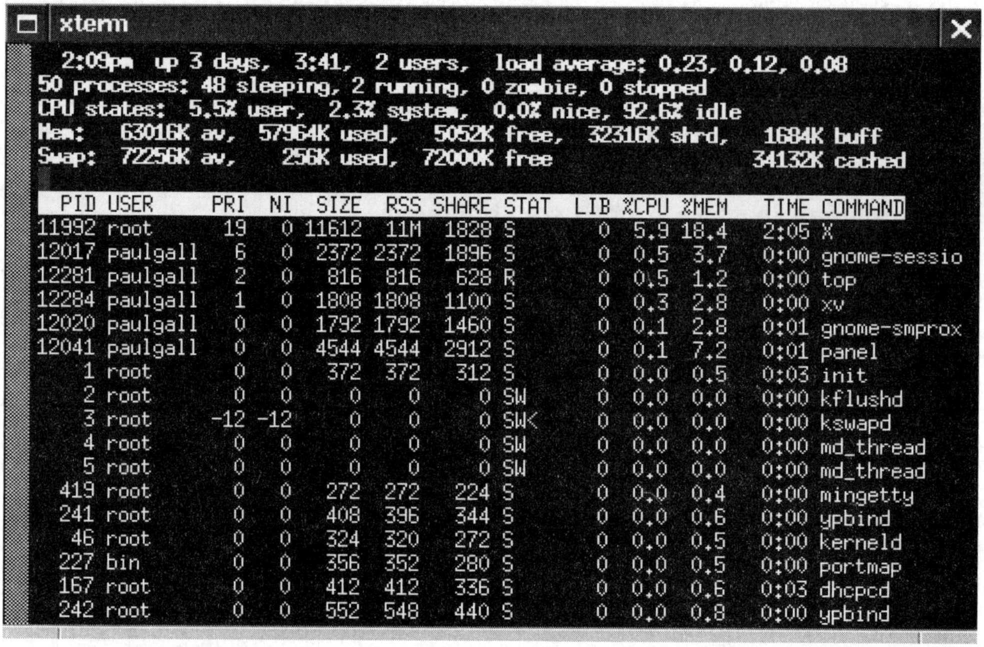

```
xterm
  2:09pm  up 3 days,  3:41,  2 users,  load average: 0.23, 0.12, 0.08
50 processes: 48 sleeping, 2 running, 0 zombie, 0 stopped
CPU states:  5.5% user,  2.3% system,  0.0% nice, 92.6% idle
Mem:   63016K av,  57964K used,   5052K free,  32316K shrd,   1684K buff
Swap:  72256K av,    256K used,  72000K free                 34132K cached

  PID USER     PRI  NI  SIZE  RSS SHARE STAT  LIB %CPU %MEM   TIME COMMAND
11992 root      19   0 11612  11M  1828 S       0  5.9 18.4   2:05 X
12017 paulgall   6   0  2372 2372  1896 S       0  0.5  3.7   0:00 gnome-sessio
12281 paulgall   2   0   816  816   628 R       0  0.5  1.2   0:00 top
12284 paulgall   1   0  1808 1808  1100 S       0  0.3  2.8   0:00 xv
12020 paulgall   0   0  1792 1792  1460 S       0  0.1  2.8   0:01 gnome-smprox
12041 paulgall   0   0  4544 4544  2912 S       0  0.1  7.2   0:01 panel
    1 root       0   0   372  372   312 S       0  0.0  0.5   0:03 init
    2 root       0   0     0    0     0 SW      0  0.0  0.0   0:00 kflushd
    3 root     -12 -12     0    0     0 SW<     0  0.0  0.0   0:00 kswapd
    4 root       0   0     0    0     0 SW      0  0.0  0.0   0:00 md_thread
    5 root       0   0     0    0     0 SW      0  0.0  0.0   0:00 md_thread
  419 root       0   0   272  272   224 S       0  0.0  0.4   0:00 mingetty
  241 root       0   0   408  396   344 S       0  0.0  0.6   0:00 ypbind
   46 root       0   0   324  320   272 S       0  0.0  0.5   0:00 kerneld
  227 bin        0   0   356  352   280 S       0  0.0  0.5   0:00 portmap
  167 root       0   0   412  412   336 S       0  0.0  0.6   0:03 dhcpcd
  242 root       0   0   552  548   440 S       0  0.0  0.8   0:00 ypbind
```

Figure 15-15: The command 'top' shows you running

processes

Here's why: Even though you may not be typing, listening to music or browsing with Netscape, your machine is still working on a variety of processes in the background. (A process is a program which is being executed. Multiple processes are running all the time on your system.)

- **Tip:** Curious to take a peek? Just go to a shell prompt and type top. You'll see the processes that are currently running (see Figure 15-15). To quit this view, type [Q].

  (To learn more about the top command, type man top at the shell prompt; to move forward a screen, press the [Spacebar]; to move back a screen, press [B]; to quit, press [Q]. You'll learn more about these "man pages" later in this chapter.)

Like a faithful assistant, your Linux system is carrying out tasks silently all the time. You can't just turn out the lights and lock the door on your assistant. Instead, you've got to give them time to put away their work and make sure everything's in its proper place before saying "good night." To shutdown or reboot while you're in GNOME, exit from your X session (**panel -> Log out**). Once you're at the login screen, left-click on **Options**, and select **Halt** or **Reboot**. You'll then be asked whether you want to stop or restart your machine. Choose Halt to shutdown your machine; choose Restart to restart, or "reboot" your machine.

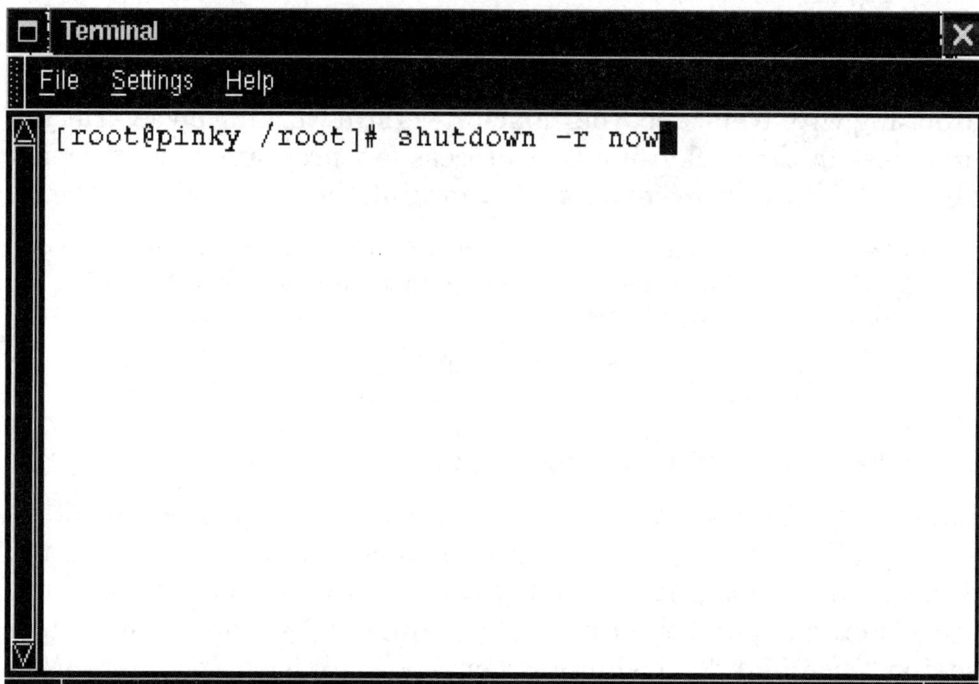

Figure 15-16: The shutdown command at the shell prompt

At the shell prompt, you can reboot or halt your system from your root account. To reboot from the prompt, type:

```
shutdown -r now
```

(See Figure 15-16.)

Or, if you want to exit from your system and turn off your machine, type:

```
shutdown -h now
```

The -r option stands for "reboot," while the -h option means "halt." Using `now`, means that you want to perform this action immediately.

> **Please Note:** Remember to save your work and exit from any applications which may be running before you perform a shutdown from the shell prompt, because you could lose work.

If you choose to halt the system, you'll see a list of messages about which services are stopping; then, you'll see:

```
The system is halted
```

Now everything's put away and it's safe to turn off your computer.

- **Tip:** Try substituting +5 for now; you'll find that you've just commanded your assistant to put everything away and stop working in five minutes.

You can learn more about the shutdown command by typing:

```
man shutdown
```

at a shell prompt. You'll be presented with a "man page," which will tell you about this command.

To go forward a screen, press the [Spacebar]; to go back a screen, press [B]; and to quit, press [Q].

- **Summary:** To shutdown or reboot from GNOME, from the log in screen, go to **Options -> Hal**t or **Reboot**. From the shell prompt: Log in as root, and type shutdown -r now (to reboot) or shutdown -h now (to halt).

Pulling Yourself Up by the Boot

When you're logged in as the root account, you might want to take a few minutes to create a fresh "boot diskette" or copy the diskette you already have. There are a number of reasons you should make a boot diskette: it can help you recover from a system failure, it can help you test a new kernel you've downloaded and compiled and it can help you share your computer with more than one operating system.

- **Tip:** You can always use a copy of the boot diskette to form the first half of a rescue disk set. You'll need a boot diskette and a rescue diskette to enter rescue mode. To read more about rescue mode, see later in this chapter.

You were given the opportunity to make a boot disk when you installed Red Hat Linux. If you chose not to make a boot disk at installation, here's your chance to start from scratch. For now, we'll make boot disks from the shell prompt while we're in an X session. Go to the shell prompt: In GNOME, for example, left-click on the **GNOME footprint** on the panel, go to **Utilities** in the menu and click on one of the items marked **xterm** or on the **GNOME terminal** item. Now, make sure you're logged in as root. At the shell prompt, if you see something like `[billy@localhost billy]`, for example, type:

```
[billy@localhost billy] su
Password: yourrootpassword
[root@localhost billy]#
```

This will allow you to change from your regular user account to the root account. **Please Note:** when you're in the root account, you are commander in chief of everything on your system, so be careful.

- **Tip:** The command su means substitute users, which lets you log in temporarily as another user.

Briefly, we'll find the Linux kernel version; then, we'll use the mkbootdisk command to make a bootable floppy from the kernel. Put a standard diskette in the floppy drive.

- **Tip:** In Linux, the floppy drive is referred to as /dev/fd0.

If you've previously used the diskette, remember: You will lose anything that had been on that diskette!

Figure 15-17: Changing directories to /lib/modules

Now, at the prompt, type:

```
cd /lib/modules
```

(Shown in figure 17.)

Now, type:

```
ls
```

The command `ls` will list the contents of a directory. (You can learn more about the cd and ls commands in Chapter 2). For now, just type the commands as you see them.)

Here, you can find the kernel version of your Red Hat Linux system. The kernel is the heart of any Linux system. Your kernel version will be something similar to:

```
2.2.x-yy
```

(there will be several numbers after 2.2, as in 2.2.2-0.1 or 2.2.5-1).

Now that you've found the kernel version, you can tell the mkbootdisk command which kernel to copy to your floppy. (If you don't tell mkbootdisk where to copy the kernel, it will default to copying to the floppy in /dev/fd0.)

Just type:

```
mkbootdisk –device /dev/fd0 2.2.5-1
```

Then press [Enter].

- **Tip:** If your screen becomes a little crowded with commands and "command not founds," you can always start with a clean slate by typing clear at the prompt.

You're done.

- **Summary:** As root, in a terminal window, cd /lib/modules; choose kernel number; then type mkbootdisk –device /dev/fd0 kernel.number. To clean the display, type clear.

A Good "Man" Is Easy to Find

As you investigate your new system, you're bound to have questions about commands and system services. One of the easiest ways to find out about how to use many commands or some applications is through the man command. The word man stands for "manual", a series of online "pages" which can tell you the purpose of many commands. In a highly condensed format, man pages provide a summary of a command's purpose, the options available and the syntax which is used to issue the command. If you count yourself among the "newbies" to Linux, you might not find man pages as useful as someone who's more accustomed to their terse delivery of information. But man pages can help steer you toward the proper way to use commands on your system. Even at this point, you can gain insight into your system by familiarizing yourself with the man pages. You'll certainly want to know how to use them eventually. There are several ways to view the man pages: from GNOME's Help Browser, from an application called xman or from the shell prompt.

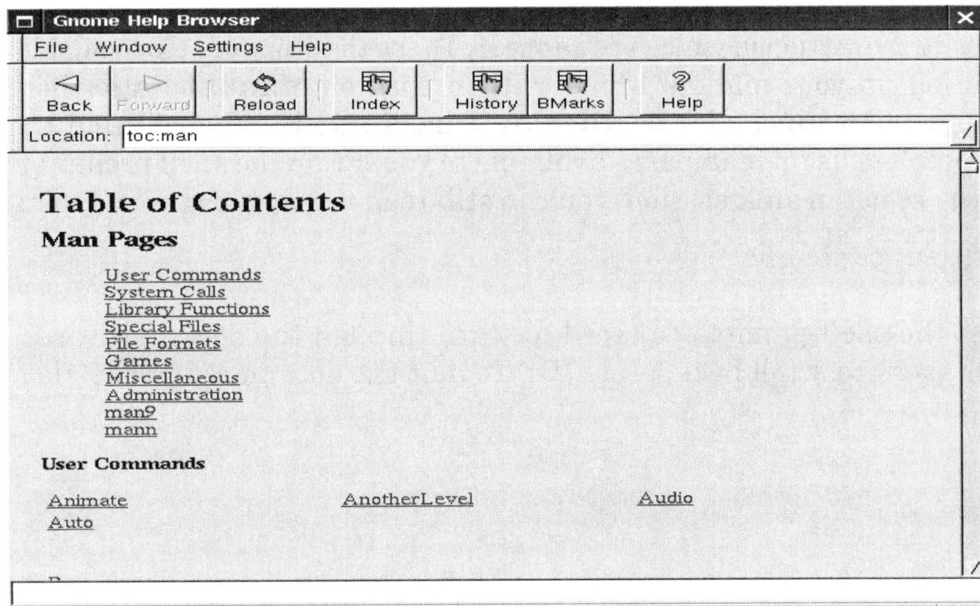

Figure 15-18: Man page index in GNOME's Help Browser

GNOME's Help browser: To start GNOME's Help Browser, go to **Panel Help system**. The GNOME Help Browser will start. On the first page, you'll find links to the man pages and to other helpful documentation.

- **Tip:** Read about how to get more from GNOME in the GNOME User's Guide, which you'll find at the official GNOME website: *www.gnome.org*. For more information about man pages, take a look at the **Finding Documentation** chapter in the Red Hat Linux Installation Guide.

From xman: Depending on your window manager, there will be different ways to access the graphical presentation of the man pages through the menus. (Window managers literally manage how the windows in your X session are presented.) A quick way to start the manual browser, however, is to go to a shell prompt and type:

```
xman
```

which will start the X Window System manual browser. When the menu appears, click on **Manual Page**. From here, you'll have a number of options from which to find a man page: You can alphabetically display all the man pages on your system; search for them by command or by the section in which they appear. To see the scope of help available, bring up your manual browser, then click on **Manual Page** then, under **Options**, click on **Display Directory**. Here, you'll find the complete list of man pages available to you. From the shell prompt: If you're not in an X session, you can still read the man pages by typing

```
man pagename
```

at the shell prompt. To scroll forward through the document, press [Space]; to scroll back, press [B]. To quit the document, press [Q].

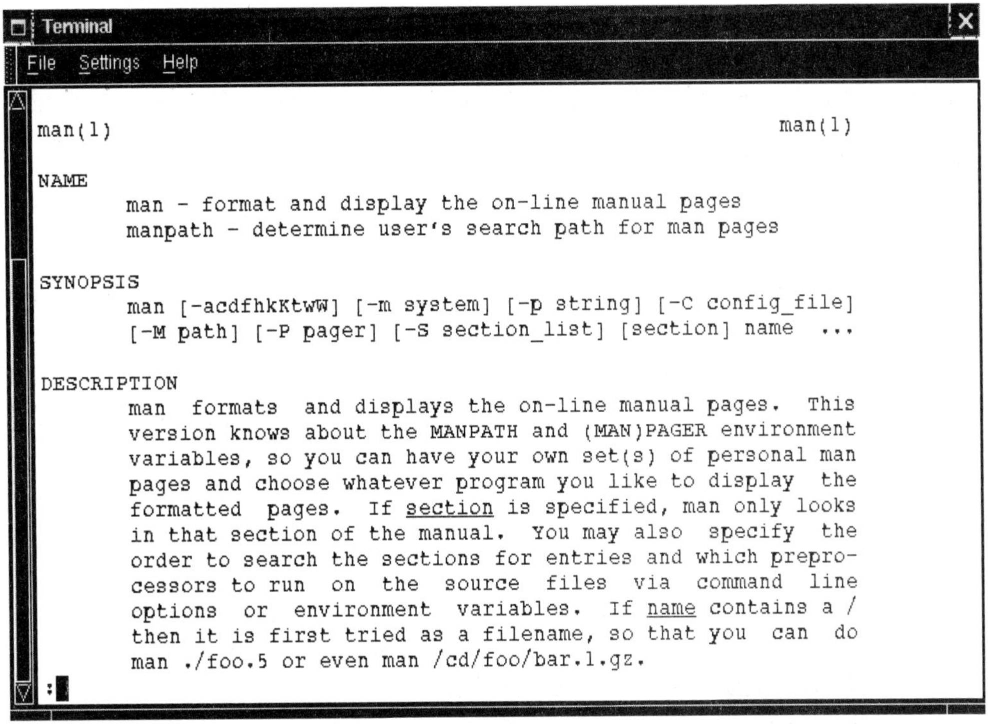

```
Terminal
File  Settings  Help

man(1)                                                        man(1)

NAME
       man - format and display the on-line manual pages
       manpath - determine user's search path for man pages

SYNOPSIS
       man [-acdfhkKtwW] [-m system] [-p string] [-C config_file]
       [-M path] [-P pager] [-S section_list] [section] name  ...

DESCRIPTION
       man  formats  and displays the on-line manual pages.  This
       version knows about the MANPATH and (MAN)PAGER environment
       variables, so you can have your own set(s) of personal man
       pages and choose whatever program you like to display  the
       formatted  pages.  If section is specified, man only looks
       in that section of the manual.  You may also  specify  the
       order to search the sections for entries and which prepro-
       cessors to run  on  the  source  files  via  command  line
       options  or  environment  variables.  If name contains a /
       then it is first tried as a filename, so that you  can  do
       man ./foo.5 or even man /cd/foo/bar.1.gz.
:
```

Figure 15-19: Reading a man page at the shell prompt

Of course, like any good help system, the man command has its own man page. At the prompt, type

```
man man
```

to display the manual page (as shown in Figure 19).

If you want to print:

Sometimes, just viewing the man page on the screen isn't enough; you may want to have a printed copy in front of you. Although you could send the page to a printer, because of certain text formatting in the man pages, you'd likely end up with a document filled with "garbage," symbols which didn't translate from your screen to the printer.

Before you print, then, you may have to "strip" the formatting from the page, which you can do with the col command. (As you might guess, there's a man page for col, also.)

For example, to print a man page for the man, type:

```
man man | col -b | lpr
```

In detail, the above command "sends" the output of the manual page entry through the col filter, which helps format the output for the printer. Then, the output from col is sent to the printer. This is called piping, and you can learn more about it in Chapter 2.

What is Rescue Mode?

Rescue mode is a term used to describe a method of booting a small Linux environment completely from diskettes. What follows in this section may help you recover from a problem at some point. A copy of these instructions is also available as rescue.txt on your Red Hat Linux 6.0 CD-ROM. As the name implies, rescue mode is there to rescue you from something. In normal operation, your Red Hat Linux system uses files located on your system's hard drive to do everything – run programs, store your files, and more. However, there may be times when you are unable to get Linux running completely enough to access its files on your system's hard drive. By using rescue mode, it's possible to access the files stored on your system's hard drive, even if you can't actually run Linux from that hard drive. Normally, you'll need to get into rescue mode for one of two reasons:

- You are unable to boot Linux, and you'd like to fix it.
- You are having hardware or software problems, and you want to get a few important files off your system's hard drive.

Let's take a closer look at each of these scenarios.

Unable to boot Linux

— Many times this is caused by the installation of another operating system after you've installed Red Hat Linux. Some other operating systems assume that you have no other operating systems on your computer, and overwrite the Master Boot Record (or MBR) that originally contained the LILO bootloader. If LILO is overwritten in this manner, you're out of luck — unless you can get into rescue mode.

Hardware/software problems

— There can be as many different situations under this category as there are systems running Linux. Things like failing hard drives and forgetting to run LILO after building a new kernel are just two things than can keep you from booting Red Hat Linux. If you can get into rescue mode, you might be able to resolve the problem — or at least get copies of your most important files. What do you need to get into rescue mode? To get into rescue mode, you'll need a rescue disk set. These are two diskettes that contain the files necessary to boot into rescue mode. If you elected to make a boot diskette while you were installing Red Hat Linux, you're halfway there! The first diskette in a rescue disk set is this boot diskette. Now on to the second diskette... The second diskette is called the rescue diskette. It is produced by writing an image file onto a diskette. The image file is called rescue.img, and is located in the images directory on the first Red Hat Linux CD-ROM. To gain access to this file, you'll first need to mount your Red Hat Linux CD-ROM. Start by inserting the CD-ROM in your system's CD-ROM drive. You'll need to do this while logged in as root. Type the following command:

```
mkdir /mnt/cdrom
```

Now, type:

```
mount /dev/cdrom /mnt/cdrom
```

You may get an error message from the first command saying that the file exists. That's fine; we just want to make sure that there is a /mnt/cdrom directory on your system. The second command should issue an informational message that /dev/cdrom is being mounted read-only. **Please Note:** Some systems may not recognize /dev/cdrom. If this is your case, you'll have to replace /dev/cdrom in the command with the appropriate device name for your CD-ROM. Next, issue the following command (again, while logged in as root):

```
cd /mnt/cdrom/images
```

then type:

```
ls
```

to list the contents of the images directory. You should see a file named rescue.img. This is the rescue diskette image file. Next, put a diskette in your first diskette drive, and enter the following command:

```
dd if=rescue.img of=/dev/fd0 bs=1440k
```

Your system's diskette drive should start writing to the diskette. After a minute or so, the dd command will complete, and you'll get your shell prompt back. Wait for your diskette drive's access light to go out, and that's it! You now have a rescue disk set. Label this diskette something like "Red Hat Linux 6.0 rescue diskette" and store it someplace safe. Let's hope you never have to use it. If you should ever need to use rescue mode, here's how. Boot your system with the boot diskette in the first diskette drive. At the LILO Boot: prompt, enter the word rescue. You will see the usual kernel messages as the Linux kernel starts up. Eventually, it will ask you to insert the next diskette, and press [Enter]. Remove the boot diskette, insert the rescue diskette, and press [Enter]. The rescue diskette will be read into memory. After a minute or so, you should see the shell prompt. That's it – you're in rescue mode! Now what? When it comes to rescue mode, that's a bit like asking, "how long is a piece of string?" What you require depends a great deal on what your system's problem is, your level of Linux expertise, and several variables we haven't even thought of yet. So we can't give you explicit instructions. But we can tell you what programs you have access to while in rescue mode. Here's the list:

```
badblocks   bash      bzip2
cat         chmod     chroot
cp          cpio      dd
e2fsck      fdisk     grep
gunzip      gzip      head
ifconfig    init      ln
ls          lsmod     mkdir
mke2fs      mknod     mount
mt          mv        open
pico        ping      ps
restore     rm        route
rpm         sed       sh
swapoff     swapon    sync
tac         tail      tar
traceroute  umount    vi
vim
```

You're likely to be unfamiliar with most, if not all of these commands. However, the commands do have man pages. Once you begin to feel more comfortable with commands, you should consider familiarizing yourself them through the man pages. (You may not have that luxury if you have to use these commands...) You've worked with some pretty useful commands for your Red Hat Linux system so far. You may not have known much about where those files were in the directory, however. For more information about the Linux filesystem, including navigation and working with other useful commands to help you understand your system, turn to the next chapter.

16 You Are Here

Let's say you want to buy a pair of sneakers at a nearby shopping mall. You may not be familiar with the mall, but that shouldn't be a problem. Why not? Because of the maps, which you can usually find near all the major entrances to the mall. The same can be said for your Red Hat Linux system: Navigation's easy once you know where you're going.

- **Tip:** Make sure you've logged into your user account! Remember that unless you like to live on the wild - and dangerous - side, using a root account for all your activities is toying with disaster. If you haven't created your user account yet, turn to Chapter 1 and do it now. Really... no kidding...

Finding Yourself With pwd

Sooner or later (probably sooner), when you start looking through directories, you're bound to ask, "Where the heck am I?" And you won't be speaking philosophically. DOS can answer that question just by showing you at the prompt like:

```
C:GAMES\Quake\ID1>
```

Your Linux system, by default, just shows your current directory.

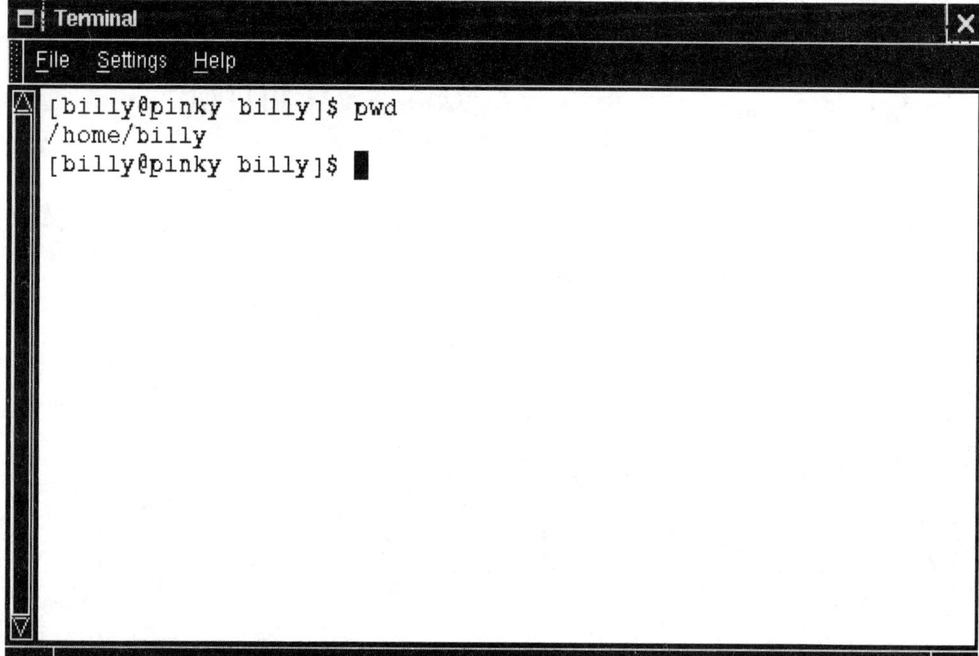
Terminal
File Settings Help
[billy@pinky billy]$ pwd
/home/billy
[billy@pinky billy]$

Figure 16-1: The command pwd shows you where you are

Try this: open an xterm window. You'll see something like:

```
[billy@localhost billy]
```

Now type:

```
pwd
```

What do you see? Something like

```
/home/billy
```

The command `pwd` stands for *print working directory*. When you typed pwd, you were asking your Linux system, "where am I?" Your system responded by "printing" the directory you're in to the monitor (as shown in Figure 16-1).

Seems easy, right? It ought to be; you'll be using `pwd` plenty as you look around. (Even Linux gurus depend on this little command.)

Getting From Here to There: cd

Whenever you want to change directories, all you've got to do is type:

```
cd
```

Go ahead, try it. In an xterm window, type:

```
cd
```

That didn't do much, did it? That's because you didn't tell your system where you wanted to go. Whether you're going to a store in a mall or to visit relatives across the country, you've got to know how to get from one point to another. That is, you'll need to know the path to follow. As with anything in life, the path — or, pathname — is basically the set of directions that takes you from one point to another. In the case of your Linux system (and in the DOS/Windows world, as well), you state a path to take you from one directory or file to another. Let's try it again.

Open an xterm window. Find yourself first with the pwd command. When you type your commands, your window will look like:

```
[billy@localhost billy] pwd
/home/billy
[billy@localhost  billy]
```

Now that you see where you are, you can start to give your system the path to follow. Well, almost... Try typing:

```
cd home
```

What happened? You know there's a directory called home, and you typed in the path. So what does this "no such file or directory" mean? It means your path is incomplete. Try typing:

```
cd /home
```

Now you've successfully changed directories and moved from your login directory into the subdirectory called home.

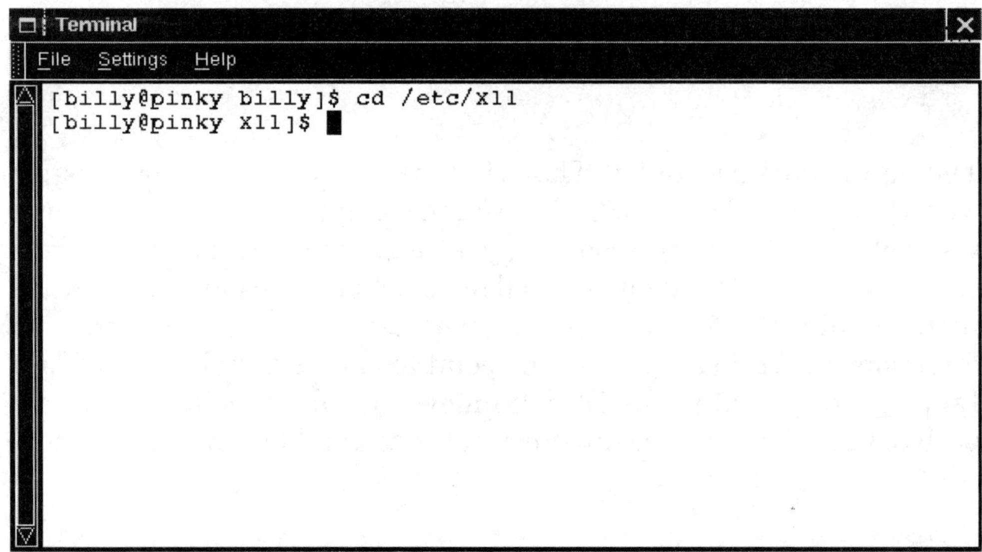
Terminal
File Settings Help
[billy@pinky billy]$ cd /etc/X11
[billy@pinky X11]$

Figure 16-2: Absolute pathnames state out the full path

The difference, of course, was adding the forward slash. Let's take a second to look at the reason adding a slash made all the difference. When you saw you were in /home/billy, you were looking at the full path — or the absolute path from the root directory. You can think of the billy directory as being located two directories "down" from the root, which is the topmost level of your system. So when you typed:

```
cd /home
```

you were actually saying "go to the root directory, then go to the directory called home, which is one directory below the root." You specified an absolute path to get to the home directory (see, for example, Figure 16-2). Now, if you type:

```
cd /
```

you'll end up with a prompt that looks like:

```
[billy@localhost /]
```

That single forward slash means you're at the root. When you're at the root, you can't go any higher on your system (the same is true in DOS/ Windows).

To get back to your login directory from the root directory by using the absolute path, just type:

```
cd /home/billy
```

You're home.

Using the absolute path is just one way to move around. Another method of getting from one point to another is by using the relative path (as in Figure 1-1).

Let's go back to the root directory:

```
cd /
```

Now, let's move *back* to your login directory using relative pathnames:

```
cd home/billy
```

Notice that the / is missing? That's because the root directory is the parent of the home directory, which means that the home directory is one step down from the root directory. Since home is the parent of the directory called billy, these two directories are separated with a /.

If you're in your login directory, you can move up one directory, to home, just by typing:

```
cd ..
```

The relative path describes the directory you want to cd to in terms which are relative to your current directory.

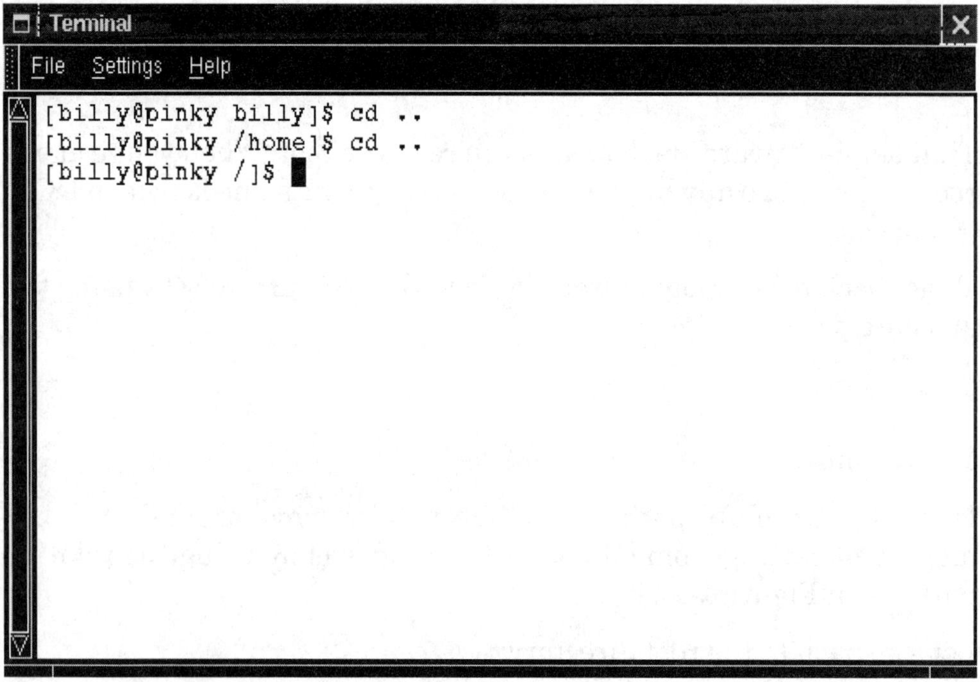

```
Terminal
File  Settings  Help
[billy@pinky billy]$ cd ..
[billy@pinky /home]$ cd ..
[billy@pinky /]$
```

Figure 16-3: Relative pathnames are 'relative' to your current position

When you typed `cd ..`, you were saying "go up one directory." The next directory up, from your login directory, was home.

- **Tip:** When speaking of directories which hold other directories, you can refer to them as parent directories. In our case, home is the parent directory of billy.

Using two dots (..) when you cd is the same as stating you want to go to the parent of your current working directory. Try using a single dot. Type:

```
cd .
```

What happened? Not much. That's because using a single dot (.) is the same as specifying your current working directory.

The differences between absolute and relative paths can sometimes be pretty striking.

Getting back to our shopping mall analogy, if you were to give directions by using an absolute path, you might say something like:

"Get your car keys. Get in the car. Start the car. Pull out of the driveway. Drive to the corner..."

...And so on, until you're finally standing inside your favorite shoe store in the shopping mall.

When you're using a relative path, you're saying something like:

"The store's a couple miles from here, in the shopping mall."

That's quite an exaggeration, but you get the idea: As long as you know where you want to go in relation to where you are, you can use relative paths.

- **Tip:** A path is absolute if the first character is a /; otherwise, it's a relative path.

You're now in the home directory, the parent of your login directory. Type:

```
cd ..
```

and you'll find yourself at the root directory.

Using relative paths, get yourself back to your login directory by typing:

```
cd home/billy
```

Doesn't look much different from absolute paths, does it? Notice, though, that there's no forward slash in front of home. In essence, you were saying, "go one directory down, to home, then go to billy, in the home directory."

- **Tip:** Whenever you want to quickly jump back to your login directory just type cd ~ anywhere in the system.

That wasn't much of a demonstration.

Try this: from your login directory, type:

```
cd ../../etc/X11
```

Now, you're in the directory X11, which is where you'll find configuration files and directories related to the X Window System.

Please Note: You can always type pwd to find out where you are in the directory tree. And you can get back to your login directory with the cd ~ command.

Take a look at your last cd command. What you were really telling your system was, "go up to the parent directory, then up to that directory's parent directory (which is the root directory), then go to the etc directory and from there, to the X11 directory."

Using an absolute path would also get you to the X11 quickly. Type:

```
cd /etc/X11
```

and you're there.

- **Tip:** Always make sure you know which working directory you're in before you state the relative path to the directory or file you want to get to. You don't have to worry about your position in the filesystem, though, when you state the absolute path to another directory or file.

Now that you're starting to get the hang of changing directories, see what happens when you change to root's login directory.

```
cd /root
```

Oops... You're not logged in as root, so you're "denied permission" to access that directory.

Denying access to the root and other users' accounts (or login directories) is one way your Linux system prevents accidental or malicious tampering. You'll find out more about file "ownership" and permissions later in this chapter.

Really want to change to the root login? Then you've got to use the su command. Type this series of commands:

```
[billy@localhost billy] su root
Password: (your root password)
[root@localhost billy]# cd /root
[root@localhost /root]#
```

As soon as you give the root password, you'll see the changes in your command prompt to show your new, superuser status: the root account designation at the front of the prompt and # at the end (as shown in Figure 16-4).

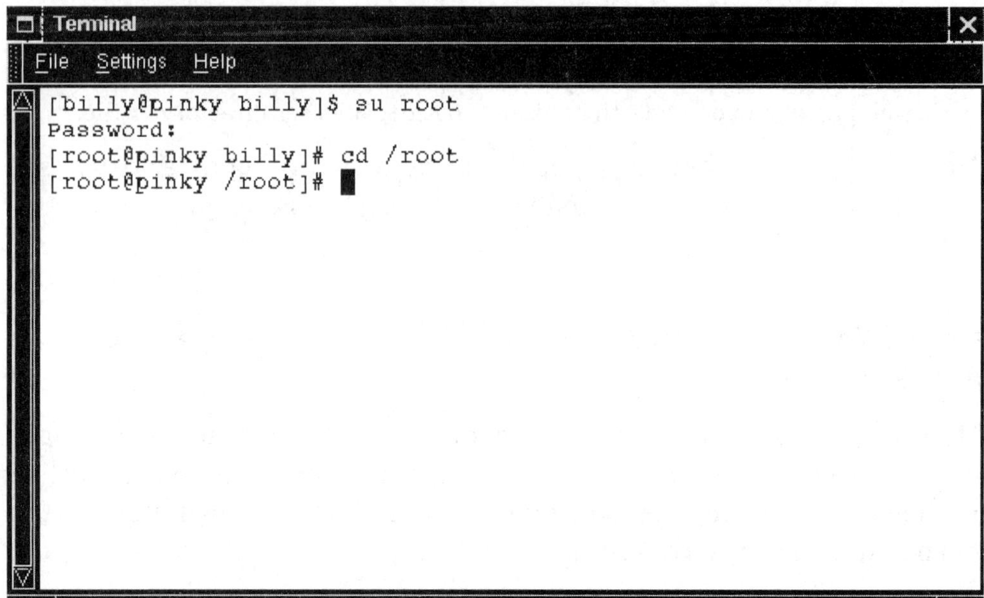
Terminal
File Settings Help
[billy@pinky billy]$ su root
Password:
[root@pinky billy]# cd /root
[root@pinky /root]#

Figure 16-4: Becoming root

Now, when you cd to root's login directory, you'll be granted access.

When you're done being root, just type exit at the prompt.

```
[root@localhost /root]# exit
exit
[billy@localhost billy]
```

- **Summary:** To change directories using absolute pathnames, type cd/ directory/directory; to change directories using relative pathnames, type cd directory to move one directory below, cd directory/directory to move two directories below, etc.; to jump from anywhere on the filesystem to your login directory, type cd ~ ; to change to the parent of the directory you're in, type cd .. Use . to refer to your current directory.

Looking Around With ls

Now that you know how to move around, it's time to take a look at what's in the directories. But first, let's make sure you've got something you can look for in your login directory before we go any further. You can start by creating an empty file. To do so, you can use a utility called touch at the shell prompt. Try it; type:

```
touch  foo.bar
```

Now, in your login directory, you've got an empty file called `foo.bar`. You'll see it in a couple minutes. Let's also create a new directory, using the mkdir command. At the prompt, type:

```
mkdir  tigger
```

Now, you've created a directory called `tigger` in your login directory. From root, your new directory's absolute pathname would be /home/yourlogin/tigger, and your directory is the parent of tigger. (You can learn more about creating — and removing — files and directories in Chapter 3.)

Now, you're ready to go.

In the DOS world, using the `dir` command will display the contents of a directory.

The same can be said of Linux — with some notable exceptions.

In Linux, `dir` won't fully display the contents of directories, and doesn't have the power or flexibility of the list command — `ls`.

In your login directory, for example, type:

```
dir
```

Now, in the same xterm window, type:

```
ls
```

Looks the same (see Figure 16-5). You see, among other contents, your new file, `foo.bar` and the new directory, `tigger`.

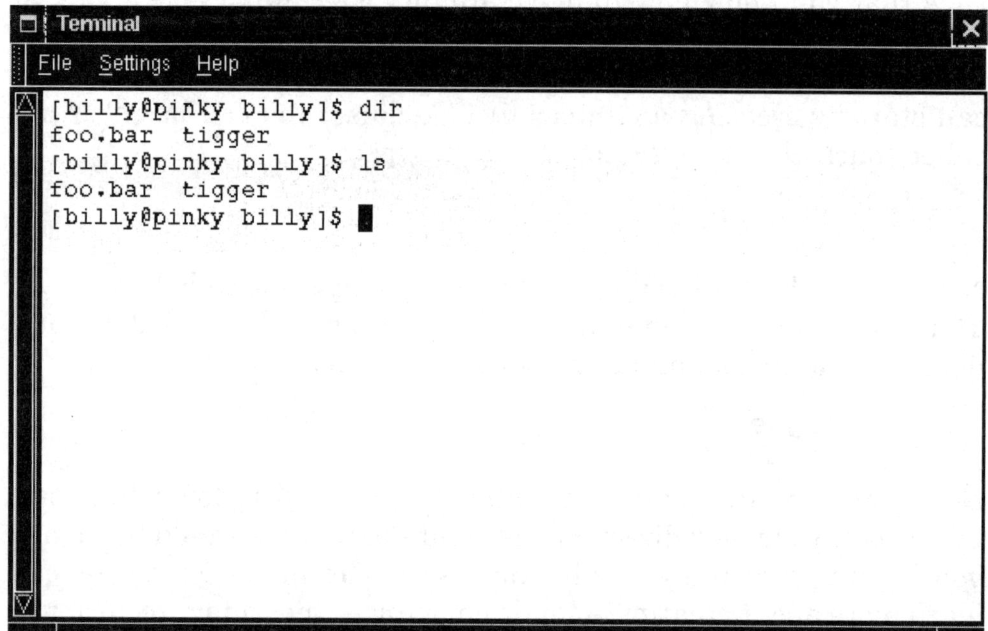
Terminal
File Settings Help
[billy@pinky billy]$ dir
foo.bar tigger
[billy@pinky billy]$ ls
foo.bar tigger
[billy@pinky billy]$

Figure 16-5: The dir and ls commands seem similar

But here the similarities end. Where dir shows you the contents of your directory, it doesn't actually show you everything. Even using the ls command, by itself, won't show you all the files in your directory. To see everything, you've got to call upon an option or two.

For example, in the same window that you'd used to type the dir and ls commands, now type:

```
ls -a
```

Quite a difference. When you added the -a option, you were specifying that you wanted to list all the files in the directory (see Figure 16-6).

In fact, there are a multitude of options available with the `ls` command.

- **Tip:** If you want to see all the options of the ls command, you can read the man page by typing man ls at a shell prompt. If you want to print the man page, type man ls | col -b | lpr at the prompt.

Why so many options? Because they can help you sort information according to your needs. For example, you can specify how files are displayed, see their permissions and much more.

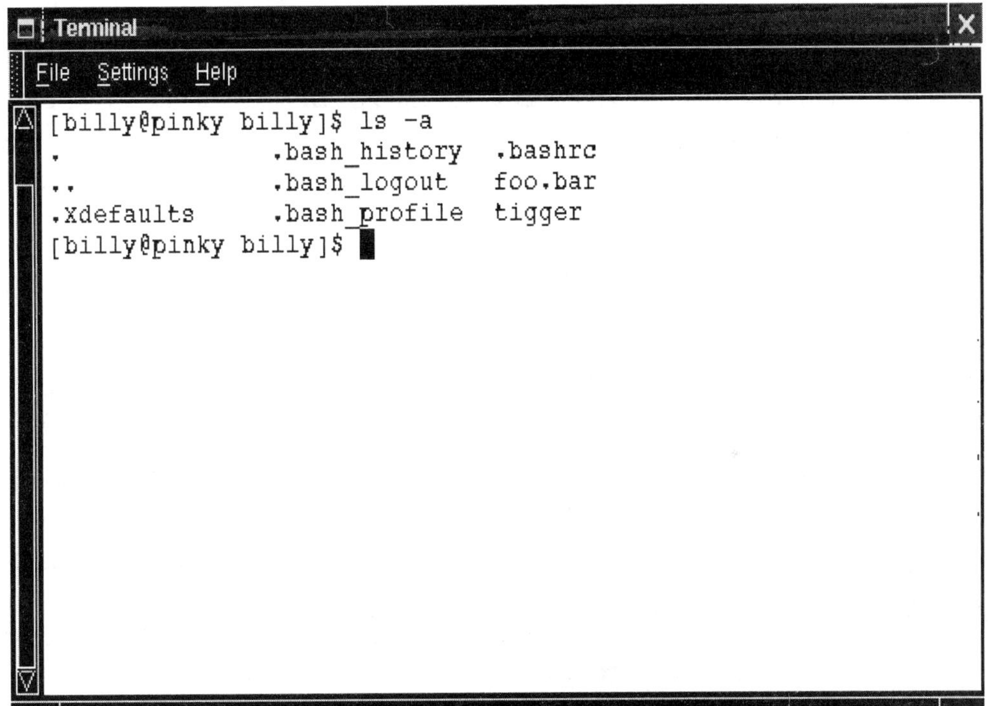
Terminal
File Settings Help
[billy@pinky billy]$ ls -a
. .bash_history .bashrc
.. .bash_logout foo.bar
.Xdefaults .bash_profile tigger
[billy@pinky billy]$

Figure 16-6: The ls command with the -a option

When you typed `ls -a`, you probably noticed the files that begin with dots. These are called *hidden files* or, appropriately enough, *dot files*.

Hidden files are mostly configuration files which set preferences in programs, window managers, shells and more. The reason they're "hidden" is to help prevent any accidental tampering by the user.

Whenever a filename starts with a dot (.), it's a hidden file, and `ls` won't list it.

Viewing all the files can give you plenty of detail, but there's more you can uncover, simply by adding more than one option. If we want to see the size of a file or directory, when it was created and more, we can just add the "long" option (-l) to our `ls -a` command. Try it. Type:

```
ls -al
```

There's quite a bit more detail now. You can see the file creation date, its size, ownership, permissions and more. You don't have to be in the directory whose contents you want to view, either. Let's see what's in the /etc directory by typing:

```
ls -al /etc
```

Here, you'll get plenty of information about the contents of the `/etc` directory. If you want to add color to your listing, just include the `--color` option.

```
ls -al –color /etc
```

To some, adding `–color` does more than add a splash of color; it gives a clue about the types of files in a directory. For example, directories might all be a royal blue, program files would be green, and so on. If you like what you see, here's how you can display the listing in color all the time. Briefly, we'll be adding one line to the `.bashrc` file in our login directory. The .bashrc file is used by your shell when you login (an example `.bashrc` file is shown in Figure 16-7). Now before we go any further...

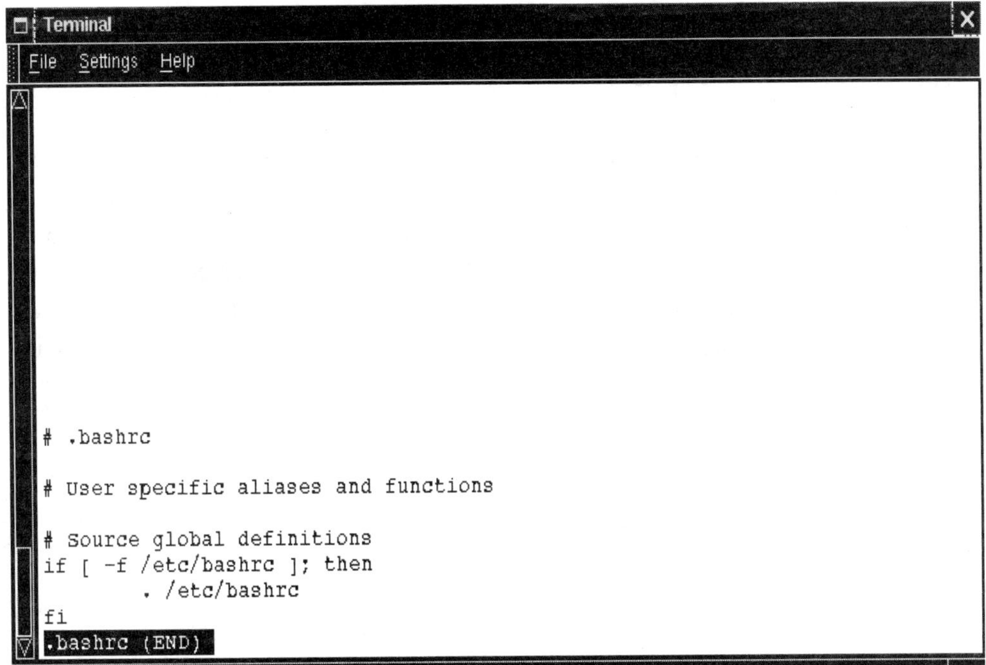
Terminal
File Settings Help
# .bashrc
# User specific aliases and functions
# Source global definitions
if [-f /etc/bashrc]; then
. /etc/bashrc
fi
.bashrc (END)

Figure 16-7: The .bashrc file

Remember that any changes you make to configuration files can cause you a world of grief if you've made a mistake and you don't have a backup copy of that file. To make a backup copy, make sure you're in your login directory and in an xterm window, type:

```
cd
```

to get to your login directory. Then copy the `.bashrc` file, keeping it in the same directory, but with a name like `.bashrc2`.

```
cp .bashrc .bashrc2
```

When you type the above command, what you're saying is, "make a copy of the `.bashrc` file and name that copy `.bashrc2`." Now, you have a backup copy of the unmodified `.bashrc` file in your login directory. If you make a mistake or have trouble, you can replace your

.bashrc file by typing:

```
cp .bashrc2 .bashrc
```

at the shell prompt. If you need to type this command, you'll be saying, "make a copy of the file .bashrc2 and name that copy .bashrc." The copy command here will overwrite the original .bashrc file — and you'll still keep a copy of the original (and untouched) .bashrc file with the name of .bashrc2. Now that we're prepared, we'll open .bashrc with Pico, a simplified *text editor*. (A text editor is a utility program that can create or modify files.) From an xterm window, type:

```
pico .bashrc
```

You should see something like this:

```
# .bashrc
# User specific aliases and functions
# Source global definitions
if [ -f /etc/bashrc ]; then
     . /etc/bashrc
fi
```

It's a pretty short file. Those hash marks (#) are comments. Any text after them is ignored by the shell, but they are put there to help guide anyone who's editing or modifying files. Bring your cursor under the line #User specific aliases and functions and type:

```
alias ls="ls -al —color"
```

So the full file ought to look something like this:

```
# .bashr
 # User specific aliases and functions
alias ls="ls -al —color"
# Source global definitions
if [ -f /etc/bashrc ]; then
```

```
    . /etc/bashrc
fi
```

See Figure 16-8 for an example in Pico.

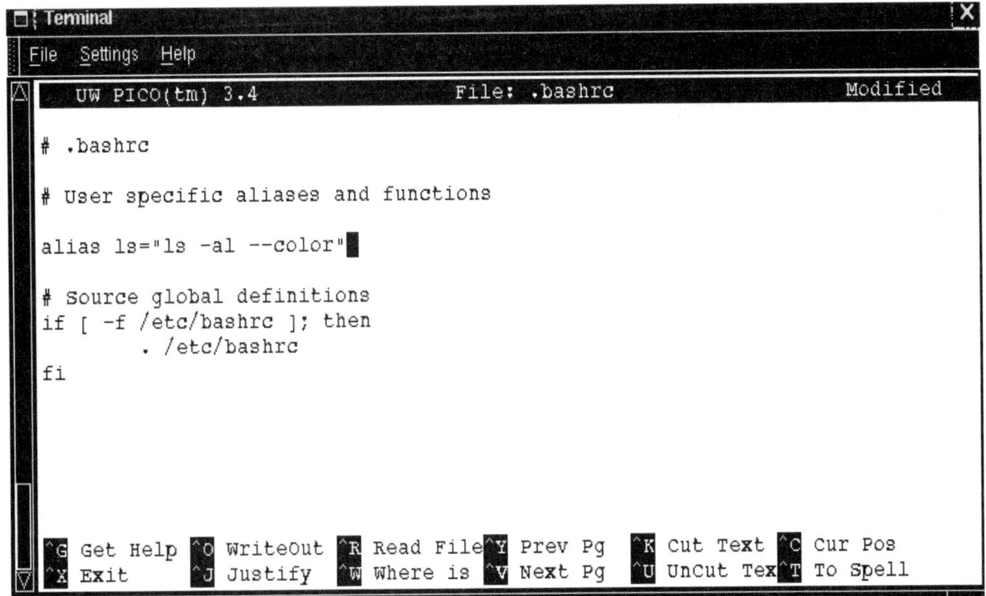

Figure 16-8: Adding an alias for the ls command to the .bashrc file

Double-check for any typos then, when you're satisfied with the changes, exit by pressing the [Ctrl] and [X] keys. You'll see, at the bottom of your editor screen, a message reading:

```
Save modified buffer (ANSWERING "No" WILL DESTROY CHANGES)?
Press [Y] for "yes."
```

Now, another message will appear at the bottom:

```
File Name to write: .bashrc
Simply pressing [Enter] will save your changes to your
.bashrc file.
```

You won't be able to see your changes take effect until you close your xterm window and open a new xterm. Once you do that, you'll see your modifications take effect.

Here's a short list of some popular options with ls. Remember, you can view the full list by reading the ls man page (man ls).

- **-a** — all. Lists all the files in the directory, including the hidden files (.filename). The .. and . at the top of your list refer to the parent directory and the current directory, respectively.
- **-l** — long. Lists details about contents, including permissions (modes), owner, group, size, creation date, whether the file is linked to somewhere else on the system and where its link points.
- **-F** — file type. Adds a symbol to the end of each listing. These symbols include / to indicate a directory; @ to indicate a symbolic link to another file; * to indicate an executable file.
- **-r** — reverse. Lists the contents of the directory from back to front.
- **-R** — recursive. This recursive option lists the contents of all directories (below the current directory) recursively.
- **-S** — size. Sorts files by their size.

A little later in this chapter, when we introduce you to pipes and I/O redirection, you'll discover that there are other ways to view the contents of a directory.

- **Summary:** To see the contents of a directory, type ls at a shell prompt; typing ls -a will display all the contents of a directory; typing ls -a —color will display all the contents categorized by color.

A Larger Picture of the Filesystem

Every operating system has a method of storing its files and directories so that it can keep track of additions, modifications and other changes. In Linux, every file is stored on the system with a unique name, in directories which can also hold other files and directories — or, subdirectories. You might think of the system as a tree-like structure, in which directories "branch off." Those directories may contain — or be the "parent" of — other directories which may hold files or directories of their own. There wouldn't be a tree without a root, and the same is true for the Linux filesystem. No matter how far away the branches, everything is connected to the root, which is represented as a single forward slash (/). It might seem confusing to have several references to "root" - the root account, the root account's login directory and the root directory (/), but think of it this way: The root login, who is the system administrator, is just as important to keeping things together in the system as the system's root (/).

- **Tip:** Even though there are other Linux distributions, your Red Hat Linux system is likely to be compatible with them. The reason is because of the Filesystem Hierarchy Standard (also known as FHS). These guidelines help to standardize the way system programs and files are stored on all Linux systems. You can read more about the FHS at its website: *http://www.pathname.com/fhs/*

As long as we're logged into our user account — which will help prevent disastrous mistakes — let's take a look around. The first stop on this tour ought to be the root directory, which will give us a larger picture of where things are. At the shell prompt, then, let's type:

```
cd /
```

We'll see a prompt which looks like:

```
[billy@localhost /]
```

Now, let's see which directories "branch off" root by typing:

```
ls
```

Doesn't look like much, does it? Well, it's a little like viewing the tip of an iceberg. These are the parent directories of other directories, in which there may be other directories... and so on.

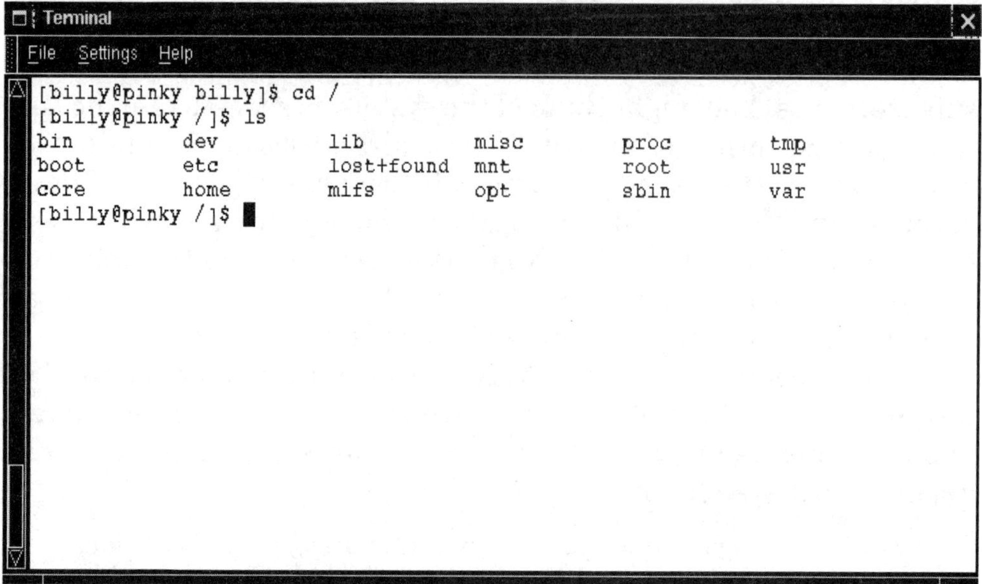
Terminal
File Settings Help
[billy@pinky billy]$ cd /
[billy@pinky /]$ ls
bin dev lib misc proc tmp
boot etc lost+found mnt root usr
core home mifs opt sbin var
[billy@pinky /]$

Figure 16-9: Getting of view of the directories from root

Here are just a few of the directories we're likely to find:

```
etc        lib       sbin
usr        var
```

There are more, but let's take a look in the `/etc` directory.

```
[billy@localhost /] cd etc
[billy@localhost /etc] ls
```

Here, among other type of files and directories, we'll find *configuration files*, which are files that help make programs work for our system, store our program and system settings and more. Among the directories in here, you'll see `/etc/X11`, which also contains directories and configuration files for the X Window System.

In the directory `/etc/skel`, you'll find skeleton user files, which are used to populate newly created user accounts with standard, commonly used files. That sounds a little gothic, perhaps, but here's what it means. When we were logged in as root, one of our first tasks was to create an account for ourselves. When our user account was created, files were taken from `/etc/skel` and placed into the new account. These files helped to "flesh out" the account (skeleton... flesh... get it?). Let's look around a little in /usr. From our current location in `/etc/skel`, we can type:

```
[billy@localhost /skel] cd /usr
[billy@localhost /usr] ls
```

In /usr, we're going to find a number of directories which hold some of our system's most important programs, and files (see Figure 16-10).

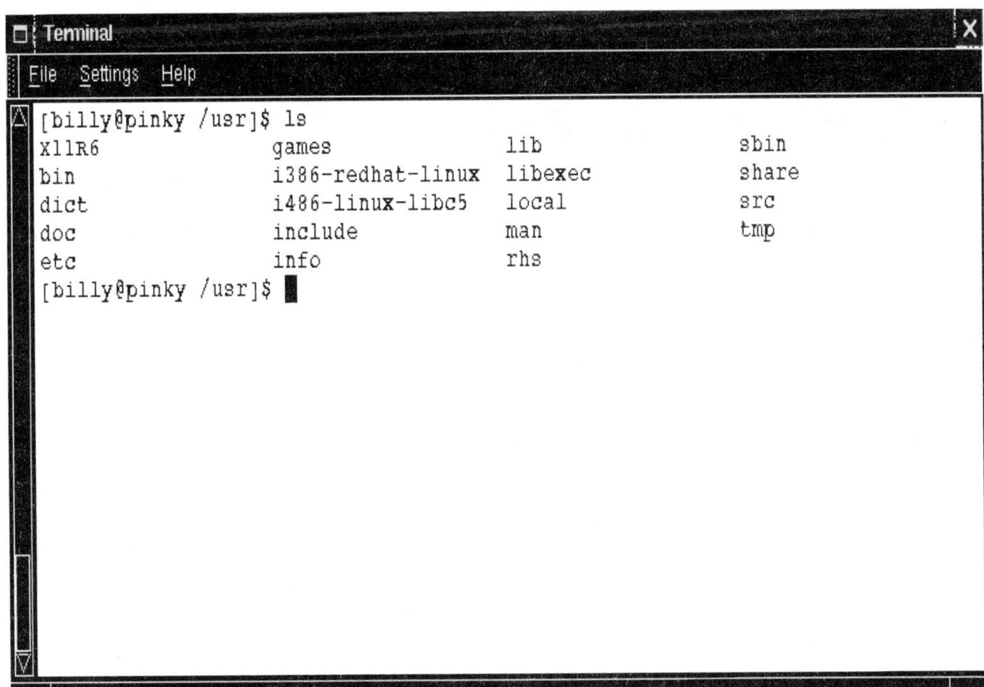
Terminal
File Settings Help
[billy@pinky /usr]$ ls
X11R6 games lib sbin
bin i386-redhat-linux libexec share
dict i486-linux-libc5 local src
doc include man tmp
etc info rhs
[billy@pinky /usr]$

16-10: The ls command in /usr

In /usr/man we'll find the system manual pages; other documentation which isn't covered by man pages will be found in /usr/doc. In /usr/X11R6, we'll find files related to the X Window System, including configuration and documentation files. Although we may think of something more literary when we hear the word "libraries," in /usr/lib we'll find files which are considered libraries for our system. In this context, libraries are files containing commonly-used snippets of code which can be shared by many programs. Red Hat Linux uses the RPM (the **R**ed Hat **P**ackage **M**anager) technology of software installation and upgrades. Using RPM, either from the shell prompt or through GnoRPM, is both a safe and convenient way to upgrade or install software. (For more on using GnoRPM, see its chapter in the Red Hat Linux Installation Guide.) However, once you become more comfortable with your system, there may be times when you'll want to install software that may not be available in RPM format. To minimize collisions with RPM-managed files, the best place to put such software is in /usr/local.

"Washing" the Window

After even one ls command in an xterm window, things might start feeling a little crowded. We can always exit from the terminal window and open a new one, but here's a quicker way to wipe the slate clean. Just type:

```
clear
```

at the shell prompt. The clear command does just as advertised: it clears the terminal screen. Sometimes, you may accidentally open a program file or some other non-text file in a terminal window. Once you close the file, you could find that the text you're typing doesn't match with the output on the monitor. In such cases, you simply have to type:

```
reset
```

to return the window to its default values.

- **Summary:** To clear clutter in a console or xterm window type clear; to return an xterm window to its default display properties, type reset.

Using cat

There's a handy utility which can help you keep short lists, gather those lists together and, at the same time, show you a little of the power behind your Red Hat Linux system. The utility is called cat, short for "concatenate," which means that it strings files together. But cat can also perform a quick demonstration of two important terms: standard input and standard output. *Standard input* and *standard output* direct input and output (often referred to as *I/O*) to the user. If a program reads from standard input, it will, by default be reading from the keyboard. If a program writes to standard output, by default it will be writing to the screen. Let's start cat to see what this means. At the shell prompt, type:

```
cat
```

The cursor moves to a blank line. Now, in that blank line, let's type:

```
stop at sneaker store
```

and press the [Enter] key.

Suddenly, your screen looks like:

```
[billy@localhost billy] cat
stop by sneaker store
stop by sneaker store
```

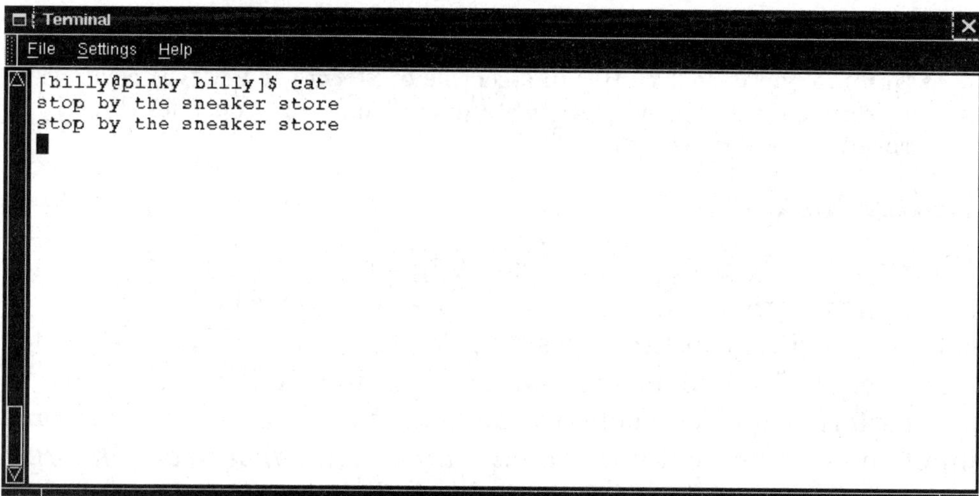
Terminal
File Settings Help
[billy@pinky billy]$ cat
stop by the sneaker store
stop by the sneaker store

Figure 16-11: cat demonstrates standard input and standard output

To quit `cat` now, just move the cursor to a blank line by pressing [Enter] then press the [Ctrl] and [D] keys at the same time. So it's not too exciting. But `cat` has just demonstrated the definition of standard input and standard output. Your input was read from the keyboard (standard input), and that input was then directed to your terminal (standard output).

- **Summary:** Standard input is often text which is entered from the keyboard. Standard output is the place where information is sent, such as your terminal (as shown in Figure 16-11).

Using Redirection

Now that we have a handle on what standard input and standard output are, it's time to expand a little. Redirection means causing the shell to change what it considers standard input or where the standard output is going. We used `cat` before to demonstrate the idea behind standard input and standard output. Now, let's use `cat` to see how standard output can be redirected. To redirect standard output, we'll use the > symbol. Placing > after the `cat` command (or after any utility or application that writes to standard output) will direct its output to the filename following the symbol. Let's try it. In an xterm window type:

```
[billy@localhost billy] cat > sneakers.txt
buy some sneakers
then go to the coffee shop
then buy some
coffee
```

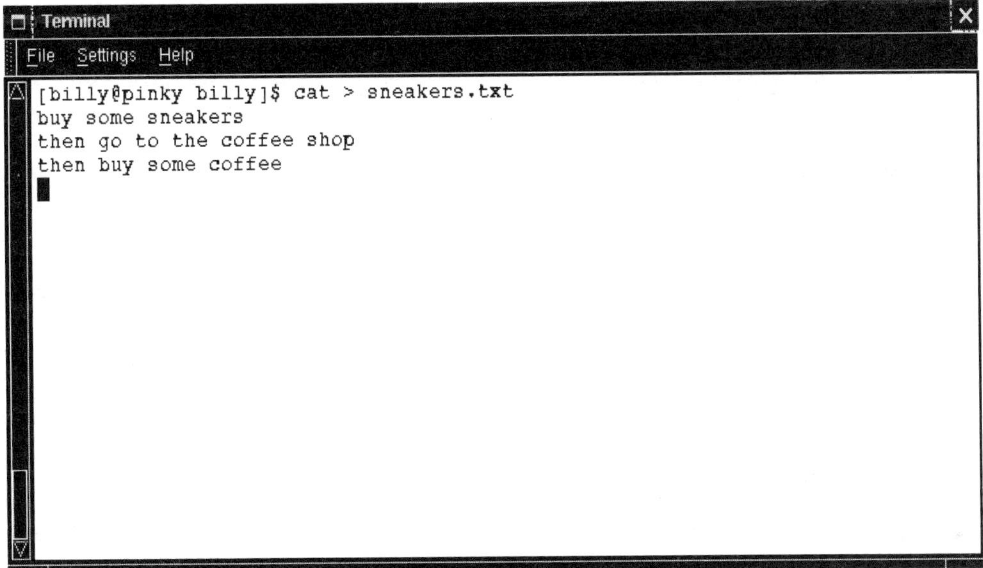

Figure 16-12: Redirecting the output to a file

Now press [Enter] to go to an empty line, and use the [Ctrl] and [D] keys to quit cat. Notice the difference (see Figure 16-12)? For one thing, there are no double entries. That's because the standard output from cat was redirected. That redirection was to a brand new file you made called `sneakers.txt`.

You can find the file in your login directory (may we suggest using `ls` if you want to see it listed?).

You can even use `cat` to read the file, by typing:

```
cat sneakers.txt
```

at the prompt.

- **Tip:** Be careful when you redirect the output to a file, because you can easily overwrite an existing file! Make sure the name of the file you're creating doesn't match the name of a pre-existing file, unless you want to replace it.

Let's use output redirection for another file and call it `home.txt`.

```
[billy@localhost billy] cat > home.txt
bring the coffee home
take off shoes
put on sneakers
make some coffee
relax!
```

Now, on an empty line, use the [Ctrl] and [D] keys again to quit cat.

We can check the file again by typing:

```
cat home.txt
```

at the prompt.

Let's use `cat` again to join `home.txt` with `sneakers.txt` and redirect the output of both files to a brand new file we'll call `saturday` (you'll find an example in Figure 16-13).

```
[billy@localhost billy] cat sneakers.txt home.txt >
saturday
```

That's it.

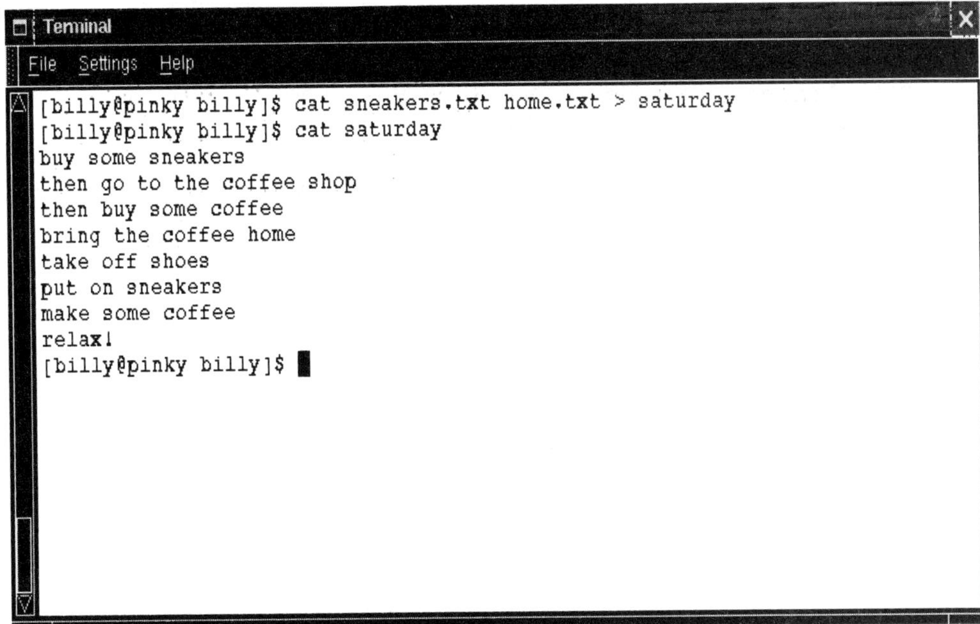
Terminal
File Settings Help
[billy@pinky billy]$ cat sneakers.txt home.txt > saturday
[billy@pinky billy]$ cat saturday
buy some sneakers
then go to the coffee shop
then buy some coffee
bring the coffee home
take off shoes
put on sneakers
make some coffee
relax!
[billy@pinky billy]$

Figure 16-13: Joining files and redirecting the output

Now it's time to check our handiwork. Type:

```
[billy@localhost billy] cat saturday
```

and you should see something like this:

```
[billy @localhost billy] cat saturday
buy some sneakers
then go to the coffee shop
then buy some coffee
bring the coffee home
take off shoes
put on sneakers
```

```
make some coffee
relax!
[billy @localhost billy]
```

You can see that cat has added `home.txt` where `sneakers.txt` left off.

- **Tip:** Creating and combining short files with cat can be a convenient alternative to using a text editor like pico.
- **Summary:** By using the output redirection symbol (>) you can send the output to a file instead of the terminal. The cat utility can be used along with output redirection to join files together into a single, unified file with one filename.

Appending Standard Output

There's a neat twist to output redirection which allows you to add new information to the end of an existing file. Similar to when you used the > symbol, you tell your shell to send the information somewhere other than standard output. However, when you use >>, you're *adding* information, rather than replacing it. The best explanation is a demonstration, so let's take two files which have already already been created — `sneakers.txt` and `home.txt` — and join them by using the append output symbol. We want to add the information in `home.txt` to the information already in `sneakers.txt`, so we type:

```
cat home.txt >> sneakers.txt
```

Now let's check the file by typing:

```
cat  sneakers.txt
```

And there it is — with the contents of `home.txt` at the end. What we were saying when we typed that command was, "append the output from the file `home.txt` to the file `sneakers.txt`." By appending the output, we've saved ourselves a step or two (and a bit of disk clutter) by using existing files, rather than creating a new file. Compare the results of the files `sneakers.txt` and `saturday` now, and you'll see that they're identical. To make your comparison, just type:

```
cat  sneakers.txt;  cat  saturday
```

The contents of both files will be displayed - first `sneakers.txt`, then `saturday` (as shown in Figure 16-14).

- **Tip:** Remember that when you append output, you've got to include the double greater-than symbols (>>). Otherwise, you'll end up replacing the very file to which you want to append information!

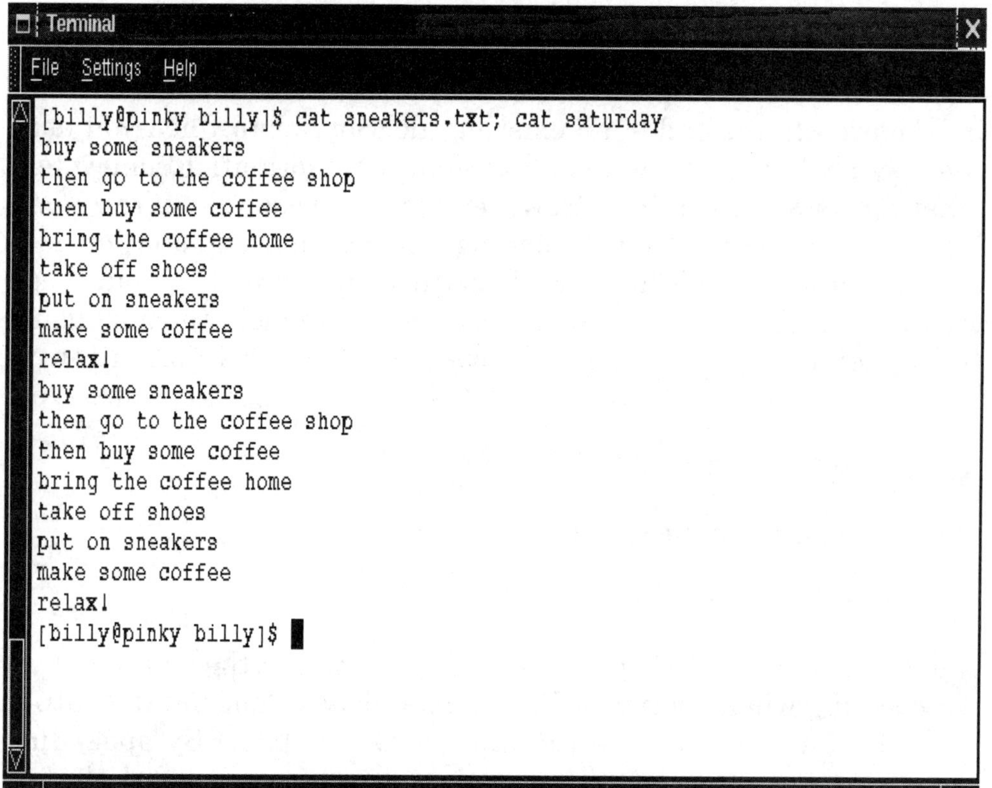

Terminal
File Settings Help
[billy@pinky billy]$ cat sneakers.txt; cat saturday
buy some sneakers
then go to the coffee shop
then buy some coffee
bring the coffee home
take off shoes
put on sneakers
make some coffee
relax!
buy some sneakers
then go to the coffee shop
then buy some coffee
bring the coffee home
take off shoes
put on sneakers
make some coffee
relax!
[billy@pinky billy]$

Figure 16-14: Stringing commands and comparing files

(By the way, if you're curious about the use of the semi-colon in that last command, read on. We'll cover that later in this chapter.)

- **Summary:** To append output, use two greater-than symbols (>>). For example: cat addthisfile >> tothisfile.

Redirecting Standard Input

Not only can you redirect standard output, you can perform the same type of redirection with standard input. Here's how it works: When you use the redirect standard input symbol <, you're telling the shell that you want a file to be read as input for a command. We can use a file we've already created to demonstrate this idea. Just type:

```
cat < sneakers.txt
```

Because we used the less-than symbol (<) to separate the `cat` command from the file, the output of sneakers.txt was read by `cat`.

Pipes

No, we're not going to start talking about plumbing here. In Linux, "pipes" connect the standard output of one command to the standard input of another command. Let's take a step back, to the ls command. There are plenty of options available with ls, but what if the contents of a directory stream by too quickly for you to view them? Let's view the contents of the `/etc` directory.

```
ls -al /etc
```

How do we take a closer look at the output before it races off the screen? One answer is to pipe the output to a utility called `less`. Known as a pager, `less`, (like `more`) allows us to view information one page (or screen) at a time. We use the vertical bar (|) to pipe the commands (as shown in Figure 16-15).

ls -al /etc | less

Now we can view the contents one screen at a time. To move forward a screen, just press [Space]; to move back a screen, press [B]; to quit,

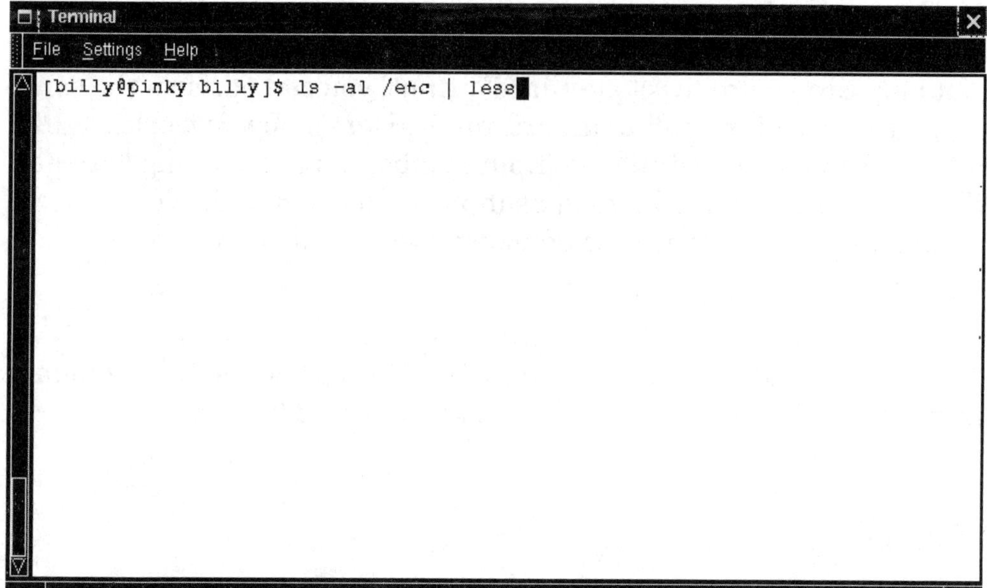

Figure 16-15: Piping the output of ls to the less pager

just press [Q].

Actually, we've already been using pipes, before we even discussed what they were. In previous references to man pages, we used the following to print out the man page entry:

```
man ls | col -b | lpr
```

Here, we're sending the output of man ls to a filter called col with an option of -b to help format the text for the printer, then we sent the output of that to the printer using the lpr command.

- **Summary:** Piping allows you to send the output of one command as the input of another command. For example: ls -al /etc | more pipes the output of the ls command to the more utility for easy viewing.

Stringing Commands Together

Linux allows you to enter multiple commands at one time. The only requirement is that you separate the commands with a semicolon. Want to see how long you've been online using Netscape? Just combine the `date` command with Netscape's command.

```
date; netscape; date
```

Remember that commands are case sensitive, so the command to start Netscape must be in lower-case to start the browser. In the `xterm` window, we'll see something like this:

```
[billy@localhost billy] date; netscape; date
Saturday Mar 27 21:26:27 EST 1999
```

We'll see the second date entry when we close out of Netscape. Then, our screen will look like this:

```
[billy@localhost billy] date; netscape; date
Fri Mar 26 13:26:27 EST 1999
Fri Mar 26 14:28:32 EST 1999
[billy@localhost billy]
```

And the prompt will return. The discrepancy between the two results from the date command shows that we were using Netscape for just over an hour

Ownership and Permissions

Earlier in this chapter, when we tried to `cd` to root's login directory, we received the following friendly message:

```
billy@localhost billy] cd /root
bash: /root: Permission denied
[billy@localhost billy]
```

That was one demonstration of Linux's security features. Linux, like UNIX, is a multi-user system, and file *permissions* are one way the system uses to protect against any type of tampering — malicious or accidental. One way to gain entry when we see we're denied permission is to su to root, as we learned earlier. That's because whoever knows the root password has complete access.

```
[billy@localhost billy] su root
Password: (your root password)
[root@localhost billy]# cd /root
[root@localhost /root]#
```

But switching to superuser isn't always convenient — or smart, since it's so easy to mistakenly mess up important configuration files. All files and directories are "owned" by the person who created them. We created the file `sneakers.txt` in our login directory, so `sneakers.txt` "belongs" to us. That means, we can specify who's allowed to read the file, write to the file or, if it were an application instead of a text file, who can execute the file. Reading, writing and executing are the three main settings in permissions. Since every user on the system is placed into a group when that user is created, then we can also specify whether certain groups can read, write to, or execute our file. Let's take a closer look at `sneakers.txt` with the `ls` command using the -l (long) option (see Figure 16-16).

```
[billy@localhost billy] ls -l sneakers.txt
-rw-rw-r— 1 billy billy 150 Mar 19 08:08
sneakers.txt
```

There's quite a bit of detail here. We can see who can read (r) and write to (w) the file, as well as who created the file (`billy`) and to which group the owner belongs (`billy`).

- **Tip:** Remember that, by default, your group was the login name you chose.

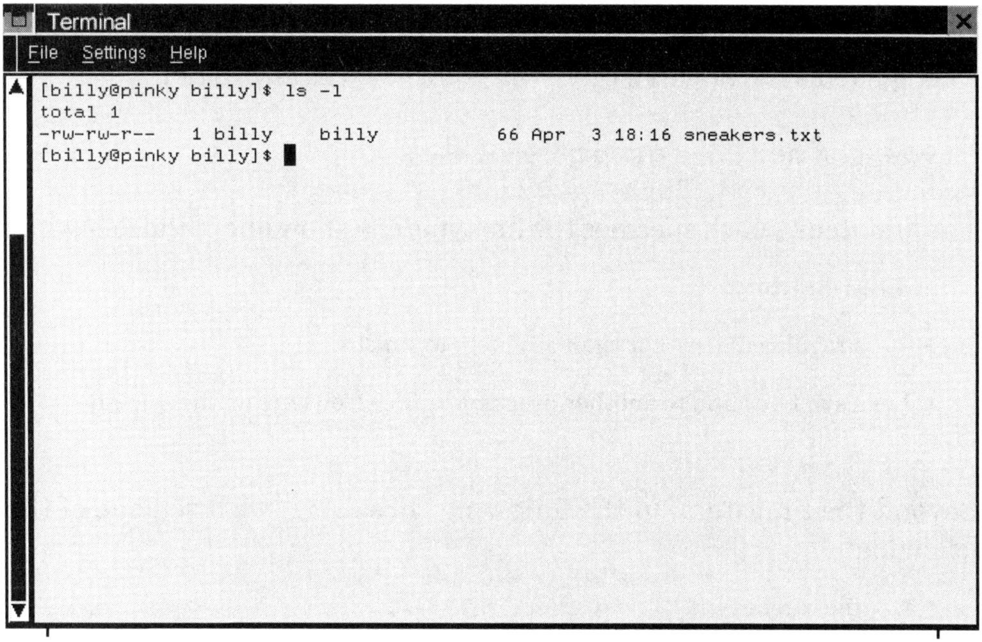

Terminal

File Settings Help

```
[billy@pinky billy]$ ls -l
total 1
-rw-rw-r--    1 billy    billy          66 Apr  3 18:16 sneakers.txt
[billy@pinky billy]$
```

Figure 16-16: Permissions for sneakers.txt

Other information to the right of the group includes the file name, date and time of its creation as well as size.

How do all those dashes and letters fit together? It's not as hard to read as it might seem. Let's take a look:

```
-rw-rw-r—
```

There are 10 slots in this column. The first slot represents the type of file. The remaining nine slots are actually three sets of permissions for three different categories of users.

Those three sets are: the owner of the file, the group in which the file belongs and "others," meaning users and groups other than owner of the file (`billy`) and those in billy's group (which is also `billy`).

Let's stretch out these file settings a bit:

```
-     (-rw)      (-rw)      (r—)     1 billy billy
|       |          |          |
type   owner      group     others
```

The first item, which specifies the file type, can show one of the following:

- **d** — a directory
- **-** — a regular file (rather than directory or link)
- **l** — a symbolic link to another program or file elsewhere on the system

Beyond the first item, in the following three sets, we'll see one of the following:

- **r** — file can be read
- **w** — file can be written to
- **x** — file can be executed (if it's a program)

When we see a dash in owner, group or others, it means that particular permission hasn't been granted. Let's look again at first column of sneakers.txt and identify its permissions. (See Figure 16-17)

```
[billy@localhost billy] ls -l sneakers.txt
-rw-rw-r— 1 billy billy 150 Mar 19 08:08 sneakers.txt
[billy@localhost billy]
```

Figure 16-17: A closer view of permissions

The file's owner, `billy`, has permission to read and write to the file; it's not a program, so billy doesn't have permission to execute it. The group, `billy`, has permission to read and write to `sneakers.txt`, as well. Similar to the program notation for owner billy, there's no execute permission for group `billy`.

In the last set, we can see that those who aren't either the user `billy` or in the group called `billy` can read the file, but can't write to it or execute it.

We can use the `chmod` command to change a file's permissions.

Let's work a bit more on `sneakers.txt` to change the permissions with the `chmod` command.

The original file looks like this, with its initial permissions settings:

```
-rw-rw-r— 1 billy billy 150 Mar 19 08:08 sneakers.txt
```

As long as we're the owner of the file — or we're logged into the root account — we can change permissions in any combination of settings for the owner, group and others.

Right now, the owner (that's us) and our group (which is `billy`) can read and write to the file.

Anyone outside of our group — for example, anyone in the adm group - can only read the file (r—).

- **Tip:** Remember that file permissions are a security feature. Whenever you allow everyone to read, write to and execute files, you may be increasing your risk of tampering. As a rule, then, you should shy away from allowing everyone to read and write to a file.

In this case, however, let's say that we want to allow everyone to write to the file, so they can read it, write notes in it and save it. That means we'll have to change the change the "others" section of the file permissions.

Since we're the owner of the file, we don't have to su to root to do it. Let's take a look at the file first. At the shell prompt, type:

```
ls -l sneakers.txt
```

which gives us this file information:

```
-rw-rw-r– 1 billy billy 150 Mar 19 08:08 sneakers.txt
```

Now, type the following:

```
chmod o+w sneakers.txt
```

To check our results, we can list the file's details again. Now, the file looks like this:

```
-rw-rw-rw- 1 billy billy 150 Mar 19 08:08 sneakers.txt
```

There's our result: Now, everyone can read and write to the file (Figure 16-18).

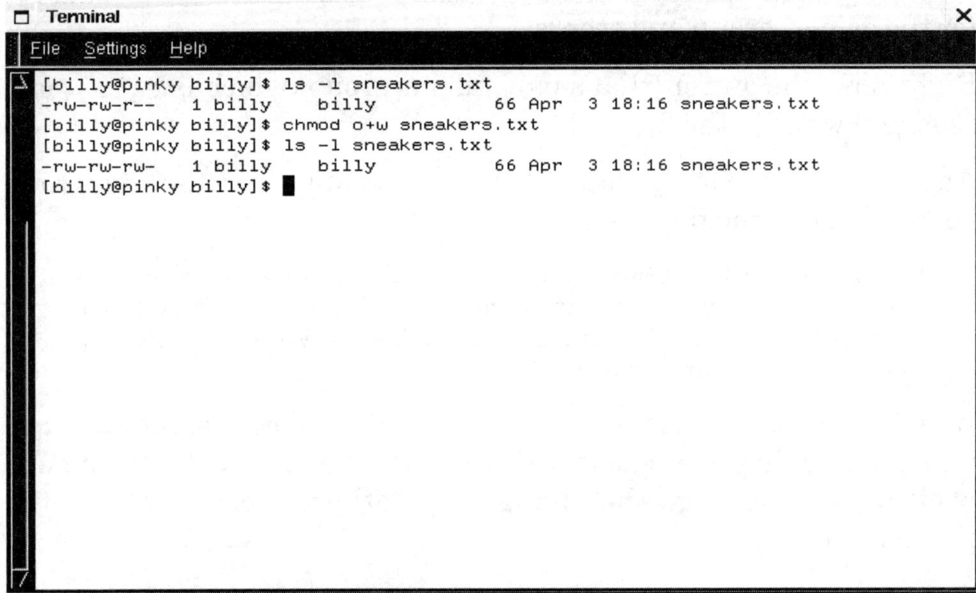

Terminal
File Settings Help
[billy@pinky billy]$ ls -l sneakers.txt
-rw-rw-r-- 1 billy billy 66 Apr 3 18:16 sneakers.txt
[billy@pinky billy]$ chmod o+w sneakers.txt
[billy@pinky billy]$ ls -l sneakers.txt
-rw-rw-rw- 1 billy billy 66 Apr 3 18:16 sneakers.txt
[billy@pinky billy]$

Figure 16-18: Changing permissions for sneakers.txt

When we typed o+w, we were saying, "for others, add write permission to the file sneakers.txt."

If we want to remove all access permission from sneakers.txt (even though it's only a sketchy shopping list), we could use the chmod command to take away both the read and write permissions like so:

```
chmod go-rw sneakers.txt
```

and the result will look like this:

```
-rw—— 1 billy billy 150 Mar 19 08:08
sneakers.txt
```

By typing go-rw, then, we were saying "for the group and others, remove read and write permission to the file sneakers.txt."

You might think of these settings as a kind of shorthand when you want to change permissions with chmod, because all you really have to do is remember a few symbols and letters with the chmod command.

Here a list of what the shorthand represents:

Identities

- **u** — the user who owns the file (that is, the owner)
- **g** — the group to which the user belongs
- **o** — others (not the owner or the owner's group)
- **a** — everyone (u, g, and o)

Permissions

- **r** — read access
- **w** — write access
- **x** — execute access

Actions

- **+** — adds the permission
- **-** — removes the permission
- **=** — makes it the only permission

Want to test it out? Let's remove all permission from `sneakers.txt` — for everyone.

```
chmod a-rw sneakers.txt
```

Now, let's see if we can read the file:

```
[billy@localhost billy] cat sneakers.txt
cat: sneakers.txt: Permission denied
[billy@localhost billy]
```

Guess it worked; even we can't get into the file. But since the file belongs to us, we can always change permission to allow us read and write access. (See Figure 16-19)

```
[billy@localhost billy] chmod u+rw sneakers.txt
[billy@localhost billy] cat sneakers.txt
buy some sneakers
then go to the coffee shop
then buy some coffee
bring the coffee home
take off shoes
put on sneakers
make some coffee
relax!
[billy@localhost billy]
```

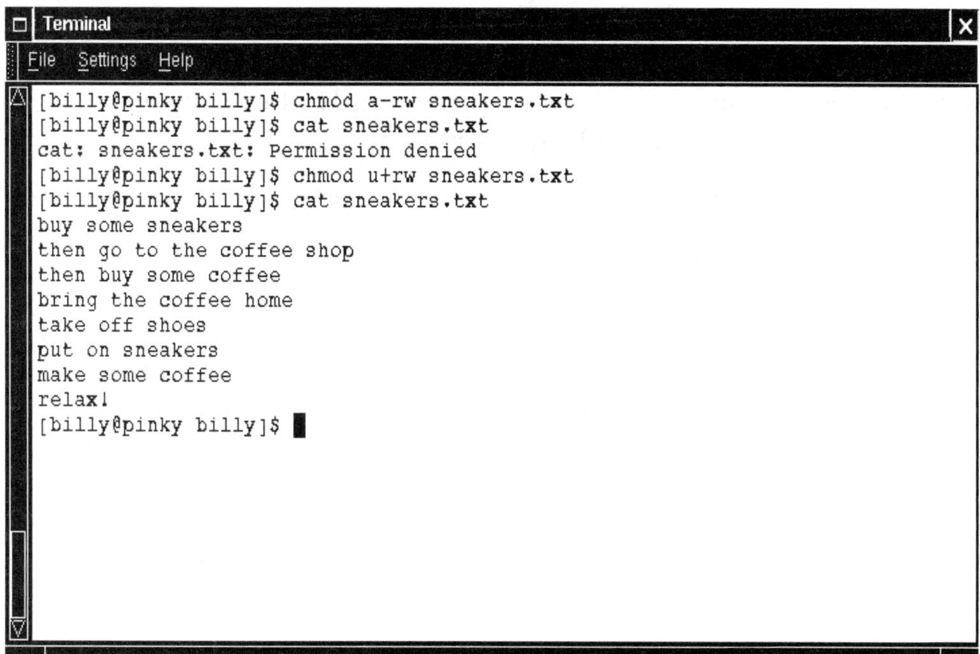
Terminal
File Settings Help
[billy@pinky billy]$ chmod a-rw sneakers.txt
[billy@pinky billy]$ cat sneakers.txt
cat: sneakers.txt: Permission denied
[billy@pinky billy]$ chmod u+rw sneakers.txt
[billy@pinky billy]$ cat sneakers.txt
buy some sneakers
then go to the coffee shop
then buy some coffee
bring the coffee home
take off shoes
put on sneakers
make some coffee
relax!
[billy@pinky billy]$

Figure 16-19: Removing, then restoring permissions

Here are some common examples of settings that can be used with chmod:

- **g+w** — adds write access for the group
- **o-rwx** — removes all permissions for others
- **u+x** — allows the file owner to execute the file
- **a+rw** — allows everyone to read and write to the file
- **ug+r** — allows the owner and group to read the file
- **g=rx** — lets the group only read and execute (not write)

By adding the **-R** option, we can change permissions for entire directory trees.

There's a slight twist, however, because we can't really "execute" a directory as we would an application. Instead, when we add or remove execute permission for a directory, we're really allowing (or denying) permission to search through that directory.

To allow everyone read and write access to the tigger directory in our login directory, we just type:

```
chmod -R a+rw tigger
```

But... If we don't allow others to have execute permission to tigger, it doesn't matter who has read or write access, because no one will be able to get into the directory — unless they know the exact filename they want.

For example, let's type:

chmod a-x tigger

to remove execute access to all.

Here's what happens now when we try to `cd` to into tigger:

```
[billy@localhost billy] cd tigger
bash: tigger: Permission denied
billy@localhost billy]
```

Let's restore ours and our group's access.

```
chmod ug+x tigger
```

Now, if we check our work with `ls -dl` we'll see that only others will be denied access to `tigger`.

Fun with Numbers in chmod

Remember when we made a reference to the "shorthand" method of chmod? Here's another way to change permissions; it may seem a little complex at first - especially if math isn't your strong suit. Let's go back to the original permissions for `sneakers.txt`.

```
-rw-rw-r– 1 billy billy 150 Mar 19 08:08 sneakers.txt
```

Each permission setting can be represented by a numerical value:

- r = 4
- w = 2
- x = 1
- \- = 0

When these values are added together, the total is used to set specific permissions - more specific than changing permissions with the alphabetical "shorthand." In `sneakers.txt`, then, here are the numerical permissions settings:

```
–       (-rw)       (-rw)       (r–)
          |           |           |
        0+4+2       0+4+2       4+0+0
```

The total for the user is six, the total for the group is six and the total for others is four. The permissions setting, then, is read as 664. If we want to change sneakers.txt so those in our group didn't have write access, but could still read the file (as shown in Figure 16-20), we'll have to remove the access by subtracting 2 from that set of numbers.

The numerical values, then, would become six, four and four — or 644.

So we can type:

```
chmod 644 sneakers.txt
```

Let's check our changes by listing the file (`ls -l sneakers.txt`):

```
-rw-r—r— 1 billy billy 150 Mar 19 08:08 sneakers.txt
```

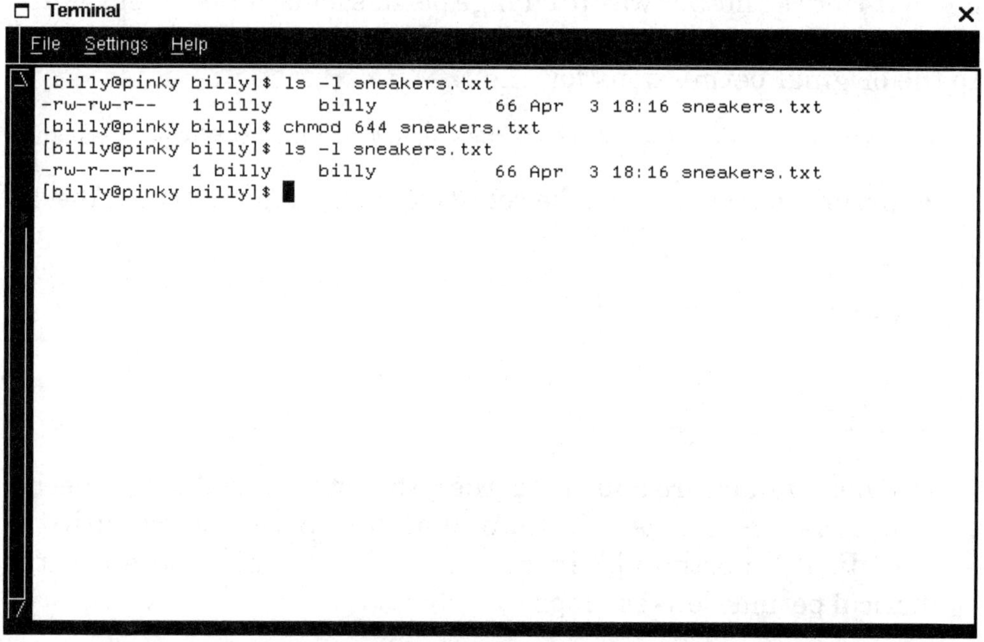

```
Terminal
File  Settings  Help
[billy@pinky billy]$ ls -l sneakers.txt
-rw-rw-r--   1 billy    billy          66 Apr  3 18:16 sneakers.txt
[billy@pinky billy]$ chmod 644 sneakers.txt
[billy@pinky billy]$ ls -l sneakers.txt
-rw-r--r--   1 billy    billy          66 Apr  3 18:16 sneakers.txt
[billy@pinky billy]$
```

Figure 16-20: Removing group write permissions

And there it is; now, neither the group nor others have write permission to sneakers.txt. To return the group's write access for the file, we can just add the value of w (2) to the second set of permissions.

```
chmod 664 sneakers.txt
```

- **Tip:** Beware 666 and 777. Biblical implications aside, either of these settings will allow everyone to read and write to a file or directory. Such settings as these could allow tampering with sensitive files, so in general, it's not a good idea to allow these settings.

Here's a list of some common settings, numerical values and their meanings:

- **-rw——— (600)** — Only the user has read and write permissions.
- **-rw-r—r— (644)** — Only user has read and write permissions; the group and others can read only.
- **-rwx——— (700)** — Only the user has read, write and execute permissions.
- **-rwxr-xr-x (755)** — The user has read, write and execute permissions; the group and others can only read and execute.
- **-rwx—x—x (711)** — The user has read, write and execute permissions; the group and others can only execute.
- **-rw-rw-rw- (666)** — Everyone can read and write to the file. Bad idea.
- **-rwxrwxrwx (777)** — Everyone can read, write and execute. Another bad idea.

Here are a couple common settings for directories:

- **drwx——— (700)** — Only the user can read, write in this directory.
- **drwxr-xr-x (755)** — Everyone can read the directory, but its contents can only be changed by the user.

- **Summary:** You can change permissions with the chmod command by using letters or numbers. Type chmod (permissions) file to change permissions of a file or directory.

You've already come quite a distance in learning about your Red Hat Linux system — from navigation to setting and changing permissions. Now, it's time to learn a little more about managing what you have on your system. The following chapter wil help you to understand a little more about file types and how to work with a variety of commands.

17 Managing Files and Directories

If you're a Linux newbie — and there are many — you may feel a little disoriented when you want to accomplish your first tasks. Relax. If you've had any experience with other operating systems, learning Linux is a bit like learning to drive in a new country: The ideas are the same, but some of the particulars are a bit different. We'll go over several of those "rules of the road" in this chapter. But there's one component of your new operating system you just can't do without: the shell. We've made numerous references to the shell — as in "shell prompt," or "bash." Now, it's time to learn a little more about this indispensable tool. But first, a little history...

Shell Collecting

In the olden days (we're talking '60s here), when AT&T's Dennis Ritchie and Ken Thompson were designing UNIX, they wanted to create a way that humans could interact with their new system.

Operating systems at the time did come with "command interpreters," which could take commands from the user and interpret them for the computer to understand.

But Ritchie and Thompson wanted something more, something which could offer better features than the command interpreters of the day.

Enter the Bourne shell (known simply as sh), created by S.R. Bourne, which fulfilled the goals of UNIX's creators.

Since the creation of the Bourne shell, other shells have been developed, such as the C shell (csh) and the Korn shell (ksh).

When the Free Software Foundation sought a royalty-free shell, developers began to work on the language behind the Bourne shell as well as some of the popular features from other shells available at the time.

The result was the Bourne Again Shell — or bash.

By now, of course, you've probably seen the word bash when you've mistyped commands at the shell prompt (as in bash: oops: command not found).

In Chapter 1, when we covered redirection and piping, we were also demonstrating the power of bash.

- **Tip:** You can learn more about bash by reading the bash man page. At the shell prompt, type man bash (or you can save the file as a text file by typing man bash | col -b > bash.txt, which you can then open to read with an editor like pico or a pager like less. You can also print the file with man bash | col -b | lpr, but be warned: it's a large file. If you want more information, O'Reilly & Associates publishes *Learning the bash Shell*, by Cameron Newham and Bill Rosenblatt.

Although your system came with several different shells, bash is the default shell for Red Hat Linux.

You might think of bash as a fleet-footed office assistant who has made a habit of keeping notes on ways to fulfill commands quickly. This assistant also keeps pointers on how you like to customize the way you work.

These "pointers" bash keeps are referred to as *environment variables*.

The shell uses an "environment" in the same way we use an environment, like a kitchen. We work in our kitchen, arrange pots, pans, and spices. We know where the dishes are, how things operate.

The same can be said for `bash` and its environment. There's a basic arrangement to `bash` as there would be to just about any kitchen. For example, we'd expect to see pots in a kitchen in the same way that we would expect to see certain commands in `bash`.

That's the idea behind environment variables.

As long as your assistant has the right pointers, he'll fulfill your commands quickly.

Let's take a look at our environment variables. At the shell prompt, type:

```
env
```

Quite a few "shortcuts" `bash` uses, aren't there?

Each one of these helps bash customize the environment for you.

Among the most important environment variables is the PATH environment variable — which defines what is known as the *default path*.

The PATH environment variable for our account billy might look something like this:

```
PATH=/usr/local/bin:/usr/X11R6/bin:/usr/bin:/bin:/usr/X11R6/
bin:/home/billy/bin
```

It looks crowded, but the PATH statement is a great signpost, which points to where programs can be found.

- **Tip:** Remember the reference in the previous chapter to the FHS (Filesystem Hierarchy Standard)? The PATH statement is set according to that standard, and programs are installed in directories in accordance with the FHS as well. The end result is that the PATH statement will enable bash to automatically find nearly any program, assuming it has been installed in accordance with the FHS.

Locating Files and Directories

There will be times when we know a file or directory exists but we won't know where to find it. Searching for a file or directory can be made much easier with the `locate` command.

With `locate`, we'll see every related file or directory which matches our search criterion. Let's say we want to search for all files related to the `finger` command.

```
locate finger
```

The `locate` command uses a database to check for files and directories which match the string finger.

- **Tip:** To learn more about locate, read the locate man page by typing man locate at a shell prompt.

It's a handy command which works very quickly — as long as the database is up to date. That database is automatically updated on a nightly basis, from `cron`. What's `cron`? It's a small program that runs in the background, performing various tasks — such as updating the `locate` database — at regularly scheduled intervals.

- **Tip:** cron is a daemon. Daemons handle tasks in the background. To read the cron man page, type man cron at the shell prompt.

So what happens if we:

- Have more than one operating system on our machine, and switch between them — causing us to halt and restart our Red Hat Linux system;
- Shutdown and turn off our machine at the end of the day.

This might mean that `cron` never has a chance to update the `locate` database. No problem. We can just update the database manually. Let's give it a try.

First, `su` to root.

Now, at the shell prompt, type:

```
/etc/cron.daily/updatedb.cron
```

After a few minutes, the locate database will be current.

Command History and Tab Completion

It doesn't take long before the thought of typing the same command over and over becomes unappealing, at best.

Linux users don't feel any differently about that, either. But in Linux, since you can string together commands at the shell prompt, one minor typo in a couple lines of a command could mean that all that typing was in vain.

So there's a solution: It's called *command-line history*. By scrolling with the up and down arrow keys, we can find plenty of our previously typed commands — including the ones with typos.

Let's try it by taking a look again at `sneakers.txt`. The first time, however, at the shell prompt, we'll type:

```
cat sneakrs.txt
```

Oops! Nothing happens, of course, because there is no `sneakrs.txt` file. No problem. We'll just use the up-arrow key to bring back the command, then use the left-arrow key to get to the point where we missed the "e." Insert the letter and press `[Enter]` again.

Voila! We now see the contents of `sneakers.txt`.

The bash shell can store up to 1,000 commands.

- **Tip:** By typing the env command at a shell prompt, we can see the environment variable that controls the size of the command-line history. The line which reads, "HISTSIZE=1000" tells us that bash will store 1,000 commands in its history.

The command-line history is actually kept in a file, called .bash_history in our login directory. We can read it in a number of ways: by using `pico, cat, less, more,` and others.

Be prepared, though: the file can be pretty long.

Let's read it with more:

```
more .bashhistory
```

To move forward a screen, press [Space]; to move back a screen, press [B]; to quit, press [Q].

Another time-saving tool is known as *tab completion*. If you type part of a file or pathname then hit the [Tab] key, bash will present you with either the remaining portion of a the file/path, or a beep. If we get a beep, we can press [Tab] again to obtain a list of the files/paths that match what we've typed so far.

So even if we do turn off the machine at the end of the day, we probably won't have to work too hard in order to remember the command to update locate's database: The chances are good that the command will be stored in the command-line history or can be completed with tab completion (as long as we remember the start of the pathname for the command).

Both tab completion and command-line history can be useful to help you use a command you've forgotten, as well.

Let's try tab completion to update locate's database. First, su to root.

Now, at a shell prompt, type the beginning of the path:

```
/etc/cr
```

Now, press the [Tab] key and tab completion will complete the path to /etc/cron (and you'll hear a beep). Press [Tab] again, and you'll be presented with a list of possible completions:

```
cron.daily cron.hourly cron.monthly cron.weekly crontab
```

So add the `.daily` to the command (or simply type the .d and press [Tab] again). Press [Tab] again, and the result will be:

```
logrotate tetex.cron tmpwatch updatedb.cron
```

And there's our `updatedb.cron` command. We can simply add it to the end of the path we've got so far (or just type u and press [Tab] yet again) and press [Enter] to run `updatedb.cron`.

Identifying and Working with File Types

If you're new to Linux, it won't take long before you begin seeing files with extensions that may seem foreign. A file's extension is the last part of a file's name, after the final dot (in the file `sneakers.txt`, "`txt`" was that file's extension).

Here's a brief listing of extensions and their meanings:

Compressed/Archived Files

- **Z** — a compressed file
- **.tar** — an archive file (short for tape archive)
- **.gz** — a compressed file (gzipped)
- **.tgz** — a tarred and gzipped file

File Formats

- **.txt** — a plain ASCII text file
- **.html/.htm** — an HTML file
- **.ps** — a PostScript file; formatted for printing
- **.au** — an audio file
- **.wav** — an audio file
- **.xpm** — an image file
- **.jpg** — a graphical or image file, such as a photo or artwork
- **.gif** — a graphical or image file
- **.png** — a graphical or image file

System Files

- **.rpm** — a Red Hat Package Manager file
- **.conf** — a configuration file
- **.a** — an archive file
- **.lock** — a "lock" file; determines whether a program is in use

Programming and Scripting Files

- **.h** — a C and C++ program language header file
- **.c** — a C program language source code file
- **.cpp** — a C++ program language source code file
- **.o** — a program object file
- **.pl** — a Perl script
- **.tcl** — a TCL script
- **.so** — a library file

But file extensions are not always used, or used consistently. So what happens when a file doesn't have an extension, or the file doesn't seem to be what the extension says it's supposed to be?

That's when the file command can come in handy.

In 1, we created a file called `saturday` — without an extension. Using the `file` command, we can tell what the file is by typing:

```
file saturday
```

and we'll see it's a text file. Any file that's designated a text file should be readable using `cat`, `more`, or `less`.

- **Tip:** To learn more about the file command, read the file man page by typing man file.

And speaking of reading files...

There are plenty of ways to read files in Linux. In the previous chapter, for example, we covered the pagers more and less — they're called pagers because you can "page" through documents one screen at a time. We also learned how we can not only view but manipulate files with the cat command.

But there are even more options when it comes time to take a look at README files, man pages or documents you've created.

You have a number of tools to help you read text files, among them, the text editors pico, emacs, and vim, the pagers more and less, and the viewers head, tail, cat, and grep.

Let's take a look at some of the features in these tools.

The less Command

In Chapter 1, we were introduced to the pager less. Less is the pager that's used to display man pages.

Let's view the man page for less to see less in action.

```
man less
```

To move forward a screen, press [Space]; to move back a screen, press [B], and to quit, press [Q].

There are other powerful features in less, as well, including the ability to scroll horizontally and specify the number of lines to scroll.

The more Command

Odd as it may seem, more offers less than less (actually, less was inspired by more).

Let's take a look at the man page for more, but this time, we'll open the page using more — by piping man's output to more.

```
man more | more
```

It may not look too different at first, but there are fewer enhancements to `more` than to `less`. Probably the most striking difference at first is the lack of a way to go backwards in a document — although moving forward by pressing [Space] and quitting by pressing [Q] are the same.

The head Command

You can use the `head` command if you just want to look at the beginning of a file. The command is:

```
head <filename>
```

`Head` can be useful, but because it's limited to the first several lines, you won't know how long the file actually is. By default, you can only read the first 10 lines of a file, although we can specify the number to see more by typing:

```
head -20 <filename>
```

Read `head`'s man page (`man head`) for more information. You'll probably find that `less` or `more` are more helpful, because you can page through the file if you find that the information you're looking for is further into the file than you originally thought.

The tail Command

The reverse of head (obviously), is `tail`. With (`tail`), you can review the last 10 lines of a file.

The cat Command

The command `cat`, short for concatenation, will dump the contents of the entire file on the screen. Using `cat` can be handy if the file is fairly short, such as when we created `sneakers.txt`. But if a file is fairly long, it will easily scroll past you on the screen, since `cat` displays the whole file.

The grep Command

The `grep` command is pretty nifty for finding specific character strings in a file. Let's say we want to find every reference we made to "coffee" in the file `sneakers.txt`, which we created in our login directory. We could type:

```
grep coffee sneakers.txt
```

and we would see every line in which the word "coffee" could be found.

- **Tip:** Unless otherwise specified, grep searches are case sensitive. That means that searching for Coffee is different than searching for coffee. So among grep's options is -i, which allows you to make a case-insensitive search through a file. Read the grep man page for more about this command.

I/O Redirection and Pipes

And don't forget about using pipes and output redirection when you want to store and/or print information to read at a later time.

You can, for example, use `grep` to search for particular contents of a file, then have those results either saved as a file or sent to a printer.

To print the information about references to "coffee" in `sneakers.txt`, for example, we just type:

```
grep coffee sneakers.txt | lpr
```

This command behaves similar to the command `ls -al /etc | more`, which you may have used in Chapter 1 to list the contents of the `/etc` directory then send the results through the `more` command for viewing on the screen.

- **Tip:** Remember the distinction of using > and >>: using > will overwrite a file, while >> appends the information to a file. Usually, unless you're certain you want to, it's safer to use >>, because you won't lose potentially valuable information (though you may have to edit the file if you didn't want to append information to it).

Wildcards and Regular Expressions

What if you forget the name of the file you're looking for? You can't say to your computer, "Find a file called 'sneak' or 'sneak-something'."

Well, yes you can, in a way. Using wildcards or regular expressions, you can perform actions on a file or files without knowing the complete filename. Just fill out what you know, then substitute the remainder with a wildcard.

- **Tip:** To read more about wildcards and regular expressions, take a look at the bash man page (man bash). Remember that you can save the file to a text file by typing man bash | col -b > bash.txt. Then, you can open and read the file with less or pico (pico bash.txt). If you want to print the file, be prepared: It's quite long.

We know the file's called "sneak-something.txt", so just type:

```
ls sneak*.txt
```

and there's the name of the file:

```
sneakers.txt
```

You'll probably use the asterisk (*) most frequently when you're searching. The asterisk will search out everything that matches the pattern you're looking for. So even by typing:

```
ls *.txt
```

or:

```
ls sn*
```

you'd find `sneakers.txt` — except that as time goes on, there will be more text files, and they'll all show up because they match the pattern you're searching for.

It helps, then, to narrow your search as much as possible.

One way to narrow the search might be to use the question mark symbol (?). Like the asterisk, using ? can help locate a file matching a search pattern.

In this case, though, ? is useful for matching a single character — so if you were searching for `sneaker?.txt`, you'd get `sneakers.txt` as a result — and/or `sneakerz.txt`, if there were such a filename.

When an asterisk, for example, just happens to be part of a filename, such as might be the case if the file `sneakers.txt` was called `sneak*.txt`, that's when regular expressions can come in handy.

Regular expressions are more complex than the straightforward asterisk or question mark.

Using the backslash (\), you can specify that you don't want to search out everything by using the asterisk, but you're instead looking for a file with an asterisk in the name.

If the file is called `sneak*.txt`, then, type:

```
sneak\*.txt
```

Here is a brief list of wildcards and regular expressions:

- ***** — Matches all characters
- **?** — Matches one character in a string (such as sneaker?.txt)
- ***** — Matches the * character
- **\\?** — Matches the ? character
- **\\)** — Matches the) character

You can also use wildcards for more than searching: they can come in handy when you want to move and rename files. And regular expressions can help you rename files with characters like * and ? in them.

For more on that, read on.

Copying, Moving and Renaming Files and Directories

By now, you've learned a little about the structure of the filesystem; and you've learned how to create files and directories. But just because you know how to create files and directories doesn't mean that you're stuck with the changes you've made. What if you want to rename and/or move files and directories? Let's start with the copy command.

Copying Files

Like so many Linux features, you have a variety of options from which to choose when you want to manipulate files and directories. You can also use wildcards when you're copying, moving, or deleting files and directories. Basically, the copy command is not much more complex than typing:

```
cp <source> <destination>
```

so to copy the file `sneakers.txt` to the directory `tigger` in your login directory, just type:

```
cp sneakers.txt tigger
```

Notice that you also used relative pathnames to copy the file. You can use both relative and absolute pathnames with cp. Our login directory is the parent of the directory `tigger`; meaning that `tigger` is one directory down from ours. Read the `cp` man page (`man cp`) for a full list of the options available with `cp`. But among the options you can use with `cp` are:

- **-i** — interactive. Prompts you to confirm if the file is going to overwrite a file in your destination. This is a handy option because it can help prevent you from making mistakes.

- **-r** — recursive. Rather than just copying all the files and directories, copies the whole directory tree, subdirectories and all, to another location.
- **-f** — force. Copies without prompting you for confirmation that the file should be overwritten. Unless you're sure you want to force the copy, you probably don't want to make friends with this option right now.
- **-v** - verbose. Will show the progress of the files being copied.

Just by using `cp` alone, you won't see much when the command is executed. Using an option, such as -i, can make the process a little more useful, because if you want to copy a file to a location that already has a file with the same name, you'll be asked first if you really want to overwrite — meaning replace — the file that's already there.

- **Tip:** Remember that among your options is -f (force), which can overwrite files without asking you if you're certain. Make sure, when you use the force option, that you really want to overwrite a file.

Now that we have the file `sneakers.txt` in the `tigger` directory, let's use `cp -i` to copy the file again to the same location.

```
[billy@localhost billy] cp -i sneakers.txt tigger
cp: overwrite 'tigger/sneakers.txt'?
```

If we want to overwrite the file that's already there, we can press [Y] and then [Enter]. If we think we don't want to overwrite the file, now's the time to press [N] and [Enter].

Moving Files

To move files, use the mv command (man mv), which is similar to the cp command, except that with mv the file is physically moved from one place to another, instead of being duplicated, as with cp. Common options available with mv include:

- **-i** — interactive. Will prompt you if the file you've selected will overwrite an existing file in the destination directory. This is a good option, because like the -i option in cp, you'll be given the chance to make sure you want to replace an existing file.

- **-f** — force. Overrides the interactive mode and moves without prompting. Unless you know what you're doing, this option doesn't play nice; be very careful about using it until you become more comfortable with your system.
- **-v** — verbose. Shows a list of the files being moved.

If you want to move a file out of your home directory and into another directory, you would type:

```
mv sneakers.txt tigger
```

or,

```
mv sneakers.txt /home/billy /home/billy/tigger
```

using absolute pathnames.

Renaming Files

Actually, we've already covered half of renaming, because when you copy or move files, you can also rename. To copy the file `sneakers.txt` from our login directory to our `tigger` subdirectory, just type:

```
cp sneakers.txt tigger
```

To copy and rename that file from `sneakers.txt` to `piglet.txt`, type:

```
cp sneakers.txt tigger/piglet.txt
```

To move and rename the file, just substitute `mv` for `cp` in the above example. If you `cd` to `tigger` and use `ls`, you'll see the file `piglet.txt`. If you just want to rename the file and keep its location, just `mv` in your current directory:

```
mv sneakers.txt piglet.txt
```

Deleting Files and Directories

We talked about creating files with the `touch` command and by using redirection in Chapter 2. And we created the directory `tigger` using `mkdir`.

But we haven't discussed how to delete files and directories.

Deleting files and directories with the `rm` command (`man rm`) is a straightforward process. Let's take our new file `piglet.txt`, and delete it from the `tigger` directory with the `rm` command:

rm piglet.txt

What happens if we didn't really want to get rid of it? Too late! Again, that's where the -i (interactive) option comes in handy, because with it, we have the chance to think about whether we really want to toss the file.

```
[billy@localhost billy] rm -i piglet.txt
rm: remove 'piglet.txt'?
```

You can also delete files using the wildcard *, but be careful, because you can easily delete files you didn't intend to throw away.

To remove a file using a wildcard, you would type:

```
rm pig*
```

You can also remove more than one file in one command, as in:

```
rm piglet.txt sneakers.txt
```

Options for removing files — and directories — include:

- **-i** — interactive. Prompts you to confirm the deletion. This is good.
- **-f** — force. Overrides interactive mode and removes the file(s) without prompting. This might not be good, unless you know exactly what you're doing.
- **-v** — verbose. Shows a listing of files as they're being removed.
- **-r** — recursive. When removing directories, will remove all of the files and the subdirectories of the specified directory. This can also get rid of an empty directory.

To remove directories with `rm`, you must specify the -r option.

For example, if you want to recursively remove the directory tigger you would type:

```
rm -r tigger
```

And if you want to combine options, such as forcing a recursive deletion, you can type:

```
rm -rf tigger
```

- **Tip:** *Be careful!* rm is a powerful command, and can delete your entire system! If you're root and you type the simple command rm -rf / you're sunk — like a snake eating its tail, the command will recursively remove everything on your system.

The safer alternative to using `rm` for removing directories is the `rmdir` command. With this command, you won't be allowed to use recursive deletions, so a directory which has files in it won't be deleted.

Read the `rmdir` man page by typing `man rmdir` to find out more about the command.

Time to Learn More

So far, you've learned to become familiar with how to create accounts, using passwords, your filesystem and more.

But what we've covered is just the tip of the iceberg. There are books, websites, and newsgroups (Linux users are second to none when it comes to helping new users) to help you find out more about your new system.

You can begin with the next chapter, in which you'll find pointers to other documentation, as well as additional post-installation configuration.

18 What Do I Do Now?

Now that you're becoming a little more familiar with your Red Hat Linux system, you might be wondering, "What do I do now?" If so, this chapter is for you. We'll start with some basic places you can go to find more documentation and help from the Linux user community. Then we'll show you how to do some post-installation configuration so you can set up things just the way you want. But before we do any of that, let's talk about documentation...

Getting the Documentation That's Right for You

It is critical to make sure you have documentation that is appropriate to your level of Linux expertise. There is no more certain way to make your experience using Red Hat Linux a failure than to not have the documentation you need, when you need it. As the name implies, *The Getting Started Guide for Red Hat Linux 6.0* is just that — a guide to taking those first steps with your newly installed Red Hat Linux system. Let's take a look at three categories of people using Red Hat Linux, and try to be more explicit in terms of the documentation you'll need. Let's start by figuring out your experience level. Here are the three basic categories:

New To Linux — Has never used any Linux (or Linux-like) operating system before, or has had only limited exposure to Linux. May or may not have experience using other operating systems (such as Windows). Is this you? If so, please turn to **Documentation For First-Time Linux Users**.

Some Linux Experience — Has installed and successfully used Linux (but not Red Hat Linux) before. Or, may have equivalent experience with other Linux-like operating systems. Does this describe you? If so, please turn to **Documentation for More Experienced Linus Users**.

Old Timer — Has installed and sucessfully used Red Hat Linux before. Are you an old-timer? If so, please turn to **Documentationfor Linux Gurus**.

Documentation For First-Time Linux Users

"A journey of a thousand miles begins with a single step." This old saying can be applied to just about any endeavor; we're going to apply it to learning to use your Red Hat Linux system. Learning to use a Linux system effectively can be a long, rewarding journey, where you find that you can easily do things that people with other operating systems can only dream of. But like all journeys, you've got to start somewhere, and take that first step. And the first step you need to take is to get yourself some documentation! This cannot be stressed enough; without documentation you will only become frustrated at your inability to get your Red Hat Linux system working the way you want. Here's what you should look for in terms of Linux documentation:

- **A brief history of Linux** — Many aspects of Linux are the way they are because of historical precedent. There is also a Linux culture that, again, is based to a great deal on past history. A bit of knowledge about the history of Linux will serve you well, particularly as you interact with more experienced Linux users on the Internet.

- **An explanation of how Linux works** — While it's not necessary to delve into the most arcane aspects of the Linux kernel, it's a good idea to know something about how Linux is put together. This is particularly important if you've been working with other operating systems; some of the assumptions you hold about how computers work may not transfer from that operating system to Linux. A few paragraphs that discuss how Linux works (and particularly how it differs from the operating system you're used to), can be invaluable in getting off to a good start with your Red Hat Linux system.

- **An introductory command overview (with examples)** — This is probably the most important thing to look for in Linux documentation. The design philosophy behind Linux is that it's better to use many small commands connected together in different ways than it is to have a few large (and complex) commands that do the whole job themselves. Without some examples that illustrate the Linux approach to doing things, you will find yourself intimidated by the sheer number of commands available on your Red Hat Linux system.

Here is some direction that may help to match all of your requirements:

- **Books** — **Linux for Dummies**, by John "maddog" Hall, published by IDG; **Using Linux**, by William H. Ball, published by Que; **Running Linux**, by Matt

Welsh and Lar Kaufman, published by O'Reilly & Associates; **Linux Volume 1: ac to zcat, the basics**, by Dale Sheetz and Mark Williams Company, published by Linux Press; **Red Hat Linux Secrets**, by Naba Barkakati, published by IDG.

- **Red Hat's website** — At Red Hat's very own website (*http://www.redhat.com*), you'll find links to the Linux Documentation Project (LDP), the Official Red Hat Linux 6.0 Installation Guide, FAQs (Frequently Asked Questions), a database which can help you search for a Linux Users Group near you, a knowledgebase of information and more. In short, you'll find a wealth of information to help you get started.
- **Newsgroups** — Linux users are second to none when it comes to helping new users understand Linux. You can find dozens of Linux-related newsgroups on the Usenet, but a quick search through Deja News (*http://www.dejanews.com)* shows: *linux.help; linux.redhat, linux.redhat.digest, linux.redhat.misc* and *linux.redhat.rpm*. Also, from the Deja News website, you can frequently search for specific information from Linux newsgroups.

As you gain more experience using your Red Hat Linux system, you'll probably find that you'll need more in-depth information. Continue reading the next section to find out more about the kinds of documentation that will help you at that point.

Documentation for More Experienced Linux Users

If you've used other Linux distributions, you probably already have a basic grasp of the most frequently used commands. You may have installed your own Linux system, and maybe you've even downloaded and built software you found on the Internet. What sorts of information will you need?

- **Task-oriented information** — Many times, you'll find that you'd like to configure your Red Hat Linux system in a certain way, but you're not sure where to begin. In this case, it's often a big help to see what others in similar circumstances have done. This is where the Linux Documentation Project (also known as the LDP) can come in handy. Each of their HOWTOs document a particular aspect of Linux, from low-level kernel esoterica, to using Linux in an amateur radio station. If you selected one of the various howto packages when you installed Red Hat Linux, you'll find the HOWTOs on your system in `/usr/doc/HOWTO`.

Documentation for Linux Gurus

If you're a long-time Red Hat Linux user, you probably already know that the following pretty much says it all when it comes to documentation:

Use the Force – Read the source! There are times when you'll just have to sit there and look at the sources to understand things. Fortunately, because of the freely available nature of Linux, it's easy to get the sources. Now if it were only that easy to understand them... Now that we've covered documentation, let's look at some other common system tasks.

The X Window System

While there are people that will use the character-cell interface present when you first log in, many people prefer a graphically-oriented user interface. For Linux systems, the graphical user interface of choice is the X Window System. In order to run X, you need to have the necessary packages installed. If you selected the "X Window System" component to be installed when you originally installed Red Hat Linux, everything should be ready to go. In that case, please refer to **XFree86 Configuration**.

If You Haven't Installed X

If you didn't select the "X Window System" component when you installed Red Hat Linux, your Red Hat Linux system won't have the necessary software installed. While it is possible to manually install the required packages, you'll probably find it easier to re-do the installation, particularly if you're new to Linux. Another possibility is to perform an upgrade of the software and select the X Window System components that you need from the package selection installation process.

XFree86 Configuration

There are three methods for configuring XFree86 on your machine:

- Xconfigurator
- xf86config
- by hand

Xconfigurator and xf86config are functional equivalents and should work equally well. If you are unsure of anything in this process, a good source of additional documentation is: *http://www.xfree86.org*

Xconfigurator is a full-screen menu-driven program that walks you through setting up your X server. xf86config is a line-oriented program distributed with XFree86. It isn't as easy to use as Xconfigurator, but it is included for completeness. If these utilities fail to provide a working

XF86Config file, you may have an unsupported card or you may need to write the config file by hand. Usually the former is the case, so check and make sure your card is supported before attempting to write the config file yourself. If your card is not supported by XFree86 you may wish to consider using a commercial X server. If you have questions about whether or not your video card is supported you can check out *http://www.xfree86.org* for information on XFree86.

The X Server

Provided you selected the proper video card at install time, you should have the proper X server installed. When later running Xconfigurator or xf86config, you need to make sure you select the same video card or the autoprobe will fail.

If you think you installed the wrong X server for your video card, you will have to install the correct one before it can be configured. For instance, if the CD is mounted on `/mnt/cdrom`, and you need to install the S3 server, enter the following commands:

```
cd /mnt/cdrom/RedHat/RPMS
rpm -ivh XFree86-S3-3.1.2-1.i386.rpm
ln -sf ../../usr/X11R6/bin/XF86S3 /etc/X11/X
```

This will install the S3 server and make the proper symbolic link.

Xconfigurator

To configure the X Window System you must first select your video card. Scroll down the list of supported cards until you locate the card in your machine. Figure 1-1 may help you determine the video server that matches your hardware. If your card is not listed it may not be supported by XFree86. In this case you can try the last card entry on the list (Unlisted Card) or a commercial X Windows server.

The next step is to select your monitor. If your monitor is not listed you can select one of the generic monitor entries or "Custom" and enter your own parameters. Custom monitor configuration is recommended only for those who have a sound understanding of the inner workings of CRT displays. The average user should probably use one of the generic selections from the list. After selecting a monitor you need to tell Xconfigurator how much video memory you have. Move the highlight to the appropriate list entry and then press [Enter] or [F12] to continue. For the next step it is recommended that you select the default (No Clockchip Setting) entry, but experienced users may want to select a specific clockchip.

Selecting your Server

If you are unsure what chipset you have, the best way to find out is usually to look at the card. Figure 18-1 lists which chipsets and boards require which servers. Pick the one that best matches your hardware.

Server	Chipset
8514	IBM 8514/A Boards and true clones
AGX	All XGA graphics boards
I128	#9 Imagine 128 (including Series II) boards
Mach32	ATI boards using the Mach32 chipset
Mach64	ATI boards using the Mach64 chipset
Mach8	ATI boards using the Mach8 chipset
Mono	VGA boards in monochrome
P9000	Diamond Viper (but not the 9100) and Others
S3	#9 Boards, most Diamonds, some Orchids, Others
S3V	Boards using the S3 ViRGE (including DX, GX, VX) chipset
SVGA	Trident 8900 & 9400, Cirrus Logic, C & T, ET4000, S3 ViRGE, Others
VGA16	All VGA boards (16 color only)
W32	All ET4000/W32 cards, but not standard ET4000's

Figure 18-1: XFree86 X Servers

Finishing Up

If later you want to increase your refresh rate for your monitor, you can edit the config file by hand or you can run Xconfigurator again and pick a monitor from our list that more closely matches the specs of your monitor.

The final configuration step consists of selecting the video modes that you want to include in your XF86Config file. Use the arrow keys to move the cursor up and down the list under each color depth (8, 16 and 24 bit). Use the [Spacebar] to select individual resolutions and the [Tab] key to move between color depth fields. When you have selected the video modes you want to use move the cursor to the "OK" button and press [Enter], or use the [F12] shortcut. An information screen will give you the most current information on selecting video modes, starting and stopping the X server.

If You've Already Installed X

If you selected the "X Window System" component when you installed Red Hat Linux, but didn't choose to start X automatically when the system boots, you're all set. All you'll need to do is to get X running. As it turns out, there are two ways to do this. You can:

- Start X manually after you log in.
- Start X automatically whenever the system boots.

Let's start with the manual procedure.

Starting X Manually

Red Hat Linux, during the installation, gives you the option of starting X automatically. If you didn't choose this option, you'll see the character-cell login prompt you saw when you first booted your Red Hat Linux system. In order to get X started, you'll first need to log in. Do so (using your non-root account), and then enter the startx command. The screen should go blank, and (after a short delay) you should see a graphical desktop with one or more windows. The appearance of the desktop you'll see will vary, depending on the packages you installed and other variables. (See Chapter 1 for more info.)

Starting X Automatically

Please Note: Make sure you verify that your X configuration works properly before making X start automatically. Failure to do so can make it difficult to log into your Red Hat Linux system. If you haven't done so already, review the previous section before continuing. It is possible to configure your Red Hat Linux system such that X will start automatically whenever the system is booted. When configured in this manner, xdm will run, which will present a graphically-oriented login screen. After logging in, you will have a regular X session running, just as if you had issued a startx command manually.

Here's a quick overview of how it's done:

- Test xdm using telinit.
- Edit /etc/inittab.
- Reboot.

Let's look at each step in more detail.

Testing xdm Using telinit — The telinit command is used to change your Red Hat Linux system's "run level." It is the run level that controls various aspects of system operation, including whether xdm should be started or not. Since xdm is started at run level 5, you'll need to issue the command:

```
/sbin/telinit 5
```

Please Note: You will need to be logged in as root in order to use telinit. Also note that you should not be running anything else on your Red Hat Linux system when you change run levels, as any running programs may be killed by the run level change. If everything is configured properly, after a short delay you should see an xdm login screen. Log in, verifying that an X desktop appears. Then log out to make sure that xdm reappears. If it does, your system is configured properly to automatically start X. If there are problems, you can go back to run level 3 using telinit (i.e., "/ sbin/telinit 3"), or by rebooting.

Editing `/etc/inittab` — The file `/etc/inittab` is used to, among other things, determine the system's default run level. We need to change the default run level from 3 to 5; therefore, we'll need to edit /etc/inittab. Using the text editor of your choice, change this line in /etc/inittab:

```
id:3:initdefault:
```

When you're done, it should look like this:

```
id:5:initdefault:
```

Please Note: Make sure you change only the number 3 to be 5! Do not change anything else, otherwise your Red Hat Linux system may not boot at all! When you've made the change, exit the editor, and use this command to review your handiwork:

```
less /etc/inittab
```

(Press the [Space] to page through the file; [Q] will exit.) If everything looks OK, it's time to reboot. Use the shutdown command to properly shut down your system, and you're done!

Exiting X

When you're done, and you'd like to leave X, select the **GNOME foot** on the panel bar, choose **Log out** and answer **Yes** to confirm your decision. You will then be logged out of your system.

Please Note: If you're running GNOME as your desktop environment, all programs that were currently running will be restarted when you log back in.

Changing Your Desktop

You can use the **Switchdesk** feature to change out your desktop environment. **Switchdesk** will present a screen which allows you to switch between any desktop environments that you may have installed

Run Programs and type switchdesk.

on your system. You will then be asked to exit and restart X. You will see your new desktop of choice after X has restarted. To use the **Switchdesk** feature you can type switchdesk at the command line of an Xterm. If you are using GNOME, click on the **GNOME foot**, choose

Virtual Consoles and X

Note that even if you're running X, you still have access to the regular character-cell user interface. That's because Red Hat Linux uses virtual consoles while X is running. To switch to a virtual console, press [Ctrl]-[Alt]-[Fn], where [Fn] is any one of the first six function keys. When switching virtual consoles, you should see a standard login prompt; at this point you can login and use the system normally on any (or all) of the virtual consoles. When you'd like to go back to your X session, simply press [Ctrl]-[Alt]-[F7].

Please Note: Some people remap keys under X; if you do this, be aware that your X keyboard mappings will only be active when in X. This can be confusing if, for example, you've swapped the [Ctrl] and [Caps Lock] keys under X, as you will have to use two different keystrokes to switch between X and non-X virtual consoles.

Handy X-Based Tools

There are several tools that can make life easier for the new Red Hat Linux user. They perform tasks that either require root access, or can only be done by memorizing arcane commands. They all require X to run, so you'll need to get that set up first. These tools are:

- **User Information Tool** – Makes it easy to update your "gecos," or basic account information. Run /usr/bin/userinfo to start it.
- **User Password Tool** – Changing passwords is simple with this tool. It's started by running /usr/bin/userpasswd
- **Filesystem Mounting Tool** – Makes mounting and unmounting filesystems simple. Every user-mountable filesystem must have the user option present in /etc/fstab (see the mount man page for more information on the user option). Run (1) /usr/bin/usermount to start it.

- **Network Device Tool** — Starting and stopping network interfaces becomes a point-and-click operation with this tool. Run /usr/bin/usernet to start this tool. Requires that every interface to be controlled by usernet is configured to be "user-controllable." This can be done by using netcfg, and selecting the interface's Allow any user to (de)activate interface checkbox.

Configuring Your Red Hat Linux System For Sound

By default, the only sound you'll hear out of your newly installed Red Hat Linux system is the ordinary, boring, default beep. If your computer system has sound hardware, chances are you can make it work under Red Hat Linux. In some cases successfully getting sound support to work requires a kernel rebuild. However, most of the time it's possible to use the modular sound drivers.

Modular Sound Drivers

Red Hat Linux 6.0 includes the standard OSS/Free sound drivers. This makes it possible to load and unload the various sound drivers without recompiling the kernel or rebooting. For additional information, please consult the README files in the rhsound documentation directory (`/usr/doc/rhsound*`), and also the files in the kernel documentation directory (`/usr/doc/kernel-doc-*/sound`). There is a mailing list associated with the modular sound drivers (*sound-list@redhat.com*). To subcribe, send mail to *sound-list-request@redhat.com*, with "subscribe" as the subject line.

Recognized Sound Cards

At this point, most sound cards should be recognized by the modular sound drivers; however, drivers for the following sound cards were among the first to be developed, and as such, have received the most testing:

- Sound Blaster 1.0
- Sound Blaster 2.0
- Sound Blaster Pro

- Sound Blaster 16
- Sound Blaster 16 PnP
- Sound Blaster AWE32/AWE64

Sound Card Configuration Tool

Also included in Red Hat Linux 6.0 is `sndconfig`, a screen-oriented utility that can properly configure modular sound card drivers. There are a few things that you should know about `sndconfig`:

> **Plug and Play Aware** — sndconfig is able to detect and automatically configure Plug and Play sound cards such as the Sound Blaster 16 PnP. The configuration information is stored in the /etc/isapnp.conf file, along with the configuration information for any other Plug and Play devices. In order to ensure that no configuration will be lost, sndconfig saves your original `/etc/isapnp.conf` file as `/etc/isapnp.conf.bak`.
>
> **Modifies /etc/conf.modules** — `sndconfig` modifies the module configuration file (2) `/etc/conf.modules` by adding information about the module options required for your sound card. Note that sndconfig saves your original /etc/conf.modules file as (3) `/etc/conf.modules.bak`.

To set up your sound card, run `/usr/sbin/sndconfig`. Note that you must be root in order to run `sndconfig`. If your system contains a Plug and Play sound card, `sndconfig` will identify it, and configure it appropriately. If you do not want sndconfig to probe for Plug and Play sound cards, run sndconfig with the —noprobe option. It is also possible to manually specify the settings for your sound card; to do so, run sndconfig with the —noautoconfig option. If sndconfig cannot automatically identify your system's sound card (or you ran sndconfig with the —noprobe option), you'll be asked to select the type of sound card you have (See Figure 18-2). Use the [] and [] keys to scroll through the different cards listed, and position the highlight on the entry that matches your system's sound card.

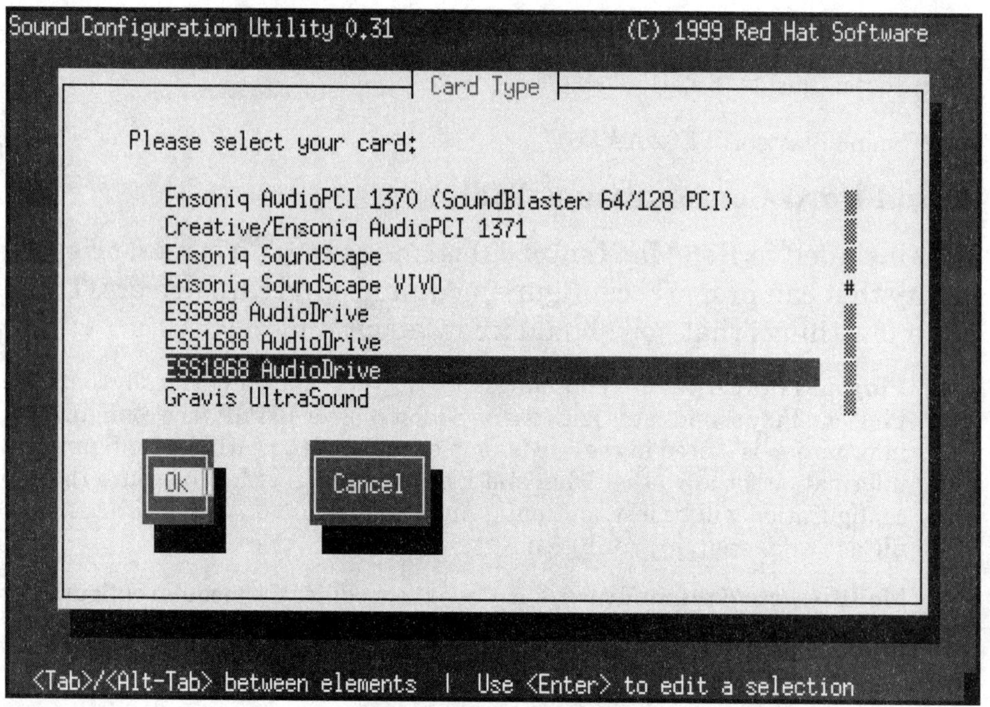

Figure 18-2: Selecting Sound Card Type

If you've run `sndconfig` with the `—noautoconfig` option, you'll see a screen similar to the one in Figure 18-3]. Here is where you can specify the settings for your sound card. Using the [Tab] key, select a field. Then use the arrow keys to select the desired setting for that field. When finished, select **Ok**, and press [Space].

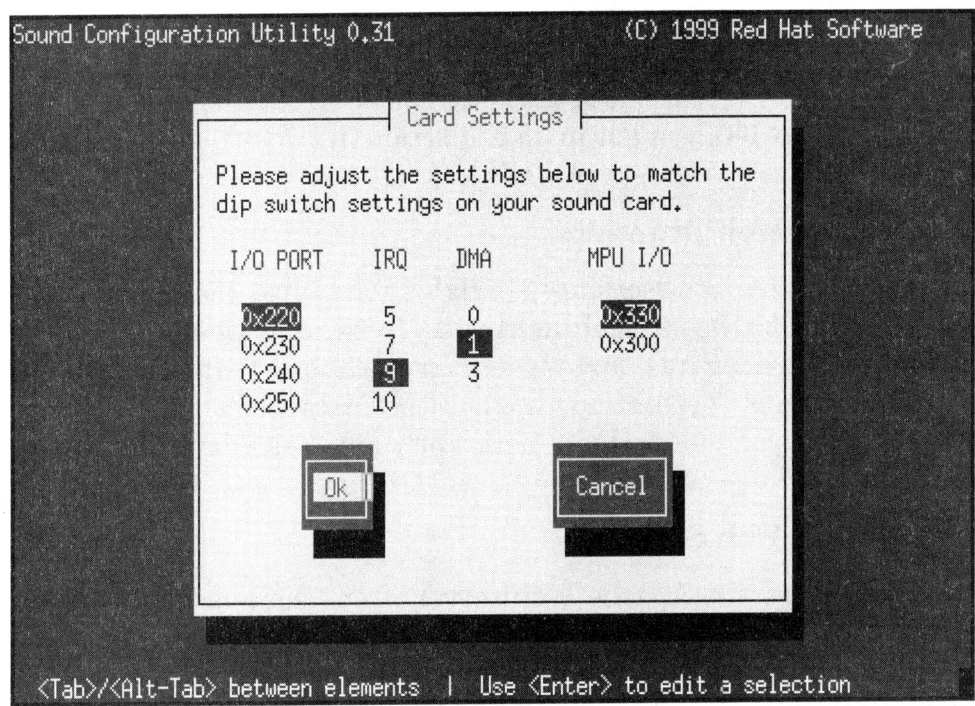

Figure 18-3: Configuring Sound Card

After this screen, you may see an informational dialog box saying that `/etc/conf.modules` already exists. Select Ok and press [Space] to continue.

Finally, `sndconfig` will attempt to play a sound sample to verify proper configuration of your sound card. If you can hear the sound sample (make sure the speaker volume is turned up), you're done!

> **Please Note:** On cards that have a recognized MIDI synthesizer, sndconfig will attempt to play a MIDI sample as well.

World Wide Web

The World Wide Web is one of the hottest aspects of the Internet today. Red Hat Linux lets you get in on the action in two ways — as a Web browser, and as a Web server. Let's look at both.

World Wide Web Browsers

A variety of Web browsers are available for Linux, including freely distributable browsers such as Arena, Lynx, and Grail. The most popular commercial browsers are those from Netscape Communications Corporation. And now they're available with Red Hat Linux 6.0! If you selected the netscape-communicator or netscape-navigator packages, you're ready to surf. Enjoy!

World Wide Web Server

If you installed the Apache Web server (from the apache package), then your Web service is already up and running! Just point your Web browser at *http://localhost*.The default page shown is `/home/httpd/html/index.html`. You can edit this file (or completely replace it) to your liking. All the CGI programs, icons, and HTML pages are stored in `/home/httpd`, but this can be changed in the apache configuration files, all of which are stored in `/etc/httpd/conf/`. Logs of all httpd activity are kept in `/var/log/httpd/`. Setting up your Web site is as easy as adding your own HTML pages and links to the `/home/httpd/html/` directory. For more information on customizing your Web server we recommend a reference such as *HTML: The Definitive Guide* by Chuck Musciano & Bill Kennedy, published by O'Reilly & Associates.

Good luck and enjoy!

As we said before, there is a wealth of information available which can help you get the most out of your your new Red Hat Linux system. We hope this guide has assisted you in your journey.

Index

Symbols

A

B

C

D